Surveillance and Control
in Israel/Palestine

Surveillance is always a means to an end, whether that end is influence, management, entitlement or control. This book examines the several layers of surveillance that control the Palestinian population in Israel and the Occupied Territories, showing how they operate, how well they work, how they are augmented, and how ultimately their chief purpose is population control. The authors look not only at the political economy of surveillance and its technological and military dimensions, but at the ordinary ways that Palestinians in Israel and the Occupied Territories are affected in their everyday lives. Chapters from renowned scholars provide an examination of surveillance and its associated technologies at several levels:

- the social sorting of populations through discursive practices involving people counting and census construction
- spatial control, urban warfare, and territorial sovereignty
- geographic mobility
- the use of various forms of technology to manage people and violence in conflict situations
- discourses of state securitization, biopolitics, and states of exception that are deployed as means of surveillance
- the role of the military–industrial–surveillance complex in promoting surveillance
- the extent to which existing privacy and other related laws protect against intrusiveness by the state, private sector, and third parties in the collection and dissemination of personal information
- how the practice of social sorting in Israel/Palestine has influenced and in turn been influenced by global considerations related to the discourse on security and terrorism.

Written in a clear and accessible style, this book will have large appeal for scholars and students of sociology, political science, international relations, surveillance studies and Middle East studies.

Elia Zureik is Emeritus Professor of Sociology at Queen's University, Canada. His published work covers the Middle East, with special reference to the Israeli–Palestinian conflict, and surveillance.

David Lyon is Director of the Surveillance Studies Centre at Queen's University, Canada. He is the author of *Surveillance Studies: An Overview* (2007) and *Identifying Citizens: ID Cards as Citizenship* (2009), and is currently researching the global growth of national ID systems.

Yasmeen Abu-Laban is Professor and Associate Chair (Research) in the Department of Political Science at the University of Alberta, Canada. She specializes in the politics of gender, racialization, migration and citizenship. She is co-author of *Selling Diversity* (2002), co-editor of *Politics in North America* (2008), and editor of *Gendering the Nation-State* (2008).

Routledge Studies in Middle Eastern Politics

Surveillance and Control in Israel/Palestine

Population, territory, and power

**Edited by Elia Zureik,
David Lyon and
Yasmeen Abu-Laban**

Routledge
Taylor & Francis Group

LONDON AND NEW YORK

First published 2011
by Routledge
2 Park Square, Milton Park, Abingdon, Oxon OX14 4RN

Simultaneously published in the USA and Canada
by Routledge
270 Madison Ave, New York, NY 10016

Routledge is an imprint of the Taylor & Francis Group, an informa business

Typeset in Baskerville
by Keystroke, Station Road, Codsall, Wolverhampton
Printed and bound in Great Britain
by MPG Books Group, UK

British Library Cataloguing in Publication Data
A catalogue record for this book is available from the British Library

Library of Congress Cataloging in Publication Data
Surveillance and control in Israel/Palestine : population, territory and power / edited
by Elia Zureik, David Lyon and Yasmeen Abu-Laban.
       p. cm. — (Routledge studies in Middle Eastern politics ; 33)
     Includes bibliographical references and index.
   1. Electronic surveillance—Israel. 2. Palestinian Arabs—Israel 3. Conflict
management—Israel. I. Zureik, Elia. II. Lyon, David, 1948- III. Abu-Laban,
Yasmeen, 1966-
HV7936.T4S87 2011
355.3′433095694—dc22   2010025054

ISBN: 978–0–415–58861–4 (hbk)
ISBN: 978–0–203–84596–7 (ebk)

Contents

Illustrations

Figures

Tables

List of contributors

Yasmeen Abu-Laban is Professor in the Department of Political Science at the University of Alberta, Canada. She specializes in the politics of gender, racialization, migration and citizenship. She is co-author of *Selling Diversity* (UTP Higher Education 2002), co-editor of *Politics in North America* (UTP Higher Education 2008), and editor of *Gendering the Nation-State* (UBC Press 2008).

Nurhan Abujidi is a Professor at San Jorge University, Zaragoza, Spain, and a researcher at COSMOPOLIS, City Culture and Society at the Vrije University of Brussels. Her research focuses on the fields of military urbanism and destruction, territoriality, sovereignty and biopolitics, urban renewal and post-war reconstruction projects and issues of identity, gender, architecture linked to armed conflict and wars, and she has several publications in these areas.

Abigail B. Bakan is Professor of Political Studies at Queen's University, Kingston, Ontario, Canada. Her publications include *Negotiating Citizenship: Migrant Women in Canada and the Global System* (with Daiva K. Stasiulis; University of Toronto Press 2005), winner of the 2007 Canadian Women's Studies Association annual book award; and *Critical Political Studies: Debates and Dialogues from the Left* (co-editor with Eleanor MacDonald; McGill-Queen's University Press 2002).

Glenn Bowman is Senior Lecturer in Anthropology at the University of Kent, Canterbury, UK, where he convenes the MA in the Anthropology of Ethnicity, Nationalism and Identity. A former editor of the *Journal of the Royal Anthropological Institute*, he has carried out extensive fieldwork in Jerusalem and the West Bank as well as in Macedonia (FYROM) and Serbia.

Hillel Cohen teaches in the Department of Middle East Studies at the Hebrew University of Jerusalem. His recent books include *Good Arabs: The Israeli Security Agencies and the Israeli Arabs* (University of California Press 2008) and *The Rise and Fall of Arab Jerusalem* (Routledge Sudies on the Arab Israeli Conflict 2010).

Nick Denes is a Ph.D. candidate in Sociology at Goldsmiths College, London University.

Michael R. Fischbach is Professor of History at Randolph-Macon College in Ashland, Virginia, USA. He specializes in the history of the Arab–Israeli conflict, particularly issues relating to land ownership and property losses, compensation, and restitution.

Stephen Graham is Professor of Cities and Society at the Global Urban Research Unit in Newcastle University's School of Architecture, Planning and Landscape. He has authored, co-authored and edited a range of books, including *Telecommunications and the City* (Routledge 1996), *Splintering Urbanism* (Routledge 2001) (both with Simon Marvin), *The Cybercities Reader* (Routledge 2004), *Cities, War and Terrorism* (Wiley 2004), *Disrupted Cities: When Infrastructures Fail* (Routledge 2009), and *Cities under Siege: The New Military Urbanism* (Verso 2010).

Neve Gordon is Professor of Politics and Government at Ben-Gurion University and author of *Israel's Occupation* (University of California Press 2008).

Usama Halabi has been a law researcher and advocate in Jerusalem since 1987. He received his law degree from the Hebrew University in Jerusalem and holds an LL.M in Law, specializing in national discrimination in Israeli law, and a second LL.M in International Legal Studies from the American University in Washington, D.C.

Ariel Handel is a post-doctoral fellow in the Minerva Center for the Humanities at Tel Aviv University. He has published several articles on movement regimes, spatial control and violence, with a special focus on Israel/Palestine. His forthcoming book, *Separation: Time and Space in Israel/Palestine* (with Cedric Parizot) will be published in Hebrew by the Van Leer Jerusalem Institute and Am Oved Publishers.

Rassem Khamaisi is an urban planner and an Associate Professor in the Department of Geography and Environmental Studies at the University of Haifa, and a senior research fellow in the Van Leer Jerusalem Institute. His work primarily focuses on geography and planning among Arabs in Israel and the Palestinians in the occupied territories and Jerusalem, as well as on public administration and public participation and urban management. He has also published on urbanization and planning among the Arabs and Palestinians.

Anat E. Leibler is a faculty member in the graduate programme of Science, Technology and Society Studies at Bar-Ilan University in Tel-Aviv. She carried out historical-comparative research on the emergence of national statistics in Canada and Israel. Her current research focuses on political demography, social sorting, economic standardization, and population management.

David Lyon is Director of the Surveillance Studies Centre at Queen's University, Canada. He is the author of *Surveillance Studies: An Overview* (Polity 2007) and *Identifying Citizens: ID Cards as Citizenship* (Polity 2009), and is currently researching the global growth of national ID systems.

Nigel Parsons is Senior Lecturer in the Politics Programme at Massey University, New Zealand, and author of *The Politics of the Palestinian Authority: From Oslo to al-Aqsa* (Routledge 2005). He is currently researching the biopolitical aspects of Zionism, Israeli institutions and infrastructure, along with associated political and institutional developments in the occupied territories.

Ahmad H. Sa'di is Senior Lecturer in the Department of Politics and Government at Ben-Gurion University of the Negev. He has published widely in refereed journals and has contributed essays to collective volumes. His work has been published in English, Arabic, Hebrew, German and Japanese. He is the co-editor, with Lila Abu-Lughod, of a volume on Palestinian memory of the 1948 war entitled *Nakba: Palestine, 1948 and the Claims of Memory* (Columbia University Press 2007).

Tamir Sorek is an Assistant Professor of Sociology and Israel Studies at the University of Florida. His scholarly interests centre on ethnic and national identities, particularly in the Israeli–Palestinian context.

Helga Tawil-Souri is an Assistant Professor at the Department of Media, Culture, and Communication at New York University. Her research deals with Palestinian internet practices, broadcasting and cinema, and contemporary spaces of social, political and technological control/resistance. She is also a photographer and documentary film-maker.

Reg Whitaker is Distinguished Research Professor Emeritus at York University and Adjunct Professor of Political Science at the University of Victoria. He has also acted as an advisor to the Government of Canada on aviation security.

Elia Zureik is Emeritus Professor of Sociology at Queen's University, Ontario, Canada. His published work covers the Middle East, with special reference to the Israeli–Palestinian conflict, and surveillance.

Preface

Elia Zureik, David Lyon and Yasmeen Abu-Laban

This volume concerns itself with surveillance in Israel/Palestine, and its implications for human population control locally, regionally, and globally. The designation "Israel/Palestine" is used to capture the contested area of land, and zone of militarized conflict, encompassing the "Green Line" (1949) Armistice boundaries established between Israel and neighboring countries after the 1948 war, as well as the territories of the West Bank and Gaza Strip and the eastern portion of Jerusalem that Israel captured and unilaterally annexed after the 1967 Arab–Israeli War.[1] As in much of the twentieth century, in the final years of the first decade of the twenty-first century the epic themes of "war" and "peace" dominated much international media coverage of the Middle East. Indeed, it is striking that mere months after Israel's 22-day war on Gaza (December 2008–January 2009) the newly inaugurated American President Barack Obama made headlines pledging his support for a two-state-focused peace process and stating "the United States does not accept the legitimacy of continued Israeli settlements" (Zeleny and Cowell 2009; Obama 2009). It is settlements that form the backdrop to *la vie quotidienne* in Israel/Palestine. A United Nations report highlights Israeli settlements, begun in 1967, as "the most important factor" driving the restrictions imposed by Israeli authorities on the freedom of movement of Palestinians in the West Bank and East Jerusalem through "physical obstacles (e.g. checkpoints, roadblocks, the Barrier) and administrative and legal measures (e.g. prohibitions, permit requirements, annexation)" (United Nations 2009: 1–2).

Close attention to the grand themes of war and peace, as well as daily life, in Israel/Palestine may highlight developments of deep interest to those in the multidisciplinary area of contemporary Surveillance Studies, with its emphasis on the human consequences of new digital technologies (Marx 1988; 2005). From the introduction in 2005 of "smart" biometric magnetic cards that Palestinians living under occupation hoped, in vain, might facilitate mobility (Hass 2007) to the Israeli Knesset's 2009 decision to introduce biometric ID cards for all Israeli citizens and legal residents, which has spawned new debates over "privacy" (Ilan 2009), there is much that fits the familiar tropes of Surveillance Studies as developed from the 1980s with attention to the United States, Britain, and increasingly other European Union countries (Murakami Wood 2009: 179–185).

As David Murakami Wood has noted, however, to speak of the "surveillance society," as is now commonly done in Surveillance Studies, is to risk invoking a monolithic construct that is insensitive to history and context (Murakami Wood 2009: 179–181).[2] It is for this reason that we feel that key elements to be found in the multidisciplinary area of Middle East Studies can be of considerable relevance in navigating the study of surveillance and its impact on population control in Israel/Palestine as a conflict zone, and emboldening the analytic power of both Surveillance and Middle East Studies. Note, for example, that analysts attuned to surveillance have increasingly paid attention, particularly after September 11, 2001, to state borders of Northern countries as sites of increasingly globalized surveillance and racialized mobility restrictions via passports, visa and airport security controls for migrants and refugees, especially from the global South (Broeders 2007; Abu-Laban 2005; Salter 2003; Andreas and Biersteker 2003). However, there is a specificity to the surveillance regime in Israel/Palestine as it concerns checkpoints, with Israeli security personnel controlling the movement of vehicles and pedestrians in the context of occupation, expanding settlements, and diminishing land and physical space for Palestinians and Palestinian development (United Nations 2009: 1–3). The attention given to modern history (or histories) in Middle East Studies may serve to underscore the relevance of colonialism, as well as the relevance of shifting geopolitical concerns in understanding contemporary Israel/Palestine as part of a region. Moreover, evolving debates in the field of Middle East Studies bring to the fore themes of knowledge, power, and control. Colonialism, geopolitics, and control therefore form important points of reference in the study of surveillance in Israel/Palestine and its implications for population management and control of land. Each of these three points of reference will be discussed in turn.

Colonialism and historical narratives

Following the collapse of the Ottoman Empire, and on the heels of the end of World War One, the entire region of the Middle East was colonized by Western powers (in particular Britain and France) despite the yearning for freedom expressed by subject populations. Through the League of Nations, Britain was granted a "mandate" over Palestine, and, stemming from the 1917 Balfour Declaration, when the Jewish settlers in Palestine constituted no more than 10 percent of the population, began to use immigration to establish there "a national home for the Jewish people," a project given increased international legitimacy and urgency thirty years later as a result of the Holocaust. Thus, while many countries of the Middle East achieved independence following World War Two, the competition for land in Palestine involved a new form of colonization, in the form of settler-colonialism. While Palestinian Arabs (Christians and Muslims) remained a majority in the area until the late 1940s, constituting two-thirds of the population, the goal of creating a Jewish state in Palestine was further developed in the 1947 United Nations Partition Plan and through violence. On May 14, 1948, an independent state of Israel was declared, and the British mandate came to an end. As a result, open warfare between the surrounding Arab states and Israel erupted. By the end of the war, Israel had taken more land than had been allotted under the Partition Plan. Israeli leaders immediately presented the new state as belonging to all the Jewish people around the world and invited immigration from them. This is codified as the Israeli state's "law of return."

The events of 1948 are subject to very different national narratives on the part of many Jewish Israelis (who refer to the period as a war of independence that made possible a national state) and Palestinians (who view the year 1948 as a disaster – in

Arabic, the Nakba – characterized by the majority of the Arab population losing homes and property and becoming stateless refugees inside and outside of historic Palestine). Today, more than sixty years after their dispersal, Palestinians comprise one of the world's largest and oldest refugee groups.

The theme of colonialism is made centrally explicit in many chapters in this volume, including those of Zureik, Lyon, Bowman, Khamaisi, and Fischbach, while the surveillance implications of commemorating the Nakba itself are addressed by Sorek.

Geopolitics: international and regional competition

After the 1948 Arab–Israeli War the competition between Arabs and Jews intensified through a series of wars in the region (1956, 1967, and 1973) as well as through the 1982 Israeli invasion of Lebanon. As such, Israeli attempts at hegemony in the region, and resistance to it, were linked to militarization, and this is the context in which Israel's "military-industrial and surveillance complex" was nurtured. Additionally, the Cold War competition between the United States and the USSR impacted the region. Many Arab countries were brought into the orbit of the USSR (e.g. Egypt, Syria, Iraq) while Israel was firmly in the American camp. As such, while Arab states/Palestinians may view many developments in relation to discourses of offense and violence, Israel/Western states may view them in relation to discourses of defense and security. The collapse of the Soviet Union and the end of the Cold War have changed certain dynamics of the region. Thus, in 2009, Russia very publicly announced a desire to purchase pilotless spy aircraft from Israel (an admission that would not have been possible during the Cold War) in an effort to learn from the technology to improve their own drones (Associated Press 2009). The relevance of developments in Israel/ Palestine on the larger regional and international environment, especially in the post-Cold War and post-September 11 periods, as well as the political economy of the Israeli surveillance industry, is explicitly considered by Graham, Gordon, Denes, Whitaker, and Abu-Laban and Bakan.

Control

Edward Said was the most prominent critic of the relationship between knowledge production and power/control in Oriental Studies historically, and Middle East Studies of the Cold War era. His insights were to have significant influence on the development of the field. Drawing from Foucault, his 1978 book *Orientalism* laid the foundation for a new way of approaching Middle East Studies from the vantage point of the knowledge/power binary, cracking open space for other kinds of scholarship sensitive to minoritized groups, including women, as well as the themes of colonialism and post-colonial theory (Kandiyoti 1996; Abu-Laban 2001). In the words of Schueller (2007: 42), the shift inspired by Said, which is reflected in several chapters in this volume, was about "the decolonization of knowledge" with deep links to independence movements globally, and anti-racist struggles in the United States specifically.

In the post-September 11, 2001 period, US Middle East Studies has become the focus of a vociferous attack that has drawn the attention of some scholars to both state- and societally based surveillance of the written and spoken words and theoretical paradigms used by Middle East studies scholars in the (American) academy (Davidson

2008; Lockman 2005; Beinin 2004). As summarized by Schueller (2007: 42), "today, with many on the Right arguing for the United States to unequivocally don the mantle of empire, anticolonial critiques have become suspect." Websites like Campus Watch, and new policies directing federal oversight of the curricula used in area studies receiving government funding, are hallmark features of what has been dubbed a new American McCarthyism when it comes to the scholarly study of the Middle East (Schueller 2007: 41; Lockman 2005: 90–102; Beinin 2004).

Extending the current focus of surveillance beyond the American academy to the geographical specificity of the Middle East and Israel/Palestine can provide new insights into questions concerning power and control in relation to social and state actors. Themes of control (as well as the relevance of Giorgio Agamben's idea of state exception) are explored in relation to this broader conceptualization of surveillance in the chapters by Sa'di, Cohen, Halabi, Tawil-Souri, Handel, Abu-Laban and Bakan, Abujidi, and Parsons in this collection. These interventions, as well as others in the volume, draw from a rich set of understandings introduced by contemporary Surveillance Studies.

The question of how power and knowledge relate to each other is an antique one but it also has some very up-to-date twists. In Israel and the occupied Palestinian territories (OPT) governmental authorities' knowledge of the Palestinian population – not to mention of Israeli citizens, too – is very tightly linked with the capacity to govern. This has been the case ever since the founding of the state of Israel and, in a sense, even before. Everything from census details that carefully construct the Palestinian population (Zureik 2001) to a system of internal monitoring by "security services" of suspected dissidents within Israeli universities (Bezalel 2009) paints a complex picture of how knowledge is a crucial component of control.

Because this power/knowledge relationship has been enhanced in modern times through bureaucratic organization, and because new technologies have added some new dimensions to the mix, it is worth focusing specifically on what is generally referred to as "surveillance" in order to understand better the dynamics of governing in the Middle East. The "architecture of occupation," as Eyal Weizman (2007) describes Israeli strategies of control, is dependent upon surveillance – to determine who is where, what areas present the largest "threat" to Israel, and where to locate checkpoints, watchtowers, and the like.

This kind of surveillance infrastructure, though not necessarily tied to colonial and occupation regimes like that in Israel, is now common across the world. In many circumstances, "assemblage" might be a better concept, because the component parts often appear together in one place without having an overall plan. They appear as the unintended consequences of commercial and administrative policy. In the case of Israel, as we shall see, some deliberate policy-making accounts for the relations between the various parts of the surveillance infrastructure, in a concerted effort to maintain the purity of the "Jewish state" and to sequester Palestinians and non-Jewish Israelis in specific zones, at specific times.

The interesting question, then, is how far the Israeli surveillance system succeeds in the aim of buttressing the dominant relations of state power. This theme is explored across a number of dimensions in the chapters that follow.

Surveillance Studies Today

In order to have a sense of how surveillance works, it is worth highlighting some key concepts and theories of what is now called Surveillance Studies.

Though a relatively recent disciplinary area, it deals with a topic that is as old as human history. And while, in its modern, bureaucratic form, surveillance became central to disciplinary power, as Michel Foucault (1977) argued, today a confluence of organizational and technological change has helped push it into a new phase.

To make his case, Foucault dusted off the prison plans dreamed up by English social reformer Jeremy Bentham for a "panopticon" or "all-seeing place." This captured the sense of self-discipline engendered by fear of being watched in a bounded context – the prison – where no inmate was ever out of sight. Even if no warder were in the central inspection tower, prisoners would still comply, thought Bentham, because they could not tell if he was there or not (due to a system of blinds obscuring his location). Of course, there are some observable panoptic effects of contemporary surveillance. One may not know for sure that the downtown video camera is switched on, but one complies, just in case (Koskela 2003). In many countries Foucault's case holds up. Brutal public punishment for misdemeanors has been replaced by expectations of self-discipline, shored up with incentives or legally based negative sanctions.

But Foucault also explored other kinds of surveillance, notably what he dubbed "biopower." Here, the knowledge in question is not simply that of the visual, or of visual images, but statistical knowledge of populations. His work suggests that bureaucratic organizations, which are characterized in part by their quest for adequate knowledge to facilitate management, actually "make up" or construct the populations they describe by placing them in categories. This is the sense mentioned above in which, in the Israeli case, Palestinian and other groups are "made up" by the census. The power/knowledge relationship here depends on statistics and on sorting out differences, real or imagined, in populations (see Bowker and Star 1999). Indeed, this is where the notion of "social sorting," now basic to much Surveillance Studies thinking, originates (Gandy 1993; Lyon 2003).

These ideas have been discussed extensively within the Surveillance Studies literature (see, e.g., Lyon 2006) and they have in some cases made important contributions to our understanding. Over the last few decades, however, further transformations have occurred in surveillance that involve both organizations and technologies, neither of which were seriously countenanced within Foucault's primarily historical work. Put briefly, surveillance has now become a primary mode of organizational practice and this, more often than not, involves the use of searchable databases and networked communications. As organizations seek new ways of maximizing opportunities and minimizing risk, they turn to data collection and analysis. The purpose of this is to categorize populations and to discriminate between them in treatment.

At the same time, the notion of security has taken on the status of a primary political and policy goal, and this is used as justification for many novel practices. This includes not only the obvious tilting towards "national security," especially in the wake of 9/11, but a general commitment to security – from personal safety to urban and even global security. This encourages recourse to risk discourses and a turn, especially in the first years of the twenty-first century, towards precaution, pre-emption and prevention (Zedner 2009). The future is colonized by the present, and insurance and actuarial practices are privileged. Now, however, several older categories start to lose their salience. Individuals are responsibilized and the social forms of security are breaking down. Surveillance is implicated in several new formations, the final results of which are as yet unclear.

Surveillance Studies has developed apace, especially in countries of the global North. Theoretical development, following Foucault in the first place but then based on the critique of Foucault or even the rediscovery of older social and political theorists, has occurred in tandem with the expansion of empirical studies. Technological development is now understood to be basic to social transformations in surveillance and this is articulated with the political economy of organization, risk management, and, in some locations, population control. Countries with highly developed surveillance infrastructures, such as the UK and the USA, have been researched extensively, with the result that there is a burgeoning market for books and a rapidly growing number of articles devoted to surveillance (see, e.g., the bibliography in Lyon 2007).

The same is not true, unfortunately, of many countries in the global South. While some of these, with their colonial or postcolonial backgrounds, or clearly non-Western or mixed political cultures – India, China, and some other Asian countries, for example – have started to receive social scientific attention, all too often the focus is still on affluent countries of the global North. Yet there are many situations in which power relations may be properly understood only in terms of surveillance analysis. Postcolonial developments in Ghana or South Korea, for instance, make sense partly in terms of the prevailing surveillance dynamics. In the former, British rule paved the way for contemporary administrative surveillance. In the latter, Japanese conquest left a legacy of military modernity that shaped today's surveillance in specific ways. But a prime example of where social and political realities may be illuminatingly construed in terms of surveillance is Israel and the OPT.

Hence the essays in this book, structured around an analysis of surveillance, should lead to a fuller understanding of power relations and population control in Israel and the OPT. And while Surveillance Studies may make contributions in terms of enhanced analysis, it is also enriched and challenged by the encounter with non-Western territories and cultures. For example, Israel not only practices surveillance on its subaltern populations but is a major supplier and a global producer of surveillance equipment. Indeed, it is second only to the USA in this respect. And Israel is also a prime example of an administration that uses tried-and-tested methods of conventional, face-to-face surveillance – informers and secret agents – alongside the highest of high-tech surveillance devices. But this is to anticipate. The chapters of the book make their own cases.

Thus, the task facing the editors is twofold: first, to provide up-to-date information about population control and surveillance in Israel/Palestine on both sides of the Green Line; second, to fuse the mushrooming discipline of Surveillance Studies in the West with theoretical and methodological considerations that have bearing on the issue of colonialism. With regard to the first, the editors assembled in a workshop held in Cyprus in December 2008 a group of international researchers with varied disciplinary backgrounds who were provided with a clear statement of purpose to situate the case study of Israel/Palestine in the context of Surveillance Studies. Papers selected for this volume were based on the workshop presentations and were directly informed by debate surrounding colonialism and Surveillance Studies. With regard to the second task, several contributions highlighted the role of colonialism in developing surveillance technologies as means to control the land and the indigenous population that lives on it. In fact, colonialism ushered in the use of the now familiar key surveillance methods – from censuses, maps, and fingerprinting to the actual implementation of Bentham's panopticon prison.

The task of fusing Surveillance Studies with colonialism resulted in several important insights. First, the neglect of colonialism and gender in Foucault's pioneering work on biopower and surveillance is treated in this volume through discussions of demography, restrictions on mobility, and land dispossession in Israel and the West Bank and Gaza. Second, by incorporating research into everyday life, it is possible to capture the nature of quotidian and face-to-face surveillance in the context of colonial occupation. Third, on the whole, current Surveillance Studies focus on the disciplining of behavior rather than consciousness. The suppression of memory and indeed the colonizing of memory (Moses 2008) have serious repercussions for Surveillance Studies in colonial and conflict zones, as demonstrated in this volume. Fourth, the racialized conception of surveillance in a colonial setting such as Israel/Palestine has ramifications for personal autonomy and the use of time by the subject (in contrast to citizen) population whose mobility is closely monitored. Finally, from a theoretical angle, the fusing of colonialism and surveillance will no doubt bring to the fore discourse on methods of resistance to control.

Notes

1   Israel would also capture the Sinai Peninsula (which was later returned to Egypt) as well as the Golan Heights (which remains an area of conflict with Syria).
2   By extension, the same could be said for the idea of the "surveillance state."

Bibliography

Abu-Laban, Y. (2005) "Regionalism, Migration and Fortress (North) America," *Review of Constitutional Studies*, 10(1/2): 135–162.
—— (2001) "Humanizing the Oriental: Edward Said and Western Scholarly Discourse," in N. Aruri and M.A. Shuraydi (eds) *Revising Culture, Reinventing Peace: The Influence of Edward Said*, New York and Northampton: Interlink Publishing: 74–85.
Agamben, G. (2005) *State of Exception*, Chicago: University of Chicago Press.
Andreas, P. and T.J. Biersteker (eds) (2003) *The Rebordering of North America*, New York: Routledge.
Associated Press (2009) "Report: Russia to Buy Israeli-made Surveillance Drones," *Haaretz.com*, 11 April. Available HTTP: <http://www.haaretz.com/hasen/spages/1077711.html> (accessed July 14, 2009).
Beinin, J. (2004) "The New American McCarthyisim: Policing Thought about the Middle East," *Race and Class*, 46(1): 101–115.
Bezalel, M. (2009) "The Ivory Watch-Tower: Security Games at Ben-Gurion University," *Jerusalem Post*, July 8. Available HTTP: <http://www.jpost.com/servlet/Satellite?cid=1246443753616&pagename=JPost%2FJPArticle%2FShowFull> (accessed July 14, 2009).
Bowker, G.C. and S.L. Star (1999) *Sorting Things out: Classification and its Consequences*, Cambridge, MA: MIT Press.
Broeders, D. (2007) "The New Digital Borders of Europe," *International Sociology*, 22(1): 71–92.

Davidson, L. (2008) "The Attack on Middle East Studies: A Historical Perspective," *Middle East Policy*, 15(1): 149–160.

Falk, R. (2007) "Academic Freedom under Siege," *International Studies Perspectives*, 8: 369–375.

Foucault, M. (1977) *Discipline and Punish*, New York: Vintage Books.

Gandy, O. (1993) *The Panoptic Sort: A Political Economy of Personal Information*, Boulder, CO: Westview.

Hass, A. (2007) "The Yearnings for a Magnetic Card," *Haaretz.com*, July 17. Available HTTP: <http://www.haaretz.com/hasen/spages/857291.html> (accessed July 14, 2009).

Ilan, S. (2009) "Plan to Introduce Biometric IDs Stirs Privacy Debate," *Haaretz.com*, March 15. Available HTTP: <http://www.haaretz.com/hasen/spages/1070793.html> (accessed July 14, 2009).

Kandiyoti, D. (ed.) (1996) *Gendering the Middle East: Emerging Perspectives*, New York: I.B. Tauris.

Koskela, H. (2003) "Cam-era: The Contemporary Urban Panopticon," *Surveillance and Society*, 3(3): 292–313.

Lockman, Z. (2005) "Critique from the Right: The Neo-conservative Assault on Middle East Studies," *CR: The New Centennial Review*, 5(1): 63–110.

Lyon, D. (2007) *Surveillance Studies: An Overview*, Cambridge: Polity.

—— (ed.) (2006) *Theorizing Surveillance: The Panopticon and beyond*, Cullompton: Willan.

—— (ed.) (2003) *Surveillance as Social Sorting: Privacy, Risk and Digital Discrimination*, London and New York: Routledge.

Marx, G.T. (1988) *Undercover: Police Surveillance in America*, Berkeley: University of California Press.

—— (2005) "What's New about the 'New Surveillance'?: Classifying for Change and Continuity," *Surveillance & Society*, 1(1): 9–29.

Moses, A.D. (ed.) (2008) *Empire, Colony, Genocide: Conquest, Occupation and Subaltern Resistance*, New York and Oxford: Berghahn Books.

Murakami Wood, D. (2009) "The 'Surveillance Society': Questions of History Place and Culture," *European Journal of Criminology*, 6(2): 179–194.

Obama, B. (2009) "Text: Obama's Speech in Cairo," *New York Times*, June 4. Available HTTP: <http://www.nytimes.com/2009/06/04/us/politics/04obama.text.html> (accessed June 5, 2009).

Said, E. (1978) *Orientalism*, New York: Vintage Books.

Salter, M. (2003) *Rights of Passage: The Passport in International Relations*, Boulder, CO: Lynne Rienner.

Schueller, M.J. (2007) "Areas Studies and Multicultural Imperialism: The Project of Decolonizing Knowledge," *Social Text*, 25(1): 41–62.

United Nations, Office of the Coordination of Humanitarian Affairs Occupied Palestinian Territory (2009) *West Bank Movement and Access Update: May 2009*. Available HTTP: <http://www.ochaopt.org/documents/ocha_opt_movement_and_access_2009_05_25_english.pdf> (accessed July 14, 2009).

Weizman, E. (2007) *Hollow Land: The Architecture of Occupation*, London and New York: Verso Press.

Zedner, L. (2009) *Security*, London and New York: Routledge.

Zeleny, J. and A. Cowell (2009) "Addressing Muslims, Obama Pushes Mideast Peace," *New York Times*, June 5. Available HTTP: <http://www.nytimes.com/2009/06/05/world/middleeast/05prexy.html> (accessed June 5, 2009).

Zureik, E. (2001) "Constructing Palestine through Surveillance . . .," *British Journal of Middle Eastern Studies*, 28(2): 205–227.

Acknowledgments

A large, successful project such as this is usually the product of collective efforts. Here we would like to acknowledge with gratitude the fruitful participation of our contributors throughout the project. We also register our thanks to Emily Smith, associate researcher of the Surveillance Studies Centre at Queen's University, whose meticulous work made the entire editing process easier to carry out. Thanks to Sarah Cheung for her timely assistance in the latter phase of the book project. To Joan Sharpe, project administrator at the Surveillance Studies Centre, we express special appreciation for her managerial skills. Finally, we acknowledge with thanks the generous financial support of the Canadian Social Science and Humanities Research Council, which made it possible to organize the workshop.

Part I
Introduction

1 Colonialism, surveillance, and population control

Israel/Palestine

Elia Zureik

> The whole desolate West Bank scene is punctuated with garrison-like settlements on hilltops. If you're looking for a primer on colonialism, this is not a bad place to start.
>
> (Cohen 2009)

At a time when the governments of industrialized nations and spokespersons of leading international organizations sing the praises of globalization, it may seem intellectually quaint – if not entirely out of place – to resuscitate a discussion of colonialism. Yet, as far back as the seventeenth century, colonialism has left an enduring mark on modern nation states, particularly those of the post-colonial variety. In discussing the "colonial present" in Iraq, Afghanistan, and Palestine, geographer Derek Gregory notes that "while they may be displaced, distorted, and (most often) denied, the capacities that inhere within the colonial past are routinely reaffirmed and reactivated in the colonial present" (Gregory 2007: 7). It is not only the territorial and economic dimensions of colonialism that left their mark; as the late Edward Said noted (1994; 1978), so did Orientalism's colonial culture and its instruments of power.

Specifically for our purpose, colonialism played a leading role in the development and adoption of surveillance and control technologies that are essential tools of governance to this day. Equally relevant is the relationship between colonialism and what Michel Foucault calls biopolitics or population management. The purpose of this chapter is to situate discussions about surveillance in Israel/Palestine in the context of the colonial experience as it relates to the control of territory and population management. The chapter will further clarify the connections between what appear to be two separate intellectual pursuits: surveillance studies, on the one hand, and a study of a regional ethno-national conflict that is the product of colonialism, on the other. To accomplish this, the chapter will take the reader into a discussion of colonialism and its applicability to Israel/Palestine, the centrality of surveillance in the study of colonialism, the ontology of surveillance, case studies of surveillance in Israel/Palestine which draw upon the contributions to this volume, resistance to surveillance, and concluding remarks.

Zionism and colonialism

The contours of colonialism

Colonialism exhibits different forms and structures. For example, it can involve the actual occupation and permanent settlement of a country or territory, such as in Australia, New Zealand, South Africa, and the Americas. In most cases a mother country provides protection and sponsorship. These large-scale projects of settler colonialism involved the displacement and at times extermination of the indigenous population, whose status was reduced from a majority to a minority – if not in numbers, at least in terms of power relations. But colonialism can also involve occupying the territory militarily without necessarily settling the country. India under British rule is a prime example. In some cases, colonialism represents a hybrid of military occupation and settlement. The French in Algeria provided an example until the French were forced out after a bloody war. Israel's occupation of the Palestinian territories since 1967 is a hybrid of military occupation, settler colonialism, expulsion, and displacement of the indigenous population. Zionist colonization patterns of Palestine starting in the late nineteenth century and continuing throughout the first half of the twentieth, first under Turkish and later British rule, have their origins in European colonialism, even though no mother country and metropolis to speak of existed. At the outset, military occupation was not involved, although there was collusion with and eventual external sponsorship of Zionist colonization, notably by Britain. In the words of Forman and Kedar, "Thus, at the onset of British rule, official documents attested to an Imperial policy of Jewish colonization, facilitating immigration, land acquisition, settlement, development, and elements of sovereignty. In addition to perceived mutual interests, the British–Zionist relationship was based on a discourse of development and modernization" (Forman and Kedar 2003: 497).

Within the colonialism model, it is possible further to identify internal colonialism, which refers to the exploitation by a dominant settler group (and its descendants) of indigenous people who are co-residents of a geopolitical entity in a post-colonial state, as for example in South Africa, Northern Ireland (Hechter 1975), and Palestine. In his contribution to this volume, David Lyon discusses at length the applicability of the internal colonialism model to Israel/Palestine. He argues that internal colonialism distinguishes between citizen and subject. Israel's control of the West Bank constitutes a form of internal colonialism, since its Palestinian residents are subjects who are territorially controlled by Israel but lack citizenship rights. I have argued elsewhere that Palestinian citizens in Israel are also internally colonized by a political regime that curtails their access to resources (mainly land, but also jobs) and the exercise of full citizenship rights (Peled 2007; Ophir and Azoulay 2005; Zureik 1979). Finally, there is neocolonialism, which involves the use of socio-economic and military power to influence the policies and internal economies of weaker (mainly post-colonial) states without physically and militarily occupying them. Critics point out that present-day rhetoric surrounding globalization conceals a new form of neocolonialism that has become widespread since the latter part of the twentieth century.

Because discussions of colonialism tend to stress its common characteristics regardless of where it takes place, there is a danger of overlooking specific features that are geographically and historically contingent. For example, Israeli colonization of the West Bank for over forty years has gradually evolved to differentiate it from other familiar forms of classical colonialism. As argued by Ariel Handel in this volume, colonization of the West Bank is less a matter of managing the population through a Foucauldian framework of biopolitics, and more a matter of controlling the resources (land, water, and airspace) while neglecting the population. Such a position, which rests on separation between the colonizer and colonized, is also espoused by Neve Gordon:

> For many years, I maintain, the occupation operated according to the colonization principle, by which I mean the attempt to administer the lives of the people and normalize the colonization, while exploiting the territory's resources (in this case land, water, and labour). Over time, a series of structural contradictions undermined the principle and gave way in the mid-1990s to another guiding principle, namely, the separation principle. By *separation* [italics in original] I mean the abandonment of efforts to administer the lives of the colonized population (except for the people living in the seam zones or going through the checkpoints), while insisting on the continued exploitation of nonhuman resources (land and water). The lack of interest in or indifference to the lives of the colonized population that is characteristic of the separation principle accounts for the recent surge in lethal violence.
>
> (Gordon 2008a: xix)

It is important to make the point that this separation and neglect, if indeed it is a neglect, should not be associated with any benign policy of live and let live. I will show in this chapter, as others have written in this volume (Denes; Bowman), that the ultimate objective of the Zionist project is to control and stifle Palestinian life from attaining any sense of normalcy. The situation is akin to adopting necropolitics in managing the Palestinian population (Wolfe 2006).

Until recently, mainstream social science was unanimous in describing Israel as a pioneering, settler-immigrant society that is democratic and has little in common with European settler-colonial ventures. While my intention is not to deal in detail with the debate over whether Israel is or is not a colonial society, it is important for this discussion to shed light on why I (and an increasing number of other writers) think Israel's original settlement policies dating back to the early part of the twentieth century exhibit features that are consonant with those of European-inspired colonial regimes (see Massad 2006). As Glenn Bowman demonstrates in this volume, the ideational manifestation in the shape of Herzlian settler Zionism and its association with European colonialism continue to shape the nature of Israeli policies and treatment of the Palestinians in historical Palestine.

Breaching the consensus

Several writers have breached the once-dominant consensus about the nature of Israel as advanced by Israeli and Western social scientists by situating its formation in the context of colonization and the ensuing conflict with the indigenous Palestinian population. Executing this intellectual reconstruction has not been easy. It was once considered "slanderous," as sociologist Uri Ram (1993) remarked, to associate Zionism in scholarly discourse with colonialism. Or, as expressed more forcefully by historian Ilan Pappe, who personally and professionally suffered as a result of his critical perspective on Zionism, "any reference to Zionism as colonialism is tantamount in the Israeli political discourse to treason and self-hatred" (Pappe 2003: 81).

A key figure in this critical school, one who is associated with the label "post-Zionism," is sociologist Gershon Shafir. In the introduction to his book *Land, Labour and the Origins of the Israeli–Palestinian Conflict, 1882–1914*, he remarked: "I came to the conclusion that, during most of its history, Israeli society is best understood not through the existing inward-looking interpretations but rather in terms of the broader context of Israeli–Palestinian relations" (Shafir 1989: xi). This relationship is to be understood by considering the "appropriateness of the model of European colonization for the Israeli case [which] is due to some structural similarities" (Shafir 1989: 10). Shafir further remarks: "At the outset, Zionism was a variety of Eastern European nationalism, that is, an ethnic movement in search of a state. But at the end of the journey it may be seen more fruitfully as a late instance of European overseas expansion, which had been taking place from the sixteenth through the early twentieth centuries" (Shafir 1989: 8).

For Shafir, though, the crux of initial Zionist colonization of Palestine revolved around the issue of land and labour, and how to implement colonization without exploiting native labour. Neither of these issues – either of land or population – was resolved without ethnic separation, exploitation, and outright dispossession. Eventually the issue of demography came to occupy a central place in Zionist public discourse, and this continues to this day; it was principally manifested in the ethnic cleansing of Palestinians in 1948 by Zionist forces and in preventing the Palestinian refugees from returning to their homes. As Jewish immigration to Palestine increased and voluntary land sales to the settlers remained minuscule, it became clear after 1948 that without confiscation and seizure of land, supported by an ideology that justifies these policies and indeed dehumanizes the indigenous population, the Zionist project could not have attained its objectives. To varying degrees, these policies and practices have been obtained since the early days of Zionist colonization of Palestine.

Gil Eyal (2006: 33–61) offers a different and sympathetic interpretation of Zionism which he sees as imbued with Orientalist rhetoric. In commenting on the works of Said, Shafir, and others, Eyal points out that settler Zionism embodied diverse and even contradictory attitudes towards the Arab population of Palestine – fascination and disgust, superiority and admiration. While not denying the colonialist attitudes of Zionist writers, starting with Herzl, he argues these attitudes reflected the need of Zionist settlers to distance themselves from the native "Oriental" population (both Arab and Jewish of Middle Eastern background) with its "primitive" culture, and establish a separate identity that is also dissociated from the European experience of stigmatizing the Jews. To this reader, such attempts by Eyal to present Zionism as a "hybrid" of multifaceted sentiments does not negate the fact that, except for a minority of binationalists among the settlers, Zionism's ultimate objective has always been to colonize the land and, in the face of Arab opposition, build a separate society fortified by what Vladimir Jabotinsky called an "iron wall" of separation from its Arab neighbours (see Lustick 2008).

In taking issue with such an interpretation, Gabriel Piterberg (2008: 62) argues that Zionism's colonialist character is manifested along three "fundamentals of hegemonic settler narratives":

the alleged uniqueness of the Jewish nation and relentless search for sovereignty in the biblically endowed homeland; the privileging of the consciousness of Zionist settlers at the expense of the colonized, and at the expense of the results of colonization by the settlers rather than their intentions; and the denial of the fact that the presence of the Palestinian Arabs on the land destined for colonization was the single most significant factor that determined the shape taken by the settlers' nation.

Surveillance and colonialism

The colonial gaze

One of the most powerful strategies of imperial dominance is that of surveillance, or observation, because it implies a viewer with an elevated vantage point, it suggests the power to process and understand that which is seen, and it objectifies and interpellates the colonized subject in a way that fixes its identity in relation to the surveyor.

(Ashcroft, Griffiths, and Tiffin 1998: 226)

The gaze metaphor in surveillance studies owes its origin to Jacques Lacan's "mirror stage" theory:

the gaze corresponds to the grande-autre [the process of Othering, whereby the colonizer's self-affirmation and identity construction is configured on the basis of stigmatizing and denigrating the identity of the Other, the colonized] within which the identification, objectification and subjection of the subject are simultaneously enacted: the imperial gaze defines the identity of the subject, objectifies it within the identifying system of power relations and confirms its subalterneity and powerlessness.

(Ashcroft, Griffiths, and Tiffin 1998: 226)

Though Othering is a convenient way of propping up one's ego and power, it is inherently fragile: it must be constantly fed by the illusory inferiority of the Other – and is thus constantly at risk of being discredited. A key feature of surveillance in colonized regions is its racialization of the "native." Yasmeen Abu-Laban and Abigail Bakan in this volume argue that surveillance in Israel/Palestine is distinguished by its racialized context and the asymmetric power relations between the colonizer and colonized in which it operates.

Academic research by social scientists and legal scholars about surveillance and security in Western countries has grown remarkably in the last couple of decades, particularly after the terrorist attacks of 11 September 2001. Yet, among key social science writers on modes of surveillance, states of exception, and securitization, empirical research about colonial and post-colonial regimes – including the Middle East – is scarce. This is peculiar since surveillance and the state of exception, in which the law is suspended for the purpose of ruling indigenous populations and territory, are common features of both colonial and post-colonial zones experiencing ethno-national conflict. The current volume makes an important contribution in this direction. Useful studies of colonial situations bearing on the central role of surveillance have mainly been provided by historians, anthropologists, media, and culture studies scholars. The insights of these researchers provide an important point of departure for our study.

Quotidian and other forms of surveillance

What distinguishes these colonial-cum-surveillance studies is the anchoring of surveillance activities, as essential instruments of ruling, in a quotidian context. Thus in Bayly's (1996) masterful work on India he shows how the gathering of information in pre- and post-colonial India involved not only data about population and territory but information gathered through informal surveillance by astrologers, physicians, marriage brokers, and holy men. Categorization and enumeration of population in pre-colonial India was carried out by local elites, and subsequently modified and implemented by the British for the purpose of ruling and taxation. From the mid-eighteenth century onward the British cultivated "colonial knowledge" that was embedded in a corpus of Orientalist trope. The stereotyping of the Other in Orientalist discourse, in as much as it is a basic staple of colonial knowledge, should not obscure the fact that, as Bayly shows, it is not always successful, and triggers resistance by the colonized. Indeed, the case of India shows how the colonized successfully used the same tools of information dissemination that were applied by the British to control them, notably the print media.

David Spurr (1993) lists twelve discursive modes by which colonial rhetoric constructs the Other. These start with surveillance, followed by appropriation, aestheticization, classification, debasement, negation, and eventually end with resistance. Spurr's list is not all that different from the one provided by Bernard Cohn (1996), who analyses colonial knowledge through six "modalities": historiographic, observational/travel, survey, enumerative, museological, and surveillance. Surveillance is not a one-way process. Mary Louise Pratt takes into account the co-presence of the colonizer and the colonized in a dialectical fashion in the context of the "contact zone," which she defines as "the space of colonial encounters, the space in which peoples geographically and historically separated come into contact with each other and establish ongoing relations, usually involving conditions of coercion, radical inequality, and intractable conflict" (Pratt 1991: 6). She argues for the need to understand how colonizer and colonized are co-constituted through these encounters.

It is significant that the basic tools of surveillance as we know them today (fingerprinting, census-taking, map-making, and panoptic prisons) were refined and implemented in colonial settings, notably by the Dutch in Southeast Asia (Anderson 1991: 164) and the British in India and other colonies. In *Colonizing Egypt*, Timothy Mitchell remarks,

> Foucault's analyses are focused on France and Northern Europe. Perhaps the focus has tended to obscure the colonizing nature of disciplinary power. Yet the panopticon, the model institution whose geometric order and generalized surveillance serve as a motif for this kind of power, was a colonial invention. The panoptic principle was devised on Europe's colonial frontier with the Ottoman

Empire, and examples of the panopticon were built for the most part not in northern Europe, but in places like colonial India.

(Mitchell 1988: 35)

For the British, Simon Cole explains, fingerprinting was "viewed as a tool for colonial governance," and "the system of fingerprinting identification actually emerged in the colonies rather than in England" (Cole 2002: 63, 75). Proponents of fingerprinting as a method of surveillance and sorting of the population into "deviants" and "normal" groups were led by Francis Galton, the British eugenicist and advocate of social Darwinism. It is no coincidence that the impetus for the British to develop a scientific method of population classification further occurred in the wake of the 1858 Sepoy Mutiny in which Hindu and Muslim conscripts rebelled against the British. Taking their cue from the experience in India, the British introduced ID cards in Palestine during the Arab Revolt from 1936 to 1939 as part of their campaign to stave off Palestinian opposition to colonial rule and illegal Zionist immigration (Cohen in this volume; Thomas 2008).

Keeping records, or "ruling by records," as Richard Saumarez Smith (1996) calls it, is a cornerstone of colonialism, as it is for any administrative body. The important distinction in the case of colonialism is that the occupier determines the configuration of land, population, and other forms of record-keeping. In his contribution to this volume, Michael Fischbach captures the constructivist nature of colonial record-keeping for governance:

> Data such as population censuses, tax lists, land records, survey maps, and so forth do not merely dispassionately represent a world – in this case, a population that the state governs – that is "out there" in a pristine, positivistic sense. The processes of sorting, categorizing, and describing help create the very population that is being observed and recorded. This represents not merely the need for simplicity dictated by bureaucratic need, but the wider "imaginings" about the nature of society.

The constructivist aspect of surveillance takes on special meaning in colonial and post-colonial regimes. The recording of census data involves interpretation and construction, according to which censuses and other population data are grouped, sorted, and labelled in ways that reflect the administrative needs of those in power. However, Fischbach notes, the British were not able to rule by records alone, and had to rely on "local knowledge" and the appointment of village leaders who facilitated the collection of population and land data. Fischbach further asks, "The question then becomes, beyond the obvious degree to which data and information helped Britain rule Palestine, did such surveillance transform the basic nature of Arab life in Palestine as a result?" His answer is: "The record would suggest that they did not, not because of any weakness in the transformative power of the data, but because of Palestinian resistance to the Mandate itself and the Zionist project, and because the British need to work with the Palestinians in implementing certain policies forced them to temper their outside, unilateral decision-making."

On the Zionist side, various organizations and individual researchers collected data about Palestinians during the Mandate period. A key organization that compiled maps of Palestine and comprehensive lists of villagers and land holdings for military and settlement purposes was Shai, the intelligence arm of the Hagana. The data compiled were instrumental during the 1948 war and the ensuing expulsion of Palestinians; after the establishment of the state the information was utilized to provide demographic data on the Palestinians who remained in Israel and were subjected to military rule. The relationship between record-keeping and power in the Israeli/Palestinian context remains very much part of Israel's system of control to this day, as recounted by an Israeli activist:

> Who was born and who died and who wants to change address and who wants to get a passport and who wants to go here or there . . . all of this – you have to register . . . in the Civil Administration. One mustn't forget that the entire registration of citizens, including in Gaza, is held by Israel. The one who registers the citizens is the one in control . . . Bureaucracy reigns supreme.
>
> (Quoted in Braverman forthcoming)

The ontology of surveillance and its forms

Fear, risk, and dignity

It is clear that surveillance involves the exercise of power. In the words of Christian Parenti, surveillance is "tied up with the questions of power and political struggle. Not only in the very direct fashion . . . but so too at the level of what Raymond Williams called 'structures of feeling'" (Parenti 2003: 3). As a feature of power, surveillance in everyday life is involved in the constitution of subjectivities at the level of desire, fear, security, trust, and risk – all of which ultimately impact upon human dignity and individual autonomy. But if we consider the meaning of "structures of feeling" in Williams's formulation, the dialectic and tension between consciousness and feelings, on one hand, and lived experience and resistance, on the other, lead us to situate surveillance in a social context and examine the role of agency and community in responding to the challenges of being watched and surveilled, especially by the state.

Following David Lyon, it is broadly accepted that surveillance refers to "the focused, systematic and routine attention to personal details for purposes of influence, management, protection or direction" (Lyon 2007: 14). Personal details usually refer to information of one type or another that nowadays most likely exist in electronic format. The assumption underlying this view of surveillance is that organizations, be they public or private, are engaged foremost in the collection of data for the sake of population management, national security, and financial transactions, among other objectives. In the process, however, there is the danger that the exhaustive collection of personal information might infringe on the privacy of individuals and groups, a major concern in advanced, industrialized countries. In colonial settings such as the occupied territories, on the other hand, exclusion through restrictions on mobility and access to territory, rather than inclusion, guide the rationale for surveillance activities. Israel as an occupying power is less interested in the management of the population (in the Foucauldian sense) than it is in controlling and appropriating the territory on which the population resides. This, however, should not minimize the importance the colonial state attaches to the collection, control, and categorization of population data, as alluded to earlier.

Immediately after 11 September 2001, fear for personal and national security figured prominently in the debate about the war on terror. In fact, according to public opinion data in the West, to question the introduction of intrusive surveillance techniques as a deterrent to terrorism was tantamount to compromising state security (Smith 2006). In time, the public has moved away from unquestioning acceptance of limitations on personal freedom and privacy that were justified through recourse to national security rationale. Yet, so pervasive has the discourse of security-cum-fear become that, according to Mike Davis (2001: 50), "the globalization of fear became a self-fulfilling prophecy." The relationship between fear and the adoption of security policies in the occupied territories is discussed by Freedman (2008). Engin Isin (2004) argues that the literature on fear is trapped in a rational conception of the subject and plays down the role of subjectivities – affect, insecurity, and emotions – which set limits on the rational subject in its liberal and neoliberal construct. He suggests adopting a conception of the individual, the so-called neurotic citizen, whose concern is to reduce risks and uncertainties in order to minimize its own insecurity:

> While on the one hand the neurotic citizen is incited to make social and cultural investments to eliminate various dangers by calibrating its conduct on the basis of its anxieties and insecurities rather than rationalities, it is also invited to consider itself as part of a neurological species and understand itself as an affect structure.
>
> (Isin 2004: 223)

What flows from Isin's comment is that governments are able to rule by capitalizing on citizens' fear, and that surveillance technologies in everyday life are marketed as necessary to reduce fear and risk. The psychological toll of surveillance points to positive correlations between intensive surveillance and feelings of paranoia and psychosis (Kershaw 2008). As Thompson (2002: 100) states, paranoia "is the inevitable result of living with intensive state surveillance." Without burdening the discussion with Freudian and psychoanalytic concepts about human nature and neurosis, most commentators agree that surveillance implies intrusiveness into one's private domain and, indeed, personal autonomy and dignity.

The contributions of Usama Halabi and Ahmad Sa'di in this volume provide clear examples of the invidious role of collaboration and surveillance by the Israeli state in the daily lives of Palestinian citizens. People's livelihoods depend on the extent to which they are willing to collaborate with the authorities in collecting information about their community members. This does not mean that the surveilled individuals are unaware of these activities, as the study by Halabi demonstrates. In the name of security, the right to privacy and personal autonomy is brushed aside by the state when it comes to the Palestinians in Israel.

Privacy and surveillance are usually considered each other's nemesis or, to quote Lucas Introna, they are "co-constitutive" of each other. This makes privacy a requisite to autonomy, for "without privacy there would be no self" (Introna 1997: 269–270). Kupfer (1987: 81–82) argues, "privacy contributes to the formation and persistence of autonomous individuals by providing them with control over whether or not their physical and psychological existence becomes part of another's experience. Just this sort of control is necessary for them to think of themselves as self-determining." The assumption is that the greater the surveillance, the lower the risk factor. Greater privacy requires greater trust, but, paradoxically, surveillance is required to produce trust. According to Richard Ericson and Kevin Haggerty (1997: 117), "Privacy can expand only with trust, but trust can only expand with surveillance." The contingent relationship among surveillance, trust, privacy, and risk must be underscored. Privacy laws are essential in order to regulate the protection of personal information and safeguard against state and other forms of intrusion. These matters become especially problematic in conflict zones where security and risk are correlated in a particular way in the shadow of the state of exception. In Agamben's words, there is a price to be paid by states that are obsessed with security: "Security reasoning entails an essential risk. A state which has security as its only task and source of legitimacy is a fragile organism; it can always be provoked by terrorism to turn itself terroristic" (Agamben 2002: 2).

Forms of surveillance

The theme of state surveillance is highlighted by Anthony Giddens (1987: 206), who singles out two main features. First, surveillance is associated with modernity and the rise of the nation state. This "remote" type of surveillance for administrative purposes involves bureaucratic and technical means such as the electronic codification and storage of information, and cross-referencing with other types of information stored in disparate databases. Second, surveillance is also non-technical and carried out under supervision in which direct, face-to-face contact is utilized for observation and the gathering of personal information. The dialectic between the two forms, which is also acknowledged by Giddens, is described by Christopher Dandeker as "mutually reinforcing," since "the very collection of information normally presupposes a certain capacity to supervise and manage behavior and vice versa" (Dandeker 1990: 39). As shown in several of the contributions to this volume, Israel's control of the Palestinians is all-encompassing, and involves both types of surveillance measure. In referring to Palestinian citizens in Israel, Adriana Kemp says that the "Palestinians stand at the centre of the state's desire for control, discipline, and regulation of the most minute levels of conduct of those who are members of the society and polity, yet do not belong to them" (Kemp 2004: 74; see also Lowrance 2005). With words that echo Foucault's notions of "capillary power" and "microphysics of power," Kemp goes on to identify the essence of the inclusion/exclusion contradiction underlying the logic of governmentality facing the Israeli state. On the one hand, discipline and surveillance are applied systematically and minutely to govern the Palestinian community in Israel, while at the same time the state limits the community's participation in the body politic as active citizens entitled to partake in the definition of the public good. In pursuit of this objective, the Israeli state has deployed surveillance assemblages since its inception sixty years ago. These comprise a collection of hard and soft technologies involving human reporting of information through the use of collaborators and spying on the everyday activities of people that is reminiscent of the East German Stasi (Sivan in Elazari 2006).

Technical surveillance extends from the use of methods such as the electronic recording of information through telephone tapping and intercepting electronic messaging, closed-circuit television, video monitoring, geopositioning systems, radio frequency identification, fingerprinting, genetic testing, DNA analysis, and retinal and facial biometric identification, to the use of less obtrusive measures, such as routine gathering of data on population in the name of governance and administration (e.g., census-taking and survey research). These technologies, which reflect an amalgam of surveillance methods involving Foucauldian "discipline" and Deleuzian "control," as we shall see later, are used by most states in governance and in day-to-day activities at airports, borders, and checkpoints (Ajana 2005: 7). Ultimately, the monitoring, recording, counting, and categorizing of people, referred to as social sorting, affect the identity of individuals and their rights as citizens and colonized subjects.

Giddens argues that there is a correspondence between citizenship rights and surveillance practices in the modern nation state. Based on T.H. Marshall's familiar threefold typology of social, political, and economic rights in the modern nation state, Giddens associates the first with policing, the second with "reflexive monitoring" by the "state's administrative power," and the third with the "management of [economic] production" (Giddens 1987: 206). By linking surveillance to rights, it is possible, according to Giddens, to appreciate the two-sided aspects of surveillance in terms of power generation: it facilitates the administration of people, thus empowering the state and organizations generally. At the same time, however, it provides citizens with certain rights with which to challenge the state. In other words, surveillance is simultaneously enabling and constraining.

Although these forms of surveillance are important, they do not capture the exclusion/inclusion dimensions, and the new demands for additional citizenship rights that are associated with colonialism, globalization (such as multicultural and group rights), and the right of movement, in which surveillance plays a dominant role. Here, the development of national identification cards, and the problems associated with their means of sorting and categorizing populations, is central to understanding the processes of inclusion and exclusion in the allocation of these rights. These forms of surveillance also fail to acknowledge the impact globalization has on the treatment of such vulnerable groups as indigenous people, immigrants, and refugees in terms of their economic, political, and social rights. The march of globalization has primarily heightened the use by Western states of intensive surveillance in order to monitor the allocation of rights and ensure that they are bestowed on rights-bearing citizens as constituted by national and supra-national regimes. In Western countries, the 11 September 2001 attacks in the United States provided further impetus for implementing stricter surveillance methods at a high personal cost to target groups (immigrants, racial groups, Muslims, political activists, etc.) who are at the receiving end of the monitoring process (Webb 2007; Bonikowski 2005).

Case studies of surveillance

If colonial surveillance is a strategy of dominance, how is this accomplished? Here I proceed by listing several key strategies that are a combination of people watching people in a quotidian context and those that involve bureaucracy and the use of surveillance technology. Altogether, I present case studies covering Israel/Palestine in the following areas: the identity problem, silencing of memory, racialized time, bureaucratic and non-technical surveillance, technical surveillance, immobility and destruction of urban space, the checkpoint, biopower, the state of exception, and resistance. I then offer some concluding remarks.

The ever-present identity dilemma

Write down!
I am an Arab
My identity card number is 50,000
I have eight children
The ninth will come after a summer,
Will you be angry?

(Darwish 1964)

Written in prison more than forty years ago, the stanzas in this epigraph are from the well-known poem "Identity Card" by the late Mahmoud Darwish, considered to be the Palestinian national poet. In this poem, Darwish refers to the ID number to remind the police interrogators that he is a citizen of the country and to protest, as the *New York Times* obituary mildly put it, "Israel's desire to overlook the presence of Arabs on its land" (Bronner 2008). From a sociological perspective, however, the poem captures a more encompassing Palestinian experience of displacement and monitoring both inside Israel and outside it. It tells the story of how Palestinians assert their claims of belonging to the land by having large families, continuous majority presence in historical Palestine, and resistance to Israeli policies. The generalized feeling by Palestinians of being watched and surveilled, the central theme of this book, is echoed more recently by historian Rashid Khalidi: "[The] quintessential Palestinian experience . . . takes place at a border, an airport, a checkpoint: in short at any of those modern barriers where identities are checked and verified" (Khalidi 1997: 1).

Current plans to introduce national identity cards in Western countries have triggered heated debates on the grounds that, in the hands of governments, cards carrying personal information could become tools of "ubiquitous surveillance" over people's lives (Bennett and Lyon 2008; Lyon 2008). In colonial and post-colonial countries characterized by histories of foreign occupation and ethnic conflict, the use of national identity cards as markers of group membership predates the current debate about privacy violations and identity theft in Western countries. As pointed out earlier, several writers have analysed how colonial and post-colonial regimes introduced maps, censuses, statistical records, and identity cards as essential ingredients in the project of ruling.

In Israel, mandatory identity cards were introduced in 1949, following the establishment of the state. The ethnic background of citizens comprised the main content of these cards. Sixty years later, over the objections of the Israeli Bar Association (Somfalvi 2008), plans are now under way to replace the old ID cards with biometric ones that will be cross-referenced with existing government databases. The regime of ID cards in the West Bank and Gaza is drastically different from the one used in Israel. The West Bank and Gaza ID cards are the product of three political environments: Israel's administrative and military rule; the Oslo Accords, which transferred the day-to-day running of the territories to the Palestinian Authority, which issued its own identity cards; and the fact that Palestinians living in Israeli-annexed East Jerusalem are governed by a third system according to which Israel issues ID cards to residents that differ from the ID cards issued to its own population within the 1967 borders (Zureik 2001; Abu-Zahra 2008a, 2008b; Kelly 2006; Loewenstein 2006). The ID card emerges as the primary surveillance tool.

Several contributions in this volume address the use of identity cards in both Israel and the occupied territories (e.g., Lyon, Tawil-Souri, Halabi). In his contribution, David Lyon argues that, generally speaking, the rationale for introducing ID cards is twofold: it lies in the state's need for securitization, and it guarantees the allocation of rights and duties to citizens. In the occupied territories ID cards are essential tools in the Israeli matrix of control. They regulate mobility and residency but do not bestow any state rights. For Tawil- Souri, the ID card is an instrument of colonial power: "At every checkpoint exists an under-theorized manifestation of a low-tech, visible, physical and tactile means of power: the ID card." Halabi, who considers the ID card as an instrument of surveillance, notes that, although from 2002 the nationality designation (Arab, Jew, Druze) was removed from the ID cards, other codes have since been instituted. In the case of Israeli citizens, eight coded stars replace the old nationality identification. Palestinian residents of East Jerusalem are issued with ID cards whose serial number starts with the digits "08," while those who reside in the occupied territories are assigned a serial number starting with "09." ID cards are also issued in different colours: ID cards for East Jerusalem are blue, while for Gaza and the West Bank they are orange (although the Palestinian Authority replaced these with blue covers after the Oslo Agreement). A further means of classification concerns those who are of so-called "mixed marriage": the offspring of an East Jerusalemite Palestinian who is married to a non-resident is given a code beginning "086," and as of 2002 the law prohibits family reunification of West Bank and Gaza residents if they marry an Israeli resident and are males under the age of thirty-five or females under twenty-five.

Silencing and suppressing memory

In line with the workings of internal colonialism, the Israeli state implemented a major instrument of surveillance during its first two decades by imposing military rule over the Arab sector. Alina Korn described the system of military rule which lasted until 1967 as follows:

> Various methods of political control were elaborated during the period of the military government and were widely used. These were designated to construct a social reality whereby the military government would be perceived as an "all-seeing, all-knowing body," even when its presence was not always evident. In order to realize this panoptic concept, a ramified network of paid agents and informers was operated. In return for the information and services provided, these agents and informers received privileged treatment. The military government awarded special favors to those who cooperated and enacted sanctions as punishment on those who did not; it employed numerous means of incentives and also pressure, in order to broaden the circle of cooperation.
>
> (Korn 2000: 168)

In addition to the far-reaching consequences of the military government outlined above, the system of surveillance and its imposition of various restrictions contributed to the criminalization of Palestinian citizens of Israel. "The means and forms of surveillance that were applied in order to broaden the political control over the Arab population brought in their wake an over enforcement of the military regulations, and as a result a rise in the convictions rates" (Korn 2000: 170).

The main edifice of surveillance erected by Israel gave rise to various categories of Arab residents. Korn describes this segmentation of the Palestinian population:

> The laws that served to expropriate lands from the Arabs, together with the restrictions on their movements, created several categories of Arab residents with different civil status: Arabs who had fled from their homes during the battles to other places within the boundaries of the State of Israel ("refugees"); Arab inhabitants that had been evacuated from their villages against their will, both during and after the war, to other places within Israel ("evacuees"); legal inhabitants or refugees that had returned legally but had lost their rights over their property because they were absent from their place of residence during the population census carried out in 1948 ("present absentees"); refugees who returned to Israel illegally, of whom some were permitted to remain, and others were refused resident permits ("infiltrators").
>
> (Korn 2000: 173)

The lasting effects of the system of surveillance are borne out by Areej Sabbagh-Khoury's current research on the military government's role in Palestinian life. Based on her interviews, she concluded that, long after the military government had been abolished in 1966, Palestinians continued to be fearful of speaking out against state policies. She remarks that they are like the prisoners in the panopticon: although they do not know whether they are being watched by the guards, they simply assume the worst, refrain from opposition, and largely remain silent (Sabbagh-Khoury forthcoming).

An example of the process of disciplining memory is illustrated by the late Emile Habibi, the Palestinian novelist, member of the Knesset, and political activist, in his classic work of short stories, *The Pessoptimist*. In one of the stories, titled "The Story of the Fish that Understands all Languages," Habibi presents the following dialogue between a mother and her son concerning silencing, as narrated by the son:

> At school you [mother] warned me: be careful in what you say. And when I told you that the teacher is my friend, you whispered as if he could be watching me! And when I heard the story of Tantura [a village near Haifa] whose Palestinian population was expelled by Zionist forces in 1948], I cursed them, and you whispered in my ear: be careful in what you say.
>
> And when I met with my friends to declare a strike, they too told me: be careful in what you say.
>
> In the morning you mother told me that I talk in my sleep, be careful in what you say! And when I hummed tunes in the shower, my father would shout at me: change the tune. The walls have ears, be careful what you say.
>
> (Habibi 2006: 151[1])

In discussing Israeli attempts to stifle the annual Palestinian commemoration of the Nakba, Tamir Sorek, in his contribution to this volume, introduces an important corollary to the current conception of surveillance. He points out that, as currently conceived, surveillance's main purview is the collection of personal data. Such a definition, he argues, is inadequate in accounting for surveillance as a process of memory disciplining and construction at the group level. The crux of his concern is the process of self-disciplining that individuals go through at the level of consciousness in order to avoid punishment and conform to the dictates of the majority. This is a form of panopticon surveillance by which people are aware that what they say and do may be observed constantly, or not at all. At one time the government's secret agents would monitor the Palestinian population. Lately, a shift has occurred whereby disciplining the Palestinian population is carried out through a "civic gaze" of ordinary people accompanied by threats from Jewish politicians to punish Palestinian citizens if they continue to commemorate the Nakba. In stressing discipline over surveillance, Sorek argues, it is possible to account for the disciplining of consciousness and memory – something current surveillance studies focused on behaviour do not address sufficiently.

The controversy surrounding commemoration of the Nakba was brought to the fore most recently when politicians belonging to parties in the right-wing coalition government of Benjamin Nentanyahu demanded that a law be passed to prohibit the Palestinian citizens of Israel from holding any public commemoration related to the Nakba. A second law is being considered that would demand an oath of allegiance by those seeking to obtain an Israeli identity card. The law of allegiance stipulates that Israel is a "Jewish, Zionist and democratic state," something that Palestinian citizens object to because the law overrides the ethnic and national feelings of one-fifth of the population of Israel. It is significant that these moves are being led by the party of Avigdor Lieberan, Israel's foreign minister (Boudreaux 2009; Glickman 2009). Further, the Israeli government approved a bill that would ban state funding of any NGOs that organize events to commemorate the Nakba (Haaretz Service 2009), and the Ministry of Education banned mention of the Nakba in Israeli school books (Black 2009).

Racialized time

> They are stealing our time. Everything takes so long!
>
> (Muna)[2]

One ontological feature that is overlooked in the study of surveillance, especially in colonial settings, is its ability to inject racialism and affect one's mastery and use of time. This is evident in detentions and searches at airports, borders, and checkpoints where monitoring is not carried out strictly in a random fashion, and does not affect all people to the same degree. Reg Whitaker shows in his chapter how citizenship, race, and national origin play important roles in determining who is profiled by Israeli security personnel. Of particular relevance for us is the relationship between surveillance and time use in a colonial context such as Israel/Palestine, which is dealt with in Nurhan Abujidi's chapter. Colonization, anthropologist Julie Peteet points out, extracts its toll from Palestinians along two important dimensions, space and time:

"Palestinian space shrinks, time slows, and mobility is constrained," while the Israeli occupiers, on the other hand, have "freedom of movement and expansion through space and control of time" (Peteet 2008: 14).

Political scientist Amal Jamal introduces the concept of "racialized time" to examine Israel's differential treatment of its Palestinian citizens and those who live in the occupied territories (Jamal 2008). His point of departure is to argue, through recourse to Martin Heidegger's work, that control over one's time is an essential human requisite: it distinguishes humans from animals. Relegating Palestinians to the margins of society by seizing control over their time, Jamal argues, places them in Agamben's state of exception. The Zionist narrative depicts time in the Jewish experience as dynamic and eternal; in the Palestinian one as empty, static, and discontinuous. Moreover, Israeli "Jewish time is distinguished from Palestinian time by adopting methods whose objective is to suppress, block, delay or keep still the flow of Palestinian time" (Jamal 2008: 376). According to Peteet, "In general, colonial regimes tend to fashion the native as occupying a different, timeless and motionless zone, distinct from the settlers' modernity and civilization" (Peteet 2008: 14).

In arguing his case, Jamal borrows from colonial and post-colonial literature (such as Frantz Fanon) in which, relative to the colonizers', native values are depicted as inferior. Israeli control of Palestinian use of time and space is thus legitimized and facilitated by surveillance in the form of closures, checkpoints, the so-called separation wall, restriction on mobility, and land use. This occurred in Israel proper at one time, but more so for the last forty-plus years in the occupied territories. Over the years, international and local human rights organizations and the media have documented numerous cases of mistreatment and humiliation of Palestinians at checkpoints. In addition, Palestinians have been denied the right to seek access to their land, places of employment, and emergency healthcare that at times resulted in death (United Nations Human Rights Council 2008). As pointed out above, of particular significance is the association of time with space in the colonial context, which Jamal sees as having significant repercussions for the quality of life in a global world dominated by advanced technology. If time is emptied of its human meaning and mobility is methodically restricted, how then can the Palestinians partake in the determination of their daily life and benefit from exposure to world cultures? Colonial rule maintains the gaps and hierarchies in the use and valuation of time between rulers and ruled. The Palestinian situation under Israeli rule is a case in point, as demonstrated in the contributions to this volume.

Non-technical and bureaucratic surveillance

Israel has made a name for itself as the invincible spy state by catching sought-after enemies, and has advanced this image as a unique form of state branding. In popular culture and diplomatic circles Israel is presented as a model of how to carry out espionage and cloak-and-dagger operations successfully, and either apprehend or pre-emptively (and sometimes mistakenly) assassinate its enemies. Few outside observers realize that the Israeli surveillance system is also a formidable *domestic* spy enterprise aimed primarily at the Palestinians under its control – in Israel and the occupied territories. To make the state surveillance system as efficient as possible, especially during the early decades, when it confiscated Palestinian land, Israel created an institutional structure that monitored the Palestinian population bureaucratically with the aid of separate divisions in various government departments and agencies (e.g., education, police, military, central bureau of statistics, intelligence agencies, and land registration).

A dominant feature of Israeli surveillance practices has been the use of old-fashioned spy networks embedded in local Arab communities. As will be shown below, these networks relied heavily on Palestinian collaborators and informers whose cooperation with Israel was more the result of personal and economic necessity than any ideological identification with the state. At times of organized dissent and violent opposition to colonial rule, this form of non-technical surveillance (see Zurawski 2005) – people watching people – also relied on special undercover units, the so-called Mista'rivim ("Arab pretenders"), to gather information and liquidate individuals deemed dangerous by the state. There was, of course, no recourse to due process. These units were widely used in the West Bank and Gaza during the first (1987–1993) and second (2000–2004) Palestinian uprisings. And they still are today. On many occasions, starting with the first Intifada, the actions of these units involved extra-judicial killings of Palestinian activists, which resulted in the death of innocent civilians (Zureik and Vitullo 1992). The practice of targeted assassinations continues in a systematic way to this day and is carried out using sophisticated surveillance technologies, such as drones that track down and assassinate Palestinians who appear on Israel's list of wanted people. It is estimated that since September 2000 Israel has assassinated 400 individuals using the extra-judicial techniques of targeted killings (Gordon 2008b). The use of drones for surveillance purposes in the West Bank and Gaza has become a central feature of Israel's targeted assassinations of Palestinian militants (Whitaker 2004; Fisk 2001).

The use of such methods dates back to the pre-state period in the 1940s, if not earlier, when Jewish undercover units operated in Palestine and in neighbouring Arab countries. At the time, these special units (the Palmach) of the fledgling Israeli army (the Hagana) gathered intelligence; engaged in acts of terror and sabotage, if necessary, to spread fear and spur Jewish immigration from Arab countries to Palestine; and countered the activities of Palestinian nationalists who opposed Jewish immigration and the selling of land to Zionist settlers. Initially, local Arabic-speaking Jews and Jews who originated from Arab countries were recruited to these units in the pre-state period (Zvika 1986). After 1948, Israel widened its domestic surveillance networks by recruiting native Palestinian informants and collaborators to gather information about the political activities of fellow Palestinians; this first applied to Palestinian citizens of Israel and was later extended to residents of the West Bank and Gaza (Cohen 2006, 2008).

Before 1948, Zionist surveillance activities centred on gathering political intelligence to secure land purchases in Palestine. Eventually, however, both before and after 1948, surveillance aimed to confront Palestinian violent opposition and frustrate Palestinian nationalism (Cohen 2008). For land acquisitions, the informer's task was to collect information about availability of land and its location, and entice landowners to sell to the Zionists. When it became clear that mounting Palestinian opposition to Zionism could not be contained through political intelligence alone, surveillance tactics changed: the target became information about Palestinian military organizations and guerrilla activities. At times, this information was shared with the British in Palestine.

As part of their opposition to Zionism, Palestinian activists sought to block the flow of information from collaborators to the Zionists through economic boycotts and assassinations of other Palestinians.[3] As Cohen demonstrates in his chapter in this volume, assassinations were also carried out by Jews against other Jews.

In the face of mounting opposition, Hillel Cohen remarks, "the Zionists increasingly used manipulation and financial and material inducements to recruit Arabs" (Cohen 2008: 158). When voluntary land sales dried up (not more than 7 per cent of the land in Palestine had been legally sold through various means to the Zionists by 1948), surveillance methods were developed to locate landowning Palestinians who were in financial distress. Offers would then be made to these individuals: in exchange for payment of their debts, they would sell their land to the Zionists. It would be an understatement to say that such collaboration caused divisions in Palestinian society and weakened its opposition to the Zionist settlers.

In his other book covering the post-1948 period, Hillel Cohen demonstrates the continuity in Israeli surveillance practices between the pre- and post-1948 periods (Cohen 2006). The networks of collaborators established in the pre-state period were subsequently expanded by adding new recruits – including those who had once resisted Israeli policies but found themselves compelled to cooperate in order to secure jobs and other favours from agents of the state. State surveillance agencies particularly sought the cooperation of Palestinian notables and heads of clans in an effort to discredit the overwhelmingly Arab Communist Party. This party, in the early decades of the state, mounted an ideological and organizational campaign to mobilize Palestinian citizens in Israel against the dominant Zionist political parties, and to expose Israeli policies of land confiscation and the military government. The deep involvement of the state security apparatus in civil society in the Arab sector reveals the extent to which the state manipulated the Arab community. Cohen shows how the domestic intelligence service (Shabak) used collaborators to intervene through threats and promises of favours to weaken the Communist Party's hold on Arab voters and strengthen the position of so-called Arab political parties affiliated with the main Zionist parties, particularly Mapai, the ruling labour party at the time. Immediately after independence, Israel took measures to prevent, at all costs, Palestinian refugees from returning to their homes. Here too the state's army of collaborators gathered information about so-called infiltrators, many of whom were killed by the Israeli army, while others were forced to return to the refugee camps.

The state exercised "intimate" bureaucratic surveillance over two additional areas of society: education and local elections. In the former, appointments of teachers were conditional upon approval of the security services, although recently the Ministry of Education has stated that it has removed from its midst the Shin Bet operatives who were responsible for screening Arab teachers for their political orientation (Khromachenko 2006). In the latter, the government continued to rely on traditional Arab social structure by appointing heads of loyal clans to run the affairs of local councils. As Cohen points out, monitoring processes run by the security services were opposed by other Zionist parties who competed for Arab votes, such as the left-wing Mapam (the United Workers Party). Mapam exposed the close connection between the security services and the ruling Mapai Party. It is not uncommon to come across cases of the state security agencies coercing Palestinians to work as collaborators in return for favours. To this day, media reports reveal cases of Palestinians from the occupied territories who are denied access to medical treatment or release from prison unless they cooperate with the Shabak (Reuters 2008; Melmen 2008).

Using archival material, Ahmad Sa'di (2005) traces the role of collaborators in aiding the state in its formative years of selectively incorporating the Palestinian minority through "minimal hegemony." That is to say, Palestinians would be able to exercise a form of citizenship not predicated on acceptance of the state's national goals as dictated by dominant Zionist ideology as long as the Palestinian minority refrained from actively opposing such an ideology. This observation is in line with Korn's (2000: 167–168) findings.

In his contribution to this volume, Sa'di methodically traces the evolution of Israel's methods of control of the Palestinian minority since the state came into being. He shows how, failing in the first decade to transfer or encourage the remaining Palestinian minority to emigrate, it became clear that the state had to devise alternative control methods. These surveillance methods had several dimensions. First, they were bureaucratic in nature and allowed the state to withhold economic and development projects from the Arab sector if its leaders did not cooperate with the state. Second, surveillance led to the ghettoization of the Arab community by breaking up its spatial continuity. By confining the Arabs to geographically designated areas, the state was able to implement its projects of land confiscation. Third, by means of "divide and rule," the Arab community was treated not as a single national unit, but rather as one divided into religious denominations, each of which was treated according to its willingness to cooperate with the state.

Technical surveillance

Israeli state surveillance is not confined to Palestinian citizens; it touches the lives of the Jewish majority as well, although it takes different forms and is not so bound up with nationalistic considerations (Yoaz 2007a; Haaretz Service 2007a; Ilan 2007; Yoaz 2007b; Michael 2007). Until 2004, the Israeli army tapped all outgoing international telephone calls. According to the latest Annual Report of the Association for Civil Rights in Israel (ACRI), "the police conducted 1,128 wiretaps in Israel in 2006 – an increase of 25% over previous years. By way of comparison, 1,839 wiretaps were conducted throughout the United States in 2006" (ACRI 2008). In 2007, the police reported that there were 1,375 wiretap cases in Israel (Ilan 2008a, 2008b; Levy 2008). What is significant about the data, in addition to the disproportionate wiretapping compared to the United States, which has a population fifty times larger than that of Israel, is that the courts in Israel almost automatically approve police requests for wiretaps. Of 400 wiretaps analysed in 2006, only three were not approved by the courts. This led Privacy International, a non-governmental watchdog of privacy practices worldwide, to comment: "[al]though the courts are supposed to weigh privacy concerns against law enforcement needs before authorizing wiretaps, authorization is, in practice, almost automatic upon request" (Privacy International 2007). In that year, of 1,255 police requests for wiretaps, only seven were rejected by the courts, according to the latest report by ACRI (2008: 54). In 2007, the courts refused eleven surveillance requests from the police out of a total of 1,375 wiretap cases (ACRI 2008: 54).

In its worldwide ranking of surveillance societies based on thirteen privacy indicators, Privacy International assigned Israel a score of 2.3 on a scale from 1 to 5

(1 was assigned to countries that practised extensive surveillance, and 5 to those with the least surveillance). Of the thirteen indicators, Israel was found to practise maximum surveillance in two areas: giving police access to personal data, and monitoring travel and trans-border data flows. No doubt as a result of 9/11, Privacy International placed the United States, the United Kingdom, Spain, and Australia in the same category (Privacy International 2007). Since these are aggregate country data, the report does not deal with the differential application of surveillance to specific societal groups, such as minorities. However, based on various reports by human rights organizations, there is no doubt that, when compared to the Jewish population, the Palestinian minority in Israel is subjected to more intensive forms of surveillance.

Political economy

State security arguments are routinely advanced to combat political activism and delegitimize claims made by nationalist and dissident groups. In the name of security, Israel rewards cooperative Palestinian citizens with security clearance to facilitate access to certain jobs, building permits, travel, and the granting of business licences, to name typical sought-after rewards. Meanwhile, it punishes those who are classified as threats to state security. As we have seen above when discussing Sa'di's work, the "carrot and stick" system does not always deliver on its promises. Nevertheless, the surveillance system has far-reaching national implications for Palestinians, beyond day-to-day matters. Journalist Amira Hass (2006) concludes, "The Israeli security services are careful to act within the framework of a clear political paradigm: maximum weakening in every possible way of the Palestinian national collective, so that it will not be able to realize its goal and establish a state worthy of the name, in accordance with international resolutions" (Hass 2006). This has been a dominant attitude of the Zionist security apparatus all along, going back to the time of the British Mandate: namely, to frustrate the national aspirations of the Palestinians (Cohen 2008: 267).

The rising obsession with security and surveillance in the West following the events of 11 September 2001 gave Israel an opening to present itself to the outside world as a successful model of a security state that is also democratic in the Western tradition. Israel seized the opportunity and marketed itself globally not only as a practitioner of surveillance but as an important global player in providing expertise that was second to none based on experience and the production and deployment of surveillance-related software and hardware. As the chapter by Whitaker in this volume demonstrates, although behavioural profiling is advanced by Israel as the "golden standard" for successful risk management against terrorism at airports, the genesis of this approach in a specific national and ethnic conflict between Israel and the Palestinians must be considered before it is adopted by other countries, together with its discriminatory consequences for human rights.

According to one estimate, 350 companies in Israel are involved in the manufacture of homeland security products (Klein 2007: 515). According to the US government, more than 400 Israeli companies are involved in the export of security-related products, with a turnover of $4.5 billion for 2007. The value of the exports reached $1.2 billion in 2007, an increase of 20 per cent from the previous year (US Department of Commerce 2009).

If Israeli state branding is traditionally associated with tourism, as the site of the Holy Land, and is portrayed as the natural home for the Jewish people worldwide, in the aftermath of 11 September 2001 Israel has emerged as a major supplier of military and security products. In the words of Naomi Klein (2009), Israel is a "twenty-four-hour-a-day showroom" which has managed "to turn endless war into a brand asset."

Israel plays an increasingly important role in the globalization of surveillance technologies, as documented by the chapters by Nick Denes and Neve Gordon in this volume about the political economy of Israel's defence industries. Israel's far-flung involvement in the production and sale of homeland security and surveillance technologies worldwide has catapulted it to a leading position among producers of such technologies. With a population of a mere seven million, Denes claims, Israel is among the five largest weapons exporters, and accounts for 10 per cent of global weapons sales; 80 per cent of its weapon production is geared for export, in contrast to the US, where exports account for only 20 per cent of military sales. Israel, known for the manufacture of sophisticated drones, controls 70 per cent of the market in unmanned aerial vehicles (UAVs), and is a world leader in border surveillance technologies, such as sensors, fences, and electro-optical applications designed to operate in the dark. These technologies have not only military but civilian applications (see Gordon in this volume).

The political economy of Israel's high-tech sector and its associated surveillance and homeland security industries, according to Gordon, is due to several factors. First, the close collaboration between the military and the industrial sector is reflected in the fact that close to half of senior officers in this sector have security-related backgrounds, a phenomenon that is unique to Israel. Second, Israel is able to capitalize on its "laboratory experience" by demonstrating the use of these technologies in its ongoing conflict with Palestinians and its Arab neighbours. Third, the close alliance between Israel and the United States has opened huge markets for Israeli products in the United States itself and Europe, as well as India and China.

With a special focus on UAVs, Denes shows that the "Zionist experience" greatly helped Israel to become a major player in the manufacture and export of weapons. This experience translates into ideological indoctrination at various levels of society, particularly in schools and the military, in which Israel is depicted as a survivalist state destined to bring an end to years of exile and persecution of the Jewish people. Israeli institutions have also successfully nourished Zionism's special attention to technology and science as requisites of successful modernization and colonization. Finally, Israel's Spartan image as a beleaguered state in perpetual war with its enemies has legitimized the claims made to external weapons customers that it has a "battlefield laboratory" unmatched anywhere else in the world.

Thus it is not surprising to see various efforts by the government and private sectors to market Israel as a unique country in terms of its hands-on experience with security policies and security products on account of its ongoing conflict with its neighbours. To cite just two such examples, consider the campaign mounted by the Israeli government to forge homeland security agreements with the United States and Canada (for Canada, see Kilibarda 2008). Spearheading the efforts to sign these agreements is Avi Dichter, previous chief of Israel's domestic spy agency, the Shin Bet, and one-time Minister of Public Security in the Kadima government (Stoil 2007a, 2007b).[4]

The publicly released agreement between Israel and Canada reads like a template for bilateral administrative agreements, although it is not clear where, how, or when Canada shared with Israel the security problems highlighted in the agreement. If anything, Israel's foreign spy agency (Mossad) has twice abused its international diplomatic prerogative. First, in 1997, it provided its operatives with Canadian passports to use in a botched assassination plot against a Hamas official in Jordan. Second, in 2004, New Zealand officials discovered that Mossad was using fraudulent passports and other documents in order to conceal the identity of its operatives. Most recently, in January 2010, Israel used fake European passports to carry out a cloak-and-dagger assassination of a Hamas leader in Dubai. Among the areas of cooperation mentioned in the Canada–Israel agreement are border management and security involving the use of biometric technology, tracking of money laundering, illegal immigration, and other areas of mutual interest. These areas, the agreement stipulates, will be facilitated through the sharing of information and expertise, research, discussion of public safety issues, and exchange of technical information, including education, training, and exercises, among others. The agreement concluded by noting that "this declaration is not intended to create legally binding obligations, under either domestic or international law" (Government of Canada 2008).

It is important to elaborate on the implications of this statement. Although this is simply an administrative agreement and as such is not legally binding, the two governments remain theoretically bound by international law in its implementation. Some would argue that the implementation of these administrative agreements is a new means to create global governance. The fact remains, however, that the agreements are not subject to accountability by elected representatives of the countries concerned. Critics have pointed out that the Canada–US Smart Card Agreement is similarly undemocratic because it is not accountable for abuse.[5]

In the case of the United States, the Department of Homeland Security has chosen a subsidiary of an Israeli security company with operations in the US "to supply technology to identity threats, to deter and prevent crossings, and to apprehend intruders along the US borders with Canada and Mexico" (Wordpress 2007). Also, the extent of Israeli involvement in US security affairs involves collaboration with individual states. According to the American Israel Public Affairs Committee (AIPAC), the premier American lobby organization on behalf of Israel, "more than 30 states have traveled to Israel to learn counter-terrorism techniques as well as homeland security preparedness and response practices" (AIPAC 2006). Individual agreements have been signed with Israel by the states of Maryland and Illinois.

Immobility and destruction of urban space

For the sociologist Max Weber, the state was distinguished by its monopoly over the legitimate means of violence, and for Karl Marx through its monopoly over the means of production. For John Torpey (1998), the globalized state now seems to be moving in the direction of exercising monopoly over the movement of people. Lyon suggests adding a fourth dimension – monopoly over the "means of identification" – to the threefold typology of monopolization of control. This entails exercising control in determining and checking personal identity claims (Lyon 2008: 122–123). As will be demonstrated below, the colonial conditions in Palestine create specific circumstances

in which mobility restriction is only one component of an elaborate system of surveillance, and cannot be understood by appealing to civilian and other bodies that
regulate the international movement of people.

A sociologically informed theorization of surveillance in the context of globalization
is undertaken by the sociologist Ronen Shamir in which he refers, by way of an
example, to Israeli practices in the occupied territories. Shamir's focus is an attempt
at "theorizing the translation of the paradigm of suspicion into actual technological
screening designed to police the mobility of those social elements that are deemed to
belong to suspicious social categories" (Shamir 2005: 197). Adriana Kemp makes a
related point, with particular focus on the Palestinian minority in Israel, when she
says, "the constitution of the Palestinian minority as a dangerous population has been
the result of a coupling between the national goals of the dominant ethnic group and
the constant preoccupation of the disciplinary state with population management and
surveillance" (Kemp 2004: 74). An interesting feature of Kemp's analysis shows how
the Israeli state, by using national security arguments, "constituted" its Palestinian
minority from the outset through management of territory and population by means
of a legal system that, although couched in universal, non-discriminatory language,
has sanctioned a state-authorized surveillance system aimed primarily at defining the
Palestinians as a dangerous minority.

While he does not state it in precisely these words, Shamir's (2005: 197) focus on
"biosocial profiling as an increasingly dominant technology of intervention" fits with
Gilles Deleuze's claim that we are witnessing a paradigm shift from Foucault's
"disciplinary society" to "societies of control" (Deleuze 1992). Societies of control are
characterized by technology-assisted digitization and conversion of the body into
binary codes. With the influx of refugees, immigrants, and displaced people, population management is facilitated by technologies that contribute to biosocial profiling.
Smart identity cards and biometrics, among others, are examples of such technologies
of social sorting and categorization.

A substantial and empirically focused analysis of Israeli surveillance of the
Palestinians in the occupied territories using speciality is provided by the architect
Eyal Weizman. In *Hollow Land: Israel's Architecture of Occupation* (Weizman 2007b), which
was preceded by *A Civilian Occupation* (Segal and Weizman 2003) and a series of articles
on the *Politics of Verticality* (Weizman 2002), Weizman describes in detail Israel's (civilian
and military) control of the movement of people in the West Bank; the development
of the landscape through zoning and building of settlements; the state's monopoly
over water resources; control of the airspace; and allocation of the electromagnetic
spectrum. As he says, these form parts of Israel's panoply of surveillance measures that
also encompasses "electronic techniques of demarcation, population control, identity
cards, inspection, currency control" (Weizman 2007b: 288) among others. What
distinguishes the occupation of the West Bank from traditional forms of colonization,
according to Weizman, is not the ideology of occupation itself, which is still driven by
a desire to dispossess the Palestinians and suppress their national aspirations, but the
forms of its implementation, its architectural contours, and the contradictions that
arise therein. The central point that underlies Weizman's work relates to his notion
of contradiction. The relationship between state power and Israel's settlement policies
is not to be understood as one-to-one correspondence, with the former determining
the latter. The relationship between space and power "is responding to many and

diffused forces and influences; space is the product of conflicting interests" (Weizman 2007a).

Using a postmodern idiom – "structured chaos," "improvisation," and "plastic geography" – Weizman describes the fields in which the various actors are involved in the contest over space. He argues that the coexistence of direct discipline and indirect forms of control no longer fits the theoretical narrative that presupposes an evolution from "disciplinary societies" to "control societies" (see Ajana 2005: 7). While it is prudent to go beyond Foucault's binary framework of power that juxtaposes the spectacle of the pre-modern against the disciplinary power of the modern, the colonial and racialized specificity of Palestine (and undoubtedly other colonial and post-colonial settings) calls for yet another amendment to this binary system. In the words of Achille Mbembe, "Late-modern colonial occupation differs in many ways from early-modern occupation, particularly in its combining of the disciplinary, the biopolitical, and the necropolitical. The most accomplished form of necropower is the contemporary colonial occupation of Palestine" (Mbembe 2003: 27).[6]

As another example of spaciality, I offer the research carried out by Haim Yacobi, who deployed Foucault's metaphor, itself derived from Jeremy Bentham's panopticon, to analyse what he calls "urban panopticism" in the city of Lod, an Arab–Jewish mixed city that witnessed a significant Palestinian population expulsion in 1948, and subsequent segregation between the Palestinian and Jewish parts of the city. Segregation is explained as an outcome of urban planning designed to retain power in the hands of the majority. According to Yacobi, "[t]he built environment in Lod cannot be seen as merely a technical division of organizing space. Rather, similar to other cultural representations it expresses, produces and reproduces power relations" (Yacobi 2004: 62).

The basic premise of this approach is to view the production of space as part of a control project that defines space in accordance with a political agenda. In this sense Yacobi took his cues from Weizman, who described the planning agenda of settlements in the West Bank as follows:

> These settlements are constructed according to a geometric system that unites the effectiveness of sight with spatial order, producing "panoptic fortresses," generating gazes to many different ends. Control – in the overlooking of Arab towns and villages – in the overlooking of main traffic arteries; self-defence – in the overlooking of the immediate surroundings and approach roads. Settlements could be seen as urban optical devices for surveillance and the exercise of power.
> (Cited in Yacobi 2004: 57–58)

A fourth example relates to the process of what Stephen Graham (2003) calls urbicide (the planned destruction of urban areas: cities and infrastructure), which refers to urban warfare in the West Bank but is equally applicable to Gaza, as documented in the latest invasion of the Strip in December 2008. An important outcome of this research is to demonstrate that military technologies of surveillance are making their way into urban settings, thus blurring the division between civilian and military sectors. However, during times of conflict – whether in Iraq, Afghanistan, or Palestine – Third World regions present an "unclean" urban terrain of guerrilla warfare in which regular armies find it difficult to operate (see Gregory 2007). According to Graham,

"Palestinian cities are portrayed as potentially impenetrable, unknowable spaces which challenge the three-dimensional gaze of the IDF's [Israel Defence Forces'] high-technology surveillance systems and lie beyond much of its heavy-duty weaponry" (Graham 2003: 70).

It is significant that Israel's brutal urban warfare strategies in Palestinian cities and refugee camps, as well as in Lebanon, have influenced American urban warfare in Iraq. In his contribution to this volume, Graham demonstrates the close connection between Israel and the United States in this regard, so much so that during Israel's major incursion in the sprawling refugee camp of Jenin in 2002, which has been condemned by international human rights organizations, American military personnel were reportedly present to observe the Israeli operation first hand. There have also been reports that the Israeli military visited the US to train the Americans, and were in Iraq to observe American conduct of urban warfare. Thus, Graham remarks in this volume, the "Israeli military and security experience in addressing these purported imperatives – as the ultimate surveillance-security state – is rapidly being exported around the world." The Israeli impact goes beyond American mimicking of Israeli urban warfare tactics to include an ideological component reflected in the "war on terror" campaign of the last Bush administration, and pre-emptive war and targeted assassinations which have been condemned by human rights organizations and experts in international law. The upshot of this, according to Graham (this volume), has been the "Palestinianization of Iraq," which "involved the various Iraqi insurgencies and militias directly imitating the tactics of Hamas or Hezbollah as well as the US military directly imitating the IDF."

Using the city of Nablus as a site for her research, Abujidi (this volume) explores the physical and socio-political structures that form parts of Israel's colonization of the West Bank. The matrix of surveillance involves curfews, regulating the use of public spaces, violating private spaces such as the home, imposed confinement, and temporary and arbitrary occupier's laws. Altogether these measures reflect what one author has called an attempt at "colonization of the mind" (Jamoul 2004). Through interviews with Nablus residents, Abujidi describes the development of daily resistance tactics rooted in counter-knowledge, commemoration, and schooling.

Glenn Bowman uses the metaphor of encystations and entombment to describe the encircling of the Palestinian populations of Bethlehem, Qalqilya, and Tulkarem by the "security wall," which has had the effect of cutting them off from the rest of Palestine. He points out that the wall's objective is to put the Palestinians beyond the sight and reach of the Israeli Jewish population, and ensure that the newly built system of bypass roads will be reserved exclusively for settler use. The encirclement of the Palestinians put the "surrounding social body at risk" (Bowman 2003: 129). The wall itself has required the expropriation of 10 per cent of Palestinian land. Bearing in mind that the West Bank and Gaza constituted 28 per cent of the area of Mandated Palestine, land expropriation for roads, the wall, and above all new settlements is expected to reduce the size of the Palestinian enclaves to no more that 45 per cent of the area of the West Bank, which is almost 15 per cent of the area of historical Palestine. The larger effects of quarantining the Palestinian population is to make life socially and economically unbearable and cause their emigration, mainly to Jordan. At one time, this was Ariel Sharon's preferred transfer solution, in line with his previous statement that "Jordan is Palestine."

I offer two further examples that, while not cast in the language of surveillance as such, illustrate the use of the census for population control and categorization. First is the study by Anat Leibler (2004; Leibler and Breslau 2005), who analyses the "co-production" (in Bruno Latour's constructivist terminology) of the first Israeli census. Leibler describes this activity, involving the government and the Israeli Census Bureau, as leading to the creation of a new category of citizens, the so-called "present absentees." These are Palestinian citizens of Israel who were subjected to a curfew at the time of census-taking and were not enumerated *in situ* in the first census. As such they were present in the country but absent from their homes during the census-taking. Although they are citizens, to this day they are prevented from returning to their original homes and live in localities that are unrecognized by the government.

Second, my own work on census construction shows biopolitics in action and explores Israel's monitoring of Palestinian population growth and movement in the West Bank and Gaza (Zureik 2001; see also Wilkins 2004). Pursuant to several clauses in the Oslo Agreement, Israel gained control over entry and exit in the occupied territories, registry of births and deaths, and residency rights. The topic of demography is central to the debate over Israeli–Palestinian relations. For example, allowing the return of Palestinian refugees to their homes in what is now Israel is opposed by the Israeli authorities on the ground that it poses an "existential threat" to the Jewish character of the state.

The checkpoint

The publication of the picture below caused controversy in Israel, where officials dismissed suggestions that the image of the Israeli soldiers was reminiscent of those of German soldiers during World War Two, who forced their Jewish victims to play instruments before they perished in the concentration camps. They were also quick to condemn the behaviour of the soldiers as boorish, and to blame the event on inexperience. Without drawing any false analogy between 1940s Germany and Israel in the 2000s, the fact remains that the checkpoints are emblematic of Israeli colonization of the West Bank. Quoting from Azmi Bishara's *Checkpoints* (2006), Weizman (2007b) remarks that Israel is best described as the "state of the checkpoints," the occupied territories are the "land of the checkpoints," the Israelis the "owners of the checkpoints," and the Palestinians "the people of the land of the checkpoints." For

Figure 1.1 A soldier checks a man's documents as he plays the violin

Source: BBC

Palestinians, the border/checkpoint is the most visible signifier of their condition in the occupied territories.[7] The movement of close to 2.5 million people in the West Bank is subjected to tight military control; encounters with soldiers at checkpoints are thus etched into Palestinians' daily experience. This does not take into account the 1.5 million Palestinians who live under constant military siege in Gaza. In excess of 600 checkpoints of various kinds, including temporary and "flying" checkpoints, have been erected in the West Bank, and there is no proof, according to a recent report by the United Nations Office of the Coordination of Humanitarian Affairs, which monitors the roadblocks, that they have been reduced in number, as the Israeli military claims (Amr 2008). Anthropologist Rema Hammami described her experience as a commuter from Jerusalem to Bir Zeit University, where she teaches, as follows:

> More commonly, soldiers would drop in at the checkpoint for a few hours, to toy with the droves of walking commuters, stopping all – or a select few – for interminable identity and baggage checks. As often, they would "organize" the drivers and peddlers by ramming their vans or stands with their jeeps. Over three years at the Sudra checkpoint, three Palestinians were shot to death by the Israeli military, another two died in accidents among the crush of vans, at least one man died of a heart attack as he was wheeled across a stretcher, two babies were born behind a rubble mound and untold numbers of young men were beaten by soldiers, often in full public view. No one has counted the numbers of injured at the demonstrations staged in futile attempts to clear the checkpoint away.
>
> (Hammami 2004: 27)

In this example, which focuses on what Pratt (1991) calls the "contact zone" between colonizer and colonized, Hammami argues that in the absence of leadership-inspired resistance, the daily encounters with Israeli soldiers forged the emergence of "public spaces" and "civic resistance" at the checkpoints. While this resistance is collectively understood, it is individually practised. Checkpoints and closures not only have devastating effects on the economy of the occupied region but rupture the flow of social relations and curtail access to education. Filling the void of organized mass resistance, Hammami focuses in this ethnographic study on the taxi drivers of minivans whose "thuggish" behaviour matched the "thuggish" behaviour of the Israeli soldiers at the checkpoints, though with a few notable exceptions. Van drivers expressed resistance by devising alternate routes to avoid military roadblocks when transporting their passengers. When soldiers blocked travel by vans, Palestinians resorted to more primitive means of transportation, such as the horse and buggy. Between the drivers and the porters of the horse and buggy, close to 500 people were eking out a living on any given day in the midst of the checkpoint chaos. Further, food vendors and other service providers also worked at the checkpoints.

Risk, uncertainty, and dehumanization

It is at the checkpoint that identity claims are checked and verified. Identity documents are a far cry from ironclad proof of one's identity; rather, they are contested texts that are subject to decisions and interpretations made by border officials on behalf of the state. Anthropologist Tobias Kelly put it aptly with his claim that "documents produce

legibility and illegibility, stability and instability, and coherence and incoherence"
(Kelly 2006: 90). It is precisely because of the unstable nature of official documents
that fear and uncertainty "penetrate the lives of Palestinians." In computerized
bureaucracies identity exists in the form of "data doubles" (Lyon 2003), in which the
persona of the individual resides in numerous databases, and where the physical and
legal presences of the identity holder are subject to different official interpretations.
For example, Kelly's case study of a village in the West Bank describes how, upon
reaching a checkpoint, the passengers of the van in which he was travelling and who
had foreign passports were let through by the Israeli soldiers, with one exception: a
traveller with a distinctly Arab name who carried a Venezuelan passport. Like the van
drivers described by Hammami, here too the passenger used a circuitous route through
olive orchards to reach his home.

Several researchers have noted the capricious behaviour of soldiers at checkpoints.
The main rationale behind this type of behaviour is to introduce uncertainty and
confusion in the mind of the surveilled. Kelly recorded his observations as follows:

> The level and type of enforcement of checkpoints shifted from day to day and
> hour to hour. Sometimes the soldiers would only let people with PNA (Palestinian
> National Authority) identity cards through and sometimes only those with Israeli
> identity cards and foreign passports. Sometimes only women were let through,
> and sometimes nobody. Occasionally the checkpoint was open all day, and at
> other times closed in the afternoon. Often no cars would be allowed through and
> people would have to pass on foot. At other times the soldiers would not let people
> pass through the checkpoint at all but would allow them to walk over the hill in
> full view. These constant shifts meant that when approaching a checkpoint, it was
> never entirely clear whether a person, even one with normally "valid" identity
> papers, would be allowed through, turned back, or detained at the side of the
> road. Much depended on the individual soldier.
>
> (Kelly 2006: 100)

Uncertainties, in turn, produce apprehension and fear among Palestinians, who never
know what to expect at a checkpoint. The reduction of such uncertainties is, to some
extent, a performative act on the part of the surveilled:

> Indications of legal status were not just restricted to documents but could also be
> produced through bodily performances. People would try to dress, talk, or walk
> in ways that they imagined would pass them off as Israeli citizens in the eyes of
> soldiers at checkpoints. In this way, legal status, whether embedded in bodies or
> documents, was brought to the front of their interaction with Israeli soldiers,
> obscuring other aspects of their subjectivity that might prevent them from passing
> through. Although identity documents were part of a system that tried to restrict
> movement, they also created opportunities for people to pass, both through the
> checkpoint and as something other than a potentially threatening Palestinian.
>
> (Kelly 2006: 99)

Kelly concludes by noting that "[a]lthough identity documents may be introduced as
part of wider 'security' measures, they produce insecurity" for the identity holder (Kelly
2006: 104).

For legal scholar Irus Braverman, the checkpoints constitute "liminal national spaces," thus accentuating uncertainty and enhancing state surveillance. If liminality is intended to signify a transitional state of being between, the experience at the checkpoint, Braverman demonstrates, is anything but transitional or temporary. Its uncertainty extends both in time and space: "[e]ventually, the prolonged state of liminality is extended to such degree that the Palestinian comes to embody it and thus carry it with him wherever he goes" (Braverman forthcoming). The main features of the newly constructed checkpoint terminals that resemble international crossing points are their claims of modernization. By modernizing the checkpoints and relying heavily on technology (e.g., through the use of scanners and sensor machines, biometric cards, advanced computer systems, turnstiles, and the deployment of private security guards in place of soldiers), Israel projects a humanizing image of its treatment of the Palestinians. Braverman draws upon Bruno Latour's (1987) actor network theory by looking at the constellation of humans and non-humans as a network in the exercise of surveillance at the checkpoints:

> In fact, the intensified utilization of things – in effect, the *de-humanization* of the border – also translates into a project of *dehumanizing* the Palestinians at the border. Through the utilization of nonhuman things at the border, Israel's move from de-humanization to dehumanization – namely, its attempt for civilization – is made to seem not only necessary, scientific, and neutral, but also positive and progressive.
>
> (Braverman forthcoming; italics in original)

The officials claim that the modernized checkpoints no longer reflect the sort of chaos Hammami reported, but Braverman asserts that this is not the case. The upshot of the transformation of the checkpoint is that the technology that appears to be neutral and scientific removes elements of discretion at a very high cost to the Palestinian users:

> In one case an Israeli officer points to the metal fences situated on the top of turnstiles to ensure that Palestinians cannot cut the queue from above. Just the other day, [the same officer continues], a Palestinian was nonetheless crushed from the pressure between the entrance to the queue, on the one hand, and the turnstile, on the other hand, and broke one of his ribs as a result. The physical technology of the turnstile, presented by Israel as decreasing human friction and promoting orderliness, thus ends up increasing other forms of friction and enhancing chaos. What Israel claims to be humanitarian in policy and design, in practice dehumanizes the Palestinian.
>
> (Braverman forthcoming)

Furthermore, she states with regard to the uncertainty that "feeds into Israel's apparatus of occupation":

> This sort of dissonance between performances is everywhere: in the outside signs welcoming the passengers and wishing them good health that are surrounded by heaps of trash and debris; in the inside signs blinking "have a pleasant stay" in a

familiar red, yet obscured by thick layers of bars and fences; and in the twelve new booths installed to serve passengers, of which only four are regularly operative. The general design of the place thus sends conflicting messages: you are a customer and as such we are here to serve you better, but you are at the same time also dangerous and living under occupation.

(Braverman forthcoming)

Biopower, refugee camps, and the politics of death

We the Palestinians are terrorists and therefore anything they do to us is legitimate. We are treated as *homo sacer* – to whom the laws of the rest of humanity do not apply.

(Shehadeh 2003: 95)

Although occupation is associated with all kinds of deprivations in daily life, the sixty-year-old refugee camp is, according to Azoulay and Ophir (2004), "not simply where Palestinians have been gathered; it is rather the space in which their existence is constantly being reduced to 'bare life.'" Azmi Bishara (2004) describes the maze of walls, barriers, gates, observation towers, barbed wire, and electrical wires slicing through villages and other inhabited areas of the West Bank as tantamount to the "recreation of the detention camp where the exception becomes the rule . . . and the state of emergency becomes permanent." It is not surprising to see several authors refer to Agamben in their discussions of the situation facing Palestinian refugees. In Agamben's work, and in Hannah Arendt's before him, the twentieth-century refugee symbolized, on the one hand, the most vulnerable person under the aegis of the nation state, and, on the other (for Arendt), the "vanguard" of a people whose identity in the twentieth century was shattered following the wars of Europe. Arendt's analysis, according to Agamben, invites us "to abandon without misgivings the basic concepts in which we have represented political subjects up to now (man and citizen with their rights, but also the sovereign people, the worker, etc.) and to reconstruct our political philosophy beginning with this unique figure [the refugee]" (Agamben n.d.). Refugee camps and refugeehood epitomize the state of exception in conflict zones. Here Palestinian refugees live outside juridical law but inside the spaces controlled by the sovereign who controls the law. To quote Agamben, "[h]e who has been banned is not, in fact, simply set outside the law and made indifferent to it, but rather *abandoned* by it, that is, exposed and threatened on the threshold in which life and law, outside and inside, become indistinguishable" (Agamben 1998: 28; italics in original). Thus bare life reflects the objectification and commodification of life where individuals are stripped of their dignity and personhood (Edkins 2008).

This is true not only of life in the West Bank and Gaza, which is controlled and directly monitored by Israel. Palestinian refugees experience this in varying degrees in other places of dispersal (such as Lebanon, Jordan and Syria), and anywhere else where they live under close surveillance by the host governments, whether in camps or outside the camps, and by the United Nations Agency for Refugees. The upshot of this, according to T.J. Demos, who echoes Agamben, is that

[t]he nation-state is the very power uniquely authorized to suspend law when it sees fit, creating a state of emergency – that zone of indeterminacy between law

and non-law that opens a space for extrajudicial brutality (e.g., torture and executions) – that is now threatening to become the rule. In reality Palestinians already exist in the shadow of the nation-state, precariously inhabiting Israel's seemingly permanent state of exception.

(Demos 2006: 79)

After Hamas won the majority of seats in the internationally supervised national Palestinian elections in 2007, Israel tightened its grip on the occupied territories and embarked on a systematic policy of cutting the flow of funds and drastically reducing food supply and other essentials to Gaza (where most of the Hamas leadership resides) – all in the name of fighting terror. Dov Weissglasse, Israel's point man in advising successive Israeli prime ministers on policy towards the Palestinians, described the choking off of the food supply and other essential goods to Gaza's population of 1.2 million people as akin to a diet regime. He quipped, "it is like an appointment with a dietician. The Palestinians will get a lot thinner, but won't die" (cited in Levy 2006). A discussion of the impact of this siege on Palestinian life in Gaza is provided by several commentators and human rights organizations (see Waugh 2008).

Palestinian refugee life has witnessed a disproportionate share of massacres and calamities, all of which are carried out under the supervision of one nation state or another. The vulnerability of Palestinian refugees in their bare life was brought into sharp relief during Israel's invasion of Lebanon in 1982, and the ensuing Sabra and Shatilla refugee camp massacres near Beirut. These massacres were perpetrated by the Christian Phalange militias, but with the full knowledge of the occupying Israeli army under the command of Ariel Sharon, Israel's defence minister at the time.[8]

Exception to the state of exception?

As a deeply divided society that is fundamentally characterized by Jewish/Arab cleavages, and whose military government has occupied the West Bank and Gaza for more than forty years and subjected its own Palestinian citizens to state of emergency laws from 1948 to 1966, Israel has developed into a laboratory of social control and population management on both sides of the Green Line. In the name of security, it is an example of a surveillance state *par excellence* or, to use Yehuda Shenhav's words, "is in a constant state of exception" (Shenhav 2006; see also Lentin 2008: 63–115). But it is not clear how far one can apply Agamben's state of exception analogy to Israel.

It is not surprising, however, that there is a great deal of interest in the applicability of Agamben's framework to Israel. In the course of attempting this alignment, several criticisms have been voiced. One criticism of Agamben's work is that he presents a passive, totalizing view of the oppressed. Nowhere do we see the colonized reacting in voice or in action to their subjugated existence (Lentin 2008: 1–22). A related cautionary note is sounded by Weizman, who questions the applicability of Agamben's binary framework regarding state of exception and argues that characterizing the West Bank and Gaza, indeed Israel itself, as primarily in a state of exception potentially obscures the complex assemblages of actors involved in contesting methods of social control, including surveillance practices (Weizman 2007a). This becomes even more apparent in discussions of patterns of resistance to surveillance. Furthermore,

Agamben's work lacks any reference to gender, particularly the role of women and how they are targeted for systemic violence in national conflict situations (Lentin 2006).

Ilan Pappe provides a different and more encompassing criticism of the applicability of Agamben's framework to Israel. This critical assessment of Agamben is shared by Abu-Laban and Bakan in their chapter in this volume (see also Ghanim 2008; Lentin 2008). Pappe argues that Israel is not a state of exception but a "state of oppression" as far as the indigenous Palestinian population is concerned. He labels this the "state of the Mukhabarat" ("intelligence state" in Arabic). Following Agamben's argument, to say it is a state of exception is to subscribe to the notion that Israel is (was) a democracy for all of its citizens and gradually has become undemocratic. Three conditions characterize a state of exception: "changes in sovereignty, amendments of constitutions and transformations on the ground, based on new legislation or de-legislation" (Pappe 2008: 155). According to Pappe, none of these prevails in the case of Israel.

With regard to the first point, Pappe points out there has been no real transition in power from the legislature to the executive, as was the case in Germany's state of exception with the rise of Hitler. In its treatment of the Palestinians, "[t]he state rests on its power to oppress – regardless of whether the power lies with the government or the parliament" (Pappe 2008: 156). The distinction between the sovereign (exec-utive) and parliament is meaningless in the case of Israel, as far as the Palestinian *homo sacre* is concerned. Their bare life is disconnected from any transition and slide to undemocratic practices. The majority Jewish population is not affected by any changes in sovereignty and the presence of Palestinian "bare life." Furthermore, "as Jewish citizens of Israel, we are disinterested in this debate, since we accept the state's racist ideological infrastructure and trust it to disallow any legal or real parallels between 'us' and 'them,' the oppressed Palestinians" (Pappe 2008: 156).

The second requirement for a state of exception to exist is when the citizenry is unaware of the diminution in the system of checks and balances governing the functioning of the government. In the case of Israel, Pappe argues, "the Israeli state of oppression [of Palestinians] is noticed, acknowledged and welcomed by its Jewish citizens who leave it in the hands of the political elite to vacillate between *de facto* and *de jure* acknowledgement" (Pappe 2008: 157). Only when the dilution in the system of checks and balances begins to affect the Jewish majority does Agamben's model of state of exception become relevant to the Israeli case.

Finally, the overarching Zionist framework of the state from the outset is designed to dispossess and oppress the Palestinians, according to Pappe. Thus, the model of state of exception fails in its applicability to the Israeli case due to the fact that, being a colonial state, from its inception Israel embodied certain laws and rules that are *sui generis* anti-democratic in their impact on the Palestinian population. Prime examples of this are the Emergency Regulations, which date back to the time of the British Mandate and are still on the books, and the Israeli Law of Return. Here Pappe concludes that Israel is an exception to the state of exception:

> The integration of these abuses of power, law and sovereignty into the ideology of a colonizing regime is beyond Agamben's discursive and analytical framework. And these elements that are basically racist and colonialist and not the outcome of a collapsing republic or democracy are far more sustainable as facts of life.

They remain so pervasive in the lives of citizens not because of laws, their interpretation or even their abuse, but because of the way the State of Israel came into being, and due to an element that is totally absent from the paradigm of the state of exception: the hegemony of the security apparatuses.

(Pappe 2008: 159)

Resistance to surveillance

Issues

No discussion of surveillance is complete without reference to counter-surveillance, dissimulation, resistance, and critical assessment of privacy legislation designed to regulate and protect the flow of information in both public and private sectors. Surveillance practices should also be weighed in terms of social justice issues and how these affect citizenship, human rights, individual autonomy, and mobility across and within borders. It is worth mentioning in this regard the place of human rights and non-governmental organizations in monitoring state activities as a form of counter-surveillance. These are crucial issues in conflict zones of the type we are concerned with, where there is extensive state surveillance of one form or another (as noted earlier) and suspension of the law, as is the fact that Israeli discourse on privacy protection is underdeveloped and fairly recent. The lack of adequate privacy protection on the internet is noteworthy, since the internet, a means of communication and major tool of both mobilization of social movements and government surveillance in most countries, registers the highest rate of diffusion in Israel compared to other countries in the region.

Below, I offer several issues to consider when thinking about researching resistance to surveillance in a colonial setting like Israel/Palestine. This will be followed by case studies of resistance to surveillance in the occupied Palestinian territories.

First, generally speaking, mainstream literature on surveillance is not as plentiful on the resistance as it is on the surveillance side. Literature on resistance is mostly theoretical; the empirical side, in addition to being largely anecdotal, tends to be Western based. In Western societies writings about counter-surveillance have focused on the role of non-governmental organizations in building privacy-advocacy groups; the introduction of legislation to protect against government and private sector intrusion into the private lives of individuals; and understanding the use of sophisticated technologies in rendering the identity of individuals transparent. (In most cases these individuals are unaware that their identity is being tracked through myriad governmental and private databases.) Even in open societies, individuals must be persistent and technologically savvy to learn how various private and public bodies collect and store information about them. Further obstacles bar those who seek to understand how this information is used and attempt to devise means to ensure privacy protection.

Second, surveillance is contextual. In discussing resistance to surveillance, one must be aware, as far as possible, of who is being surveilled, when and where the surveillance is taking place, who is carrying it out, and with what effect. It is one thing to talk about countering surveillance in Western countries, where there is legal (though not necessarily constitutional) recourse to privacy protection. It is a different story entirely to discuss surveillance in a colonized region under military occupation, such as the West Bank and Gaza. There, surveillance is racialized and carried out as part of a larger control mechanism whose details are cloaked in secrecy and whose practice is carried out in the name of national security.

Third, the conception of privacy in Western writings is individually based and conceived as the right of the individual to be left alone. The debate on privacy in Western scholarship anchors its intellectual roots in individualism. This presents methodological problems in devising means of documenting surveillance practices directed at a national group engaged in national struggle on a daily basis. In a collectivist, third world society such as Palestine, it is an unknown luxury to access – let alone enforce – non-existent privacy protection laws. It is almost superficial to talk about privacy violations in isolation from what is going on in the rest of society, particularly when the population is subjected to wide-ranging forms of collective punishments involving, as we have seen, dispossession, deprivation, and even death.

Fourth, researching counter-surveillance in Palestine requires researching collective forms of resistance. This is not to ignore the fact that surveillance also affects individuals *qua* individuals. It is the individual cases that come to light through occasional media reporting – such as spying, humiliations at checkpoint, and the targeting of individuals for extrajudicial assassinations – that bring to light the national dimensions of surveillance. In other words, surveillance in zones that are riddled with ethnic and national conflict must be considered an integral part of the system of domination. In the case of Palestinians this is the Israeli state occupation apparatus in the territories and a parallel system of close monitoring in Israel itself. Further, it would be theoretically unjustifiable to look in an isolated fashion for individual privacy violations as proof of surveillance.

Fifth, defining what constitutes resistance goes beyond acts aimed at thwarting and opposing individual surveillance. It also includes national and group actions of resistance. Resistance to surveillance is part and parcel of the panoply of resistance tactics used by the Palestinians. Resistance must be understood in its quotidian, everyday aspects, which may not appear, at first glance, to be acts of resistance at all. Whether it is the checkpoint, the wall, the prison, closures, or other forms of surveillance, it is clear that in the face of asymmetrical power relations and the might of the Israeli occupying forces, military and violent acts of resistance will be met with crushing responses, and will prove unproductive, as the disproportional ratio of Palestinian to Israeli deaths during the last eight years shows. The turn to analysing everyday acts of resistance proved a productive undertaking. Anthropologists and ethnographers have resorted to documenting ethnographies of resistance to reveal the nuances of how people cope, resist, and adapt to their circumstances.

Case studies of resistance

Besides the discussions of resistance in chapters in this volume, I have chosen three ethnographic case studies involving resistance to demonstrate how Palestinians adapt, survive, "get used to" their circumstances, and "get by" while living under occupation. The underlying methodological orientation of these anthropological perspectives is to reveal patterns of resistance that are part of everyday life but may not be detected or labelled as resistance by others. Lori Allen parts ways with Foucault's position that "[t]he existence of power relationships depends on a multiplicity of points of resistance which are present everywhere in the power network. Resistances are the old terms in relations of power: they are inscribed in the latter as irreducible opposite" (Foucault 1979: 95–96). She argues that if "power [and resistance – in original] is everywhere then it can be nowhere" (Allen 2008: 460). Such an expanded definition of power and resistance, Allen claims, is unable to reveal agency's liminal position: it is neither submissive nor confrontational; resistance is neither military nor organized on a mass basis. Thus she notes how Palestinians consider their sumud (steadfastness on the land) as an act of resistance:

> Palestinians sometimes called these practices "sumud," a nationalistically inflected form of stoicism. In these conditions where the routine and assumptions of daily life are physically disrupted, purposefully and as part of the political program of Israeli colonialism, everyday life in Palestine – in its everydayness – is itself partly the result of concerted, collective production. There is something beyond political motives and awareness that inspire the incorporation of disorder into a quotidian order, however. The necessities of survival, and the physical and psychological capacities that people have to learn and adapt to sustain themselves in changing circumstances also feed into a kind of agency that is no doubt quite prevalent in situations of ongoing violence, but that scholars have yet to adequately explore.
>
> (Allen 2008: 456–457)

Like Allen, who was critical of Foucault's conceptualization of power, Julie Peteet examines resistance through the cultural prism of "ritual performances." In a series of perceptive articles, she provides theoretical insights on space, place, culture, and identity as possible sites and resources of mobilization for dealing with both ontological insecurity (what she calls lack of trust) and the production of resistance in the lives of Palestinian refugees:

> Resistance to exile itself and resistance to the legal designation "refugees" are central motifs of Palestinian exile culture. Resistance as an analytic concept is a point of entry to understanding these refugee communities. They insist on specific connection between space, place, culture and identity. Yet this connection between a time and a place in the past and contemporary struggles to return to it should not gloss over the experience of exile itself, which also evinces a clear connection between place, space, and culture. Palestinians are desirous of a specific territorialization of place, space, culture and power, one rooted in the past but oriented toward the future. Reterritorialization is only conceivable through resistance and empowerment.
>
> (Peteet 1995: 171)

Peteet's subaltern research about Palestinian refugees in Lebanon shows that the discourse which portrays refugees as hapless and dependent individuals is rejected by them in favour of a discourse of resistance in which refugeehood is replaced with the refugees' call for their "right of return" to their homeland. But resistance is not only discursive but performative. In an article devoted to the torture of male Palestinian prisoners in Israeli jails, Peteet approaches the body not as "site of a text, a site of inscription," in Foucault 's sense, but as an active and creative subject that challenges asymmetrical power relations and makes history. For Palestinian male prisoners, torture and its inscription of the body undergoes a reversal in the meaning intended by the Israelis. It becomes a "rite of passage into manhood":

> Mobility, safety, and daily routine are out of the control of Palestinians under occupation. Occupation is a daily shared experience that is subject to continuous questioning and widespread rejection. A prominent mode of embedding the power of the dominant group is to beat, daily and publicly, Palestinian male bodies. Like monarchal spectacles of public torture, the public beating, widespread during the Intifada, is a representation of the power of the occupier, encoding and conveying a message about the consequences of oppositional expressions and practices.
>
> (Peteet 1994: 33)

As her interviews with Palestinian ex-prisoners – all of whom are working-class "subaltern youths" – reveal, the torture produced the opposite effect. The body became a site for "transformation and empowerment, not humiliation and pacification," and "[t]hese experiences have been construed as rites of passage into manhood, with its attendant status and responsibilities, and concomitantly as vehicles of entry and, to a large extent, initiation into underground political leadership. For the community under occupation, the signs inscribed on the individual bodies were read as a collective assault and a commentary on suffering" (Peteet 1994: 33). Contra Foucault, punishment, beatings and torture of Palestinians remain public spectacles. In response to the first Intifada, in January 1988 Defence Minister Yitzhak Rabin ordered his troops to use "might, power, and beatings" to "break the bones" of Palestinians. The public actions of soldiers who were captured on camera and broadcast worldwide triggered condemnation. The use of the camera as an instrument of dissimulation and counter-surveillance made headlines more recently, too, when an Israeli special unit's deadly activities on the West Bank were captured by a Palestinian on a camera provided by B'Tselem, the Israeli human rights organization (A. Lyon 2008).

Finally, Iris Kline-Jean adds to the repertoire of everyday resistance a discussion of nationalism that is localized and at the micro-level. Her point of departure is that the suspension of everyday life is a "form of resistance" manifest in a "duplex political initiative." At one level resistance emerged as an outcome of the "nationalizing efficacy of ordinary people's daily exercises of neighborhood, household, kinship, and self" (Kline-Jean 2001: 83). On another level, that self-nationalization, which rejected the accounts of the elites, managed to remain congruent with the national objectives.

Concluding remarks

I have approached the subject of researching the Palestinians under Israeli control from a new angle by situating the position of the Palestinians within the emerging fields of surveillance studies and biopolitics. Treating the Palestinians as an object of Israeli surveillance, whether in Israel proper or the occupied territories, clearly raises theoretical, methodological, and empirical issues. At the theoretical level, the *mainstream* literature on surveillance does not address colonial and post-colonial regions. I pointed out that the current debate in the surveillance literature is based on Western scholarship, and tends to be Eurocentric. The concept of surveillance, as used in this study, stresses the management of population and territory, including both technical and non-technical aspects. I have outlined how the Israeli state manipulated the Palestinian minority in its midst by deploying an array of spy networks and collaborators who served the interests of the state by providing information about the political activities of fellow Palestinians. In contrast to the focus of surveillance research in the West, I did not deal with topics such as identity theft, credit card fraud, and consumption, issues that are of great interest to Western researchers. The scarcity of publicly available data on the use of high technology for surveillance purposes (such as biometrics, RFID, and data mining) made the task of incorporating these in the current study difficult. I did provide some publicly available data on telephone tapping, but this refers to the state as a whole and does not single out the Palestinians. I also provided anecdotal and isolated cases of privacy violations, such as searches at airports, borders, and checkpoints.

In relation to the critical – but understudied – topic of resistance to surveillance, I have summarized some ethnographic studies by anthropologists of everyday surveillance to show how crucial and promising these studies are. From a theoretical angle, the chapter draws attention to the need to rethink the use of Agamben and Foucault in the context of Israel/Palestine, and find ways to augment their important insights to capture the specificities of surveillance in a colonial zone.

Finally, but not least, there is a need to widen the scope of empirical research in this area for two reasons. First, the situation of the Palestinians under Israeli control, whether in Israel proper or the occupied territories, calls for bringing into sharper relief that gambit of control exercised by Israel, including the use of discursive and other means of surveillance in the area of biopolitics. Second, Israel being, as it is, a surveillance state *par excellence*, it behooves us to include Israel/Palestine in mainstream surveillance studies, so as to expand current research from its Eurocentric focus to incorporate colonial and post-colonial zones. To this end, this book makes an important contribution.

Notes

1 Translation from the original Arabic is by the author.
2 A Palestinian in the West Bank who was interviewed by anthropologist Julie Peteet (Peteet 2008: 15).
3 For a discussion of extrajudicial killings of Palestinians by Palestinians in the occupied territories, see Be'er and Jawad (1995).
4 It is interesting to note that in December 2007 Dichter had to cancel a trip to Britain for fear he would be arrested and prosecuted for war crimes. Dichter was also in the news recently for a gun attack directed at him as he led a Canadian group on a tour of the outskirts of Gaza (Harel 2008).
5 The author is grateful to Professor Art Cockfield at Queen's University Law School for clarifying this point.
6 A similar point is made by Derek Gregory (2004) and, along similar lines, Honida Ghanim (2008).
7 The experience with borders and checkpoints is not confined to the OPT. It extends to the rest of the Arab world, where Palestinian refugees took shelter after their 1948 dispersal. This is clearly depicted in Palestinian literature, poetry, paintings, and, most recently,

cinematic art. A classic Palestinian novella of this genre is Ghassan Kanafani's *Men in the Sun*, which portrays the tragic experience of three Palestinians who were smuggled in an empty water tank of a truck on their way to Kuwait, and perished in the scorching heat of the sun at the Kuwait/Iraq border while the guards were interrogating the driver. See also his translated other works, where the theme of refugees and exile dominates: *Palestine's Children: Returning to Haifa and Other Stories*. A poignant film that focuses on the checkpoints – Elia Suleiman's *Divine Intervention* (2002) – was nominated for an Oscar and won an award at the Cannes film festival.

8   The Israeli official report, known as *Report of the Commission of Inquiry into the Events of the Refugee Camps in Beirut – 8 February 1983*, laid "indirect responsibility" on Ariel Sharon for making it possible for the Phalange units to enter the camps and massacre hundreds of refugees. The Appendix of the report remains classified to this day. For a contrary view, which lays the blame squarely on the Israeli government, and in particular Sharon, see MacBride (1983).

Bibliography

Abunimah, A. (2009) *Anti-Arab Racism and Incitement*, Palestine Center Information Brief, No. 161. Online. Available HTTP: <http://www.thejerusalemfund.org/ht/display/ContentDetails/i/2242/displaytype/raw> (accessed 25 March 2009).

Abu-Zahra, N. (2008a) "Identity Cards and Coercion in Palestine," in R. Pain and S.J. Smith (eds) *Fear: Critical Geopolitics and Everyday Life*, Burlington, VT: Ashgate.

—— (2008b) "IDs and Territory: Population Control for Resource Expropriation," in D. Cowen and E. Gilbert (eds) *War, Citizenship, Territory*, New York and London: Routledge.

Agamben, G. (1998) *Homo Sacer: Sovereign Power and Bare Life*, Stanford, CA: Stanford University Press.

—— (2002) "Security and Terror," *Theory and Event*, 5(4): 2.

—— (n.d.) "Georgio Agamben on Hannah Arendt's 'We Refugees.'" Online. Available HTTP: <http://roundtable.kein.org/node/399> (accessed 11 August 2009).

Ajana, B. (2005) "Surveillance and Biopolitics," *Electronic Journal of Sociology*. Online. Available HTTP: <http://www.sociology.org/content/2005/tier1/ajana_biopolitics.pdf> (accessed 10 August 2009).

Allen, L. (2008) "Getting by the Occupation: How Violence Became Normal during the Second Palestinian Intifada," *Cultural Anthropology*, 23(3): 453–487.

American Public Affairs Committee (AIPAC) (2006) "United States Looks to Israel for Homeland Security Expertise," Issue Brief, 6 December.

Amr, W. (2008) "UN Says Israel's West Bank Roadblocks Increasing," *Reuters*, 30 September. Online. Available HTTP: <http://uk.reuters.com> (accessed 30 September 2008).

Anderson, B. (1991) *Imagined Communities. Reflections on the Origins and Spread of Nationalism*, London and New York: Verso.

Ashcroft, B., Griffiths, G. and Tiffin, H. (1998) *Post-Colonial Studies: The Key Concepts*, London and New York: Routledge.

Association of Civil Rights in Israel (ACRI) (2008) *The State of Human Rights in Israel and the Occupied Territories, Annual Report 2007*, Jerusalem: ACRI.

Azoulay, Y. (2007) "Civilians from the Military Firms to be Trained to Operate Flying Drones," *Haaretz*, 26 December.

Azoulay, A. and Ophir, A. (2004) "On the Verge of Catastrophe," paper delivered to the Politics of Humanitarianism in the Occupied Territories Conference, Van Leer Institute, Jerusalem, 20–21 April.

BBC (2004) "Israel Army Forces Violin Recital." Online. Available HTTP: <http://news.bbc.co.uk/2/hi/middle_east/4043299.stm> (accessed 4 Februray 2010).

Bayly, C.A. (1996) *Empire and Information: Intelligence Gathering and Social Communication in India, 1780–1870*, Cambridge: Cambridge University Press.

Be'er, Y. and Jawad, S. (1995) *Collaboration in the Occupied Territories: Human Rights Abuses and Violations,* Jerusalem: B'Tselem.

Bennett, C. and Lyon, D. (eds) (2008) *Playing the Identity Card,* London and New York: Routledge.

Bishara, A. (2004) "A Short History of Apartheid," *Al-Ahram,* 8–14 January.

—— (2006) *Checkpoints: Fragments of a Story,* Tel Aviv: Babel Press [Hebrew].

Black, I. (2009) "1948 No Catastrophe Says Israel, as Term Nakba Banned from Arab Children's Textbooks," *Guardian.* Online. Available HTTP: <http://www.guardian.co.uk> (accessed 22 January 2009).

Bonikowski, B. (2005) "Flying while Arab (or was it Moslem? Or Middle Eastern?): A Theoretical Analysis of Racial Profiling after September 11th," *The Discourse of Sociological Practice,* 7(1–2): 315–328.

Boudreaux, R. (2009) "Israeli Legislation Raises Issue of Loyalty," *Los Angeles Times,* 26 May.

Bowman, G. (2003) "Israel's Wall and the Logic of Encystation: Sovereignty Exception or Wild Sovereignty?," *European Journal of Anthropology,* 50: 127–136.

Braverman, I. (forthcoming). "Civilized Borders: A Study of Israel's New Border Regime," *Antipode: A Radical Journal of Geography.*

Bronner, E. (2008) "Mahmoud Darwish, Leading Palestinian Poet, Is Dead at 67," *New York Times.* Online. Available HTTP: <http://www.nytimes.com/2008/08/11/world/middle east/11darwish.html> (accessed 11 August 2008).

Cohen, H. (2006) *Good Arabs: The Israeli Security Services and the Israeli Arabs,* Yerushalayim: Keter 'Ivrit [Hebrew].

—— (2008) *The Army of Shadows,* Berkeley: University of California Press.

Cohen, R. (2009) "Clinton's Mideast Pirouette," *New York Times,* 27 April. Online. Available HTTP: <http://www.nytimes.com/2009/04/27/opinion/27iht-edcohen.html?ref=global home> (accessed 10 August 2009).

Cohn, B.S. (1996) *Colonialism and Its Forms of Knowledge: The British in India,* Princeton, NJ: Princeton University Press.

Cole, S. (2002) *Suspect Identities: A History of Fingerprinting and Criminal Identification,* Cambridge, MA: Harvard University Press.

Dandeker, C. (1990) *Surveillance, Power, and Modernity: Bureaucracy and Discipline from 1700 to the Present Day,* New York: St Martin's Press.

Darwish, M. (1964) "Identity Card." Online. Available HTTP: <http://electronic intifada.net/v2/article9754.shtml> (accessed 19 July 2010).

Davis, M. (2001) "The Flames of New York," *New Left Review,* November/December: 34–50.

Deleuze, G. (1992) "Postscript on the Societies of Control," *October,* 59: 3–7.

Demos, T.J. (2006) "Life Full of Holes," *The Grey Room,* 24: 72–87.

Edkins, J. (2008) "Biopolitics, Communication and Global Governance," *Review of International Studies,* 34: 211–232.

Elazari, J. (2006) "Filmmaker: Israel Regime Like East German Stasi." Online. Available HTTP: <http://www.ynetnews.com> (accessed 11 December 2006).

Ericson, R.V. and Haggerty, K.D. (1997) *Policing the Risk Society,* Toronto and Buffalo: University of Toronto Press.

Eyal, Gil. (2006) *The Disenchantment of the Orient: Expertise in Arab Affairs and the Israeli State,* Stanford, CA: Stanford University Press.

Fisk, R. (2001) "Death by Remote Control as Hit Squads Return," *Independent,* 13 April.

Forman, G. and Kedar, A. (2003) "Colonialism, Colonization, and Law in Mandate Palestine: The Zor al-Zarqa and Barrat Qisarya Land Dispute in Historical Perspective," *Theoretical Inquiries in Law,* 49: 491–530.

Foucault, M. (1979) *Discipline and Punish: The Birth of the Prison,* New York: Vintage Books.

Freedman, S. (2008) "Culture of Fear," *Guardian,* 22 June. Online. Available HTTP: <http://www.guardian.co.uk/commentisfree/2008/jun/22/israelandthepalestinians.fear> (accessed 19 August 2009).

Fulghum, D.A. and Wall, R. (2002) "Israel Refocuses on Urban Warfare," *Aviation Week and Space Technology*, 13 May.

Gerber, H. (2003) "Zionism, Orientalism, and the Palestinians," *Journal of Palestine Studies*, 33(1): 23–41.

Ghanim, H. (2008) "Thanatopolitics: The Case of the Colonial Occupation in Palestine," in R. Lentin (ed.) *Thinking Palestine*, London: Zed Books.

Giddens, A. (1987) *The Nation-State and Violence*, Berkeley: University of California Press.

Glickman, A. (2009) "Ministerial Committee: Ban Nakba Day." Online. Available HTTP: <http://www.ynetnews.com> (accessed 24 June 2009).

Gordon, N. (2008a) *Israel's Occupation*, Berkeley: University of California Press.

—— (2008b) "Shadow Plays," *The Nation*, 24 March.

—— (2009) "Avigdor Lieberamn, Israel's Shame," *Guardian*, 25 March. Online. Available HTTP: <http://www.guardian.co.uk> (accessed 25 March 2009).

Government of Canada (2008) "Canada and Israel Sign Declaration to Cooperate on Public Safety". Online. Available HTTP: <http://www.publicsafety.gc.ca/media/nr/2008/nr 20080323-eng.aspx> (accessed 12 August 2009).

Graham, S. (2003) "Lessons in Urbicide," *New Left Review*, January–February: 63–78.

Gregory, D. (2004) "Palestine and the War on Terror," *Comparative Studies of South Asia, Africa and the Middle East*, 24(1): 185–198.

—— (2007) *The Colonial Present*, Oxford: Blackwell.

Haaretz Service (2007a) "A Major Invasion of Privacy" [editorial], *Haaretz*, 19 December.

—— (2007b) "IDF Facility Tapped all Calls from Israel to Abroad until 2004," *Haaretz*, 4 February.

—— (2008) "IDF Troops Film Themselves Humiliating Bound Palestinians." Online. Available HTTP: <http://www.haaretz.com> (accessed 7 October 2008).

—— (2009) "Ministers Okay Bill to Ban Funding of Nakba Events." Online. Available HTTP: <http://www.haaretz.com> (accessed 19 July 2009).

Habibi, E. (2006 [1974]) *The Secret Life of Saeed, the Ill-Fated Pessoptimist*, Haifa: Arabesque Publishing House [Arabic].

Hammami, R. (2004) "On the Importance of Thugs: The Moral Economy of a Checkpoint," *Middle East Report*, 231: 26–34.

Harel, A. (2008) "Qassam Rocket Fired from Gaza Strip Lands Near Ashkelon," *Haaretz*. Online. Available HTTP: <http://www.haaretz.com/hasen/spages/971823.html> (accessed 12 August 2009).

Hass, A. (2006) "In the Name of Security, but Not for Its Sake," *Haaretz*, 20 September.

Hechter, M. (1975) *Internal Colonialism: The Celtic Fringe in British National Development, 1536–1966*, London: Routledge and Kegan Paul.

Hertzl, T. (1997) *The Jewish State (1896)*, Northvale, NJ: Jason Aronson.

Higgs, E. (2001) "The Rise of the Information State: The Development of Central State Surveillance of the Citizens in England, 1500–2000," *The Journal of Historical Sociology*, 14(2): 175–197.

Ilan, S. (2007) "Knesset Okays Establishment of 'Big Brother' Database for Police," *Haaretz*, 18 December. Online. Available HTTP: <http://www.haaretz.com/hasen/objects/pages/ PrintArticleEn.jhtml? itemNo=935812> (accessed 19 July 2010).

—— (2008a) "Police Wiretaps Climb Sharply in Peripheral Areas," *Haaretz*, 18 June. Online. Available HTTP: <http://www.haaretz.com/hasen/objects/pages/PrintArticleEn.jhtml? itemNo=984365> (accessed 19 July 2010).

—— (2008b) "Under 'Big Brother Law,' Telecom Firms Would Tell All to Police," *Haaretz*, 14 August. Online. Available HTTP: >http://www.haaretz.com/print-edition/news/ under-big-brother-law-telecom-firms-would-tell-all-to-police-1.251864> (accessed 10 August 2010).

—— (2009) "Plans to Introduce Biometric IDs Stirs Privacy Debate," *Haaretz*, 13 March. Online. Available HTTP: <http://www.haaretz.com/hasen/objects/pages/PrintArticle En.jhtml?itemNo=1070793> (accessed 19 July 2010).

Introna, L.D. (1997) "Privacy and the Computer: Why We Need Privacy in the Information Society," *Metaphilosophy*, 28(3): 259–275.

Isin, E.F. (2004) "The Neurotic Citizen," *Citizenship Studies*, 8(3): 217–235.

Isin, E.F. and Turner, B.S. (2007) "Investigating Citizenship: An Agenda for Citizenship Studies," *Citizenship Studies*, 11(1): 5–17.

Jamal, A. (2008) "On the Troubles of Racialized Time," in Y. Shenhav and Y. Yona (eds) *Racism in Israel,* Jerusalem: Van Leer Institute and Hakibutz Ha-Meuhad [Hebrew].

Jamoul, L. (2004) "Palestine: In Search of Dignity," *Antipode*, 36(4): 581–595.

Kanafani, G. (2000) *Palestine's Children: Returning to Haifa and Other Stories* (trans. Barbara Harlow and Karen E. Riley), Boulder, CO: Lynn Rienner.

Kelly, T. (2006) "Documented Lives: Fear and the Uncertainties of Law during the Second Palestinian Intifada," *Journal of the Royal Anthropological Society*, 12: 89–107.

Kemp, A. (2004) "'Dangerous Populations': State, Territoriality and the Constitution of National Minorities," in J. Migdal (ed.) *Boundaries and Belonging: States and Societies in the Struggle to Shape Identities and Local Practices*, Cambridge: Cambridge University Press.

Kershaw, S. (2008) "Culture of Surveillance May Contribute to Delusional Condition," *International Herald Tribune*, 29 August.

Khalidi, R. (1997) *Palestinian Identity: The Construction of Modern National Consciousness*, New York: Columbia University Press.

Khromachenko, Y. (2006) "Shin Bet Will No Longer Scrutinize Arab Educators" *Haaretz*, 6 January.

Kilibarda, K. (2008) *Canadian and Israeli Defense – Industrial and Homeland Security Ties: An Analysis*. Online. Available HTTP: <http://www.surveillanceproject.org/files/Canadian%20and %20Israeli%20Defense%20Industrial%20and%20Homeland%20Security%20Ties.pdf> (accessed 12 August 2009).

Klein, N. (2007) *The Shock Doctrine: The Rise of Disaster Capitalism*, Toronto: Alfred A. Knopf.

—— (2009 [2007]) "Laboratory for a Fortressed World," *The Nation*, February. Online. Available HTTP: <http://www.naomiklein.org/articles/2007/06/laboratory-fortressed-world> (accessed 10 August 2010).

Kline-Jean, I. (2001) "Nationalism and Resistance: The Two Faces of Everyday Activism in Palestine during the Intifada," *Cultural Anthropology*, 16(1): 83–126.

Korn, A. (2000) "Military G|overnment, Political Control and Crime: The Case of Israeli Arabs," *Crime, Law & Social Change*, 34(2): 159–182.

Kupfer, J. (1987) "Privacy, Autonomy, and the Self-Concept," *American Philosophical Quarterly*, 24(1): 81–89.

Latour, B. (1987) *Science in Action: How to Follow Scientists and Engineers through Society*, Cambridge, MA: Harvard University Press.

Leibler, A. (2004) "Statistician's Ambition: Governmentality, Modernity and National Legibility," *Israel Studies*, 9(2): 121–149.

Leibler, A. and Breslau, D. (2005) "The Uncounted Citizenship: Citizenship and Exclusion in the Israeli Census of 1984," *Ethnic and Racial Studies*, 28(5): 880–902.

Lentin, R. (2006) "*Femina Sacra*: Gendered Memory and Political Violence," *Women Studies International Forum*, 29: 463–73.

—— (ed.) (2008) *Thinking Palestine*, London and New York: Zed Press.

Levy, G. (2006) "As the Hamas Team Laughs," *Haaretz*, 22 February.

—— (2008) "Stop Watching, Big Brother," *Haaretz*, 7 August. Online. Available HTTP: <http://www.haaretz.com/hasen/spages/1009392.html> (accessed 12 January 2010).

Loewenstein, J. (2006) "Identity and Movement Control in the OPT," *Forced Migration*, 26: 24–26.

Lowrance, S. (2005) "Being Palestinian in Israel: Identity, Protest, and Political Exclusion," *Comparative Studies of South Asia, Africa and the Middle East*, 25(2): 487–499.

Lustick, I. (2008) "Abandoning the Iron Wall: Israel and 'the Middle East Muck,'" *Middle East Policy*, 15(3): 30–56.

Lyon, A. (2008) "Reuters North American News Service." Online. Available HTTP: <http://www.kibush.co.il/show_file.asp?num=28637> (accessed 20 August 2008).

Lyon, D. (2003) "Surveillance as Social Sorting: Computer Codes and Mobile Bodies," in D. Lyon (ed.) *Surveillance as Social Sorting: Privacy, Risk and Digital Discrimination*, New York: Routledge.

—— (2007) *Surveillance Studies: An Overview*, Cambridge: Polity Press.

—— (2008) *Identifying Citizens: ID Cards as Surveillance*, Cambridge: Polity Press.

MacBride, S. (1983) *Israel in Lebanon: The Report of the International Commission to Enquire into Reported Violations of International Law by Israel during its Invasion of Lebanon*, London: Ithaca Press.

Massad, J.A. (2006) *Persistence of the Palestinian Question: Essays on Zionism and the Palestinians*, London and New York: Routledge.

Mbembe, A. (2003) "Necropolitics," *Public Culture*, 15(1): 11–40.

Melmen, Y. (2008) "Shin Bet to Palestinian: Collaborate or Go to Jail," *Haaretz*, 4 September.

Michael, B. (2007) "Stupid Big Brother: New Law Will Enable Police to Create Monstrous Database, but Won't Make It Any Smarter". Online. Available HTTP: <http://www.ynetnews.com> (accessed 25 December 2007).

Mitchell, T. (1988) *Colonizing Egypt*, Cambridge: Cambridge University Press.

Ophir, A. and Azoulay, A. (2005) "The Monster's Tail," in M. Sorokin (ed.) *Against the Wall*, New York: The New Press.

Pappe, I. (2008) "The *Mukhabarat* State of Israel: A State of Oppression is Not a State of Exception," in R. Lentin (ed.) *Thinking Palestine*, London: Zed Books.

—— (2009) "Dummy or Real," *London Review of Books*, 14 January.

—— (ed.) (2003) *The Israel–Palestine Question*, New York: Routledge, e-Library.

Parenti, C. (2003) *The Soft Cage: Surveillance in America, from Slave Passes to the War on Terror*, New York: Basic Books.

Peled, Y. (2007) "Citizenship Betrayal, Israel's Immigration and Citizenship Regime," *Theoretical Inquiries in Law*, 8(2): 603–628.

Peteet, J. (1994) "Male Gender and Rituals of Resistance in the Palestinian Intifada: A Cultural Politics of Violence," *American Ethnologist*, 21(1): 31–49.

—— (1995) "Transforming Trust: Dispossession and Empowerment among Palestinian Refugees," in V.E. Daniel and J. Knudsen (eds) *Mistrusting Refugees*, Berkeley: University of California Press.

—— (2008) "Stealing Time," *MERIP*, 248: 14–15.

Piterberg, G. (2008) *The Returns of Zionism: Myths, Politics and Scholarship in Israel*, London and New York: Verso.

Pratt, M.L. (1991) *Imperial Eyes: Travel Writing and Transculturation*, New York: Routledge.

Privacy International (2007) "PHR2006 – State of Israel." Online. Available HTTP: <http://www.privacyinternational.org/article.shtml?cmd%5B347%5D=x-347-559526> (accessed 12 August 2009).

Rabinowitz, D. (2001) "The Palestinian Citizens of Israel, the Concept of Trapped Minority and the Discourse on Transnationalism in Anthropology," *Ethnic and Racial Studies*, 24(1): 64–85.

Ram, U. (1993) "The Colonization Perspective in Israeli Sociology: Internal and External Comparisons," *Journal of Historical Sociology*, 6(3): 327–350.

Reuters (2008) "World Health Organization: Israel Turning Away Sick Gazans who Die in 'Avoidable Tragedies,'" *Haaretz*, 18 January.

Rosenfeld, H. (2002) "The Idea is to Change the State, Not the 'Conceptual' Terminology," *Ethnic and Racial Studies*, 25(6): 1083–1095.

Sabbagh-Khoury, A. (forthcoming) *Palestinian Predicaments: Jewish Immigration and Refugee Repatriation.*

Sa'di, A. (2005) "The Politics of Collaboration: Israel's Control of National Minority and Indigenous Resistance," *Holy Land Journal*, 4(10): 7–26.

Said, E.W. (1978) *Orientalism*, New York: Pantheon Books.

—— (1994) *Culture and Imperialism*, New York: Vintage Books.

Segal, R. and Weizman, E. (2003) *A Civilian Occupation*, London and New York: Verso Press.

Shafir, G. (1989) *Land, Labour and the Origins of the Israeli–Palestinian Conflict, 1882–1914*, Cambridge: Cambridge University Press.

Shamir, R. (2005) "Without Borders? Notes on Globalization as a Mobility Regime," *Sociological Theory*, 23(2): 197–217.

Shehadeh, R. (2003) *When the Birds Stopped Singing*, Hanover, NH: Steerforth Press.

Shenhav, Y. (2006) "The Imperial History of 'State of Exception,'" *Theory and Criticism*, 29: 205–218 [Hebrew].

Smith, E. (2006) "Privacy in the USA," background paper commissioned by the Globalization of Personal Data Project (GPD), Queen's University, Kingston, Ontario. Online. Available HTTP: <http://www.queensu.ca/sociology/Surveillance/?q=node/78> (accessed 10 August 2009).

Smith, R.S. (1996) *Rule by Records: Land Registration and Village Custom in Early British Panjab*, Delhi: Oxford University Press.

Somfalvi, A. (2008) "Biometric Database to be formed in Israel." Online. Available HTTP: <http://www.ynetnews.com> (accessed 8 August 2008).

Spurr, D. (1993) *The Rhetoric of Empire: Colonial Discourse in Journalism, Travel Writing and Imperial Administration*, Durham, NC: Duke University Press.

Stoil, R. (2007a) "Israel, Canada Sign Security Accord," *Jerusalem Post*. Online. Available HTTP: <http://www.jpost.com> (accessed 29 October 2007).

—— (2007b) "Israel, US Sign Homeland Security Pact," *Jerusalem Post*. Online. Available HTTP: <http://www.jpost.com> (accessed 7 February 2007).

Thomas, M. (2008) *Empires of Intelligence: Security and Colonial Disorder after 1914*, Berkeley: University of California Press.

Thompson, S. (2002) "Returning the Gaze: Culture and the Politics of Surveillance in Ireland," *International Journal of English Studies*, 2(2): 95–107.

Torpey, J. (1998) "Coming and Going: On the State of Monopolization of the Legitimate 'Means of Movement,'" *Sociological Theory*, 16(3): 239–259.

United Nations Human Rights Council (2008) *Annual Report*. Online. Available HTTP: <http://domino.un.org/UNISPAL.NSF/9a798adbf322aff38525617b006d88d7/fd246b9c33182c72852573ed005001d2!OpenDocument> (accessed 1 February 2008).

United States Department of Commerce, US Commercial Service (2009). Online. Available at HTTP : <http://www.buyusa.gov/israel/en/> (accessed 19 January 2009).

Wagner, M. (2007) "Eliyahu Advocates Carpet Bombing Gaza," *Jerusalem Post*. Online. Available HTTP: <http://www.jpost.com> (accessed 30 May 2007).

Waugh, L. (2008) "Diary: Living in Gaza," *London Review of Books*, 5 June. Online. Available HTTP: <http://www.lrb.co.uk/v30/n11/waug01_.html> (accessed 5 June 2008).

Webb, M. (2007) *Illusions of Security: Global Surveillance and Democracy in the Post-9/11 World*, San Francisco, CA: City Lights Books.

Weizman, E. (2002) *The Politics of Verticality*. Online. Available HTTP: <http://www.opendemocracy.net> (accessed 23 April 2002).

—— (2007a) "Beyond Colonialism: Israeli/Palestinian Space." Online. Available HTTP: <http://www.re-public.gr/en/> (accessed 27 September 2007).

—— (2007b) *Hollow Land: Israel's Architecture of Occupation*, London and New York: Verso Press.

Whitaker, B. (2004) "Assassination Method: Surveillance Drone and Hellfire Missile," *Guardian*, 23 March.

Wilkins, K.G. (2004) "The Civil Intifada: The Process and Politics of the Palestinian Census," *Development and Change*, 33(5): 891–908.

Wolfe, P. (2006) "Settler Colonialism and the Elimination of the Native," *Journal of Genocidal Research*, 8(4): 387–409.

Wordpress (2007) "Homeland Security Selects Israeli Company to Keep US/Mexico Border Safe." Online. Available HTTP: <http://www.mlyon.01.wordpress.com/2007/09/13> (accessed 13 September 2007).

World Tribune (2008) "Israel Activates Unmanned Video-Directed Machine Gun Stations on Gaza Borders," 3 April. Online. Available HTTP: <http://www.worldtribune.com/worldtribune/WTARC/2008/me_israel0017_04_03.asp> (accessed 12 August 2009).

Yacobi, H. (2004) "In-Between Surveillance and Spatial Protest: The Production of Space of the 'Mixed City' of Lod," *Surveillance-and-Society*, 2(1): 55–77. Online. Available HTTP: <http://www.surveillance-and-society.org> (accessed 11 August 2009).

Yoaz, Y. (2007a) "Court in Session in the Wake of Big Brother," *Haaretz*, 6 December.

—— (2007b) "Secret Clause Lets Shin Bet Get Data from Cell Phone Firms," *Haaretz*, 24 September.

Zurawski, N. (2005) "People Watching People," *Surveillance and Society*, 2(4): 498–512. Online. Available HTTP: <http://www.surveillance-and-society.org> (accessed 11 August 2009).

Zureik, E. (1979) *The Palestinians in Israel: A Study in Internal Colonialism*, London: Routledge and Kegan Paul.

—— (2001) "Constructing Palestine through Surveillance Practices," *British Journal of Middle Eastern Studies*, 2: 205–227.

Zureik, E. and Vitullo, A. (1992) *Targeting to Kill: Israel's Undercover Units*, Jerusalem and Washington, D.C.: Palestine Human Rights Center and the Center for Policy Analysis on Palestine.

Zvika, D. (1986) *The "Arabists" of the Palmach*, Tel Aviv: Hakibutz Hameuchad [Hebrew].

Part II

Theories of surveillance in conflict zones

2 Identification, colonialism, and control

Surveillant sorting in Israel/Palestine

David Lyon

The concept of an "Israeli Arab" is a fictitious one – there should be no such concept. There are only Palestinian Arabs. We must restore to the Arab in Israel his true identity, instead of robbing him of it.

(A.B. Yehoshua, Haifa University, 1977, cited in Zureik 1979: 178)

The roadblocks, the separate roads, the fence and the prohibitions against entering the country for everyone who is not Jewish are different levels in this system of separation. The "smart" cards fit into the picture in a natural way that strikes fear in anyone who understands that "separation" and peace are contradictory terms.

(Amira Hass, "The yearnings for a magnetic card," *Haaretz*, May 9, 2007)

I long for the day I'll finally get an ID card. I want to pass through each and every checkpoint in the West Bank, just to show everyone I have an ID card. Sometimes I feel that death will be the only solution to my problem. In the afterlife I'm sure no one gets asked about his ID card.

(Muhannad al-Khafash, 2008)

Introduction

Why, in Amira Hass's words, does the "magnetic ID card" fit into the picture of separate development of Israeli and Palestinian people in such a "natural way"? And why, furthermore, might this "strike fear in anyone who understands that 'separation' and peace are contradictory terms"? The answer lies in the ways that colonialism was imposed in Israel, sorting the population by ethnic categories and using various identification cards (hereafter "IDs"; see Lyon 2009) as markers of citizenship. This is a practice that has been documented in several situations of "internal colonialism," including South Africa, and these comparative examples throw light on the Palestinian experience both before and after 1967. But going beyond this, IDs also "fit naturally" in two other senses: first is that IDs are increasingly in evidence in a process dubbed by Nikolas Rose the "securitizing of identity" (Rose 1999) in which the condition of freedom – whether economic or political – is the production of some legitimate identification; second is that the use of surveillance and security technologies such as IDs is likely to expand proportionately to the experience of widening gaps of opportunity and access.

This chapter focuses on just one dimension of surveillance, population control and states of exception: identification practices. In Israel and the occupied Palestinian territories (OPT), as anywhere else, identification practices – ID for short – are crucially important and consequential for other areas of governance as well. Indeed, identification is a vital dimension of many surveillance practices. But they are not all the same. The ID regimes in Israel and the OPT are different, for example. As with a number of other surveillance techniques, ID is also subtle as a mode of discrimination and may not immediately conjure up the same negative responses as might the presence of a "security wall" or "armed checkpoints."

IDs have become more and more central to the systems of governance in Israel and the OPT. As Amira Hass (2006) says, "You exist if the Israeli computer says so." Elaborating, she asserts that Israel's control of Palestinian freedom of movement is not reflected merely in roadblocks and border passes: "It derives first and foremost from controlling the Palestinian population registration. Identity numbers, births, deaths, marriages, changing addresses – if these details have not been updated in Israel's Interior Ministry computers, they don't exist."

The parallel systems for Israel and the OPT may be summarized as follows. Israeli citizens and permanent residents hold an ID (the *Teudat Zehut*) bearing an Israeli coat of arms, issued by the Interior Ministry. It comes in a blue plastic casing. Who counts as a Jew and whether this should be on the card are controversial issues and this datum has not been included on the card since 2005. Until the creation of the Palestinian Authority (PA) in 1994 non-Israeli residents of the West Bank and Gaza Strip carried a card in an orange casing bearing the Israeli Defence Forces insignia, although Palestinians barred from entering Israel had green casings on theirs. Since 1994 the PA has issued Palestinian IDs to its residents with Israeli approval. Otherwise identical to the old Civil Administration cards, they now bear the PA insignia, are in a dark green casing, and Arabic, not Hebrew, is the first language. However, control over the population registry is a grey area, even though the PA assigns the numbers. Control is vested in the "Israeli side." (See Chapter 11, this volume, on the symbolic significance of these ID cards.)

I begin by offering a few comments to clarify what is being argued here. Having already used such words as "surveillance" and "discrimination," I should make clear that neither of these is necessarily negative. Surveillance is an activity undertaken by all kinds of organizations, not only governmental ones, in order to keep track of populations and to ensure that benefits, entitlements and indeed rights, as well as debts or obligations, are appropriately distributed. Today, such surveillance is usually computer-assisted, not to mention statistically sensitive, and often operates in pursuit of purposes such as security or risk-management in governmental contexts, or profit or market maximization in more commercial ones. Indeed, organizations today rely on systematic surveillance as never before, as a standard operating principle (Lyon 2007).

Whether for marketing, risk management or yet other purposes, surveillance generally involves discriminating between different population groups in order to treat those groups differently, according to their needs and desires, or to what is deemed appropriate by those administering the system concerned. So, for example, surveillance carried out by Amazon.com is intended to discriminate between classes of readers in order to bring the most relevant books to the attention of online surfers with the maximum potential interest in those titles. Databases of personal information, gleaned from brokers of commercial data, combined with statistical analysis, provide instant suggestions to each surfer of books that "other customers have bought" which are similar to the one she happens to be viewing.

Personal identification is also sought as never before, and in many life-spheres (Rose 1999). This includes nation-states, which seek to establish stable identification systems; again, this is not necessarily negative. While it is true that in a number of countries where new electronic national ID systems have been proposed or introduced civil liberties groups and privacy advocates have raised objections and launched public protest (see, e.g., Bennett and Lyon 2008; Lyon 2009; Bennett 2008), the process of registration itself may be seen as protecting civil liberties. It is one means of ensuring equality before the law and of underpinning access to rights and benefits for all citizens. Indeed, Simon Szreter argues that identity registration functioned from 1538 to facilitate social security and a mobile labour market in early modern Britain and that it should be a contemporary priority in poorer nations to turn the "liberal rhetoric" of rights into a reality of empowered individuals (Szreter 2007). By 1948 the UN recognized this as a human right.[1]

So what might be said about identification in relation to surveillance and citizenship in Israel and the OPT? The question hints at the answer. It is an ambiguous relation. Identity registration, where the individual's record is maintained by the state, is a means of surveillance. Fates hang in the balance depending on the holding and the status of the ID. At the same time, the use of identification cards, relating to the state record, is a means of demonstrating citizenship and thus of claiming rights to its benefits. It has been so since the invention of identification documents (Abercrombie *et al.* 1983), which means that these are highly significant items, for better or worse, both for the nation-state and for the individual, whether a citizen or not. In the case of Israel and the OPT, not all ID cards are of equal value and the colour-coding affects life-chances quite differently. At the same time, to have an ID at all confers definite advantages. As Elia Zureik says, "the identity card is one of the most coveted documents sought after by the highly monitored Palestinian population" (Zureik 2001: 224).

IDs for Israelis and Palestinians

IDs have been in use from the instituting of the state of Israel in 1948. At that time, they distinguished between Palestinian residents[2] and Jewish settlers and were based on statistics from the British Palestinian Mandate. They certainly fit with the basic population categories of "Jew" and "non-Jew" used in the census which was basic to the idea of constructing a "Jewish" state. This follows the practice expressed in the Balfour Declaration of 1917, promising a Jewish "homeland" in Palestine, and referring to the 90 per cent of the existing population as "non-Jewish communities" (Zureik 2001: 214). The label "Jew" offers privileged status and until 2002 this was also written into personal ID cards, the visible markers of the bureaucratic reality. Thus the Zionist project, implicitly supported by the British colonial administration (Shalev 2002), finds a crucially significant symbol in the ID card.

The 1982 Identity Card Carrying and Displaying Act made clear that all residents over sixteen must carry the card at all times and present it on demand to police officers, heads of municipal authorities or members of the armed forces. Access to guarded offices or areas may depend on presenting ID, which is also valid for participation in elections. Various personal details are found on the card, including, until 2005, ethnicity. This has since been replaced by eight asterisks. However, Jewish status may still be determined by checking if the birth date is written in Hebrew.

The year 1967 was a watershed. From 1948 to 1966 passes and ID cards were issued as part of Israel's military rule over its Palestinian citizens to regulate spatial location and movement. After 1967 Israel began issuing IDs to residents of the West Bank and Gaza Strip after the occupation. Although officially the PA now issues IDs to Palestinians, it does so only with Israeli approval. It appears that Israel controls the population registry according to the Interim Agreements under the Oslo Accords, assigning numbers for Palestinian cards. According to the Palestinian Ministry of Social Affairs, over 50,000 Palestinians have been waiting for more than eleven years for their ID cards to be approved by Israel. Thus they cannot travel and are considered "illegal" in their own place of residence.

From looking at government and commercial sources it is clear that in Israel at least the long-term aim is to use a single smart card ID system as part of an overall "identity management" programme. This will bring Israel in line with several other countries that have recently adopted (e.g., Spain and Italy) or developed (e.g., France) advanced "national" IDs (see Bennett and Lyon 2008). Preliminary ideas for a smart ID were shelved in 1985 partly because of a lack of international experience. In 1998–1999 a decision was made to go ahead with a partial programme of Requests for Proposals but 2008 saw the vendors compete for procurements and firm commitments to pursue a fully fledged smart ID system (Ishai 2008). In July 2008 the Interior Ministry proposed that the new IDs contain fingerprints and a biometric photo, which was accepted in cabinet despite some doubts about ways this might impinge on people's rights (Haaretz Service 2008).

By December 2008 the Ministry of the Interior had awarded Hewlett-Packard (HP) the contract to make 5 million smart cards for the Israeli population, in a project advertised as an e-government identity management initiative. Israeli citizens will be able to perform online functions using the new card, obtaining access to government departments and authenticating forms with a digital signature. It is also seen as a measure to contain the forgery of IDs, which reportedly is a growing phenomenon. The biometric database on which the ID will depend may become the subject of political controversy, even though the Ministry of the Interior is assuring citizens that it is both necessary and, largely through encryption and the authority of a ministerial committee, safe (Lillian 2008). No mention has been made of any such programme for the OPT.

Although IDs were used earlier as a means of controlling the Palestinian population (see below), since 1967 Israel has had a monopoly in civil registration and issuing ID for Palestinians. It also administers entry visas and work permits for Palestinian non-ID holders in the OPT. In September 1967 a snap census in the OPT caused tens of thousands of Palestinians studying, working or travelling abroad to lose their right to residency or identification. Following the Oslo Accords, issuing IDs became the responsibility of the Palestinian Authority, but because Israel retained its hold on the population registry, Israel in fact still determines all rights and statuses of those in the OPT.

Personal details, including name, age, date and place of birth, political affiliation and security record, are held in a central database accessed by Israeli officials at checkpoints and borders. The card also carries a photo of the bearer and is written in English, Arabic and Hebrew. ID holders in the West Bank and Gaza may change their card colour to the green of the PA although East Jerusalem dwellers still carry blue IDs. ID holders may live legally in the OPT but are citizens of no land (Lowenstein 2006: 24), thus making travel tiresome and sometimes impossible.

The ID system appears arbitrary to the Palestinians, especially those born in the Gaza Strip but for some reason living in the West Bank. Gaza Strip students wishing to study in West Bank universities have a particularly hard time. Also, Palestinians without IDs have had to leave for a neighbouring country every three months in order to return and apply for a new tourist visa. But since April 2006 many such have been denied re-entry, despite having family members – or even being married to someone – in the OPT. According to Jennifer Lowenstein (2006), this is a means of keeping out "foreign" activists and limiting the resident population to Palestinians, against whom Israeli forces can use live ammunition. These ID policies render Palestinians stateless and severely restrict movement. Because they may not return if they leave, those without IDs are virtual prisoners in their zone. Even those with IDs confront a permit regime more "complex and ruthlessly enforced than the pass system of the apartheid regime" (Lowenstein 2006: 25). This does irreparable damage to family life and livelihoods, and of course it denies access to property.

It is important to recognize that ID documentation comprises two main items: the ID card itself and the population registry, which today is generally a searchable computer database (Lyon 2009). Gérard Noiriel (1996) thus distinguishes between the "card" and the "code," where the latter is the registration database. From 1969, for example, following military occupation, all Palestinians in the West Bank were issued with identification numbers by the Israeli Ministry of the Interior. Now updated, these are the means of access to the personal details in the registry, which Palestinians themselves may not see but which are visible on the screen of the "lowest ranking soldier at the most remote checkpoint in the West Bank or on the computers at the Erez [Gaza] crossing point" (Hass, cited in Abu-Zahra 2007: n.p.).

The ID cards, however, serve to limit mobility and indeed access to other aspects of daily life as well, much as John Torpey (2000) argues with respect to the passport. The obligation to display IDs gives police, soldiers and other authorities powers to limit mobility. One knows where physical barriers exist; to be stopped randomly is much less predictable (see Lyon 2005). As Nadia Abu-Zahra points out, mobility checks depend both on the IDs and their being matched to zoned areas from which certain cardholders are banned, at least at certain times. So, for instance, in 1971 the General Exit Permit No. 5 was issued, allowing some Palestinians living in the OPT to enter Israel, but not between 1 and 5 a.m. (Abu-Zahra 2007: 306).

The realities of IDs for Palestinian life are brought home with particular poignancy by Eyal Weizman in his book *Hollow Land*. He demonstrates how architectural features of the checkpoints into the West Bank and Gaza involve colour-coded lanes and sub-lanes, "dividing passengers according to destinations defined by the geography of the Oslo Accords" (Weizman 2007: 139). Passengers are met by Palestinian police officers who take their IDs, but they pass them to Israeli officials hidden behind a one-way mirror. Unlike Foucault's description of the panopticon, where power is "visible but unverifiable," at places like the Allenby Bridge the power is not even visible. The system is intended to give the impression that power is in Palestinian hands but in fact – as Palestinians soon discover – it is in Israeli hands (see Zureik 2001).

Interestingly, Weizman shows how the language of Oslo substituted merely instrumental "management" for "occupation," thus giving the appearance of a purely bureaucratic administrative structure. This could be mistaken for Gilles Deleuze's "control society." The checkpoint valves do indeed modulate the flow of people using IDs in their architectural setting, but in so doing in fact set up a kind of "international border" that simultaneously is a border of sovereignties. If Foucault does not quite work here, nor does Deleuze. Weizman points out that the Oslo process obliges Palestinians to identify themselves not only "as *objects* exposed to military power but also as political *subjects* of another" (Weizman 2007: 144; italics in original). Thus the systems of direct discipline and indirect control coexist, layered the one on the other.

But not only mobility is restricted by the use of IDs. Nadia Abu-Zahra gets close to this when she observes that "The Israeli state has monopolized not only the 'legitimate means of movement' but many other aspects of life also. ID is needed for high school matriculation, applying for a driver's licence, a marriage contract or a birth certificate. It is needed for travel and for 'family reunification.'" As a result, she continues, "Palestinians have no choice but to undergo whatever is necessary to register and obtain an ID" (Abu-Zahra 2007: 316). In other words, "life is impossible" (Cook, Hanieh and Kay 2004: 32, cited in Abu-Zahra 2007: 316) without ID. Amira Hass (2006) clearly has it right when she says, "You exist if the Israeli computer says so."

In less extreme contexts, one could argue that IDs are increasingly used not merely as a means of controlling mobility but as a means of access to many benefits and opportunities, both commercial and government-sanctioned. Indeed, I have suggested that today's IDs represent not so much a monopoly (by the state) in the means of movement (as Torpey proposes) but an *oligopoly* on the very *means of identification*. It is the identification itself which is required not only for travel but for transactions, whether the latter are associated with credit cards or with, say, government-provided welfare or medical benefits. And it is an oligopoly because today, through out-sourcing and the dependence of government on private sector expertise and technical knowledge, others than the state play roles in establishing and maintaining control, using IDs. In Israel, however, the state is clearly prominent, through its various organs, and IDs are required for access to basic human necessities; or, as Giorgio Agamben would put it, "bare life" (Agamben 1998).

Identification, colonialism and categories

What is the connection between the colonial roots and conflict zone fruits of identification processes in Israel? Identification is vital to surveillance and especially so in colonial situations where the categories – ethnic, religious and so on – are so consequential for political power and for governance in general. In this section, after a brief look at consequential British colonial practices in Palestine, the concept of "internal colonialism" is discussed critically, not merely to characterize the Israeli treatment of Palestinians, both in Israel and the OPT, but to draw some telling comparisons with other situations where IDs have been central to the maintenance of power. As I shall argue, IDs may be used both to distinguish between cardholders through different citizenship assignments and, by withholding IDs altogether from some members of the population, to deny those persons access to basic rights and amenities.

As noted above, the British colonial administration under the Palestine Mandate created the original "modern" census and this defined the population in prejudicial fashion. Such categorization was highly effective in a number of other colonial projects, such as those of the British in India and Africa, even though many such categories have been criticized in retrospect as little more than "racist myths" (Berman 2008). Their effectiveness is shown in the ways that they were used to maintain power. This occurs, as Ian Hacking (1986) suggests in his concept of "dynamic nominalism," as those categories constitute an active intervention that help shape social circumstances. The labelling helps to create new identifications which, even though they may be rejected by those to whom they are applied, still serve to define the new "reality." Thus, as Bruce Berman (2008: 22) says, colonial powers "mapped out the axes of ethnic conflict in ways that live on today."

The role of identification in population control in the new state of Israel began early, as Ilan Pappe points out. In a chapter titled "Occupation and its ugly face" he observes that the hardships for the Palestinians were far from over once the "ethnic cleansing" operations were largely completed in 1949. They were physically abused, their houses were "looted, their fields confiscated, their holy places desecrated and Israel violated such basic rights as their freedom of movement and expression, and of equality before the law" (Pappe 2006: 200). But that was not all.

They were also subjected to "inhuman imprisonment" following closure orders on villages and towns. Importantly, Pappe notes, in the dreaded interrogations of "illegal" suspects, "The worst offence was not being in possession of one of the newly-issued identity cards, which could result in a prison term as long as a year and a half and immediate transfer to one of the pens to join other 'unauthorized' and 'suspicious' Arabs found in now Jewish-occupied areas" (Pappe 2006: 201). ID cards had been issued to the 150,000 Palestinians who had not been expelled – thus creating the "Israeli Arab" minority – in order to prevent the imminent return of the 800,000 refugees and their descendants now outside the country.

A key concept, linking surveillance and identification practices, is "internal colonialism." This is a theory of the distribution of power and advantage within states. Developed in the first instance by theorists such as Antonio Gramsci (in his essay on the "Southern Question"; Gramsci 2006 [1926]) to describe the persistent underdevelopment of some Italian regions, it later came to connote situations of both economic disadvantage and cultural distinctiveness. Michael Hechter (1998 [1975]) argued that in the UK economic power and resources were concentrated in the centre, which subordinated the "Celtic fringe" to the latter's disadvantage. It has also been used, for example, to describe the situation of Mexicans in the US after the Mexican War of 1846–1848. In the case of Israel/Palestine, internal colonialism seems to have taken over where the ID categorization of British Palestine Mandate colonialism left off.

Of course, the concept of internal colonialism immediately runs into trouble in the case of Israel/Palestine, as that term – "Israel/Palestine" – indicates so clearly. A territory called "Palestine" does not exist officially as far as the Israeli government is concerned. Equally, for some Palestinians, Israel has no legal right to exist. So, one might logically object, what is "internal" here? Well, for the purposes of this analysis, it makes sense to retain the term "internal colonialism" because of its resonance with similar situations, and not because it accurately describes the state of affairs in the region. The occupied territories are landlocked within the settler state of Israel and, in this purely geographical sense, could be thought of as "internal colonies" of native Palestinians under the control of Israel.

One situation with which ours has some resonance is the former Soviet Union. The concept of internal colonialism is used explicitly by Marc Garcelon in relation to this "surveillance order," the "administrative fulcrum" of which from 1932 was the "internal passport" (Garcelon 2001: 83). This document was central to the system because it was required both for residential housing permits and for work-books to secure employment. Unlike external passports, says John Torpey, internal passports act as "a state's principal means of distinguishing among its subjects in terms of rights and privileges . . . [and] may be used to regulate the movement of certain groups of subjects, to restrict their entry into certain areas, and to deny them the freedom to depart their places of residence" (Torpey 1998: 254).

For Garcelon, the Soviet case shows how "above all" internal colonialism entailed "*administrative differentiation* such that there are both citizens and subjects, as dictated by the colonial analogy" (Garcelon 2001: 84; italics in original). Thus those who could show themselves to be embracing the Soviet ideology generally had access to the benefits that were dependent on the internal passport – notably, access to the dynamic urban areas of "closed cities" – while others, such as Chechens, found that their internal passports "effectively condemned them to the marginal ranks of physical laborers, internal exiles, and labor camp inmates" (Garcelon 2001: 87). Thus while the internal passport was used by police, its disciplinary power was probably more significant, according to Garcelon. Not only were different groups classified by these documents; denying them to the majority of the peasantry effectively tied that group to within a few kilometres of their collective farms.

The Soviet passport carried biographical information on "class background," nationality, military service, criminal record, place of work and residence and the issuing authority. From 1937 they also carried photos. They could thus be used by both police and state administrators, and by the 1960s they were, very effectively, throughout the country. They were the main means of restricting access to goods and services available in the closed cities and of containing rural–urban migration. In these ways they bear a remarkable similarity to many aspects of both the South African passbook under apartheid and Israel.

Elia Zureik drew illuminatingly on the term "internal colonialism" in his classic study of *The Palestinians in Israel* (1979) in order to illustrate the ways in which the colonial "settler" society of Israel dominated the Palestinian population, and his usage also ties in neatly with the work of Garcelon. In Zureik's original study, however, less attention was devoted to the surveillance dimensions of internal colonialism, something that his more recent work addresses. This more recent work demonstrates how surveillance practices construct the "Palestinians" and how land and demography, expressed in administrative classification and census categories, are at the heart of the Palestinian–Israeli conflict (Zureik 2001).

Several key features of internal colonialism stand out in the case of Israel. First, asymmetrical relations between settlers and the native population, achieved by superimposing a capitalist mode of production on a traditionally peasant social order and displacing the latter from their land, and maintained by closing off indigenous access to educational, cultural and residential facilities. Second, metropolitan centres are dominated economically and politically by settlers, along with some pockets within the mainly native underdeveloped hinterland. Third, a justificatory ideology – complete with negative stereotypical images of Arabs – is created, based on the dehumanization of the indigenous culture and way of life (Zureik 1979: 28–29).

The particular "justificatory ideology" is of special interest in the case of Israel, of course. It centres on Zionism and on the attempt to create a "Jewish state." This religiously rooted ideology does make the Israeli case distinct from other examples of internal colonialism, and until 2002 it made Israeli ID cards the only ones in the world to declare the religion of the bearer as the criterion of citizenship. As such, of course, it is deeply controversial. Not only are some Israelis not Zionist, but Palestinian ("Arab") Israelis may be of various religious stripes or none, and Christian residents may or may not be sympathetic to Zionism.[3] So while there may be some important parallels with other forms of internal colonialism, this quasi-religious feature – Zionism – does make it distinctive with respect to national identity and citizenship.

Nonetheless, the features of Israeli internal colonialism spelled out above would also seem to fit another society with which contemporary Israel is frequently compared: South Africa under apartheid. This chapter does not attempt to make a systematic case for or against the usefulness of this analogy. Only the issue of modes of identification is in question. For, in this case, even more relevantly than in the Soviet example, asymmetric relations between settlers and natives, metropolitan domination of the hinterland, and a justificatory ideology are all reflected in a specific means of identification, the infamous passbooks.

Identification under apartheid

From one point of view, possible parallels between South African apartheid and Israeli racist policies might come as no surprise. What makes the Israeli internal colonialism case distinctive is the mobilizing of religious beliefs, which formed part of the core components of Zionism, to justify the "separate development" of different communities. But in fact religious belief was also profoundly implicated in the South African case (which is why religiously committed people were so deeply embroiled in the apartheid struggles, *on both sides*, and why one mechanism for mutual understanding was the "Truth and Reconciliation Commission"). As Donald Akenson argues:

> What events in Ulster and South Africa since the seventeenth century, and in the state of Israel in the twentieth century, have in common is that they can be understood only by direct reference to the very oldest strands in the cultural fabric that is shared by Western societies: the memory of events that occurred as much as four millennia ago and are recorded sometimes in blurred form and other times with eerie sharpness, in the scriptures.
>
> (Akenson 1992: 5)

Both the content of these beliefs and the confidence and tenacity with which they are held may well be part of the reason for the apparent intractability of political positions in these conflict zones, but that issue is not pursued here.

In 2006 Jimmy Carter published *Palestine: Peace Not Apartheid*, which sparked major controversy, even though paradoxically he says very little about apartheid in the book. Despite this, it seems to have stimulated others to use the analogy more freely. The notion of comparing Israel's policies to apartheid was far from new, however. As Elia Zureik observed more than thirty years ago, "While official *de jure* apartheid of the South African variety does not exist in Israel, national apartheid on the latent and informal levels . . . is a characteristic feature of Israeli society" (Zureik 1979: 16). In an insightful review of Carter's book, Joseph Lelyveld points out that the "basic issue is one of control, which was the point of the settlements in the first place" (Lelyveld 2007). But how is this control achieved?

By taking a sideways glance at South Africa under apartheid as a possibly parallel case, the dynamics of identification and power may be traced in the Israeli treatment of Palestinians especially pre-1967. Control is achieved in both cases by a variety of means, but the use of an ID system is central. The pass system in South Africa, with its religiously sanctioned racialized categories, meant that "Africans," "Coloureds" and "Asians" had to carry identification when outside their designated areas of work or residence. The system provided a potent means of control and was deeply resented and resisted. IDs would take on new meanings in what came to be called the OPT.

Until 1966, so-called Israeli Arabs lived under the military administration that permitted detention without trial, imposed curfews, restricted where they could live and work and required them to carry passes to move around the country. In colonial and apartheid South Africa, 87 per cent of the land was reserved for whites. South Africans were categorized by an array of racial definitions that determined who could live where, under the Population Registration Act. Long before, the Native Land Act of 1913 had driven non-whites off their ancestral lands by outlawing black property-holding. Similarly, "Israeli governments reserved 93% of the land – often expropriated from Arabs without compensation – for Jews through state ownership, the Jewish National Fund and the Israeli Lands Authority" (McGreal 2006). Unlike in South Africa, it is true, some small compensations were offered, but for various reasons – some on nationalist grounds, and some because the compensations were low – many Palestinians refused to accept them. In any case, the majority of owners of seized lands are refugees living outside Israel, for whom compensation is still a dominant concern.

The Population Registry Act, by distinguishing between nationality and citizenship, permitted Arabs to be "citizens" of the state but not the nation. And this "nationality" appears on IDs, earlier in name, now in numeric code, and determines permitted residential zones, access to welfare programmes, and the kind of treatment the bearer may expect from civil servants and police officers. Unlike South Africa under apartheid, no official doctrine of inferiority/superiority appeared in the Population Registry Act. However, the implied inferiority of "Arabs" within Israeli bureaucratic practices and in public opinion leads to Palestinians being treated as if they are second-class citizens. Reviewing the debate over whether Israel and the OPT represent a form of apartheid, with regard to the specific case of identification systems, throws light on the broader issue of ID, colonialism and control.

In her article questioning the use of "apartheid" as an analogous way of describing the Israeli treatment of Palestinians, Susie Jacobs (2005) acknowledges that the use of permits and IDs is similar to the pass system in South Africa under apartheid. The Pass Laws enabled social and political control on a massive scale and were both resented and resisted, especially by "Africans." In the seam zone between the Green Line and the wall, Palestinian residents of the OPT require special permits to live in their own homes, farm their own land and make family visits. The IDF controls entry, but often the zone is not open at scheduled times, so children cannot get to school, farm-workers to the fields or the ill to hospital.

In a response to this, Greg Dropkin (2005) insists that Jacobs underplays the Pass Law similarities and argues that in fact the situation for Palestinians is in some ways worse. He cites the *One Big Prison* report (Lein 2005), mentioning in particular the "Divided Families Procedure" that requires, for example, female residents or citizens of Israel married to male residents of Gaza to leave their IDs at the Erez District Coordination Office on entering the Strip. Then they pick up a permit to enter the PA, which they have to leave behind on exiting, even if it is still valid. Another application is needed for a further visit. Today, for example, Palestinians from Israel who marry people from the OPT and live in Israel now have to separate from their partners, who are sent back to the OPT.

UN Special Rapporteur John Dugard (a South African) notes that "The South African pass laws were administered in a humiliating manner, but uniformly," whereas the Israeli laws are administered humiliatingly but not uniformly. He continues, "the arbitrary and capricious nature of their implementation imposes a great burden on the Palestinian people" (Dugard 2004). In 2007, Dugard updated his UN report, arguing that the situation was much worse than it had been three years earlier. He did not mince words: "It has become abundantly clear that the wall and checkpoints are principally aimed at advancing the safety, convenience and comfort of settlers" (Dugard, cited in McCarthy 2007).

The internal colonialism argument makes much sense of the experiences of Palestinian residents of Israel and the OPT. In particular, the ID systems reflect and reinforce the existing political and economic asymmetries that are felt especially in restrictions on mobility (as in the former Soviet Union). The comparison with apartheid also throws light on the centrality of IDs for maintaining power, especially through making daily life a burdensome reality, through disrupting normal family life and by reducing some to "bare life."

To what extent, then, is this situation likely to continue? Will IDs continue to be the nexus of power relations and will Palestinians continue to find that acknowledgement of their very existence depends on some Israeli computer? There are two important reasons why ID systems are likely to continue to be significant players in the desperate drama being worked out in Israel and the OPT. One, already alluded to, is that, globally, new biometric ID systems requiring massive searchable population registry databases are being adopted, even in quite poor (e.g., Angola and the Ivory Coast) as well as in rich countries. The "securitizing of identity" and the quest for "identity management systems" that often combine governmental and commercial functions are becoming basic to information infrastructures.

The other reason why IDs are likely to continue to be significant is that, especially in situations where there are growing visible inequalities of access to resources, there is a trend towards strengthening "social defence technologies." Given the variety of such techniques already in existence in this part of the world – the security fence, for instance – and the considerable Israeli surveillance technology capacities, other developments, such as the biometric smart card identifier, come as no surprise. The final part of this chapter discusses the role of surveillance, and especially IDs, from a Durkheimian perspective.

Social divisions and intensified surveillance

The paradox of IDs is that they are both a means of social control and exclusion, and a desired means of access and inclusion. They are increasingly the nexus of power and governance, especially in situations of conflict and zones of struggle. They operate on at least two levels. The meanings and benefits attached to holding an ID differ, depending on how the bearer is identified. This produces one kind of social sorting. But another kind of sorting occurs between holders and non-holders of IDs. To hold an ID at all admits the bearer to places or privileges generally denied to the non-holder.

Either way, as IDs – especially "national" IDs – are used more frequently and intensively, they are likely to operate for good or ill within a larger assemblage of surveillance technologies (Haggerty and Ericson 2000). The rise of surveillance as an organization device and as a means of governance may be traced to several factors: the generally increasing information-intensiveness of administration, the availability of both infrastructural and discrete surveillance technologies, a dependence on risk management and precautionary ideologies as well as, arguably, growing disparities of access to opportunities and resources (Lyon 2007, 2009).

The latter argument is worth exploring in more detail. Although it applies in the relatively affluent societies of the global North, one might venture to suggest that its relevance would increase in less affluent countries and especially where there is ongoing conflict and struggle over land, resources or opportunities. It could well be relevant to countries in Africa, Latin America and Asia. Following Durkheim's theory of crime (Durkheim 1982), when inequalities are becoming more marked, groups at opposite ends of the social spectrum perceive each other to be a growing threat to their own security. In particular, the more privileged groups will see the activities of subordinate groups as enlarging risks and challenging their position.

In response to more desperate activities undertaken by subordinate groups (the less well-off, in his theory of crime), Durkheim predicts that the dominant group will demand ever more draconian measures and that further categories of behaviour should be treated as inadmissible or as crimes (Perri 6 2005). This response may be popular with the dominant group even in the absence of evidence that effective governance of risks will occur. The dominant group will also seek new technological "solutions," says Durkheim, to secure spatial segregation from the groups perceived as a threat, thus reinforcing their exclusion and the division of that society into rival enclaves. Perri 6 extends Durkheim, suggesting that we might "expect to see increased surveillance, increased checking of people seeking access to public spaces, and this would be disproportionately used for categories of person deemed suspect, possibly reinforcing stigma of groups" (Perri 6 2005: 35).

Long term, this Durkheimian perspective would suggest that simply adding more defensive surveillance technologies is unlikely to improve the situation in question. Durkheim viewed such governance as monological, being basically one-way communication, and thus likely to be self-disorganizing due to the false assumption that everything can be controlled. For Durkheim, only the introduction of what he thought of as political ritual activities, which are inherently dialogical in character, can halt the downward spiral of instrumentality, with its self-reinforcing tendency to increase the disappointment and frustration of subaltern groups. Such rituals carry the hope of respect, which must surely be the only way out of the mire of resentment (compare Sennett 2003). The Truth and Reconciliation Commission in South Africa was one such "healing" ritual but it took place *after* the dismantling of political apartheid had begun. What the appropriate rituals might be *prior* to the dismantling of occupation is as yet unclear.

The relevance of a Durkheimian analysis to the case of IDs in Israel and the OPT is evident. The registration and identification systems in place are already flashpoints of social, political, economic and ethnic division. While efforts to establish properly dialogical and thus mutually respectful means of finding just settlements in Israel and the OPT still seem a distant hope, the actual gaps in life experiences and expectancies continue to grow. The resort to technical, and thus, for Durkheim, merely mono-logical, means of maintaining separate "development" for different groups in Israel and the OPT will in the long run tend to exacerbate rather than address the pressing issues of human rights in this region. Given the technical expertise available, and the growing number of other countries that use new IDs, the chances are that biometric IDs with corresponding databases will be crucial to that quest for social defence technologies. And in the relatively small region of Israel and the OPT, there is less reason than in some other countries – such as contemporary South Africa (Breckenridge 2005a, 2008) – to think that they might not be workable.

Conclusion

Identification systems have been vital to the project of creating Israel, ever since 1948. Although the character of these IDs has altered, notably after 1967 and after 1994, and although the ID systems of Israel and the OPT are different in some respects, their role as a nexus of power is still crucial. When seen against a backdrop of other situations, such as the use of internal passports in the internal colonialism of the former Soviet Union, or the use of passbooks in South Africa under apartheid, this makes a great deal of sense. For ID systems, including both the "code" and the "card," have proved to be effective means of reproducing the basic social divisions that their organizational categories express (even when the bureaucracy supporting them lacks basic efficiency; see Breckenridge 2005b).

Clearly, in the case of Israel and the OPT, IDs operate as a means of restriction on movement and, indeed, they appear to follow the path proposed by Torpey in relation to passports, in that they are a (state) monopoly in the means of movement. As such, the system that sanctions them is the cause of much hardship and harm that violates human rights. However, they speak of more than movement. As several examples have shown, the ability to participate in normal family, educational and work life, not to mention in recreational or political activities, is curtailed, with IDs used as the medium. In some cases, as we have seen, Palestinian people are reduced to "bare life" through the use of IDs or ID denial. So it seems that the identification process itself, not just movement, is in question. You exist if the (Israeli) computer says that you do.

Let us return to the question with which we began: why, in Amira Hass's words, does the smart card fit into the picture of separate development of Israeli and

Palestinian people in such a "natural way"? And why, furthermore, might this "strike fear in anyone who understands that 'separation' and peace are contradictory terms"? The "magnetic" ID card fits so naturally because of the social, economic, political and *religious* setting that gives it its meaning (see Heidegger 1977; Lyon 2009: ch. 3). And, I have argued, the electronic ID card will appear to be even more natural in the future. This is, first, because electronic ID systems are becoming increasingly important to both government and commercial administration throughout the world and, second, because (if the extrapolation from Durkheim is correct) IDs operate as an essential social defence technology in situations where gross socio-economic and political inequalities are growing in a palpable manner.

That this might also "strike fear in anyone who understands that 'separation' and peace are contradictory terms" should also be evident from the foregoing. It is beyond the scope of this chapter, not to mention the competence of this author, to elaborate on this in detail. I should note, however, that other approaches than the mere resort to technical means are possible. Indeed, given the political-religious underpinning of ID systems in Israel, Zionism itself would have to be confronted as a provider of the crucial category of citizenship identification before the issues could in any way be justly resolved. And that could not take things further than from an obsession with mere "technical means." Nonetheless, I have hinted at how, again, in a Durkheimian frame, the respect that accompanies dialogic political ritual is still worth hoping for, and one might add (going beyond Durkheim) that the fears engendered by monological tendencies may be countered by relational approaches. This would not necessarily entail the rejection of ID systems because, as we have also seen, they may express as well as deny basic human rights. But it does mean that ID systems would require reconstruction to embody peace and not separation.

Notes

1   Article 24, clause 2 of the UN International Covenant on Civil and Political Rights (ICCPR).
2   The official Israeli designation is "Israeli Arab."
3   For a Christian account of Israeli–Palestinian conflicts that is decidedly non-Zionist and with which this author has some sympathy, see Chapman 2002.

Bibliography

Abercrombie, N., S. Hill and B.S Turner (1983) *Sovereign Individuals of Capitalism*, London: Allen and Unwin.

Abu-Zahra, N. (2007) "IDs and territory: population control for resource expropriation," in D. Cohen and E. Gilbert (eds) *War, Citizenship, Territory*, London and New York: Routledge.

Agamben, G. (1998) *Homo Sacer: Sovereign Power and Bare Life*, Stanford, CA: Stanford University Press.

Akenson, D. (1992) *God's Peoples: Covenant and Land in South Africa, Israel and Ulster*, Ithaca, NY: Cornell University Press.

Al-Kafash, M. (2008) "Residency and family separation," Israeli Information Center for Human Rights. Available HTTP: <www.btsleem.org/eng/Family_Separation/20080529/Unregistered_persons.asp/>.

Bennett, C. (2008) *Privacy Advocates: Resisting the Spread of Surveillance*, Cambridge MA: MIT Press.

Bennett, C. and D. Lyon (eds) (2008) *Playing the Identity Card: Surveillance, Security and Identification in Global Perspective*, London and New York: Routledge.

Berman, B. (2008) "Who are you? Let me tell you! Western colonial states and the formation of group identities," paper presented at Ethnicity Democracy and Governance Workshop, Queen's University, September 18. Available HTTP: <http://www.queensu.ca/edg/>.

Breckenridge, K. (2005a) "The biometric state: the promise and peril of digital government in the new South Africa," *Journal of South African Studies*, 31(2): 267–282.

—— (2005b) "Verwoerd's bureau of proof: total information in the making of apartheid," *History Workshop Journal*, 59: 1.

—— (2008) "The elusive panopticon: the HANIS project and the politics of standards in South Africa," in C. Bennett and D. Lyon (eds) *Privacy Advocates: Resisting the Spread of Surveillance*, Cambridge, MA: MIT Press.

Carter, J. (2006) *Palestine: Peace Not Apartheid*, New York: Simon and Schuster.

Chapman, C. (2002) *Whose Promised Land?: The Continuing Crisis over Israel and Palestine*, Oxford: Lion.

Cook, C., A. Hanieh and A. Kay (2004) *Stolen Youth: The Politics of Israel's Detention of Palestinian Children*, London: Pluto Press.

Dropkin, G. (2005) "Israel, apartheid and sanctions: in response to Susie Jacobs," June 13. Available HTTP: <http://www.labournet.net/other/0506/isaparth1.html>.

Dugard, J. (2004) *Report*. Available HTTP: <http://stop-us-military-aid-to-israel.net/b2/index.php?m=200412/>.

Durkheim, E. (1982) *The Rules of Sociological Method*, New York: Free Press.

Garcelon, M. (2001) "Colonizing the subject: the genealogy and legacy of the Soviet internal passport," in J. Caplan and J. Torpey (eds) *Documenting Individual Identity: The Development of State Practices in the Modern World*, Princeton, NJ: Princeton University Press.

Gramsci, A. (2006 [1926]) *The Southern Question*, Toronto: Guernica Editions.

Greenstein, R. (1995) *Genealogies of Conflict: Class, Identity and State in Palestine/Israel and South Africa*, Hanover, NH: Wesleyan University Press.

Haaretz Service (2008) "Who's afraid of fingerprints?," *Haaretz*, July 8. Available HTTP: <www.haaretz.com/hasen/objects/pages/PrintArticleEn.jht.../>.

Hacking, I. (1986) "Making up people," in T. Heller, M. Sosna and D.E. Wellbery (eds) *Reconstructing Individualism: Autonomy, Individuality, and the Self in Western Thought*, Stanford, CA: Stanford University Press.

Haggerty, K.D. and R.V. Ericson (2000) "The surveillant assemblage," *British Journal of Sociology*, 51(4): 605–622.

Hass, A. (2006) "You exist if the Israeli computer says so," *Haaretz*, November 6. Available HTTP: <www.imemc.org/article/22481?print_page=true/>.

Hechter, M. (1998 [1975]) *Internal Colonialism: The Celtic Fringe in British National Development*, New York: Transaction Books.

Heidegger, M. (1977) *The Question Concerning Technology and Other Essays*, New York: Harper Torchbooks.

Ishai, O.Y. (2008) "Identity management in Israel." Available HTTP: <www.ict-hanoi.gov.vn/Israel-E-id%20in%20Israel-520Mimshak%20Ltd20%20%ver%20.0%2006062007/>.

Jacobs, S. (2005) "Israel=Apartheid? A comparison and critique," *Engage*. Available HTTP: <www.engageonline.org.uk/archives/index.php?id=12/>.

Lein, Y. (2005) *One Big Prison* [B'Tselem and HaMoked report]. Available HTTP: <www.btselem.org/English/Press_Releases/20050329.asp/>.

Lelyveld, J. (2007) "Jimmy Carter and apartheid," *New York Review of Books*, March 29. Available HTTP: <www.nybooks.com/articles/19993/>.

Lillian, N. (2008) "Smart card project underway," *Ynet News*, December 1. Available HTTP: <www.ynetnews.com/articles/0,7340,L-3631644,00.html/>.

Lowenstein, J. (2006) "Identity and movement control in the OPT," *Forced Migration Review*, 26: 24–25.

Lyon, D. (2005) "The border is everywhere: ID cards, surveillance and otherness," in E. Zureik and M. Salter (eds) *Global Surveillance and Policing*, Cullompton: Willan.

—— (2007) *Surveillance Studies: An Overview*, Cambridge: Polity Press.

—— (2008) "Identification practices: state formation, crime control, colonialism and war," in K. Franko Aas, H.O. Gundhus and H.M. Lomell (eds) *Technologies of InSecurity*, London and New York: Routledge.

—— (2009) *Identifying Citizens: ID Cards as Surveillance*, Cambridge: Polity Press.

McCarthy, R. (2007) "Occupied Gaza like apartheid South Africa says UN report," *Guardian*, February 23. Available HTTP: <www.guardian.co.uk/world/2007/feb/23/israeland thepalestinians.unitednations/>.

McGreal, C. (2006) "Worlds apart," *Guardian*, February 6. Available HTTP: <www. guardian.co.uk/world/2006/feb/06/southafrica.israel/>.

Noiriel, G. (1996) *The French Melting Pot: Immigration, Citizenship and National Identity*, Minneapolis: University of Minnesota Press.

Pappe, I. (2006) *The Ethnic Cleansing of Palestine*, Oxford: Oneworld Publications.

Perri 6 (2005) "The governance of technology," in C. Lyall and J. Tait (eds) *New Modes of Governance: Developing an Integrated Approach to Science, Technology, Risk and the Environment*, Aldershot: Ashgate.

Rose, N. (1999) *Powers of Freedom*, Cambridge and New York: Cambridge University Press.

Sennett, R. (2003) *Respect in a World of Inequality*, New York: Norton.

Shalev, T. (2002) *One Palestine, Complete: Jews and Arabs under the British Mandate*, London: Abacus.

Szreter, S. (2007) The right of registration: development, identity, registration and social security – an historical perspective, *World Development*, 35(1): 67–86.

Torpey, J. (1998) "Le contrôle des passeports et la liberté: le cas de l'Allemagne au XIXe siècle," *Genèses* 30: 53–76.

—— (2000) *The Invention of the Passport: Surveillance, Citizenship and the State*, Cambridge: Cambridge University Press.

Weizman, E. (2007) *Hollow Land: Israel's Architecture of Occupation*, London and New York: Verso.

Zureik, E. (1979) *The Palestinians in Israel: A Study in Internal Colonialism*, London: Routledge and Kegan Paul.

—— (2001) "Constructing Palestine through surveillance practices," *British Journal of Middle Eastern Studies*, 8(2): 205–227.

3 A place for Palestinians in the *Altneuland*

Herzl, anti-Semitism, and the Jewish state

Glenn Bowman

Too often one finds oneself attempting to use *realpolitik* to make sense of Israeli policies towards the Palestinians of Israel and the territories it has occupied since 1967. Here I will argue that such policies, rather than being based on practical political strategies, are founded on an ontological project, operating from the earliest days of the Zionist project, in which the non-Jewish population of a Jewish state is treated, at best, as invisible and, more generally, as an internal enemy which must be contained, controlled, and eventually expelled. I contend that, before we can consider "matrices of control" or "states of exception," we need to assess the distinctions on which practices of inclusion and exclusion are based; those between what Giorgio Agamben would term *bios* (human life) and *zoe* (bare or animal life).[1] In this chapter I will, by examining the work of Theodor Herzl and its legacy to the state it played a key role in generating, show that Israel was initially conceived as a strategy for the extirpation of anti-Semitism via the isolation and reformation of a particular category of Jew. In this the local non-Jewish populations were to be extraneous, expelled wherever possible and ghettoized when that proved impossible. In time Herzl's program of producing the "new Jew" was to backfire, producing in the contemporary times a "Jewish state" so internally heterodox that the category "Jewish" can be given commonality only through a politics of fear based on the constant invocation of anti-Semitism. It is here, I will contend, that the state's Palestinian population became essential to its functioning, being conceived as an antagonistic interiority whose threat had constantly to be revealed, counteracted and, one might say, provoked.

One of the founding myths of the Zionist settler project was that it intended the indigenous non-Jewish population to benefit from the economic and cultural development European Jews would bring to the region.[2] Although subsequent phrases – such as Golda Meir's "there were no such thing as Palestinians" (1969)[3] elaborated on by apologists such as Joan Peters in *From Time Immemorial* (1984)[4] – might lead one to question how local peoples were to be helped if they weren't to be recognized, there has been an assumption, informing, for instance, Britain's Mandate period policies, that Zionism was meant to provide not only Jews with a homeland but a vanguard mechanism for improving the living standards and rights of the resident Arabs.

Often cited as evidence is Theodor Herzl's *Altneuland* (1902), a utopic portrayal of a future Jewish state in Palestine (*sic*). At one point in that novel Rachid Bey, a Muslim neighbor of David Litwak, the Jew who guides the Prussian aristocrat Kingscourt around Haifa, responds to Kingscourt's query "what happened to the old inhabitants of the land who possessed nothing – the tenantry?":

Those who had nothing could only gain. And gain they did: employment, better food, welfare. There was nothing more wretched than an Arab village of *fellaheen* at the end of the nineteenth century. The tenants lived in buildings not fit for cattle. The children were naked and uncared for, their playground the street. Today things are changed indeed . . . people are far better off than before; they are healthy, they have better food, their children go to school. Nothing has been done to interfere with their customs or their faith – they have only gained by welfare . . . The Jews have brought us wealth and health; why should we harbour evil thoughts about them? They live among us like brothers; why should we not return their kindly feelings? . . . We Mohammedans have always been better friends with the Jews than you Christians.

(Herzl 1960 [1902]: 95, 100)

This progressivist portrayal of a Muslim who had studied at the University of Berlin and was a full and active member of the Zionist "New Society" suggests that Herzl's conception of relations between Jews and Palestinians in the future Zionist state was antithetical to the later vision of those who founded Israel on ethnic cleansing and expropriation and built it into the militaristic, oppressive and racist state it is today. This incommensurability suggests either that Herzl's heirs have radically subverted the legacy of the man popularly known as the "Father of Zionism" or that *Altneuland* was deceptive in its intent, meant by Herzl to mask his real purpose in launching the Zionist state-building project.[5]

I want to argue here that the situation is more complicated, and that Herzl's own conception of the Jewish state was fundamentally split, with one trajectory – perhaps his real *desideratum* – seeking to give rise to a state which, while nominally Jewish, would promote the rich cosmopolitan modernism of the Vienna he loved, and the other – albeit the dominant one – leading to a racialist Jews-only state. Understanding this split perspective will involve a critical reading of his life and his writings (in particular his 1895 text *Der Judenstaat*), but in setting forth this reading I intend to do more than simply throw light upon some biographical specificities and textual incompatibilities. In particular, in looking into the relation of Herzl to Vienna, Zionism, and his imaginings of a Jewish state, I intend critically to assess what led the Zionist project to mirror the anti-Semitism it was designed to counter. Exposing the contradictions and contingencies which resulted in Herzl's futurisms giving rise to a state in numerous ways opposed to that which he had imagined will, I hope, give support to those, inside and outside the Zionist "new society," who believe that Israel and the Jewish community it claims to represent do not need to base Jewish rights and security on the destruction of the rights and lives of others.

There are, of course, methodological problems with treating an individual's life and work as somehow emblematic of the culture of a larger collectivity, but in a number of ways it seems viable to see Herzl – whose charismatic figure looms over the Zionist Congresses (see Berkowitz 1993) – as someone who spoke to and for many European Jews: "Herzl's experience was emblematic of that of a large number of Central European Jews, which is why his resolution of his ambivalence through Zionism resonated so powerfully in others of his generation" (Kornberg 1993: 3). That so many identified themselves with the scenarios of identity, antagonism, and deliverance sketched by Herzl in his speeches, his journalistic work, and his famed *Der Judenstaat* suggests that this particular interpellation (Althusser 1971: 160–165) played a substantial role in shaping Zionism's earliest forms. Although later articulations of Zionism, for instance those of the Labor and Socialist Zionist movements, diverged from and critiqued Herzl's model, I will argue that Herzl's program of creating a "new Jew" to displace the "ghetto Jew" remained latent in all Zionisms (when it was not overt) and thus that the structure of Herzl's identity discourse is paradigmatic for Zionism as a general movement. For this reason I want first to consider the conflicts and contradictions which gave rise to Herzl's image of Jewish identity and the Zionist project.

Great strides were taken towards the full assimilation of Jews into mainstream European society in the wake of the French Revolution. Although impediments to full integration were frequently encountered on that path there was a generalized optimism throughout Central and Western European Jewry in the latter half of the nineteenth century that assimilation was the inevitable fate of the Jewish people. Most Jews in Austria, France, Germany, and Great Britain were urbanized and had discarded the cultural distinctions which, further to the east, signaled the Jewishness of those confined to ghettos in Eastern Europe and in and around the Russian "Pale of Settlement." For assimilating Jews, religion was a private affair (if not an atavism which had no hold on them at all) which might be discarded in exchange for the benefits of full incorporation into European civilization. Conversions from Judaism to Christianity had increased significantly in the nineteenth century, either pragmatically or through intermarriage.[6] Heinrich Heine, who in 1825 became Christian so as to be able to qualify for a law degree, called baptism an "*entréebillet zur europäischen Kultur* [entry ticket to European civilisation]" and queried "who would let a mere formality stand between him and European civilisation?" (Laqueur 2003: 9).

Herzl, until the early 1890s, considered himself primarily a journalist and a playwright; and, while aware of his Jewishness, he strove for full incorporation into the hegemonic culture of Vienna (to which his family had moved from Budapest when he was eighteen). As a law student he belonged to – and enthusiastically engaged with – two radical German nationalist organizations, the Akademische Lesehalle (Academic Reading Hall) and the Albia fraternity (a dueling club). Later he identified strongly with Vienna's artistic circles, affecting an aristocratic aestheticism as a means of distancing himself from the commercial taint of common journalism. Jacques Kornberg, in a powerful study of Herzl's ambivalent relation to his Jewishness, argues that these were attempts to "distance himself from his Jewish Hungarian origins" (Kornberg 1993: 49) by shedding Jewish traits and becoming part of the "Germandom" of the surrounding culture.[7] Viennese culture, until the rise of racial nationalism in the 1890s, was both assimilationist and anti-Semitic; a Jew could "pass" as a full member of European (Christian) society precisely by showing no evidence of what Christian Europeans saw as stereotypical "Jewishness." Herzl identified with the values of that environment, aspiring to be the "new man" of the Enlightenment while sharing its disdain for the stereotypical ghetto Jew whose atavistic religiosity and provincialism were antithetical to enlightened cosmopolitanism.

Herzl's struggle through the 1880s to gain recognition as a literary artist coincided with an increase in populist anti-Semitism sparked by financial crisis and fueled by accusations that Jewish financiers had corrupted the market. This found resonance in the anti-Enlightenment *völkisch* racial nationalism which was simultaneously emerging (Laqueur 2003: 28–30; Zimmerman 2001: 137–146). Between 1883 – when he withdrew from Albia because of its policy shift from promoting the assimilation of Jews into the German nation to advocating their exclusion as racially alien – and 1895 – when the election of the anti-Semitic Christian Socials to power in the Vienna City Council spurred his realization that Jewish emancipation could take place only in a Jewish polity – Herzl worked for recognition as a fully assimilated and successful individual against the prejudices which saw him not as a man and an artist but as a "Jew."

Part of his strategy for overcoming prejudice was a discursive splitting of the Jew into two distinct personifications. One type of Jew, with which he identified, was the enlightened cosmopolitan who carried his Jewishness in the same way as an Austrian or a Frenchman bore his national origin – as an evident yet fundamentally irrelevant aspect of an all-round educated person deporting himself with grace and self-possession. The other Jew, whom he loathed and in whom he believed anti-Semites found the font of their stereotypes of the Jew, was the *Ostjude* ("Eastern Jew") who dwelled in and had been shaped by the ghetto. For Herzl, the ghetto Jew – isolated from participation in European national movements as well as from modernization and enlightenment – had developed a self-serving mentality focused on economic gain and manifest in an obsessive money hunger and a self-debasing humility behind which lurked a crafty arrogance. Herzl, like Freud and other assimilated Western Jews,[8] looked with repulsion upon this Jew, whom they called *mauschel* (usually rendered into English as "yid"):

> We've known him for a long time, and just merely to look at him, let alone approach or, heaven forbid, touch him was enough to make us feel sick. But our disgust, until now, was moderated by pity; we sought extenuating, historical explanations for his being so crooked, sleazy, and shabby a specimen. Moreover, we told ourselves that he was, after all, our fellow tribesman, though we had no cause to be proud of his fellowship . . . who is this Yid, anyway? A type, my dear friends, a figure that pops up time and again, the dreadful companion of the Jew, and so inseparable from him that they have always been mistaken for one for the other. The Jew is a human being like any other, no better and no worse . . . The Yid, on the other hand, is a hideous distortion of the human character, something unspeakably low and repulsive.
>
> (Herzl, "Mauschel," *Die Welt*, 15 October 1897, quoted by Pawel 1989: 345)

The *mauschel* was, however, more than a Jewish other for Herzl. It was an antagonist – something which endangered the very ground of his identity by its presence.[9] The Eastern Jew, by providing the bases for the stereotypical images with which anti-Semites legitimated excluding and persecuting all Jews, not only put at risk Herzl's social identity and status but, by sharing a "tribal" identity with him, subverted at its foundations his laboriously achieved sense of self. This dual threat devolved from Herzl's anxiety that others, to whom he would present himself as a European, might reject his self-presentation and reduce him to the Jew he and they despised ("You may think that you are like everybody else but you're just a Jew").

Herzl responded to this threat by throwing up barriers – both ontological and social – between himself and the *mauschel*. He rendered foreign the bloodline he saw as spawning the *mauschel*, suggesting that "at some dark moment in our history some inferior human material got into our unfortunate people and blended with it" (Herzl, quoted by Kornberg 1993: 164). In order to protect Western Jews from the stigmas arising from being associated with the Eastern Jew, Herzl, in 1893, proposed to cut the ties of name and religion that associated them. He argued in his journalistic work for a mass enlistment of Jews in the project of Austrian socialism which – nominally anti-Semitic in its hostility to Jewish distinctiveness – would eradicate that distinctiveness by making Jewish socialists an integral part of the German culture it promoted as a norm for all of Central Europe. He later proposed an even more explicit cessation of the stigma of Jewishness by suggesting an orchestrated mass baptism of Austrian Jews into the Catholic Church (see Pawel 1989: 186–188). The self-deputed last generation of Jewish fathers would accompany its sons to Vienna's cathedral, where a great collective baptism of the latter would take place. In this manner the last Austrian Jews would gain the respect of the gentiles as they proudly extinguished their community by transforming their sons into full Europeans. The threat posed to the Western Jew by the *mauschel* would be obviated by denying the Jewish religion which bound one to the other.

Herzl was finally forced to abandon strategies grounded on confidence that Enlightenment Europe would welcome Jews into its community if Jews discarded the Jewishness that rendered them distinct when – after three decades of Liberal rule – the Christian Socials, an overtly anti-Semitic party which had begun its climb to power the previous decade, won a firm majority in the 1895 Vienna city council elections. The Christian Socials instituted policies of Catholic revivalism and Jewish exclusion, and Herzl (already sensitized by the Dreyfus Affair to the resurgent appeal of anti-Semitism in Europe) was forced to acknowledge that no matter how un-Jewish or un-*mauschel* he and other Jews would become – no matter how much they worked to transform themselves to effect assimilation – they would never be allowed to coexist within European society except as ghettoized others barred from entry into the institutions of the dominant culture. In the new racial discourse a Jew was a Jew, even when he was a Christian.

Herzl responded quickly with an elaboration of the fundamentals of the program he called Zionism. The speed of invention seems less surprising when it is recognized that all Herzl did was displace the policies of Jewish transformation he'd already developed to a site – *any* site – outside of the bounds of a Europe that would not accept them. Herzl's Zionist state was not informed by the Jewish religion but simply one in which Jewish citizens could function as full citizens without suffering exclusionary discrimination in any domain of social activity. In effect, he argued that as Jews were made "Jewish" by exclusion and Europeans could only see Jewishness when it saw Jews (henceforth insisting on maintaining the exclusionary policies that made Jews "Jewish"), Jews would have to leave Europe in order to stop being "Jewish" and reveal themselves as European. The Zionist state, wherever it was to be established, would be a place where Jews could act just like – and thus become just like – other Europeans.[10]

In the wake of the election which tolled the death knell of his ambitions of direct assimilation, Herzl – still at heart an assimilationist – announced a program for establishing a European state outside of Europe: "In the election the majority of non-Jewish citizens – no, all of them – declare that they do not recognize us as Austro-Germans. All right, we shall move away; but over there too we shall only be Austrians" (Patai 1960: I, 246–247).

The Jewish state Herzl had in mind was a reconstitution in another place of the best elements of pre-Christian Social Viennese society, with Jews making up the citizenry and anti-Semitism rendered unviable by Jewish "normalization." The geographical displacement envisioned in his diaries and journalism becomes, in the "New Society" of the future, not only spatial but temporal. Nonetheless, the "doubling" of pre-1890s Vienna evident in his earlier writings continues to be played out in the novel: Herzl's image of the New Society of *Altneuland* is one of idealized pre-anti-Semitic Vienna projected into a future in which an intellectual vanguard opens the way to prosperity and security for all members of a multi-ethnic society. Herzl presents *Altneuland* as an opportunity to try again to create the cosmopolitan enlightenment which the Christian Socials and the forces of anti-Semitic intolerance sabotaged.[11] It monumentalizes the assimilationist aspiration which drove Herzl's early attempts to dissolve Western Jews into the Enlightenment European society which surrounded them. Here the new Jew, modeled on the enlightened Christian European, provides the norm for a social order mirroring Europe – if Europe could be imagined as being without anti-Semitism. However, although in *Altneuland* anti-Semitism is "left outside" in old Europe, the concept of normalization, so central to Herzl's earlier drive towards Jewish assimiliation, internalizes an equivalent malignancy in his *Der Judenstaat* and in so doing introduces a fatal fissure into the conception – and future – of the Jewish state. The *mauschel*, haunting and threatening Herzl's conception of Jewish assimilation, proves foundational to his idea of a Jewish state and, in playing such a fundamental role, divides his concept of the state in two,[12] sowing the seeds for its eventual realization as a racist ethnocracy.

A careful reading of *Der Judenstaat* reveals – behind the rhetoric predicting "a great upward tendency [which] will pass through our people" providing "ambitious young men . . . a bright prospect of freedom, happiness and honours" (Herzl 1993: 70, 9) – an accompanying scenario intended to overcome the antagonism the Eastern Jew posed to Herzl and, in his eyes, to Jews in general. For Herzl, the exposure of "Christian citizens" to "wandering Jews", displaced from the ghettos and emigrating into countries in which assimilated Jews already peacefully coexist, "either introduce[s] Anti-Semitism where it does not exist, or intensif[ies] it where it does." A Jewish state would eradicate anti-Semitism by gathering in and settling these "faithful" and "foreign" Jews (Herzl 1993: 18). It would isolate Eastern Jews – those provokers and amplifiers of anti-Semitic feeling – and, through a carefully rationalized program of "relief by labor," use their unremunerated work both to transform them from "good for nothing beggar[s] into . . . honest bread winner[s]" (Herzl 1993: 39)[13] and to render the country habitable. Only after that hard labor of dual transformation had been carried out would other Jews even consider leaving Europe and emigrating to Palestine:

> We shall not leave our old home before the new one is prepared for us. Those only will depart who are sure thereby to improve their position; those who are now desperate will go first, after them the poor, next the prosperous, and, last of

all, the wealthy. Those who go in advance will raise themselves to a higher grade, equal to that whose representatives will shortly follow. Thus the exodus will be at the same time an ascent of the classes.

(Herzl 1993: 20)

The plan for a Jewish state was thus a plan to quarantine Eastern Jews from their nominal Western "brethren" and, through that isolation and a well-regimented regime of work and social engineering, to raise them gradually to the "level" of assimilated Western Jews. This process would sweat from them, and later from the Jewish *parvenu* who had brought the stench of the market into the drawing rooms of the Western Jewish "aristocracy" (see Kornberg 1993: 71–76), all traces of the ghetto.

It is indicative that this labor of human and spatial transformation is elided in *Altneuland*, where a twenty-year gap falls between Kingscourt's and Loewenberg's first viewing of "the ancient land of the Jews" – "dirty and neglected, full of motley oriental misery [where] [p]oor Turks, dirty Arabs and shy Jews lounged around" (Herzl 1960 [1902]: 30) and their return to a "marvellously changed" Palestine filled with people "more civilized" than they (Herzl 1960 [1902]: 42). The masking of this immense labor – which Herzl is at pains to detail in the earlier *Der Judenstaat* – suggests that the Palestine of the state-building project of that text, and that of *Altneuland*, may not at all be the same country. The utopic character of the New Society of *Altneuland* is implied in *Der Judenstaat*'s indication that Western Jews will, in effect, have no reason to emigrate to the redeemed Palestine:

> The movement towards the organisation of the State I am proposing would, of course, harm Jewish Frenchmen no more than it would harm the "assimilated" of other countries. It would, on the contrary, be distinctly to their advantage. For they would no longer be disturbed in their "chromatic function,"[14] as Darwin puts it, but would be able to assimilate in peace, because the present Anti-semitism would have been stopped for ever . . . They would be rid of the disquieting, incalculable, and unavoidable rivalry of a Jewish proletariat, driven by poverty and political pressure from place to place, from land to land. This floating proletariat would become stationary.

(Herzl 1960 [1902]: 42)

The future Jewish state would not affect fully assimilated Jews at all, except to free them from the curse of anti-Semitism; some might choose, as members of a wealthy elite, to emigrate to Palestine once it had been fully developed, while others, like the "Jewish Frenchmen" described above, "would certainly be credited with being assimilated to the very depths of their souls if they stayed where they were after the new Jewish state, with its superior institutions, had become a reality" (Herzl 1993: 18). After all, anti-Semitism would, in Herzl's scenario, disappear with the disappearance of that which had provoked it. Herzl's project would eliminate the last barrier to Jewish emancipation and assimilation by exterminating the *mauschel*, by transformation or worse:

> In our own day, even a flight from religion can no longer rid the Jew of the Yid. Race is now the issue – as if the Jew and the Yid belonged to the same race. But

go and prove that to the anti-Semite. To him, the two are always and inextricably linked . . . And then came Zionism! . . . We'll breathe more easily, having got rid once and for all of these people whom, with furtive shame, we were obliged to treat as our fellow tribesmen . . . Watch out, Yid. Zionism might proceed like Wilhelm Tell . . . and keep a second arrow in reserve. Should the first shot miss, the second will serve the cause of vengeance. Friends, Zionism's second arrow will pierce the Yid's chest.

(Herzl, "Mauschel," *Die Welt*, 15 October 1897, quoted by Pawel 1989: 346)

Herzl's plan to establish a Jewish state outside of Europe seems, at first glance, to promise Jews – blocked within Europe from becoming fully European by the racism of the new nationalist anti-Semitisms – a place in which they can develop their full *human* (read "European") potential without impediment. A closer reading reveals that while it appears to be a design for the eventual abolition of anti-Semitism, it is in itself profoundly anti-Semitic, blaming the "Jewish" characteristics of one sector of the "Jewish" population for the hatred of the Jews felt by non-Jews. Not only does Herzl see Jewishness through the eyes of the anti-Semitic non-Jew,[15] but he contends that anti-Semitism can be extinguished only by exterminating those Jewish characteristics (and if necessary their bearers) which provoke it. Behind the abstract image of the Jewish state as a machinery for constructing a new humanity via an "ascent of the classes" lurks a concrete plan for a detention camp which, via the forced labor of draining the malarial swamps and otherwise redeeming the land,[16] might bio-engineer a new Jew out of the coarse old Jew of the *shtetls* of Eastern Europe and the slums of the West.

Herzl was an Austrian who wanted to remain Austrian in Austria and conceived, in the face of rising anti-Semitism, that the only way of so doing was to abolish anti-Semitism. Instead, however, of challenging anti-Semitism at the core of its logic (as, for instance, Sartre (1948) does in *Anti-Semite and Jew*), Herzl accepted that anti-Semites were justified in their loathing of the "all-too-Jewish" *Ostjude* (a loathing he himself, like many assimilated Western Jews, shared) and proposed to end anti-Semitism by disappearing the *Ostjude*. In at least the short term the purpose of the state he proposed to establish was to gather, hold, and remake the *mauschel*. The New Society envisaged in *Altneuland* would have to wait until that work of reformation was completed, if it were not in fact to take shape back in Europe, led by a vanguard of assimilated Jews.

Herzl's charisma, and the appeal to both Western and Eastern European Jews of his vision of an extra-European Jewish state untroubled by anti-Semitism, enabled him to play a leading role in the articulation of the Zionist program which would evolve into the Labor Zionism of the founding fathers of the state of Israel. Insofar as the activists of the Zionist Congresses were not looking to practice their "chromatic function" in Europe but were anxious to lay the foundations both of a new state and a new Jewry, they enthusiastically adopted the project of *aliyah* and the colonial settlement of Palestine. Herzl, although profoundly disappointed by a visit to Palestine in 1898 (Laqueur 2003: 110), fervently embraced the leadership of the movement despite its goals being somewhat disjunct from his own.[17] In part because of the significant and increasing contribution of Russian Jews to the early Zionist Congresses,[18] the explicit focus on the *Ostjude* was dropped, but what remained central to the project was the extirpation of the "old Jew" and the creation, through manual labor and secular education, of the muscular "new Zionist man" (Berkowitz 1993: 99–118).

Zionism, as elaborated by Herzl and adopted by the Zionist movement, grounded modern Jewish identity on two platforms: one was recognition of the anti-Semitism which prevented Jewish assimilation into the European mainstream; the other was the project of abolishing the pre-modern "Jewishness" which spurred that anti-Semitism. Both of those supports to identity were imported into the Jewish state founded in Israel, although, as in Herzl's own program, the policy of rooting out of the "old Jew" took precedence. The pre-state Zionist cadres that settled in Palestine before 1948 fervently worked to dig out the remnants of "atavistic" practices, beliefs, and deportment. Contemporaneously the Nazis and their sympathizers exterminated most of the remaining *Ostjuden* practices by the systematic genocide of Jewish populations in Poland, Russia, and other regions of Eastern and Central Europe. While to a large degree the original focus of the program had disappeared by the time Israel was founded, modernization remained a central platform of the new state. This was manifest in educational policies such as the eradication of Yiddish and its replacement with Hebrew, but it was most evident in policies towards communities that came to be seen as equivalent to the *Ostjuden* – those of the Jews of the Arab world.

Israel, in the early years of its existence, endeavored to "gather" Jews from their worldwide diaspora, but particular attention was paid to Jews who had lived – in some cases for millennia – in the countries of the Middle East. Some of these were Sephardim – Jews originally from Spain who, after its fifteenth-century *reconquesta* and its attendant religious "purification," had been scattered throughout North Africa – while others were Mizrachim [im] Jews who had, in many cases since the time of the Babylonian exile, lived in Egypt, Iran, Iraq, Yemen, and as far afield as Ethiopia. Israel worked out various ways of bringing these "Eastern Jews" out of their natal countries and into the new world in which they were to be transformed into Israelis; in some cases it negotiated population transfers by economic and political trade; in others, as with Iran and Iraq, it organized covert activities to promote emigration amongst communities that were loath to leave.[19] When these people arrived in Israel, often in mass population transfers, they were treated as *mauschel* – Jews with no sense of modernity, identity, or civilisation – and the state immediately set in train processes of turning them into "modern" Jews.[20] Yet they were not what modernizing Zionism needed them to be. Wrenched out of societies in which they had often belonged to well-integrated, sophisticated, and relatively wealthy urban elites, they were plunged into state-orchestrated collective projects designed to transform them into something approximating the pathetic, unsophisticated, and uncivilized anachronisms the modernizing project needed as raw material. Giladi provides a transcript of an interview with an Iraqi woman brought to Israel in 1948 which succinctly expresses this process, and the violence it entailed:

> We were wearing our Sabbath clothing. We thought as the plane landed that Israel would welcome us warmly. But goodness how wrong we were. When the plane had landed at Lod airport, a worker approached us and sprayed us all over with DDT, as if we were lice-infested. What sort of welcome was that? We thought they were spitting in our faces. When we disembarked from the plane, they herded us into a train, which was so crowded that we were stepping on each other and

our fine clothes were dirtied. My husband was crying and so was I. Then the children started crying and our sobs went up to heaven and cast a pall over the train. Since it was a freight train it had no electric light, but as it sped along we thought of the death trains which had taken European Jews to the Nazi camps. Finally we reached the "Sha'ar Ha'aliya" camp and we were taken in with other families, then they wrote down our names and "gave" us new Hebrew names. "Said" became "Hayyim," "Su'ad" became "Tamar," and I was renamed "Ahuva" and so on.

(Giladi 1990: 103)[21]

This treatment of non-Ashkenazi Jews would eventually backfire, producing political and communal solidarities around the rage non-European Jews felt at being discriminated against and denigrated on the grounds of their cultural and religious beliefs and practices. The growing influence of such alliances not only led to very different politics after Labor lost power in 1977 but placed "Israeli identity" in question, revealing the state as composed of a series of discrete, often mutually antagonistic, constituencies.

The problematic fragmentation of Jewish identity in the wake of the politicization of non-Ashkenazi Israelis, in particular immigrants from Morocco, not only curtailed the project of Jewish transformation which was so central to Herzl's project but raised real questions about, to borrow a phrase from Israeli discourse, "who is a Jew?" If Israel were to be made up, on the one hand, of secularized Jews who, in abandoning traditional culture (including all but the formal vestiges of religion), had become indistinguishable from Europeans (and Americans) and, on the other, of others whose powerful assertions of distinct cultural and religious identities rendered them antagonistic to the core tenets of the Zionist project, then the meaning of "Jewish" in "Jewish state" was thrown into radical contention.[22] Friedland and Hecht's (1996) ethnography of the "civil war" between Orthodox and secular Jews in Jerusalem shows that what is at stake in this dispute over the meaning of "Jewish" might be the survival of a collectivity called "Jewish."

The "solution" adopted has proved to be a shift of focus from the creation of the "new Jew" to an emphasis on anti-Semitism as the negativity which, in effect, constitutes a Jewish positivity. While Zionism's initial project had at its core a problematic internalization of Austro-Hungarian racism, it nonetheless attempted to counter anti-Semitism with a work of communal modernization meant to make possible eventual assimilation into the Enlightenment project. The contemporary enactment of Zionism abandons that transformative project, essentializing Jewishness as "that which suffers anti-Semitism" and establishing as its central project the proof of an omnipresent and threatening antagonism. In part this is evidenced in the increasing amplification of public assertions by the state and its agencies that Jews, wherever they live in the modern world, are subject to an ever-rising tide of anti-Semitic persecution which can be countered only by a retreat behind the protective walls of the Jewish state (see Bowman 2009: 300–302). More virulent, and more salient to the topic of this book, is the escalating demonization – and provocation – of Palestinians within Israel and the occupied territories and Arab populations in the surrounding nations.

It is interesting, and symptomatic, that despite *Altneuland*'s wonderfully civilized Rachid Bey there was never any real attempt, in the realized Zionist state, to assimilate

Palestinian Arabs into the New Society. From the earliest days of the Zionist project Palestinians were meant to exist outside the Jewish collectivity, even if they were allowed to remain within the erstwhile (though never declared) borders of the state.[23] Thus, for instance, Ben-Gurion's policy of *avodah ivrit* ("Hebrew labor"), elaborated early in the second *aliyah*, which demanded that Jewish property not be worked by non-Jews. (Despite this, the Israeli economy was dependent on Palestinian labor right until the Oslo Accords.[24]) Thus too the uncanny phantom position after 1948 of *nokhehim nifkadim* or "present absentees" (Piterberg 2001: 42–43) – Palestinians living within Israel without legal status (or rights). Debates within the Foreign Office, which dealt with "Internal Refugees," centered in the early 1950s on whether these "phantoms" should simply be forced to emigrate or subjected to what Alexander Dotan, chair of the Advisory Committee on Refugees, described as "a secular Jewish cultural mission" (quoted by Piterberg 2001: 45) to make them over as non-Jewish Jews, obliterating any Palestinian identity and rendering them culturally, but not juridically, assimilable. Although Dotan rhetorically linked his plan to the policies of assimilation employed with Jewish newcomers – talking of using education policies like those of the *ma'abarot* or transition camps built for Jewish immigrants – it was in fact designed not to assimilate Palestinians but to neutralize and render them invisible. It was nonetheless overruled by Josh Palmon, Ben-Gurion's advisor on Arab affairs, who, with the aim of impelling "Arabs" to emigrate, perpetuated the harsh military regime established after the war until 1966.

While anyone who could be considered "Jewish" was grist for the modernizing mill of the Jewish state, Herzl's and the founding fathers' conceptions of the Jew – which vacillated between being defined as a racially distinct entity and one constituted by anti-Semitism – meant that in the early decades of the state non-Jews within it were in effect incidental and, functionally, invisible. Palestinians were quarantined outside the national project, kept before 1967 in militarily sealed village ghettos from whence they might be granted permission to exit to provide labor for Jewish businesses and *kibbutzim* (see Lustick 1980). After the 1967 war and the consolidation of the Palestine Liberation Organization under the leadership of Fatah, Palestinians – on the outside – began to play a more significant role as an external antagonism which could be shown to be (in large part for external international consumption) a threat to the survival of the Jewish state and thus a reason why it should receive substantial international and diasporic support. (Israel, before the first Intifada, shared the PLO's disdain of the "inside," monitoring it for dissent while mining it for markets and labor.)

It was only in the wake of the 1977 elections and the burgeoning of the identity politics of Israel's newly politicized Jewish constituencies that the Palestinians within the borders of the territories Israel claims as its own came to play a significant role in the nation's conception of itself. The collapse of the Zionist project of making the "new Jew" (a collapse brought about in part by its success and in part by its generation of antagonistic "other" identities) threatened Israeli Jewish identity itself with collapse – a collapse which could render the national project unviable. The solution has been to draw Jews within the borders of Israel as well as in the diaspora together defensively in the face of what they are told are ever-present threats to their personal and collective survival as Jews. In the absence of a convincing external enemy (with European and American anti-Semitism in serious decline, the PLO driven out of Jordan and Lebanon, and the surrounding Arab states stilled by treaty or internal crisis) the

Palestinians "inside" had to be demonized. The first Intifada, in which the Israeli military was unable successfully to repress a popular uprising, revealed the "phantom" Palestinian population as more powerful than had been assumed and led to moves – initially effected by Oslo – to bring all Palestinians, including the PLO cadres who "returned" from Tunisia and Yemen, together behind checkpoints within Gaza and the West Bank. Subsequent policies have in large part functioned as provocations – increased land confiscations and house demolitions, massively expanded settlement programs, targeted assassinations and widescale arrests, desecrations of religious sites (the Ibrahimi Mosque and the Haram es-Sharif), failure to fulfill treaty obligations, and so on – meant to ensure that Jews are constantly aware of the rage of Palestinians and their non-Palestinian supporters, a rage that, by being defined as anti-Semitic, clearly defines a Jewish "us" opposed by an ever-expanding field of "them."

I am arguing, perhaps counter-intuitively, that current Israeli practices of surveillance, control, and walling are not meant to protect the Jewish civilians and state institutions from attack by a hostile non-Jewish population, but more vitally to protect Jewish identity, and the state which has founded itself on it, from dissolution from within. By "encysting" Palestinians – quarantining them in enclaves as "'matter' held to put the surrounding social body at risk" (Bowman 2009: 295) – Israel stages for its own population a continuous performance of threat on their own doorsteps, forcing that population to huddle together defensively despite its own radical heterogeneity, while simultaneously guaranteeing that the contained and curtailed Palestinians (and their supporters) produce dramatic yet relatively impotent gestures of resistance. Any questioning of state policies, and of the politics of fear, from within the Jewish community is deemed treasonous, suicidal, and the result of Jewish self-hatred. Meanwhile, criticism of Israel from "outside" is viewed, simply and purely, as anti-Semitic. All of these attacks serve to fortify further the walls the Jewish state and its "supporters" have thrown up around an essentialized, and finally incohesive, Jewish community. Herzl might be shocked to see that his *Altneuland* has become, to borrow the title of another of his works, *Das Neue Ghetto* (*The New Ghetto*), but he is not absolved of culpability.

Notes

1 On matrices of control, see Halper 2000. On states of exception, *bios*, and *zoe*, see Agamben 1998 and 2005.
2 "It was one of the most strongly held beliefs of early Zionists that Jewish settlement in Palestine, regardless of the dispossession, would be to the benefit of Jews and Arabs alike" (Rose 2005: 61).
3 *Sunday Times*, 15 June 1969.
4 Peters 1984. For a critique, see Finkelstein 1988.
5 Leonhard wrote: "*Altneuland* was written primarily for the world, not for Zionists. It had propagandistic aims; Herzl wanted to win over non-Jewish opinion for Zionism" (Leonhard and van der Hoeven 1971 [1960]: 119).
6 See Laqueur 2003: 3–39 on intermarriage and integration in Western and Central Europe.
7 See Kornberg 1993: 46–51 on German nationalism and pp. 60–66 on aesthetic culture.
8 Freud, in a letter to Fluss of 18 September 1872, described a family of *ostjude* he had seen recently (he refers to their accent as *mauscheln*): "he was cut from the cloth which fate makes swindlers when the time is ripe: cunning, mendacious, kept by his adoring relatives in the belief that he is a great talent, but unprincipled and without character . . . I have enough

of this lot. Madame Jewess and family hailed from Meseritsch: the proper compost heap for this sort of weed" (quoted in Gilman 1993: 13). See also Laqueur 2003: 56–61 and Kornberg 1993: 22–24). Even Bernard Lazare, who subsequently was to take a stand against the Jewish state project, referred in 1894 in *L'Antisémitisme* to "these coarse and dirty, pillaging Tatars, who come to feed upon a country which does not belong to them" (quoted in Piterberg 2008: 6).

9 The concept of antagonism, drawn originally from Hegel, is productively developed by Ernesto Laclau and Chantal Mouffe in *Hegemony and Socialist Strategy* (1985: 95–148).

10 As opposed to Russian movements, which contended that when Jews gathered together as self-sustaining groups a real and undistorted Jewish spirit would emerge, Herzl's Zionism contended that the state – operating according to principles mapped out for it by an enlightened minority – would shape a new Jew: "the notion that Jewish faults stemmed from their exclusion from the political sphere and could be cured by full citizenship was a keystone of this ideology" (Kornberg 1993: 161).

11 That the Jewish nationalist Geyer brings anti-Semitism (directed at that other Semitic population – the Palestinians) back on to the scene as a threat to the well-being of the community emphasizes the parallels between Vienna in the 1880s and the future Jewish state (as in fact does the oxymoronic title "Old New Land").

12 The play of meaning between the two possible translations of *Der Judenstaat* – "the Jewish state" and "the state of the Jews" – may here have unintentional significance.

13 The policy of unpaid labor of the Jewish Company (that agency charged with developing the infrastructure of the coming state) ensures that the worst traits of the *mauschel* will be extinguished: "The company will thus make it impossible from the outset for those of our people, who are perforce hawkers and pedlars here, to re-establish themselves in the same trades over there. And the company will also keep back drunkards and dissolute men" (Herzl 1993: 37). "Redemption through labor" was a major plank of Zionism, evident, for instance, in the central tenet of Poale Zion, the Russian Zionist movement that only a return to the soil could redeem the Jewish people. For the Jews of the Second Aliya, the first Zionist emigration to Palestine (1904–1906), "manual labour . . . was not a necessary evil but an absolute moral value, a remedy to cure the Jewish people of its social and national ills" (Laqueur 2003: 281).

14 "Chromatic function," the Darwinian conception of adaptive mimicry, was a topic of contemporary debate and discussion. Nietzsche wrote in 1881 of how "animals learn to master themselves and alter their form, so that many, for example, adapt their colouring to the colouring of their surroundings (by virtue of the so-called 'chromatic function'), pretend to be dead or assume the forms and colours of another animal or of sand, leaves, lichen, fungus (what English researchers designate 'mimicry'). Thus the individual hides himself in the general concept 'man,' or in society" (Nietzsche 1982: 20).

15 Here mimicking the anti-Semitic attitude to Jews to the extent of racially othering the *Ostjuden* by attributing their negative qualities to the result of miscegenation with some "inferior human material." He also, as his comments on "chromatic function" make clear, accepts that Jews, as an integral entirety, are racially distinct from other Europeans.

16 See Sufian 2007 for a richly researched study of this dually redemptive process.

17 Laqueur, following Schorske, believes that "the narcissistic streak in his character played a great part in it. Herzl relished the role of Messiah-King which he was to assume in the years to come" (Laqueur 2003: 97). Max Nordau's insistence on the democratic assemblies of the Zionist Congresses weakened the impact of his specific programmatic positions without reducing his role as figurehead of the movement.

18 "Of great importance for the future of the movement was his meeting with the representatives of Russian Jewry, who with seventy delegates had constituted the strongest contingent [of the First Zionist Congress of 1897] in Basle. Herzl was impressed by the calibre of these men, of whose existence, with very few exceptions, he had been only dimly aware" (Laqueur 2003: 107). See also pp. 112–113 on the growth of the Russian Zionist movement by the Fourth Congress of August 1900.

19 See Giladi 1990 and Gat 2000 for differing views on the character of this activity.

20 See, on these communities and their treatment on arrival in Israel, Alcalay 1993: 37–59; Bowman 2002: 461–463; Giladi 1990; and Swirski 1989.

21 Compare Herzl from *Der Judenstaat* on the reception into the Jewish state of new immigrants: "Clothing, underlinen, and shoes will first of all be manufactured for our own poor emigrants, who will be provided with new suits of clothing at the various European emigration centres . . . Even the new clothing of the poor settlers will have a symbolic meaning. 'You are now entering on a new life'" (Herzl 1993: 46).
22 See Golden on dilemmas raised in representing Israel in Tel Aviv's Museum of the Jewish Diaspora: "how many 'facets' can be contained within one culture before it becomes two or three or indeed as many cultures as the 'facets' themselves?" (Golden 1996: 237).
23 As early as June 1895 Theodor Herzl wrote in his diary regarding the indigenous population: "The private lands in the territories granted us we must gradually take out of the hands of the owners. The poorer amongst the population we try to transfer quietly outside our borders by providing them with work in the transit countries, but in our country we deny them all work. Those with property will join us. The transfer of land and the displacement of the poor must be done gently and carefully. Let the landowners believe they are exploiting us by getting overvalued prices. But no lands shall be sold back to their owners" (quoted in Haneghi *et al.* 1971: 14).
24 Initially (1907) this exclusionary labor policy was meant to apply only to lands owned by the Jewish National Fund, but by 1920 Ben-Gurion was calling for its extension to the entire economy (see Shafir 1996: 78–90).

Bibliography

Agamben, G. (1998) *Homo Sacer: Sovereign Power and Bare Life*, trans. Daniel Heller-Roazen, Stanford, CA: Stanford University Press.
—— (2005) *State of Exception*, trans. Kevin Attell, Chicago, IL: University of Chicago Press.
Alcalay, A. (1993) *After Jews and Arabs: Remaking Levantine Culture*, Minneapolis: University of Minnesota Press.
Althusser, L. (1971) "Ideology and Ideological State Apparatuses (Notes towards an Investigation)," in *Lenin and Philosophy and Other Essays*, trans. Ben Brewster, London: Verso, pp. 121–173.
Berkowitz, M. (1993) *Zionist Culture and Western European Jewry before the First World War*, Chapel Hill: University of North Carolina Press.
Bowman, G. (2002) "'Migrant Labour': Constructing Homeland in the Exilic Imagination," *Anthropological Theory*, 2(4): 447–468.
—— (2009) "Israel's Wall and the Logic of Encystation: Sovereign Exception or Wild Sovereignty?," in Bruce Kapferer and Bjørn Enge Bertelsen (eds) *Crisis of the State: War and Social Upheaval*, New York and Oxford: Berghahn Books, pp. 292–304.
Finkelstein, N. (1988) "Disinformation and the Palestine Question: The Not-So-Strange Case of Joan Peters's *From Time Immemorial*," in Edward Said and Christopher Hitchens (eds) *Blaming the Victims: Spurious Scholarship and the Palestine Question*, London: Verso, pp. 33–69.
Friedland, R. and R. Hecht (1996) *To Rule Jerusalem*, Cambridge: Cambridge University Press.
Gat, M. (2000) "Between Terror and Emigration: The Case of Iraqi Jewry," *Israel Affairs*, 7(1): 1–24.
Giladi, G. (1990) *Discord in Zion: Conflict between Ashkenazi and Sephardi Jews in Israel*, trans. R. Harris, London: Scorpion.
Gilman, S. (1993) *Freud, Race and Gender*, Princeton, NJ: Princeton University Press.
Golden, D. (1996) "The Museum of the Jewish Diaspora Tells a Story," in Tom Selwyn (ed.) *The Tourist Image: Myths and Myth Making in Tourism*, New York and London: John Wiley & Sons, pp. 223–250.
Halper, J. (2000) "The 94 Percent Solution: A Matrix of Control", *Middle East Report*, 216: 14–19.
Haneghi, H., M. Machover and A. Orr (1971) "The Class Nature of Israeli Society," *New Left Review*, 1(65): 3–26.

Herzl, T. (1960 [1902]) *Altneuland*, trans. Paula Arnold, Haifa: Haifa Publishing Company.
—— (1993 [1895]) *The Jewish State: An Attempt at a Modern Solution of the Jewish Question*, 7th edn, trans. Sylvie D'Avigdor, London: Henry Pordes.
Kornberg, J. (1993) *Theodor Herzl: From Assimilation to Zionism*, Bloomington: Indiana University Press.
Laclau, E. and C. Mouffe (1985) *Hegemony and Socialist Strategy: Towards a Radical Democratic Politics*, trans. Winston Moore and Paul Cammack, London: Verso.
Laqueur, W. (2003) *A History of Zionism*, London: Tauris Parke.
Leonhard, L. and M.C. van der Hoeven (1971 [1960]) "Shlomo and David, Palestine, 1907," in Walid Khalidi (ed.) *From Haven to Conquest: Readings in Zionism and the Palestine Problem until 1948*, Washington, D.C.: Institute of Palestine Studies, pp. 115–124.
Lustick, I. (1980) *Arabs in the Jewish State: Israel's Control of a National Minority*, Austin: University of Texas Press.
Nietzsche, F. (1982) *Daybreak: Thoughts on the Prejudices of Morality*, trans. R.J. Hollingdale, Cambridge: Cambridge University Press.
Patai, R. (ed.) (1960) *The Complete Diaries of Theodor Herzl*, New York: Herzl Press and Thomas Yoseloff.
Pawel, E. (1989) *The Labyrinth of Exile: A Life of Theodor Herzl*, New York: Farrer, Strauss and Giroux.
Peters, J. (1984) *From Time Immemorial: The Origins of the Arab–Jewish Conflict over Palestine*, New York: Harper and Row.
Piterberg, G. (2001) "Erasures,", *New Left Review*, 10, July–August: 31–46.
—— (2008) *The Returns of Zionism: Myths, Politics and Scholarship in Israel*, London: Verso.
Rose, J. (2005) *The Question of Zion*, Princeton, NJ: Princeton University Press.
Sartre, J.P. (1948) *Anti-Semite and Jew*, trans. George Becker, New York: Schocken.
Shafir, G. (1996) *Land, Labor and the Origins of the Israeli–Palestinian Conflict, 1882–1914*, Berkeley: University of California Press.
Sufian, S. (2007) *Healing the Land and the Nation: Malaria and the Zionist Project in Palestine, 1920–1947*, Chicago, IL, and London: University of Chicago Press.
Swirski, S. (1989) *Israel: The Oriental Majority*, trans. Barbara Swirski, London: Zed Books.
Zimmerman, A. (2001) *Anthropology and Antihumanism in Imperial Germany*, Chicago, IL: University of Chicago Press.

Part III
Civilian surveillance

4 Ominous designs

Israel's strategies and tactics of controlling the Palestinians during the first two decades

Ahmad H. Sa'di[1]

Introduction

There is likely no setting where the centrality of the population in governance is as crucial as it is in colonial settler regimes. The size, natural growth, structure, migration, and spatial distribution of the indigenous population and the settlers are of fundamental importance to the functioning – and even the very survival – of these regimes. Moreover, since these regimes are premised on racial/national domination, they devise different, even opposing, principles of governmentality for natives and settlers. Intentionality, elaborate planning, and learning, therefore, are at the heart of how these regimes handle populations. Generally speaking, such regimes have dealt with the problem of biopower through strategies reminiscent of the ways in which European societies treated "abnormal" populations (namely, through exclusion, quarantining, or surveillance) (Foucault 1991). These strategies, according to Foucault (2000: 332), work simultaneously at the collective and individual levels. In colonial settler regimes, they took the form of removal through expulsion or genocide, ghettoization, or the imposition of surveillance and control techniques. These latter techniques were intended to mold the indigenous population's identity, culture, consciousness, and modes of economic activity, most noticeably through regular (and occasionally mundane) practices aimed at keeping them subordinate. Yet, these strategies should be viewed as archetypes, and the emergence of hybrid models in various colonial settings, such as Israel, is highly likely (see, e.g., Abernethy 2000; Judd 2004; Fieldhouse 1981).

Ethnic cleansing, as evidenced in the history of the political thinking of Zionist leaders and Israeli practices during the 1948 war, was doubtless Zionism's favored strategy (Shahak 1989; Masalha 1992; Pappe 2006). Success, however, was mixed: about 160,000 out of 900,000 Palestinians remained on the territory upon which Israel was established. The question of the regime's strategies of handling this population has rarely been posed in a thoroughgoing manner. Rather, it has been mostly piecemeal, resulting in a fragmented and disconnected essence which the regime intends to alter through well-devised strategies. This is the subject of the ensuing discussion.

In fact, the very existence of such strategies has been denied by Israeli scholars and the Israeli public. Expressing the view widely held among Israelis, Benziman and Mansour (1992: 211) write: "State's leaders have not discussed systematically the fundamental questions regarding Jewish–Arab relations inside the Green-line, they have neither set for themselves long or medium term objectives nor did they devise plans for the achievement of these goals." Even the sole article on the state's policy of controlling the Palestinian minority written by an Israeli academic did not depart from this conception, thus its author stated:

> The establishment itself has, nevertheless, neither the interest nor the time to deal with Arab matters. Since it has no positive expectations of them, such as becoming equal and active partners in Israeli society, it does not define this situation as a state concern that requires planning, allocation of resources and ongoing daily care.
>
> (Smooha 1982: 75)

Since 1990, Smooha has become less interested in Israel's policy of control. Instead, in a series of articles (Smooha 1990, 1997, 2002), he has argued that domination on racial/national grounds is part of a democratic regime he labels "ethnic democracy."

Few scholars have thus far discerned elaborate state strategies for dealing with the Palestinians minority. Of them, the most important are Zureik (1979), who employed a model of internal colonialism, and Lustick (1980), who analyzed the regime's practices through a system of control comprised of three mutually reinforcing components: segmentation, cooptation, and dependency. Yet, Lustick described his model as a theorization of actual practices rather than part of a defined state strategy:

> The system metaphor . . . helps avoid the suggestion of comprehensive conspiracy by permitting analysis of how specific policies, because of the structural and institutional contexts within which they are adopted, tend to have *unanticipated* consequences which also reinforce one or another component of control. Thus the "system of control" described and analyzed in this study is offered as an analytical construct for interpreting a complex social, economic and political reality.
>
> (Lustick 1980: 78–79)

However, recent research by Cohen unveiled a set of tactics laid down as early as 1920 – when the Jewish population comprised a mere 10 percent of the population – which aimed to destabilize and disorganize the indigenous Arab community by instigating conflicts among various groups (Cohen 2004: 18). Techniques of social sorting, data collection, and surveillance – of the population and its property, particularly land – were widely employed by specialized Zionist bodies (Danin 1987; Pappe 2006; Fischbach 2008).

In this chapter I shall discuss Israeli strategies and objectives regarding the Palestinian minority in chronological order. The first section therefore deals with the formative stages during which various strategies evolved. The second section discusses the first state's comprehensive plan to deal with the Palestinians, along with some of the plan's implications. The third section presents the maturation of the control design.

The formative stage: the first decade

During the 1948 war, Israeli leaders endeavored to achieve the ethnic cleansing of the majority of Palestinians. Through the statistical-bureaucratic means of registration, the emerging demographic reality was to be objectivized, and the population was divided into categories characterized by hierarchies of entitlements and rights to citizenship. Thus, during November 1948, the first census – doubling as a registration process – was carried out. Although presented as a "snapshot" of the population at a given point in time, it was in fact constitutive of the social reality. Its major aim was to present a coherent legal position to deny refugees the right of return at the end of the war, as Leibler and Breslau (2005: 892) explained:

> If now, in late 1948, all those remaining in the country, Jews and Arabs alike, were universally granted citizenship, it would be possible to observe international norms [of territory-based citizenship] while turning the distinction between Arabs who had stayed and who had left into a permanent, legal divide.

In an administrative move that was indicative of future state strategies, the census/ registration also aimed to create the political basis for a hierarchical system of citizenship in Israel according to which Jewish settlers from pre-1948 were placed at the top while Palestinian "present absentees" were relegated to the bottom (Leibler and Breslau 2005: 896–897). The main binary of Jews versus Arabs (i.e., dominants versus subordinates) was underscored by the "present absentees" category, which includes only Arabs. It is comprised of Palestinians who resided, on 27 November 1947, on the territory upon which Israel was established, but who were not registered as citizens in the census/registration. This group includes Palestinians who, in response to the fighting, fled to safer areas inside the territories controlled by Israel or to areas that were captured later. It also includes Palestinians who simply were not present when the registration took place and Palestinian refugees who managed to return. This categorization allowed the state to expropriate their property, particularly their land, and prevent their return to their villages. In 1949 they numbered 81,000 (Leibler and Breslau 2005: 896).

The 1948 war ended with the demographic transformation of Palestine. A Jewish state was established on 77.8 percent of Palestine's territory; out of 900,000 Palestinians who lived in this territory, only 156,000 eluded the ethnic cleansing campaign launched by Jewish forces (Pappe 2006). Even so, Israeli leaders viewed this minority with apprehension and abhorrence. Early debates on how to handle the minority lamented the incompleteness of the transfer campaign. Yitzhak Ben-Zvi, who was to become Israel's second president, observed that "there are too many Arabs who remained in the country" (Segev 1998: 46). Other Mapai leaders made similar observations. Eliyahu Carmeli, a Knesset Member (KM), pointed out, "I'm not willing to accept a single Arab and not only an Arab but any gentile. I want the state of Israel to be entirely Jewish." Yehiel Duvdevany, KM, maintained, "If there was any way of solving the problem by way of a transfer of the remaining 170,000 Arabs we should do so." And Zeev Onn, another Mapai leader, commented, "The landscape is more beautiful – I enjoy it, especially when traveling between Haifa and Tel-Aviv, and there is no single Arab to be seen" (Segev 1998: 47). This approach would later be translated into plans to decrease the minority population through various means, including transfer.

Indeed, the first state's set of goals, which was formulated in 1949, focused on three issues that would comprise the basis of state's future strategy: decreasing the size of the minority population; rearranging its spatial distribution; and subjecting it to a tight regime of control and surveillance. The state's objectives were articulated as follows:

1   To prevent the return of Palestinian refugees and expel those who succeeded in returning.
2   To relocate (and occasionally to transfer) the population of partly empty villages and neighborhoods, and Palestinian villages residing adjacent to the new borders, and transfer of Palestinian-owned lands to Jewish settlements.
3   To establish political control over the Palestinians and segregate them from the Jewish majority.

(Segev 1998: 52)

David Ben-Gurion, the first prime minister of Israel and its founding father, adopted these goals, and his directions would ensure their implementation. The following describes how these goals were put into practice.

While the issue of the refugees is multifaceted and was fought on various fronts, one way of blocking Arabs' return to Israel was to settle Jewish immigrants on their land and, in many cases, in their houses. This was part of a policy later labeled "Judization." Indeed, according to Peretz (1958: 143): "of 370 new Jewish settlements established between 1948 and 1953, 350 were on absentees' property. In 1954 more than one third of the new immigrants (250,000) settled in urban areas abandoned by Arabs."

The second goal led to the development of two processes: the continuation of transfers, and the spatial rearrangement of Palestinians. As to the first, research on the expulsion of the Palestinians usually refers to the massive ethnic cleansing of Palestinians during 1947 and 1948. However, this process continued intermittently and on a smaller scale until 1959, eleven years after Israel's establishment. The most well-known cases are the expulsion of the inhabitants and refugees from Faluga and Iraq al-Manshiya (3,100 people in 1949); the transfer of Al-Majdal's residents – numbering some 2,600 – mostly to Gaza during February–October 1950 (Morris 2004: 528–529); and the expulsion of 12,000–15,000 refugees who remained in the "Triangle" area following its handover from Jordanian to Israeli rule in accordance with the 1949 Rhodes armistice agreement (Morris 2004: 529–533). The last documented expulsion was the deportation of hundreds of Bedouins from the al-'Azazma tribe to Jordan and Egypt in 1959 (Cohen 2006: 223; Jiryis 1976: 82). According to Morris (2004: 536), Israel's policy of cleansing the borders of Palestinians resulted in the expulsion of 30,000–40,000 people.

These overt and coercive transfers were accompanied by silent initiatives as well. The Higher Council for Arab Affairs (a coordinating body of state control–surveillance agencies, established in July 1952) estimated that the aggressive stick-and-carrot policy intended to elicit massive Palestinian migration had led, by 1965, to the exodus of some 3,000 Palestinians (Cohen 2006: 120). Various unsuccessful clandestine attempts at transfer were revealed some years later by scholars and journalists; others might still be hidden, either because they have not yet been discovered or because they were not formalized or put on paper. The best-known transfer plan, under the codename "Operation Yohanan," aimed at transferring Galilee Christians and settling them in Brazil and Argentina. The plan began to take shape in the autumn of 1950 but culminated in failure in early 1953. It was engineered by Yosef Weitz, the director of the Jewish National Fund's Land Settlement Department, and he received the active collaboration of Foreign Minister Moshe Sharett as well as the blessing of Prime Minister Ben-Gurion. Various tactics regarding the management of the transfer were devised. A letter from Sharett to Weitz of 4 November 1952 discloses some of these:

> In reply to your letter dated 6 October [1952] and after I have consulted the Prime Minister and other colleagues in the Foreign Ministry, who accepted my opinion, I here inform you that we approve of the implementation of the plan, which it has been agreed to call "Operation Yohanan" (the emigration of Christian Arabs from the Upper Galilee to Argentina and Brazil). It seems to us that it is absolutely desirable to keep this matter secret for the time being. In any case, we should promote matters in a way which would enable us, at a time of need, to present this movement [publicly] as emigration of individuals conducted on the initiative and responsibility of those concerned – similar to the emigration of the Maronites from Lebanon – and not as a government operation. We assume in advance that the departees would leave and arrive at their destination as subjects of Israel and until their naturalization in the new country the Israeli embassy would extend to them all the required assistance. Thus the permission to begin implementation has been given and I ask you to inform me about any progress.
>
> (Quoted in Masalha 1996: 30)

These tactics carry the fingerprints of Israeli diplomacy. They aimed to absolve the Israeli state of liability for the actions of its agents.

Another unfulfilled plan was hammered out by Ariel Sharon in 1964. Then an IDF colonel, he planned to expel some 300,000 Palestinians residing in the Galilee in the course of a war that would be waged with Syria. The plan reached the operational level as he enquired about the number of vehicles needed to carry out the deportation (Melman and Raviv 1988).

The second process of spatial rearrangements comprised the emptying of some villages in order to cleanse the border areas of Palestinians or transfer their land to Jewish settlements. The research on Palestinians' relocation inside Israel has remained patchy and inconclusive. The most famous cases are the displacement of the residents of the villages of Iqrit (7 November 1948), Kafr Bir'im (13 November 1948), and Ghabsiya (24 January 1950). Although the inhabitants of these three villages were promised early return, this has still not materialized, despite official promises and several verdicts by the High Court of Justice (Pappe 2006: 185–187; see also Sa'di 2005; Morris 2004: 509–516). Another widely known case is the forced movement of Haifa's Palestinian residents from the upper and western parts of the city to a concentrated area in the old Wadi Al-Nisnas neighborhood. Haifa's model was followed in Jaffa, Lydda, Acre, and Al-Majdal (until the expulsion of its citizens) (Pappe 2006: 207–208; Morris 2004).

Having transformed the country demographically and constructed a ring of Palestinian-free areas along the new borders, the state had isolated Palestinians in Israel from the refugees and the rest of the Arab world. The third goal, then, was to govern them through an effective control and surveillance system. They were to be governed not by the ordinary state bureaucracy, but rather by a military government and through the British Mandatory Emergency Regulation, primarily enacted to fight Jewish terrorism. Besides the spatial isolation of Palestinians, their institutional segregation aimed to enhance the effectiveness of the technologies of surveillance through which they were to be governed. A letter from Foreign Minister Sharett to his fellow ministers, dated 24 February 1950, underscored the need to maintain this segregation:

> There is a growing number of cases of Arab citizens of Israel applying directly to members of the government and the central offices not via the authorized officials, i.e., the military governor or the local officers in charge of Arab affairs . . .
>
> When there is a direct application by Arabs who are residents of Israel, your offices should firstly verify the details of the case in question with the appropriate local military authorities and not respond to the applicants until the matter has been clarified, and then do it in full cooperation with the authorized local government. Also, it would be preferable if the answer would not be given to the applicants directly, but that the final decision should be transmitted via the local military governor or the regional officer for Arab Affairs.
>
> (Quoted in Segev 1998: 65)

Three years after the formulation of these objectives, Mapai's political committee reformulated them in a way that would reflect the new reality. By 1952 it became clear that a mass expulsion of Palestinians along the 1948 lines was impossible. This, however, did not mean that the idea or the planning for transfer was abandoned; as a case in point, "Operation Yohanan," mentioned above, was under way when these objectives were formulated.

Thus, the new objectives altered the emphasis from transfer to control and surveillance. These objectives, and the reality on which they were based, were:

1   The expulsion of the Arabs is impossible.
2   The activities of the [Mapai] party and the government must be increased (among the Arab population).
3   The existing separate institutional frameworks . . . should be strengthened in the interest of the state and the party.

> (Wiemer 1983: 37)

In addition to the shift of emphasis, these objectives reflected the growing synchronization of various control and surveillance apparatuses (CSA), which included: the Office of the Prime Minister's Advisor on Arab Affairs, the military governors, Mapai's Arab Department, the Histadrut's Arab Department, the police, the General Security Services (Shin Bit), and the army. This synchronization also reflected the Mapai leadership's view of the affinity between the state and Mapai goals.

The second decade: the first comprehensive plan[2]

Almost ten years after the establishment of the state, a committee composed of central figures in CSA was established to study and analyze the state's strategy and goals towards the Palestinian minority and to present a comprehensive plan for dealing with

sideration when making decisions pertaining to their political activity and everyday behavior. They also supervised the political discourse in their communities and responded to deviations from the "proper" national discourse. A pupil from the village of Tamra had first-hand experience of this. He gave a speech congratulating the state and its leaders on Independence Day 1954, and a few days later he received a death-threat letter signed by the "Palestinian underground."[9] Such incidents were common and attest to the nature of the double surveillance experienced by the Arabs in Israel.

The West Bank and Gaza Strip under Israeli occupation

The Palestinians in the West Bank (WB) and Gaza Strip (GS) came under Israeli sovereignty as a result of the occupation of these areas in the Six-Day War (1967). After nineteen years of living under Jordanian (West Bank) and Egyptian (Gaza) rule, they were, in a sense, already accustomed to living with political surveillance as both countries had placed limits on political activity. The Jordanian security agencies used informers in mosques, within political parties, in clubs, and in many other organizations to control opposition activity. When Israel occupied the West Bank, capturing the archives of the Jordanian intelligence agencies was among its first actions. This proved to be fruitful not only because Israel had thus acquired intelligence on political activists and organizations all over the WB but because it identified Jordanian intelligence informers, some of whom agreed to continue their activities under their new masters. In addition, the military control of the WB enabled the Israelis to enhance the permissions-in-exchange-for-information strategy, which had already been so central to the control system over the Palestinians in Israel. Yet there were important differences between the methods used west and east of the Green Line, which derived from the basic fact that the Palestinians in Israel were Israeli citizens, while those in the WB and GS were not. Thus, unlike the Palestinians in Israel, who were encouraged to adopt the Zionist symbols (even if not to identify with them) and not to express the Arab nationalist narrative publicly, there was no such attempt *vis-à-vis* the Palestinians in the occupied territories.

The main goal of the state's surveillance was to prevent subversive activity. In this context it is important to note a relatively unknown fact: Israeli Arabs of all religious backgrounds were recruited by the Israeli security agencies in the territories – military government, police, civil administration, and, to a lesser degree, the *Shabak* – and they have had a significant role in the surveillance system developed in the WB and GS since 1967. This demonstrates that, to a certain extent, the division between the occupier and the occupied is drawn not only on ethno-religious lines but on citizenship.

The armed struggle and the competing surveillance systems

The first step the Israeli army took after taking over the West Bank and Gaza Strip was to collect weapons remaining in Palestinian hands. This task was more difficult to achieve in the Gaza Strip, where units of the Palestinian Liberation Army (an organ of the PLO) had been organized under Egyptian command before the war. But in both areas it required the cooperation of the local population. As in the Galilee in 1948 and the Triangle in 1949, mukhtars and potential informers were summoned to the military authorities and were required to provide information on subversive activity and on individuals who possessed weapons. The first weeks after the war saw a mass collection of weapons, but then the pace slowed.

Israel was not the only one seeking to consolidate its control over the residents of the territories. The Fatah movement saw the occupation of the area by Israel as a golden opportunity to act more freely in the territories, where the Hashemites had hitherto restricted their activity. Arafat and his colleagues decided to relocate their headquarters to the territories. Their grand plan was to mobilize the population into civil disobedience, while Fatah's trained recruits would launch a guerrilla war. The date chosen for the second *intilaqa* – as this outbreak of resistance was termed – was 28 August 1967, and Fatah cells primed themselves for this day. However, the population's support for this "popular war" was rather limited, and many Fatah members were arrested before the *intilaqa* or just after, sometimes without having participated in even a single operation. In the last months of 1967 the Palestinian organizations were engaged in a battle for survival, and Fatah was forced to withdraw its headquarters to Jordan. This was an important success for the Israeli security services in the West Bank and its impact was apparent for many years. Despite this, some cadres of Fatah and the Popular Front for the Liberation of Palestine (PFLP), which was established in December 1967, as well as other organizations, remained in the territories and continued their activities on a smaller scale.

The situation that emerged in the territories was similar in many ways to what was happening inside Israel: the population at large, regardless of its political views, was placed under conflicting surveillance systems. The Israelis aimed at preventing the Palestinians from supporting the armed struggle and participating in civil disobedience; PLO factions implemented surveillance in order to prevent the population from cooperating with Israel (not to mention with Jordanian intelligence, which was also active in the first years after the occupation). However, as we shall see, "cooperating with Israel" had different meanings for different factions in different periods.

Informing on armed activists has been considered treason since the inception of the Arab national movement and continues to be regarded as such in the present day. Nevertheless, since the very first days of the occupation, informers have played a key role in the Israeli surveillance system. They were instrumental in the breakdown of the *intilaqa* of 1967 and enjoyed Israeli protection. However, they, in turn, were placed under strict Palestinian surveillance. Palestinian intelligence networks were set up by local activists in the territories and by the PLO's headquarters in Jordan for the purpose of gathering information on Palestinian informers as well as on members of the general population. Suspects were warned and sometimes attacked. The goal of the nationalists was to create an atmosphere in which collaboration would be deemed socially unacceptable.

They had some success, as the attempt on the life of an informer from Aqraba, east of Nablus, in November 1967 illustrates. The attack was carried out by an armed group that infiltrated from Jordan. But the Israeli authorities reached the conclusion that the mukhtar of the village also supported it. According to the testimony of the informer's daughter, the mukhtar had told her – apparently with glee – two weeks before the attack that her father had been sentenced to death because he had informed on individuals who possessed weapons.[10] Such a case, which was by no means unusual, demonstrates the reality in the villages, whereby some people worked with the Israelis while others – probably more – sided with the Palestinian militants. Even those who tried to distance themselves from the political and military scene were approached (and scrutinized) by both sides.

In the Aqraba case, the mukhtar sided with the *fidayeen*, as the Palestinian combatants were termed at the time. This was not always the case, though, and some mukhtars – identified as an influential group and targeted by both the Palestinian activists and the Israeli agencies – chose to collaborate with Israel. Soon after the occupation, the Israeli commander of the WB published a booklet entitled "The Roles and Authorities of the Mukhtars." As during British and Jordanian rule, each and every mukhtar was required "to keep the security in his area; to inform the authorities of any stranger or suspect who enters the area . . . to supply the authorities with immediate information about any crime or any danger to the security of the area," and so on.[11] Many of them adapted themselves to the new regulations. Some tried to play both sides. Some supported the Palestinian national movement. Some remained loyal to Jordan (at least in the first decade after the occupation).

The mukhtars were not the only ones singled out for scrutiny by all parties. As previously mentioned, surveillance was experienced by the population as a whole. In September 1967, Israel launched a census of the population, which serves until the present day as the official source determining who has the right of residency in the territories (and who does not) and who would receive an identity card (and who would not). It was a very useful aid in tracking the *fidayeen* who entered the occupied territories illegally. In the summer of 1969, Fatah also initiated a detailed survey of Palestinian towns and villages in the West Bank. Palestinians from the WB who visited Jordan were requested to answer a detailed questionnaire on site, or to take it with them to their villages and look for the required information. The questionnaire contained questions on the population of each village, the political and military activity it conducted, names of martyrs and prisoners from the village, demolished homes, names of prominent people in the villages (such as mukhtars and teachers), attitudes of the local population towards Jews in general and their relationship with the Israeli army in particular, and names of collaborators. The information was arranged in villages' files under the supervision of Fatah's intelligence officers (Ghazi al-Husseini was one of them). Some of these questionnaires were captured by the Israeli security agencies, which were alarmed by the systematic nature of Fatah's work.[12]

Another form of surveillance and control was distributing leaflets against informers and (in some periods) against working in Israel. Such leaflets became part of the political scene during the early 1970s in Jerusalem, the WB, and Gaza.[13] Here also the aim was to give the population as a whole the feeling that the eyes and ears of the Palestinian organizations were open, and all moves were watched.

The surveillance of the population by Palestinian groups was more severe in the Gaza Strip, especially between 1969 and 1971. During this time, hundreds of Palestinians who were accused of collaboration were attacked and killed by Palestinian militants (Sayigh 1999: 287). Not all of them were collaborators, however. In some cases members of one organization killed members of another (the main competition was between the PFLP and the Palestinian Liberation Forces), accusing them of being informers. Day-laborers who worked in Israel were also attacked, since doing so was defined as treason.[14] One can argue that the Palestinian surveillance system in the Gaza Strip was, in a sense, self-destructive and damaged support for the resistance activity.

However, one should not forget the context of this activity – the Israeli military occupation – which was built on both practical and symbolic violence. During the first five years of the Israeli occupation, hundreds of Palestinians were killed by Israel (most of them *fidayeen*, who were killed after they had infiltrated Israel through the Jordan Valley; others were residents of the GS and WB), hundreds were placed in administrative detention, thousands were convicted and sent to jail, hundreds of homes were demolished, and dozens of Palestinians – if not more – were deported by Israel. State violence was used by Israel in the following years, usually termed "restoring law and order," which is the privilege of rulers.[15]

The Israeli measures proved effective and by the mid-1970s the territories witnessed some changes in both the political and military fields. The level of Palestinian armed resistance decreased dramatically (after 1972 armed activity was quite rare), but the PLO gained greater support among the population, especially after it was recognized by the Arab League as the sole legitimate representative of the Palestinian people at the League's Rabat conference of 1974. This, in turn, led the PLO to declare that anyone who did not support it was a traitor,[16] and to put in place mechanisms for political surveillance of the population.

Political surveillance

In the first half of the 1980s both sides continued to use political surveillance. This was happening as support for the PLO was growing and it affected most of the population. Following the peace treaty between Israel and Egypt (which ignored the PLO), and with the inception of negotiations on Palestinian self-rule in the occupied territories, the PLO was determined to prevent any local leadership from acting independently. This was a continuation of its old policy: initiatives by local leaders in the WB and Gaza to negotiate with Israel about the establishment of a Palestinian state in the occupied territories were forcefully rejected and oppressed by the PLO. There were two main reasons for this. First, the PLO did not recognize Israel and demanded the establishment of a Palestinian democratic state in the whole of mandatory Palestine; and, second, the PLO wanted to be the sole representative of the people. As early as summer 1968, a Fatah member had been arrested by the Israeli security services and told his interrogators that he was recruited in Karame, in the East Bank, and was sent by Yasser Arafat to assassinate two people who promoted the idea of an independent Palestinian state: Aziz Shehadeh and Khalil Janho. [17] Over the following years Janho was attacked several times and his cars were set on fire, while Shehadeh was murdered in 1985 (although not necessarily because of his political views).

The gradual establishment of the Village Leagues – Palestinian organizations based on traditional leaders and local activists who were not part of the PLO and were supported by Israel – from the late 1970s enraged the PLO. Members of the Leagues were under constant PLO surveillance; they were harassed, and sometimes attacked, by local activists; and Israel supplied them with weapons to protect themselves. Their names and activities were reported to the PLO and to Jordan, which also opposed them.[18] Several assassinations took place: for instance, in November 1981 the head of the Leagues in the Ramalla area, Yusef al-Khatib, was shot,[19] a murder which highlighted the degree to which the Leagues were being scrutinized. In September

1984 a Gazan Fatah cell killed the mayor of Rafah, Abd al-Hamid Qishta, as he emerged from the mosque, and also tried but failed to kill Qalqilia's mayor. From the point of view of the PLO, all of these figures were guilty not only of over-moderation but of acting outside (or against) the national movement. Interestingly, this Gazan cell also conducted inter-organizational surveillance: they pursued the evolving Islamic movement in the Gaza Strip, and assassinated one of its leaders, the dean of the Islamic University, Isam'il al-Khatib.[20]

These were the cornerstones in the implementation of the PLO's surveillance-and-control system. It existed alongside the Israeli one. Another form of surveillance developed by Israel, aimed at improving its understanding of the general atmosphere in the occupied territories, was the censoring of letters. Every week, the Israeli authorities read and analyzed thousands of letters that were sent from the WB and GS, and reports were dispatched to various official bodies. It seems that this practice replaced the method whereby informers documented comments and statements, which had been commonly used in the Arab communities of Israel. In the first week of 1968, for example, 3,300 letters were read and analyzed. Many of them included harsh criticism of Israel's conduct in the territories. However, many others included positive comments. Some prayed for a new war that would bring about the destruction of the Jewish state, while others wished for peace between the nations.[21] This gave the Israeli authorities an insight into the people's attitudes. It should be noted that the same practice was also used by the military censor, who read letters sent by Israeli soldiers from 1948 until very recently – and for the same reasons.

Different forms of surveillance were directed at preventing political activities. These included restrictions on reading material (lists of "forbidden books" were published every so often by the military command), declaring various organizations illegal, tracing activists who spoke against the military rule, and, after 1978, arresting activists who participated in the campaign against the Egyptian–Israeli peace agreement.

In the West Bank and Gaza the clear winner in the battle for political allegiance was the PLO. The first Intifada (which began December 1987) was unequivocal proof of this. The Intifada opened a new arena for surveillance. Indeed, in times of intensive conflict, surveillance also intensifies. Hamas, which was established at that time, created its security apparatus to deal with collaborators; Fatah had already established its own, known as the "strike forces," in almost every village and neighborhood, and the leftist organizations did the same. Everyone persecuted informers, forcing some to abandon their activities and killing hundreds who allegedly refused to comply. The Israeli surveillance system, which was based on informers, was therefore undermined.

But this success was only temporary. Israel managed to rebuild its network of informers, and again the Palestinian population as a whole was placed under double surveillance: by the (numerous) Palestinian groups, on the one hand, and by Israel, on the other. A new situation emerged after the signing of the Oslo Accords, and the establishment of the Palestinian Authority (PA) in 1994, and yet another change occurred as a result of the 2006 elections and the victory of Hamas. However, most Palestinians in the PA areas still live under double, if not triple, surveillance.

Conclusion

The experience of life under foreign rule, either as a national minority or as a member of an occupied society, entails subjection to at least two layers of surveillance. In the Palestinian case, this situation prevailed during the British Mandate, then continued under Jordanian and Egyptian rule between 1948 and 1967 and as a minority in Israel, as well as later under military occupation in the territories. The Zionists and the Palestinian national movement have both used surveillance in order to shape and control political conduct, military activity, consciousness, and identities. As a result, the Palestinians have not been free to make personal decisions over where to work, what to buy, or to whom to sell their land; nor were they free to act in the political field, whether they were pro- or anti-Israel.

A glance at the majority group reveals that it too has been under constant surveillance of various kinds, both in-group and out-group. First, as it does in the occupied society, the majority implements in-group surveillance in order to prevent its members from defecting from the struggle or acting against the colonial/settlement project. Political surveillance was particularly pronounced in the 1980s when Israelis who defied the law prohibiting contact with the PLO were intensely scrutinized. In more recent years, Israelis who actively oppose the occupation are placed under surveillance by the Israeli security services.[22]

The full matrix of surveillance also includes state surveillance over right-wing activists: over the years, Israel has placed several radical activists in administrative detention and has barred them from entering the occupied territories, especially during tense periods. At the same time, the state itself is under surveillance by human rights organizations, intelligence agencies of various countries, and UN agencies. The monitoring of settlement activity by the left-wing organization Peace Now is another example of the state of Israel being under surveillance (and it is worth mentioning that this project is funded by foreign bodies). Moreover, Israeli officials can be subjects of surveillance by Palestinian groups. The assassination of the Israeli minister Rehav'am Ze'evi in October 2001 is a reminder that this form of surveillance should also be taken seriously.

This assassination came at a time when attempts were supposedly being made to coordinate the surveillance conducted by Israel and the PA under the terms of the Oslo Agreements. The Palestinian security agencies were supposed to support the Israelis in their struggle against Hamas and other militant groups that violently opposed the agreements. Since the establishment of the PA, Israeli–Palestinian intelligence cooperation (under the auspices of the US) has had its ups and downs. The Palestinians who participated in it were accused by the opposition of treason, and PA intelligence officers were themselves put under surveillance by Hamas, especially (but not exclusively) in the Gaza Strip. Indeed, the security cooperation can be analyzed as an Israeli success to recruit elements within the occupied territories to protect Israeli interests (as is suggested by Hamas) – a typical action by colonial rulers. Alternately, one can suggest that the united surveillance effort is the only way for Palestinians to achieve their declared national goal of establishing a state in WB and GS with Jerusalem as its capital, because preventing terror might facilitate full Israeli withdrawal from the occupied territories. The acceptance of the "mini-state" idea by the mainstream PLO – and the latter's readiness to participate in joint surveillance to achieve that goal – testifies to the power relations between Israel and the Palestinians, to the acknowledgment by the PLO that Israel is in the Middle East to stay, and to the PLO's need for an ally against Hamas. But it has also increased the tension between Fatah and Hamas, and has led to an intensification of the surveillance activity by both parties. Thus it is safe to assume that the Palestinians in the territories will continue to live under competing surveillance systems for the foreseeable future.

Notes

1 Reports based on this survey are in Central Zionist Archive (hereafter CZA), S15/357; Z111/39; L4/16; Z4/566.

2 Arab intelligence activity was under the surveillance of the Zionist institutions, thus information about their activity can be found in Zionist (and British) intelligence sources. See, for example, reports of the Information Office of 1920 in CZA, L4/739. Reports by Palestinian activists can be found in the files of the Arab Higher Committee, captured by Israel in 1948. See, for example, Israel State Archives (hereafter ISA), 65, 337/1064.

3 See testimony of Israel Avni, recorded 10 December 1970, in the Oral History Division, Harman Institute of Contemporary Jewry, Hebrew University of Jerusalem (hereafter OHD-HU), 57 (7); and testimony of Hiram Danin, 1 December 1970, OHD-HU, 57 (6c).

4 The head of the Arab Executive, Musa Kazem al-Husseini, called upon all Arab residents of Palestine to participate in the census of 1931 and to supply the officials with required details (residency, landownership, etc.). He defined participation in the census a national duty. See "An Announcement to the Arab Nation," 25 June 1931, in ISA 65, 987/129. On the role of Arif al-Arif in carrying out the census among the Bedouins in the Negev, for both improving British control and Arab national reasons, see Assaf Likhovski, *Law and Identity in Mandate Palestine* (Chapel Hill: University of North Carolina Press, 2006), 192ff.

5 See, for example, in ISA 2, SF (Special Files) of the mandatory government, file 215/40, a report by the Palestinian "National Fund" to the High Commissioner, 26 August 1945, which exposes names of *samasira* and includes a demand that the government evacuate Jews who settled illegally in areas where they were forbidden to purchase land.

6 The Committee for Guarding the Rights of the Arabs to Hasan . . ., 24 March 1961, ISA 79, 202/5 and Hasan's testimony to the police in the same file.

7 An undated letter, January 1958, ISA 79, 82/19.

8 Israel Police, Special Branch Safad to Special Branch Jezreel, "Info," 25 May 1967, ISA 79, 318/4.

9 Military Governor North the Israeli Police/Northern District, 11 August 1954, ISA 79, 119/11.

10 Report of IDF, Division 5, 20 November 1967, ISA 79, 323/4.

11 IDF Command of the WB, "The Roles and Authorities of the Mukhtars" (n.d.), ISA 79, 315/5. The military commander also issued an ordinance (no. 153 for 1968) in which owners of hotels were required to report details of their visitors every day to the police, and people who let their homes were also required to provide the names of their tenants.

12 IDF, Division 5/Intelligence to Border Police/Intelligence Officer, "Intensification of PLO's Intelligence Activity in Judea and Samaria," 19 June 1969, ISA 79, 323/4; see also Husseini 2006.

13 For example, see Brigade 5/Intelligence, "Capture of a Terrorist Group Near Qabatia: Initial Report," 14 April 1970, ISA 79, 368/10. For leaflets from this period, see ISA 79, files 358/1 and 374/1. On a bomb near an informer's house in Jerusalem, see, Brigade 16/Intelligence to IP/Southern District, 17 August 1968, ISA 79, 374/3. For threats issued by Fatah against merchants, see Israel Police/Samaria, "Summary of Intelligence, Events and Coordination," 29 November 1967, ISA 79, 430/11.

14 See the testimony of member of the PLF, Gaza SD to IP HQ, 14 February 1971, ISA 79, 369/8.

15 According to the IDF spokesman on 10 December 1971, there were 700 administrative detainees in mid-1971; more than half of them were released that year. Among the first deportees were members of the newly established Supreme Muslim Council. In the 1980s most deportees were PLO supporters.
16 *Filastin al-Thawra*, 117, 10 November 1974, p. 10.
17 Israel Police/Judea to Southern District, "Ahmad T. . .," 17 June 1968, ISA, 451/17.
18 Israel, in its turn, sentenced the activists who passed the information to the PLO. See, for example, file 1105/82 of Hebron Military Court (military attorney *vis* Abdalla al-Rajoub).
19 See Military Court, Ramalla, file 4142/83, in which the assassins were sentenced.
20 Military Court, Gaza, file 350/85, contains the testimonies of the assassins.
21 Bureau of the Chief Censor, "Weekly Reports out of Letters," 10 January 1968, ISA 79, 464/3-5
22 A recent request from the IDF to the *Shabak* to gather intelligence on left-wing activists was reported in *Haaretz*, 7 November 2008, p. 1.

Bibliography

al-Hout, B.N. (1984) *Al-Qiyadat wal-Mu'asasat al-Siyasiyya fi Filastin 1917–1948* [*The Political Leadership and Institutions in Palestine, 1917–1948*], Acre: al-Aswar.
"British Mandate for Palestine" (1923) *The American Journal of International Law*, 17(3): 164–171.
Cohen, H. (2008) *Army of Shadow: Palestinian Collaboration with Zionism 1917–1948*, Berkeley: University of California Press.
——(2010) *Good Arabs: The Israeli Security Agencies and the Israeli Arabs 1948–1967*, Berkeley: University of California Press.
Danin, E. (1984) *Teudot u-Dmuyot* [documents and characters from the archives of the Arab gangs in the 1936[-]1939 riots], Jerusalem: Magnes [Hebrew].
Fanon, F. (1978) *The Wretched on the Earth*, trans. Constance Farrington, New York: Grove Press.
Glazer, S.A. (2001) "Picketing for Hebrew Labor: A Window on Histadrut Tactics and Strategy," *Journal of Palestine Studies*, 30(4): 39–54.
Husseini, G. (2006) Transcription of an interview with al-Jazeera, 22 May. Online. Available HTTP: <http://www.aljazeera.net/NR/exeres/D7203784-2B0B-43C6-B5DF-9C76AD1C91C2.htm#> (accessed 21 November 2008) [Arabic].
Khalidi, R. (1997) *Palestinian Identity: The Construction of Modern National Consciousness*, New York: Columbia University Press.
Lapidoth, Y. (1994) *Ha-Sezon: Tseid Ahim* [*The Hunting Season: Chasing Brothers*], Tel Aviv: Jabotinski Institute [Hebrew].
Likhovski, A. (2006) *Law and Identity in Mandate Palestine*, Chapel Hill: University of North Carolina Press.
Mandel, N. (1976) *The Arabs and Zionism before World War _*, Berkeley: University of California Press.
Sayigh, Y. (1999) *Armed Struggle and the Search for State*, Oxford: Oxford University Press.
Zimmerman, T. (1994) *Bein Patish ha-Knesset le-Sadan ha-Memshala* [*Between the Knesset Rock and the Government Hard Place*], Tel Aviv: Institute for Studying Israeli Society and Economy [Hebrew].

6 The changing patterns of disciplining Palestinian national memory in Israel[1]

Tamir Sorek

The representation of the past is a major sphere of contestation in Israel/Palestine; more specifically, it is a battleground between the state of Israel and its Palestinian citizens. This chapter deals with the attempts of the state and groups in the mainstream Jewish population to shape the way Palestinians remember their past. In this context, I argue that "surveillance," as it is commonly conceived in surveillance studies, is insufficient for analyzing the way collective memory is controlled and disciplined. If surveillance is indeed "the focused, systematic, and routine attention to personal details for purposes of influence, management, protection or direction" (Lyon 2007: 14), the term too heavily emphasizes the collection of personal of data, giving only secondary importance to discipline as one of its potential purposes. Discipline, however, can be achieved by alternate means that do not necessarily include the collection of personal data.

Transferring the focus from "surveillance" to "discipline" would allow us, first, to move beyond the level of individuals in analyzing the control of collective phenomena such as collective memory. In a later reference to his influential panopticon metaphor, Michel Foucault downplayed the political importance of the focus on the individual in the panopticon: "what appeared now, is not the idea of a power which would take the form of an exhaustive surveillance of individuals . . . but the set of dispositifs which, for the government and those who governed, make relevant very specific phenomena which are not exactly individual phenomenon" (quoted and translated by Bigo 2008: 100). This rethinking by Foucault might explain his consent to translate the title of his related book *Surveiller et Punir* to "Discipline and Punish" (Foucault 1977) in English. What lies at the core of the panopticon metaphor is not the collection of data, but the potential to instill self-discipline by making the subject aware that he/she is being watched. My aim is not to reinstate a "pure" Foucauldian perspective, but to emphasize that the collection of personal data in itself lacks political meaning if it does not have the power to affect the subject and shape its behavior.

A second purpose of emphasizing discipline over surveillance is to invite a discussion of the attempts to shape consciousness, rather than bodies or behavior. Although influencing the subject's consciousness is a major goal of governments, existing technologies are not yet effective in monitoring consciousness. Surveillance studies therefore say little about attempts to discipline consciousness, including collective memory. Instilling self-discipline does not require collecting data on subjects' behavior: it is enough to let them know that they are being watched. That is, the visibility of the surveillance apparatus and the constant reminder of the existence of the gaze are as important as the visibility of the subject and the focused collection of individual data.

In this chapter I illustrate how, in the course of specific historical developments, "surveillance" as a mechanism to discipline Palestinian national commemoration inside Israel has been losing its centrality (although not disappearing entirely), while alternative disciplinary practices have emerged. There has been a shift from the reliance on strict monitoring by authorized security agencies to a combination of two increasingly important elements: the "civic gaze" of ordinary people; and sporadic public intimidation by politicians.

In *Discipline and Punish*, Foucault described a historical change in the disciplinary means in France between the seventeenth and the nineteenth centuries. One dimension of this change was "the state-control of the mechanisms of discipline." Foucault argued that, while in England private religious groups continued to carry out social discipline, in France the most important aspects were taken over by the police apparatus (Foucault 1995 [1975]: 214). The growing emphasis on civic gaze at the expense of direct state surveillance, as described below, can be considered a privatization of the disciplinary agency and, therefore, an inversion of the dynamics which represented and shaped the rise of modernity, according to Foucault. Interpreted thus, we are witnessing a "post-modern" and "post-state" form of discipline. This privatization, however, does not signal a weakening of the nation-state. Rather, it reflects the internalization of the state's ideology by individual Jewish citizens who voluntarily serve as its agents in imposing the official narrative. In addition, the civic gaze is backed by public intimidation directly performed by state agents, and its efficiency is derived from the state's power.

The rules have changed

On December 9, 1992, a heated debate in the Knesset dealt with a proposal to outlaw Campus, the Arab students' association at Haifa University. One of the major concerns of Gonen Segev, the Knesset Member from the right-wing Tsomet Party who initiated the discussion, was a calendar distributed by the student organization. The calendar referenced key dates in the Palestinian national narrative. Segev protested:

> Some of the dates mentioned in this calendar: the anniversary of the Palestinian revolution; Land Day; the Deir Yassin massacre; the partition plan; the anniversary of the trauma of 1948 (and I know this is the day when the war of liberation of my people erupted) . . .; the Balfour declaration is mentioned there as well and also the Intifada anniversary. The anniversary of the Palestinian revolution and Palestinian Independence Day – the day is mentioned at Haifa University as a holiday.

> Honorable Speaker, Knesset members, I am talking about students at Haifa University and not about students in Beir-Zeit or an-Najah. I am talking about Arab students born in Israel in its limited pre-1967 borders. You call them Israelis. They call themselves first of all Palestinians. They mention the dates of the Palestinian people and make our national holidays days of mourning. This is the main problem.

Member of Knesset (MK) Tawfik Zayad (Democratic Front for Peace and Equality): There is no contradiction.

MK Gonen Segev: The day when the state was declared is considered by them as a day of mourning . . . Yesterday a sticker was distributed at Haifa University which says: "today is the fifth anniversary of the blessed Palestinian Intifada. On the same day three victims of the Intifada were buried . . .

MK Zayad: Send them to jail. What do you want?

MK Segev: If we will not bash the head of the snake while it is still young, a latent Intifada will erupt among the Arab Israelis and we will not know how to stop it. I am calling on the Minister of Education to impose order on the chaos which prevails in the institutions of higher education and in schools. I would like to remind everyone that we live in the Land of Israel, in the home of the Jewish people. I demand that Campus be outlawed and that the activity of Campus members in the universities in Israel be forbidden.

(Knesset 1992)

As a cycle of holidays specifically designed to commemorate socially marked events, the calendar year often encapsulates the conventional master-narratives constructed by mnemonic communities from their history, and therefore demonstrates the most sacred events in a group's collective past. Moreover, the calendar symbolically reproduces the national past: by blurring the boundary between present and past, the past stays alive in the present (Zerubavel 2003). This is exactly what brought the calendar distributed at Haifa University to a parliamentary session, whose proceedings were symptomatic of the evolving atmosphere in Israel in the 1990s.

For many years Israeli–Zionist hegemonic collective memory has de-legitimized public discussion about the tragic price the Palestinians paid for the establishment of the Jewish state, the destiny of the Palestinian refugees, and the drastic change in the country's landscape following the war (Raz-Krakotzkin 1994). Since this past is perceived by state agencies as challenging the legitimacy of the state of Israel (Swedenburg 1995: 38–75; Benvenisti 2002), and since keeping this past alive could have meant the persistence and validation of a Palestinian national identity within the state of Israel, attempts to commemorate it by the Arab-Palestinian citizens of Israel – especially the commemoration of 1948 – were carefully monitored.

Arab formal education might be the extreme example. The official curriculum in history has ignored the Palestinian national narrative. Teachers with a nationalist orientation were not hired or were fired once this political tendency was discovered (Al Haj 1995). Approaches to both curriculum and hiring have seen a gradual liberalization; however, their contemporary character still reflects a fear of the Palestinian national narrative (see below).

Another strictly monitored sphere has been political commemoration. For the military government officers and the *Shabak* (General Security Services) in the 1950s and 1960s, the celebration of Israel's Independence Day was the ultimate test of loyalty, a litmus test which enabled the state to rank Arabs according to levels of obedience. Every year, all state institutions in Arab towns and villages were required to perform festive ceremonies and raise the Israeli flag (Al Haj 1995; Bauml 2001; Robinson 2005; Cohen 2006). Police informants received detailed instructions to report on the atmosphere in their villages on Independence Day. "Negative" attitudes, such as removing or vandalizing flags and pictures of leaders, or speeches which referred to the "tragedy of the Palestinian people," were followed by police investigations and arrests (Bauml 2001). Interestingly, the end of the military government in 1966 did not immediately change this policy. Although since the 1970s Arab citizens have not been brutally forced to celebrate Israel's Independence Day, authorities still show strong concern for how Arabs behave on that day.

Since the mid-1980s, however, the state's motivation and ability to discipline Palestinian memory has rapidly waned, a result of several interrelated socio-political processes in the state and among both Jewish and Arab societies. The strengthening of the liberal discourse of citizenship and the increased power of the Israeli Supreme Court, which defended this discourse (Shafir and Peled 2002), created a wider range of freedom of speech. Furthermore, among certain elements of the Jewish Israeli academic elite and related circles, publications of the "new historians" partially legitimized public discussion about Israel's responsibility for the Palestinian tragedy (Ram 1998). The exclusion of Egypt from the Arab-Israeli military conflict, and the dismantling of the Soviet Union – the major strategic ally of Israel's enemies – also reduced the siege mentality by abating existential anxieties and increasing the collective self-confidence of Jewish society in Israel. Later, the Oslo process intensified this dynamic and introduced some "post-conflict" attitudes among the Israeli elite, who conveniently adopted the view in the late 1990s that the conflict had virtually ended.

At the same time, Arab society gained confidence with the emergence of new circles of educated elites, which led to the founding of an independent Arabic press in the 1980s (Caspi and Kabaha 2001), formalized leadership in the form of the Follow-Up Committee (Lajnat al-mutaba'a) and its sub-committees, and massive commemorative rituals interwoven with political protest, such as Land Day (Yiftachel 2000). Moreover, Arab local governments gradually gained more autonomy (Rosenfeld and Al-Haj 1990). This was especially important in the field of high school education, since local councils nominate teachers for these schools. One major development that represents this changing political atmosphere was the establishment in the early 1990s of several committees formed by the second generation of internal refugees to protect the rights of the displaced Israeli (Arab) citizens of 1948, to "cultivate the heritage," and commemorate the lost (Benvenisti 2002: 268; Cohen 2003). These signified the growing confidence to deal publicly even with the most sensitive subject of the 1948 war and Palestinian refugees.

As a result of these broader trends, in 1992 Arab students were already confident enough to distribute a calendar that referred to the establishment of the state as a "tragedy." It seems that for some Jewish politicians the mere existence of this narrative was a surprise, while for others its public appearance was a threat. The sarcastic reaction of MK Zayad (i.e., "jail them") clarified that the arsenal of legitimate methods to confront this narrative was by then limited. The Knesset voted against Segev's demand,[2] and for the next nine years there was no recorded attempt by legislators to clip the wings of Palestinian national commemoration inside Israel.

The implications of October 2000 and the second Intifada

The change described above does not mean that during the 1990s Palestinians in Israel were free to write their own narrative or to commemorate their national past without interruption. Arab formal education continued to be monitored. Despite the introduction of some changes in the 1970s, the official curriculum still ignored the Palestinian national narrative (Al Haj 1995). The new spirit of the 1990s was reflected in the attempts of three education ministers from the left-wing Meretz Party to reduce the *Shabak*'s involvement in authorizing nominations of teachers and school directors, but their success was only partial. Similarly, organized visits to the ruins of Palestinian villages in the 1990s sometimes faced police interference, and violent confrontations developed (Benvenisti 2002: 268).

The tension between the "1990s spirit" and its backlash reached its peak around the time of the fiftieth anniversary of Israel's establishment and the *Nakba*. In March 1998, the Higher Follow-Up Committee (FUC) decided to commemorate the *Nakba* in a series of events. This decision provoked both explicit and implicit threats from the Israeli government. The Minister for Arab Affairs in Netanyahu's government, Moshe Katzav (later elected as Israel's president in 2000), described the FUC's decision as one that was "dangerous and might damage Jewish–Arab co-existence" (*Al-Ittihad* 1998). Minister of Interior Eli Yishai threatened to cut governmental funding of any local authorities that financed the *Nakba* commemoration. In the same year, massive rallies and processions to and within abandoned Arab villages did not result in the authorities' interference. However, officials of the Israel Land Authority embarked on a large-scale operation of fencing off abandoned Arab structures and erecting large signs that warned against "trespassing" (Benvenisti 2002: 268).

Before the eruption of the second Intifada, these public threats were vague and relatively minor in their tone. This dynamic prevailed, however, only as long as it was accompanied by a decline in the level of existential anxiety on the Jewish side. The events of October 2000 and the second Intifada interfered with the coherence of these two processes. Historian Tom Segev, who celebrated post-Zionism in a book published shortly before the Intifada, wrote: "Palestinian terrorism seems to push Israelis back into the Zionist womb" (Segev 2002: 151), and the "Zionist womb" resists Palestinians commemorating their tragic past. At the same time, socio-political developments have made it impossible to restore the old practices of disciplining memory.

In addition, some processes among the Arab-Palestinian society in Israel made their own contribution. First, during the 1990s Palestinian civil society inside Israel grew and became institutionalized to create a strong web of self-confident civil activism. Many organizations directly or indirectly deal with establishing the public presence of a Palestinian national narrative. Second, new communication technologies (e.g., internet and satellite TV) have made the flow of information more difficult to control. In a survey I conducted in July–August 2008 with representative samples of the Jewish and Arab populations in Israel, I asked respondents to identify the main source of their historical knowledge.[3] Among the Arab respondents, 24 percent mentioned television and 16 percent mentioned the internet; among the Jewish respondents, only 14 percent mentioned television and just 6 percent mentioned the internet. These gaps suggest that, for the Arab citizens, new technologies were especially important, given their mistrust of the state-sponsored school system.

The implications of the Intifada on Arab citizens, and especially the events of October 2000, were equally dramatic. During late September and early October 2000, with the beginning of the Palestinian uprising, flames spread inside the 1967 Green Line, and the country witnessed a wave of demonstrations, stone-throwing, blocked roads, and police gunfire against demonstrators. Inside Israel, police killed thirteen Palestinian Arabs (twelve of them Israeli citizens). These events triggered a political earthquake among Arab citizens. The unbearable ease with which demonstrators were killed and the indifferent reaction of the frightened Jewish public to the police brutality invoked widespread frustration and a growing awareness of the fragility of the civil and political rights of Arabs in Israel. This awareness has translated into the removal of self-imposed barriers on political protest, as well as on public displays of the Palestinian national narrative (Sorek 2008).

The following story illustrates the inability of the old disciplinary mechanism to deal with these new developments. A major source of power among the Palestinian community in Israel is the relative autonomy of local councils that support and sometimes initiate commemorative events. In Israel, when a local council or mayor fails to run their town or city, the Ministry of the Interior is authorized to dismantle the council or fire the mayor, and to nominate a temporary committee or a temporary mayor. Only Jewish temporary mayors are appointed to run failed Jewish councils; in Arab localities most of the appointees are Jewish as well.

On December 25, 2007, due to the complete failure of the local council of Kafr Kana, an Arab town, the Minister of the Interior nominated Ilan Gavrieli as temporary mayor. In May 2008 the local branch of the Islamic Movement planned to celebrate the birthday of the Prophet Muhammad (*mawlid an-nabi*) and to commemorate the *Nakba* at the same event in the local stadium. It submitted a routine request to the local council and to the police, and received the latter's approval. However, it was astonished to receive a negative answer from the nominated council. According to the council, "this is a political event and it is forbidden by the law" (Rofe-Ophir 2008a). The furious activists organized a protest and distributed a flyer that read: "we will not allow the military government to return to Kafr Kana." They also appealed to the district court in Nazareth to overrule the council's decision. The appeal was accepted and the event took place as planned.

The majority's disciplining civic gaze

The court's decision clarified that the old methods used to discipline Palestinian memory had lost their legitimacy. However, certain forces in Israeli society have been trying to reinstate the undermined disciplinary power. These attempts are carried out by an increasingly present voluntary "civic gaze" of ordinary citizens, backed by public intimidation by certain functionaries in the legislative and executive branches.

For Foucault, the gaze imposes disciplinary practices that inscribe identities upon docile bodies (Foucault 1995 [1975]). Foucault's original thesis referred to specific agents, specialized in specific kinds of surveillance, who direct their scrutinizing gaze to specific individuals. Foucault's panopticon metaphor, which symbolizes this ever-present institutional gaze, certainly fits the reality of the military government. Furthermore, the military government's long shadow still deters Palestinians in Israel from approaching "sacred cows" of the Zionist ethos (Sorek 2008; Sabbagh-Khoury forthcoming). The Jewish civic gaze on Arab public behavior, however, is much less institutionalized and its sources are more vaguely identifiable. The civic gaze should not be confused with the phenomenon of self-appointed informers – namely, citizens who voluntarily report other citizens to the security services. The agents of the civic gaze themselves act to correct the subject's behavior. In addition, the civic gaze is not focused; rather, it is a consistent, random scrutinizing of the public sphere without pre-determined attention to specific individuals. Nevertheless, as I will illustrate later, it is still effective as a disciplinary mechanism.

The civic gaze in practice

The majority's disciplinary gaze is as old as the state, and it has been functioning from the very moment Arabs met Jews amid the post-1948 balance of power. Because of the effectiveness of state-controlled disciplinary practices in the specific field of political commemoration, most Jewish citizens have never encountered the commemorative events organized by Arab citizens. With the exception of university settings, Palestinian political commemoration has been carried out exclusively inside Arab towns and villages. Since 2000, however, Jewish citizens gradually and increasingly have been paying attention to these events. Since Palestinian political memory has become increasingly public and more determined to broach topics sensitive for the Jews in Israel, it has been watched not only by the authorities but by gazing civic eyes, ready to correct "diversions" from the dominant Zionist narrative. Even until 2005, opposition was concentrated mainly in the universities, where sporadic clashes between Arab and Jewish students – especially around *Nakba*/Independence Day – occurred. More recent years, however, have witnessed confrontations between Arab commemorators and Jewish counter-demonstrators in other contexts.

On June 17, 2005, about 150 people, most of them Arab-Palestinian citizens, marched in a memorial parade from the old prison in Acre to the Muslim cemetery in the city. They were commemorating the seventy-fifth anniversary of the execution of three Palestinians by the British authorities (Rabed 2005). The three were the first to gain the status of Palestinian national martyrs in Palestinian national mythology (transmitted from parents to sons and daughters), and are considered anti-colonial heroes. In the early years after their execution the Arab Higher Committee organized massive commemorative rallies of national protest; decades later the parade organizers from the Tawfiq Zayad Institute intended to renew this tradition.

On their way to the cemetery, the parade participants were surprised to encounter a group of Jewish-Israeli protesters waving Israeli flags and holding large signs bearing the word "traitors." From a Jewish-Israeli perspective, this commemoration was outrageous: the three men had been sentenced to death for their part in the massacre of Jews in Hebron and in Safad/Tsfat in August 1929, an event which became a constitutive myth of victimhood in the Zionist narrative (*pra'ot tarpat*). Moreover, although the parade did not directly refer to the *Nakba*, it was a reminder that the Palestinians in Israel are remnants of a viable national community that existed before the state was established, and whose destruction was a precondition for the existence of a Jewish state. Subsequent short reports about the parade on some Hebrew news websites sparked furious reactions from Jewish readers (see, for example, reader's comment on Rabed (2005)).

In recent years, the *Nakba* has also been commemorated in mixed Arab–Jewish towns. The modest event organized in Lid/Lod in 2006 faced a Jewish counter-demonstration organized by some right-wing members of the local council under the title "Flags for Israel." One member wrapped in an Israeli flag addressed the participants and warned:

> Commemorating the *Nakba* by the Arabs of Israel is a denial of the mere existence of the state of Israel, and whoever denies our right to live in peace and security cannot complain that we do not accept him for a job, cannot complain that he is not allowed family unification, cannot be surprised that we check him from head to toe when he enters the bus and should not be surprised if he is not welcome to live near us.
>
> (Ganei Aviv and its Residents 2006)

Interestingly, every element in this multidimensional threat has been identified by Sabbagh-Khoury (forthcoming) as a deterrent to Palestinian citizens in Israel from protesting against issues considered taboo by Jewish-Israelis: the economic dependency on the Jewish side, the tendency to give priority to issues concerning their daily lives, and, finally, the fear of another expulsion, shaped by the trauma of the *Nakba*.

On May 8, 2008, group of Jewish activists came for the first time to confront the annual Return Parade, the central event of *Nakba* Day among the Palestinian citizens of Israel. At the invitation of a new organization named ha-Shomer he-Hadash (the New Guardian), several hundred people attended a massive picnic at the Jewish settlement of Tsipori. The *Nakba* parade route was obstructed since, on its way to the destroyed village of Safuriye, it went through Tsipori, which had been established in 1949 on Safuriye land.

Ha-Shomer he-Hadash was founded in early 2008 by Jewish ranchers who felt that the state had failed to protect them against trespass and looting. Although their point of departure seems to be related to mere protection of private property, their struggle is articulated in the typical ethno-nationalist discourse of a settler society, and it is consciously contextualized in the history of the Israeli–Palestinian conflict. Their name echoes the name of a pre-state paramilitary organization, ha-Shomer, founded to substitute Arab guards in the Jewish settlements with Jewish guards. Symbolically, their first country-wide meeting was scheduled for Land Day (March 30) 2008. At this meeting, the chair, Yoel Zilberman, said: "An all-out war is managed every day and every hour over the national land of all of us, there is a need to return the national pride, patriotism and Zionism and make sure that the ranchers learn to be courageous and proud" (*Maariv* 2008).

Several weeks later, ha-Shomer organized the protest against the *Nakba* commemoration in Tsipori. The event deteriorated into a violent confrontation between the Arab participants and the police. There were injuries on both sides, and thirty-one Arab demonstrators were arrested. It is noteworthy that counter-demonstrations in front of parades commemorating post-1948 events such as Land Day or the October 2000 uprising had never been documented before. These new counter-demonstrations signal to Arab citizens that they are touching a very sensitive nerve in the collective ethos of Jewish citizens.

Public intimidation

This civic gaze has no power of its own. In order for it to be effective, everyone involved must be aware that it represents the interests of the state, which is, for its part, ready to use its own disciplinary mechanism. Therefore, the gaze is complemented by more formalized steps.

Post-2000, the Arab-Palestinian minority has increasingly been seen by the authorities as an existential threat to the Jewish state. The level of anxiety is manifest in the description of the current processes in Arab society in Israel as the "real strategic danger in the long term." This assessment comes from a private discussion of *Shabak* senior advisers with Prime Minister Ehud Olmert, and was carefully chosen for release to the press (Caspit and Hilleli 2007). Nevertheless, the post-2000 modes of disciplining memory are not necessarily part of an organized and coordinated plan. Their main characteristic is their public visibility. Politicians, whether in office or aspiring to office, make public declarations which have the potential to deter Palestinian citizens from organizing or participating in commemorative events. Sometimes these declarations are explicit threats, but the intimidator cannot always follow through, so their main effect is to create an intimidating public environment.

For example, in May 2001, before the first Independence Day after the eruption of the second Intifada, the new Minister of National Infrastructure, Avigdor Lieberman, instructed his ministry's functionaries to avoid any contact with public figures who participated in *Nakba* commemorations. The Ministry of National Infrastructure has a large budget, and denying access to its resources could seriously impede Arab municipalities. Lieberman justified his decision by the need to "punish public figures who turn the Day of Independence into a day of holocaust" (Nir 2001). Three months later, the Minister of Education, Limor Livnat, declared that she was considering making allocation of bonuses and extra funding to schools conditional on their being "loyal to the state." Livnat explained that "schools that commemorate *Nakba* Day, or raise the Palestinian flag and celebrate after terrorist attacks, should not receive bonuses" (Trabelsi 2001).

Livnat went to the media with her new ideas before consulting the ministry's legal advisors (Trabelsi 2001). In both cases, the legality of the newly declared policies was dubious,[4] and there is no evidence that either policy was officially implemented. However, as I asserted earlier, the importance of these statements lies mainly in the atmosphere they create.

Although Lieberman and Livnat were the most explicit in linking commemoration of the past to the distribution of resources in the present, their attitude represents a wider spectrum of the "carrot and stick" policy frequently articulated by Israeli cabinet ministers. For example, as part of the preparations for the celebration of Israel's sixtieth Day of Independence, the Israeli government tried to convince Arab municipalities to take part. Arab political leaders were promised that the "celebrations will include money investment in the infrastructure of the Arab localities" (Inbari 2007). Although we could classify this policy as a "carrot," the poor infrastructure of most Arab towns and the desperate need for funding for public projects should have made them high priorities on the government's list of supported projects regardless. Therefore, making the support they deserve conditional on obedient political behavior should be seen more as another form of threat.

Although the FUC leadership publicly rejected these attempts to "bribe" Arab mayors, in some municipalities the "carrot and stick" policy seems to have been effective. Orsan Yassin, mayor of Shefa-'Amr from 1998 to 2008, organized an official Independence Day celebration in his town. He explained his political philosophy on several occasions: for example, "I had enough of the extremists. We, the moderates, will overpower them. I expect that the Prime Minister will support the moderate Arabs more significantly" (Retner 2000). In another interview to the Hebrew media he complained:

> This is our state and we should be part of it. The FUC positions only hurt our lives. We have to find a good way to educate the children to be part of the state . . . The problem is that in spite of what I am doing for the state, I am not being backed up. The relation [of the government] to Shefa-'Amr is like [its] relation to Umm el-Fahm. We should receive different treatment so everyone will go in my direction.
>
> (Vitkon 2008)

It is noteworthy that in 1998, the newly elected Yassin destroyed a new monument for the *Nakba* martyrs that had been erected in his town (Sorek 2008). Yassin might be extreme in his overt instrumentalism, but he could also represent a wider phenomenon. For example, the government was able to recruit two Arab-Muslim mayors to sit on the advisory board of the sixtieth anniversary celebrations (Sami I'sa from Kafr Qasim, and Talal al-Kirnawi from Rahat).

Some public intimidation inhabits the twilight zone of bizarre politics and potential crimes against humanity. On December 3, 2007, the Israeli Knesset gathered for a special festive session to celebrate the sixtieth anniversary of the UN decision to partition Palestine into Jewish and Arab states. The Arab MKs boycotted this event, provoking furious reactions from some Jewish MKs. Two days later, the FUC chair, Shawki Khatib, informed the Israeli government that the Arab municipalities would not take part in the celebration of Israel's sixtieth Independence Day: "We are not part of these festivals because, in our view, the State of Israel was founded on the ruins of the Palestinian people and because of the expulsion of 80 percent, if not more, of the Palestinian residents who lived then in Palestine" (Inbari 2007). Following this decision the Public Security Minister and former head of the *Shabak*, Avi Dichter, declared, "Whoever cries about the *Nakba* year after year shouldn't be surprised if they actually have a *Nakba* eventually." He called on Israeli-Arab leaders to reconsider their decision not to take part in the celebrations. In the same context, he attacked the mere use of the term *Nakba*, and argued that it harms the Arab public: "From the *Nakba* they will not get any better education, from the *Nakba* they will not get better economic opportunities" (Rabed 2007).

These threats were made before an Arab audience at the opening ceremony of the first Arab branch of the Kadima Party in a non-Jewish locality, in Shefa-'Amr. Meron Benvenisti (2007) wrote in *Haaretz* that "only paranoia and a repressed feeling of guilt could produce" Dichter's declaration. Only seven years earlier, in 2000, Ami Ayalon, Dichter's predecessor in the *Shabak* (1996–2000), recognized that "their [the Palestinians'] *Nakba* accompanies them as a trauma in the same way that the Holocaust accompanies us" (Mifneh 2001), an empathic statement that was diametrically opposite to Dichter's view. Although the difference between these two statements is related to differences in personality and politics, it might well indicate the changes in the level of "*Nakba* anxiety" in Israel's main surveillance agency over the last decade.

Recognizing that the authorities' ability to discipline commemoration of the *Nakba* is restricted by the rule of law, right-wing politicians have been involved in recurrent attempts to outlaw *Nakba* commemoration. In July 2001, four MKs from different right-wing parties submitted a bill aimed at amending the Independence Day Law. According to the proposed amendment, a person who commemorated Israel's Day of Independence as a day of mourning would be jailed for one year or fined 100,000 NIS. The bill was rejected by the Knesset, was resubmitted in March 2003 (Knesset 2003) and failed again. A third attempt was made in January 2005. This time it was barely rejected in the preliminary vote: 29 against 22 (Knesset 2005). Although the government opposed it, this time the amendment was supported not only by the Israeli extreme right but by the mainstream Likud Party. The strongest support came from the centrist Shinuy Party (all nine MKs of that party who attended the session voted in favor), a strong indication of the popularity of the idea in Israeli mainstream politics. Interestingly, discounting the seven Arab MKs who opposed the amendment, it would have been a tie between the Jewish MKs who supported it and those who opposed it. The same amendment was rejected again in January 2008, but in May 2009, following the establishment of a new right-wing coalition, it was adopted for the first time by the Ministerial Committee for Legislation. Later, the government backtracked and proposed an amended bill, according to which the Minister of Finance is authorized to halt public funding for organizations (read: Arab municipalities) who support the "negation of Israel as a Jewish state" (read: mourn at the Day of Independence). The new bill was approved by the Knesset on July 19, 2009.

Although calls to ban Palestinian commemoration have usually been limited to *Nakba* Day, they were recently extended to include another event: Land Day (Rofe-Ophir 2008b). This development is also related to the intensified political activism following October 2000, since in recent years Land Day has been celebrated not only in Arab areas but in mixed Arab–Jewish towns. As a result, Land Day, which is usually rich in symbols of Palestinian nationalism, became more visible to the Jewish public. In Lid, the Land Day rally in 2006 raised concerns among Jewish residents which propelled them to demand the banning of a similar rally on *Nakba* Day (Channel 7 2006).

Measuring the effectiveness of the new disciplinary modes

Nur Masalha argues that "the more the state policies were focused on suppressing *Nakba* memory and dissolving the internal refugees problem, the more the indigenous resistance to that policy became stronger and the more visible *Nakba* commemoration and actual direct action became" (Masalha 2005: 43). Indeed, judging by the public visibility and salience of the *Nakba* commemoration practices, one might argue that the new disciplinary mechanisms mostly failed to achieve their goal. The *Nakba* is frequently discussed in the Palestinian press, and it is commemorated annually in rallies and visits to the depopulated villages. In some schools the *Nakba* has become part of the unofficial curriculum, reluctantly ignored by the Ministry of Education. For a fuller picture, however, one should take a look not only at the presence of national commemoration but at its absence.

We will never know how many Arab mayors have considered commemorating the
Nakba in their towns but were deterred by the above-mentioned public intimidation.
What we can do is look at the ways in which Arab citizens of Israel answer questions
about the *Nakba* and attempt to assess the level of their concern and hesitation based
on these answers. Before proceeding, I should point out that I make the following
assumptions:

1   The *Nakba* is the major anchor of the contemporary Palestinian national narrative.
2   In the Palestinian national narrative the *Nakba* is a direct result of the aggression
    of the Jewish military forces in 1948.
3   The establishment of the state of Israel is the major anchor of the contemporary
    Israeli national narrative (as demonstrated by Schuman *et al.* 2003).

In the survey I conducted in July–August 2008 (see above), interviewees were asked:
"In 1948, hundreds of thousands of Palestinians became refugees. According to your
opinion, who is responsible for that?" Respondents were offered five options, ranging
from complete responsibility of the Jewish side to complete responsibility of the Arab
side. The answers given allow us to assess the extent to which Arab respondents dare
to adopt the Palestinian national narrative in conversations with anonymous
interviewers (all of whom were Palestinian citizens of Israel). Since the Israeli national
narrative is compatible with the authorities' expectations, it was expected that Jewish
citizens would feel free to express that narrative in conversation with a stranger.
Therefore, the data from the Jewish sample will be presented as a point of reference.
Finally, since the youngest generation (eighteen–twenty-nine) has been exposed
primarily to the more recent disciplinary modes, we can learn about their efficacy if
we compare the level of adoption of the Palestinian national narrative among different
generations.

There are some indications that respondents saw the question about responsibility
as a threat. Some of them made wry comments, such as "That sounds like a *Shabak*
question." More significant were the relatively high percentages of safe, "middle of
the road" answers, which indicated equally shared responsibility, and the refusal to
apportion responsibility to either side, which together totaled 51 percent. In the Jewish
sample, these options represented only 39 per cent.

Interestingly, only 23 percent of Arab respondents answered that Jews are the main
or only party responsible, while 26 percent blamed the Arab side, fully or primarily.
Among Jewish respondents, 54 percent blamed the Arab side fully or primarily, while
only 7 percent said that the Jews were mostly or fully responsible. This was despite
the fact that the Jews, as a majority and victorious in the war, might have been
expected to feel more confident to practice self-criticism.

Even more telling is the gap between generations (see Table 6.1). Among the third
generation, the percentage of those who followed the Palestinian national narrative
was more than three times that of the first generation. And the percentage who refused
to apportion any responsibility was more than six times higher in the first generation than in the third generation. There are two likely explanations for this: on the
one hand, the "long shadow" of the military government, which continues to dictate
caution among the first generation; and, on the other, the dramatic impact of the
events October 2000 on individuals who were teenagers at the time. In the Jewish

sample there was almost no comparable difference between the generations (see Table 6.2), emphasizing that the Arab generational gap is related to the Arab status as a surveilled minority. Still, given the centrality of the *Nakba* in the Palestinian national narrative, and given the popular image of the young generation as the "Stand-Tall Generation," a term coined by Rabinowitz and Abu-Baker (2005), the percentage of those who emphasize Jewish responsibility remains suspiciously low. This suggests that personal memories of the military government are not necessary to prevent the adoption, or at least the presentation, of a Palestinian national narrative.

Another interesting comparison is between the results of the phone interviews and a study based on face-to-face interviews that asked a similar question (Zureik 1999). This comparison is presented in Table 6.3. The gaps between the answers in face-to-face interviews and phone interviews are remarkable. They imply that the interviewees were concerned that they might be "tested" by the authorities in phone interviews (or that the authorities were tapping the phone lines), a concern that might have been significantly reduced by sitting with the interviewer in their own homes.It

Table 6.1 Who is responsible for the creation of the Palestinian refugee problem in the 1948 war? (Arab sample)

	The Jewish side is the only or the main party responsible	*Equal responsibility of Jews and Arabs*	*The Arab side is the only or the main party responsible*	*No answer/ everyone/ no one/ a third side*
Third generation (18–29)	31.7%	44.3%	19.0%	5.0%
Second generation (30–59)	17.7%	37.6%	30.1%	14.7%
First generation (60+)	9.6%	26.9%	32.7%	30.8%
Total	22.6%	39.3%	25.8%	12.2%

Table 6.2 Who is responsible for the creation of the Palestinian refugee problem in the 1948 war? (Jewish sample)

	The Jewish side is the only or the main party responsible	*Equal responsibility of Jews and Arabs*	*The Arab side is the only or the main party responsible*	*No answer/ everyone/ no one/ a third side*
Third generation (18–29)	10.6%	28.7%	54.3%	6.4%
Second generation (30–59)	6.0%	34.3%	50.6%	9.2%
First generation (60+)	6.6%	24.6%	58.1%	10.8%
Total	53.7%	30.1%	7.0%	9.2%

Table 6.3 Who is responsible for the creation of the Palestinian refugee problem in the 1948 war? (A comparison of answers obtained by face-to-face and phone interviews)

	The Jewish side is the only or the main party responsible	Equal responsibility of Jews and Arabs	The Arab side is the only or the main party responsible	No answer
Phone interviews (Sorek, 2008)	22.6%	39.3%	25.8%	12.2%
Face-to-face interviews (Zureik, 1999)	73.6%	9.6%	5.4%	0.6%

is noteworthy that the concern about surveillance seems to be salient only when it comes to suggesting Jewish responsibility for the *Nakba*. In other questions from the same questionnaire, respondents were not deterred from openly displaying Palestinian identity and pride. For example, in response to the question, "To what extent do you feel proud of being Palestinian" (possible answers: "very proud", "proud to a certain extent", "not so proud", "not proud at all"), 58.3 percent chose "very proud." The first generation (age sixty and above) even led this tendency, with 74.5 percent. When asked about their pride in Israeli identity, only 19.3 answered "very proud." These numbers suggest that merely displaying Palestinian pride or a critical attitude toward the state is not widely perceived as risky behavior. However, many Arab citizens still feel that directly blaming the Jewish side for the expulsion of 1948 skirts too close to, or even crosses, the threshold of tolerance of the state or the Jewish majority.

Conclusion

The anxiety of the Jewish public in Israel regarding the public appearance of a Palestinian national narrative has led to continuous attempts to discipline the public display of Palestinian political memory. In the first decades after 1948 this discipline was imposed mainly by strict monitoring by the security services and even forcing Arabs to display the Zionist narrative publicly. As the Jews' siege mentality abated and Arab self-confidence and organizational ability increased in the 1980s and 1990s, the Palestinian national narrative, and especially the commemoration of the *Nakba*, gained more public visibility. The second Intifada reversed the direction of Jewish anxiety in Israel, but it was too late to restore the old modes of disciplining memory. Instead of strict monitoring by the security services, however, Palestinian memory in Israel is still shaped by the watchful civic gaze of ordinary citizens and by public intimidation by government officials. Recurrent attempts to use legislation to outlaw memory of the *Nakba* have failed so far, but they are now supported by forces from the center of the Israeli political map. It is thus feasible that these attempts could succeed in the future.

Findings from a nationwide survey were used to assess the readiness of Arab citizens of Israel to display the Palestinian national narrative. A surprisingly low number of Arab respondents in the survey adopted the conventional Palestinian national narrative in their answers. The fact that less than 10 percent of the respondents of the first generation and only 17 percent of second generation blamed the Jewish side, fully or mostly, for the creation of the Palestinian refugee problem implies that even in 2008 a significant proportion of the population did not feel comfortable in making the *Nakba* an actual political issue.

Among the third generation the proportion of those who blamed the Jewish side was much higher, but it was still less than a third of all respondents in that age group. This is far lower than the percentage of those who blamed the Arab side in the parallel Jewish cohort. These findings suggest that, although the contemporary disciplinary modes are not as influential as those of the military government period, their effect should not be underestimated.

Notes

1   This chapter is based on research funded by a Fulbright-Hays Faculty Research Abroad Fellowship and by a grant from the Lucius N. Littauer Foundation.
2   Segev himself later became a symbol of corruption. In September 1995 his vote in the Knesset was crucial to the approval of the second stage of the Oslo Accords. In exchange for his support of Rabin's government he became the Minister of Energy. In 2005 he was jailed for attempting to smuggle Ecstasy pills into Israel using his expired diplomatic passport.
3   530 Arabs and 502 Jews were interviewed by phone in their native language (Arabic, Hebrew, or Russian) by interviewers from their respective ethnicities. The survey was carried out by the B.I. Lucille Cohen Institute for Public Opinion Research at Tel Aviv University.
4   The Association for Civil Rights in Israel sent letters to both Lieberman and Livnat to protest and explain the problem of their proposal from a legal point of view. See <http://www.acri.org.il/SearchResults.aspx?type=0&group=0&topics=0&text=ggg16g ggg11ggg02ggg05&cb1=False&cb2=False&results=1 [Hebrew]>.

Bibliography

Al Haj, M. (1995) *Education, Empowerment, and Control: The Case of the Arabs in Israel*. Albany, NY: State University of New York Press.
Al-Ittihad (1998) Interview with MK Muhammad Baraka, March 30 [in Arabic].
Bauml, Y. (2001) *The Attitude of the Israeli Establishment toward the Arabs in Israel: Policy, Principles, and Activities: The Second Decade, 1958–1968*, Ph.D. Dissertation: University of Haifa [in Hebrew].
Benvenisti, M. (2002) *Sacred Landscape: The Buried History of the Holy Land since 1948*, Berkeley, Los Angeles and London: University of California Press.
—— (2007) "Time to stop mourning," *Haaretz*, December 23 [in Hebrew].
Bigo, D. (2008) "Security: A Field Left Fallow," in M. Dillon and A. Neal (eds), *Foucault on Politics, Security and War*, New York: Palgrave Macmillan: 93–114.
Caspi, D. and M. Kabaha (2001) "From Holy Jerusalem to the Spring," *Panim*, 16: 44–56 [in Hebrew].
Caspit, B. and Y. Hilleli (2007) "Increase in the identification of the Arabs of Israel with Iran," *Maariv*, January 3. Available HTTP: <www.nrg.co.il/online/1/ART1/555/618.html> (accessed December 1, 2008) [in Hebrew].
Channel 7 (2006). "Demand in Lod: to prevent *Nakba* Day from happening," May 7. Available HTTP: <http://www.inn.co.il/News/News.aspx/147981> (accessed December 1, 2008) [in Hebrew].
Cohen, H. (2003) "Land, memory, and identity: the Palestinian internal refugees in Israel," *Refuge: Canada's Periodical on Refugees*, 21(2): 6–13.

—— (2006) *Good Arabs*, Jerusalem: Keter and Ivrit.

Dayan, A. (2004) "Ministers of Education are changed – the *Shabak* representative always stays," *Haaretz*, September 29 [in Hebrew].

Foucault, M. (1977) *Discipline & Punish: The Birth of the Prison*, New York: Pantheon Books.

—— (1995 [1975]) *Discipline & Punish: The Birth of the Prison*, New York: Vintage Books.

Ganei Aviv and its Residents (2006) "Lod refuses to surrender," May 15. Available HTTP: <http://aviv7.co.il/redac_i/redact10i.htm>(accessed December 1, 2008) [in Hebrew].

Inbari, I. (2007) "The Arab boycott," *Maariv*, December 6. Available HTTP: <http://www.nrg.co.il/online/1/ART1/668/029.html> (accessed March 14, 2010) [in Hebrew].

Knesset (1992) "The 35th assembly session of the 13th Knesset, December 9, 1992: Arab students association in Haifa University." Available HTTP: <http://www.knesset.gov.il/Tql//mark01/h0019364.html#TQL> (accessed December 1, 2008) [in Hebrew].

—— (2003) "Bill no. 7727203: Independence Day Law (amending – forbidding *Nakba* Day)." Available HTTP: <http://www.knesset.gov.il/privatelaw/data/18/2286.rtf> (iaccessed December 1, 2008) [in Hebrew].

—— (2005) "Electronic votes in the Knesset Assembly – meeting no. 211, vote no. 4, January 15, 2005." Available HTTP: <http://www.knesset.gov.il/vote/heb/Vote_Res_Map.asp?vote_id_t=3869> (accessed December 1, 2008) [in Hebrew].

Lyon, D. (2007) *Surveillance Studies: An Overview*, Cambridge: Polity.

Maariv (2008) "Whose Land Day?," March 30. Available HTTP: <http://www.nrg.co.il/online/1/ART1/715/868.html> (accessed December 1, 2008) [in Hebrew].

Masalha, N. (2005) *Present Absentees and Indigenous Resistance: Catastrophe Remembered: Palestine, Israel, and the Internal Refugees*, London and New York: Zed Books: 23–56.

Mifneh (2001) "Interview with Ami Ayalon," *Mifneh*, 32. Available HTTP: <http://www.kibbutz.org.il/mifne/articles/20010101_yisrael.htm>.

Nir, O. (2001) "Lieberman will disconnect the contact between his ministry and mayors commemorating the Nakba," *Haaretz*, May 21 [in Hebrew].

Rabed, A. (2005) "Acre: parade in memory of the 'martyrs' who murdered Jews in 1929," *Y-net*, June 17. Available HTTP: <http://www.ynet.co.il/Ext/App/TalkBack/CdaViewOpenTalkBack/0,11382,L-3100396,00.html> (accessed December 1, 2008) [in Hebrew].

—— (2007) "Dichter: whoever cries about the *Nakba* will have a Nakba," *Y-net*, December 17. Available HTTP: <http://www.ynet.co.il/articles/0,7340,L-3483382,00.html> (accessed December 1, 2008) [in Hebrew].

Rabinowitz, D. and K. Abu-Baker (2005) *Coffins on Our Shoulders: The Experience of the Palestinian Citizens of Israel*, Berkeley: University of California Press.

Ram, U. (1998) "Postnationalist pasts," *Social Science History*, 22(4): 513.

Raz-Krakotzkin, A. (1994) "Diaspora in sovereignty: towards a criticism of 'the negation of diaspora' in Israeli culture," *Teoria Uvicoret*, 4: 23–55 [in Hebrew].

Retner, D. (2000) "Go to the monument and find the reasons for the flare-up," *Haaretz*, May 9 [in Hebrew].

Robinson, S.N. (2005) "Occupied citizens in a liberal state: Palestinians under military rule and the colonial formation of Israeli society, 1948–1966," Ph.D. dissertation, Stanford University.

Rofe-Ophir, S. (2008a) "Kafr Kana residents: why are we forbidden from commemorating the *Nakba*?," *Y-net*, April 26. Available HTTP: <http://www.ynet.co.il/articles/0,7340,L-3536017,00.html> (accessed December 1, 2008) [in Hebrew].

—— (2008b) "Thousands in Land Day events: danger of fascism," *Y-net*, March 30. Available HTTP: <http://www.ynet.co.il/articles/0,7340,L-3525348,00.html> (accessed December 1, 2008) [in Hebrew].

Rosenfeld, H. and M. Al-Haj (1990) *Arab Local Government in Israel*, London: Westview Press.

Sa'ar, R. (2001) "A *Shabak* man nominates Arab directors in the Arab sector," *Haaretz*

December 6 [in Hebrew].

Sabbagh-Khoury, A. (forthcoming) "Palestinian predicaments: Jewish immigration and Palestinian repatriation," in R. Kanaaneh and I. Nusair (eds) *Displaced at Home: Ethnicity and Gender among Palestinians in Israel*, New York: SUNY Press.

Schuman, H., V. Vinitzky-Seroussi and A.D. Vinokur (2003) "Keeping the past alive: memories of Israeli Jews at the turn of the millennium," *Sociological Forum*, 18(1): 103–136.

Segev, T. (2002) *Elvis in Jerusalem: Post-Zionism and the Americanization of Israel*, New York: Metropolitan Book.

Shafir, G. and Y. Peled (2002) *Being Israeli – The Dynamics of Multiple Citizenship*, Cambridge and New York: Cambridge University Press

Sorek, T. (2008) "Cautious commemoration: localism, communalism, and nationalism in Palestinian memorial monuments in Israel," *Comparative Studies in Society and History*, 50(2): 337–368.

Swedenburg, T. (1995) *Memories of Revolt: The 1936–1939 Rebellion and the Palestinian National Past*, Minneapolis and London: University of Minnesota Press.

Tawfiq Zayad Institute (2005) "From Akka Prison . . . the venerable parade pulled away to the tombs of the martyrs Jamjum, Hijazi, and Al-Zir." Available HTTP: <http://www.zayyad.com/index0.asp?f=oldnews.asp&m=menu0.asp&t=frontmenu0.asp> (accessed on March 24, 2008) [in Arabic].

Trabelsi, T. (2001) "Livnat to Arab schools: give loyalty – get money," *Y-net*, August 19. Available HTTP: <http://www.ynet.co.il/articles/0,7340,L-1029929,00.html> (accessed on December 1, 2008) [in Hebrew].

Vitkon, A. (2008) "The Likud Mayor of Shefa-'Amr," *Makor Rishon*, November 3. Availble HTTP: <http://www.makor1.co.il/makor/Article.faces;jsessionid=3edb07230d53f61715f8a00483a9feaa868dc8124fb.e34Mc3aTbNiTby0LaxmNbxqRchmMe0?articleId=35394&channel=1&subchannel=5> (accessed on December 1, 2008) [in Hebrew].

Yiftachel, O. (2000) "Minority protest and the emergence of ethnic regionalism: Palestinian-Arabs in the Israeli 'ethnocracy,'" in S. Ben-Ami, Y. Peled and A. Spectorowski (eds) *Ethnic Challenges to the Modern Nation State*, London and New York: Macmillan and St Martin's Press: 145–180.

Zerubavel, E. (2003) "Calendars and history: a comparative study of the social organization of national memory, " in J.K. Olick (ed.) *States of Memory: Continuities, Conflicts, and Transformations in National Retrospection*, Durham, NC: Duke University Press: 315–337.

Zureik, E. (1999) *Public Opinion and Palestinian Refugees*, report submitted to the International Development Research Centre, Ottawa.

Part IV

Political economy and globalization of surveillance

7 Laboratories of war

Surveillance and US–Israeli collboration in war and security

Stephen Graham

Introduction: learning from Jenin

> In America, Palestine and Israel are regarded as local, not foreign policy, matters.
> (Said 2003)

In April 2002, in a dramatic shift in strategy, the Israeli Defence Force bulldozed a 40,000-square-metre area in the centre of the Jenin refugee camp in the northern West Bank. A UN report estimated that some 52 Palestinians were killed in the attack, about half of them civilians. In a detailed investigation, Human Rights Watch found that several civilians, including a disabled man, were crushed to death in their homes, because Israeli forces failed to allow relatives the time to help them escape; others were used as human shields by the advancing Israelis. In Jenin, Operation Defensive Shield (*Mivtza Homat Magen* in Hebrew), which involved major military operations against other Palestinian cities, left 140 multi-family housing blocks completely destroyed, 1,500 damaged and some 4,000 residents homeless, out of a population of 14,000. During the operation, lesser demolitions were also carried out in Nablus, Hebron and Ramallah. Destruction of material infrastructure and cultural and administrative facilities was also widespread.

Michael Evans (2007), an Australian urban warfare specialist, has highlighted the pivotal importance of the Defensive Shield operations, as exemplars of a new kind of "asymmetric" war pitting high-tech state militaries against insurgents, and surrounding civilians, within closely built, urban terrain. Along with learning negative lessons from the US defeat in Mogadishu and Russia's humiliation during their attempts to annihilate the Chechen capital of Grozny in the mid-1990s, Israeli "successes" here have been widely interpreted as combining high-tech surveillance and targeting with the techniques of World War Two urban warfare for erasing space and penetrating into the core of resistant cities. "In operations in Jenin in April 2002," Evans (2007) writes:

> The Israelis mixed information-age battlespace preparation by state of the art reconnaissance drones and UAVs [Unmanned Aerial Vehicles] with industrial-age techniques of mouse-holing through walls to avoid enfiladed streets. Caterpillar D9 armoured bulldozers complete with "mine plows" were employed to clear away fortified buildings, IEDs and booby trap nests thus allowing tank–infantry squads to manoeuvre through streets more easily. Despite the

application of new technology systems, operations in Jenin and Ramallah still required the kind of small unit tactics and combined arms organisation that would have been familiar to veterans of World War II city fights.

By learning directly from these new urban wars, the US military worked very hard, from the mid-1990s, to improve its ability to pacify and control the cities that were now deemed the main foci of its adversaries. "Significant theoretical analyses were completed by RAND Corporation scholars focusing on the technical and tactical peculiarities involved in conducting military operations inside cities" (Evans 2007).

The processes through which US forces sought to exemplify and imitate Israeli experience during Defensive Shield were already under way as the bulldozers made their way through the built spaces of the Jenin camp. US military observers were already there, getting a first-hand perspective on the Israeli doctrine in action as a useful input into the detailed planning for the invasion of Iraq's cities the following April. Eyal Weizman (2004: 83) writes that "an Israeli paratrooper who participated in the battle of Jenin told me that there were US officers (dressed in IDF uniform) present as spectators within the rubble of the refugee camp as the last stages of the 'battle' unfolded."

On 17 June 2002, the *US Army Times* reported that "while Israeli forces were engaged in what many termed a brutal – some even say criminal – campaign to crush Palestinian militants and terrorist cells in West Bank towns, US military officials were in Israel seeing what they could learn from that urban fight." Lt. Col. Dave Booth – who oversees US Marine–IDF exchanges on urban warfare – reported in another article in the *Marine Corps Times* that the Marines wanted "to learn from the Israeli experience in urban warfare and the recent massive search-and-destroy operations for Palestinian insurgents in the West Bank" (quoted in Evans 2007).

The US Marines' Warfighting Lab quickly used these detailed exchanges – which culminated in a Joint Chiefs of Staff delegation to Israel between 17 and 23 May 2002 – to "make changes to the Corps' urban war-fighting doctrine to reflect what worked for the Israelis" (quoted in Evans 2007). A major consultation then occurred between Israeli and Pentagon specialists on urban warfare at a Defense Policy Advisory Group meeting in Washington in early June.

In September the Joint Chiefs of Staff laid out a new doctrine for urban operations, taking account of lessons learned from Jenin and elsewhere, with a view to an impending attack on Iraq. Seymour Hersh (2003) also observed in the *New Yorker* in December 2003 that, "according to American and Israeli military and intelligence officials, Israeli commandos and intelligence units have been working closely with their American counterparts at the Special Forces training base at Fort Bragg, North Carolina, and in Israel to help them prepare for operations in Iraq." In the same month Julian Borger (2003) reported in the *Guardian* that, "according to two sources, Israeli military 'consultants' have also visited Iraq."

General Vane, then Deputy Chief of Staff for Doctrine Concepts and Strategy at the United States Army Training and Doctrine Command, admitted in July 2003 that Israeli experience was pivotal as US forces tried to confront the proliferating urban insurgencies on the streets of Iraq's cities that followed the easy military defeat of the state's military forces in 2002. "[Israeli] experience continues to teach us many lessons," he wrote. "And we continue to evaluate and address those lessons, embedding and incorporating them appropriately into our concepts, doctrine and training" (cited in Filkins 2003).

So emerged a complex set of circles of imitation, partnership, trade and bi-partisan rhetoric linking Israeli policies of securitization, military urbanism, and intensifying surveillance intimately – indeed, almost seamlessly at times – into the United States' "global war on terror." Crucial here was the Bush administration's perception that the central geopolitical conflicts in the world now emanated from, and operated through, the Middle East – a "new strategic environment [was] characterized, first and foremost, by the asymmetrical threats stemming from rogue states and terrorist networks, driven by nihilistic ideologies bent on massive destruction at all costs" (Freilich 2006).

At the core of this purported geopolitical challenge are new imperatives of sur-veillance and (attempted) social control: how pre-emptively to identify, track, target and destroy fighters, insurgents and terrorists who are effectively indistinguishable from the mass of urban civilians who surround them. Such a challenge, moreover, is deemed by mainstream security and military theorists now to pertain both to the challenges confronting neo-colonial urban warfare on the urban periphery of Baghdad or Gaza and to the counter-terrorist, border-security or "homeland" security domains within the cities or territories at the core of US, Western or Israeli power.

In such a broad context, this chapter, which draws on a new book (Graham 2010), argues that Israeli military and security experience in addressing these purported imperatives – as the ultimate surveillance–security state – is rapidly being exported around the world. The chapter explores the circuits of exemplification and imitation through which this is occurring. To get to the root of these, however, it is necessary to move well beyond discussions about purchases of particular Israeli military equipment by US forces or of Israeli firms selling border surveillance or unmanned drone systems to Western countries (both of which are now common). Rather, we need to understand the emergence of the broader legal, political–economic, biopolitical and geopolitical context within which such imitations and appropriations become normalized. It is to this task that the current chapter is addressed.

Crucial here is the way in which the legal and discursive bases for the "war on terror" – within which the adoption of military-standard surveillance pre-emptively targeting civilian domains within states of legal exception and biopolitical securitization takes place and is normalized – closely imitate Israeli experience and doctrine. As well as outlining such imitation, this chapter demonstrates that, in addition to mimicking Israeli discourse about the need to suspend international law because of the unique challenges of this "new war," the US military has widely imitated the experience, technology and doctrine of Israeli forces in tailoring itself to the challenges of urban colonial and counter-insurgency warfare. The chapter also argues that the Israeli economy has, in turn, been boosted as it profits from its new status as the global exemplar of maximum securitization and high-tech urban control.

Legal limitations: reciprocal states of exception

> The security challenges of Israel are the security concerns of the United States writ small.
>
> (Henriksen 2007)

A central element in the recent high-tech economic renaissance of Israel in what Naomi Klein (2007a: ch. 20) has called the "standing disaster Apartheid state" has been the gradual convergence between US military doctrine in post-Invasion Iraq and the long-standing Israeli techniques of repression, incarceration and the fragmentation of geography in the occupied territories. The Bush administration's justification for the use of extra-judicial and pre-emptive assassination within his "war on terror," for example, was clearly heavily influenced by Israel's earlier justification of its use of such methods. Central here was the assertion that "this war was 'unprecedented' and thus constituted a legal *terra nulla*" (Hajjar 2006: 32). Lisa Hajjar (2006: 32) observes that such a claim has a direct Israeli precedent: "the Israeli military at the start of the second intifada had already characterized its war on terror in the West Bank and Gaza as a legal *terra nulla*."

Perhaps the most glaring similarity between US government's justification of its "war on terror' and Israeli legitimation of its treatment of the Al Aqsa Intifada has been the strategic idea of "pre-emption" and "preventative war." Here it is clear that the Bush administration's obsession with "pre-emption" was heavily influenced by emerging Israeli doctrine in Defensive Shield. Azmi Bishara (n.d.) has suggested that the whole idea of the "war against terror," especially the "pre-emptive invasion of Iraq," represented what he terms "globalized Israeli security doctrines." These conceptions, he writes, "are actually Israeli conceptions, including understanding 'terrorism' as the 'main enemy.'"

In a simplistic and Manichean division of the world into two hermetically sealed groups – "terrorists" and "non-terrorists" – Bush therefore followed a long-standing Israeli strategy for the same ends: to allow coalitions of convenience, with all manner of dubious allies, to entrench their sovereign power against a generalized, demonized enemy whose geopolitical claims are radically delegitimized and whose subhuman, monster-like status means that political negotiations will never be necessary.

The "war on terror's" reliance on the construction of a series of legal and geographical grey zones as means to justify the suspension of norms of international law finds direct precedence in Israeli practice in the occupied territories. Here, as Darryl Li (2006: 38) puts it, "Israel has assiduously waged a campaign to deny the applicability of international law to the territories, especially insofar as the law interferes with processes of demographic engineering."

The international legal scholar Lisa Hajjar (2006: 32) provides a particularly nuanced discussion of the similarities between US and Israeli practice here. "Comparing the Israeli and American alternative legalities," she writes, "one finds some clear commonalities" in the detailed legal justification for the state of exception and the irrelevance of international humanitarian law. Hajjar notes, first, that "the Israeli description of the status of the West Bank and Gaza as *sui generis* in order to assert that IHL [international humanitarian law] does not apply resembles the US claim that IHL was inapplicable to the war in Afghanistan because it was a 'failed state'" (Hajjar 2006: 32). Second, Hajjar (2006: 32) underlines that "both governments have argued that the statelessness of their enemies translates into rightlessness under IHL, and these interpretations have been based on the notion that IHL allocates rights only to states and their Citizens" and not to adversaries located in "failed states." Such a legal trick has been used to legitimize mass incarceration without trial in both cases. Finally, "both have utilized national laws to authorize practices that contravene IHL norms and rules, thereby domesticating international law in adverse ways" (Hajjar 2006: 32).

Biopolitical imitations: Israel and the "Palestinianization" of Iraq

As the US military task in Iraq quickly morphed in late 2003 from the relatively simple task of defeating an infinitely inferior state military to one of pacifying complex urban insurgencies, so Israel's direct involvement in shaping the doctrine, weaponry and military thinking of US occupying forces has grown – with corresponding pay-offs for the Israeli economy. "What had initially been termed a 'conventional armed conflict' had become a 'counter-insurgency conflict' that came to bear striking resemblances to Israeli operations in the second Intifada" (Hajjar 2006: 34–35).

In launching its "global war on terror," the Bush administration directly used Israeli history, especially during the second Intifada, "as a salient – and in some ways explicit – model for the United States's 'new paradigm'" (Hajjar 2006: 22). Hajjar (2006: 22) observes that "the second Intifada and the US global war on terror, though quite different, both involve asymmetrical warfare that pits powerful states with powerful militaries against stateless individuals and groups and non-state organizations in the midst of dense, urban concentrations of civilian populations." Makram Khoury-Machool (2003) describes this process as the "Palestinianization" of Iraq. Importantly, such a process has involved the various Iraqi insurgents and militias directly imitating the tactics of Hamas or Hezbollah as well as the US military directly imitating the IDF (Weizman 2004: 84).

The United States' imitation of Israeli tactics and strategy has not operated wholesale, however. The US added some of its own new concepts in an attempt to "legalize" its actions within the context of a wholesale withdrawal of the traditions of international humanitarian law and the Geneva Convention. One example here was the invention of the concept of the "illegal combatant" who could be incarcerated indefinitely without right to trial but did not, at the same time, warrant the status of a prisoner of war (Hajjar 2006: 22).

In a detailed analysis of the lessons of Israeli practice for US special forces, Thomas Henriksen, a Hoover Institution fellow, is unequivocal about the direct imitation of Israeli policy in developing US strategy, doctrine and weaponry for the "global war on terror." He writes:

> The Israeli Defense Forces' (IDF) military actions have been – and are – a crucible for methods, procedures, tactics, and techniques for the United States, which now faces a similarly fanatical foe across the world in the Global War on Terror . . . Israeli experiences offer an historical record and a laboratory for tactics and techniques in waging counter-insurgencies or counterterrorist operations in America's post-9/11 circumstances.
>
> (Henriksen 2007)

By August 2004, as complex insurgencies raged across Iraq's cities, Toufic Haddad was able to observe that "US techniques in Iraq" were already "unmistakably similar to Israeli techniques in the 1967 Occupied Territories" (International Socialist Review

2004). This, he noted, was "because of the active cooperation between Israeli military advisers and the Americans on the ground." His diagnosis of similarities was, indeed, striking:

> the use of aggressive techniques of urban warfare with an emphasis on special units, house-to-house searches, wide-scale arrest campaigns (almost 14,000 Iraqis are now in prison), and torture; the erecting of an elaborate system of watchtowers, military bases, checkpoints, barbed wire, and trenches to monitor, control, and restrict transportation and movement; the clearing of wide swaths of land next to roads; the use of armored bulldozers to destroy the houses of suspected militants; the razing of entire fields from which militants might seek refuge; the heightened relevance of snipers and unmanned drones; and the attempted erection of collaborator networks to extract information from the local population about resistance activities – both military and political.
>
> (International Socialist Review 2004)

On the back of the argument that the US in Iraq was effectively facing a scaled-up version of what the Israeli military had long experienced in Palestine, the US Army War College undertook a major workshop titled "Shifting Fire" in 2006. This was explicitly designed to draw US lessons on the challenges of managing propaganda and other "information operations" within counter-insurgency warfare from Israeli experience in the occupied territories. The Israeli–Palestinian conflict was even used as a "proxy" for the US invasion of Iraq. This was done because it "allowed for a freer debate of key issues, and avoided putting participants in the position of having to discuss specific US-led operations or the more political aspects of current US policy in Iraq and Afghanistan" (USAWC 2006).

Space as exemplar: the Gaza lab

These complex processes of US imitation of Israeli practice relate closely to the particular status of the Gaza Strip as a "laboratory" of new techniques of urban control, pacification and counter-insurgency warfare within the Israeli military. According to Darryl Li (2006: 38), even after notional Israeli "disengagement" from the area in 2005, the Gaza Strip has continued to act as a

> space where Israel tests and refines various techniques of management, continuously experimenting in search of an optimal balance between maximum control over the territory and minimum responsibility for its non-Jewish population ... Because the Gaza Strip represents a stage of concentration and segregation that is unprecedented in the conflict, it can be seen as a space in which the "pure" conditions of laboratory experimentation are best approximated.

The example of the "urban warfare laboratory" of Gaza is especially interesting to Israeli and US forces because it is based on the idea of "control at a distance," through militarizing boundaries, continuous raids, regular wholesale invasions (as in winter 2008–2009), assassination strikes and intense aerial surveillance, rather than control through the continuous presence of occupying armies. "Closure in the Gaza Strip is enforced with less military manpower and less 'friction' (i.e. direct contact) with the civilian population, entailing less exposure to attack and less potential for negative publicity" (Lee 2006: 43). Following the building of the separation barrier in the West Bank, there is evidence that Israel is trying to instigate Gaza-style regimes of control there, too, with each Palestinian enclave turned into a "mini-Gaza" with a much more hermetic approach to "closure."

Geographical imitations: divide and rule

> When the wall around the American compound in Baghdad looks as if its components are leftovers from Jerusalem, when "temporary closures" are imposed on whole towns and villages with earth dykes and barbed wire, when larger regions are carved up by roadblocks and checkpoints, when homes of suspected terrorists are leveled, when Apache helicopters are used in civilian areas, and when "targeted assassinations" are re-introduced into a new militarized geography, it is not only because these have become parts of a joint military curriculum written by Israeli training officers, but because they spread out through a process of mimicry, at whose center the West Bank functions as a laboratory of the extreme.
>
> (Weizman 2004: 83)

There is little doubt that US attempts in early 2007 forcibly to reconstruct the urban geographies of Baghdad and other Iraqi cities deemed especially troublesome, to reduce opportunities for insurgents to move around and launch their attacks, were directly modelled on Israeli experience in the occupied territories. Certain towns were completely sealed off with razor wire or walls. Biometric identity cards were enforced for all adults. And, eventually, massive urban wall complexes, with associated "security buffer zones," were enforced across 30 of Baghdad's 89 official districts (Fisk 2007).

In these cordoned-off towns and urban districts, civilians quickly found themselves inhabiting what Robert Fisk (2007) calls "a 'controlled population' prison." As in the occupied territories, this notion of "security" "requires putting [the population that is deemed threatening] behind a wall." This, in turn, is seen to demand its own geography of cleared "security buffer zones" through which artificial separations can be imposed on complex and mixed-up urban geographies: "The ideal way to secure a barrier is through a vacant 'buffer zone,' whose emptiness allows a handful of soldiers to monitor relatively large areas and to respond quickly, decisively, and overwhelmingly to any perceived infiltrators, all while ensconced in fortified positions" (Li 2006: 45). Once "security" or "buffer zones" are "cleared," Li notes that "they become effective 'free-fire' areas." In the occupied territories, "Palestinians enter [these] at their own risk and dozens if not hundreds have died doing so" (Li 2006: 45).

Such partitioning of Iraqi cities and urban districts by US forces inevitably resonates powerfully with the erection of massive concrete barriers in the West Bank and the increasingly militarized borders and "shoot to kill" zones in and around Gaza. Checkpoints, buffer zones, enforced identity cards, collective punishments, bulldozing, mass incarcerations without trial, imprisonment of suspects' relatives, and associated landscape clearances and demolitions of buildings deemed to be sheltering enemies – all of these smacked of direct imitation of Israeli policy in the occupied territories (while also resonating with earlier counter-insurgency wars in Algeria, Vietnam and elsewhere). Such a conclusion would have been supported further by the sale by Israel to US combat engineers of twelve of the massive D-9 caterpillar armoured bulldozers used so extensively since Operation Defensive Shield in 2002. (Perhaps "re-sale" would be a better description, as these machines are manufactured in the US by the Caterpillar Corporation.)

Such similarities were not lost on Iraqi urban residents coming to terms with such familiar, but shocking, new "security" geographies. "I see no difference between us and the Palestinians," one Iraqi man, Tariq, screamed at Dexter Filkins, a *New York Times* reporter, in December 2003. "We didn't expect anything like this after Saddam fell" (Filkins 2003). Reidar Visser was especially critical of the way that the new archipelago of fenced-off enclaves worked to reaffirm sectarian violence and identity, rather than working against it:

> When will Westerners realize that most Iraqis – with the exception of many Kurds and a few noisy parliamentarians from other communities – view sectarianism as a perversion and not as a legitimate basis for organizing the country politically and administratively? It is highly disturbing that physical separation schemes of this kind should appear to be a priority of the Bush administration in early 2007, at the expense of the political track towards national reconciliation.
>
> (Visser 2007)

Thomas Henriksen says that Israeli experience with checkpoints was directly imitated by US forces in Iraq. He remarks that these, as well as road patrols, "have proven . . . effective in limiting terrorism. Thus a near-saturation of territory seems effective." However, he argues that there were problems in "upscaling" Israeli doctrine developed in small and tightly packed cities like Gaza to the much larger and more complex urban geographies in Iraq (Henriksen 2007).

Vertical geopolitics: dronespace

> The effectiveness [of Israel's aerial assassination policy] is amazing. The State of Israel has brought preventative assassination to the level of a real art. When a Palestinian child draws a sky nowadays, he will not draw it without a helicopter.
>
> (Avi Dichter, Israel's then Internal Security Minister, quoted in Elmer 2005: 4)

The development by the CIA and US special forces of targeted assassination programmes in the "war on terror" has also been a direct imitation of the long-standing Israeli policy of "pre-emption" by extra-judicial state killing, usually by helicopters or unmanned and remotely piloted drones armed with missiles.

Graham Turbiville (2007), in a report for the US Joint Special Operations University, is absolutely clear about the direct imitation here: "In the post-9/11 security environment the targeting of terrorist and insurgent leaders and cadres by US military and intelligence resources has advanced in many ways – some publicly reported and visible – and have been accompanied by notable successes." Israeli practice is highly lauded as something to strive to imitate among US special forces. Turbiville (2007) notes, "certainly, Israeli [assassination] actions against Palestinian, Hezbollah, and other terrorist leaders and support infrastructure since independence . . . constitutes the gold standard for the systematic conceptual and operational consideration it has received from the Israeli Government and military and security bodies."

The United States began employing assassination tactics for the first time in November 2002, even though they had been directly prohibited by US executive orders since 1977. To justify this policy, as Lisa Hajjar (2006: 31) has argued,

> [US o]fficials utilized Israeli-like reasoning to justify the assassination of Ali Qaed Sinan al-Harithi [the first target] and five others (including a US citizen) in Yemen by a pilotless drone, proclaiming that because Harithi was allegedly a member of al-Qa'ida and because arrest was impossible, assassination was a legitimate tactic, even against a person located in a country not at war with the United States [i.e., Yemen].

By December 2003, US drone-based assassinations had been combined with aggressive special forces operations inside Syria through which US forces attempted to kill jihadists ostensibly on their way to fight in Iraq. IDF urban warfare specialists helped train these special forces at Fort Bragg in North Carolina (Borger 2003). As well as generating a robust response from anti-war campaigners and humanitarian law specialists, some US intelligence officials decried both the policy and its direct imitation of Israel. "This is basically an assassination programme," one former senior US intelligence official told Julian Borger: "That is what is being conceptualised here. It is bonkers, insane. Here we are – we're already being compared to [then Israeli Prime Minister] Sharon in the Arab world, and we've just confirmed it by bringing in the Israelis and setting up assassination teams" (Borger 2003).

Israel's use of drones for extra-judicial assassinations is especially important as as an exemplar for the United States' assassinations in the "war on terror" (see Weizman 2006: ch. 9). "The evolution of the occupation of the Gaza Strip is perhaps best manifested in Israel's use of airpower, especially since the beginning of the al-Aqsa intifada . . . Use of airpower is positively correlated with territorial isolation and segregation" (Li 2006: 34). In Gaza, drone-based assassinations are a primary mechanism for the new model of "external control" without the occupation of permanent armies that is such an influence on US policy. Israel is a global pioneer in the use of aerial drones for the persistent and ubiquitous surveillance of subject populations in "low-intensity conflicts" (a situation, as we shall see, that it exploits fully on the international arms markets). Overwhelmingly, once again, Gaza has been the laboratory for this new doctrine and weaponry: "Some 90 percent of the assassinations in the Gaza Strip during the intifada have been executed from the air" (Li 2006: 48).

Aerial assassinations, then, are but one element of a much broader strategy of what Israeli planners term "urban area domination" – a doctrine which is having considerable influence on the US military (Sanders n.d.). Indeed, although rarely publicized, US and Israeli efforts to perfect armed unmanned drones are now very closely integrated. Ralph Sanders reports that the United States'

> AAI Corporation is making the Israeli-designed Pioneer UAV for both the [US] Army and Navy. IAI [Israeli arms giant Israeli Aerospace Industries] has assisted

TRW Avionics and Surveillance Group [two other US companies] to produce the Hunter UAV [also for the US military], which was originally developed by IAI. Since this cooperation began, Malat [a division of IAI] ... [has also] developed more advanced battlefield UAVs in collaboration with US partners.

(Sanders n.d.)

As part of the broader strategy of aerial domination, Israel has modified its state-on-state war machinery for the so-called "low-intensity conflict" of permanently dominating dense urban areas, using unmanned drones and satellites, from above. New, specialized missiles have been developed, known as "Spikes," which are specifically designed for urban assassination raids. These allow drone pilots to detect and destroy "targets" very quickly, a process absorbed within the euphemism "closing the sensor-to-shooter cycle" or, more honestly, "accelerating the kill chain" (Sanders n.d.).

By 2007, such weaponry was being just as widely adopted by Western state militaries. Spike missiles we already fitted to France's new generation of armed drones (Tran and Opall-Rome n.d.). The US, British and Singaporean militaries then ordered the Hermes armed drones made by the Israeli arms corporation Elbit (UAV Blog 2006). And, most controversially of all, the same company was awarded a major contract by the US Department of Homeland Security to patrol the US–Mexico border and to target immigrants passing through this increasingly militarized zone. By 20 July 2007, the Border Patrol was claiming that there had been "42 apprehensions [of immigrants] directly attributable to UAV surveillance" (Israeli Weapons.Com 2007). As early as 2004 it was being envisaged that such patrols would be extended to the US–Canadian border.

Here again, then, we confront the role of (post-Israeli-"withdrawal") Gaza as an exemplary field in the experimentation of new architectures, geographies and technologies of control-at-distance, which are becoming widely imitated and exemplified elsewhere. Here emerges a verticalized Orientalism within which the racialized subjects of colonial power are continually scrutinized, tracked and targeted from above through the dominating apparatus of Western techno-scientific power (see Graham 2003). In Gaza, as Eyal Weizman (2008: 325) writes:

> the geography of occupation has thus completed a 90-degree turn: the imaginary "Orient" – the exotic object of colonization – was no longer beyond the horizon, but now under the vertical tyranny of Western airborne civilization that remotely managed its most sophisticated and advanced technological platforms, sensors and munitions above.

New architectures of power: raids at a distance for the "Long War"

More recently, Israel's growing use of continuous raids and temporary invasions, rather than wholesale, colonial invasions and occupations, is also now widely seen as a paradigmatic lesson for US military policy. Such tactics are seen by many US military theorists to be perfectly suited to the US military as it seeks to develop its doctrine for what the Pentagon has, since 2005, called the "Long War" – more or less permanent and globally scattered use of pre-emptive raids against its purported adversaries. Such arguments for a shift towards "control at a distance" through raids, targeted killings and persistent surveillance by unmanned drones and satellites are especially strong after the disastrous failure of the full military invasion of Iraq. The widespread US adoption of drone-based bombing raids within Pakistani territory since 2007 – a highly controversial policy that has resulted in many civilian casualties within an ally state – is one example of the US imitation of Israel's new models of (attempted) control at a distance.

"The Israeli approach to combating terrorism over the long haul affords an example of a counterterrorism strategy" to US forces, writes Thomas Henriksen (2007). In the context where the US seems unlikely to be able to pursue wholesale invasions against states deemed to be sources of terrorism, Israeli doctrine is again likely to provide vital lessons and models to imitate. According to Henriksen (2007), what he terms these "denied areas" or "ungovernable spaces" – where "American counterinsurgency strategies" cannot be utilised – now "lend themselves to the Israeli way of war."

Henriksen (2007) notes that Israel

> has relied over the years on raids, sometimes fairly long-distance strikes, as prevention, preemption, deterrence, and punishment for terrorism perpetrated on its territory or against its citizens abroad . . . The United States might find that it . . . must dispatch commando raids, capture terrorists for intelligence, assassinate diabolical masterminds, and target insurgent strongholds with airpower, missiles, or Special Operations Forces from bases around the globe rather than undertaking enormous pacification programs and nation-building endeavors in inhospitable lands. Military offensive operations must not be surrendered; they must be applied so as to marshal our resources for a protracted conflict.

Here Henriksen suggest that *both* Israeli and US societies are now best suited to continuous warfare through long-distance "preventative" aerial raids and assassination programmes, rather than full-scale invasion. The United States, he argues, must thus strive ever more to model its strategy on that of Israel. Both "Israeli and American societies are better at sustaining low-profile counterattacks that are launched in the name of prevention, deterrence, and retribution than full-blown offensive wars such as Israel's 1982 Lebanon intervention or America's Iraq and Afghanistan invasions" (Henriksen 2007). A US Air Force report identifying Israeli lessons for future US warfare strategy concludes, similarly, that such an approach "may include accepting the value of targeted killing of an adversary's leaders, something the Israeli military has learned to do quite successfully" (Larsen and Pravecek 2007: 4).

Selling the security state: political economies of surveillance

It is no coincidence that the emergence of Israel as a unique global exemplar of urban militarism and securitization has been closely associated with the dramatic resurgence in its national economy that occurred before the international financial meltdown in 2008. Between 2000 and 2003, the Israeli economy experienced a major recession. This was due both to the global collapse of internet stocks and to the Al Aqsa Intifada, which started in September 2000, and was marked by devastating suicide attacks against Israeli targets. Imri Tov (2003), writing in *Strategic Assessment*, the pro-Israeli Jaffa Centre for Strategic Studies' journal, characterizes the early 2000s as

> one of the worst economic periods in the country's history . . . the conflict has reached its current peak, at which the two sides are trying to exhaust each other. The visible economic consequences over the thirty months of escalation in the conflict are a cumulative result of the conflict itself; its long duration, unlike any previous escalation of violence in Israel; and a number of other factors. All these have joined to produce the current recession, which now claims the dubious honor of 50–60 billion shekels ($10–13 billion) in accumulated damages.

Israel's increasingly high-tech economy has been marshalled towards the challenges of selling high-tech security systems and urban warfare machinery to a rapidly growing global market, using its "combat-proven" status to advantage. This has been so successful that, according to *Jane's Defence Weekly*, Israel made more than $3.5 billion in arms sales in 2003 alone and in that year exported arms and security equipment on a level which matched Russia (reported in *USA Today* 2003). If after-sales services are included, Israel is now the world's third-largest arms and security equipment exporter. If not, it is in fifth place. By 2007, Israeli defence exports had climbed to more than $4 billion (Krauss 2007). In 2004, *Business Week* magazine labelled Israel as one of the world's "rising innovation hotspots" because of its strength in high-tech communications, chips, software and sensors. All of these benefit heavily from military research and development. Between the downturn in 2002 and 2005, foreign industrial investment in Israel rose from $1.8 billion to $6.1 billion (Goldberg 2007).

As a result, "the IDF has become a secondary customer for almost all" major Israeli arms and security companies (Sadeh 2004). Israel now sells $1.2 billion defence and security products to the United States (Klein 2007b). The rapid integration of US and Israeli security technology sectors has been powerfully assisted by the very high level of cross-investment and ownership between the high-tech industries in the two nations. Israel, for example, has more companies listed on the high-tech Nasdaq stock market than any of the advanced countries of Europe: by January 2008, there were more than 75 Israeli companies, worth a total of $60 billion, listed on the Nasdaq (Snyder 2008).

With the 9/11 attacks, and the deepening integration of Israeli strategy into the "urban warfare" aspects of the "war on terror" discussed above, Israeli capital, with considerable support from the US and Israeli governments, has worked intelligently to project its skills, expertise and products beyond the more obvious markets surrounding urban warfare, towards the much broader and ever-extendable areas of global securitization, surveillance and counter-terrorism. The advantage of this is that virtually any high-tech company – from biotechnology, through computing, to telecommunications, electronics and new materials technology – can easily project itself as a "security" company, such are the infinite ways in which the everyday spaces and infrastructures of cities can be deemed insecure in the contemporary world.

At a talk in Tacoma in May 2007 designed to forge US–Israeli links in high-tech security industries, Bernel Goldberg, executive director of the Washington Israel Business Council, was unequivocal:

As a top national priority, Homeland Security in Israel is more than just an exportable commodity. Israel's self-reliance has created a diversified and cutting edge security industry, adding innovation to existing technologies as well as developing new ones. Israel today has earned its worldwide reputation for providing leading security solutions and continues to successfully partner with key world players to protect airports, seaports, government offices, financial institutions, recreational centers, international events and more.

(Goldberg 2007)

Israeli firms have been able to use this context and reputation to re-brand themselves in a post-9/11 context better and faster than any other companies. Their systems, standards and practices are fast emerging as global exemplars, to be imitated, copied or bought up outright. As a result, "Israel's long history of government spending on the war on terror has produced standards, methodologies and concepts that are only now emerging around the world" (Fairfax County Economic Development Authority 2007).

Consequently, "suddenly new profit vistas opened up for any company that claimed it could spot terrorists in crowds, seal borders from attack and extract confessions from closed-mouthed prisoners" (Klein 2007b). The exploitation of these opening vistas of securitization was, of course, made possible by the long-standing receipt of over $84 billion in military grants from the US state between 1976 and 2007. Then the Bush administration added extra aid in 2007 – to help Israel "fight terrorism" – thus pump-priming Israel's security firms for their assault on global markets even more heavily.

The success of this strategy was a major factor in Israel's dramatic economic renaissance in 2007–2008. By February 2008, the *Israel High-Tech Investment Report* (2008) was able to boast:

> in the aftermath of the war in Lebanon in 2006, Israel has experienced one of its best economic years. Venture capital investments flowed in and could reach $1.7 billion. Foreign investments were strong. The Tel-Aviv Stock Exchange gained nearly 30%. 2007 marked the year that Israel became the world's fourth largest defense supplier.

Security "showroom": a global exemplar

Indeed, the very Israeli identity and branding of the new techniques and technologies of urban securitization and militarization have been major selling points here. As Naomi Klein (2007b) observes, "many of the country's most successful entrepreneurs are using Israel's status as a fortressed state, surrounded by furious enemies, as a kind of twenty-four-hour-a-day showroom – a living example of how to enjoy relative safety amid constant war."

To visitors, this "showroom" is essentially a place of hyper-militarized urbanism – a process of urban life where every movement and action involve scrutiny and the negotiation of architectural or electronic passage points to prove legitimate rights of access or presence. In effect, Israel has generalized the sort of security architecture, and intense profiling practices, more usually reserved for airports to a whole system of cities and everyday infrastructure. The aforementioned US Air Force report, assessing the lessons that the US might learn from Israel, points out that, in Israel, "nearly every upscale restaurant has private security at the door, including metal detectors and bomb sniffing sensors. All public buildings, including shopping malls and bus and train stations, have armed guards and metal detectors at their gates" (Larsen and Pravecek 2007: 14).

Israel's Ministry of Industry, Trade and Labor (n.d.) boasts that many of the "leading edge" security systems being sold around the world by Israeli firms are

> based on systems developed for the Israel Defense Forces. No other country has such a high percentage of former army, security forces and police officers with experience in combating terrorism who can act as consultants in developing security concepts and systems for each unique situation . . . [Israeli companies] have pioneered leading edge systems that combine CCTV with the latest software, communications, command and control solution packages.

They offer the most effective "intruder detector systems based on motion detectors, infrared barriers," and remain unrivalled in the more architectural aspects of military urbanism: "In defense against terrorist or criminal activity the first line of protection remains good fencing" (Israeli Ministry of Industry, Trade and Labor n.d.).

Crucially, then, Israel has been able to marshal its techniques of hyper-militarization to match and exploit global trends towards the militarization of everyday spaces, infrastructures and sites. The key markets here are not merely the more formal technologies of control and killing – militarized borders, unmanned drones, weapons designed for use in dense urban areas, and missiles for pre-emptive assassination. Rather, they extend to the whole gamut of urban surveillance and securocratic war: passenger profiling software, biometrics and checkpoint systems. As Naomi Klein (2007b) points out, all of these systems and architectures are "precisely the tools and technologies Israel has used to lock in the occupied territories."

Israeli companies, such as Rafael, heavily stress the ways in which the everyday systems and infrastructures of cities are now sites of "low-intensity conflict" requiring radical securitization (using their expertise and technology, of course). "In wartime conditions," runs the spiel in their "anti-terror homeland security solutions" marketing brochure,

> Rafael systems provide defense against intruding military forces, intelligence and terrorist units. In times of peace, these systems prevent the border crossing of illegal immigrants, smugglers, drug traffickers and terrorists. During Low Intensity Conflicts (LIC), Rafael technologies serve as shields against intruding intelligence or terrorist units. They also provide smart screening of pedestrians, vehicles and cargo at border check points.
>
> (Rafael Corporation n.d.)

In 2006, for the first time, Israeli firms exported over $1 billion worth of "homeland security" equipment and services – up 20 per cent on the 2005 figure. David Arziof, director of the Israeli Exports Institute (IEE) – an Israeli government body – estimated that exports would increase a further 15 per cent during 2007, to reach $1.15 billion (Kravitz 2007). The $39 billion US market loomed large in these growing exports, as did the projected global growth of homeland security markets – from $46 billion in 2005 to $178 billion by 2015 (with the US accounting for half of that total) (Carafano *et al.* 2006).

However, "combat-proven" Israeli security products and services were also enticing growing global interest, as the status of Israel as a global exemplar of securitization spread around the world. In 2007 the IEE was "preparing to host dozens of foreign delegations from the sector this year. Among these, an international group with representatives from the US, Singapore, Kenya, Canada and Belgium" (Kravitz 2007). Such visits often encompass joint training exercises, as well as visits to archetypal examples of Israeli military urbanistic "best practice." One delegation from the US state of Maryland, for example, visited "Ben Gurion Airport, the port of Ashod, a commuter rail line and rail station, and a hospital for mass casualties" (Pockett 2007: 16).

Security–industrial complexes: joint ventures

Complex joint ventures between US and Israeli companies, and central and local governments, are emerging, aimed at furthering the integration between US and Israeli security companies and profitably generalizing Israeli experience. Driven by the perception that "the United Sates, as well as the entire international community, can learn much from Israel's efforts in the homeland security arena" (Pockett 2007: 150), in March 2004 the US and Israel signed a joint Homeland Security Foundation Act. This "set aside $25 million for research and development of new homeland security technologies conducted jointly by American and Israeli companies" (Pocket 2007: 147). Pump-priming US and Israeli security companies to allow them to exploit global markets, in the hope that this will "have positive economic effects in both states," is a major goal of the act, as is developing new security products for US and Israeli markets (Israeli Ministry of Public Security 2007).

On announcing the news, Curt Weldon, a Republican Representative for Pennsylvania, underlined the economic spin-offs of joint Israeli–US securitization efforts:

> If we expect to win the war on terrorism, we have to cooperate with our friends and allies, and I can think of no better partner than Israel. The Israelis are experts in preventing and responding to terrorism, and I am confident that by working together, this proactive legislation will foster the kind of research and development that will propel private industries to develop the technology that will help protect us from terrorism.
>
> (Cited in Pockett 2007: 148)

In addition, the US–Israel Science and Technology Foundation (USISTF), a joint organization founded to promote high-tech development, set up an initiative in 2004 to encourage US and Israeli firms to develop comprehensive security systems to protect key buildings and infrastructures (Charlaff 2004).

US local governments also see the enrolment of Israeli security firms as a way of furthering their own development as hot-beds of research and development in the burgeoning and lucrative security industry. In January 2008, for example, the local economic development authority for Fairfax County in Virginia – a locality at the heart of one of the largest concentrations of high-tech US defence and security capital centred on the Beltway around Washington, D.C. – hosted a senior delegation of representatives from major Israeli security and defence corporations. The declared aim of the conference was to convince these companies to set up offices in the area (to complement the sixty-five which, by 2007, already had offices in and around Washington) and to entice them to work on joint ventures with US firms based there. Gerald Gordon, president and CEO of the Fairfax authority, described the rationale clearly:

> Homeland security covers such an enormous range of services given the need to protect our air, land and water borders. We don't have the sufficient experience to cover everything [in the US] and Israel has to be the first place to look for these. Because of the close alliances the US has with Israel, the conference takes on a second layer in how to tap into government contracts.
>
> (cited in Kravitz 2007)

The Israeli firms' presence at the Fairfax event demonstrates the extent to which the detailed experience of securitization and repression in the occupied territories lies at the heart of Israel's push to be the global exemplar of military urbanism. DefenSoft Planning Systems, for example, boast of their unrivalled experience in "buffer zone protection planning," covering "airports, seaports, industrial campuses, urban zones, and other strategic infrastructure sites." One of their recent contracts has involved "planning new [sensor] deployment around Gaza Strip" (see DEFENSOFT 2010). Meanwhile, Mate CCTV, which has received grants from the Israel–US Bi-national Industrial Research and Development Foundation (BIRD), offers "intelligent video surveillance," including an automated "behaviour watch" function. Finally, Suspect Detection Systems' specialism is a system that, the makers claim, automatically "identifies malicious intent at border control and other checkpoints" (Fairfax County Economic Development Authority 2007).

These joint ventures are already accruing major contracts in US and global securitization. The Israeli firm Elbit, for example, is working with Boeing under a controversial Department of Homeland Security contract to build a high-tech surveillance system along the US–Mexico border. This will utilize the expertise Elbit has acquired "protecting Israel's borders . . . to keep Americans safe," according to the Israel21c marketing service (Goldman 2006). Elbit's president, Tim Taylor, claimed that "the strategic and technological strengths that we bring to the project will help restore the safety and security that Americans have known for so long. Detecting threats along 6,000 miles of border in the US is not the place for experimentation" (cited in Goldman 2006).

Conclusion

> Clearly, Israel no longer has reason to fear war.
>
> (Klein 2007a: 241)

This chapter has demonstrated that the security–industrial complexes of Israel and the United States are in the process of integrating seamlessly with the military–

industrial complexes of those nations. This is occurring within a context marked by widespread imitation of the legal, geopolitical, geographical and technological means which the Israeli state has mobilized to fight permanent "assymetric warfare" against non-state enemies at home and abroad. The centrality of Israeli doctrine as an exemplar underpinning the so-called "war on terror," in particular, has meant that the security–military–industrial complexes of the United States and Israel are becoming intimately connected, to such an extent that it would perhaps make more sense to consider them as one transnational unit. Fuelled by the closely related ideologies of permanent war emanating from the US and Israeli administrations – within the infinitely flexible and extendable confines of the "global war on terror" – these processes of exemplification, experimentation, imitation and justification are forging the rapid integration of the permanent war economies of both Israel and the United States.

The US–Israeli security–industrial bubble – a rare area of growth amid recession-prone stocks and a global economic downturn – is based firmly on the generalization and imitation of doctrines and technologies of "security" forged during the long-standing lockdown and repression of Palestinian cities by Israeli military and security forces. Through this, there is a danger that Israeli practices of urban hyper-militarism are being generalized and normalized across transnational scales.

Such a prospect raises key questions about the global political economies of the security industries that surveillance studies has barely started to address. It challenges critical scholars to address the way legal, socio-technical, geopolitical and political–economic aspects of imitation relate within broad, global trends towards intensifying surveillance and securitization. And it forces scholars to address the often neglected links between increasingly militarized spaces of civilian surveillance and experimentation with "urban warfare" on colonial frontiers. Michel Foucault (2003: 103) wrote:

> It should never be forgotten that while colonization, with its techniques and its political and juridical weapons, obviously transported European models to other continents, it also had a considerable boomerang effect on the mechanisms of power in the West, and on the apparatuses, institutions, and techniques of power. A whole series of colonial models was brought back to the West, and the result was that the West could practice something resembling colonization, or an internal colonialism, on itself.

It is now necessary for critical surveillance scholarship to excavate the Foucauldian "boomerang effects" that surround the blurring of US and Israeli military and security doctrine. Here particular attention needs to be paid to how such boomerang effects are constituted through complex circuits of exemplification and imitation.

Bibliography

Bishara, A. (n.d.) "On the Intifada, Sharon's Aims, '48 Palestinians and NDA/Tajamu Stratagem," *Between the Lines*. Available HTTP: <http://www.azmibishara.info/interviews/btl_sharonaims.htm>.

Borger, J. (2003) "Israel Trains US Assassination Squads in Iraq," *Guardian*, 9 December. Available HTTP: <http://www.guardian.co.uk/Iraq/Story/0,2763,1102940,00.html>.

Carafano, J., Czerwinski, J. and Weitz, R. (2006) "Homeland Security Technology, Global Partnerships, and Winning the Long War," *The Heritage Foundation*, 5 October. Available HTTP: <http://www.heritage.org/Research/HomelandSecurity/bg1977.cfm>.

Charlaff, J. (2004) "Joint Israeli–American Initiative to Streamline Homeland Security Management," Israel21c, 28 November. Available HTTP: <http://www.usistf.org/download/Israel%2021c.htm>.

DEFENSOFT (2010) *A Global Leader in Boundary Security Planning*. Available HTTP: <http://www.defensoft.com/>.

Elmer, J. (2005) "Maple Flag, the Israeli Air Force and 'the New Type of Battle We Are Being Asked to Fight,'" *Briarpatch*, December: 3–8.

Evans, M. (2007) *City without Joy: Urban Military Operations into the 21st Century*, Canberra: Australian Defence College Occasional Series No. 2, ISSN 1834-772X. Available HTTP: <http://www.strategicstudiesinstitute.army.mil/pdffiles/of-interest-7.pdf>.

Fairfax County Economic Development Authority (2007) "Special Event United States–Israel HLS Technologies Conference and B2B (Business to Business) Meetings between Israeli and US Companies, January 16–18." Available HTTP: <http://www.fairfaxcountyeda.org/israel_event_0107.htm>.

Filkins, D. (2003) "A Region Inflamed: Tough New Tactics by US Tighten Grip on Iraq Towns," *New York Times*, 7 December. Available HTTP: <http://query.nytimes.com/gst/fullpage.html?res=9E0CE1DC133DF934A35751C1A9659C8B63>.

Fisk, R. (2007) "Divide and Rule – America's Plan for Baghdad," *Independent*, 11 April. Available HTTP: <http://www.independent.co.uk/news/fisk/robert-fisk-divide-and-rule – americas-plan-for-baghdad-444178.html>.

Foucault, M. (2003) *Society Must be Defended: Lectures at the Collège de France, 1975–6*, London: Allen Lane.

Freilich, C. (2006) "'The Pentagon's Revenge' or Strategic Transformation: The Bush Administration's New Security Strategy," *Strategic Assessment*, 9(1). Available HTTP: <http://www.tau.ac.il/jcss/sa/v9n1p5Freilich.html>.

Goldberg, B. (2007) "Introduction, Washington Israel Business Council Washington State and Israel: Investment and Trade Opportunities World Trade Center Tacoma, May 4th, 2007." Available HTTP: <http://www.wtcta.org/index.php?CURRENT_PAGE_ID=627-288k>.

Goldman, L. (2006) "Israeli Technology to Keep US Borders Safe," Israel21c, October 15. Available HTTP: <http://www.israel21c.org/bin/en.jsp?enDispWho=Articles%5Ell450&enPage=BlankPage&enDisplay=view&enDis>.

Graham, S. (2003) "Vertical Geopolitics: Baghdad and after," *Antipode*, 36(1): 12–19.

—— (2010) *Cities under Siege: The New Military Urbanism*, London: Verso.

Hajjar, L. (2006) "International Humanitarian Law and 'Wars on Terror': A Comparative Analysis of Israeli and American Doctrines and Policies," *Journal of Palestine Studies*, 36(1): 21–42.

Henriksen, T. (2007) *The Israeli Approach to Irregular Warfare and Implications for the United States*, Hurlburt Field, FL: JSOU Press, Joint Special Operations University Report 07-3. Available HTTP: <https://jsoupublic.socom.mil/publications/jsoupubs_2007.php>.

Hersh, S. (2003) "Moving Targets: Will the Counter-Insurgency Plan in Iraq Repeat the Mistakes of Vietnam?," *New Yorker*, 15 December.

International Socialist Review (2004) "Iraq, Palestine, and US Imperialism." Available HTTP: <http://www.isreview.org/issues/36/toufic.shtml>.

Israel High-Tech Investment Report (2008). Available HTTP: <http://ishitech.co.il/0208ar11.htm>.

Israeli Ministry of Industry, Trade and Labor (n.d.) "Applying Israel's Homeland Security Experience Worldwide." Available HTTP: <http://www.tamas.gov.il/NR/exeres/7A26C75C-2C31-4E80-8E09-B4D465C721A3.htm>.

Israeli Ministry of Public Security (2007) "An Israel–USA Homeland Security Fund." Available HTTP: <http://www.mops.gov.il/BPEng/OnTheAgenda/Israel-USAcollaboration/>.

Israeli Weapons.Com (2007) "Hermes 450." Available HTTP: <http://www.israeli-weapons. com/weapons/aircraft/uav/hermes_450/Hermes_450.html>.

Khoury-Machool, M. (2003) "Losing the Battle for Arab Hearts and Minds," *Open Democracy*, 2 May. Available HTTP: <http://www.opendemocracy.net/media-journalismwar/article_ 1202.jsp-51k>.

Klein, N. (2007a) *The Shock Doctrine: The Rise of Disaster Capitalism*, London: Allen Lane.

—— (2007b) "Laboratory for a Fortressed World," *The Nation*, 2 July. Available HTTP: <http://www.thenation.com/doc/20070702/klein>.

Krauss, L. (2007), "Analysis: Israel Defense Exports Strong," UPI.com, 13 December. Available HTTP: <http://www.upi.com/International_Security/Industry/Analysis/ 2007/12/13/analysis_israel_defense_exports_strong/7255/>.

Kravitz, A. (2007) "US Homeland Security Market Beckons," *Jerusalem Post*, 18 January. Available HTTP: <http://www.jpost.com/servlet/Satellite?cid=1167467758745&page name=JPost%2FJPArticle%2FEMail>.

Larsen, J. and Pravecek, T. (2007) "Comparative US–Israeli Homeland Security," USAF Counterproliferation Center, Air University, Maxwell Air Force Base, AL: Counter-proliferation Papers Future Warfare Series No. 34.

Li, D. (2006) "The Gaza Strip as Laboratory: Notes in the Wake of Disengagement," *Journal of Palestine Studies*, 35(2): 38–49.

Pockett, C. (2007) "The United States and Israeli Homeland Security: A Comparative Analysis of Emergency Preparedness Efforts," USAF Counterproliferation Center, Air University, Maxwell Air Force Base, AL: Counterproliferation Papers Future Warfare Series No. 33.

Rafael Corporation (n.d.) "Anti-Terror Homeland Security Solutions." Available HTTP: <http://www.rafael.co.il/marketing/SIP_STORAGE/FILES/2/782.pdf>.

Sadeh, S. (2004) "Israel's Defense Industry in the 21st Century: Challenges and Opportunities," *Strategic Assessment*, 7(3). Available HTTP: <http://www.tau.ac.il/ jcss/sa/v7n3p5Sad.html>.

Said, E. (2003) "Dreams and Delusions: The Imperial Bluster of Tom Delay," *CounterPunch*, 20 August. Available HTTP: <http://www.counterpunch.org/said08202003.html>.

Sanders, Ralph (n.d.) "Israel Practice New Concepts for Airborne, Urban Area Domination: An Israeli Military Innovation," *Defense Update*. Available HTTP: <http://www.defense-update.com/features/du-1-06/feature-urban-il.htm>.

Snyder, D. (2008) "Israel's Technology Creates an Investment Goliath," *Fox Business*, 16 January. Available HTTP: <http://www.foxbusiness.com/article/israels-technology-creates-investment-goliath_429161_49.html>.

Tov, I. (2003) "Economy in a Prolonged Conflict: Israel 2000–2003," *Strategic Assessment*, 6(1). Available HTTP: <http://www.tau.ac.il/jcss/sa/v6n1p5Tov.html>.

Tran, P. and Opall-Rome, B. (n.d.) "French UAV to Carry Israeli Missiles," Rafael Corporation. Available HTTP: <http://www.rafael.co.il/marketing/SIP_STORAGE/ FILES/0/600.pdf>.

Turbiville, G. (2007) *Hunting Leadership Targets in Counterinsurgency and Counterterrorist Operations Selected Perspectives*, Hurlburt Field, FL: JSOU Press, Joint Special Operations University Report 07-6. Available HTTP: <https://jsoupublic.socom.mil/publications/jsou/JSOU 07-6turbivilleHuntingLeadershipTargets_final.pdf>.

Unmanned Aerial Vehicles Blog (2006). Available HTTP: <http://www.livingroom.org.au/ uavblog/archives/cat_uav_news.html>

USA Today (2003) "US Military Employs Israeli Technology in Iraq War," 24 March. Available HTTP: <http://www.usatoday.com/tech/world/iraq/2003-03-24-israel-tech_x.htm>.

USAWC (2006) *Shifting Fire: Information Effects in Counterinsurgency and Stability Operations*, US Army War College, Carlisle Barracks, PA: Workshop Report USAWC 10. Available HTTP: <http://www.carlisle.army.mil/usacsl/Publications/ShiftingFireMenu.pdf>.

Visser, R. (2007) "Baghdad Zoo: Why 'Gated Communities' Will Face Opposition in the Iraqi Capital," Historiae.org, 23 April. Available HTTP: <http://www.historiae.org/gated.asp>.

Weizman, E. (2004) Note in J. Crandall (ed.) *Under Fire – The Organization and Representation of Violence*, Rotterdam: Witte de Witte.

—— (2006) *Hollow Land*, London: Verso.

—— (2008) "Thanotactics," in Michael Sorkin (ed.) *Indefensible Space: The Architecture of the National Security State*, New York: Routledge.

8 Israel's emergence as a homeland security capital

Neve Gordon

In preparation for the 2008 Beijing Olympics several Israeli companies won contracts to provide security during the games. Nice Systems was selected to upgrade the security network in subway stations in Beijing. Nice currently boasts over 24,000 customers in 100 countries, with 85 of the *Fortune* 100 companies on its list. American Express, JP Morgan and Federal Express are among its clients, as are an array of police departments, the Federal Aviation Authority in the United States and the European Space Agency. All incoming telephone calls to the Los Angeles and New York City police departments are recorded on Nice technology, as are roughly 90 percent of the transactions at brokerage firms worldwide. In 2007, the company's revenues reached $519 million, well above the $418 million revenues of 2006. A company press release noted that in Beijing Nice would connect the subway stations to a security system to give "security personnel the power to identify risk, make optimal decisions, and take action that improves security" (Nice Systems 2006).

DDS was awarded the contract to supervise access control in ten Olympic facilities. Since its foundation in 1986, DDS has installed over 45,000 systems in 40 countries. Its clients include major international firms and organizations, such as Airbus Industries, Lucent, Motorola, Intel, Nokia, City Bank and Oxford University. In Beijing, DDS installed its one-card-solution managing system (smart cards) in 2,000 doors (DDS 2009). ClickSoftware Technologies, which has headquarters in Israel and Massachusetts, and offices in Europe and Asia Pacific, was also contracted by the Chinese government; its responsibility was to manage the field activities of hundreds of telecommunication technicians during the Olympics. The company provides mobile workforce management and service optimization software, and it has over 100 customers across a variety of industries and geographies. In Beijing, its software was used to optimize the scheduling operations of several hundred technicians responsible for break/fix, installation and maintenance work (ClickSoftware 2009).

The fact that Israeli companies were chosen to supply such services is a reflection not only of Israel's military relations with China but of the visibility of Israeli security firms in the global arena. Indeed, the Olympics is merely one of many international areas in which Israeli homeland security (HS) and surveillance companies are routinely involved (see Invest in Israel 2009). Their customers include governments, police and security agencies, banks and commercial corporations, airlines, oil, energy and utility companies as well as private consumers in well over a hundred countries (Israexport 2005c; Invest in Israel 2009). Israel, in other words, has successfully positioned itself as a global HS capital.

In this chapter, I describe some of the key internal processes that enabled Israel to secure such a prominent place in this global market. The difference between Israel and the other newly established high-tech capitals – e.g., Ireland, India, and Taiwan – which do not have a robust HS industrial sector is, I argue, due to the salient impact of the Israeli military and the state-owned military industry on the country's high-tech sector. More specifically, I show that the Israeli high-tech industry was initially propelled by local demand, primarily from the military and security establishments; this helped shape the orientation of the high-tech industry in its first stages. In addition, both the military and military industry served as conveyor belts for literally thousands of programmers for the high-tech industry, who played a vital role in converting products and ideas from military to commercial use. The military has also created a "collaborative public space" (Breznitz 2005) that facilitates the sharing of ideas and collective learning oriented towards the invention and improvement of security products and services, while the incorporation of security personnel who have had experience in combat opens both political and economic doors and provides credit to the products and companies they represent. Finally, I maintain that the use of the occupied Palestinian territories, Lebanon and Israel itself as laboratories and showcases for the products that are developed is crucial for Israel's marketing efforts. Considered together, all these factors help explain how Israel became a homeland security capital.

The military industry

Israel's HS and surveillance industry is firmly linked to the shift in demand following the terrorist attacks of 9/11 and the ensuing war on terror as well as to political, economic, social and cultural global processes relating to the increasing movement of people, goods and services across political borders; these latter processes include ongoing attempts of different government agencies and businesses to find ways of decreasing the risk of smuggling, theft, drug trafficking, counterfeiting, illegal entry, disruption to global supply networks, and so on (Stevens 2004: 18). They also include mechanisms that aim to help governments and businesses conduct their operations more efficiently and cost-effectively, thus suggesting that while the HS and surveillance products and services may have been developed to monitor an array of activities relating to terrorism and criminal threats, currently they are extensively deployed by governments, corporations, financial institutions, gated communities, hospitals and schools to manage populations, consumers, employees, as well as an array of transactions and interactions (Lyon 2003).

While such global events and processes are no doubt crucial for understanding the impressive achievements of Israel's HS industry, one cannot really make sense of the industry's expo-nential growth without taking into account numerous internal factors, among them the central role played by military industry and the military.

The foundation of the military industry can be traced back to the pre-state Zionist struggle. The production of weapons and ammunition

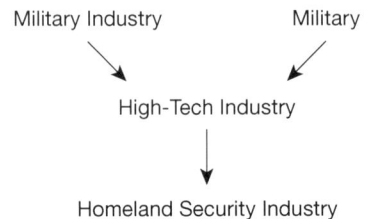

Figure 8.1 Historical roots of the homeland security industry

had already begun in the 1920s, and in 1933 TAAS, which was later renamed Israeli Military Industries (IMI), was officially established in order to manufacture rifles, mortars, hand grenades and ammunition in underground workshops. Israel Aerospace Industries (IAI, originally called the Bedek Aviation Company) was founded in 1953 and is currently Israel's largest military exporter, boasting a record high of $2.8 billion in sales during 2006. In addition, some privately owned firms were established in the 1950s, and are currently responsible for 25 percent of Israel's arms sales. Israel, one should add, was recently ranked as the sixth-largest military exporter (SIPRI 2008).

The military industry's success is intricately tied to the establishment of a research and development division – which was subsequently called RAFAEL (Armament Development Authority) – in the early 1950s as part of the state-owned military industry. From the outset, the military industry was relatively large, employing until the mid-1960s about 15,000 workers, or roughly 2 percent of Israel's full-time workforce. Following the June 1967 war, the industry underwent a dramatic change. Charles de Gaulle declared a military embargo on Israel due to France's decision to ally itself with the Arab countries. France had been Israel's major supplier of weaponry, including nuclear technology, and de Gaulle's decision put Israel in a bind, since it desperately needed to acquire critical weapons. Following the war, the Israeli government decided to shift vast amounts of resources to Israel's military industry in order to reduce the country's dependency on other states for military equipment. Accordingly, the Israeli government designated the military industry a national priority sector and channeled large sums of money both directly to the industry and to the military, which then purchased products from the industry (Vekstein and Mehrez 1997). By 1975, the number of people employed in the military industry had tripled, reaching approximately 45,000, or 5.5 percent of the full-time workforce (Central Bureau of Statistics 2007d; Dvir and Tishler 2000).

As a way of maintaining regional superiority, Israel's military industry focused on high-tech development, concentrating on computer and electronic technologies, electro-optics, aeronautics, mechanical design and metalworks, as well as chemical and software engineering. The Israeli government was always heavily involved in the military industry, both as owner of a large segment of this industry and as the industry's main customer (through the military) (Dvir and Tishler 2000: 198). For about a decade the size of the industry's workforce remained relatively static, but in the mid-1980s it was downsized (Justman 2002). The downsizing was originally precipitated by an economic crisis in Israel and later by the end of the Cold War and the dramatic decrease in weapons trade (Azulay, Lerner and Tishler 2002). As can be seen in Figure 8.2, a "deliberate reduction in domestic defense procurement after 1985 released tens of thousands of workers into the labor market, providing an abundant supply of skilled labor for an emerging high-tech sector and allowing more efficient exploitation of the commercial potential of Israeli R&D" (Justman 2002: 2).

Despite the downsizing, the military industry was able to expand its markets. This remarkable trend has to do with the fact that in the 1970s certain corporations (most prominently IAI) decided to shift their research and production interests from major platforms to technologically advanced systems and components, and to begin focusing on civilian as well as military markets (Azulay, Lerner and Tishler 2002). By 1999, IAI reported that 39 percent of its revenues came from the civilian sector. Another important factor leading to the industry's ongoing success involves the relationships

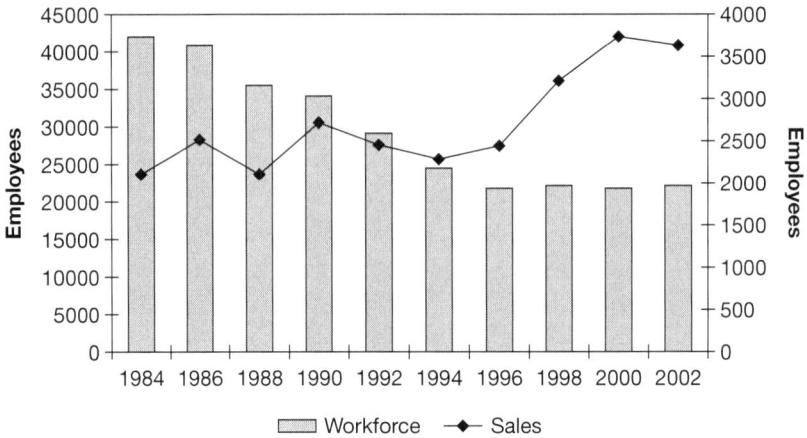

Figure 8.2 Israeli state-owned military industries – employees and exports
Note: Figures include subsidiaries, but exclude former employees on companies' payrolls
Source: Sadeh 2004

it established with US, German and French industries, with which it shared technological knowledge and carried out trade (Avnimelech and Teubal 2004). We now know that the strategic decision to concentrate on military R&D with an emphasis on technologically advanced systems proved advantageous, since it ultimately served to facilitate the foundation of a solid technology-orientated economic base for Israel. Many engineers, scientists and managers who were initially employed in the state-owned military industries eventually moved into the private sector, where they applied the knowledge and training they had acquired in new projects.

The military

Not unlike the military industry, the Israeli military also provided a fertile breeding ground for future generations of high-tech workers and entrepreneurs. In order to understand the impact of Israel's military on its high-tech industry and, more specifically, its HS industry, it is vital to examine the military's role in Israel's computing history. In 1960, nine years before the first computer science programs were introduced in Israeli universities and before the official birth of Israel's software industry in 1969, the Israeli military was already developing software in a newly established military unit called MAMRAM (a Hebrew acronym for the Center of Computers and Automated Recording) (Ariav and Goodman 1994). MAMRAM rapidly became the largest and most sophisticated computing center in the country (Breznitz 2005). Integral to its operations was an internal training unit, which became independent in the second half of the 1990s and is now known as the School of Computer-Related Professions. This is the main programming, software-engineering and computer-users training unit in the military. The School for Computer-Related Professions trains about 300 programmers each year, and they end up serving a minimum of five years in the military. By the age of twenty-one, the average

MAMRAM programmer has extensive experience and has worked on multiple projects, where he or she will have served as a team leader (Breznitz 2005: 48). In addition to MAMRAM, the air force, 8200 (i.e., the electronic warfare unit) and other military intelligence agencies have their own computer training programs, which are not as big as MAMRAM, but still train hundreds of young Israelis each year.

Thus, the military has served as a conveyor belt for literally thousands of programmers and application instructors, most of whom join the Israeli high-tech industry. A study conducted in 1998 by the Center for Technological Forecasts at Tel-Aviv University estimated that 35 percent of the start-up entrepreneurs in Israel were trained in R&D during their military service and that 57 percent of these entrepreneurs had served as officers in the military (Dvir and Tishler 2000: 38). All of this helps explain the orientation of Israel's high-tech industry and its emphasis on communications and security.

Silicon Wadi

Like Japan, Israel lacks natural resources. Its economy is consequently dependent on human capital, which over the past two and a half decades has been channeled into the high-tech industry. Early on, a few foreign multinational corporations identified the potential of human capital in Israel. In 1964, Motorola opened an R&D branch there, while IBM, Intel, Digital Equipment and numerous others followed suit in the 1970s and 1980s (Avnimelech and Teubal 2004: 40). The homegrown industry, however, received its first real boost only in 1984, with the enactment of an R&D law that supported knowledge-intensive industries, which significantly increased Israel's R&D grants to science and technology infrastructure. This change coincided with the economic restructuring processes within Israel and the ensuing downsizing of the workforce in Israel's military industries (Avnimelech and Teubal 2004). While the workers who left the industry and the thousands of Israelis who completed their military service in high-tech-related jobs did indeed serve as the necessary core for the private high-tech surge throughout the 1990s, their move from military to civilian enterprises does not tell the whole story.

One cannot fully understand the growth of Israel's high-tech industry without taking into account the role of Israeli universities and the immigration of scientists and engineers from the former Soviet Union. Over the years the universities had developed cutting-edge computer science departments and were training hundreds of programmers each year. And although homegrown talent was no doubt crucial, more engineers emigrated to Israel from the former Soviet Union in the 1990s than Israel's Technion University had produced since its foundation in 1924 (Schwartz 2005). This immigration helps explain why Israel claims the highest proportion of scientists and engineers with postgraduate education in the world: 135 per 10,000 compared with 78 per 10,000 in the US (Israel Export and International Cooperation Institute 2007a).

All these developments help explain why a distinct private high-tech sector was able to emerge in the late 1980s and early 1990s. By the year 2000, an estimated 3,500 to 4,000 start-ups were operating in Israel, more than one start-up per 1,500 people. From 1990 to 2000 there was a fivefold increase in high-tech exports – from $2.2 billion to $11 billion. In 2000, however, the upward trend halted as a result of the second Intifada and the bursting of the global tech bubble. But in 2002 the high-tech industry began climbing back up and it has grown rapidly ever since. Currently, Israel boasts the highest concentration of high-tech start-ups per capita, and the second largest in the world in absolute numbers, after Silicon Valley. The Israeli potential was not missed by venture capitalists, as can be seen by the dramatic increase in the number of venture capital funds investing in the industry: from two in 1991 to over a hundred in 2001. In 2007, 462 Israeli high-tech companies raised $1.76 billion from local and foreign venture investors, 31.5 percent above 2005 levels (Israeli Venture Capital Research Center 2008). The Israeli high-tech industry's presence in the international arena is also notable: on Nasdaq, for example, 67 out of the 298 non-US listed companies are Israeli, putting Israel in first place among foreign nations on the index.[1]

One should also note that, despite the global economic recession, Israeli homeland security companies continue to do well. In the first three months of 2009, Aeronautics Defense Systems signed a $50 million contract for its Aerostar Tactical UAV with the Dutch Ministry of Defense, while South Korea awarded Elisra a $25 million contract to supply an "integrated electronic warfare suite." Israel's Aeronautics struck a $22 million deal to deliver air surveillance equipment to Mexico's national police force, and Transnet Port Terminals, the largest cargo terminal operator in South Africa, expanded Nice's IP video surveillance environment at Durban Car Terminal and Ngqura. Elbit Systems announced that it had won a $40 million contract from the Israeli Ministry of Defense to supply UAVs to the Israeli military, and MATE Intelligent Video, a technology leader in intelligent video surveillance systems and video analytics, announced that its Trigger analytic video encoder had been chosen by CCTV Center, a leading distributor in Spain, to protect several local solar fields. These are just a few examples of the contracts secured by Israeli companies at the height of the global recession.[2]

The emergence of a homeland security industry

Clearly not all or even a majority of Israel's high-tech companies focus on HS and surveillance. And yet, Israel's "High-Tech Knowledge Portal" maintains that, after telecommunications, HS is the second-largest high-tech subsector in terms of number of companies.[3] Interestingly, in terms of the number of HS/surveillance companies and the revenues these companies accrue, there is no comparison between Israel and countries like Ireland, Taiwan and India, all of which have enjoyed a similar high-tech boom but have not developed an HS sector within their high-tech industries.[4] Only two other countries appear to have such robust HS and surveillance high-tech sectors: the United States and the United Kingdom. The difference between Israel and the other newly established high-tech capitals reflects the impact of the internal forces and processes that led to the creation Israel's HS industry.

Military conversion and technological spin-offs

There is no dispute that many of Israel's homegrown technological skills were honed inside secret military labs and that military research has given Israel a clear lead in vital aspects of telecommunications and software technology. According to one government institute, "what grew out of a direct military need with a high-tech edge has developed into a core element of the Israeli economy and placed Israel at the forefront of the global security and HS industry" (Israel Export and International Cooperation Institute 2007b). Thus, the military and military industry are not only responsible for providing a skilled labor force to Israel's high-tech industry but have equipped it with specific technological knowledge that has enabled private entrepreneurs to manufacture a variety of spin-offs.

A well-known example of private conversion involves Given Imaging, a Nasdaq-listed Israeli company that is currently redefining the field of gastrointestinal diagnosis. Given Imaging developed PillCam, a disposable miniature video camera contained in a capsule that can be easily ingested by the patient. The capsule transmits high-quality color images of the gastrointestinal tract, which allows physicians to see the small intestine and esophagus while sparing the patient the ordeal of an endoscopy (Given Imaging 2008). The tiny camera was originally developed as a device to transmit images from missiles (Schwartz 2005). Given Imaging's story is typical of many high-tech firms in Israel, some of which produce gadgets for medical supervision, and many of which create products for HS and surveillance.

Haifa-based Fibronics was founded by engineers who had worked together in military intelligence. The company got off to a good start in the 1980s with a data-networking technology called the Fiber Distributed Data Interface, but since it lacked a US distribution arm it was eventually taken over by Elbit Computers. Enigma did better. Founded by veterans of a military intelligence unit, the company developed software that provides maintenance information about complex products, such as jet engines, construction machinery, automobiles and telecommunications equipment. It currently boasts annual sales in the hundreds of millions of dollars (Enigma 2008).

A survey of Israel's high-tech industry reveals that these stories are not coincidental, and that various applications developed by private HS companies started life in military R&D in the areas of sensors, information-gathering technologies, image enhancements, video and audio compression applications, high-speed image analysis and optical inspection systems (Dvir and Tishler 2000; Gordon 2009).

Collaborative public space

Contrary to the commonly held view, which sees the military and military industry as mere suppliers of skilled labor and technological spin-offs to the private high-tech sector, Dan Breznitz (2005) adds a whole new dimension to the discussion. He shows that the military plays an additional role in shaping the high-tech industry by providing it with what he calls "collaborative public space." The notion of a collaborative public space adds a spatial dimension to existing theories that emphasize the importance of social networking, systems of flexible production, and the creation of formal and informal institutions for the development of technological innovation.

By collaborative public space, Breznitz means a

> structured social space imbued with high mutual trust within which different actors and groups regularly study, cooperate, share information, and partake in collective learning. Collaborative public spaces are, therefore, the institutions that both stimulate and enable the different actors and organizations in a system to

meet, discuss, transfer, interpret, and develop ideas, knowledge, and information that are inherent to their industry.

(Breznitz 2005: 36)

The existence of such vibrant public space where people from different walks of life meet enhances not only the capabilities and economic capacities of individual actors but the industrial sector as a whole. Participation in these meetings, Breznitz adds, helps diffuse information throughout the industrial system through formal and informal transactions and collaborations between individual actors, which augments the capacity for collective action and spurs ideas for public policy. It also facilitates a sense of a shared future. To be sure, this collaborative space fosters elite formation and the crystallization of social class formations. However, it is "public" only in a limited sense – that is, to those who are Jews, have the necessary military experience, and can utilize the old-boy network. Even Jews who do not have the correct type of military experience have a hard time joining this "collaborative public space."[5]

The close relationship between the military and civilian sectors in Israel is not limited to the common denominator of compulsory military service; it also rests on the constant cultivation of this relationship during the long years of service in the reserves that many Israelis carry out. Every Israeli citizen who has served in the military is required to serve for up to thirty days a year as part of their reserve duty. Men usually serve in non-combat units until between the ages of fifty and fifty-six. Women are usually exempt, except for those who have specific skills and training; these are usually called to reserve duty until the age of twenty-six. The crux of the matter is that the military sponsors multiple activities of collective learning by creating and disseminating IT teaching and learning materials among the reserve soldiers. The School for Computer-Related Professions, which has at its disposal around 400 reserve personnel (which amounts to about 12,000 days of reserve duty per year), serves as a point of contact for the reserve personnel, regular duty personnel and students, creating a strong multi-cohort network which is rare among teaching institutions. Small project teams composed of active-duty soldiers and civilian experts from a multitude of firms and academic institutions, doing their reserve duty, are gathered together in order to share their knowledge in a way that would be impossible outside the military (Breznitz 2005). Furthermore, the reserve personnel are constantly exposed to the knowledge produced in the military, knowledge that they then utilize in their private firms or in the universities. Finally, the military also serves as an important point of contact for knowledge acquired from foreign software tools and IT technology development companies, such as Oracle, Sun, Novell, Cisco and Microsoft.

Security network and military credit

The military has facilitated the exponential growth of Israel's HS and surveillance industry not only by enhancing the technological capabilities of this high-tech sector but as a result of the penetration of people with combat-related experience into the industry. Of the 237 surveillance companies I examined, a total of 166 provided a list of members of either the management team or the board, and 156 of these provided short biographical notes for each person. Of these, 102 companies mentioned on their

for roles ranging from shipping-lane and forest-fire monitoring to glacier melt and human migration surveillance. They are being assigned not only a central role in transforming the spaces and forms of violence and control which shape contemporary military practice, but a pivotal role in mapping and monitoring the fundamental human and environmental processes shaping our world. Focusing on combat applications, Stephen Graham (2010: 321) submits an account of the "visual display of war as spectacle" involving "God's-eye maps with diagrammatic and satellite-imaged 'targets.'" This cosmological metaphor for absolute aerial and electro-optical domination attains even greater currency when the ubiquity of UAV monitoring systems in civilian as well as military fields is accepted.

Invested exports: moral economies and techno-nationalism

UAV exports and Israeli "border" experience

Histories of military UAVs recognize but understate Israel's role in their development. The standard account is one of US trials for bombing reconnaissance in the Vietnam War, followed by declining development while research took off in Israel between 1967 and 1982, culminating in the decisive role played against Syrian defences in the Lebanon War which cemented the UAV's status (see Clark 1999; Glade 2000). What is less commonly foregrounded is the extent to which Israeli designs have come to dominate the UAV export market. According to (incomplete) data from the Stockholm International Peace Research Institute, of all UAV systems transferred internationally between 2001 and 2005, 68 per cent were Israeli-supplied (SIPRI 2001–2006). Israeli and US UAVs are integral to the SBI, the UK's Israeli-built Watchkeeper programme is the largest system currently coming into service (2010), India's border with Pakistan is continuously monitored by Israeli-built UAVs, and states from Finland to Botswana are deploying Israeli systems in a range of surveillance theatres. With the US's Predator and Pioneer models based on Israeli designs, and IAI and Elbit cornering most of the remainder of the export market, transfers today overwhelmingly involve Israeli designs.

These transfers occur primarily within larger packages of bespoke "security solutions" that are tailored to meet client needs. Here, the idea of the border, the homeland, and their hermetic closure represents a recurrent trope. Israeli exporters package UAVs as part of such "tailored operational solutions" as "Border Control and Management Systems" (Elbit), "Anti-Terror Homeland Security Solutions" (Rafael), or "Integrated Border Protection Systems" (IAI). Thus, while sovereign territorial state borders are being subjected to the perforating effects of liquid war/homeland defence, Israel's own boundary systems and experiences are suggested as a model. When Elbit secured UAV contracts for initial phases of the SBI, success was attributed to its proven border-security work in Israel. Press releases stressed the link: "The talent and expertise that Elbit Systems has employed for years in protecting Israel's borders will now be put to use on US borders to keep Americans safe" (Goldman 2006).

This invocation of Israel's "border-security" experience as somehow embodied in its UAV exports is strikingly consistent, resurfacing in diverse settings as clients attach themselves to a securitized imaginary organized around mythical oppositions and a narrative of Israel's frontline condition. Even in Muslim Indonesia, officially opposed to trade links with Israel, Defence Minister Juwono Sudarsono defends the purchase of Israel's UAVs by wielding an image of an embattled Israel warding off an inchoate "Arab" exterior: "This is the world's most sophisticated UAV and has been tested for years while doing the job along Israel's borders with Arab countries" (Sudarsono 2006).[3] Of course, UAV transfers involve more than symbolic exchange and the transmission of nationalist tropes; the operational principles of systems interoperability and the strategic privileging of bilateral collaboration engender pronounced levels of services cooperation, as evidenced in the proliferation of "joint task forces" and "bilateral working groups" which attend increased NWTS transfers. For India, already deploying Israeli UAVs along its borders, IDI technical provision is increasingly coupled to such projects. In mid-2007, a year after Israel's Gaza Strip and Lebanon perimeters were breached, a delegation led by Deputy Chief of Staff Moshe Kaplinsky arrived in India "to instruct the Army on how to stop infiltrations into Jammu and Kashmir from across the Pakistani border" (Raghuvanshi 2007).

This submission of Israel's "borders" as indices of desirable security levels overlooks the ambiguities of Israel's territoriality. The debate which erupted in 2006, when Minister of Education Yuli Tamir proposed indicating in school atlases what she (creatively) termed the "Green Line," descended into farce when neither she nor her opponents could coherently describe a cartography adequate for what Tamir conceded was the "scrambled situation" of a state "truly distinctively formed in this world" (Knesset Committee on Education, Culture, and Sport 2007). However defined, Israel's "border" control systems have repeatedly failed to prevent even lightly equipped guerrillas from operating either side of them. The West Bank wall is a monument to the failure of Israeli NWTS to secure a notional perimeter – even one on which Israel's ground forces have been deployed (on both sides) for decades.

But if such borders offer a poor paradigm for "traditional" ideas of state security, they do provide a touchstone for powerful resonances which go beyond "traditional" ideas of territoriality. Identification with Israel's "borders" as the imperilled vanguard of a global conflict suggests a wider affinity and commonality with Zionism's claims and ideals, and by direct implication permits a localized arrangement of positionality relative to the global war's binaries and "border" security logics. The IDI's UAV exports provide not only the new and "creatively liberating" technological architecture for military revolutions undertaken in the prosecution of localized wars but a repository of assertions about difference, virtue, and threat through which to arrange and articulate these conflicts in terms of the wider cartography of global war.

In the following pages, I return to the specific and the national – to the "Zionist experience." Drawing on interviews with nationalist engineers involved in UAV development and export, I suggest that throughout these processes a series of national, moral, and oppositional claims are attached to the UAV as a meaningful artefact. Exported as a techno-conceptual assemblage, I argue that the UAV emerges resonant with meanings deriving from the Zionist project, redolent of the battlefield "experience" from which it emanates and whose logic it proposes.

Resonances of the national in IDI success

Reading the IDI as a hub of techno-scientific practice, but also as a site where national meanings are given substance, reflects several tropes emerging from readings of Zionism.

IDI success and specificity can be broadly associated with three core themes. First, the small-scale, close-knit, and militarized nature of Jewish-Israeli society fosters the high levels of personnel integration, low levels of bureaucracy, and informal mechanisms of organization upon which a fast development cycle depends. It does so while providing – via the integration of high-school, military, university, and industry knowledge bases – what one admirer has described as a "tailor-made, vertically integrated system for identifying, recruiting, training and exploiting" industry personnel (Grant 2006: 30). Second, Zionism's valorization of the scientific as an expression of self-reliance, "modernity," and "post-exilic" identity has historically invested institutions and positions of technical expertise with national kudos (Efron 2007: 224),[4] constructing the technician as what Derek Penslar calls a "Zionist ideal type, the embodiment of the relentlessly pragmatic spirit that Zionists toiled to instil" (Penslar 1991: 154).[5] Finally, the setting for this "relentless pragmatism" has been one of conflict. On the one hand, the setting of permanent war provides themes of survival, expedience, and self-sacrifice which inflect the industry throughout; on the other, the actual prosecution of permanent war provides the much-vaunted "battlefield laboratory" in which to develop, beta-test, and demonstrate innovations in the crafts of war and surveillance. During interviews conducted with scientists following the 2006 Lebanon War, these themes were pronounced. They often emerged with claims about moralities and civilization to suggest forms of national specificity – economies organizing boundaries and oppositions in this state of constant war and military innovation.

Compact, mobilized, at war: IDI scientists explain Israeli R&D

> [E]veryone knows someone from somewhere. And they can call them and say "look, I need this" – and he will.
>
> (Weihs 2007)

The IDI is not only the fastest-growing NWTS exporter. Crucially, it has significantly faster R&D-to-test cycles than other major defence industries. David Stavitsky, chief scientist at Elbit, links this to a relatively small community of specialists: "Israel is a small country and this is a good thing for development, because people know each other and the knowledge circles can be cut in various ways" (Stavitsky 2007). Professor-General Yitzhak Ben-Israel, a Member of the Knesset, Tel Aviv University scholar, ex-director of MAFAT (the military R&D directorate), and head of Israel's Space Agency, embodies this intersecting of competences. He also adds a spatial dimension: "I go to a meeting and I see almost everyone. You need to talk with the government in Jerusalem – it's 40 minutes' drive; you want to speak with the IDF Chief of Staff – 15 minutes. It's a smaller country" (Ben-Israel 2007).[6]

The IDI's densely knit knowledge economy extends in its orbit to the laboratories and professionals of academia, with the mobilization of training and research institutions integral to the industry. Israel's leading aeronautics scholar, Daniel Weihs of the Technion, has decades of experience working within the IDI as engineer, consultant, and board member. Having also worked extensively abroad, he concludes that there "is a unique situation here," in Israel: "I would say that 70–80 per cent of engineers in this industry – in aerospace – are graduates of the Technion. So, even if I don't remember them personally, they would remember me" (Weihs 2007).

Haim Russo of Elbit's electro-optics division (ELOP) credits university laboratories and training with "standing behind this whole vast industry" (Russo 2007). The current president of Tel Aviv University (TAU), Zvi Galil, concurs, declaring himself "awed by the magnitude and scientific creativity of the work being done behind the scenes at TAU that enhances the country's civilian defense capabilities and military edge." He describes TAU, Israel's largest university, as being on "the front line of the critical work to maintain Israel's military and technological edge" (Galil 2008–2009: 4). This relationship between military industrial and academic research is often unequal. Weihs (2007) goes on to describe military needs trumping generic research at the Technion: "We have a wind tunnel lab here in this department, and in many cases basic research has been pushed aside by urgent projects that had to be tested in the wind tunnels . . . [e]xternal projects . . . funded by IAI, Elbit."

What might otherwise produce a corrupt, inefficient, and unstable condition characterized by poorly regulated interests cutting across institutions and sectors is purportedly tempered by nationalist commitment. Asked about the effects of "brain-drain" on the IDI, Ben-Israel (2007) contends that career-oriented emigration to the US or EU is "a smaller phenomenon than in other countries because of the environment around us and [because] people are more attached to the country." This "environment" of low-intensity conflict is perceived as the motor of innovation and the principal check on rampant market competition and its attendant problems for rapid R&D. Shlomo Nir (2007), CEO of electro-optics company CONTROP, describes permanent war as "the primary drive for accomplishing good products" and links this in turn to a particular work ethic: "I used to think that we have [more] intelligent people, but I've seen intelligent people all over, so maybe it's a question of more dedication and that we are in war and have to work hard and give a bit more thought to what we are doing and being good at it." He suggests a link between this pragmatic wartime commitment and a notion of "Jewish" character, arguing: "Jewish people all over have always strived to learn more and more; that's really why we do what we do."

Stavitsky (2007) describes an Israeli "way of doing things" which extends out of this mobilized ethos to produce a refined model for R&D: "I think it's a psychological thing. Countries that are continuously at war . . . are thinking about tomorrow and the day after. Countries that are not at war think about the day after. And this is a different state of mind . . . the [research-to-test] cycle depend[s] on how close you are to a conflict." Despite accountability to Elbit's shareholders, this continuous war setting means Stavitsky's ultimate goal remains that "winning development that will maybe overcome my enemy with minimal risk to my people." Both he and his counterpart at IAI, Leah Boehm, cited the 2006 Lebanon War as an example of national commitment exceeding commercial priorities. Boehm (2007) recalled an arrangement involving UAVs:

> There was a shortage of UAVs; there was a shortage of payloads like radar systems and electro-optical systems, which we had for another customer. It was "on the shelf," I would say. And we loaned it to our troops because it was an emergency. They didn't necessarily buy it because of a shortage of budget . . . When it's a crisis or a war, we don't make such decisions based upon profit. It's a national emergency and I don't think it has to do with the fact that we are a government-owned company.

Asked if something similar might happen in the United States, Boehm (2007) replied that it would not:

> That's the United States and we are Israel . . . Israel is in a survival situation . . . I lived in the States for six years, so I know the mentality there. Here, when it has to do with helping our defence forces . . . there are no questions. And I am sure that even a [private] company like Elbit – maybe they did the same.

Elbit did indeed do much the same. Stavitsky (2007) described the war as an opportunity to test new systems:

> All the equipment that was in the [Lebanon] war, regardless of whether it was logistic or frontline, goes through evaluation continuously . . . Our people were involved in pushing things that were almost ready for service right to service in order to make sure it would get exposure in the fight. Even though it was not 100 per cent ready – let's say equipment that was new, that wasn't tested yet, but should be ready in three or five months – we managed to finish it just to put it into the battle in order to test it . . . Afterwards we learned lessons about the equipment . . . [and] generated new requirements in order to supply for the next battle.

This interdependency between continuous war and the IDI can take extreme expression. Shlomo Nir (2007) recalled the late-Oslo period as a time of industry concern: "We passed through the years . . . 1998, 1999, 2000, 2001, and at that time the violence was very low [*sic*] and there was some expectation that there might be peace and Israel wouldn't spend money on defence. In this company we were not very happy about it." Reflecting on the present, he noted, "the potential is really huge. Especially now, with al-Qaeda almost everywhere."

National mentalities and techno-moralities

A tendency to generalize from the industry to the national is pronounced in these accounts. Shlomo Nir posited a connection to a "Jewishness" characterized by intellectual inquiry; David Stavitzky spoke of broad "Israeli" qualities of improvization and urgency; and Yitzhak Ben-Israel reified a militarized national value system. Like Leah Boehm, most proposed a distinctive "Israeli" mindset. Shlomo Nir (2007) said: "there is in the US people's minds – which are made in a certain way – an ability to solve certain problems. And then there is the Israeli type of mind, which is different. And they are set to solve different problems."

Stavitsky (2007) put the IDI's ability to compete with larger states and manufacturers down to Israelis' ability to "use some kind of ingenuity." For Ministry of Trade and Industry Chief Scientist Eli Opper, success boils down to a "spirit of entrepreneurship" rooted in the Zionist narrative: "those who were fighting for independence – even eighty years ago – understood that they should take care about science and technology. And obviously, since Independence Day, the investment has been really high . . . The effect is that we are relying on our brain power in an ultimate way" (Opper 2007).

Ben-Israel (2007) invoked a classic image of David and Goliath while instating the scientist as national defender and Zionist emblem. As for the academic reserves, "We use them for solving problems that we don't know how to solve concerning the fact that we are only seven million people surrounded by hundreds of millions of Arabs. And if you want to count Muslims – it is over 1 billion."

The shift from assertions about an ingenious, but imperilled, Israeli particularism to claims about a moral divide between Israel and its foes is a slight one. Daniel Weihs (2007), speaking of the 2006 Lebanon War, gave examples of weapons available but not used out of a commitment "at least [to] try to play according to the rules. I won't say that about the other side. Or they are playing according to different rules."

Shlomo Nir left Cairo as a child following the 1956 Suez War:

> Most people think if we are good with the Arabs they will make peace with us – it's not true. I was born in Egypt and I know exactly what the Arab mentality is. If you are not strong then they snatch. You have to be very strong in order to address that . . . if you don't have this [technical] edge you won't survive.
>
> (Nir 2007)

Lior Tabansky, a former student of Ben-Israel, left Moscow at the age of fourteen. He compared the situation in Israel with that of the Russian army in Chechnya. While both Israel and Russia face a "terrorist" problem, he suggested the two countries' different strategies reflect differing values:

> Now, when you are faced with this kind of problem . . . one of the obvious things to do is to go and send the whole army there, encircle the whole area, kill everyone in your way, and so on. That's one way. Russia can afford it in Chechnya but no one really wanted to do so [here]. So that's where the technology comes in.
>
> (Tabansky 2007)

Productions of NWTS as an index of moral, technical, and civilizational distinctiveness are not unique to Israeli RMA discourse; they inherit logics from European modernist schemes of progress, social Darwinism, and colonialism, positively correlating the technical and the ethical to produce hierarchies and a meritocratic rationale for violence.[7] However, ubiquitous securitization in Jewish-Israeli society, and the scope of the IDI as a national asset, lends use of the weapon as synecdoche for the national a degree of prominence (see JPPPI 2006: 98).[8] Discerned through these scientists, scholars, and officials, the IDI's self-definition is one of self-abnegation for the national good – of placing "the people" before profit, of attachment to the country, and of technical as well as moral superiority over an amorphous, billion-strong enemy. It is an industrial culture deemed to obey higher purposes than those normative commercial, career, or personal pursuits associated with market competitors. And it is an industry shaped in the crucible of a powerfully constructed "war for survival," where a close-knit, loyal, and motivated force of problem-solvers forever proves its worth against an unsophisticated enemy that does not play by the rules. The overarching trope of "crisis" sees vague notions of intelligence, dedication, and ingenuity overcome formalities and bureaucracies, producing IDI R&D on the always-urgent cohering frontline of scientific innovation and national survival.

These accounts of IDI specificity are reinforced by others produced in uncritical secondary literature on the IDI. A number of biographies, often self-published, lionize figures behind the IDI's growth and transformations. Arnold Sherman's *High-Tech in Israel: A Dream Realised* consciously invokes Herzlian lore to chronicle the career of Uzia Galil, founder of what became Elbit. Galil is an "incorrigible overachiever doomed to personal restlessness" who has a "strange dream about building a high-tech industry in Israel, premised on the postulate that a little nation with few national resources . . . could compete one day with the electronics giants of the world" (Sherman 1988: 87, 125). Dalit Milstein's *Efi Arazi: His Way* tells the story of self-described "visionary" Efraim Arazi, founder of SCITEX and frontrunner in the harmonizing of military and civilian ICT sectors. Arazi, who began his career in the US, is described "abandoning the fleshpots of America and returning to Israel" in June 1967, when "the feeling of urgency and unit pride that gripped the citizens of Israel tipped the balance" and prompted him to establish SCITEX (Milstein 2005: 73–74). Less hagiographic but nonetheless celebratory accounts of the IDI invoke similar motifs. Alex Bloch's history of attempts to manufacture the French Fouga fighter in Israel contrasts "drunk" French technicians with a disciplined and motivated Israeli force evincing "intense involvement with the security of the country" (Bloch 2004: 11, 21). Ralph Sanders grants the IDI "an almost mystical power to fashion and build just about any modern, high-technology weapon that Israel decided it needed for its defense" and contrasts the "financial strength" of Israel's weapons patron, the US, with the "physical and human strength" of Israeli technicians (Sanders 1991: 355–356).

Speaking about weapons R&D involves performances of *Israeliyut*, the "Arab mentality," the nature of permanent war, and a moral economy distinguishing Israel from its enemies. Yet, the IDI is foremost an export industry, involving bilateralism and end-user applications occurring far from IDI sites of battlefield "experience." The local encoding of exports thus enters uncertain processes of translation in transposition from the local laboratory to the client theatre; Zionism's specificities yield to increasingly generic techno-moral bifurcations positing ingenuity, resilience, and science against numerically stronger, ethically inferior, and technically primitive "enemies" assembled at the figurative gates of a globally mapped "civilizational" frontier.

The battlefield "showcase"

Universalizing Zionist "experience" – concepts and practices

> What do you mean by terror? Is it an Israeli thing? . . . We don't do things for the Palestinians. We fight terror, and terrorism is as universal as anything else.
> (Ben-Israel 2007)

A tension exists in the IDI between generating sufficiently specialized technologies to meet the army's immediate needs and ensuring R&D meets the requirements of foreign clients. In theory, resolution demands a compromise whereby longer-term R&D produces system cores, to which multiple modifications are made to produce bespoke designs. Ben-Israel (2007) lends the principle vivid substance in describing Israel's shifting application of "precision" bombing:

The technology is seldom tailored to a very specific need. For example, we built . . . the concept of what is now called precision strike: smart bombs, very accurate technologies, ending with an accuracy of centimetres. We did it . . . to cope with the Syrian, Egyptian military forces. Now we use it [for assassinations]. The technology is the same; you have to locate the target and direct a weapon to hit the target. The target may be a tank or a wheelchair – if you remember Sheikh Yassin – but the technology is the same. There is nothing tailored for wheelchairs; you use the technologies that you have.

But the shift from targeting tanks on the battlefield to targeting wheelchairs in the home signals more than a shift in technical application; it reflects shifts in the imagining of warfare; and it produces particular power effects. Foremost of these is the assertion of omnipresence and the closing down of the sensor–shoot loop separating the moment of surveillance from the moment of death. The conceptual transformation of "precision bombing" from a devastating but temporally and spatially discrete form of violence to the deployment of "precision bombing" to construct the imminence of death as the condition of life in the Palestinian home is vast. Israel's ability to wield this moment rests on a marriage of conceptual and technical innovations. It is the UAV which now provides for this perpetually looming violence. The shift from tank to wheelchair signals a shift along the continuum of the "border," from the territorial frontiers of colonial expansion to the internal frontiers of colonial subjugation which produce occupied Palestinian lives as inadmissible internalities – disavowals of an avowedly *Jewish* "nation-state."

In arguing that exporting the "Zionist experience" through the transfer of UAVs involves the translation of oppositional logics inhering in particular nationalist narratives, I have shown how NWTS emerge resonant with ideological economies of difference. I have argued that their production and export are attended by powerful suggestions about a social Darwinian struggle between a technologically sophisticated and mobilized frontline of scientist-soldiers and a "primitive," but dangerous, immoral horde. Such propositions travel well within a militarized political economy in part due to their versatility. Their content sustains a logic of difference and a rationalization for oppression which can be translated into diffuse geopolitical contexts. But while broad assertions of oppositionality are intrinsic to the "experience" narrated within the IDI, it is in *practice* that this notion of "experience" gains purchase over the military imaginary. Israel's use of NWTS is both an illustration of military technologies and a lesson in their application. The UAV, in particular, gains its power as a "conceptual enabler" in facilitating a "doctrine of disproportionality" entailing the army's purposive departure from the norms and laws of war. For client forces and joint developers looking to effect their own revolutions in the multiplying "wild places" of the GWoT, Israel's UAV deployments, in Lebanon or Gaza, offer a model for increasingly permissive forms of war conducted not between states but across divides in which civilians cease to hold rights, and combatants cease to be human.

Doctrinal innovation and technology tests: Gaza 2008–2009

Following the 2006 Lebanon War, senior strategists embarked on a re-evaluation of the ways in which Israel's overwhelming military superiority had been exercised. Core to the doctrinal developments they arrived at was the decision henceforth explicitly to target civilian populations while eschewing confrontations with insurgent or resistant forces. In the build-up to the 2008–2009 Gaza offensive, military advisors and strategists outlined the new approach. They declared that Israel should "refrain from the cat and mouse games of searching for Qassam rocket launchers . . . [and] not be expected to stop the rocket and missile fire against the Israeli home front through attacks on the launchers themselves" (Siboni 2008: n.p.). War was now to be aimed at achieving "the destruction of the national infrastructure, and intense suffering among the population" (Eiland 2008: 16). Referring to a perceived failure to impress a sense of defeat upon Hizbollah in 2006 by killing its cadres, Giora Eiland, ex-chair of the National Security Council, reasoned that "the suffering of hundreds of thousands of people are consequences that can influence Hizbollah's behavior more than anything else." He noted that this shift to overt targeting of civilians might "incur international pressure" but claimed "high level professional military dialogue between Israel and . . . military leaders" would generate "the requisite support" (Eiland 2008: 16). Eiland's colleague at the Institute for National Security Studies, Gabriel Siboni, also proposed deploying force "that is disproportionate to the enemy's actions and the threat it poses . . . [and] aims at inflicting damage and meting out punishment to an extent that will demand long and expensive reconstruction processes . . . [This] approach is applicable to the Gaza Strip as well [as Lebanon]" (Siboni 2008: n.p.).

The Gaza offensive which followed these developments concluded with more than 1,400 Palestinians dead and over 5,000 wounded, many permanently. Over half the dead were civilians, with 400 of them women or children (PCHR 2009). These figures corresponding chillingly with those predicted by the Israeli Chief of Staff prior to the attack (Harel 2009). Throughout the offensive, during the ceasefire, and following the redeployment of Israeli forces, Qassam missiles continued to fall, the hostage Gilad Shalit remained captive, the Hamas regime retained power, and the southern tunnels providing a lifeline for Gazans continued to operate. Yet, Ben-Israel (2009) now declared that, for the Palestinians, "it appears that the path of resistance has failed, big time." As doctors and investigating teams reported on the use of experimental anti-personnel munitions on Gaza's dense urban–human fabric (including highly carcinogenic (when not immediately lethal) "dense inert metal explosives", white phosphorus, and cluster munitions; see Hallinan 2009), Ben-Israel (2009) heralded a "milestone that would be etched in the historic memory of the Middle East for many years." Defence Minister Barak reassured Israelis that they "have the most moral army in the world" (Somfalvi 2009). While this army blocked bodies investigating war crimes from gaining access to Gaza (B'Tselem 2009), the military spokesperson's office released images designed to cement the techno-moral distinction between dead Palestinians and victorious Israeli forces. Images of crude explosives fashioned out of empty pharmaceutical containers were distributed to the media. Despite undermining claims of Hamas being a highly equipped Iranian proxy, the pictures were given as evidence of Palestinians' "cynical use of humanitarian supplies to attack Israel" (Katz 2009). In contrast, Israel's UAV-anchored battlefield command, munitions delivery, and target reconnaissance were described as an unparalleled demonstration of futurewar proficiency. International security and military experts participated in this construction. *Aviation Week* described the offensive as centring on a "hunter–killer" operation that involved scanning the entire Gaza area using UAVs" (Eshel 2009).

Homeland security journals announced in "no other conflict have UAVs been integrated more deeply into both surveillance and attack missions" (*HS Daily Wire* 2009b). The Israeli army credited the UAV with keeping them "one step ahead" (IDF 2009). In place of the Palestinians' crude "medical grenades," proving at once their unworthiness of humanitarian assistance and their techno-scientific primitivism, an Israeli force which had killed over 700 civilians in 22 days (three Israeli civilians were killed in the same period) was celebrated as an integrated machine at the frontline of progress. Journals enthused over "gear making its combat debut" such as the "unprecedented, coordinated use of the one-ton Mk84 Joint Direct Attack Munition" and "a range of laser-guided bombs and missiles" (*HS Daily Wire* 2009a).

In the field of homeland security and GWoT geostrategic planning, the Gaza offensive was scrutinized as a proving ground for innovative NWTS and the "evolving" operational doctrines attending their deployment. Without questioning Israel's overt pursuit of intense civilian suffering, the "contest" in Gaza was submitted as an index of Western techno-moral distinctiveness and as a demonstration of the types of war to come. Zionism's latest "experience" was thus packaged and translated as a universal paradigm for success, with the UAV functioning as both the symbolic and operational centrepiece in a model signalling the overwhelming domination of "progress" over a Luddite pre-modern enemy epitomized in the crude, undetonated "medical grenades" plucked from the corpses of dead Palestinians.

Exporting the unapologetic use of force

Translations of the Zionist experience

In this chapter, I have argued that Israel's NWTS exports, symbolically and operationally centred on UAV transfers, offer a means of arranging the imprecise cartographies of diffuse conflict theatres in line with a techno-moral cosmology supposing a bifurcated world struggle. They flow within, and help compose, emerging strategic and diplomatic alignments, providing both a weapons architecture for absolute domination and a doctrinal paradigm for the exercise of unchecked state violence. In setting what Stephen Graham (2008) terms the "gold standard" for contemporary surveillance and combat praxis, Israel submits its battlefield laboratories as showcases in the effective application of the technologies it develops, deploys, and exports. Its client states often opportunistically harness their own strategic concerns to an ideal of Israel as a "frontline" polity. They do so in recognition that Israel's military extremes are not only tolerated by dominant powers, but rewarded economically and diplomatically.

In prosecuting its conflict with indigenous Moro insurgents alongside US forces, the Philippines' Arroyo regime has consciously linked its purchase of Israeli UAVs to the mapping out of an oppositional divide between a sophisticated US ally and jungle-dwelling extremists. IDI NWTS are invested with a mystical power to fix the local conflict in line with this binary: "In need of dramatic results in its war against the extremists, the Armed Forces are banking on technology to help them out. To the rescue: an Israeli unmanned aerial vehicle (UAV) that can see through foliage and buildings – and pinpoint the location of hostile forces" (*Philippine Star* 2001).

In Thailand, where the highest echelon of the military and parliament represents increasingly coterminous alignments, dissident politicians advocating autonomy in the southern Malay provinces oppose what they see as the ubiquitous deployment of Israel as a model for modern state form. After three decades of Israeli counter-insurgency training and arms provision, they claim that Israel has emerged as an idealized model of prosperity and might:

> When it comes to the issue of an example *par excellence*, it's always Israel that's being brought up by the [Thai MPs]. How they turned the deserts into a heaven of agriculture; how they manage such a voluntary and civic society in which everybody participates. And they marvel at the ability of the Israelis to crush the Arabs, you know . . . So the Israelis are looked upon as having a state *par excellence*.
> (Choonhavan 2008)

India's vast investment in the "Zionist experience," its rapidly expanding network of Israeli UAV "border" security systems, and the proliferation of bilateral planning bodies such as the India–Israel Joint Working Group on Counter-Terrorism, are now explicitly linked by senior politicians and RMA architects to placing the two states in "the same camp that fights terrorism" (Sahgal 2003) and thereby attaining "the political will and moral authority to take bold decisions" (Shahin 2003). Brigadier Arun Sahgal, overseeing India's RMA, has linked the arrival of new Israeli UAV systems to a more belligerent stance on Pakistan, arguing, "the sale of an advanced weapons system . . . means de-hyphenating Indo-Pakistani relations and recognition of India's preeminent position in the region" (Sahgal 2003). His former colleague, Subhash Kapila (2000), makes the broader argument that "[i]n terms of strategically educating itself from the Israeli experience, India could learn to have the will to use power, unapologetically."

Each of these diverse contexts "evolves," alongside numerous others (e.g. Turkey, Georgia, Iraq, Afghanistan, Indonesia), within the interconnected cartography of violence and uncertainty in which I have attempted to situate Israel's UAV and NWTS exports. I have described a series of intersecting revolutions undertaken in the global mapping of "border" security logics, in the organization of military structures, and in the doctrinal conduct of war. I have argued that throughout these dynamic shifts in geostrategy and warfare, the primacy of the UAV as a "transformative" device and conceptual "liberator" is pronounced and constant. And I have shown that it is, to a great extent, within Israel's mobilized R&D industries, and in its dynamic battlefield showcases, that this nodal architecture for futurewar and surveillance is being invested with potent conceptual and doctrinal meaning.

Operating at a powerfully constructed ideational and military frontline between a "progressive" space of stability and an unsited space of primitivism and recalcitrance, I have argued that Israel's battlefield innovations hold out a twofold allure to client states and regimes. On the one hand, they offer new means for effecting low-risk domination over civilian populations and lightly equipped subversives while legitimizing this asymmetry via techno-moral claims. On the other hand, they propose new modes for exercising this domination unapologetically, while accruing diplomatic latitude and positional recognition through increased affinity with the US's pre-eminent ally. This is clearly a dialectic process involving opportunism and intersecting interests rather than a simple linear process of transmission. Yet, as developer, deployer, and exporter of the paradigmatic surveillance and combat technology of the revolutions being conducted in force structure, operational theatre, and doctrinal framework, Israel's battlefield showcases resonate with profound significance from Indonesia to Iraq. They posit a fusion of claims and practices deemed definitional of the moralities, modernities, and "genius" of the state forms to be defended and expanded in the wars to come.

And yet the underlying peculiarity of the Zionist "experience" *vis-à-vis* the Palestinians should not be altogether lost in raising the notion of a "universalizing" in IDI NWTS export dynamics.

Epilogue: can genocide be translated?

Israel's military experience ultimately accumulates within a pronounced genocidal mathesis. As Patrick Wolfe (2006: 388) shows, pure settler-colonial genocide "destroys to replace." Its "relationship of war" is, in Foucault's sense, "total": "If you want to live, the other must die" (Foucault 2003: 256–257). Unrequited "demographic interest" lends this "inherently eliminatory" logic "continuity through time," producing genocidal "structure rather than . . . event" (Wolfe 2006: 390). IDI architectures of subjugation, expulsion, and killing are developed in a "live laboratory" peopled by unwanted lives. While the demographic "miracle" of 1948's purge erodes under territorial expansion and remnant natality, Zionist eschatology attaches to Palestinian life: "Above all hovers the cloud of demographics. It will come down on us not in the end of days, but in just another few years" (Olmert in Glick 2004). Zionism's geostrategists recognize retrieving nation-state purity from co-presence means "we cannot play nicely when it comes to demography" (Soffer 2007); politicians summon necro-therapeutics for lives that "resemble a cancer" (Housing Minister Effi Eitam cited in Ibrahim 2005: 21); the army launches "the second half of 1948," coded "chemotherapy" (Reinhardt 2001; Katriel 2002). Less bellicose "liberals" champion extruding Palestinian bio-waste via bilateralism with proxy militias; the Jewish-Israeli public overwhelmingly support (Ghanem 2003; Ben-Meir and Shaked 2007) denaturalizing a disorder whose closely scrutinized births comprise a "threat to the ideological foundations of the Zionist state" (Berkovitz 1997: 616).

Israel's military, directly subjugating this unwanted, pathogenic life for all but six months of its sixty-three years, is meanwhile the state's central institution, inaugurated as "the forge of Jewish fraternity" (Ben-Gurion 1949: 21), to play "a major partner in the nation's construction" (Soen 2008: 72), as inculcator and epitome of "the essence of Israeli citizenship and identity" (Eisenstadt 1967: 396). Interchangeable aphorisms "The People's Army" and "A Nation in Uniform" disclose a boundary-erasure haunting the army's "total structure" status (Soen 2008), enjoying far higher levels of Jewish-Israeli public confidence than Supreme Court, parliament, or media (Tami Steinmetz Center for Peace Research 2002–2009). IDI R&D occurs where this total structure meets the Palestinian body in a condition of total war to advance a demographic policy which amounts to military-experimental "anti-natalism." It is this definitive genocidal calculus which finally determines the nature of the IDI's battlefield laboratories and of the Zionist "experience" cumulatively inscribed in the techno-conceptual artefacts of the NWTS industry. And yet the uniquely savage arithmetic of this underlying dynamic (perhaps necessarily) becomes invisible to the extent that Zionist "experience" is posited generic and replicable – to the extent that genocide's serial declensions of death and expulsion are made sufficiently transparent to accommodate the diverse reappropriations and reinscriptions of clients.

While the Israeli army's war against Palestinian civilian life in Gaza was being waged, journalists observed the RMA's principle of diffuse command autonomy in practice, noting "lots of manoeuvring room for field commanders" (Harel 2009). UAV operators, the human nodes at the centre of this fluid killing system, attested to power – "If I say this man is armed, they'll bomb. If I say stop the attacks, they stop" (Shachtman 2009) – but also to exhilaration: "It feels like hunting season has begun. Sometimes it reminds me of a PlayStation game. You hear cheers in the war room after you see on the screens that the missile hit a target, as if it were a soccer game. The Palestinians are completely transparent to us" (Harel 2009).

Palestinian life undergoes a double seizure to transparence in the IDI's death labs; the initial denial in the mathesis of demographic total war is consolidated in a secondary seizure to plasma display and electro-optical acquisition. The intensity of Zionism's "hunting season" experiences derives from, and is sustained in, this double transparency, this emptying of Palestinian life. It is this which explains the staggeringly high, and consistent, level of Jewish-Israeli public support for an offensive avowedly lacking in military-strategic goals and producing utter civilian carnage (Ben-Meir 2009).[9] The extent to which such dehumanization can accrue within and survive the migrations of the IDI's techno-conceptual apparatuses remains uncertain. But it would be imprudent to assume the horrors of Gaza inimitable outside Zionism's genocidal matrix.

When the architects of Israel's latest doctrine identified "high-level professional military leaders" as a source for generating the "requisite support" for killing civilians, they identified an imperative to harness not public relations or diplomacy *per se*, but the interests of a network of strategists coalescing around a desire to overhaul the norms of war worldwide. This was intuitive and successful. For instance, in Britain, Richard Kemp (2009) outdid politicians and advocacy professionals with claims there had never "been a time in the history of warfare where any army has made more efforts to reduce civilian casualties than the IDF is doing today in Gaza." Perhaps excessive, this was not obtuse propagandizing such as evidenced in sections of the media or academia (e.g., Aaronovitch 2008; Hirsh 2009). Kemp is an ex-commander of UK forces in Afghanistan, an ex-member of the UK's Joint Intelligence Committee, and a prominent counter-terrorism strategic advisor. Championing the "milestone-etching" operation reflected self-interest. Perceiving the RMA's liberating power impeded by moral and legal obstacles, forces agitating for more permissive conduct in war observed in Gaza both model and wellspring for a missing element in ongoing RMA "co-evolution." To be fully unleashed, future-force's "new" armies, pitted against "new" enemies – those stubbornly transgressing civilian–combatant distinctions – need to operate in "new" moral–legal environments that are "cultivated" in the ever-evolving battlefield.

The International Legal Department (ILD) of the Israeli army obeys an enticing mandate for such interests: "Our goal is not to fetter the army, but to give it the tools to win in a lawful manner" (Feldman and Blau 2009). Shortly after the Gaza offensive, the director of the ILD for two decades, Daniel Reisner, described the "co-evolving" dynamic of experience-norm, following Ben-Israel by pointing to Israel's move from tanks to wheelchairs – and that local movement's global translation:

If you do something for long enough, the world will accept it. The whole of international law is now based on the notion that an act that is forbidden becomes permissible if executed by enough countries. International law progresses through violations . . . We invented the targeted assassination thesis and we had to push it. At first there were protrusions that made it hard to insert easily into the legal molds. Eight years later, it is in the center of the bounds of legitimacy.

(Chassay 2009; Bisharat 2009)

Six months after Gaza, Kemp joined US and Israeli lawyers, officers, and strategists at an event intended to forge "solutions to legal problems" in "the practical experience of the nations" (Dinstein in Izenberg 2009): the Limitations of International Law in Handling the War on Terrorism and International Law and Military Operations in Practice Conference at the Jerusalem Centre for Public Affairs. The Israeli conveners of the event – which was conducted in English and had video links to the US – were not its primary beneficiaries. As one dissident Israeli lawyer noted at the time, in Israel, distinctions "between types of conflicts or between civilians and combatants no longer exist . . . Instead of legal advice and international humanitarian law minimizing suffering, they legitimize the use of force" (Naftali in Feldman and Blau 2009).

The Palestinian has been made manifestly easy to kill in the Zionist "experience" (becoming a "transparent" life-form in the military, public, and legal gaze well before the "PlayStation" effect of UAV warfare effected its final seizure to produce a mere electro-optical "event"). The disposability of this life ultimately derives from genocidal demographic interests particular to a certain settler–colonial calculus. But a desire for ever-more permissive means of exercising violence against civilian populations is global and widespread, sustaining alignments of interests across diverse strategic, operational, and jurisprudential settings from the Pentagon to Waziristan, Delhi to Balikatan. This objective currently represents the third dimension of the futurewar vision, one "co-evolving" in the battlefield laboratory alongside (and in dynamic exchange with) the formative "techno-conceptual" dyad of the RMA. The Zionist experience, and hence the Palestinian body, represents a key venue in this latest evolutionary juncture, as underscored by the intense technical, strategic, and legal scrutiny attending Israel's 2008–2009 experiments in Gaza.

In the Zionist experience, a move has been emphatically realized from tank to wheelchair, combatant to civilian, immorality to legitimacy, humanity to transparency. And this movement, in all its allure for the architects of new forms of warfare at the shifting "borders" of today's scalar homelands, is being achieved with the UAV as its celebrated "enabler."

Acknowledgment

The author would like to thank Emily Smith and Sarah Cheung for their assistance in preparing this chapter for publication.

Notes

1 The Ministry of Defence announced exports of $4.4 billion for 2006 (10 per cent of global arms exports), with sales to India accounting for upwards of $1.5 billion (Israeli Ministry

of Defence 2007). Figures for 2007 indicated new contracts worth $5.6 billion (Dagoni 2008).

2   This disavowed sovereign border is produced in turn as an effect of the enemy's refusal to obey the logics of juridical–territorial enclosure. Thus, the US Department for Homeland Security (2004) claims: "In a world where terrorists do not respect traditional boundaries, our strategy for homeland security cannot stop at our borders."

3   Responding to suggestions that he was betraying Muslim sensitivities, Sudarsono (2006) added, "The people of Israel are the offspring of the people of Abraham just like Muslims, so this does not pose a problem."

4   Noah Efron (2007) notes Chaim Weizmann's dual appointment as President of Israel and the Sieff (later Weizmann) Research Institute reflected an understanding of scientific and governmental fields as "harmonious enterprises". Ben-Gurion (1948: 8) certainly saw science as an extension of Zionist "pioneering": science, he wrote, "means the domination of nature by man; '*khalutziyut*' [pioneering] means domination of man over himself."

5   See also Penslar 2000 and Hart 2000.

6   Ben-Israel's former student and scholar of high-tech weapons use during the second Intifada, Lior Tabansky (2007), is more blunt: "the defence industry and the army are pretty much the same people and what helps to get new ideas quickly and usually informally into the army is this . . . That's what makes the whole [development] process way faster."

7   The claim accompanying this techno-moral imaginary runs counter to the oft-repeated logic proposing expanding access to technologies as a means of global integration and a rationale for expanding new orders. It is a claim instead of proprietorship; one which supposes techno-scientific progress as a defining "Western" attribute to be jealously guarded from those who would use it against its rightful guardians. The US's National Security Strategy (2002–2006) thus warns that "[t]errorists are organized to penetrate open societies and to turn the power of modern technologies against us" and that the "gravest danger our Nation faces lies at the crossroads of radicalism and technology." In this sense, the normative deployment of technological progress as a barometer of moral superiority is soon suspended when that progress is obtained by the "wrong" people – the case of the Iranian nuclear programme provides a clear example.

8   Suggesting "civilizational" superiority through NWTS saw Defence Minister Amir Peretz (JPPPI 2006) map Israeli–Palestinian difference across a weapons differential, pitting Israel, "with an edge in sophisticated defense technologies, against unsophisticated and dangerous weapons of fundamentalist Islam, including suicide bombers and 'Kassam' rockets."

9   Polls at the offensive's start showed 90 per cent support; as the (potentially riskier) ground phase commenced, 94 per cent "strongly supported"; when first mooted, a 13 January poll found only 26 per cent desired a ceasefire; after one was called, the first division appeared, with 48 per cent feeling the army should have "conquer[ed] all of the Gaza Strip" and the remainder accepting the decision to halt. Ninety-four per cent felt the army's performance was "very good" or "good" (Ben-Meir 2009).

Bibliography and author interviews

Aaronovitch, D. (2008) "That's Enough Pointless Outrage about Gaza," *The Times*, 30 December.

Air Force Technology (2009) "UK Envisions Pilotless Air Force," 2 March. Online. Available HTTP: <http://www.airforce-technology.com/news/news50621.html> (accessed 16 March 2010).

Alcalá, R.H. (1994) "Guiding Principles for Revolution and Continuity in Military Affairs," *Whither the RMA? Two Perspectives on Tomorrows Army*, Carlisle Barracks, PA: Army War College, Department of Defense Strategic Studies Institute.

Barilli, S. (2006) "Unmanned Aerial Vehicles for the Swiss Air Force," monograph, Alabama: Maxwell Airforce Base.

Beit-Hallahmi, B. (1987) *The Israeli Connection: Who Israel Arms and Why*, New York: Pantheon Books.

Ben-Gurion, D. (1948) "Facing the Future, Address to Hakibbutz Hameuhad," *Jewish Frontier*, 15(12), pp. 5–10.

—— (1949) "To the Young Commanders," *Jewish Frontier*, 16(1), pp. 20–23.

Ben-Israel, Y. (2007) Interview with the author, 19 November.

—— (2009) "New Rules of Play: Strategic Importance of Gaza Operation Much Greater than We Assume," *YNet*, 30 January. Online. Available HTTP: <http://www.ynetnews.com/articles/0,7340,L-3664189,00.html> (accessed 16 March 2010).

Ben-Meir, Y. (2009) "Operation Cast Lead: Political Dimensions and Public Opinion," *Strategic Assessment*, 11(4), n.p.

Ben-Meir, Y. and Shaked, D. (2007) *The People Speak: Israeli Public Opinion on National Security: 2005–2007*, Tel Aviv: INSS.

Berkovitz, N. (1997) "Motherhood as National Mission: The Construction of Womanhood in the Legal Discourse in Israel," *Women's Studies International Forum*, 20(5/6), pp. 605–619.

Bisharat, G. (2009) "Israel Changing the Rules of War," *San Francisco Chronicle*, 1 April.

Bloch, A. (2004) "The Fouga Airplane Project," *Israel Studies*, 9(2), pp. 1–33.

Boehm, L. (2007) Interview with the author, 7 September.

B'Tselem (2009) "IDF Denies Human Rights Watch, B'Tselem Access to Gaza," press release, 22 February. Online. Available HTTP: <http://www.btselem.org/English/press_releases/20090222.asp> (accessed 16 March 2010).

Bush, G.W. (2001) "Address to the Nation," 20 September.

Caldwell, J. (2002) "The Road to Objective Force," presentation at the Tactical Wheeled Vehicles Conference, Office of the Secretary of Defense.

Chassay, C. (2009) "Cut to Pieces: The Palestinian Family Drinking Tea in Their Courtyard," *Guardian*, 23 March.

Choonhavan, K. (2008) Interview with the author, 24 June.

Clark, R. (1999) "Uninhabited Combat Aerial Vehicles: Airpower by the People, for the People, but not with the People," unpublished thesis, Maxwell Airforce Base, Alabama.

Cohen, J. and Giddens, G. (2006) "Statement for the Record: Jay Cohen Under Secretary for Science & Technology & Gregory Giddens Director, Secure Border Initiative Program Executive Office before the US House of Representatives Committee on Science." Online. Available HTTP: <http://www.dhs.gov/xnews/testimony/testimony_1158761362944.shtm> (accessed 13 September 2010).

Coren, O. (2007) "IAI Wants Defence Firm Merger," *Haaretz*, 21 November.

Customs and Border Protection Agency (2008) "Protecting our Borders against Terrorism," bulletin, 14 May.

Dagoni, R. (2008) "Defense Exports Reach Record," *Globes*, 28 May.

Dalby, S. (2007) "The Pentagon's New Imperial Cartography: Tabloid Realism and the War on Terror," in D. Gregory and A. Pred (eds) *Inhuman Geographies: Spaces of Terror and Political Violence*, New York: Routledge, pp. 295–308.

Daniel, W. (2007) Interview with the author, 10 September.

Department of Homeland Security [DHS] (2004) *Securing Our Homeland: US Department of Homeland Security Strategic Plan*, Washington: DHS.

—— (2006) "Secure Border Initiative: Program Guide," supplement to *Washington Technology GCN*, 18 September. Available HTTP: <http://www.trezzamediagroup.com/uploads/sbi_supplement.pdf>.

Dun (2008) "Dun's 100 Database – Israel's Largest Enterprises." Online. Available HTTP: <http://duns100.dundb.co.il/2008/514421098/index.asp> (accessed 16 March 2010).

Efron, N. (2007) *Notes on Judaism and Science: A Historical Introduction*, Westport, CN, and London: Greenwood Press.

Eiland, G. (2008) "The Third Lebanon War: Target Lebanon," *INSS Strategic Assessment*, 11(2), pp. 9–17.

Eisenstadt, S.N. (1967) *Israeli Society*, New York: Basic Books.

Eshel, D. (2009) "Gaza Strip Tactics Examined," *Aviation Week*, 28 January. Available HTTP: <http://www.aviationweek.com/aw/blogs/defense/index.jsp?plckController=Blog&plckScript=blogScript&plckElementId=blogDest&plckBlogPage=BlogViewPost&plckPostId=Blog:27ec4a53-dcc8-42d0-bd3a-01329aef79a7Post:23447214-40e2-4beb-b191-32bf39a99766>.

European Network Against Arms Trade (2007) *European Credit Export Agencies and the Financing of Arms Trade*, Holland: ENAAT.

Feldman, Y. and Blau, U. (2009) "Consent and Advise," *Haaretz*, 29 January.

Foucault, M. (2003) *Society Must Be Defended: Lectures at the Collège de France, 1975–76*, New York: Picador.

Galil, Z. (2008–2009) *Tel Aviv University Review: Winter 2008–9*, Tel Aviv: TAU Press.

Ghanem, A. (2003) "Zionism, Post-Zionism and Anti-Zionism in Israel: Jews and Arabs in the Conflict over the Nature of the State," in E. Nimni (ed.) *The Challenge of Post-Zionism: Alternatives to Israeli Fundamentalist Politics*, London: Zed, pp. 98–116.

Giddens, G. (2007) "Testimony before the US House of Representatives Committee on Oversight and Government Reform," 8 February.

Glade, D. (2000) "Unmanned Aerial Vehicles: Implications for Military Operations," Occasional Paper No. 16, Alabama: Maxwell Air Force Base.

Glassman, J. (2007) "Imperialism Imposed and Invited: The 'War on Terror' Comes to Southeast Asia," in D. Gregory and A. Pred (eds) *Inhuman Geographies: Spaces of Terror and Political Violence*, New York: Routledge, pp. 93–109.

Glick, C. (2004) "The Demographic Bomb is a Dud," *Jerusalem Post*, 14 January.

Goldman, L. (2006) "Israeli Technology to Keep US Borders Safe," Israel21c, 15 October. Online. Available HTTP: <http://web.israel21c.net/bin/en.jsp?enDispWho=Articles^ll450&enPage=BlankPage&enDisplay=view&enDispWhat=object&enVersion=0&enZone=Technology&> (accessed 16 March 2010).

Graham, S. (2008) "Laboratories of War: US–Israeli Collaboration in 'Asymmetric Warfare' and Urban Securitisation," paper presented at the States of Exception, Surveillance and Population Management: The Case of Israel/Palestine Workshop, Larnaca, 6–8 December.

—— (2010) *Cities under Siege: The New Military Urbanism*, London: Verso.

Grant, I. (2006) "Israel's Security Crucible," *InfoSecurity Today*, 3(2), pp. 28–32.

Gregory, D. and Pred, A. (2007) *Violent Geographies: Fear, Terror, and Political Violence*, New York and London: Routledge.

Hallinan, C. (2009) "Gaza: Death's Laboratory," *Foreign Policy in Focus*, 11 February. Online. Available HTTP: <http://www.fpif.org/fpiftxt/5862> (accessed 11 February 2009).

Harel, A. (2009) "Cast Lead Expose /What Did the IDF Think Would Happen in Gaza?," *Haaretz*, 28 March.

Hart, M. (2000) *Social Science and the Politics of Modern Jewish Identity*, Stanford, CA: Stanford University Press.

Hirsh, D. (2009) "Some Things Worth Reading on the Conflict between Israel and Hamas in Gaza," *Engage*, 1 January. Online. Available HTTP: <http://engageonline.wordpress.com/2009/01/01/some-things-worth-reading-on-the-conflict-between-israel-and-hamas-in-gaza/> (accessed 16 March 2010).

HS Daily Wire (2009a) "Israel Uses New ISR Systems, Ordnance," 15 January. Online. Available HTTP: <http://hsdailywire.com/single.php?id=7246> (accessed 16 March 2010).

—— (2009b) "UAV War over Gaza," 22 January. Online. Available HTTP: <http://hsdailywire.com/single.php?id=7295> (accessed 16 March 2010).

Ibrahim, T. (2005) *One Gunman, Many to Blame: Israel's Culture of Racism Prior to the Shefa'amr Massacre and the Role of the Attorney General*, Nazareth: Arab Association for Human Rights.

Innocenti, M., Giulietti, F. and Pollini, L. (2002) "Intelligent Management Control for Unmanned Aircraft Navigation and Formation Keeping," paper presented at RTO/AVT [NATO] Course on Intelligence Systems for Aeronautics, 13 May.

Israel Defence Forces (IDF) (2009) "UAVs Are One Step Ahead in Gaza," 15 January. Online. Available HTTP: <http://dover.idf.il/NR/exeres/537834F5-35B8-4928-A743-659AE7FCDEBF.html> (accessed 16 March 2010).

Israeli Ministry of Defence (2007) "Israel's Defence Export Contracts Break All Time Record," 9 January. Online. Available HTTP: <http://www.mod.gov.il/pages/dover/doverEnglish.asp?systype=3> (accessed 16 March 2010).

Izenberg, D. (2009) "Legal Experts Say Int'l Law Will Adjust to War against Terrorism," *Jerusalem Post*, 23 June.

Jewish People Policy Planning Institute [JPPPI] (2006) "Annual Assessment 2006," Jerusalem: Jewish People Policy Planning Institute.

Kapila, S. (2000) "India–Israel Relations: The Imperatives for Enhanced Strategic Cooperation," Occasional Paper No. 131, South Asia Analysis Group. Online. Available HTTP: <http://www.southasiaanalysis.org/papers2/paper131.html> (accessed 16 March 2010).

Katriel, I. (2002) "Drunk with Power and out of Shame," *Counterpunch*, 5 September.

Katz, Y. (2007) "2006: Israel Defense Sales Hit Record," *Jerusalem Post*, 1 January.

—— (2009) "Hamas Threw 'Medical Grenades' at IDF," *Jerusalem Post*, 2 February. Online. Available HTTP: <http://www.jpost.com/servlet/Satellite?cid=1233304770155&pagename=JPost per cent2FJPArticle percent2FShowFull> (accessed 2 February 2009).

Kemp, R. (2009) Interview with BBC World, 9 January. Online. Available HTTP: <http://www.youtube.com/watch?v=WssrKJ3Iqcw> (accessed 16 March 2010).

Knesset Committee on Education, Culture, and Sport (2007) Protocol of Knesset No. 112, 1 January.

Kolenda, C. (2003) "Transforming How We Fight: A Conceptual Approach," *Naval War College Review*, 56(2), pp. 100–121.

Marshall, A. (1993) "Memorandum for the Record: Some Thoughts on Military Revolutions, Second Version," Washington, D.C.: Department of Defense.

Milstein, D. (2005) *Efi Arazi: His Way – A Biography*, Tel Aviv: Daniella De-Nur Publishers.

National Security Strategy of the United States of America (2002-2006). Online. Available HTTP: <http://slomanson.tjsl.edu/NSS_2006.pdf> (accessed 16 March 2010).

Neuman, S. (2006) "Arms Industries and Global Dependency," *Orbis*, Summer, pp. 429–451.

Nir, S. (2007) Interview with the author, 11 July.

Office of the Secretary of Defense (2002) "Unmanned Aerial Vehicles, 2002–2027," Washington, D.C.: Department of Defense.

—— (2003) "Military Transformation: A Strategic Approach," Washington, D.C.: Department of Defense.

Opper, E. (2007) Interview with the author, 21 August.

Palestinian Centre for Human Rights (PCHR) (2009) Press release, 12 March.

Penslar, D. (1991) *Zionism and Technocracy: The Engineering of Jewish Settlement in Palestine, 1870–1918*, Bloomington and Indianapolis: Indiana University Press.

—— (2000) "Technical Expertise and the Construction of the Rural *Yishuv*, 1882–1948," *Jewish History*, 14, pp. 201–224.

Persico, O. (2003) "Arms unto the Nations," *Globes*, 29 April.

Philippine Star (2001) "This Time It's Tech-Power vs the Abu-Sayyaf," 25 July.

Raghuvanshi, V. (2007) "Israelis Share Anti-Infiltration Lessons with Indian Army," *Defense News*, 14 June.

Reinhardt, T. (2001) "'The Second half of 48' – The Sharon–Ya'alon Plan," *Yedioth Aharonot*, 10 June.

Russo, H. (2007) "70 Years of Electro-Optics in Israel," paper presented at Tel Aviv Workshop for Science, Technology, and Security on Electro-Optics in the Battlefield of the Future, Tel Aviv University, 20 December.

Sahgal, A. (2003) "Israel and India Join Forces," *Asia Times*, 9 September. Online. Available HTTP: <http://www.atimes.com/atimes/South_Asia/EI09Df07.html> (accessed 16 March 2010).

Sanders, R. (1991) "The Lavi: Israel's Limits to Weapons Development," *Technology in Society*, 13, pp. 345–358.

Shachtman, N. (2009) "Robot Planes, Life-and-Death Choices over Gaza," *Wired*, 29 January.

Shahin, S. (2003) "India's Startling Change of Axis," *Asia Times*, 13 May. Online. Available HTTP: <http://www.atimes.com/atimes/South_Asia/EE13Df01.html> (accessed 16 March 2010).

Sherman, A. (1988) *High-Tech in Israel: A Dream Realized*, Jerusalem: Israel Economist Publications.

Siboni, G. (2008) "Disproportionate Force: Israel's Concept of Response in Light of the Second Lebanon War," *INSS Insight*, 74, n.p.

SIPRI (2001–2006) "Yearbooks," Stockholm: Stockholm International Peace Research Institute.

Soen, D. (2008) "All Able-Bodies, to Arms! Attitudes of Israeli High School Students toward Conscription and Combat Service," *European Journal of Social Sciences* 6(4), pp. 72–82.

Soffer, A. (2007) Interview with the author, 27 May.

Somfalvi, A. (2009) "Barak: Hamas Liable for Death of Gaza Physician's Daughters," *YNet*, 5 February. Available HTTP: <http://www.ynetnews.com/articles/0,7340,L-3667218,00.html>.

Stavitsky, D. (2007) Interview with the author, 12 July.

Sudarsono, J. (2006) "Israel High-Tech and Investment Report," November. Available (in edited form) HTTP: < http://www.ishitech.co.il/>.

Tabansky, L. (2007) Interview with the author, 27 June.

Tami Steinmetz Center for Peace Research (2002–2009) *Peace Index*, Tel Aviv: Tel Aviv University.

Tice, J. (2007) "UAV Operators Now Can Get Aviation Awards," *Army Times*, 4 April. Available HTTP: <http://www.armytimes.com/news/2007/04/army_UAV_awards_07 0403w/> (accessed 19 August 2010).

Turner, B. (2006) "Borders, Boundaries and Bodies: The Rise of the Overpopulation Warriors," *HAGAR*, 6(2), pp. 5[en[20.

United States Defense Science Board [USDSB] (2004) *Unmanned Aerial Vehicles and Uninhabited Combat Aerial Vehicles*, Washington, D.C.: Department of Defense.

United States Office of the Secretary of Defense [USOSD] (2002) *Unmanned Aerial Vehicles, 2002–2027*, Washington, D.C.: Office of the Secretary of Defense, Department of Defense.

Van Blyenburgh, P. (2008) "Unmanned Aircraft Systems: The Global Access Initiative," paper presented at the UAV–DACH Symposium, Berlin Air Show, May.

Warrick, J. and Wright, R. (2008) "Unilateral Strike Called a Model for US Operations in Pakistan," *Washington Post*, 19 February.

Weihs, D. (2007) Interview with the author, 10 September.

Wolfe, P. (2006) "Settler Colonialism and the Elimination of the Native," *Journal of Genocide Research*, 8(4), pp. 387–409.

Part V

Citizenship criteria and state construction

10 Legal analysis and critique of some surveillance methods used by Israel

Usama Halabi

Introduction: surveillance in Israel

It is no secret when I say that tens of our Palestinian society leaders inside [i.e. within Israel] have been targeted. And who targets them is not a legendary ghost, but a known authority . . . that has abilities that might cause children's hair to turn gray. It would tape our telephone conversations, detect our movements while up the road, secretly listen from a great distance to our public and private meetings using highly sensitive surveillance tools, and is able to determine each of our exact locations through our mobile phones. One funny incident that happened to me after my release from jail is this: I was traveling with Dr. Suliman. We were fasting and it was about the time of "iftar," so we decided to eat in Restaurant X, but before we entered we called Sheikh Kamal through his mobile phone and invited him to join us. A few minutes later, we arrived at Restaurant X. After a short time a stranger entered and sat at a nearby table. A few minutes passed and another stranger entered and sat at a different nearby table. Out of either caution or curiosity, I asked the restaurant's owner, "Are these two strangers journalists?" He smiled and answered, "I don't know. This is the first time they have entered my restaurant!" I said to myself, "I know who they are. They arrived after our conversation with Sheikh Kamal. The conversation was tapped, which is nothing new."

(Salah 2008: 20)

These are the words of Sheikh Ra'ed Salah, head of the northern faction of the Islamic Movement in Israel. Is his story a paranoid delusion or a reflection of reality? Maybe the two strangers entered the restaurant coincidentally, each for his own reason, and had nothing to do with the sheikh and his colleagues. Nevertheless, the surveillance methods described here certainly do exist and, as we shall see below, are used by security authorities and agencies in Israel.

This chapter reviews a few of the surveillance methods used by the state of Israel, analyzes their legality, and discusses their implications for human rights generally, and the right to privacy in particular. The methods to be discussed are:

1 The use of special data and distinct serial numbers on ID cards issued by the Israeli Ministry of the Interior to indicate cardholders' status and national and geographical affiliation.

2   Closed circuit television (CCTV) located in civilian neighborhoods (such as the old city of Jerusalem).
3   The secret gathering of communication data from communication companies by "investigation authorities." Such data include, for example, customers' names and addresses, as well as their phone numbers and locations. Also included in this section is the wiretapping of private phone conversations and hacking into private computers.
4   The planned use of "smart" identification methods, including biometric documents and databases.

Since its establishment, Israel has used various forms of surveillance. These include non-technical surveillance through which direct contact is utilized to observe and gather personal information. This includes what Zureik calls "old-fashioned spy networks embedded in local Arab communities" (Chapter 1, this volume) which relied heavily on Palestinian collaborators and informers (Cohen 2008). Technical surveillance, on the other hand, requires no direct contact. As aptly described by Zureik (Chapter 1, this volume), it

> extends from use of methods such as recording information electronically through telephone tapping and intercepting electronic messaging, closed circuit television, video monitoring, geopositioning systems, Radio Frequency Identification, fingerprinting, genetic testing, DNA analysis, and retinal and racial biometric identification, to the use of less obtrusive measures such as routine gathering of data on population in the name of governance and administration (e.g., census taking and survey research).

Israel has used both forms of surveillance to gain and maintain control over Palestinians: those who remained in the 1948 areas and have become Israeli citizens, and those who live in the West Bank, Jerusalem, and Gaza and have come under its occupation and control since 1967. However, the use of some of these forms of surveillance (mainly technical methods, such as police wiretapping) has not been limited to the Palestinian Arabs living under Israel's jurisdiction: they have also been used on Israeli Jewish citizens (see "Forms of state surveillance" below).

These methods of surveillance will be discussed in the context of the legal framework that either enables or facilitates their deployment. Further, this chapter provides commentary on how such methods – again aided by both legislation and legislators – allow Israeli state authorities to make clear distinctions between groups, most notably Israeli and Palestinian groups. As will be discussed below, these distinctions often have a greater detrimental effect on Palestinians, even though all residents are subject to the same surveillance and legal regime.

In order to clarify the relevant legal framework of this discussion and review the legality of the methods discussed, the chapter will refer to relevant existing and proposed Israeli laws and regulations. Recent and proposed legislation, in particular, appears to indicate, unfortunately, more serious future limitations on freedom of movement, freedom of speech, and the right to privacy. Among these laws is the newly enacted *Law of Criminal Procedures (Enforcement Powers – Communication Data)*, 2007, which empowers the Israeli police secretly to obtain from telecommunications companies such information as customers' names; phone specifications; and details of incoming and outgoing calls, including the duration and locations of people using mobile phones or personal computers.

In addition, several questions shall be addressed:

1   Under what circumstances (if ever) should surveillance be tolerated?
2   What is the status of the right to privacy under Israeli law? What threats to privacy result from various methods of surveillance?
3   What is the real reason for employing surveillance: imminent risk to state security or political suppression?
4   What is the state of exception in Israel that justifies surveillance?
5   To what extent does surveillance breach basic rights to dignity, privacy, and freedom of movement, as recognized in both the Israeli legal system and in international law?

When should state surveillance be tolerated?

What is the current situation in Israel? Does it balance the duty of the authorities to prevent crime and limit its scope, on the one hand, and respect and protect the right to privacy, on the other? This is essential to a system that does not needlessly overreach into residents' lives.

A possible starting point is to establish what level of surveillance is either necessary or tolerable in society. While a "close observation of a person suspected of being a spy or a criminal" (*Collins Essential English Dictionary* 2006) might be tolerated as part of a state investigation carried out in relation to a *specific offense*, gathering information as part of a general intelligence activity (a type of "data mining") directed at a group of persons *not* suspected of having committed a *specific offense* should not be allowed. In other words, a clear distinction should be made between *specific legitimate goals* that justify surveillance (e.g., protecting public safety by preventing a specific criminal activity, or locating and rescuing a person injured in a motor vehicle accident), and other *illegitimate undefined goals* (e.g., closely monitoring people or groups because of their political activity, or gathering information on a certain religious group or neighborhood and exposing all members or residents to 24/7 CCTV surveillance because one or a few *might* be engaged in criminal activity). In any case, the number of people given authority to access databases containing recorded material should be restricted, and access itself should be recorded and/or registered to minimize privacy threats.

Israel is not unique in having a system of laws and regulations that attempts to regulate and account for its citizens and residents. Doing so inevitably demands that state authorities gather, store, and perhaps share information. Who is accountable for ensuring that information-gathering is safe and accurate? What kinds of information are deemed to be sensitive, and what protective mechanisms are available? All of these questions inform states' approach to protecting the privacy of their citizens, at both the domestic and the international levels.

The right to privacy in Israeli and international law

The right to privacy is one of the most important of human rights (Criminal Appeal 1302/92: 353). It is recognized in international law under Article 12 of the *International Declaration of Human Rights*, Article 17 of the *International Covenant on Civil and Political Rights*, 1966, and Article 8 of the *European Convention on Human Rights*.

Protection of Privacy Law, *1981*

Israeli law also recognizes the right to privacy as an important human right. In 1981, the Israeli Parliament (the Knesset) enacted the *Protection of Privacy Law*. Article 1 forbids any "invasion of privacy," which includes, *inter alia*, close observation of a person that might harass him/her, intercepting and wiretapping private conversations, photographing a person in a private place, and a statutory secrecy obligation regarding a person's private matters. The statute allows the maintenance and use of databases under certain prescribed conditions. For example, a database must be registered in the Databases Registry if it includes data on more than 10,000 people, if it includes sensitive information (i.e., concerning a person's personality, state of health, financial status, opinions and beliefs), if it includes information provided by third parties (i.e., not the subjects of the data), or if the database belongs to a public institution (Article 8 of the statute) The law also provides that the Council for Privacy Protection must submit an annual report to the Knesset Constitution, Law and Justice Committee. This report, prepared by the Privacy Registrar, must provide information on observation and enforcement activities aimed at protecting the right to privacy (Article 10A of the statute).

It is worth noting that, according to the original Article 24 of the *Protection of Privacy Law* (repealed in 2005), the *transfer* of data among organs of the state, local authorities, and other public institutions was allowed unless forbidden by law, regulations, or disciplinary rules. The focus of the law, however, has shifted. Currently, according to Article 23B, *release* of data/information by a public institution is forbidden unless it was publicly published legally, or the subject of the data has consented. Violating the right to privacy is treated as both a civil tort (Article 4 of the statute) and as a criminal offense that could be punished by up to five years' imprisonment (Article 5 of the statute). Yet, Article 19 releases from responsibility any person who has acted within his/her powers as provided by law. It also grants immunity to any "security authority" (i.e., the Israeli police, the intelligence department of the Israeli army and the military police, General Security Services, and the Mosad) and its personnel if the "harm was caused in a reasonable way" and in the course of duty (Article 19(b) of the statute). In addition, the law provides that a nominal violation (i.e., a "violation with no real substance" – "*Pgia'ah shel-ma-Bechach*," in Hebrew) is not actionable under either civil or criminal law (Article 6). Moreover, the law provides a list of possible defenses ("*HAGANOT*") that, if applicable, could remove all civil and/or criminal liability (Article 18).

Basic Law: Human Dignity and Freedom, *1992*

In 1992 the right to privacy was upgraded to a basic right/constitutional right after the enactment of the *Basic Law: Human Dignity and Freedom*. The Israeli Supreme Court described it thus: "This right constitutes one of the basic rights of a person in Israel. It is one of the freedoms that designs the character of the regime in Israel as a democratic one and is one of the rights that establish the dignity and the freedom for which a human being is eligible" (Criminal Appeal 2963/98). Article 7 of the *Basic Law*, which deals specifically with protecting the right to privacy, was interpreted to include protections to computer communication, telephone communication, and the identity of persons with whom a person communicates, as well as websites a person has visited (Criminal Appeal 6640/90). In another ruling of the Israeli Supreme Court, issued on September 4, 2005, the Court ruled that "an invasion to one's personal computer is as bad as an invasion to his home." (Criminal Appeal 7368/05). In addition, Chief Justice Durit Benesh stated in one of her decisions that "the apocalyptic vision of George Orwell as the 'big brother' might easily come true if there are no boundaries to access to data reservoirs and their use" (Civil Service Appeal 6843/01: 924).

Have these statutory provisions and judicial pronouncements provided failsafe protection of the right to privacy of ordinary Israeli citizens and residents in general, and of Palestinian Arabs in particular? Unfortunately, the question must be answered in the negative. There is an undeniable gap between the legal theories reflected in laws, and court decisions, and the reality of day-to-day life. One reason for this is the near-continuous state of emergency/security in Israel.

The state of emergency in Israel is not a state of exception

It seems that the ongoing state of emergency in Israel, in effect since its establishment, has created a fertile environment for the growth of justifications for state conduct against "non-Jews." Among such conduct and activities are those technical and non-technical surveillance methods utilized by the Israeli police – mainly the General Security Service (GSS) – against the Palestinian Arab minority in Israel in order to maintain and ensure the state's control over them. To review and understand the Israeli official justification for the near-permanent state of emergency, despite its harsh consequences for human rights, we refer to Israel's national report, submitted on September 25, 2008 to the UN Council for Human Rights. Under the section entitled "State of Emergency" the report reads:

98 *A State of Emergency has existed in Israel since 19 May 1948, due initially to the basic threat and realization of hostilities directed by neighboring states, both aimed at Israel's existence.* The on-going struggle against acts of violence and terrorism committed by extremist groups and individuals in centers of civilian life, including public markets and means of transport, has compounded the problem and obliged the Government to take measures to meet the exigencies of the situation, both for the defense of the State as well as for the protection of life and property. *Such a need was addressed by the declaration and maintenance of the state of emergency, which included the exercise of powers of arrest and detention.*

99 *In 1992 the Knesset approved the* Basic Law: The Government *which provided that a state of emergency could only apply for one year and could only be renewed by vote in the Knesset.* This altered the pre-existing situation in which a continuing state of emergency had existed ever since the establishment of the State.

Consequently, *a state of emergency is no longer necessarily a permanent situation, but is subject to annual parliamentary debate and scrutiny.*

100 In recent years, Israel has been considering refraining from extending the state of emergency any further. However, *the actual termination of the state of emergency could not be executed immediately, as certain fundamental laws, orders and regulations legally depend upon the existence of a state of emergency.* These acts of legislation must be revised, so as not to leave crucial matters of the State unregulated when the state of emergency expires.

101 Following the present extension of the state of emergency, the Israeli Government and the Knesset have embarked on a joint program to complete the necessary legislative procedures required in order to end the state of emergency. As a result, measures toward removing the linkage to the state of emergency have been taken. Over the past few years, several laws have been amended, and they are no longer linked to the state of emergency, and a number of other bills are now before the Knesset. In addition, the *Military Service Law* (1951) was amended. As a result, none of its articles are now linked to the state of emergency.

102 *Since January 2000, the Government has decided to ask the Knesset to extend the state of emergency for a reduced period of six months, and not for a year, the maximum period prescribed under section 49(b) of* Basic Law: The Government, as was the former practice. In a recent petition to the High Court of Justice, there was a demand to pronounce the declaration regarding the existence of a state of emergency void, or alternatively, order that it is to be immediately terminated. *The petitioners claim that the ongoing state of emergency poses a threat to democracy and to civil rights and that in the present circumstances it is no longer vital. At present, the matter is still pending before the High Court of Justice. The Government has submitted to the Court, upon its request, a comprehensive estimated schedule regarding the measures required in order to replace the acts of legislation linked directly to the state of emergency.*

("Israel's National Report . . ." 2008; emphasis added)

Despite the language used in this report, there has been no real decrease in the infringement of human rights resulting from the state of security/emergency. Specifically, Israel's assertions that since 1992 the "state of emergency could only apply for one year and could only be renewed by vote in the Knesset" and that "a state of emergency is no longer necessarily a permanent situation, but is subject to annual parliamentary debate and scrutiny" have not been realized. On the contrary, statutes that violate Arab citizens' human rights continue to exist, and are renewed from time to time based on the renewal of the state of emergency. The most recent and obvious example of such laws is the *Nationality and Entry into Israel Law*, 2003 (temporary order), approved by the Knesset in March 2007. This law, argues Adalah, the Legal Center for Arab Minority Rights in Israel, "denies Palestinian citizens the right to acquire residency or citizenship status in Israel for their Palestinian spouses from the OPT" ("Summary Prepared by the Office of the High Commissioner . . ." 2008). Although the law is defined as a "temporary order," it has now been extended eight times. The amendments have expanded the law to exclude spouses from "enemy states" and have extended the ban to "anyone living in an area in which operations that constitute a threat to Israel are being carried out" in the opinion of the security services. In June

2008, the Gaza Strip was added to this list, thereby "nullifying the limited possibilities for any family unification between citizens of Israel and residents of Gaza" ("Summary Prepared by the Office of the High Commissioner for Human Rights . . ." 2008).

Moreover, various UN bodies have "noted with concern that the *Nationality and Entry into Israel Law* of 31 July 2003 had a disproportionate impact on Arab Israeli citizens wishing to be reunited with their families in Israel. The UN Committee on the Elimination of Racial Discrimination (CERD) and the UN Human Rights Committee recommended that Israel revoke the Order and reconsider its policy on family reunification" ("Compilation Prepared by the Office of the High Commissioner for Human Rights . . ." 2008). Nevertheless, the law continues in force and, on July 11, 2008, its validity was extended to July 31, 2009.

Forms of state surveillance

Thus far, this chapter has laid the foundation for a more in-depth discussion of surveillance by focusing on the statutory framework and the governmental attitudes that underpin it. Israeli and international laws aspire to the protection of privacy, and recognize that individuals value their privacy. It is even lifted to the rank of a basic human right. How strong is this legal foundation, however? Is it as subject to erosion as the same human right – the right to privacy – that it purports to protect? In this section, I explore four distinct methods legitimized and utilized by the Israeli state to conduct surveillance of residents and citizens. Some of these – such as the new biometric identification card and the "Big Brother" law – include the application of laws that, at least in theory, will affect all residents and/or citizens indiscriminately. The privacy-eroding effects of others – namely the ID cards/serial numbers and the CCTV system in Old Jerusalem – are felt more strongly by Palestinians.

ID cards and ID numbers as surveillance

According to Article 24 of the *Population Registry Law*, 1965, every person aged sixteen and above and registered in the Population Registry in the Israeli Ministry of the Interior must obtain and hold an identification card (ID card). Article 2 of the same law provides that thirteen pieces of information about every Israeli resident must be included in the Registry:

*   family name, given name, and former names;
*   names of parents;
*   date and place of birth;
*   sex;
*   nationality;
*   religion;
*   marital status (single, married, divorced, or widowed);
*   name of spouse;
*   names of children, and each one's date of birth and sex;
*   citizenship or citizenships (current and previous);
*   address;
*   date of entry to Israel; and
*   date residency in Israel established.

For many years the Ministry of the Interior adopted and acted on a bizarre policy according to which it transferred, with virtually no limitations, personal information from the Population Registry to various authorities and banks. The computers of the latter were even directly connected to the computerized database of the Ministry. Finally, on May 10, 2004, the Israeli Supreme Court put an end to this irresponsible conduct (HCJ 8070/98). The Court held that the Ministry of the Interior is not allowed to continue transferring information to the Tax Authority, the Broadcast Authority, and the National Insurance Institution, until the matter is regulated by specific regulations or administrative by-laws. As to the banks, the Court ordered that the transfer of information must cease and that suitable legislation be enacted. The Court gave the respondents six months to comply with its ruling. Thus, the Ministry of the Interior was forced to initiate an amendment to the *Population Registry Law* to regulate the transfer of information to other public authorities and the banks. On March 28, 2007 the *Population Registry Law* was amended, with Article 29A being added. However, the Ministry continued to transfer data to banks and other private institutions illegally (Pinchuk 2009), leading Israel's State Comptroller and Ombudsman to state in his 2008 annual report that the Population Authority at the Ministry had failed to protect Israeli citizens' right to privacy (State Comptroller and Ombudsman 2008).

Like Article 2 of the *Population Registry Law*, Article 2 of the *Population Registry Regulations* of 1990 provided, until early 2002, that an ID card must include all the information listed above, with the exception of religion and date of entry and residence in Israel. The *Regulations* additionally require Israeli citizens to state their citizenship, although it gives the opportunity to decline to do so.

Based on the *Population Registry Law* and *Regulations*, the ID cards issued by the Israeli Ministry of the Interior have reflected the nationality of their holders, whether Arab or Jewish. Therefore, until the beginning of 2002, any policeman or clerk could easily know, based on an ID card, whether the holder was a Jew or an Arab. Moreover, the card also betrayed to which sect an Arab belonged (i.e., if they were Druze or not). Israeli police are not blessed with special powers of perception; rather, the Ministry of the Interior, as part of Israel's "divide and rule" policy, treated the Druze as a separate nationality. Thus, the term "Druze" – not "Arab" – appeared on the ID card under "nationality" (Halabi 1989).

On March 25, 2002, the *Population Registry Regulations* were amended to delete the term "nationality." Since then, eight small stars appear in the space for "nationality." However, this amendment did not reflect a change in the Israeli policy towards its citizens, and the state of Israel has not become either more democratic or more sensitive to their right to privacy. Moreover, the Inspector General of the Israeli Police opposed the proposed amendment, and his representative to the Knesset Constitution, Law and Justice Committee argued, "this tool [i.e., disclosing the nationality of ID card holder] is helpful for the police to carry on its job especially in these mad days" (Ben-Haim 2002). The reason for this amendment was an attempt to overcome an "internal Jewish problem:" then-Minister of the Interior, Eli Shai of the Shas Party, refused to follow a decision of the Israeli Supreme Court, sitting as High Court of Justice, which had instructed him to register as "Jewish" any people converted to Judaism through reformist and/or conservative rabbis, and not only those converted through Orthodox rabbis (Ben-Haim 2002).

Israel's use of ID cards as a surveillance tool is the norm not only in Israel proper but in the occupied Palestinian territories. While serial numbers on ID cards issued by the Israeli Ministry of the Interior for Palestinians living in East Jerusalem start with the digits "08" and indicate permanent resident status, the serial numbers on the ID cards issued by the Israeli Civil Administration in the West Bank and Gaza start with "09." And while the cover of ID cards issued in Jerusalem is blue, the cover of those issued in the West Bank and Gaza was orange (changed to green by the Palestinian National Authority (PNA) following the signing of the Oslo Agreement between Israel and the PLO). Yet, the serial ID numbers issued by the PNA have not changed – they continue to start with "09" – and their holders are forbidden from entering "Unified Jerusalem" (or any other part of Israel) without a permit. If they do, they will be treated by the Israeli authorities as criminals, charged with an "illegal stay" and most likely sent to prison (Article 12 of the *Entry into Israel Law*, 1952, as amended in 1985). In addition, the serial numbers used by Israel in East Jerusalem enable any Israeli official easily to ascertain whether its holder was born "in Israel" (i.e., in Jerusalem) to an "Israeli parent," and whether the holder acquired his/her parent's status through ordinary registration or as a result of family unification. The explanation is simple: the serial numbers given to Palestinian adults who acquired permanent or temporary residency status by family unification always start with the digits "086."

The *Nationality and Entry into Israel (Temporary Order) Law*, 2003 replaced an Israeli Government decision of 12 May 2002. This was enacted in a bid to reduce the number of "non-Jews" (especially Palestinians) becoming Israeli residents through family unification, and thus to prevent them from accomplishing "their right of return through the backdoor" (Ministry of the Interior 2002). This law underscores the complicated situation in which Palestinian families live, and has resulted in the break-up of many Palestinian "mixed" families. For example, it prevents Palestinians from the West Bank and Gaza from applying for family unification if they are married to an Israeli resident and are males under the age of thirty-five or females under twenty-five. Another provision authorizes the Minister of the Interior to extend the validity of an existing status but forbids him from upgrading it (e.g., from temporary resident to permanent resident) (Article 4). Furthermore, sometimes members of the same nuclear family have different statuses: a father is a resident of the West Bank and holds a permit to stay in Israel (without any additional rights); a mother who is a permanent resident of Israel; and a child who is a temporary resident of Israel. In other nuclear families, the father might have temporary resident status; the mother, permanent resident status; one child under the age of fourteen the mother's status; and another child older than fourteen a permit to stay in Israel with no status (and therefore no social and health rights) (Halabi 2007).

To illustrate this, Figure 10.1 shows an ID card of a permanent resident woman married to a Palestinian-American. Her ID number starts with "080," the ID numbers of two of her sons (who acquired their residency status through a family unification process) start with "086," and the ID number of a third son born in Jerusalem and registered "normally" starts with "331."

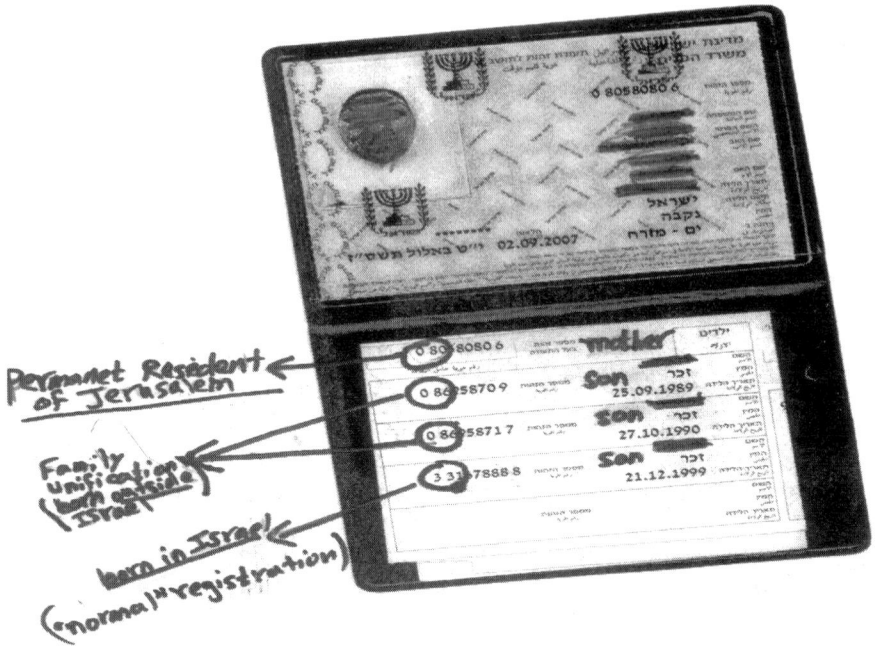

Figure 10.1 ID card of a permanent resident woman married to a Palestinian-American

The Inclusion of Biometric Identification Tools and Biometric Identification Information in Identification Documents and in Database Law

At the time of writing, it appeared that Israel would continue to use ID cards as a surveillance tool. However, old ID cards will be replaced by new biometric ("smart") ID cards. This technology will also be incorporated into other identification documents.

In June 2008 the Legal Advisor of the Ministry of the Interior circulated to various public figures and institutions, including the Israeli High Court Chief Justice, the Government Legal Advisor, and the deans of the law faculties of Israeli universities, copies of the *Governmental Memorandum Concerning Biometric ID Card, Travel Document and Database* and asked for feedback (*Governmental Memorandum* . . . 2008). As stated in the memorandum, the new ID cards and passports would contain two "flat" fingerprints of the two index fingers and a photograph of facial features (Article 2). In addition, a biometric database would be established to enable various authorities (including clerks of the Ministry of the Interior, soldiers, and policemen) to make quick comparisons between the biometric data in the ID and those in the database, for the purpose of identification. Including such biometric data would require amendments to existing laws, including the *Population Registry Law* and *The Law of Passports* of 1950. On August 3, 2008, the Israeli government approved the memorandum and called for the establishment of a biometric database by the Ministry of the Interior and the Public Security Ministry.

On October 27, 2008, a draft government bill was published under the title *The Inclusion of Biometric Identification Tools in Identification Documents and in Database.*

On October 29, this bill passed its first Knesset reading, with eighteen Knesset members voting in favor; only MK Dov Khenin (Hadash) voted against the bill. At the time of writing it had to undergo further legislative work in the Knesset's Constitution, Law and Justice Committee (Ronen 2008).

The reason for establishing the biometric database, as stated in the memorandum, is to create another method of preventing terrorist attacks ("*pigo'im*") and other offenses (mainly felonies), and allowing quick identification/authentication during major disasters. However, as stated in the brief accompanying the bill, its foremost goal is to detect forgery: "The advantage of using biometric features in order to ascertain someone's identity stems from the fact that biometric information is constantly 'on' your person, as opposed to other types of identification measures, which may be subject to alterations and a limited ability to detect forgeries." This is why, the brief explains, the bill provides that any citizen or resident who refuses to give biometric samples could face up to one year in jail (Article 29(a)).

This bill has been criticized by opposition Knesset Members and by the Israeli Bar for violating civil rights – mainly the right to privacy (Ronen 2008). Also, in its 2008 *State of Human Rights in Israel and the Occupied Territories* report, the Association of Civil Rights in Israel (ACRI) criticized the bill and described it as "dangerous":

> In October 2008, another dangerous bill passed its first reading in the Knesset – to set up a biometric data bank to include the fingerprints and facial features of Israeli citizens and residents. According to the Ministry of the Interior, the data bank is necessary for the issuing of passports and "smart" identity cards – *a claim that has been refuted by many experts in the field, including experts in the service of the Ministry of the Interior itself.* In none of the western democracies, not even in those that have introduced biometric identity cards, is there a data bank of such a nature. *The great danger posed by a biometric data bank stems from the fact that this is personal information that cannot be altered or substituted; if it falls into the wrong hands or is used for unauthorized purposes, irreversible damage may be caused.*
>
> (ACRI 2008, emphasis added; see also Or-Haf 2008)

The European Court of Human Rights has judicially commented on the retention of biometric data. In a December 2008 judgment (*S. and Marper v. the United Kingdom (Applications nos. 30562/04 and 30566/04)*), it held that it is unconstitutional for authorities to retain such data after criminal proceedings have ended in acquittals or discontinuances:

> 68 The Court notes at the outset that all three categories of the personal information retained by the authorities in the present cases, namely fingerprints, DNA profiles and cellular samples, constitute personal data within the meaning of the *Data Protection Convention* as they relate to identified or identifiable individuals. The Government accepted that all three categories are "personal data" within the meaning of the *Data Protection Act 1998* in the hands of those who are able to identify the individual . . .
>
> 85 The Court accordingly considers that the retention of fingerprints on the authorities' records in connection with an identified or identifiable individual

may in itself give rise, notwithstanding their objective and irrefutable character, to important private-life concerns . . .

125 In conclusion, the Court finds that the blanket and indiscriminate nature of the powers of retention of the fingerprints, cellular samples and DNA profiles of persons suspected but not convicted of offences, as applied in the case of the present applicants, fails to strike a fair balance between the competing public and private interests and that the respondent State has overstepped any acceptable margin of appreciation in this regard. Accordingly, the retention at issue constitutes a disproportionate interference with the applicants' right to respect for private life and cannot be regarded as necessary in a democratic society . . .

126 Accordingly, there has been a violation of Article 8 of the Convention in the present case.

Judicial pronouncements such as this motivate some to urge Israel not to establish a database that includes, indiscriminately, biometric information on all its citizens. Beyond the obvious privacy concerns, they warn that such a move could seriously harm Israel's foreign trade with EU states (Klinger 2008). However, the Israeli government was intent on bringing the bill to second and third readings and to make it law. As expected, on December 7, 2009, the *Inclusion of Biometric Identification Tools and Biometric Identification Information in Identification Documents and in Database Law* was enacted by the Knesset.

CCTV in the old city of Jeruslaem

Technology is being deployed against individuals through the collection of biometric information. For nearly a decade, however, another form of technology has been utilized to observe people going about their everyday lives. In 1999, the Ministry of Internal Security published a tender for building a closed circuit television (CCTV) system in the old city of Jerusalem. According to the Ministry, the system was destined to serve the police and security forces and to help them prepare for "scenarios and dangers" that are "likely" to occur in the old city, and also to deal with "threats" that might emerge from the Christian, Muslim, and Jewish communities (Danon 1999). Based on this general reasoning, hundreds of cameras now form a CCTV system, known as "Mabat 2000," covering almost every yard and lane of the square kilometer of the old city of Jerusalem.

According to the Israeli police's website (www.police.gov.il), Mabat 2000 can "continually scan streets and sensitive places in old Jerusalem" and save the data/scenes "caught" by the cameras. The system has been functioning "around the clock" since the end of 1999 and is managed by a control center with online screens housed in Keshleh police station, near the Jaffa Gate.

Mabat 2000 has arguably occasionally helped secure the convictions of criminals "caught" by the cameras. However, one main question remains: is it desirable and acceptable to keep thousands of innocent people under strict daily surveillance because a few crimes might be spotted by some of these cameras? This question becomes even more important when one considers the locations of some of the cameras, which enable them to scan not only public markets and streets but the main entrances of

Figure 10.2 Mabat 2000 control room in the old city of Jerusalem
Source: www.police.gov.il

houses facing the narrow lanes of the old city. This is certainly the case in the Muslim Quarter.

I contacted the office of the legal advisors to the Jerusalem police to ascertain what they view as the legal basis for deploying the Mabat 2000 system, and whether a code of practice prescribes its purpose, use, management, and monitoring. In response, they referred to the general powers given to the police under Article 2 of the *Police Ordinance (New Version)*, 1971, which include, *inter alia*, to "maintain the public order and safety of man and property." However, they did not refer to any code of practice that was specifically relevant to the system. For comparison, the City of Westminster in the UK, where a very advanced fixed and mobile CCTV system services "a network of 33 cameras in the West End as well as separate schemes in Church Street, Oxford Street and Belgravia," has developed a detailed code of practice for its use, a copy of which can be found on the council's website (www.westminster.gov.uk). Article 1.1 of this code "explains the purpose, use, management and monitoring of the various CCTV Systems that are currently deployed and are in operation around Westminster." The code also explains the objectives of the system and the principles of the code itself, among them "to ensure that the System is operated fairly, impartially and within the law." In addition, the code defines the scope of allowable and forbidden activities. For example, Article 2.4 provides, "cameras shall not be used to look into private residential or commercial property." Moreover, the images transmitted to the central control room can be viewed and stored in a digital archive for just thirty-one days (Article 2.6.1).

The "Big Brother" Law: a real danger to privacy and dignity

CCTV systems, especially those operated without regard for policy or limits, can be disconcerting and insidious. At least, however, the existence of the system is publicly known, and those who live, work, and travel in Jerusalem's old city know they are likely to be under surveillance. They have been put on warning by the public nature of the system, no matter how they may chafe at and resent it. Much more worrying is the possibility that the authorities might execute surveillance on unwitting individuals. This possibility is becoming a reality through the legitimizing action of the new so-called "Big Brother" Law.

Until recently, when secret wiretapping was an investigative necessity, the relevant authority (usually the Israeli police) would apply to magistrates' court and obtain a warrant based on the powers given to it by the *Secret Wiretapping Law* of 1979. However, not just any offense justified an application for a surveillance warrant. A wiretap for "police purposes" could be approved only if the offense under investigation was a felony (Article 6). Nevertheless, statistics show a significant rise – to 1,375 – in the number of surveillance warrant applications in 2007 (Ilan 2008) as compared with those in 2006 (1250; Ilan 2007a). Another worrisome fact is that, out of 400 secret wiretapping applications submitted to district courts in Israel in 2006, 397 were approved (Ilan 2007c). Moreover, in 2007 the Israeli courts refused only 11 applications out of the total of 1,375 (Ilan 2008).

An even more worrisome legal development occurred on December 17, 2007, when the *Law of Criminal Procedures (Enforcement Powers – Communication Data)* (also known as the *Communication Data Law*), was enacted by the Knesset. It has been in force since June 27, 2008. Initiated by the Ministry of Justice and the Ministry of Interior Security, it has come to be known as the "Big Brother" Law (Ilan 2007b).

The *Communication Data Law* allows investigative authorities to open a wide window and stare into the private lives of Israeli citizens and residents in the name of crime prevention. It authorizes the Israeli police and six other investigative authorities to receive "telecommunication data" from all telecommunication companies, including internet providers, concerning any of their clients/subscribers. Article 1 of the law divides this telecommunication data into the following sub-categories:

1   "Identification data": name, ID number or number of company, address, and telephone number.
2   "Location data": concerns intercepting supplies that are found with subscribers.
3   "Subscriber data": type of telecommunication service provided to the subscriber; name, address, and ID number of subscriber; details concerning the subscriber's means of payment; the address at which a telecommunication supply was set up for the subscriber; identification data of a subscriber's telecommunication supply.
4   "Transmission data": type of telecommunication transmission massage; identification data of a telecommunication supply which is the source of the telecommunication transmission or the address the transmission goes to or from; the line of the telecommunication transmission; identification data of the subscriber who is the source of the telecommunication transmission or its recipient; time of sending or receiving the telecommunication transmission; the duration and volume of the telecommunication transmission.

The definition of "telecommunication data" does not explicitly include the *content* of the telecommunication transmission. However, as Dr Michael Birnhack of Tel Aviv University rightly argues, "in a time where the abilities of data possessing are not a fiction but rather a daily tool reachable and easy to use, it is possible to learn from the telecommunication data about the content of the call/conversation and about the parties to that call/conversation" (Birnhack cited in HCJ 3809/08: sec. 22).

At first glance, conditions and limitations built into the *Communication Data Law* appear to mitigate intrusion and provide a balanced formula to protect citizens' right to privacy from serious – and sometimes deadly – violations. However, a deeper review reveals that the law suffers from at least four main deficiencies that weaken the suggested limits and thus create real threats to human dignity and privacy. Despite the purported legislative intent of achieving positive goals, such as preventing crime, innocent people might unwittingly be placed under surveillance, and might be harmed without justification. These fears have led ACRI to file a petition with the Israeli Supreme Court, sitting as a High Court for Justice, against seventeen respondents, including the Israeli police, the Knesset, the Minister of Justice, and nine telecommunication companies. ACRI also claims that some provisions of the law are unconstitutional (HCJ 3809/08).

The first deficiency is the possibility of obtaining an *ex parte* surveillance warrant (i.e., without notice to the subject) without establishing a "proper cause." Article 3(a) empowers a police officer or a "representative of another investigation authority" (such as the Taxes Authority, the Military Police Investigation Unit, Authority for Business Restrictions, or the Equities Authority) to apply and obtain an *ex parte* warrant that allows receipt of telecommunication data from telecommunication companies and internet providers. Before issuing the requested warrant, the court must be convinced that the purpose of the application is to achieve one of the four following objectives:

1   Rescue or protect human life.
2   Uncover, investigate, and prevent offenses.
3   Uncover offenders and bring them to trial.
4   Forfeiture of property according to law.

However, such important terms as "reasonable basis" as a minimum legal prerequisite for justifying the initiation of surveillance activity are missing. In comparison, such terms do appear in other laws that allow limitations to be imposed on human rights, such as freedom of movement, when a specific offense has allegedly been committed. For example, Article 25 of the *Criminal Procedural Ordinance (Arrest and Search) (New Version)*, 1969, authorizes the police to enter any house or other place without a search warrant if they have a "reasonable basis to assume that an offense is committed there, or has just been committed." And Article 23 of the *Criminal Procedural (Enforcement Powers – Arrests) Law*, 1996, authorizes the police to arrest a person if they have a "reasonable basis to suspect that the person committed an offense" that justifies arrest.

Therefore, the "Big Brother" Law, without strict scrutiny, might pave the way for the police and other investigative agencies to obtain *ex parte* warrants that allow them to receive telecommunication data concerning personal computers and mobile phones without establishing "probable cause" (i.e., specific reason to believe that a specific offense has been committed that justifies investigation, including surveillance). In other words, the law may be misused to initiate general intelligence activity for information "fishing," rather than investigating specific offenses.

Another deficiency of the *Communication Data Law* (Article 1) is that it applies not only when a *felony* has allegedly been committed (i.e., a serious and severe offense, such as murder (mandatory life sentence), rape (up to twenty years' imprisonment), or robbery (up to twenty years' imprisonment)) but when a *misdemeanor* is suspected (i.e., a much less serious offense, including insulting a public servant, and traffic, negligence, and defamation offenses, for which punishment ranges from three months' to three years' imprisonment, sentences which may be suspended). Since most of the offenses in the Israeli *Criminal Law* of 1977 are misdemeanors, the range of potential persons that might be affected by surveillance – even when a relatively minor offense has allegedly been committed – becomes so wide that it raises the question of whether the potential violation of the right to privacy of so many people is justifiable. ACRI has rightly argued (HCJ 3809/08: sec. 32) against such an application two reasons. First, receiving telecommunication data through secret surveillance violates the privacy not only of the suspect but of anyone he or she contacts by mobile phone or e-mail, even when such contact has nothing to do with the alleged offense, and even when it is unknown whether a charge will ultimately be filed. Second, warrants for surveillance are issued secretly, in the presence of the investigative authority only, and the magistrates' courts cannot be relied upon to exercise their discretion appropriately. Many innocent people could be hurt as a result of the issuance of a surveillance warrant, and they do not have an opportunity to appeal against such a warrant. Moreover, while the *Communication Data Law* allows surveillance even on suspicion of a misdemeanor, Article 6 of the *Secret Wiretapping Law* of 1979 states that a wiretap for "police purposes" may be approved only if the offense under investigation is a felony.

A third deficiency of the *Communication Data Law* is found in Article 4. This article empowers a police officer, based on a request of another officer, to issue a permit *without a court warrant* to obtain telecommunication data from the data bank of a telecommunication company "in an emergency" (i.e., if the officer is convinced of the urgent need to prevent a felony, to discover its perpetrator, or to save a life). This article is not consistent with Article 3(b), which states that if the subscriber is a person who has immunity according to the law (such as a lawyer, a psychiatrist, a physician, or a journalist), the court must be convinced, based on clear information included in the application for the surveillance order, that there is a basis to believe that such a person is him/herself suspected of committing an offense. Article 4 allows this immunity to be violated without a court of law having the opportunity to review and scrutinize whether claimed public interest justifies the violation. Based on this article, the police may, without a court order, secretly wiretap phone calls made to and/or from lawyers' offices in an attempt to intercept information related to suspects or accused persons they represent. Moreover, the police may invade the privacy of journalists and those who contact them. (For more detailed arguments, see ACRI's petition in HCJ 3809/08: secs. 55–56.)

The fourth deficiency relates to Articles 6–9. These articles deal with the automatic transfer of whole "information data banks," which could include restricted telephone numbers, from telecommunication companies to the Israeli police. This mechanism is an attempt by the police to create an information reservoir that will include the telephone numbers and other information of all telephone subscribers in Israel.

Restricted numbers might be used for illegal activities and even for committing serious and severe offenses, thus the investigative authorities' desire to access the details of a *specific* phone owner in order to investigate a *specific* offense is understandable. However, this authority already exists under Articles 3 and 4. Therefore, the general authorization given to the head of the Police Investigation Department in Article 6 – to transfer, in the absence of a specific investigation into any specific offense, all telephone numbers in Israel, including restricted ones, and information concerning the exact locations of all telecommunications antennas serving mobile phones and the areas they cover, without limiting the number and positions of those having direct access to these vast stores of data – is unreasonable and overly broad, and thus unconstitutional.

In addition, it is important to note that the distinction made by supporters of the *Communication Data Law* between the harm caused to privacy as a result of wiretapping and that caused as a result of receiving telecommunication data is artificial. That is, if the telecommunication data reveal that a journalist called a certain source, it may be possible to ascertain to a significant degree the content of the call from the mere fact that it was made. Similarly, if telecommunication data indicate that a married person is staying overnight in a certain place with his/her lover, this is not mere technical information. Rather, it constitutes substantive information, the receipt of which violates the right to privacy of that person. Furthermore, how could a list of internet websites that a certain person has visited, by computer or mobile phone, be treated as technical telecommunication data rather than a clear violation of the right to privacy?

Finally, it is very worrisome – though not surprising – that two months after the *Communication Data Law* entered into force, the Israeli police started to violate the law by demanding that telecommunication companies send them information and data that are not covered under its terms. For example, the police sent a written document to the Cellcom telecommunication company demanding the following information that is not listed in the Law: the name of the agent who arranged the service (i.e., sold the mobile phone); the type of mobile phone; classification of mobiles according to generations; the date on which the subscribers were connected to the service; and how account payments were made. This illegitimate attempt to gather information was revealed after Cellcom complained to the Knesset Constitution, Law and Justice Committee. The committee's chairperson responded to the police representative's claim that the document sent to Cellcom and other companies was an "unfinished working paper" with the comment: "To my eyes, it is very serious that the police have been acting with no authorization . . . Tomorrow you will come to us and ask us to approve laws with similar types of privacy violation, such as the Biometric Data Law, and I am not convinced that we will agree" (Knesset Constitution, Law and Justice Committee 2008).

Closing remarks

The right to privacy resides at the core of human rights. The loss of privacy, and becoming subject to general, continuous state surveillance methods, renders life intolerable: individuals cannot maintain their autonomy, while the groups to which they belong lose any sense of dignity and become mesmerized by the state. Such an unpleasant and worrisome situation has been rightly criticized by Michael Birnhack (2008): "A surveillance-state that knows everything about its citizens assimilates in them the feeling of being followed, until there will be no need to watch them closely: the citizens will censor themselves. This is how it was in USSR, in East Germany, and this is how Orwell described the state of the big brother." As Birnhack says, most people have "some information that they do not want made known to the public: a phone call to the center of mental health support, a call made by a married person to his or her lover, a conversation between a source and a reporter, a conversation of businessmen that examines the possibility of a future deal that it is best not to discuss in the meantime, and more."

Furthermore, all people wish to – and should – have the basic right to maintain a personal and family life. Any state aspiring to be a place residents gladly call "home" must find a way to balance the duty to protect *all* its residents from real and imminent danger, limit (if not prevent) crime, and maintain public safety and order with the duty to protect and ensure respect for *all* its residents' fundamental rights and freedoms – led by the right to privacy and the freedoms of speech and movement. In order to become such a state, Israel has to become the "state of all its residents," regardless of their race, sex, religion, and nationality. As a serious and meaningful step in this direction, Israel must amend – or revoke – a long list of laws that have been used to achieve political and "national" goals (i.e., Zionist goals that have no or limited benefit for "non-Jews"). Only then will residents feel they are living in a society where all members are equal "sisters" and "brothers" rather than disconnected individuals in a state controlled by a biased "big brother."

Bibliography

Association of Civil Rights in Israel (ACRI) (2008) *The State of Human Rights in Israel and the Occupied Territories*, Jerusalem: ACRI. Available HTTP: <http://www.acri.org.il/pdf/state 2008.pdf>.

Basic Law: Human Dignity and Freedom, Compilation of Laws of Israel [*Sefer Hakhukim*], No. 1391, March 25, 1992: 150.

Ben-Haim, Avishi (2002) "The Constitution Committee: The Nationality Clause Shall be Omitted from ID Cards," *YNet*, March 13. Available HTTP: <http://www.ynet.co.il/ Ext/Comp/ArticleLayout> [Hebrew].

Birnhack, Michael (2008) "The *Communication Data Law*: Selling Human Right for One Shekel Ninety Agurot," *YNet*, July 28. Available HTTP: <http://www.ynet.co.il> [Hebrew].

Civil Service Appeal 6843/01, *Ben Davis v. Civil Service Commissioner, Compilation of Israeli Supreme Court Decisions* [*Piski Din*], 51(2): 918, 924 [Hebrew].

Cohen, Hillel (2006) *Good Arabs: The Israeli Security Services and the Israeli Arabs*, Jerusalem: Ivreet [Hebrew].

—— (2008) *The Army of Shadows*, Berkeley: University of California Press.

"Compilation Prepared by the Office of the High Commissioner for Human Rights, in Accordance with Paragraph 15(b) of the Annex to Human Rights Council Resolution 5/1" (2008), report submitted to the Human Rights Council Working Group on the Universal Periodic Review, Third Session, Geneva, December 1–15, A/HRC/WG.6/3/ISR/2. Available HTTP: <http://www.ohchr.org>.

Criminal Appeal 1302/92, *State of Israel v. Nahmias, Compilation of Israeli Supreme Court Decisions* [*Piski Din*], 49(3): 309, 353 [Hebrew].

Criminal Appeal 2963/98, *Galam v. the State of Israel*, June 13, 1999 [Hebrew].

Criminal Appeal 6640/90, *Krokhmel v. the State of Israel*, September 7, 2006 [Hebrew].

Criminal Appeal 7368/05, *Zlotovskil v. the State of Israel*, September 4, 2005 [Hebrew].

Criminal Procedural (Enforcement Powers – Arrests) Law, 1996, *Compilation of Laws of Israel* [*Sefer Hakhukim*], No. 1592, May 12: 338.

Criminal Procedural Ordinance (Arrest and Search) (New Version), 1969, *Compilation of Laws of Israel* [*Dene Medinat Israel*], No. 12: 284.

Criminal Procedures (Enforcement Powers – Communication Data) Law, 2007, *Compilation of Laws of Israel* [*Sefer Hakhukim*], No. 2122, December 27: 72.

Danon, Yetzhak (1999) "A Settlement in the Police Tender for CCT: Megason and Epcon – Subcontractors," *Haaretz*, August 26 [Hebrew].

Entry into Israel Law, 1952, as amended on August 7, 1985, *Compilation of the Laws of Israel* [*Sefer Hakhukim*], No. 1156: 213.

Governmental Memorandum Concerning Biometric ID Card, Travel Document and Database (2008). Available HTTP: <http://my.ynet.co.il/pic/computers/04.06.2008/Copy%20of%20biometri.pdf>.

Halabi, Usama (1989) *The Druze in Israel from a Sect to a Nation?* Jerusalem: Academic Association in the Golan Heights [Arabic].

—— (2007) *Israeli Laws and Judicial System as a Tool for Accomplishing Political Objectives in Jerusalem*, Jerusalem: Civic Coalition for Defending the Palestinians' Rights in Jerusalem.

HCJ 8070/98, *Association for Civil Rights in Israel v. Ministry of Interior and 6 Others*, *Compilation of Israeli Supreme Court Decisions* [*Piski Din*], 58(4): 842 [Hebrew].

HCJ 3809/08, *Association for Civil Rights in Israel v. the Israeli Police and 16 Others*. Available HTTP: <http://www.acri.org.il> [Hebrew].

Ilan, Shahar (2007a) "Data: About 1250 Wiretappings Were Conducted in 2006, 20 Times More on Average per Person than in the US," *Haaretz*, July 23 [Hebrew].

—— (2007b) "Knesset Approves the Establishment of 'Big Brother' Database for Police," *Haaretz*, December 18 [Hebrew].

—— (2007c) "Out of 400 Applications for Secret Wiretapping Submitted by Police to District Courts in Jerusalem, Haifa and Bier Shiva, Only 3 Were Rejected," *Haaretz*, June 10 [Hebrew].

—— (2008) "Police Wiretappings Climb Sharply in Peripheral areas," *Haaretz*, May 18 [Hebrew].

Inclusion of Biometric Identification Tools and Biometric Identification Information in Identification Documents and in Database Law, 2009, *Compilation of the Laws of Israel* [*Sefer Hakhukim*], No. 2217: 256.

Inclusion of Biometric Identification Tools in Identification Documents and in Database Bill, 2008, *Compilation of Governmental Bills* [*Hatsaot Khok*], No. 408: 1.

"Israel's National Report Submitted in Accordance with Paragraph 15(a) of the Annex to Human Rights Council Resolution 5/1" (2008), report submitted to the Human Rights Council Working Group on the Universal Periodic Review, Third Session, Geneva, December 1–15, A/HRC/WG.6/3/ISR/1. Available HTTP: <http://www.ohchr.org>.

Klinger, Jonathan (2008) "Establishing a Biometric Database Might Harm Israel's Foreign Trade," *2JK*, December 5. Available HTTP: <http://2jk.org/praxis/?p=1673>.

Knesset Constitution, Law and Justice Committee (2008) "The 'Big Brother' Law: The Israeli Police Demanded from Communication Companies Data that Law Does Not Allow in Order to Build a Data Bank," press release, August 13.

Ministry of the Interior (2002) *Emigration and Settlement of Foreigners in Israel*, Jersualem: Ministry of the Interior.

Nationality and Entry into Israel Law, 2003, *Compilation of the Laws of Israel* [*Sefer Hakhukim*], No. 1901: 544.

Order Concerning the Nationality and Entry into Israel Law (Temporary Order), 2008, *Israel Official Gazette*, No. 6692, July 15: 1134.

Or-Haf, Dan (2008) "Israel: A New National Biometric Database Threatens Privacy," *Law.co*. Available HTTP: <http://www.law.co.il/en/articles/privacy>.

Pinchuk, Avner (2009) "Ministry of Interior Promises to Protect Biometric Data – In the

Meanwhile it Transfers Illegally Private Information." Available HTTP: <http://acri-antibiometric.blogspot.com/2009/01/blog-post_22.html>.

Passports Law, 1950, *Compilation of the Laws of Israel [Sefer Hakhukim]*, No. 102: 160.

Police Ordinance (New Version), 1971, *Compilation of Laws of Israel [Dene Medinat Israel]*, No. 17, March 21: 390. Available HTTP: <http://www.police.gov.il/mehozot/manat/pshia/Pages/mabat2000.aspx>.

Population Registry Law, 1965, *Compilation of the Laws of Israel [Sefer Hakhukim]*, No. 466: 270.

Population Registry Law (Amendment No. 11), 2007, the *Compilation of the Laws of Israel [Sefer Hakhukim]*, No. 2092: 2297.

Population Registry Regulations, 1990, *Compilation of Israeli Regulations [Kovitz Ha-Takanot]*, No. 5243, December 21: 370.

Population Registry Regulations, 2003, *Compilation of Israeli Regulations [Kovitz Ha-Takanot]*, No. 6160, March 25: 584.

Protection of Privacy Law, 1981, *Compilation of the Laws of Israel [Sefer Hakhukim]*, No. 1011, March 3: 128.

Ronen, Erez (2008) "The Biometric Database Bill Passes First Vote," *YNet*, October 29. Available HTTP: <http://www.ynetnews.com/articles/0,7340,L-3614965,00.html>.

S. and Marper v. the United Kingdom (Applications nos. 30562/04 and 30566/04). Available HTTP: <http://www.bailii.org/eu/cases/ECHR/2008/1581.html>.

Salah, Sheikh Ra'ed (2008) "The Optimistic Observer," *Kul Al-Arab Weekly*, March 6 [Arabic].

Secret Wiretapping Law, 1979, *Compilation of Laws of Israel [Sefer Hakhukim]*, No. 938, February 12: 118.

State Comptroller and Ombudsman of Israel (2008) *Annual Report*. Available HTTP: <http://www.mevaker.gov.il/serve/folderAdmin.asp?id=57&sw=1024&hw=698>.

"Summary Prepared by the Office of the High Commissioner for Human Rights, in Accordance with Paragraph 15(c) of the Annex to Human Rights Council Resolution 5/1" (2008), report submitted to the Human Rights Council Working Group on the Universal Periodic Review, Third Session, Geneva, December 1–15, A/HRC/WG.6/3/ISR/3. Available HTTP: <http://www.ohchr.org>.

11 Orange, green and blue

Color-coded paperwork for Palestinian population control

Helga Tawil-Souri

Introduction

As any traveler within Israel and the occupied Palestinian territories knows, and particularly as any Palestinian knows, the Israeli state practices, and arguably perfects, a logic of territorial and population control, monitoring and surveillance. One form is technological: computer databases, drones, x-ray machines, cameras, radars and hi-tech surveillance techniques that instill both fear and awe (Parsons and Salter 2008; Denes 2008; Gordon 2008). Another form is physical and geographically violent: walls, fences, checkpoints, turnstiles, settlements, bypass roads, bulldozers and machine guns (Bowman 2008; Abujidi 2008; Hanafi 2008; Segal and Weizman 2003; Weizman 2007; see Figure 11.1).

At the same time, Palestinians in the West Bank, Gaza Strip and Israel itself claim that the state of Israel, through various methods, simultaneously attempts to thwart, isolate, fragment, transfer and erase them: slowly kill them all; send them off to neighboring Arab countries, such as Jordan; strangle them geographically, politically, economically and militarily until they accept their subordination. This is not a chimerical claim of ethnic cleansing (Pappe 2006; Bowman 2008), but a reality that can be analyzed as a technical problem of the geopolitical conditions of Palestinians' status. It is no secret that "the mere existence of the Palestinian people is a major strategic impediment to the realization of classical Zionist ambitions;" and thus

Figure 11.1 Geographic violence: a bulldozer and Israeli soldiers moving concrete, with wall and tower in the background (Qalandia checkpoint, 2005)

exclusion "forms the logical background of a segregational policy that erects defensive walls of legal, institutional, and physical kinds to prevent Palestinians access to land, institutions, or other rights that could threaten Jewish hegemony" (Butenschon 2000: 20–21).

These two realities come together to form a cognitive dissonance: on the one hand, the Israeli state is accused of trying to get rid of Palestinians; on the other, the state institutes an impressive infrastructure of control and containment. Against the background of transfer, fragmentation and erasure exists an institutional logic of keeping Palestinians where they are: subjects of continued, if changing forms of, occupation and oppression. In other words, there may very well be a practice of fragmenting, isolating, transferring and erasing Palestinians, but they still need to be counted, documented, monitored and controlled first. The clearest way to grapple with this disconnect is to reconsider the familiar experience of traveling through a checkpoint, as was – and in many parts still is – common in the early 2000s throughout the occupied Palestinian territories (OPTs). At every checkpoint exists an under-theorized manifestation of a low-tech, visible, physical and tactile means of power: the ID card.

Identification cards – by which I mean specifically both the *hawiyya* (the physical card) and the *tassrih'* (the paper permit) – form an important nexus of power. They are the physical and visible symbols of a widespread surveillance mechanism. ID cards are also low-tech material artifacts of the everyday experience of how and where theoretical and technical concerns about surveillance intersect. As described below, every Palestinian must hold an ID card which is necessary for much more than crossing checkpoints. IDs are the spaces in which Palestinians meet, confront, accept and sometimes challenge the Israeli state (and, to a lesser extent, the Palestinian Authority too).

In what follows, I trace the development of the modern-day incarnation of the Palestinian ID card, since the establishment of Israel, and situate IDs in the tradition of a modernist state bureaucracy. Then I argue that ID cards, as material artifacts, function as a form of media: they are contradictory, interpreted in various ways, and are records of a particular culture at a particular time. As has already been seen, the

Figure 11.2
Checking IDs at the Huwwara checkpoint (2003)

chapter also relies on photographs to explore how control and surveillance are manifested, offering readers visual examples of these material artifacts above and beyond a description and analysis of them.

Color-coded bureaucracy

During one of my research trips, in early 2003, I lost my wallet; so, in a busy downtown Gaza City market, I bought a bright orange ID carrying case to use as a temporary holder for my money. Soon afterwards, on a visit to Tel Aviv, I was having dinner with a Jewish-Israeli acquaintance, Itamar, an active member of left-wing Israeli peace groups. As we reached for our respective wallets, Itamar shrieked at the sight of my orange case: "Where did you get that?" He explained that in his network of peaceniks, it was a sign of anarchy and honor to defy Israeli state laws and use an orange case rather than the blue one assigned to Israelis. Orange carrying cases were hard to come by in Israel proper, so I happily gave Itamar an extra one I had purchased. This particular case had the IDF insignia on it, in Hebrew.

While I had noticed the different colors in my time in Israel, the West Bank and the Gaza Strip, it had not occurred to me that certain colors held political and symbolic significance. So it was that I learned of a color-coded bureaucracy: residents of the Gaza Strip were assigned orange cases, residents of the West Bank were assigned green ones, and residents of Israel were assigned blue ones. The cards themselves, issued by Israel's Ministry of the Interior, were all a dull white, but they were universally known by the color of the casing in which they were obliged to be housed.

Behind a confusing colored history lies a system of population surveillance whose roots can be traced to a longer tradition of a key component of state power and ability to control who enters or leaves a territory and who moves within it (Torpey 2000; Caplan and Torpey 2001). Thanks to bureaucratic and technical advances, passports, as early forms of ID cards, emerged in the nineteenth century and gave rise to the panoptic and totalizing power of the state. Citizenship itself emerged in the eighteenth and nineteenth centuries as a political mechanism combating class-based social inequalities. Increasingly, citizenship – and its paper form of passports and IDs – also became a site of struggle for different minorities (Kook 2000). Identification papers also became necessary ritual aspects of the state and gave rise to differing responses on the part of various citizens. The orange ID case that Itamar desired held a certain kind of symbolic capital for him and his fellow peaceniks, but it also represents a range of issues, some particular to Israel/Palestine, some not.

State-issued ID cards were introduced in Israel in 1949 after the November 1948 census (Davis 1997; Kassim 2000; Leibler 2008). All Jews – whether having resided in Palestine prior to May 1948 or arriving from elsewhere – were given cards. ID cards were issued to the 165,000 or so Palestinians not expelled from within what would become Israel (thereafter commonly referred to as the "Arab-Israeli" population). They were given the cards not so as to incorporate them into Israeli civic and political life *per se*, but so as to *prevent* the return of the 750,000-plus Palestinian refugees who had been expelled or fled, who were then considered "absentees" and thus denied Israeli citizenship and any possibility of return. Palestinian residents of Israel had to prove continuous residence in Israel between 1949 and 1952 in order to qualify for Israeli citizenship, which was eventually granted, in theory at least, in 1952 (Davis

1997). As Ilan Pappe notes, "the worst offence [for an "Arab-Israeli" during the late 1940s and early 1950s] was not being in possession of one of the newly-issued identity cards" (Pappe 2006: 201). Although the cards were mandatory before then, it was not until the Population Registration Law of 1962 that every person aged sixteen and above had to be registered in the Population Registry, administered by the Interior Ministry, and to carry an ID card at all times.

From 1952 until 1967, only Palestinians within the Israeli state were issued cards. Those residing in the West Bank and the Gaza Strip were issued Jordanian passports (downgraded to travel documents in 1988, after Jordan relinquished its claim to the West Bank) and Egyptian *laissez-passer* documents, respectively. After Israel's occupation of the Palestinian territories in 1967, all Palestinians there were issued orange ID cards – the one Itamar was so keen on having. Any Palestinian barred from entry into Israel (usually, but not always, a person with a previous arrest record) was issued a green card. Whether orange or green, these cards did not serve as travel documents or grant Palestinians any political rights.

The cards themselves contained the usual information such cards hold globally (name, date of birth, place of residence, etc.), with the unique Israeli addition of "nationality." Here, one was identified as Jewish, Arab, or Druze; alternatively, the country of origin was indicated for those who were neither Jewish nor Palestinian. From the beginning, Israel was established "through an inborn *distinction* between country, statehood, and citizenship" (Kook 2000: 267; original emphasis), whereby the national identity of Israel's citizens and the state itself were determined by religious identity. Judaism became the basis of political and national identity. Until 2005, ID cards stated the bearer's "nationality," wherein only "Jewish" was the criteria for full citizenship. As David Lyon (2008) notes:

> the Population Registry Act, by distinguishing between nationality and citizenship, permitted [Israeli] Arabs to be "citizens" of the state but not the nation. And this "nationality" appears on IDs, earlier in name, now in numeric code, and determines permitted residential zones, access to welfare programs, and the kind of treatment the bearer may expect from civil servants and police officers.

Although "nationality" is today marked only with eight asterisks, some details still allow an official to know whether the card-holder is a Jew, such as the date of birth (given in Hebrew for Jews) and the numbering system (Halabi 2008), which denotes whether the holder is Jewish or Palestinian. As such,

> Israel . . . [is a] good example of a case where citizenship does not necessarily serve as an inclusionary mechanism and where citizenship is actually incapable of seriously combating the structures of social inequality. Indeed, citizenship itself, its contents and parameters, embody the structure of social inequality.
> (Kook 2000: 267)

After the Oslo Accords, the responsibility of issuing ID cards to Palestinian residents in the OPTs was handed over to the Palestinian Authority (PA) in 1994, but with final approval maintained by the Israeli Interior Ministry. The new carrying cases were green, with Arabic script and the PA insignia on the cover. (The PA might have opted for green because this color symbolizes Palestinian land on the Palestinian flag, although no official reason for the choice has ever been given.) The numbering system and the final permission for issuing ID cards remained with the Israeli Interior Ministry, although an applicant had to go through the motions with PA officials – another example of Israel's subjective occupation and the post-Oslo "charade of prosthetic sovereignty" assigned to the PA (Weizman 2007: 159). Some Palestinians did not bother to get green carrying cases, since the "new" cards were functionally no different than the old ones. Also, green carrying cases were introduced by the PA in the West Bank first, so one sees more there than in the Gaza Strip – thus it just *seems* that those from the West Bank were issued green and those from Gaza were issued orange. (There was a brief moment in the early 1990s when day-laborers from Gaza were issued red cards by the Israeli administration, but this was abandoned after border and police officials confused these cards with diplomatic passports.)

While newer cards may not immediately identify who is Jewish and who is not, their color-codedness still does, for every Palestinian from the OPTs carries an orange or green card. Put another way, every Jewish-Israeli, no matter if one lives in Israel proper or in an illegal outpost deep in the West Bank, carries a blue ID card. A number of contradictions arise from an unevenly spread color-coding. First, there is a deep-seated irony in recognizing – on paper, no less – that Palestinians actually live in the OPTs, and by issuing those residents a different color, the state of Israel is implicitly recognizing that the OPTs are not unproblematically part of *Eretz Israel*. Second, different laws apply to Jewish-Israelis which do not affect territorial jurisdiction; settlers, especially, enjoy a kind of mobile sovereignty accompanying them wherever they go or reside in Israel/Palestine. The legal distinction between those who are due the protection of the Israeli state is ultimately based on an ethno-national category demarcated by orange, green and blue. (Israel's Ministry of the Interior has recently begun issuing new biometric cards for all residents of Israel/Palestine that no longer have to be carried in specific carrying cases. While the colors will fade with this new technology, the differentiations marked on the cards themselves will continue, most notably in the numbering system and the printed language.) Third, in similar vein, while the Israeli state's boundaries are contested, borders are being instituted on paper in the form of colored ID cards. On the one hand, this system speaks to the recognition of the porosity of borders in a globalized world (where Jews in the OPTs, although illegally there, carry blue ID cards); on the other, it is also a mechanism of instituting hard, concrete boundaries and barriers for others (Palestinians in the OPTs). Thus the borders erected through colored IDs serve as the frames for actual Palestinian communities. Colored carrying cases are the encasing mechanisms determining the geographic limits of Palestinians' open-air prisons.

There is one further level of contradiction, which is that the Arab-Israeli population and the Palestinian residents of Jerusalem after 1967 were issued blue cards (although they may be given the option of whether to adopt an Israeli passport – not that they are provided with an alternative if they turn one down). Thus, although some Palestinian communities are "covered by blue," they are still unequal citizens and are differentiated on their IDs according to their ethno-nationality. The limits imposed on Palestinians within Israel are painfully evident:

at once included via the mechanism of formal citizenship and excluded from the community of fate, regarded as right-bearing citizens and serialized state subjects and simultaneously criminalized as "usual suspects" of disloyalty and unfaithfulness, *Palestinians stand at the center of the state desire for control, discipline, and regulation* of the most minute levels of conduct of those who are members of the society and polity yet do not belong to them.

(Kemp 2004: 73–74; emphasis added)

For the Palestinians within Israel, discipline and surveillance are applied systematically in order to limit the community's participation in civic politics (see Zureik 2001, 2008). The colors of control may be different for Palestinians in Israel and those in the OPTs, but the underlying logic of each is similar: to use ID cards as instruments of control and surveillance. ID cards symbolize another form of Israel's policy of ethnically and territorially segregating its Palestinian population(s), whether within Israel or in the OPTs (see Zureik 2001, 2008; Segal and Weizman 2003; Weizman 2007; Hanafi 2008).

Modernist subjects of "state" administration

ID cards share a common history with other systems of registration, such as censuses and passports, in that they are a modernist instrument of control, stemming from a larger need for state surveillance. Surveillance itself is associated with modernity and the rise of the nation-state, in which state-authorized surveillance mechanisms (of which ID cards are but one) are couched in the universal, non-discriminatory language of security, safety and technological/bureaucratic advancement (Scott 1998; Caplan and Torpey 2001; Lyon 1994, 2007). Thus ID cards emerge from a longer historical tradition, based on the need of a modern industrial state, and especially a colonial-like one, to control its territory and population. They amount to mobile and tactile versions of the "files" states use to store information about their subjects, which are "crucial in states' efforts to embrace their citizens" (Torpey 1998: 245); or crucial in making subjects "legible" (Scott 1998). ID cards reflect the state's need to supervise growth, supervise spatial distribution and the social composition of its population, and control movement within its territory.

Once ID cards become mandatory for everyone, they easily become a requirement for legitimate movement *within* a state's territory, as well as in and out of that territory. In the words of Torpey, "states *must* embrace societies *in order to* penetrate them effectively. Individuals who remain beyond the embrace of the state necessarily represent a limit on its penetration. The *reach* of the state, in other words, cannot exceed its *grasp*" (Torpey 1998: 244; original emphases). This is the way to understand the cognitive dissonance between Israel's plans to erase or stultify its Palestinian population and at the same time issue it mandatory ID cards. If Israel is going to "penetrate" the Palestinians, whether to keep tabs on them or to get rid of them, the latter first need to be within Israel's grasp. ID cards, along with an array of other controlling and encasing mechanisms described throughout this volume, provide Israel with precisely that kind of power. They achieve a central goal: supervising the Palestinian population, neither (immediately) liquidating it nor integrating it into the fabric of Israeli society, but controlling it and rendering it manageable to state power.

Adriana Kemp describes this contradiction as follows: "while the ethnonational drive is to exclude and segregate the 'Other,' the governmentality logic strives toward an ever more total incorporation of the minorities as subjects of the bureaucratic, disciplinary, and administrative mechanisms of the state" (Kemp 2004: 80).

ID cards are part of a larger process to "deprive people of the freedom to move across certain spaces and to render them dependent on states and the state system for the authorization to do so" (Torpey 1998: 239). As such, they enforce multiple levels of hegemony. First, they necessarily lead to an acceptance of a modern form of subjectifying on the part of their bearer; simply because in order to survive and access basic civic needs, one needs an ID card. Second, they lead to an acceptance of Israel's control of Palestinian population movement, since the state "embraces" its subjects (not all of whom are citizens) and monopolizes their means of legitimate movement (Torpey 1998; Lyon 1994, 2001; see also Bornstein 2002; Kelly 2006a; Abu-Zahra 2008). ID cards represent the effort of Israel to "grasp" the Palestinian population and monopolize control over its legitimate movement. Moreover, IDs bespeak the power of the Israeli state: "legitimized with reference to population registration, the creation of ID cards is a strict monopoly" (Abu-Zahra 2008: 177) that only the state can impose upon subjects. ID cards necessarily lead to an acceptance of Israeli state domination. No matter what a Palestinian's perspective is on Israel, occupation, negotiations, peace, the legitimacy of the state, or any other contentious issue, she or he must in the end accept the terms of control instituted by Israel. A Palestinian must turn into a modernist subject of state administration in order to function within both the Israeli state and the Palestinian proto-state. ID cards are thus one of the most tactile, everyday, mundane yet fundamental experiences of agreeing to Israel's terms of domination. Card numbering, card colors, the issuing of cards and the issuing of *tassarih'* all necessitate Palestinians' acknowledgment of the system of Israeli control (and occupation) as the mechanism of approval (see Figure 11.3).

The mechanism of approval is not simply political, but functions economically as well. The color-coded bureaucracy of ID cards is tied to economic power and conditions, particularly relations of economic dependency. ID cards serve the economic needs of the Israeli state. If we re-analyze settlements, roads, checkpoints and other

Figure 11.3
Women trying to pass the Qalandia checkpoint during Ramadan: while they may be openly defying the policies of the Israeli state by refusing to leave the closed check-point, by virtue of owning an ID card they are also subjects of the Israeli state and its forms of domination (2006)

structures as means of building gated communities in a new neo-liberal order (Segal and Weizman 2003; Weizman 2007), then ID cards and especially *tassarih'* are means by which to ensure lower wages to Palestinians individually and to preserve a core–periphery relationship collectively. Not long after the 1967 occupation, Israel ordered a mandatory collective permit over all Palestinians to enter Israel. The blanket law rendered Palestinians dependent on the Israeli economy (Roy 1999), thereby maximizing the cost of resistance (Farsakh 2005) and served Israel's need for cheap labor (Bornstein 2002; Nitzan and Bichler 2002). A Palestinian from the OPTs cannot enter Israel without a *tassrih'*. Moreover, without a patron in Israel to begin the process of permission, a Palestinian is perpetually imprisoned in the OPTs. This system reinforces dependency on individual Israeli employers, increases the potential for unfair labor practices, and thus results in further cheapening the already cheap labor that Palestinians provide (Bornstein 2002; Farsakh 2005; Kelly 2006a). The exploitability of Palestinian laborers for employers' benefits in this case results from a complex political and bureaucratic process. Thus, here, the surveillance practice of ID cards does not simply prevent entry into Israel but functions as a way to discipline Palestinians to work hard and accept low wages. The maintenance of a border regime, of which ID cards and permits are imperative, renders Palestinian workers vulnerable to exploitation by Israeli employers. A Palestinian is tolerated as a unit of labor, while explicitly stigmatized as a person, or as a member of a family or community. Although the following quote by John Torpey was meant in terms of its political consequence, it is equally relevant for its economic connotation: "in order to extract the resources they need to survive . . . states must embrace – that is, identify and gain enduring access to – those from whom it hopes to derive those resources" (Torpey 1998: 246).

There is at least one other way in which ID cards function as means of subjectifying people as pawns of state power, which I shall not elaborate on here. Suffice to say that people become dependent on a state for the possession of an "identity" (Torpey 1998; Kelly 2006a, 2006b), so ID cards "reveal a massive illiberality, a presumption of their bearers' guilt when called upon to identify themselves" (Torpey 1998: 255).

ID cards lead to both deprivation and entitlement, to an automation of privilege and exclusion. In the case of Israel, the uneven issuing of colored ID cards stems from a larger strategy of accounting for and controlling different populations differently and unevenly. As Anis Kassim notes of the larger project of the state of Israel, so it is for the practice of issuing color-coded and numerically coded ID cards: "if the creation of a Jewish state was intended to 'normalize' the status of Jews, it also ironically resulted in 'abnormalizing' the status of the Palestinians" (Kassim 2000: 202). Palestinians have been subject to ongoing attempts to make them more legible, accessible, embraceable, for the "security" interests of Israel. But the manner in which Israel has dealt unevenly with the issuing of color-coded (or more recently numerically coded) ID cards brings into question the very nature of the state of Israel, its supposed democratic ethos, and its responsibility as an occupier. Torpey argues that the use of internal passports in contemporary times (which function in the same manner as Israel/Palestine's green and orange cards) to control movement within state boundaries "bespeaks illegitimate, authoritarian governments lording it over subdued or terrorized populations. Internal passports and passes constitute a reversion to practices generally abandoned by democratic nation-states by the twentieth century" (Torpey 1998: 254–255). Torpey also argues that when state controls on movement operate within a state, and especially when done so to the detriment of a particular "negatively privileged" group, such as the Palestinians in Israel/Palestine, "we can reliably expect to find an authoritarian state (or worse)" (Torpey 1998: 243). In this case, the "worse" is still up for debate: what kind of oppressive state is Israel: an apartheid state (Davis 1989), an ethnocratic state (Yiftachel 2006), or a racist state (Lentin 2008)?

As much as ID cards have been necessary for the Israeli state to control and surveil Palestinian populations, they have also, since the Oslo Agreements, been necessary for Palestinian Authority bureaucracy. The very system that allowed for Israeli hegemony has led the way for PA control over Palestinians. (A similar argument is made about the inheritance of economic controls by the PA from Israel by Sara Roy (1999).) More importantly in the context of the post-Oslo OPTs, ID cards became necessary not just for crossing checkpoints or "trespassing" between territories, but for all the necessities of life and internal bureaucracy. "The document held by individuals as 'ID' . . . corresponds to an entire series of files chronicling movements, economic transactions, familial ties, illnesses, and much else besides – the power/ knowledge grid in which individuals are processed and constituted as administrative subjects of states" (Torpey 1998: 248). In other words, an ID card becomes a principal mean for discriminating (positively and negatively) among subjects in terms of rights and privileges. Accessing basic human necessities, or, if one prefers, accessing "bare life," today requires an ID card.

It is impossible to enumerate all the rights and privileges that an ID card affords a Palestinian "citizen," but we can list a few. ID cards are mandatory for a range of financial needs: opening a bank account, withdrawing money from a teller, applying for a credit card. They are asked for when applying for jobs, especially government or NGO jobs, which have become almost the only viable careers for Palestinians (see Figure 11.4). Many companies and government institutions remit employee salaries through banks which require an employee to show his or her ID. Any governmental and/or civil transaction requires an ID: registering a marriage, death or birth; accessing healthcare benefits; high school matriculation; establishing residency; paying taxes; or obtaining a permit for private construction needs, such as extending one's home. In order for Palestinians to vote, be it in parliamentary or presidential elections, they must submit their ID cards to PA election authorities. Refugees who need to apply formally to the UNRWA – whether for food supplies or to register children at the local school – will be asked for their *hawiyya* (above and beyond their UNRWA-issued cards). A Palestinian who wishes to perform the Hajj will also be asked for an ID card. As noted earlier, Palestinian laborers who depend on blue-collar jobs inside Israel require an ID, and one is also necessary for those within the territories who have been separated from their families by barricades, walls, checkpoints or other mechanisms and wish to apply for the arduous "family reunification" plan. In fact any form of travel that takes a Palestinian out of his or her Bantustan, and certainly out of Israel, necessitates an Israeli-issued ID card.

Identification papers are also necessary for more mundane, but in some cases importantly political, reasons. For example, an ID functions as a legal proof of birth, so Palestinians who were born within "1948 Palestine" proudly show their cards to substantiate that they are from Haifa, Jaffa or Ramleh and thus fortify their claims to those cities. (This is particularly meaningful in the case of Palestinians born in towns

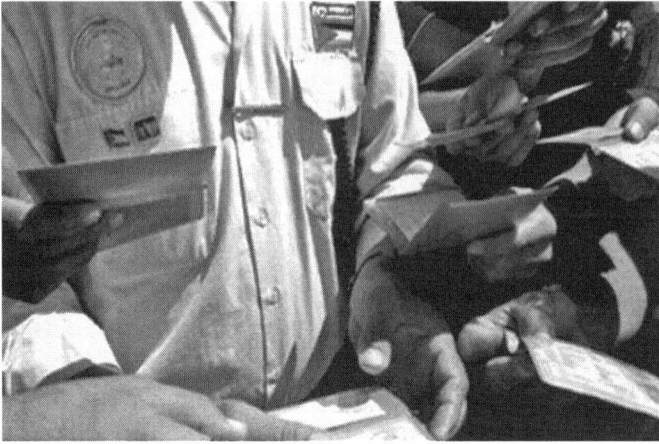

Figure 11.4 Young men handing over ID cards to a Palestinian
policeman in the hope of getting a job (West Bank, 2006)

and villages that no longer exist.) ID cards also function as proof of a person's age. Miriam Amash, an Arab-Israeli, was recently recorded as the world's oldest living person, born in 1888. While she may not look over 120 years old, her ID clearly indicates that she is.

In short, life without an ID for any Palestinian adult would be impossible, for it provides a "citizen" with the necessary access to circuits of civility. ID cards function as both necessities for "bare life" and as a means of condemning Palestinians to their lesser status in a perpetual "state of exception" (since not all ID cards are created equal in the eyes of the Israeli state). On the one hand, Palestinians need ID cards for every aspect of life, from movement to retrieval of income; on the other, with an orange or green ID card in hand (or blue with an identifying serial number, in the case of Arab-Israelis), Palestinians end up as subjects of Israeli bureaucratic domination that may very well serve the end purpose of "transferring" them.

ID cards "produce legibility and illegibility, stability and instability, coherence and incoherence in the interactions between those who speak in the name of the Israeli state and those subjected to their force" (Kelly 2006a: 90). For Palestinians in the OPTs, the implications of holding a *hawiyya* and a *tassrih'* are central to their life chances, as they enable them to move around and gain access to resources and rights. Simultaneously, Tobias Kelly shows that

> the implications of holding identity documents are always partial and unstable, as the laws and regulations that give them meaning are often incoherent . . . the result is that even as people try to gain a measure of security through holding the right documents, these same documents also mean that their lives are shot through with fear and uncertainty.
>
> (Kelly 2006a: 90)

Media and material artifacts

In the words of Michel Foucault, an ID card, as a modern system of identification, fixes identity to a bureaucratic need, "places individuals in a field of surveillance [and] situates them in a network of writing: it engages them in a whole mass of documents that capture and fix them" (Foucault 1979: 189). As mentioned earlier, an ID card represents a technical and tactile response to the geopolitical "problem" of Palestinian presence throughout Israel and the OPTs. The bureaucracy embedded in the ID card – the institutions such as the Ministry of the Interior, the national and global discourse about security and modernity, the cards' colors and number structures, what kind of information is encoded on them – exemplifies a particular institutional logic of modern-day Israel: to count, document, monitor and control Palestinians. Moreover, as Nadia Abu-Zahra succinctly puts it, "IDs are part of the materiality of coercion and control" (Abu-Zahra 2008: 177). The previous sections and the photographs that are reproduced throughout this chapter demonstrate the cards' role in the coercion and control of Palestinians. But Abu-Zahra also calls them part of a materiality, evoking Foucault's statement of ID cards being materialized in a mass of paperwork (sometimes a mess of paperwork). In the following sections I focus on this "network of writing," the materiality that both Foucault and Abu-Zahra describe. For ID cards function as material artifacts of a people being erased, a recorded form of media – printed on paper, and more recently on plastic – that is evidence of Palestinians' presence during the last half of the twentieth century and the beginning of the twenty-first.

To focus on ID cards' materiality and argue that they function as media does not suggest that we ought to spotlight our gaze microscopically on them as nothing but written documents. Media and material artifacts are not simply abstract entities but significant parts of the wider institutional and political context in which they are produced, take effect, and evoke meaning. Tobias Kelly argues – and demonstrates in his own research – that

> this means looking directly at documents in order to analyze how they are experienced by their subjects and used to mediate social and political relation-ships. It also means looking beyond documents to examine the conditions of their production and reception in very particular historical contexts.
>
> (Kelly 2006a: 92; emphasis added)

In order to understand how ID cards are a form of media, it is important to keep in mind that they symbolize the modern method in which identity has become anchored in law and policy. More important is to recognize the technique in which identity has become inscribed on paper. In the case of Israel/Palestine, the label of "nationality" has become an ascribed status which cannot be established without reference to a piece of paper that constructs and sustains enduring identities for administrative purposes. It is not simply that identity is fixed to a person and one's body but that it becomes fixed on paper – a paper without which one cannot exist, either literally or metaphorically.

The materiality of ID cards determines the identity of Palestinians – that is, gives meaning to, provides a limit for, and fixes conclusively – and any ensuing rights and privileges, or lack thereof. As such, ID cards serve as a point of physical and tangible contact between Palestinians and the state of Israel. Whenever a Palestinian hands over their ID card to an Israeli border patrol, soldier or police officer, the card becomes the physical substance through which their relationship is mediated (see Figure 11.5). In some cases the physical contact is humiliating: when Palestinians are taken away in a surprise raid from their homes at night, they are often escorted in nothing but their underwear, in which their ID cards are safely tucked. ID cards are the spaces where the Israeli logic and bureaucracy of population control, state securitization and surveillance meets Palestinians. The card becomes the mediated space where Israeli power over Palestinian geographic mobility and freedom is practiced (see Figure 11.6).

ID cards in the context of Israel/Palestine are not estranged from actual experience, as they may be elsewhere. They are decisive, and sometimes they prove fatal. Israeli officers have the unique power to determine one's "identity" and decide whether one is "guilty" or "innocent," whether one should be allowed to pass a checkpoint or arrested. Sometimes IDs are cross-checked against computer databases or printed sheets of "threatening" individuals (see Figure 11.7), but sometimes not. Almost every Palestinian and foreign traveler in the OPTs has experienced being turned away at a checkpoint without even having had the opportunity to show their ID.

Figure 11.5
Inspecting an ID card: a physical substance through which the relationship between a Palestinian and the state of Israel is mediated (West Bank, 2003)

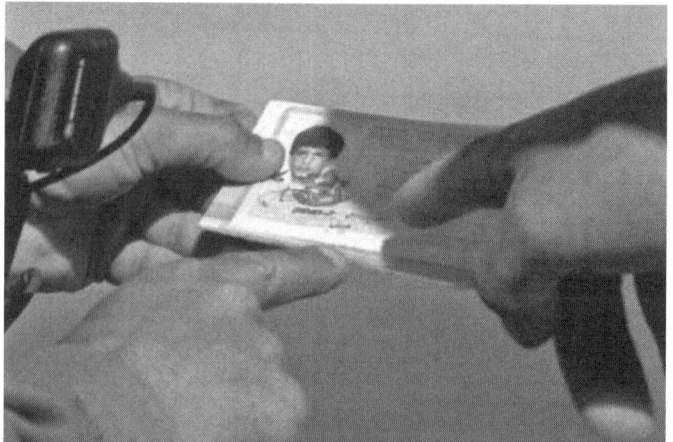

Figure 11.6
Inspection of a teenager's ID card: where paper meets flesh; where identity becomes fixed (Jerusalem, 2005)

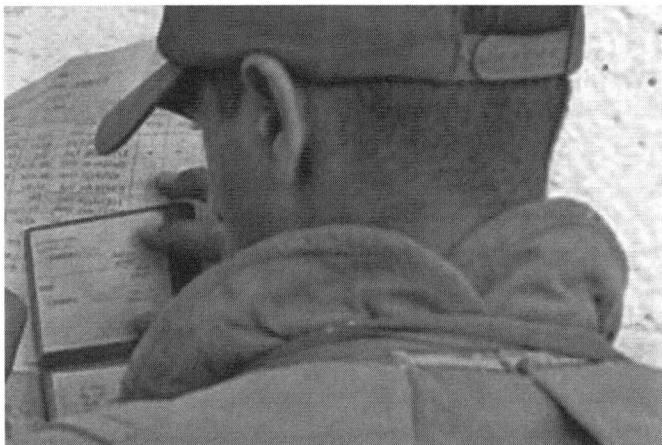

Figure 11.7
Israeli soldier
cross-checking a
Palestinian ID card
(West Bank, 2003)

As artifacts, ID cards function as a form of human interaction, mediating different social and political relationships. Contradictory, polysemic, material objects of a particular culture – there are numerous ways in which they function as media. By "media," I do not mean the entertainment/information institutions which surround us in our contemporary age. I am using the term in a more fundamental, basic and broad manner: as a tool used to store and deliver information or data; a mode of communication that incorporates multiple forms of information content and processing. Also as a mechanism by which we learn and internalize the values, beliefs and norms of our culture, and the material device in which is encoded the dominant (or hegemonic) beliefs and norms of our society, serving as a powerful socializing/ politicizing agent. Media are also bound up with the process of social relations, mediating our relationship with various institutions, affecting how we relate to the world of politics, for example. Approached in this way, the influence of media both in *content* and in *process* on areas of contemporary life is undeniable, as is the impact of the ID card on the social, political, economic and geographic life of a Palestinian.

ID cards are media in a number of differing ways. First, they are standardized, reproduced and personalized, as are increasing forms of media today, such as newspapers (standardized and reproduced), popular music and broadcast programming (reproduced), TiVo settings (standardized and personalized), and web portals such as Google and Yahoo! (standardized, reproduced and personalized). Second, ID cards are media in the sense that interaction between Palestinians and the state of Israel is what David Lyon (2008) – following Emile Durkheim – calls "monological": through an instrumental and tactile power of color and paper rather than human interchange. As such, ID cards are a form of one-way communication (keeping in mind that a state officer determines their meaning), which only increases the frustration and alienation of the subaltern group. Third, ID cards serve ritual needs, especially those of the state. For example, the state of Israel holds ceremonies in which new Jewish immigrants are given their blue ID cards by a leading government official. Similarly, in August 2008 the Hamas government awarded forty-seven Palestinian diplomatic passports to foreign peace activists from the Free Gaza Movement in a public ceremony. Hamas was honoring the docking of the first of the group's ships filled with such humanitarian assistance items as hearing aids, which had sailed from Cyprus to Gaza without Israeli circumvention, thus breaking a siege on Gaza that was in effect at the time (Silverstein 2008; see also the *Free Gaza Movement* Website).

As media, ID cards are cultural/ideological manifestations of power. They serve the national goals of a dominant group – Israel – and the constant preoccupation of the disciplinary state with surveillance or keeping its subjects in check. The regime of IDs and permits enables the "border" to be shaped not simply on the territory itself but on the people residing in it. Media function in a similar fashion by determining the borders of the state and keeping audiences/citizens preoccupied with (sometimes nationalistic, often hegemonic) programming and defining the "imagined community" of a particular nation (Anderson 1991). Moreover, ID cards, as argued earlier, serve particular economic and financial needs of dominant groups, as do many forms of media.

ID cards are also discursive constructs: contested texts subject to interpretation by police officers, border officials and soldiers, on behalf of the state; and open to differing interpretations on the part of their bearers. Cultural, ideological, political and economic all at once, the production and verification of identity documents opens spaces for contestation and disruption. Palestinians are never sure how their ID cards will be interpreted, since it is often at the whim of the soldier manning the checkpoint, for example, to decide whether one is a threat to Israeli security or not. As others have demonstrated in their research, ID cards are simultaneously legible and illegible, stable and instable, coherent and incoherent (Kelly 2006a: 90; specifically for Israel/Palestine, see: Davis 1997; Kassim 2000; Kook 2000; Zureik 2001; Bornstein 2002; Kemp 2004; Abu-Zahra 2008; and more generally see: Scott 1998; Torpey 2000; Caplan and Torpey 2001; Lyon 2001; Migdal 2004; Bennett and Lyon 2008).

ID cards play a contradictory role in the lives of Palestinians in the OPTs and of Palestinian communities within Israel, but as mediated forms they are also open to interpretation. The clearest fashion in which differing (and sometimes anti-hegemonic) readings are manifested is through forms of art that IDs have inspired. The famous British graffiti artist Banksy, whose work has adorned some of the security wall in the West Bank since 2005, stenciled a graffito on a Bethlehem building of an Israeli soldier checking a Christmas donkey's ID card (see Figure 11.8). Situated next to Manger Square, the piece is an ironic take on the politics surrounding the city of Jesus' birth and forms part of an exhibit titled *Santa's Ghetto*. Since its appearance in December 2007, the graffito has been painted over after some residents found it offensive, construing it as equating Palestinians with donkeys (see *Santa's Ghetto* Website). Another example lies outside of the Aida refugee camp in the West Bank, where a group of anonymous Palestinians painted a mural interpretation of an ID card. It depicts many a Palestinian's view of important facets of identity: 1948 is given as the birthday; the father is listed as a prisoner; the mother as murdered; the grandfather simply as "Palestinian." Under "Registration" is written "UN Resolution 194," referring to refugees' right of return (see Figure 11.9). The ID card has also made it into the most famous of Palestinian nationalist poems: Mahmoud Darwish's "I Am an Arab" (1964) begins with the lines "Write down!/I am an Arab/My identity card number is fifty-thousand."

The poem and the Aida mural are Palestinian assertions of identity thrown in the face of a hostile oppressor as expressions of challenge. With Banksy's graffito, the mural

Figure 11.8
Banksy's mural of
an Israeli soldier
checking a
donkey's ID card
(Bethlehem, 2007)

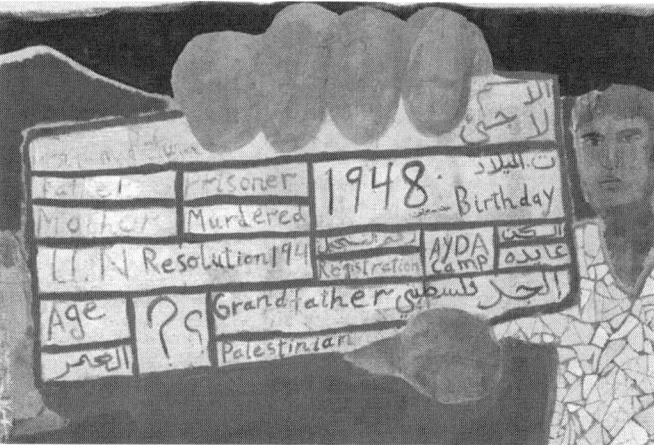

Figure 11.9
Mural art of an ID
card (Aida refugee
camp, 2006)

and the poem, along with other forms of artistic reappropriation, attempt to establish a Palestinian presence, however limited, in the face of an Israeli bureaucracy premised on its denial. These interpretations are just a few examples of how ID cards have been renegotiated and reappropriated by their subjects, conjuring up social and political experiences of great complexity. There are numerous other examples from the media, such as pamphlets, YouTube videos and blogs through which citizens challenge the hegemonic forces of their society.

Finally, as with all media technologies, ID cards also hold within them the possibility of failure, or of a reverse control. In the language of media technology, this is often termed "unintended consequences," suggesting that technologies are not simply determined by their architecture and creators but also by end-users. For example, in June 2006, a Jewish settler was abducted in Gaza. Shortly after his disappearance, a spokesman of the Popular Resistance Committees (PRC) held a press conference to claim responsibility for the settler's abduction and subsequent execution, at which the group distributed photocopies of the abductee's ID card. The PRC had also printed homemade posters (similar to the martyr posters that are familiar across the OPTs) in which the photocopy of the settler's ID card was placed over a background of a blue sky, with a Palestinian flag and the PRC logo atop the page, and camouflaged, armed resistance fighters floating on each side of the card (see Waked 2006 for a photograph and a detailed account of the events). The PRC's use of the ID serves as another example of how mediated forms of communication are open to interpretation and, depending on the powerful agent's perspective, failure. Here, a straight-forward play on "identity" is turned into political challenge using the dominant group's own tools.

Given their ubiquity and necessity among Palestinians, there has been a rise in the practice of forging ID cards. (This is a research area that is difficult – and perhaps dangerous – to explore, but it merits attention.) There are also cases of people lending their cards to friends who look similar to themselves; others who have taken the risk of replacing the photograph on an issued card. In similar vein, especially since the emergence of checkpoints all over the OPTs, Palestinians are increasingly attempting to obtain citizenship from elsewhere and to use those foreign passports to pass checkpoints (see Kelly 2006a). Certainly, circumventing the bureaucracy of Israeli-issued IDs would be one way for a Palestinian to challenge the control and surveillance mechanism more effectively. It is no doubt in response to the traditional ID cards' "user-friendliness" (the ease of changing them through photocopying, forging, replacing photographs, exchanging them with friends) and the desire for foreign passports among Palestinians that Israel is now pursuing the development of biometric cards.

While ID cards give rise to a range of interpretations – Itamar's use of the orange casing as a sign of left-leaning politics, Banksy's satirical representation of a donkey being checked, the PRC photocopying an abducted Israeli's card, Darwish's poem, the rise in contraband cards – they still maintain within their materiality the meaning attributed to them by the Israeli state at a particular political/cultural moment: the Israeli practice of controlling, surveilling and subjugating Palestinians. While Palestinians may be in the process of being silenced and erased, they are well documented; of that there is no doubt. As is typical in colonial situations, the documentation is not instituted by Palestinians themselves but by their oppressors. These documentations function as material artifacts, a printed form of media that attests to Palestinians' continued existence and problematic status within Israel/Palestine. As material artifacts, the cards also serve as proof of existence – in the same way that the settler was proven to have been abducted by virtue of his ID being photocopied by the PRC.

Conclusion

Against the hi-tech fantasy and development of Israeli surveillance (Gordon 2008; Denes 2008; Parsons and Salter 2008; Chapter 7, this volume), and against the state's desire to deploy "advanced technological systems that will minimize human friction" (Israel Ministry of Defense, quoted in Weizman 2007: 150), lies the fundamental need of one of the most low-tech yet highly systematic means of fixing identity to the body.

ID cards remain one of the most effective means of surveillance and an important nexus of power. Behind the sophisticated technological and physical/violent Israeli measures of control and surveillance lies a messy practice of paperwork. Israel may be a highly modernist, capitalist state, but it continues and will continue to rely on certain low-tech means to deal with its political and technical "problem" of the Palestinians.

ID cards function as a materiality of control and surveillance. They are also a form of media, a low-tech interaction that relies on print and paper (or plastic) that can be used by the state for particular means, but can also be used by its subjects in counter-hegemonic ways. Part of the significance of ID cards is precisely their function as media and material artifacts. They serve as a space where the Palestinian subject meets Israeli control. While ID cards operate as one means of population management and surveillance, they continue to rely on a most fundamental, invisible, ubiquitous and modern practice of paperwork. Paperwork does not break, does not need to be backed up, is relatively low cost and is "user-friendly" (in that everyone knows how to handle it and one does not need to read a manual to learn how to use it). In fact, paperwork is at the very heart of governing in a territorial state (Scott 1998). One need only think of various other state controls that rely on it: maps, landownership registrations, license plates, government documents, trade agreements and so forth.

ID cards are a means of both social/political control and social/political exclusion; a way of ensuring access and denying it. As such, they speak directly to that cognitive dissonance that many Palestinians experience: fearing that the Israeli state wants them to disappear, yet simultaneously feeling that they are political subjects of the state's bureaucratic machine. Particular to Israel, but also part of wider patterns of control, disorder and suspicion, ID cards are part of a growing trend of surveillance and the rise of a form of bureaucracy and administration needed for a nation-state, especially in colonial and conflict zones where control and surveillance serve a dual purpose of managing the territory and subjecting the population. There is no dissonance, there is simply the modern practice of control and surveillance; for, as John Torpey (1998) argues, in order to control or penetrate a population, even for the purpose of erasing it, the state must first "embrace" it. (Similarly, ID cards played an important role in differentiating between Hutus and Tutsis during the 1994 genocide in Rwanda; see Longman (2001). See also Lyon (2008) for a comparison of the Palestinian case to that of South Africa.) There is no contradiction, then, between being documented and fearing being "erased," since documentation is very much at the heart of a modernist state's need to control its population and territory, even for the purpose of ridding that territory of a particular subaltern group.

ID cards have played a central role in Palestinian life since the beginning of the twentieth century. Palestinians were subjects of the Ottoman Empire, which issued them travel documents. Under the British Mandate, they became "Turkish subject[s] habitually resident in the territory of Palestine," holding Mandate identity cards (Davis 1997: 44). With the creation of Israel, they were issued blue ID cards, while those in the West Bank and the Gaza Strip received temporary documents from Jordanian and Egyptian authorities, respectively. After 1967 Palestinians in the OPTs were issued green or orange cards. ID cards have been instrumental in the control of Palestinian populations. The same is true of some Palestinian populations outside of Israel/Palestine, most painfully in Lebanon, where Palestinian refugees are issued their own cards to designate them as non-citizen/refugees (Butenschon 2000). This has led Kassim to suggest that "one of the most enigmatic sociolegal phenomena in contemporary studies is the definition of a Palestinian" (Kassim 2000: 203), which is manifested in the fact that the "quintessential Palestinian experience . . . takes place at a border, an airport, a checkpoint: in short at any of those modern barriers where identities are checked and verified" (Khalidi 1997: 1).

A low-tech surveillance technique that relies on monological interaction, a technology to discipline political subjects, a manifestation of the Israeli state's logic of securitization, the ID card will continue to be highly significant in Palestinians' lives, if for no other reason than simply to provide proof of their problematic existence.

Bibliography

Abujidi, N. (2008) "The Palestinian Occupied Territories as Laboratories of the 21st Century Spatial Order," paper presented at the New Transparency Research Workshop on States of Exception, Surveillance and Population Management: The Case of Israel/Palestine, Larnaca, December.

Abu-Zahra, N. (2008) "Identity Cards and Coercion in Palestine," in R. Pain and S.J. Smith (eds) *Fear: Critical Geopolitics and Everyday Life*. Burlington, VT: Ashgate, pp. 175–191.

Anderson, B. (1991) *Imagined Communities*. New York: Verso.

Bennett, C.J. and D. Lyon (eds) (2008) *Playing the Identity Card: Surveillance, Security and Identification in Global Perspective*. New York: Routledge.

Bornstein, A. (2002) *Crossing the Green Line between the West Bank and Israel*. Philadelphia: University of Pennsylvania Press.

Bowman, G. (2008) "Israel's Wall and the Logic of Encystation," paper presented at the New Transparency Research Workshop on States of Exception, Surveillance and Population Management: The Case of Israel/Palestine, Larnaca, December.

Butenschon, N.A. (2000) "State, Power, and Citizenship in the Middle East," in N.A. Butenschon, U. Davis and M. Hassassian (eds) *Citizenship and the State in the Middle East*. Syracuse, NY: Syracuse University Press, pp. 3–27.

Butenschon, N.A., U. Davis and M. Hassassian (eds) (2000) *Citizenship and the State in the Middle East: Approaches and Applications*. Syracuse, NY: Syracuse University Press.

Caplan, J. and J. Torpey (eds) (2001) *Documenting Individual Identity: The Development of State Practices in the Modern World*. Princeton, NJ: Princeton University Press.

Darwish, M. (1964) "I Am an Arab." Online. Available HTTP: <http://www.barghouti.com/poets/darwish/bitaqa.asp> (accessed December 1, 2008).

Davis, U. (1989) *Israel: An Apartheid State*. New York: Zed Books.

—— (1997) *Citizenship and the State: A Comparative Study of Citizenship Legislation in Israel, Jordan, Palestine, Syria and Lebanon*. Reading: Ithaca Press.

Denes, N. (2008) "Universalizing the Unique: Israeli UAV Exports, Border-Security Doctrines and Global War," paper presented at the New Transparency Research Workshop on States of Exception, Surveillance and Population Management: The Case of Israel/Palestine, Larnaca, December.

Farsakh, L. (2005) *Palestinian Labour Migration to Israel: Labour, Land, and Occupation*. New York: Routledge.

Foucault, M. (1979) *Discipline and Punish: The Birth of the Prison*. New York: Vintage.

Free Gaza Movement Website. Online. Available HTTP: <http://www.freegaza.org/> (accessed February 18, 2009)

Gordon, N. (2008) "The Art of Homeland Security: The Political Economy of Israeli Experience," paper presented at the New Transparency Research Workshop on States of

Exception, Surveillance and Population Management: The Case of Israel/Palestine, Larnaca, December.

Halabi, U. (2008) "Legal Analysis and Critique of Some Surveillance Methods Used by Israel," paper presented at the New Transparency Research Workshop on States of Exception, Surveillance and Population Management: The Case of Israel/Palestine Larnaca, December.

Hanafi, S. (2008) "Spacio-cide: Surveillance, Bio-politics and State Exception in the Palestinian Territories," paper presented at the New Transparency Research Workshop on States of Exception, Surveillance and Population Management: The Case of Israel/ Palestine, Larnaca, December.

Kassim, A.F. (2000) "The Palestinians: From Hyphenated to Integrated Citizenship," in N.A Butenschon, U. Davis and M. Hassassian (eds) *Citizenship and the State in the Middle East: Approaches and Applications*. Syracuse, NY: Syracuse University Press, pp. 201–224.

Kelly, T. (2006a) "Documented Lives: Fear and the Uncertainties of Law during the Second Palestinian Intifada," *Journal of the Royal Anthropological Institute* 12(1): 89–107.

—— (2006b) *Law, Violence and Sovereignty among West Bank Palestinians*. Cambridge: Cambridge University Press.

Kemp, A. (2004) "'Dangerous Populations': State Territoriality and the Constitution of National Minorities," in J. Migdal (ed.) *Boundaries and Belonging States and Societies in the Struggle to Shape Identities and Local Practices*. New York: Cambridge University Press, pp. 73–98.

Khalidi, R. (1997) *Palestinian Identity: The Construction of Modern National Consciousness*. New York: Columbia University Press.

Kook, R. (2000) "Citizenship and its Discontents: Palestinians in Israel," in N.A. Butenschon, U. Davis and M. Hassassian (eds) *Citizenship and the State in the Middle East: Approaches and Applications*. Syracuse, NY: Syracuse University Press, pp. 263–287.

Leibler, A. (2008) "Surveillance, National Registration and Citizenship Rights," paper presented at the New Transparency Research Workshop on States of Exception, Surveillance and Population Management: The Case of Israel/Palestine, Larnaca, December.

Lentin, R. (ed.) (2008) *Thinking Palestine*. New York: Zed Books.

Longman, T. (2001) "Identity Cards, Ethnic Self-Perception, and Genocide in Rwanda," in J. Caplan and J. Torpey (eds) *Documenting Individual Identity: The Development of State Practices in the Modern World*. Princeton, NJ: Princeton University Press, pp. 345–357.

Lyon, D. (1994) *The Electronic Eye: The Rise of Surveillance Society*. Minneapolis: University of Minnesota Press.

—— (2001) *Surveillance Society: Monitoring Everyday Life*. Philadelphia, PA: Open University Press.

—— (2007) *Surveillance Studies: An Overview*. Malden: Polity Press.

—— (2008) "Identification, Colonialism and Control: Surveillant Sorting in Israel/Palestine," paper presented at the New Transparency Research Workshop on States of Exception, Surveillance and Population Management: The Case of Israel/Palestine, Larnaca, December.

Migdal, J.S. (ed.) (2004) *Boundaries and Belonging: States and Societies in the Struggle to Shape Identities and Local Practices*. Cambridge: Cambridge University Press.

Nitzan, J. and S. Bichler (2002) *The Global Political Economy of Israel*. Sterling, VA: Pluto Press.

Pain, R. and S.J. Smith (eds) (2008) *Fear: Critical Geopolitics and Everyday Life*. Burlington, VT: Ashgate.

Pappe, I. (2006) *The Ethnic Cleansing of Palestine*. Oxford: Oneworld Publications.

Parsons, N. and M.B. Salter (2008) "Israeli Biopolitics: Closure, Territorialisation and Governmentality in the Occupied Palestinian Territories," *Geopolitics* 13: 701–723.

Roy, S. (1999) "De-Development Revisited: Palestinian Economy and Society since Oslo," *Journal of Palestine Studies* 28(3): 64–82.

Santa's Ghetto Website. Online. Available HTTP: <http://www.santasghetto.com/> (accessed February 18, 2009).

Scott, J. (1998) *Seeing Like a State: How Certain Schemes to Improve the Human Condition Have Failed.* New Haven, CT: Yale University Press.

Segal, R. and E. Weizman (eds) (2003) *Civilian Occupation: The Politics of Israeli Architecture.* New York: Verso.

Silverstein, R. (2008) "The Free Gaza Movement," *Nation*, September 18. Online. Available HTTP: <http://www.thenation.com/doc/20081006/silverstein> (accessed November 14, 2008).

Torpey, J. (1998) "Coming and Going: On the State Monopolization of the Legitimate 'Means of Movement,'" *Sociological Theory* 16(3): 239–259.

—— (2000) *The Invention of the Passport: Surveillance, Citizenship and the State.* New York: Cambridge University Press.

Waked, A. (2006) "PRC: Kidnapping Settler Teen Was Easy," *YNet*, June 29. Online. Available HTTP: <http://www.ynetnews.com/articles/0,7340,L-3269003,00.html> (accessed January 19, 2009).

Weizman, E. (2007) *Hollow Land: Israel's Architecture of Occupation.* New York: Verso.

Yiftachel, O. (2006) *Ethnocracy: Land and Identity Politics in Israel/Palestine.* Philadelphia: University of Pennsylvania Press.

Zureik, E. (2001) "Constructing Palestine through Surveillance Practices," *British Journal of Middle East Studies* 8(2): 205–227.

—— (2008) "State of Exception, Surveillance and Population Management: The Case of Israel/Palestine: An Overview of Research," paper presented at the New Transparency Research Workshop on States of Exception, Surveillance and Population Management: The Case of Israel/Palestine, Larnaca, December.

12 "You must know your stock"

Census as surveillance practice in 1948 and 1967

Anat E. Leibler

Introduction

In 1948, the newly established Jewish state was at war with both the local Arab population of Palestine – the Palestinians – and the neighboring Arab countries. It was a year marked by demographic upheaval: while the Jewish community in Palestine comprised less than a third of the total population toward the end of the British Mandate, beginning in December 1947 many Palestinians either fled or were driven from their homes, leaving the country with a Jewish majority – some 85 percent of the total population. Yet while this numeric balance was considered one of the achievements of the war, the military and political leadership of the new state feared that Palestinians who were driven out or had fled to the surrounding countries might return to Israeli territory, reversing the demographic trend. Despite international pressure to repatriate a large number of Palestinian refugees, Israel was determined to prevent them from returning to their former homes and lands. To this end, the government took several steps under the banner of a "war on infiltration," including razing some of the Arab villages that had been abandoned since the war, and quickly moving to resettle Jewish immigrants on the sites of others. Based on the Emergency Regulations formulated in 1945 by the British Mandate, a Military Government was established to control the Palestinians who had remained in Israel and restrict their movements within the country.

Demography and population management have been central concerns of Israel's leaders since 1948. One of the dominant institutions established in 1948 to assist leaders in their demographic and administrative decisions was the Israeli Central Bureau of Statistics (CBS). Although the CBS played an active role in nation-building and state-formation processes, it has been absent from the social and historical studies of the immediate post-1948 period. In addition to the CBS, a temporary policy-making body named the "Committee Alongside the Military Government" (hereafter the Committee) was nominated to combat the phenomenon of what the Military Government viewed as Palestinian infiltration from outside the Israeli borders, as Robinson (2005) describes in her study. One of the Committee's roles was to plan and conduct a census of the local Palestinian population through which a clear line could be drawn between the remaining Palestinians and the so-called "illegal returnees," enabling the government to determine who was and who was not entitled to citizenship (Robinson 2005: n. 10). The CBS, however, had already begun to plan its first major undertaking – a census and the establishment of a population registry of all the residents living within the borders of the new Jewish state. Later, this registry would become the basis upon which Israeli citizenship was first granted.

The CBS thus enshrined some basic principles of surveillance, principles whose logic and value to successive Israeli regimes would become clearer as time went on. Rather than considering the census as a direct means of discipline by which Palestinians would be kept in a state of subjection – as in Michel Foucault's analysis of panoptic surveillance – the census may be thought of as a key means of "biopower" (see Zureik 2001). In what follows, it is argued that surveillance is carried out through statistical means in order to make populations legible. As such, the census is seen as a "technology of power" through which the state may manage or control an entire population.

Governmentality and the science of populations

The body of literature that studies national statistics as a particular practice of knowledge production by the state explores three major themes. The first is the role of statistics in rendering groups legible and demarcating the population as unified and standardized, on the one hand, and in reinforcing or solidifying ethnic status, on the other hand (Anderson 1999; Kula 1986; Leibler 2004; Scott 1998). The second theme that is evident is the development of statistics as intertwined with processes of nation formation (Bourguet 1987; Curtis 2001; Leibler and Breslau 2005; Mitchell 2002; Nobles 2000; Patriarca 1996; Prakash 1999; Zureik 2001), and with the bureaucratization and rationalization of the centralized state (Desrosieres 1998; Hacking 1990; Porter 1986). Finally, a third major theme concerns how censuses, identity numbers and identity cards are mechanisms through which the right to access circuits of civility is constantly scrutinized; these mechanisms have constituted the *civil subject*, as described in contemporary accounts of governmentality (Caplan 2001; Rose 1999; Torpey 2000, 2001).

At the heart of social studies of population management is the Foucauldian concept of "governmentality." It has inspired surveillance studies, by enabling the integration of two different levels of analysis – the subject and the population. Governmentality is also a concept in which "science" and "state" intersect, hence its centrality in inquiries on national statistics and demography. Foucault asks to relocate power not in the domain of sovereignty – which exercises power on territory and, as a consequence, on the inhabitants – but on men (subjects) and "their links, their imbrications with those other things which are wealth, resources, means of subsistence, the territory with its specific qualities, climate, irrigation, fertility . . . customs, habits, ways of acting and thinking" (Foucault 1991: 93). By doing so he provides an account of the connection between statistics and the art of government. Procedures, population enumeration, calculations and analyses allow the operation of a very specific form of power: biopower (Foucault 1991: 102; Foucault 1980: 140).

Two main points of criticism should be considered in relation to the case at hand. First, conceptually, governmentality furnishes a wide range of studies of surveillance practices; yet, it is limited when one comes to analyze the operation of these practices in conflict zones. It has been criticized for ignoring variations of surveillance in different geographical areas; the answer to the question of how it was manifested in locales other than France is not elaborated in Foucault's account. I argue here that local manifestations of governmentality vary from one place to another, especially when colonialism, or internal colonialism, are involved.

The second problem with Foucault's conceptualization of governmentality is his refusal to analyze state institutions characterized by distinct types of struggle. As a result of Foucault's metaphorical intention to "cut off the head of the king" in political science, the institutional aspect of governmentality, in the realm of the state, is problematically absent. Bruce Curtis, in his study of the politics and practices of pre-Confederation census-making in nineteenth-century Canada (Curtis 2001), analyzes the practices of governmentality and the social relations of subjection prior to 1867. At the same time, he argues that "population" should be understood in relation to a variety of ways in which social relations are subjected to authoritative categorization by state agencies: "one cannot triangulate power around sovereignty–discipline–government in the case of the configuration of social relations as population without an account of state formation and political administration – two domains in which Foucault's analytics are of far less help than they might be" (Curtis 2001: 43). Curtis draws from the important and influential insights of Philip Abrams (1988), in which Abrams problematizes the way we should study "the state." Abrams' theoretical position is neither to eliminate the state from scholarly study nor to reify it. Instead it is suggested that the unified appearance of the state should be challenged by conducting empirical work to reveal the state's capacities to exercise violence, extract economic resources and frame representations of social relations (Curtis 2001: 36–37).

Similarly, the theoretical underpinning of this chapter seeks neither to ignore the state nor to reify it. Following several works in social studies of science and the state (Abrams 1988; Curtis 2001; Ezrahi 1990; Jasanoff 2004; Mitchell 2002; Mukerji 1997) I wish to avoid presenting the "state" as a subjective actor with a will of its own. Rather, as Mitchell succinctly puts it, while other approaches are "concerned with the way modern states have misused the powers of science, and distinguishes this misuse from proper science," more relevant concerns are "the kinds of social and political practice that produce simultaneously the powers of science and the powers of modern states" (Mitchell 2002: 312, n. 77). I see a more critical use of governmentality as expanding its logic explicitly to state institutions, and thereby creating room for a more explicit consideration of specific practices of state-formation and nation-building in works dealing with the intersection of political power and science and technology.

CBS – a boundary organization

While one might argue that the first census was conducted under extreme circumstances of war and hence had exceptional characterizations, the next census that was carried out in the context of yet another war, that of 1967, strengthens the argument that the Israeli CBS is an organization that is intimately connected to mechanisms of surveillance and citizens' rights allocation. Shortly after the Six-Day War, during August and September 1967, Israel conducted a general census in the occupied territories. Every person present at the time of the census was recorded in a population registry, received the status of permanent resident of the occupied territories, and was issued an identity card. The status of permanent resident permitted the holder to live in the occupied territories, to work and have property rights. Those who were not present during the census lost these rights.

The population registration had far-reaching consequences for the Palestinians. Since, once again, as in 1948, the census was conducted right after a war, many Palestinians had been expelled or had left the territories; others were living in other countries during the war for various reasons. The estimated number of Palestinians who lost these permanent residence rights as a result of the 1967 census is 300,000. One consequence, as discussed in various reports on conditions in the occupied territories, is that the decision to allocate rights to residency and an ID card only to those who were present at the time of the census caused the separation of families. Palestinians who were absent on census day were defined by Israel as illegal residents and could not be legally unified with their families.

The 1967 census was surprisingly similar to the first Israeli census and population registration: both were taken under curfew and determined which resident would be allocated citizenship or residency rights. The role that the CBS played in both of them raises many questions about the relationships between a scientific organization, like a central bureau of statistics, and state practices of surveilling political minorities. At first glance, it seems that the CBS was an administrative tool in the hands of state institutions, perhaps including the army. The statisticians in the two censuses, however, were far from mere technocrats. Indeed, while the political conception of Israeli citizenship, which was based on the 1948 census, was affected by the coercive power of governmental institutions, such as the Military Government's control over national minorities, the less studied contribution of the CBS to the census was also extremely relevant.

The CBS's role emerges more strongly when one considers the fact that since its establishment in 1948, it has gained high professional status as an autonomous organization that has apparently been able to remain indifferent to political pressure. This was achieved through the CBS's organizational centrality and professional exclusivity concerning the means of producing national statistics (Leibler 2004). While the focus of this chapter is the 1948 census, both it and the 1967 census can be studied virtually under laboratory conditions because each was a one-time action carried out in a closed area and on a separated population. These conditions are unique when compared to census-taking in the Western world. At the same time, they furnish a rare opportunity to learn the way scientific organizations and state institutions co-produce knowledge as well as the political, social and economic order (Ezrahi 1990; Jasanoff 2004).

As will be shown in relation to the 1948 census, the CBS functioned as an organization that bridged two different spheres – the political world in which the interests of the state for territorial and demographic control are at the center, and the world of then-regnant rational discourse which included such values as objectivity, universality and impartiality. The tension between the two worlds was expressed in negotiations between two bodies – the CBS and the Committee – regarding the question of whether to hold a separate census for the Military Government, and, if so, under what terms. The CBS statisticians wanted to count the population using one questionnaire for all the residents, without regard to national, religious or ethnic grouping. In contrast, the Committee's members were interested in the populations of particular geographic areas, and wanted to ask questions about Palestinians' property and relatives who had returned to their villages since the initial wave of flight in late 1947/early 1948. The negotiations between the sides reflected two divergent sets of interests and commitments: while the CBS's foremost statisticians were academic figures, the Committee members were political figures from various ministries. The statisticians' primary allegiance was to the statistical discipline and rationalization of the state. The politicians were committed to practices related to state security and the surveillance of specific populations deemed to be hostile. In practice, the statisticians' position gradually eroded, and the two groups grew closer. Though the statisticians were professionally in conflict with the politicians and their representatives, they ultimately found a way of satisfying the politicians' needs in a more universal form.

Based on the Israeli case of the 1948 census, I suggest that organizations that are dealing with knowledge production at the same time are state institutions functioning as "boundary organizations." The concept of a boundary organization refers to the idea that an organization can be a regulatory agency that mediates between politics and science in conflictual environments. Such an organization operates at the interface between politics and science and therefore influences actors from both worlds. Professionals in these organizations have a main role as mediators. In states with different levels of political participation of minority groups, I argue that this particular type of organization is needed to facilitate state actions aimed at increasing surveillance over citizens and non-citizens, without losing legitimacy – especially the legitimacy that comes from being perceived as a rational state.

Practicing science, administrating the state

One of the main characteristics of the first census in Israel, carried out in November 1948, was that it was conducted jointly with a full registration of the population. In the transition from a voluntary institutional system of the Jewish community in Palestine to a formal bureaucracy of a new state, a full registration was a means of applying the sovereignty of the new state on its residents. Each resident was given an ID number, which represented the resident in all of his/her institutional encounters. At a practical level, counting residents, at that census, meant including them in the citizenry by assigning an identity card and a number, which would function as a certificate for voting and getting food rations that were being distributed at the time. At a formal level, it meant granting civil rights. These uses of the census were made possible only because it was conducted through an exhaustive enumeration of the population and under a seven-hour curfew, as proposed by the CBS. The idea was to take a snapshot of the population at a particular moment and to grant civil rights only to those who were present during the curfew.

In spite of the fact that the CBS stated on different occasions that the census and registration would include all of Israel's residents present at their homes, several non-Jewish groups were not counted – the entire Bedouin population as well as several geographic areas populated by Palestinians. Since the government conditioned granting ID cards and numbers upon participation in the census, those who were not counted during the curfew lost their right to get Israeli citizenship. While, as we shall see, not all Palestinians who were counted ultimately received Israeli citizenship, those who were not counted had no chance of receiving it. Consequently, the population was roughly divided into two groups – people who had property and voting rights (mostly the Jewish population) and people who did not have these rights (most of the Palestinians) (Leibler and Breslau 2005). The census was a major mechanism through which certain citizenship rights were or were not accorded to the formal process of making Palestinians citizens and its statistical categories legalized and institutionalized the appropriation of Palestinian lands in 1948. This makes the Israeli case a telling example of the dark side of Foucault's surveillance through "biopower." Because biopower is devoted to maintaining the "life" of a certain population – in this case a nation – groups identified as a threat to such life may be ignored or even eradicated.

In what follows, I focus on the statisticians' role in the variable extension of citizenship rights to Palestinians and their position with regard to the "counted" and "uncounted" Arab residents of the new state. The basic assumption guiding this part of the discussion is that the CBS is both a state institution and a scientific institution, whose knowledge – its set of political, economic and demographic categories and classifications – forms the epistemological basis of "the nation," both within its territorial boundaries and beyond them. The history of the development of this organization lends credence to this claim. In the years following its establishment, the CBS enjoyed a growing degree of prestige among different sectors of the Israeli public, such as universities, industry, economic institutions, politicians and government agencies; its statistical measurements and classifications were rarely disputed. Furthermore, the CBS's foremost statistician, Professor Roberto Bachi, had established the first two statistics-related departments at the Hebrew University. Finally, the CBS's statisticians belonged to various academic and scientific societies, and published articles in academic journals.

The CBS's establishment in August 1948 was followed by a transformation of national statistics from a fragmented array of statistical departments of various pre-state institutions to a centralized office. Bachi and Dr. Pinhas Hamburger were selected to head up the system of Israeli national statistics. As former statisticians under the British Mandate with no affiliation with the Labor Settlement Movement (LSM), the nomination of Bachi and Hamburger was contrary to the demands of LSM members to dominate the new bureaucracy and exert their influence on national statistics.[1] The perception among the Zionist organizations was that statistics should serve as a means to political ends. The use of statistics by political organizations during the period prior to the establishment of the state led to a general distrust of statistical figures among the Jewish and Palestinian populations. The establishment of a centralized system served as both a rejection of these demands and a reaction to this instrumental view of statistics. Israeli statisticians took a number of steps to expand their monopoly over the means of statistical production; one of these steps was to separate the CBS from all other government offices, instead making it directly answerable to the Prime Minister.[2]

The Committee: "You must know your stock"

Preliminary discussions on Israel's first census commenced in January 1948. The census was scheduled for November 1948, to take place simultaneously with a full registration of the population. In the transition from a system of voluntary institutions to the formal bureaucracy of a new state, a full registration was also a means of applying the sovereignty of the new state over its residents. Each resident was to be issued an identification number, which would represent the resident in all of his or her institutional encounters. Residents counted in the census would become part of Israel's citizenry, both practically (since an identification card and number enabled the bearer to vote and to obtain food rations) and formally (in terms of civil rights). These uses of the census were made possible only by an exhaustive enumeration of the population, which, at the behest of Bachi, was to be conducted under a seven-hour curfew. The goal was to capture the state of the population at a particular moment and to grant civil rights only to those who had been present at that moment.

The CBS conducted a public campaign to urge residents to cooperate with the enumerators, while explaining the census's importance to government offices, both before and after the enumeration. The CBS also decided on the details concerning identification cards which would be distributed later, as well as the questions that would appear in the census questionnaire. Yet, although it is clear that the CBS was widely respected as the architect of the census by its audiences, as we shall see, the members of the Committee failed to see Bachi's bureau as having exclusive jurisdiction over national statistics.

An analysis of the process by which Bachi became a major player sheds light on the intimate relationship between those who belong to the political sphere and those who belong to the professional and scientific sphere, as seen through Bachi's interaction with the Committee. It can enable us to see the negotiations between the two groups, as well as the practices employed by statisticians to gain legitimacy as the authoritative group for all matters statistical. This aspiration to professional exclusivity, as this author has described elsewhere (Leibler 2004), was comprehensive and affected other statistical departments that had existed before the establishment of the state, as well as all government offices.

The armed conflict between the military forces of the Jewish community and various Palestinian forces, which broke out even before the British had left the area, was the driving force behind the shift in the demographic balance in Palestine. In the course of this conflict, Israel occupied territories beyond those accorded to it by the 1947 UN resolution calling for the partition of Palestine. Benny Morris divides the expulsion of the Palestinians into four waves, noting that in the first wave, which took place in early 1948, Palestinians fled their homes not due to premeditated decisions, but as a result of sporadic battles between Palestinians and the Haganah, the major military wing of the *Yishuv* (Morris 1987: n. 54). In the second wave, between April and June of the same year, the vast majority of Palestinians were driven out of the country as a result of Plan D, an "active defense" operation of the Haganah (Morris 1987: 17, n. 92). Although Plan D was not part of a plan to change the demographic balance of the state of Israel, it included a clear and explicit order to expel Palestinians from their villages (Morris 1987: 273–277). In the fall of that year, it was already clear to the leaders of the new state that a Jewish majority had been reached in all of the areas controlled by Israel and that the "demographic problem" – the prospect of a large and partially hostile Palestinian minority interspersed among the main centers of the Jewish population – had been solved.

The Committee was to address concerns about a possible demographic reversal. It included the head of the Military Government, the Prime Minister's Advisor on Arab Affairs, representatives from the Middle East Division of the Foreign Ministry and the Ministry of Minorities. The Committee's members sought Palestinian demographic information and an accurate picture of the location of every Palestinian, making their freedom of movement within Israel contingent upon the collection of such information. This was expressed very clearly in a protocol of the Committee's first meeting. In this meeting, Ezra Danin of the Middle East Division of the Foreign Ministry voiced concern about the situation in Nazareth and its adjacent neighborhoods in the wake of the "infiltration" of refugees and displaced Palestinians. His office objected to Palestinian freedom of movement and establishing any demographic facts on the ground before the office could present a coherent demographic policy. He argued:

> It is necessary to count all the refugees and displaced people by conducting a specific census, identifying [each Arab] and obtaining details on their property. The census needs to be clear and detailed, so we can get an accurate picture about [the Arabs'] condition; then we will know how many families were separated and what property they owned. Only after conducting this job will we be able to think of a system to allow these people to move [within the borders of Israel].3

Ya'akov Shim'oni, an official from the same division, added that the census was necessary both in the struggle against infiltration and in order to identify Israel's Arab residents. He also referred to the question of Palestinian property, arguing that the census would solve this problem. "It is very common in [the] world," he stressed," that during a census, the population's movement is frozen; this is even more important in this special case." Therefore, he maintained, "we emphasized that movement within the territory of the state would be allowed only after the census was carried out."4 Interestingly, the idea suggested by Shim'oni – a census under curfew – was similar to the one proposed by Bachi in a meeting with the Interior Minister. Yet, unlike Bachi, Shim'oni wanted to restrict Palestinians' movements for considerably more than seven hours. Subsequently, curfew became the most common method of controlling Palestinians in the first decade of the state (Medding 1990: 25; Lustick 1985; Benziman and Mansour 1992: 103–114).

The question of the use of a census to identify Palestinian residents was raised by several participants in the Committee's meetings, and was of unique importance. The Committee's members needed specific information about the number of Palestinians living in particular areas – that is, in Israeli territory and in the territories occupied by Israel's military – which would come to form the borders of the state. They also wanted to know the status of these Palestinians – how many might be categorized as having "infiltrated" the borders of Israel, and how many of those who had done so had returned to their original homes. Lastly, they wanted to know which Palestinians had owned land.

Although the CBS plan to conduct a census had already been discussed as early as January of that year, the Committee wished to change this original plan and envisioned a separate census to be carried out before the general census, which was then still tentatively scheduled for September 15. The Committee's members did not feel that the planning of the census and its questionnaire should be the responsibility of the CBS, since they viewed the census as an immediate answer to the unique need for surveillance of populations.5 They believed that they could conduct the census quickly, and that officials at the Foreign Ministry and Ministry of Minority Affairs could compile the questionnaire themselves. The Committee also suggested employing people to conduct the census, whose task would be to register and nationalize Palestinian lands and properties within the borders of Israel after the Palestinians' exodus. This consisted of representatives of the Jewish National Fund, the Settlement Office and the Land Registry (Tabu), which was in charge of registering Palestinian land as "state land." These people were not statisticians or officers trained in conducting surveys; they specialized in administrating the expropriation of Palestinians' lands and assets.

By viewing the members of the Committee as representatives of the political sphere and the statisticians as representatives of science, or at least as the technocrats of the new government, one encounters a rather instrumental perception of the role of censuses as an immediate answer to the perceived need for national security and overseeing of minorities. According to this division, the purpose of censuses and the interests of the Committee coincided: "If statisticians' main reasoning in their first documents was determined by what they call the 'needs' of statistics,"[6] the Committee's interest was in having maximum control over the Palestinian population. The census was just one of the means of achieving this, alongside the establishment of the Military Government and long-term curfews. Moreover, the Committee viewed the census subjects, the Palestinians, as merchandise to be surveyed. When Avner, the representative of the Military Governor, expressed his trepidation at the thought of conducting the survey in a rush, Danin replied: "You must know your stock."[7]

Who has the right to count Palestinians?

Although the original intention of the Committee was to plan and conduct the census of Palestinians using its own people, Foreign Minister Moshe Shertok (Sharett) referred fellow Committee members Shim'oni and Danin to Bachi and Aharon Gertz, the administrative manager of the CBS, to see if the latter could provide the number of displaced Arabs. They wanted to determine the general size of the Arab population within the borders of Israel that had remained following the mass exodus of Palestinians.[8] Several days after the meeting, they contacted the CBS for this information;[9] a week later, at the Committee's third meeting, Bachi's preference for two separate censuses was already represented, though not as a major voice.[10]

For its part, the Committee felt that Bachi should comply with whatever the Committee asked of him. In a reply to a letter sent by the Middle East Division in the Foreign Ministry, Bachi stated that the CBS already planned to conduct such a census, but that it was not a high priority:

> Concerning your letter from September 2, I would like to inform you that a study of the Arab population is already included in the Bureau's plan, and we have even started collecting data on this problem. This matter, however, is very complicated, and since we have many other urgent commitments in relation to the registration of the population, we will not be able to pursue this issue in the immediate future.[11]

A census, claimed Bachi, was not a military operation, but a field of study and knowledge. Nor was it a sporadic answer to an immediate need, but part of a general, broader plan of counting the population. In other documents from 1948, Bachi emphasized the scientific and bureaucratic necessity of the first census. His insistence on ascribing scientific attributes to CBS practices was a common theme in all the places in which he discussed the role of the CBS during the crucial period of the state's establishment.[12] Bachi therefore rejected a direct link between the census and military needs or the needs of national security.

The Committee expressed its expectation that Bachi and Gertz would obtain the information they demanded by creating two separate questionnaires, to be distributed in one census: one for Arabs (Christian, Muslim and Druze) and another for Jews. The Committee's members saw the census as a means of obtaining sensitive information and it focused on two main questions. The first was about members of each family and their relatives – who lived in each household, and who had joined recently. The second related to the property each family owned. The Minister of Minority Affairs wrote to Bachi:

> [T]he state, and especially the Middle East Division [in the Foreign Ministry] is interested in clear information, to the greatest extent possible, on the number of Arabs who abandoned their property and are [now living] outside of Israel's borders, their property that remained inside the borders of Israel, and details about minorities' movements inside of Israel and its occupied territories.[13]

The Committee held at least five meetings to discuss this issue; Bachi was not present, but his position was represented. In the third meeting, the participants discussed the demand to conduct one census using two different forms. Bachi felt that such a format would be discriminatory towards the Arab population. His objection to asking part of the population direct questions about property and absent relatives was also based on the concern that this would lead to distrust among Palestinians toward the intentions of both the census's architects and the statistical enterprise in general. Thus, he maintained, the two censuses should not be conducted on the same day. Danin replied: "Professor Bachi needs to find a way to conduct the census according to our needs."[14] Facing Bachi's objection, the Minister of Minority Affairs had an original idea of how to solve the problem of trust:

> We will prepare an additional questionnaire: a regular questionnaire for all residents, and a special form for [the needs of] the Interior Minister, the Ministry of Minority Affairs and the Military Governor. [Then,] while we fill in the regular form [designed for Jews], we could add the details we are interested in to the second questionnaire [for Arabs] without them noticing that we are asking additional questions.[15]

The minister suggested bypassing the issue of Palestinians' sensitivities by asking them ostensibly innocent questions that would appear equally addressed to all members of the population. Of course, his idea did not satisfy Bachi's demand to keep the census universal and not discriminate against any national group.

When the Committee's members insisted on one, split, census, Bachi pointed out that the regulations of the Interior Ministry on the format of questionnaires and the kinds of question they could include applied to them as well. Although the Committee recognized the importance of convincing Bachi of the necessity of a split census, they also discussed the option of conducting the census using their own people, should they fail to convince him.[16] The legal advisor to the Ministry of Minority Affairs reported that the special questions were added to the general questionnaire, as Bachi had initially suggested, with the exception of two of them – one about relatives, the other about property.[17] In late September, Bachi told the Ministry of Minority Affairs that the census form was ready. He wrote that the requisite questions about absent relatives and property had been concealed in this form.[18] However, the Committee misunderstood Bachi, assuming that the two questions would be part of a special form to be attached to the general one, and that the two censuses would be carried out on the same day. As a result, the Minister of Minority Affairs sent a letter to key ministers of the new government, including the Prime Minister, asking for funding to conduct the split census.[19] In his reply to the Interior Minister, Bachi wrote:

> These studies [on absentees and Palestinians' property] were suggested by the Foreign Ministry and the Ministry of Minority Affairs – in addition to the registration of the population. In meetings with these offices' representatives I made it clear that: a. One cannot differentiate between Jews and non-Jews in the registration, such that these questions [on absentees and property] cannot be part of the general registration form. b. If you want to ask these questions, a special study will have to be conducted ... d. One cannot complicate the general registration, nor jeopardize its success by asking sensitive questions ... Therefore, the Bureau suggests conducting these special studies after the general registration, through the bureaucratic mechanism already in place.[20]

Bachi's reply is consistent with other records, in which he declared that the administration of a population registration at a time of war, during a mass exodus of the Palestinian population, was scientifically problematic. However, he promised that the CBS would make sure that residents of all religious, national, sex and age groups were included in the registration:

> Although the present registration cannot be considered a pure and scientific census, the CBS will fulfill the main criteria for demographic censuses. Therefore, we will make sure that every person in Israel – without regard to religion, nationality, gender or age group – is included in the registration, that no one is registered more than once, and that the registration provides a "snapshot" of the population at the moment it is taken.[21]

We may read these exchanges between members of CBS and the Committee as attempts by each group to exert its authority over the other. In other words, the initial position of the Committee's members was the urgent need for demographic information, but Bachi did not acquiesce, refusing to submit to the demand to treat Arabs differently and grant the matter first priority. It appears that the political demand for surveillance could not be reconciled with Bachi's insistence on planning the census in as universal, rational and scientific a manner as possible. For officials at the Military Government and the Foreign Ministry, the relationship between science and politics was quite simple – science should serve those who represent the existential needs of the state. Conversely, the first Israeli statisticians sought to protect their field of practice from political abuse – that is, anything that could challenge its scientific credibility and compromise the perceived disinterestedness of the census as a technology of the rational state.

Representation practices and the political order

Ultimately, the CBS designed a two-part form for registration of the population, the second part of which was attached as an addendum to the general form. This addendum was itself divided into two parts. The first was entitled "Information on Absent [i.e., at the time of the census] Relatives." The second was entitled "Information on Property of Family Members (present or absent)."[22] In this form, Bachi addressed the Committee's demand for specific information on the Palestinian population during the general census. Surprisingly, the solution at which he ultimately arrived was quite different from his initial position of two separate censuses, and rather similar to the solution suggested by Minister of Minority Affairs. Thus there were different forms for different populations in one census, as opposed to the single universal questionnaire Bachi had championed. By indirectly addressing the issue of property in the general questionnaire, Bachi alleviated the anticipated distrust of Palestinians, but he did not solve the problem of discrimination to which he had so vehemently objected in his letter to the Interior Minister.[23]

The question remains: did the CBS capitulate in this conflict? And if so, why? In other words, did the CBS struggle with competing loyalties – to scientific principles and to the Military Government's need for security and to oversee its national minority – before ultimately choosing the latter over the former? It seems that the CBS did not have the ability to impose its authority while positioning itself as the main agency of statistical representation of the population, since the phenomenon in question – the Palestinian population – was not given to numerical definition at that particular moment in time, which was so fraught with demographic upheaval. But by allowing the Committee members' ministries to seek alternative means of conducting a split census, the stature of the CBS as the sole statistical agency of the state of Israel would have been jeopardized. Yet it was in the interests of the Israeli administration to foster the illusion of the CBS's independence.

On several occasions during the 1948 census discussions, Bachi indicated that the CBS anticipated the Palestinians' unwillingness to be observed by the state. For example, when he portrayed the organization of official statistics of the new state, he wrote: "The poisoned political atmosphere in our country has had a damaging influence on the regularity of the statistical work . . . The general understandable distrust in the politics of the [British] government is also manifested, of course, in a baseless distrust toward enterprises that have no political intention or technical defect."[24] The document explained the Palestinians' anticipated objection by suggesting that they were suspicious of the new Jewish state in general and by stating that they were "Oriental" and therefore lacked the capacity to understand science and its application.[25] However, scientific illiteracy was not the CBS's main problem. Rather, the difficulty it faced during the census and for several months thereafter was the inability to enumerate the entire Palestinian population and present a complete statistical picture, since the "phenomenon" itself was so unstable. Even as the exodus of Palestinians was continuing, some of them found their way back into Israel as what the state deemed "illegal returnees," making it difficult to account for them using standard demographic tools. Ultimately, then, several populations were not counted.

In addition to a group of Palestinians who were classified as "present absentees," due to their absence from their homes during the seven-hour census curfew, other Palestinians who were present in the country were not included in the census. Referring to several sources, authors present various estimates of the number of "present absentees": Grossman (1992: n. 64) puts the number at 81,000; Shafir and Peled (1998: n. 110) give a figure of 90,000; while Lustick (1985: 64–72, n. 16) makes it 75,000. As Bachi would write several years after the census, while the size of the Arab population was put at 69,000, several geographical areas populated by Palestinians, such as Western Galilee and the Negev, were not visited by the surveyors due to the war.[26] Although these areas would be enumerated later, at the beginning of 1949, the data on the Arab population would remain incomplete even thereafter. Bachi offered several explanations for the incomplete figures for the numbers of Palestinians and Bedouins. These included, first, that the conditions of the war and the population exchanges among Palestinians prevented a full account of the non-Jewish population. Second, at the beginning of 1949, the territorial changes to Israel as a result of the war increased the non-Jewish population by 30,000. Finally, Bedouins were hard to count, due to their nomadic lifestyle. Robinson (2005: 15), who studied the naturalization process of Palestinians during and after the 1948 war, cites three major groups that were omitted:

> The Israeli census bureau counted roughly 69,000 Palestinians in November 1948. This figure excluded the 13,000–15,000 Bedouin residents of the Naqab/ Negev desert, whom the Interior Ministry's Registration Division secretly left out of the population registry altogether. It also excluded roughly 5,000 men and teenage boys then interned in Israel's POW camps, roughly 14 percent of all Palestinian males left in the country between the ages of 15 through 60. Most of them were picked up by the IDF upon the occupation of their home locale simply because they were of "military" age. The third major group that was not counted in the first census was some 40,000 residents of the Upper Galilee villages which the army had conquered just over a week before.

Robinson argues that the first census was initially motivated by an urgent plan, based on a fear of demographic reversal – the authorities wanted to distinguish between those who were in the country during the census and those who had infiltrated afterwards. Why, then, were so many Palestinians and Bedouins not counted, if the motivation for counting them, as suggested by Robinson, was the struggle against infiltration? Based on the evidence presented earlier in this chapter, common sense would dictate that the authorities did everything in their power to include all the residents during the seven-hour curfew in the census, so as to avert future demands of Palestinians who were not registered to be included. The Committee's entire reason for contacting the CBS was to secure reliable numbers that could offer a clear picture of the Palestinian population at the particular moment of the census, which could then be used as a means of identifying those who should be deemed infiltrators and deported from Israel.[27] The Committee's members, who expected to receive these numbers after the census, were surprised to learn that they did not exist. When Shim'oni, for example, understood that his office could not use the census data to identify infiltrators, he wrote a letter to five different ministries, alerting them to the potential threat to the state's authority in not completing the registration process:

> Since in the last few weeks there has been an increased [level of] illegal Arab infiltration – something which is dangerous and likely to cause complications, and since it is impossible to distinguish local residents from infiltrators in order to be able to act against the latter after the registration, it is our opinion that the infrastructure of the registration is harmful and dangerous and that we must do everything possible to carry out the registration immediately and without any delay.[28]

The ability to take steps against "infiltrators," then, depended on a complete registry of the population. In that case, such infrastructure can be quite powerful, and its categories may be seen as objective over time. On the other hand, if the registry is incomplete, a state could mistakenly act against those who are rightfully entitled to citizenship, weakening the state's authority. Shim'oni's concern was over the inability to use the population registry as a clear-cut legal criterion for excluding infiltrators. The Minister of Minority Affairs expressed the same concern when he wrote to officials at the various branches of his ministry that, in the absence of registration data, they should prepare a detailed report on every settlement of minorities as well as abandoned villages.[29] Paradoxically, if the CBS had conducted the census in accordance with the Committee's demands – namely that all the villages and settlements of Palestinians and Bedouins in the country be included – the vast majority of Palestinians would have been eligible for citizenship, or, at the very least, it would have been exceedingly difficult to maintain exclusionary policies.

Robinson rightly argues that the intentions of the Committee in relation to the census were exclusionary. They wanted to delineate the Palestinian population and prevent people whom Israel considers to be illegal returnees from obtaining citizenship. Yet, Robinson's detailed account also convincingly demonstrates the way in which entire populations of Palestinian villages were subject to random eviction and expulsion, even when their residents held registration certificates, meaning that they had been registered and counted during the census (Robinson 2005: 15). Moreover, in order to continue the policy of not granting citizenship to those Palestinians who were counted (i.e., to legalize the practice of not granting them citizenship), the Prime Minister's Advisor on Arab Affairs worked with the Military Government to create a new system of demographic regulation. This was the Temporary Residency Permit, later known as the "red identification card," as opposed to the blue identification cards held by most Israelis. The permit would enable the government to freeze the legal status of its Palestinian bearers (Robinson 2005: 69).

Still, Robinson's assertion that the registration of Palestinians was the sole or central motive for conducting the census fails to consider the role of the CBS and its statisticians as a separate group, with interests distinct from those of both the Committee and the "state." The statisticians were not merely extensions of the "will of the state"; among the mundane motivations for conducting the census at the particular moment when it was conducted – first elections, taxes and military conscription – was the desire to create a rare representation of a very unique moment in the history of Israeli society, after the mass exodus of Palestinians and before the mass immigration of the Arab-Jews, while consolidating the country's Jewish citizenry. However, the fact that the Palestinians were not fully represented in the census limited the CBS's ability to create a coherent and well-defined statistical object. Yet this fact was not mentioned in most of the documents of the CBS describing both the establishment of the CBS in general, and the first census in particular. By glossing over the serious methodological limitations regarding the enumeration of the Palestinians in the history of the CBS, the latter contributed to its own status as the exclusive and the most comprehensive statistical agency in Israel.

Conclusion

The political and demographic situation of Israel/Palestine in 1948 (and again in 1967) afforded the CBS a central role in the mapping and management of the population. Though its role in the formalization of Israeli citizenship is nowhere to be found in the historiography and sociology of Israeli society, the CBS was central in the formation and definition of Israel's citizenry, determining who was to be included and who excluded. Its statisticians were agents of biopower *par excellence*. This was not a result of a premeditated decision; the political conception of Israeli citizenship was affected by the coercive power of governmental institutions, such as the Military Government's control over national minorities, as well as the more mundane practices of such agencies as the CBS.

This chapter has sought to call attention to negotiation practices, methodological difficulties and the scientific ambition – common enough in those days of optimistic empiricism – to create a pure scientific object that could be perceived as a reflection of society, *sui generis*, rather than an artifact motivated by political interests.

The case at hand illustrates the way in which a government agency, in this case the Central Bureau of Statistics, can be subjected to some of the same expectations as any scientific laboratory, namely the expectation to produce "objective knowledge," which may be compromised by any of a number of factors: political pressure to interfere with the statistical representation, or simply the complexity of an unstable and uncertain phenomenon. These factors can interact with the practice of statistics, and can even play a role in censuses (Porter 1995). The ethnic complexity of Israel/Palestine prior to and during 1948 lent a certain political charge to the numerical representation of each national group. Ethnic diversity also influenced methodological considerations, as can be seen in the decision to conduct an exhaustive enumeration of the population, under curfew, at a time when sampling was already a widely used technique in censuses worldwide. Yet it was nevertheless impossible to cover the entire population of the country in the census. This weakens the exhaustiveness of the census and its claim to "truth." For the CBS, the perceived variability of the Arab population was an obstacle to precision in representing the population, and undermined the objectivity of the data it produced.

Notes

1 On the objection to Bachi's selection, see Israel State Archives (hereafter ISA): rg 41/112/12, February 1948; rg 41/117/37, March 1948. On a general review of the statist

ideology of those days, led by Prime Minister David Ben-Gurion, see: Medding 1990: 134f., 173; and Yanay 1987.

2　Central Zionist Archives (hereafter CZA) S25/9686, January 1948: 7–8, 16; ISA: rg 43/5458/29; rg 43/5458/29; rg 43/5459/2; rg 94/3562/4.

3　ISA: HZ 2564/11, August 29, 1948: "First Meeting of the Committee Alongside the Military Government" [Hebrew]. This and all other Hebrew-language archival sources quoted in English are the author's translation.

4　Ibid.

5　August 29, 1948, ISA: HZ 2564/11.

6　CZA S25/9686, January 1948: "Preparation for Establishing the State" [Hebrew]; ISA: 10/111/3560 February 1948.

7　August 29, 1948, ISA: HZ 2564/11 [Hebrew].

8　August 30, 1948, ISA: HZ 2564/22. Note written by Shim'oni on August 25, 1948 in which he suggests more ambiguity in presenting the number of Palestinians.

9　September 2, 1948, ISA: G 110/302.

10　September 9, 1948, ISA: HZ 2564/11.

11　September 21, 1948, ISA: G 110/302 [Hebrew].

12　January 1948, ISA: rg 41/107/18; January 1948, CZA S25/9686; see also interviews with Bachi in *Davar*, January 11, 1948 and August 9, 1948; *Haaretz*, August 9, 1948. Also, author's personal interview with Bachi, March 1992.

13　October 10, 1948, ISA: G 110/302 [Hebrew].

14　September 9, 1948, ISA: HZ 2564/11 [Hebrew].

15　Ibid.

16　September 14, 1948, ibid.

17　September 23, 1948, ibid.

18　September 26, 1948, ISA: G 302/110.

19　October 10, 1948, ibid.

20　Ibid. [Hebrew].

21　R. Bachi (1948) "Population Registration in the State of Israel," File no. 172, Ben-Gurion Archives, not dated [Hebrew].

22　Not dated, ISA: GL 19/3559.

23　October 10, 1948, ISA: G 302/110.

24　CZA S25/9686, January 1948: 2. Also, author's interview with Bachi, March 1992.

25　R. Musam, one of the first Israeli statisticians and a former statistician of the British Mandate, wrote on the estimate of the population living in the northern region of the country: "This number shouldn't be considered as very far from reality, because it is based on the population census of 1931 which was no doubt accurate as much as accuracy can be expected in an oriental country as ours" (Non-Jewish Population of the Jewish State – Statistical Review," ISA: GL 3559/19, not dated).

26　Bachi, R. (not dated) "Conducting the Population Registration" [November 8, 1948; Hebrew], File no. 44, Ben-Gurion Archives. See also October 10, 1948, ISA: 130.15(2), HZ 2564/22; October 24, 1948, ISA: HZ 2564/2; November 29, 1948, ISA: HZ 2564/22; November 28, 1948, ISA: 49: G 302/110; December 28, 1948, ISA: HZ 2564/22.

27　See, for example, letter from the Foreign Ministry prior to the census: October 12, 1948, ISA: G 302/110; October 14, 1948, ibid.

28　December 20, 1948, ISA: G 302/110; emphasis in original [Hebrew]. See also December 7, 1948, ibid.

29　December 24, 1948, ISA: G 302/110.

Bibliography

Abrams, P. (1988) "Notes on the Difficulty of Studying the State," *Journal of Historical Sociology*, 1(1): 57–84.

Anderson, B. (1999) *Imagined Communities*, Tel-Aviv: The Open University of Israel.

Ben-Eliezer, U. (1995) *Derech Hacavenet: Hivatzruto Shel Hamilitarism Hayisraeli, 1936–1956*, Tel-Aviv: Dvir Press.

Ben-Gurion, D. (1969) *Medinat Yisrael Hamechudeshet*, Tel-Aviv: Am-Over Press.

Benziman, U. and A. Mansour (1992) *Subtenants: Israel's Palestinians, Their Status and the Policy toward Them*, Jerusalem: Keter.

Bourguet, M.N. (1987) *Decrire, Compter, Calculer: The Debate over Statistics during the Napoleonic Period*, Cambridge, MA: Bradford Books, MIT Press.

Caplan, J. (2001) "'This or That Particular Person': Protocols of Identification in Nineteenth-Century Europe," in J. Caplan and J. Torpey (eds) *Documenting Individual Identity: The Development of State Practices in the Modern World*, Princeton, NJ: Princeton University Press.

Carroll, P. (2006) *Science, Culture, and Modern State Formation*, Berkeley: University of California Press.

Central Bureau of Statistics (1955) *Special Publication No. 36: Registration of Population, Settlements, and Regions*, Jerusalem: CBS Publications.

Curtis, B. (1995) "Taking the State back out: Rose and Miller on Political Power," *British Journal of Sociology*, 46(4): 575–589.

—— (2001) *The Politics of Population: State Formation, Statistics, and the Census of Canada, 1840–1875*, Toronto: University of Toronto Press.

—— (2002) "Surveying the Social: Techniques, Practices, Power," *Histoire sociale / Social History*, 35(69): 83–108.

Desrosieres, A. (1998) *The Politics of Large Numbers: A History of Statistical Reasoning*, Cambridge, MA: Harvard University Press.

Eliav, B. (1976) *Hayeshuv Biyemey Habait Haleumi*, Jerusalem: Keter Press.

Ezrahi, Y. (1990) *The Descent of Icarus: Science and the Transformation of Contemporary Democracy*, Cambridge, MA: Harvard University Press.

Foucault, M. (1980) *The History of Sexuality: An Introduction*, New York: Vintage.

—— (1991) "Governmentality," in G. Burchell, C. Gordon and P. Miller (eds) *The Foucault Effect: Studies in Governmentality*, London: Harvester Wheatsheaf.

Grossman, D. (1992) *Nochachim Nifkadim*, Tel-Aviv: Hakkibutz Hameuchad Press.

Hacking, I. (1990) *The Taming of Chance*, Cambridge: Cambridge University Press.

Jasanoff, S. (2004) *States of Knowledge: The Co-production of Science and Social Order*, London and New York: Routledge.

[em[em] (2005) *Designs on Nature: Science and Democracy in Europe and the United States*, Princeton, NJ: Princeton University Press.

Kula, W. (1986) *Measures and Man*, Princeton, NJ: Princeton University Press.

Leibler, A. (2004) "Statisticians' Reason: Governmentality, Modernity, National Legibility," *Israel Studies*, 9(2): 121–149.

Leibler, A. and D. Breslau (2005) "The Uncounted: Citizenship and Exclusion in the Israeli Census of 1948," *Ethnic and Racial Studies*, 28(5): 880–902.

Lustick, I. (1985) *Arabs in the Jewish State*, Haifa: Mifras.

Medding, P. (1990) *The Founding of Israeli Democracy, 1948–1967*, New York: Oxford University Press.

Mitchell, T. (1991) "The Limits of the State: Beyond Statistic Approaches and Their Critics," *American Political Science Review*, 85: 84–96.

—— (2002) *Rule of Experts: Egypt, Techno-Politics, Modernity*, Berkeley: University of California Press.

Morris, B. (1987) *The Birth of the Palestinian Refugee Problem, 1947–1949*, Cambridge: Cambridge University Press.

Mukerji, C. (1989) *A Fragile Power: Scientists and the State*, Princeton, NJ: Princeton University Press.

—— (1997) *Territorial Ambitions and the Gardens of Versailles*, Cambridge and New York: Cambridge University Press.

Nobles, M. (2000) *Shades of Citizenship: Race and the Census in Modern Politics*, Stanford, CA: Stanford University Press.

Patriarca, S. (1996) *Numbers and Nationhood: Writing Statistics in Nineteenth-Century Italy*, Cambridge and New York: Cambridge University Press.

Peled, Y. (1992) "Ethnic Democracy and Legal Construction of Citizenship: Arab Citizens and the Jewish State," *American Political Science Review*, 6(2): 432–443.

Porter, T. (1986) *The Rise of Statistical Thinking 1820–1900*, Princeton, NJ: Princeton University Press.

—— (1995) *Trust in Numbers: The Pursuit of Objectivity in Science and Public Life*, Princeton, NJ: Princeton University Press.

Prakash, G. (1999) *Another Reason: Science and the Imagination of Modern India*, Princeton, NJ: Princeton University Press.

Robinson, S.N. (2005) *Occupied Citizens in a Liberal State: Palestinians under Military Rule and the Colonial Formation of Israeli Society, 1948–1966*, Princeton, NJ: Princeton University Press.

Rose, N.S. (1999) *Powers of Freedom: Reframing Political Thought*, Cambridge: Cambridge University Press.

Scott, C. (1998) *Seeing Like a State: How Certain Schemes to Improve the Human Condition Have Failed*, New Haven, CT: Yale University Press.

Shafir, G. and Y. Peled (1998) "Citizenship and Stratification in an Ethnic Democracy," *Ethnic and Racial Studies*, 21(3): 408–427.

—— (2002) *Being Israeli: The Dynamics of Multiple Citizenship*, Cambridge: Cambridge University Press.

Torpey, J. (2000) *The Invention of the Passport: Surveillance, Citizenship and the State*, Cambridge: Cambridge University Press.

—— (2001) "The Great War and the Birth of the Modern Passport System," in J. Caplan and J. Torpey (eds) *Documenting Individual Identity: The Development of State Practices in the Modern World*, Princeton, NJ: Princeton University Press.

Yanay, N. (1987) "Hatfisa Hamamlachtit Shel Ben-Gurion," *Cathedra*, 45: 169–189.

Yiftachel, O. (1999) "'Ethnocracy': The Politics of Judaizing Israel/Palestine," *Constellations*, 6(3): 364–390.

Yurman, P. (1983) "Otzer – Velo Begzirat Habritim: Perek Bechevley Hahityatzvut Shel Hamedina," *Hauma*, 70–71: 90–101.

Zureik, E. (2001) "Constructing Palestine through Surveillance Practices," *British Journal of Middle Eastern Studies*, 28(2): 205–227.

—— (ed.) (1979) *The Palestinians in Israel: A Study in Internal Colonialism*, London: Routledge & Kegan Paul.

Part VI

Surveillance, racialization, and uncertainty

13 Exclusionary surveillance and spatial uncertainty in the occupied Palestinian territories[1]

Ariel Handel

Introduction

Since the outbreak of the second Intifada in 2000, residents of the occupied Palestinian territories (OPT) have been subjected to extremely harsh movement restrictions, affecting all daily activities. Figure 13.1 shows how the West Bank is divided into dozens of "land cells" by the blocks array (the manned checkpoints, physical blockades, restricted roads, and the Separation Wall), which affects nearly every attempted movement (see also Chapter 16, this volume; Handel 2009). It is therefore surprising to note the very low numbers of permits distributed by Israel in 2004 (one of the most restricted years). According to human rights organizations' reports, only 3,412 Palestinians (out of 2.3 million; i.e., 0.14 percent) held a valid permit for passage through internal checkpoints in the West Bank (B'Tselem 2004), while throughout the whole of 2004 only 2.45 percent of West Bank inhabitants held any kind of permit (Machsom Watch and Physicians for Human Rights–Israel 2004).

These numbers are this chapter's point of departure. I shall attempt to show that the ridiculously low numbers subvert the basic political logic of the permits. I argue that the surveillance carried out in the OPT differs from the surveillance dealt with in most surveillance studies, which have a Western (liberal/democratic) bias. Surveillance is usually related, especially since Michel Foucault's *Discipline and Punish* (Foucault 1979) and *The History of Sexuality* (Foucault 1990), to ways of "appropriating" people and constructing "normal" citizens. Observations, registrations, categorizations, drawings, and data comparisons to the "norm" are thought of as an orthopedic practice, aimed at repairing and improving human beings. Other writers, from Deleuze (1992), through Giddens (1985), to Torpey (1998), shed light on the ways in which surveillance is used by the state in order to "embrace" its citizens. Authorities can know citizens down to the most minute details, and thus equip them with the necessary certifications and permits (passports, identity cards, and other "belonging documents") that symbolize identity and grant access to some rights. In contrast to that type of surveillance, which I call "inclusive surveillance," I pit "exclusionary surveillance," which uses the same power/knowledge practices not to "embrace" its citizens but rather to exclude unwanted populations. Like an insurance company that misuses a contract's "small print" for its own good by limiting the insured's rights and benefits, the Israeli authorities use surveillance as a tool to eliminate rights, physical space, or presence, and even – in extreme cases – life.

Paraphrasing Freud's famous remark that "sometimes a pipe is just a pipe," I argue that a tower is not always a *surveillance* tower; that a checkpoint is not always a

Figure 13.1
The "land cells" map in the West Bank

Sources: Based on the UN Office for the
Coordination of Humanitarian Affairs'
closure map from January 2006 (see
www.ochaopt.org) and on analysis of the
Palestinian forbidden roads (B'Tselem
2004); see also Handel (2009)

check-point; and so on. An examination of technologies – mainly technologies of control – must be done in context. What are they made of? What form do they create? How do they work? And what goal are they meant to achieve?

I argue that in the OPT there is an extensive production of uncertainty as part of spatial control practices, and that the main role of the array of blocks, checkpoints, permits, and Israeli District Coordination Offices (DCOs) is not routine data collection and surveillance but blocking *per se* and prevention of movement. Instead of using spatial management to raise the friction level – namely the number and quality of interactions between the authorities and inhabitants, in order to collect and cross-check data – it is used mainly to prevent movement and freeze everyday life. In the following pages I will analyze the special features of surveillance in the OPT, especially in the second Intifada, from the point of view of surveillance *practices*. I will ask why there are so few permits; what the checkpoints check; and what is seen and written down. The political-theoretical frame is an attempt to make sense of seeming anomalies.

The first part of this chapter distinguishes between three types of surveillance: *colonial/founding*, *inclusive/bio-political*, and *exclusionary*. The second part discusses the surveillance and population management arrays in Israel/Palestine. After a brief historical description of their function in the years 1948–2000, I will devote most of this part to a discussion of the situation during the second Intifada. The last part examines the connections between spatial management by means of uncertainty production and the surveillance arrays. I thus claim that Israel becomes indifferent towards the Palestinians: it matters little what they are doing there, as long as they stay there.

Three types of surveillance

Since the rise of the modern state, three ideal types of state surveillance have generally flowed in chronological order. They are not clearly demarcated one from the other; rather, they merge together at times. Nearly every established regime combines the three, either towards different populations or in the practices used towards the same population. Each of the three types also characterizes a specific relation between the state and the subjects.

Colonial/founding surveillance

Colonial and postcolonial research relies on the surveillance, categorization, and investigation that were used by colonial states in their penetration of new territories. Classifying the population into different, mostly imagined, categories was a major part of the production of the new territory and of its daily control (see, for example, Anderson 1994; Cohn 1996; Mamdani 2002). But the colonial type of surveillance was implemented not only "across the sea" but in Europe itself in the early stages of new states' establishment.

From the Middle Ages to the seventeenth century, sovereignty was thought of as sovereignty over territory, and over the population only as one of its derivations. Foucault writes that sovereignty's classic problem was to conquer territories and hold on to them. The main question with which sovereigns had to deal was "how can the territory be demarcated, fixed, protected, or enlarged? In other words . . . the safety of the territory, or the safety of the sovereign who rules over the territory" (Foucault 2007: 65). With the rise of population and cities – especially in the post-Westphalian era that demanded clear definitions of territories, borders, and populations – the authorities aspired to deepen their knowledge of the territory and its elements. If until the seventeenth century the sovereign had to know only the laws and the art of politics, from that point on he also had to know the different elements of the state: the territory, the population, and its sources of power and weakness, in order to be able to defend it from external conquerors or internal threats (Foucault 2007: 274). New administrative arrays – as well as new observation, registration, and research practices – were developed to enable the sovereign to know "his" territory, count "his" subjects, and so on. That new science was called "statistics": namely, the science of the state, or the science of controlling the state. Michel Crozier's (1964) research on the bureaucratic phenomenon observes the tight connection between the measure of certainty and the level of power. Crozier argues that control and power belong to the group that succeeds in simultaneously making its actions and rationale unclear to the other groups, and understanding the actions and the reasons of the latter. In that way, "most power is exercised by such units as manage to remain the sources of other units' uncertainty" (Bauman 1998: 34).

This governmental stage in new European states – or at the same time and later in the colonies – was characterized by antagonistic relations between the sovereign and the population. The ruler studied the population from the outside. The surveillance was meant to deepen knowledge of the population in order to improve control over it. Of greatest importance was the sovereign itself, which was still synonymous with the territory and the political entity, and not the society – the *res publica*, as it was conceived later, especially after the French Revolution and the rise of the nation-state.

Inclusive / bio-political surveillance

This is the type of surveillance of which we usually speak in the modern era. Its political beginnings can be found in the French Revolution, when a new layer was added to the identification between the state and territory, and the territorial state became a "nation-state." The concept of the nation-state is rooted in the presumption of an overlap between a homogeneous group of people ("the nation") and a defined sovereign geographical space ("the state"). From then on, the society is the heart of the political entity and is the one to be defended (see Foucault 2003). The governmental principle moves from control over territory to control over population. The territory does not lose its significance – it still defines the boundaries of the *demos* – but it becomes one of the control array's attributes and not its initial principle.

Instead of a sovereign and eruptive power characterized mainly by the right to kill, a new governmental form is rising: a bio-political form that focuses on the management of life. This bio-political form is a continuous, consecutive, regulative, and fixing mechanism. Thus the role of surveillance changes: it is not meant only to study the population as a resource or as a danger, but to gain knowledge in order to fix norms and goals for development and improvement. The disciplinary form of government aspires to fix people and convert "bad" (people/actions) into "good" by means of tight control over the minutest acts and behaviors. As for surveillance practices, the disciplinary array acts on the bodies of individuals. It analyzes and disassembles persons, times, places, and actions. Disciplinary institutions – schools, hospitals, factories, prisons, military bases, and more – function as laboratories just as much as centers of correction.

According to Foucault, the disciplinary mode gave way in the eighteenth century to the *security* mode; and the flow of regulation mechanisms replaced, at least partly, the disciplinary institutions. Foucault distinguishes among the three types of control: "sovereignty is exercised within the borders of a territory, discipline is exercised on the bodies of individuals, and security is exercised over a whole population" (Foucault 2007: 11). Surveillance is not applied towards discrete atoms in prison cells or school classes, but towards society as a whole. According to Foucault, the surveillance has changed over time. The schools still transmit societal norms, but in subtler ways that do not break the society into atoms to be dealt with separately. Foucault compares authorities' reactions to the plague in the seventeenth century and the management of a smallpox eruption a century later. The plague was characterized by closure, division, isolation, and pointed treatment; during the smallpox eruption the main tools were statistic assumptions about the risks of contagion, mortality rate, after-effects, and so on. The disease was not conceived as a deviation from the norm, but part of it, which must be understood in order to improve the sum of flow, life, and mortality in the population as a whole. In the apparatuses of security there are no defined codes of permits and restrictions, but a constant effort to study the systems as they are in order to remove obstacles and encourage growth. *Laissez faire* is therefore the classic example of the security way of thinking of encouraging the "natural" flows of the economy and society (Foucault 2007: 45–47). We should emphasize here the central and important role of the freedom concept, and especially the freedom of movement of both people and goods. Surveillance systems require fewer laboratories than whole-population effective statistical arrays. This means that when examining how surveillance actually *works* we will see a difference between the disciplinary loci that meant to delay and watch (as in laboratory) and the security apparatuses that wish to observe and analyze without delaying and without breaking apart (people and actions).

Gilles Deleuze wrote about the shift from discipline societies to control societies. In discipline societies the individual passes from one closed place to another (from the family to school, military, factory, hospital, or prison, if needed) every time a project ends and another one begins. In modern societies these are continuous and smooth projects. Professional training, outpatient clinics, electronic handcuffs, electric gates, and credit cards: all these tie themselves subtly around the person, limiting, surveying, and following just as they are enabling and opening. Deleuze (1992: 5) writes of a city, imagined by Felix Guattari, in which "One would be able to leave one's apartment, one's street, one's neighborhood, thanks to one's dividual electronic card that raises a given barrier; but the card could just as easily be rejected on a given day or between certain hours; what counts is not the barrier but the computer that tracks each person's position."

That is exactly the array of which John Torpey (1998) writes in his research on the passport and the "legitimate means of movement." Torpey argues that, after expropriating the freedom of movement, modern states redistribute the means of movement as a means of controlling and appropriating people. [2] He rightly claims that the metaphor of a "penetration" of the state into society is not always accurate: it is better to say that the state "embraces" its citizens. The "penetration," which was an apt description in the colonial/founding stage, and also partly in the discipline society, does not always fit in modern states. Surveillance and administrative acts "hold" more than they "penetrate" society: "Systems of registration, censuses, and the like – along with documents such as passports and identity cards that amount to mobile versions of the 'files' states use to store knowledge about their subjects – have been crucial in states' efforts to embrace their citizens" (Torpey 1998: 245).

The redistribution of movement permits has two goals: gaining control and surveillance of subjects' movements and actions, and being perceived as benefiting the population. Hannah Arendt's (1973) famous words about the paperless people, deprived of the right to rights, reflect this clearly: holding a "statist" paper – be it an ID card or a passport – is a right, not a duty. Clearly, the state's interest is to reach as many citizens as possible in order to give them the right to rights – and embrace them at the same time.

Another type of surveillance is "big brother." Four million CCTV cameras in Britain catch the average citizen 300 times a day; in addition, cellular location, credit card spending and internet surfing habits, and so on, are subject to surveillance. That surveillance is supposedly a parallel to people's daily lives. It does not demand ID or attendance at an office: the citizen is passive. The surveillance is portrayed in such a way that only those who have something to hide will encounter problems; "decent" citizens will be fine.

To sum up the types of surveillance – discipline, security, control, embrace, and "big brother" – all have similar characteristics that distinguish them from the other types (colonial/founding and exclusionary). First, the relation between the state and the population is not antagonistic. Society is the body of the nation and is to be defended. Second, surveillance is part of the population's daily life. It does not penetrate or interfere; it is part of the everyday power and ideology apparatuses. Third (from the point of view of the surveillance practices), *the state needs the subjects to pass through as many inspection points as possible.* These can be schools and clinics; credit cards and cellular phones; ID cards and passports; or CCTV cameras. The state requires friction points with the population in order to study, follow, and embrace. The rationale is one of free movement – but one that needs coordination and cooperation with the authorities. The dialectics of free movement and high friction (a "smooth friction" that does not block the flow, but rather "accompanies" it in order to watch and regulate it) are central to my argument, as I shall show.

Exclusionary surveillance

This type of surveillance is connected to the dark side of nation-states, and to their way of differentiating populations within the territory – mainly citizens from non-citizens.[3] Most of all it symbolizes the withdrawal of the state from responsibility to its subjects, or to part of them. If colonial/founding surveillance is over territory, and inclusive surveillance is over the population as a whole, then exclusionary surveillance is meant to divide and to separate specific population groups from the general *demos* (to which inclusive surveillance is still applied) even though all groups live in the same territory.

While colonial/founding surveillance targeted the population as part of the territory's resources – and inclusive surveillance was interested in it for itself, as the main control object – exclusionary surveillance *ignores* specific populations. It is, to paraphrase the terminology of insurance companies, "small print surveillance": its main goal is to reduce the state's responsibility towards the subjects. The state does not "chase" its subjects in order to catalog and embrace them; rather, it chases them and spies on them in order to prove that they *do not* belong to it. When the Israeli population registry surveys the East Jerusalem Palestinian inhabitants who "move their life center" to another location for a certain time, its aim is not to embrace them but to deprive them of rights. The "struggle over demography" – particularly in Jerusalem, although the same is true of Israel/Palestine generally – is meant to keep some imagined demographic *status quo*, and is characterized by rights deprivation, removal, and misuse of statistical data against those surveyed.

Exclusionary surveillance differs from colonial/founding surveillance, although in both an antagonistic relation between the state and the population prevails. The colonial/founding regime's relation to the population was inclusive. Even when the population was conceived only as one of the territory's attributes, it was still inseparable from and an integral part of it; subjects were part of the territory's strength (or weakness) and comprised one of its natural resources.

However, when certain populations are conceived as unnecessary, surplus, or redundant, the route to rejecting them out of hand is short. Examples abound: indigenous groups – Native Americans, Aborigines – were not needed when settlers in the colonies developed their economic systems (see, for example, Lamar and Thompson 1981); huge slum populations, living in half-independent, informal, unregistered micro-economies, exist on the edges of society (Davis 2006); and refugees fleeing from the horrors of war or natural catastrophe to neighboring countries are similarly peripheral (Arendt 1973) – the fact that they are surplus to requirements leads the state to seek to avoid responsibility for them.

For this reason, we cannot reduce the three types of surveillance to the dichotomy of citizen/non-citizen. First, surveillance practices are partly constitutive of citizenship, and in the colonial/founding stage even precede the modern concept of citizenship. Second, there are cases of inclusive practices towards non-citizens (as in some colonies and towards workers who are needed in the contemporary West), and vice versa (exclusionary practices towards (citizen) slum or underprivileged populations or, in the specific case of Israel, towards the Bedouins living in "unrecognized villages"; Yiftachel 2009). The main questions are those of necessity, on the one hand, and the sensation of danger or threat, on the other. These factors – not the legal titles of citizenship – determine "difference." The necessity-versus-threat factors usually crystallize around racial/ethnic/national lines, creating racism, ethnocentrism, and extreme nationalism.[4]

An example of a combination of two types of surveillance as derived from the question of necessity can be found in the South African apartheid regime. In spite of the desire for racial separation and the wish to take the blacks out of the whites' spaces, it was well known that the South African economy was based on the cheap black labor force. The black population was therefore divided between the "needed" and the "redundant." Surveillance apparatuses first had to distinguish one from the other: an exclusionary surveillance was directed towards the "redundant," who were expelled from the urban space to distant and poor Bantustans (where they were "independent" – that is, not the white South African government's problem any more), while an inclusive (although still oppressive and tough) surveillance was aimed at the "needed." The latter were surveyed and delineated, but kept in proximity to the white public space. In order simultaneously to preserve the needed labor force near the city yet make it as invisible as possible, blacks were placed in closed and supervised dormitories, and certain routes and times were specified for movement from the dorms to the workplaces (Christopher 1984: 189). Architects developed systems in various scales – from the house to the full city – that separated movement routes and calculated sight perspectives in order to avoid unwanted meetings and interactions (Bremner 2005).

The supervision of movement was executed mainly through the Pass Laws and their derivations, which regulated daily movement in and between the different zones. Non-whites had to carry documents and permits for nearly every move. These documents, or "reference books," functioned not only as identity cards but as labor documents that included work histories and any rules violations. Over 250,000 people were tried each year for Pass Laws violations. Employers participated in the state's efforts by reporting even the smallest violations. A significant part of the white population was employed by that administrative army, comprising 1.2 million workers at its peak (Dayan 2009). The bureaucracy supervised and controlled every movement of non-whites, and a reference book revocation led to expulsion.

What I emphasize here is authorities' seeming need to control and regulate movement. Here as well the goal was to reach every person and not leave any corner unseen by the surveillance arrays: routes were defined, permits printed and handed out, passes registered, and people tried. All of these efforts marked the administration in the physical space as well as on the bodies of passengers. These elements are mostly absent from the contemporary surveillance and population management arrays in the occupied territories.

Surveillance and population management in Israel/Palestine

It is beyond the scope of this chapter to describe in detail the characteristics of surveillance and population management deployed by Israel on the Palestinian population across time, but we can still point to some significant landmarks. First, there was the general census taken by the nascent state of Israel in 1948 (see Chapter 12, this volume). The census (I refer here only to the counting of the Palestinian population in Israel) had a dual role: studying the population, on the one hand, and reducing and negating it, on the other. The decision to impose a curfew, and to count the people *in situ*, was intended to hold each person in his or her "true" place – just as it was intended to reduce the number of those counted. Approximately 20 percent of the Palestinian population that stayed in the new state's territory were away from home on census day. Therefore, they were not counted and were deprived of rights, and their property was expropriated. Some of them were later described as "present absentees," others as "infiltrators" who have no rights in the state of Israel.

After that first filtering, the Arab population was put under an inclusive disciplinary surveillance array. Until the end of the military government in December 1966, Israel employed a branched administrative system characterized by movement limitations, tough policing and monitoring, tight and continuous surveillance, and staged and conditional development. General Security Services (GSS) reports contained detailed information on "subversive" political conferences as well as a count of the number of Israeli flags raised on Independence Day. Special attention was paid to the education system and its employees. The aim was to educate the Palestinian population in Israel to remain quiet and cooperate with the state. It was a disciplinary system *par excellence* (see Chapter 4, this volume; Cohen 2006).

As for the territories occupied in 1967, the situation was already different. Prime Minister Levi Eshkol famously referred to the wish of separating the bride (the Palestinian population) from the dowry (the occupied territories). This principle of separation between population and territory stands at the base of the Israeli control system over the last four decades (see Gordon 2008; Azoulay and Ophir 2008).

Shortly after the 1967 war, the Minister of Defense at the time, Moshe Dayan, who was personally responsible for designing many of the characteristics of the occupation's early stages, decided not to copy the military government and its apparatuses in the OPT. In opposition to the intended interference policy applied by the military government, Dayan insisted that "the tendency should be that an Arab in the Territories would be able to live his life normally without needing and without seeing an Israeli government worker" (Gazit 1985: 152). Dayan wrote in his diary a week after the war that "we must take out the army units from the Arab cities' centers . . . and reduce their upsetting presence in the population . . . above the Israeli commander office there is an Israeli flag, and there is no reason that every Arab walking in the street will become angry seeing the flag" (Gazit 1985: 185). This type of control, known as "invisible occupation," is the opposite of inclusive surveillance. It does not create symbols of identification; nor does it police subjects' thoughts and actions. It seeks neither to contain the Palestinian population in the OPT nor expel it. Rather, it could be termed "indifferent" surveillance: as long as the population remained quiet, the control array cared for neither it nor its actions. Still, it is more akin to colonial surveillance: the population is necessary to the economy, but can also be a source of danger. Israel never thought seriously of including the Palestinian population in the Israeli *demos*, and never intended to give them Israeli IDs and voting rights.[5] However, since the population was needed as unskilled, cheap labor, it was included *de facto* in the economic system and accepted in the Israeli public space.

This type of control functioned reasonably in the first years of the occupation, but was found to be insufficient as the level of Palestinian resistance rose. The "cheap occupation" times had passed; the control array had to elevate the level of surveillance to make it tighter, more invasive, and more violent. The GSS and the Israel Defense Forces (IDF) penetrated the Palestinian spaces and populations in large numbers and with great force. Checkpoints, raids, and initiated clashes became part of the Palestinian landscape as the numbers of Palestinians killed and injured rose dramatically. And yet, although more antagonistic, surveillance during the first Intifada was still not exclusionary.

Dealing with the first Intifada, James Ron (2003) defines two types of relationship between the state and a population conceived as "dangerous." His point of departure is the question: why did Serbia implement *ethnic cleansing* in Bosnia, while Israel *policed* the occupied territories? His answer distinguishes between two spatial patterns: *frontier*, a peripheral region unincorporated into the state's legal zone of influence, which thus tends to suffer from a lawless, nationalist violence; and *ghetto*, a zone of unwanted and marginalized populations but which is still included within the dominant state's legal sphere of influence, classifying them as quasi-members of the polity. While Bosnia was a frontier *vis-à-vis* Serbia, the West Bank and the Gaza Strip were ghettoes within the state of Israel. Thus, although Israel did not wish to include Palestinians, those quasi-members of the polity, it could not exclude them altogether. Israel still felt some kind of responsibility and therefore continued the life management – even if violent and harsh.

With the signing of the Oslo Accords and the beginning of "outsourcing" the major part of civil responsibility to the Palestinian Authority, institutional relations between Israel and the Palestinians weakened. As Israel was less responsible for the Palestinians it became easier for Israel to neglect them and their problems. Further, the necessity for Palestinian workers in Israel declined dramatically with the re-establishment of the Green Line at the time of the first Gulf War, suicide-bomber attacks in Israel's cities (mainly in the second half of the 1990s), and extensive labor immigration. The wane in necessity, coupled with the closures that physically separated Palestinians from Israelis and distanced the former from the sight and public space of the latter, heralded indifference. Thus, when the second Intifada broke out, straight fighting and violence took the place of population management and policing (Gordon 2008).

Surveillance and population management in the second Intifada

During the second Intifada, Palestinians were no longer conceived as part of the Israeli polity. The guiding principle of relations between Israel and the Palestinians was that of separation (Gordon 2008). Now, there is no inclusive/bio-political surveillance in the OPT. If there is a defining feature of the second Intifada (excluding the Seam Zones and East Jerusalem, as I will show later), it is the *lack* of paperwork: a significant and near-total absence of administration and management activity. As discussed, the first two types of surveillance require as much friction as possible with the subjects. Checkpoints facilitate identification, registration, and surveillance. Pass permits require people to visit offices and register, and they "embrace" the population. In the Israeli military government years of 1948–1966, movement permits were the ultimate "carrot." Cooperators received permits for their services, and the whole population had to pass through government offices in order to register, identify themselves, and answer questions in order to receive the awaited permit.

In present-day Israel, on the other hand, checkpoints are intended not to raise the friction level but to stop Palestinian movement as much as possible (see Chapter 16, this volume). In most of the inner checkpoints, nothing is written down, and no data are cataloged or transmitted. Passage regulations are unclear and in constant flux, making it nearly impossible for the controlled population to behave "correctly." Permits are printed and dispersed in ridiculously small numbers, and the DCOs that issue the permits go to great lengths to be inaccessible and uncooperative. All of this indicates the profound difference between the current situation and the types of surveillance discussed previously.

First, the checkpoints. In the West Bank there are 103 manned checkpoints and 592 physical barriers. Excluding the 40 "closure" checkpoints[6] that have a different rationale (see below), there are 63 permanent manned checkpoints in the West Bank and an average of over 100 "flying"[7] checkpoints per week. These places – the manned roadblocks – should have been the core of the surveillance array in the OPT. In practice, though, most roadblocks are improvised facilities, lacking computers or even operation diaries. Passage through them resembles more a piece of theater than an administrative act. Palestinians try to convince soldiers – holders of near-limitless discretion regarding the decision on passage – that they are sick, that they must pass through for this or that reason, showing all kinds of documents without knowing which is relevant (see, for example, Kelly 2006). Arbitrariness is the rule rather than the clear and well-known passage regulations towards which other modern administrations tend. *The checkpoints' friction is meant not to survey but to limit movement.* The purpose is to make the passage experience unpleasant, if not impossible, in order to encourage Palestinians to avoid it altogether. There is also a "bingo" practice at the checkpoints, which contrasts with purposive surveillance.[8] Those refused passage, in most cases, are not detained or investigated; they simply return to their point of origin. There is no follow-up or purpose to the exercise: the delayed are delayed, the refused are refused; nothing is written down either way, and there is no long-term supervision.

The passage regulations, instead of being clear and known (like the citizenship laws in a modern civilized state, for example) are a mystery. Sometimes passage is granted only to women over forty or boys under fifteen; sometimes it is granted to residents of Nablus, but they are then not allowed to return. Palestinians cannot know in advance whether they can pass through a checkpoint (let alone how many "flying" checkpoints will pop up *en route*), and therefore they often prefer to avoid the checkpoint altogether. In that way the rationale of checkpoints as *check*-points is dismantled. A B'Tselem report notes that the movement restrictions in the OPT are never written down (in marked contrast to the system that operated in apartheid South Africa): not in law books or pamphlets, and not on signposts along the restricted roads themselves (B'Tselem 2004).

The surprisingly small number of permits (discussed above) is the best proof of the lack of administrative friction. [9] The DCOs, the only sources of permits, apparently do all they can to prevent people from using their services. Procedures for securing a permit are vague and inconsistent; working hours and access routes to the DCOs change constantly; and the permits are often not respected at the checkpoints in any case. A Machsom Watch report (2004) recounts a few problems:

> Bureaucratic preventions with different, irrelevant, excuses . . .the people who apply to the DCO are usually sent away with false pretexts: come now/go now, today's closed, the officer isn't here, you need more documents . . . the bureaucratic failure is so transparent that it seems clear that the purpose is not to give the service . . . Many times the DCO's location is a trap in itself: to reach it the Palestinian needs a special permit which he can get only in that DCO.

But what seems "inefficiency" is actually a very efficient system. It creates a state of "effective ineffectiveness" (Berda 2006). Another report states clearly:

> When decisions are apparently random, control becomes absolute. No one can be sure that he or she has not been – or will not be – "prohibited for reasons of security." The reasons are so numerous, and the use made of them so changeable, that uncertainty becomes the ultimate system of control within the framework of the certainty of the occupation.
> (Machsom Watch and Physicians for Human Rights-Israel 2004)

It should be clear: the checkpoint is not a surveillance apparatus but an uncertainty production post that is designed to control Palestinian movement – not to *regulate* it but to *minimize* it.

Another example of the uncertainty production at the micro-level of the checkpoint is "the imaginary line":

> Among the many delayed persons there are two taxi drivers . . . "They passed the 'green line'" says the checkpoint commander . . . it turns out that it is an imaginary line next to a green signpost pointing the way to Nablus. The signpost

is found about 200 meters from the checkpoint, and marks the line taxi drivers shouldn't pass. A driver that diverges from this imaginary line is detained.

(Machsom Watch 2004)

The imaginary line is, according to Merav Amir and Hagar Kotef (forthcoming), an apparatus with an inherent failure system. It is produced in order to ensure that the passengers will always fail, and will never understand the system or its rationale; they can never prepare themselves for the checkpoint. The imaginary line produces *a priori* guilt: Palestinians will always fail and can therefore always be blamed and punished for something. But at its most basic, it is an uncertainty tool that is meant to impose self-restrictions on movement. An example of the efficiency of the method is reflected in another testimonial:

> Anabta 12/12/05: the flying checkpoint that was in the junction disappeared . . . the gate is wide open . . . two taxis are coming from both sides and change passengers. Just as if there is a checkpoint. But there isn't. Why did they change then? The driver says that just ten minutes ago it was closed and they might close it again, therefore people manage as if there is a checkpoint.
>
> (Amir and Kotef forthcoming)

The spatial uncertainty makes nearly every movement dangerous or at least problematic. The checkpoints' friction becomes unbearable and encourages people to stay at home. One of many examples is that of Samer Sada, from the village of Jit, near Nablus:

> We are arrested here. My kids didn't leave the village for four years. Four months since I was in Nablus. Why should I go out? A soldier would tell me "show permit." I have a magnetic card to Barkan [an industrial zone near the settlement of Ariel], but there is a soldier nervous about Arabs, nervous about I don't know what, who will tell me "pull over." So why should I go? I prefer to stay at home, not to go out.
>
> (Levy 2007)

The goal of spatial uncertainty is to minimize Palestinian movement. The "war on terror" is currently the only feature of Israeli's relations with Palestinians. The easiest solution to the problem of "terror export" (or attacks on settlers in the settlements or on West Bank roads) is to freeze all Palestinian movement. The more Palestinians are frozen in one place, the safer Israelis feel (see Handel 2010). The lack of economic necessity, on the one hand, and the lack of a sense of responsibility, on the other, create a severe imbalance between the two societies' needs: a total preference for Israeli interests at the expense of Palestinians' daily life and freedom of movement.

To sum up the relation between space management and movement policing: in the sovereign regime the main function was that of deduction – tax collection on bridges, men forcibly recruiting for the army in villages or along roads, and so on (see Foucault 1990: 136). In the modern, bio-political regime the main principle is that of friction and maximum interaction between the subject and the state. In the exclusionary regime the main principle is friction reduction, as responsibility decreases. *The exclusionary regime prefers movement prevention to movement regulation.*

Another important point, although one on which I cannot elaborate fully at this time, is the distinction Israel makes between land and people. Israel simultaneously excludes people and includes land – *de facto* and *de jure*. One classic case of conjunction between the two is the "black list" of Palestinians who own land, mainly in the Jordan Valley, but were not allowed to return to the West Bank after 1967 (Eldar 2006). It is a classic paperwork act meant to exclude people and include land. There are currently 700,000 dunams of "survey lands" in the West Bank; of those, around 2,000 dunams are declared "state lands" each year (Benn 2004). It probably goes without saying that Israel does not do the same for people: that is, declare them "state people" and include them in the polity.

The Seam Zone

One place that *is* rigidly supervised, requires significant volumes of paperwork, and is subjected to seemingly classic surveillance systems is the Seam Zone (i.e., the region between the Separation Wall and the Green Line). The first article in the order creating the Seam Zone states that "no one may enter the Seam Zone or stay in it" and that "anyone in the Seam Zone must leave it immediately."[10] The next article allows all other "kinds of people" into the Zone, aside from its Palestinian inhabitants.

In the closed area, every entry and stay requires a permit. Zone villagers must have a "permanent resident permit," which must be renewed every three months, in order to continue to live in their own houses. Non-inhabitants wishing to enter the Zone must request a special permit from the DCOs. Specific categories of people may request a permit: agricultural workers, teachers, irrigation technicians, and others. In general, the permit gives its holder the right to stay within the Zone only during the day; sleeping in the Zone requires separate approval. A permit is valid only at the specific entrance gate that is named on it.

A "spatial table" is thus constituted in the Seam Zone. Each item is put in its specific place, according to the rational justification of the narrow categories set by Israel. Movement, allowed only at one named gate and only during its specific hours of operation, is also bound to specified patterns. The other aspect of the table is its ability to exclude and eliminate. The moment an item fails to fit into its prescribed location, it is considered dispensable and is discarded.

Unique to the Seam Zone is the physico-geographical existence of this table. The translation of bureaucratic documents on to a concrete territory makes classification much more violent than it ordinarily is. The method prepares the ground (or at least produces the potential) for a gradual "bureaucratic exclusion" by which the land will be emptied of its inhabitants by reducing the number of permits and tightening the criteria for eligibility. The spatial imposition of the table allows not only the removal of a person's papers from a drawer but the removal of the individual from the land (see, for example, B'Tselem 2003). The surveillance method in the Seam Zone is classically exclusionary. Each person entering or living passes through a detailed identity check, in order to prove that he or she is *ineligible* – and thus should be excluded from the area. The difference between the Seam Zone and the rest of the

West Bank lies in the wish to keep the border areas "purified," because of the fear of mixture and interpenetration (Sibley 1995: ch. 3).

The only locations at which there is classic inclusive surveillance are the "terminals" separating the OPT from Israel proper. These new facilities are designed as interstate border crossings, and tend to apply the same kind of surveillance.[11] The only people to be supervised "inclusively" are the workers in Israel and the settlements. There are 60,000 Palestinian workers who are economically necessary.[12] While this is not a negligible number, it is still small when compared to the total number of Palestinians. If these workers could be replaced by labor immigrants or Israeli workers, they too would be discharged and excluded from the Israeli surveillance interest.

Even the seemingly most significant example of Israeli surveillance – control over the Palestinian population registry – is actually intended to exclude: to identify a Gazan inhabitant in the West Bank; to identify illegal Palestinians who lack legal status for whatever reason (in the OPT themselves, not in Israel); to prevent people from coming from Jordan or Egypt.

There is, of course, also the surveillance conducted by the GSS: supervising and recording the smallest details, intercepting phone calls, placing agents within the population, and so on. But this is precisely the peak of exclusionary surveillance: temporal exclusion (to prison) or permanent exclusion (liquidation). There is no interest in the population as a whole, and as long as there is no "terror exportation" there is no concern shown for the inhabitants at all.[13]

State of exception

The state of exception is the suspension of the law but also, always, an exception of people. The exception has two aspects: distinguishing between a friend and an enemy; and defining how the law treats and relates to each of them. Exclusionary surveillance is the state of exception's operative tool. It is exclusionary surveillance that separates the people who are part of the *demos* from those who are excluded from it – a separation that stands at the base of the population management practices in the modern-day OPT.[14]

Instead of supervising the population in order to identify specific problems and violations, permanent uncertainty creates a mechanism of *a priori* guilt unconnected to real and specific actions. The extensive deployment of checkpoints and roadblocks is meant to limit movement and to create a state of basic and permanent guilt. Dani Rubinstein (2002) wrote:

> The movement limitations are not only impossible and harsh decrees, but also ones that automatically turn most of the Palestinian population into criminals. Nearly every Palestinian that leaves his house in order to reach work, school, shopping, medical treatment, or to visit relatives, must bypass a checkpoint and therefore becomes a violator of the movement regulations set by Israel.

Criminalization reaches its highest levels in the Seam Zone and in East Jerusalem, where people require a permit even to live in their own homes. Thus the person is always guilty, without the possibility of justification or correction (since there is no rule and exception, right and wrong). The person is guilty just because he lives, moves, and acts; no correction is possible, and therefore no correcting-inclusive surveillance practices are needed.

Zygmunt Bauman (1998) writes about Pelican Bay Prison in California. The inmates live in windowless cells and have nearly no interaction with the guards or their fellow prisoners. They do not work and have no access to any social activity. The guards are enclosed in their own areas; they manage the jail through loudspeakers and are seen by the prisoners only rarely. Their only mission *vis-à-vis* the prisoners is to ensure that they are locked in their cells (Bauman 1998: 108). The improving and correcting dimensions of the disciplinary prison are totally absent in Pelican Bay. All that is left is separation and closure. In contrast to the panoptic prison which aimed to teach behavior and work habits by watching every action, "what the inmates of the Pelican Bay prison *do* inside their solitary cells *does not matter*. What *does matter* is that *they stay there*" (Bauman 1998: 113; emphasis in original). This is a surveillance-free prison. Guards do not look into cells or supervise – all they do is keep prisoners locked in and alive; they have no other duties. There is neither "correction" nor "rehabilitation" – just locking and removing. The state does not embrace the prisoner in any way – it merely expels him for a specified period.

In a similar way – though for an unspecified period – Israel controls the Palestinians in the OPT. They are kept alive and blocked in their archipelago of isolated cells. What do Palestinians do in their cells? Israel no longer even seems to care.

Notes

1 I would like to thank Cedric Parizot, Yehouda Shenhav and Ronen Shamir as well as the volume editors for their excellent comments on earlier versions of this chapter.
2 Torpey follows Marx's argument about the expropriation of the means of production from workers by capitalists, and Weber's argument about the state's monopoly over the legitimate means of violence.
3 The non-citizen is a person who lives permanently in a specific state, but is not considered part of the state's collective, and many times is conceived as a problem or danger to the common safety and wealth of the national collective. A UN report estimates that there are 175 million non-citizens in the world in 2004. See: <http://www.justiceinitiative.org/activities/ec/ec_noncitizens>.
4 One can think on the rise of the "loyalty" discourse in the 2009 elections in Israel, with Avigdor Lieberman's slogan "No Loyalty – No Citizenship." This tendency to see a whole population of citizens as a threat shows that citizenship and inclusion do not always overlap.
5 Compare this to the Israeli (failed) attempt to force the Golan Druze to accept Israeli IDs after the area's annexation in 1981. In that case Israel used threats and punishments in order to impose its sovereignty on the Golan's 13,000 inhabitants (Azoulay and Ophir 2008: 78). A comprehensive comparison of the Golan with the OPT is beyond the scope of this chapter
6 The checkpoints that supposedly separate the West Bank from "Israel proper" – although all but one are located a few kilometers from the Green Line and into the OPT.
7 The "flying" checkpoint usually consists of a jeep or an armored vehicle and a small number of soldiers. It can be opened and closed in a few minutes.
8 Once a few passengers have passed through, in a totally random manner, the soldiers will delay one person and pass his name and ID number to their headquarters, and from there to the GSS offices. This process can take anything up to an hour. The important point is that most of the time, even in a case of "bingo" (i.e., some information is unearthed), the soldiers neither detain nor investigate the delayed people; they simply bar them from passing so they must turn back.

9 Compare this to the first years of the occupation, when "[t]elevisions, refrigerators, and gas stoves were counted, as were livestock, orchards and tractors. Letters ... were checked, registered and examined ... Even eating habits were scrutinized, as was the nutritional value of the Palestinian food basket ... An intricate permit regime was introduced requiring licenses to build houses, open businesses, sell produce ... or work in the public sector" (Gordon 2008: 9–10).
10 Order Regarding Defense Regulations (Judea and Samaria) (No. 378), 1970, Declaration Regarding Closure of Area No. s2/03 (Seam Area).
11 For an excellent analysis of the "terminals," see Braverman (forthcoming).
12 And they are always interchangeable. For every "entry prohibited" worker there are many competitors, so the system therefore has no obligation to any specific person.
13 Ariella Azoulay and Adi Ophir (2008) argue that the Israeli control array's responsibility towards Palestinians is reduced to the prevention of a humanitarian catastrophe. Its bio-political task is therefore to keep the Palestinian population on the verge of catastrophe: as weak as possible, but still alive.
14 See also Didier Bigo's (2006) concept of ban-opticon. Bigo speaks about surveillance as a tool of exception in the Western post-9/11 context. While he concentrates on the West and on the ways of profiling the individuals who cross its borders, this chapter deals with populations in a semi-permanent state of occupation/colonization.

Bibliography

Amir, M. and H. Kotef (forthcoming) "On Imaginary Lines: Biopolitics, Disciplinary Apparati and Sovereign Violence at the Checkpoints."

Anderson, B. (1994) *Imagined Communities*. London and New York: Verso.

Arendt, H. (1973) *The Origins of Totalitarianism*. New York: Harcourt, Brace and Company.

Azoulay, A. and A. Ophir (2008) *This Regime Which is Not One: Occupation and Democracy between the Sea and the River (1967–)*. Tel Aviv: Resling [in Hebrew].

Bauman, Z. (1998) *Globalization: The Human Consequences*. Cambridge: Polity Press.

Benn, A. (2004) "'State Land' Loophole Allows Appropriation," *Haaretz*, September 26.

Berda, Y. (2006) "The Bureaucracy of Occupation – Bare Life and Security Theology," paper presented at the Bare Life Conference, Van Leer Institute, Jerusalem, September.

Bigo, D. (2006) "Security, Exception, Ban and Surveillance," in D. Lyon (ed.) *Theorizing Surveillance: The Panopticon and Beyond*. Devon: Willan Publishing, pp. 46–68.

Braverman, I. (forthcoming) "Civilized Borders: A Study of Israel's New Border Regime," *Antipode*.

Bremner, L. (2005) "Border/Skin," in M. Sorkin (ed.) *Against the Wall: Israel's Barrier to Peace*. New York and London: The New Press, pp. 122–138.

B'Tselem (2003) "Nu'man, East Jerusalem: Life under the Threat of Expulsion," report, September.

—— (2004) "Forbidden Roads Regime in the West Bank," report, August.

Christopher, A.J. (1984) *Colonial Africa*. New Jersey: Barnes and Noble.

Cohen, H. (2006) *Good Arabs: The Israeli Security Services and the Israeli Arabs*. Jerusalem: Ivrit-Hebrew Publishing House [in Hebrew].

Cohn, B.S. (1996) *Colonialism and its Forms of Knowledge: British Rule in India*. Princeton, NJ: Princeton University Press.

Crozier, M. (1964) *The Bureaucratic Phenomenon*. London: Tavistock.

Davis, M. (2006) *The Planet of Slums*. New York and London: Verso.

Dayan, H. (2009) "Principles of Old and New Regimes of Separation: Apartheid and Contemporary Israel/Palestine," in A. Ophir, M. Givoni and S. Hanafi (eds) *The Power of Inclusive Exclusion: Anatomy of Israeli Rule in the Occupied Palestinian Territories*. New York: Zone Books, pp. 281–322.

Deleuze, G. (1992) "Postscript on the Societies of Control," *October*, 59, pp. 3–7.

Eldar, A. (2006) "The Valley's Black List," *Haaretz*, March 14.

Foucault, M. (1979) *Discipline and Punish: The Birth of the Prison*. New York: Vintage Books.

—— (1990) *The History of Sexuality, Vol. 1*. New York: Vintage Books.

—— (2003) *Society Must Be Defended*. New York: Picador.

—— (2007) *Security, Territory, Population*. New York: Palgrave Macmillan.

Gazit, S. (1985) *The Stick and the Carrot: The Israeli Administration in Judea and Samaria*. Tel Aviv: Zmora Bitan [in Hebrew].

Giddens, A. (1985) *The Nation-State and Violence: Volume Two of a Contemporary Critique of Historical Materialism*. Cambridge: Polity Press.

Gordon, N. (2008) *Israel's Occupation*. Berkeley: University of California Press.

Handel, A. (2009) "Where, Whereto and When in the Occupied Palestinian Territories: An Introduction to Geography of Disaster," in A. Ophir, M. Givoni and S. Hanafi (eds) *The Power of Inclusive Exclusion: Anatomy of Israeli Rule in the Occupied Palestinian Territories*. New York: Zone Books, pp. 179–222.

—— (2010) "Gated/Gating Community: The Settlements Array in the West Bank," in A. Lehavi (ed.) *Gated Communities in Israel*. Tel Aviv: Tel Aviv University, pp. 493–536.

Kelly, T. (2006) "Documented Lives: Fear and the Uncertainties of Law during the Second Palestinian *Intifada*," *Journal of Royal Anthropological Institute*, 12, pp. 89–107.

Lamar, H. and L. Thompson (1981) *The Frontier in History: North America and Southern Africa Compared*. New Haven, CT: Yale University Press.

Levy, G. (2007) "What Are You Doing for the Holiday?," *Haaretz*, January 5.

Mamdani, M. (2002) "Making Sense of Political Violence in Postcolonial Africa," *Identity, Culture and Politics*, 3(2), pp. 1–24.

Machsom Watch (2004) "Mabat Mineged" [Opposite Gaze], report [in Hebrew].

Machsom Watch and Physicians for Human Rights–Israel (2004) "The Bureaucracy of Occupation: The District Civil Liaison Offices," report.

Ron, J. (2003) *Frontiers and Ghettos: State Violence in Serbia and Israel*. Berkeley: University of California Press.

Rubinstein, D. (2002) "A Land of Roadblocks and Barriers," *Haaretz*, November 3.

Sibley, D. (1995) *Geographies of Exclusion*. London and New York: Routledge.

Torpey, J. (1998) "Coming and Going: On the State Monopolization of the Legitimate 'Means of Movement,'" *Sociological Theory*, 16(3), pp. 239–259.

Yiftachel, O. (2009) "Theoretical Notes on 'Gray Cities': The Coming of Urban Apartheid?," *Planning Theory*, 8(1), pp. 88–100.

14 The "Israelization" of social sorting and the "Palestinianization" of the racial contract
Reframing Israel/Palestine and the war on terror

Yasmeen Abu-Laban and Abigail B. Bakan

Introduction: social sorting and Israel/Palestine

As an emerging and multidisciplinary field, surveillance studies draws our attention to how people are seen (Lyon 2007: 1). Surveillance is ubiquitous, particularly in the contemporary information age, when both corporations and states make use of new technologies that allow for the rapid collection and flow of data within and across national boundaries (Lyon and Zureik 1996: 4–5; Whitaker 1999: 80–122). As a consequence, while surveillance arguably may be understood as a characteristic of human communities across both time and space, today there is both a qualitative and a quantitative escalation (Lyon 2007: 100). Moreover, while the ubiquity of surveillance was established well before September 11, 2001, the post-9/11 period has allowed for a steep intensification of surveillance processes (Lyon 2003; Todd and Bloch 2003; Zureik and Salter 2005). There is an increasing legitimacy of state-supported and state-promoted surveillance as an acceptable form of maintaining "security" (Ong 2006; Agamben 2005), broadly framed in terms of a post-9/11 model. This security model is ostensibly motivated to protect an innocent public citizenry associated with states of the global North from "terrorists"; and these "terrorists" ostensibly originate from and/or find safe haven in states of the global South, or seek, or have sought via immigration, to enter states of the global North.

Our particular interest in surveillance studies relates to understanding unequal power relations and sites of resistance. From this perspective the concept of "social sorting" (rather than merely "privacy") serves as a compelling point of critical entry into contemporary surveillance studies, not least in relation to Israel/Palestine and the post-9/11 period. As David Lyon argues, social sorting underscores the fact that surveillance is not a neutral process, and that people may be categorized and treated differently as a result of gender, race, ethnicity, religion, class and age, among other forms of difference (Lyon 2007: 177). Considering the post-9/11 period as a pivotal marker, we examine the manner in which a particular form of social sorting has moved from an apparently unique condition in the context of Israel/Palestine, often seen as *sui generis*, to one that has "gone global." We suggest that what could be considered a certain "Palestinianization" has occurred in liberal democracies, generalizing a sense of fear and threat in response to those who are socially sorted as "terrorists." This sorting, similar to the manner in which Palestinians have been separated and socially sorted from Israelis in the Middle East context, rests on ideologically constructed markers of difference (Islamic beliefs, Arabic origins, and/or racial stereotypes) that are frequently assumed to be visible through ascribed phenotypical characteristics. Racialized patterns of social sorting are not new. Rather, they are a feature of what Charles Mills (1997) has usefully termed the "racial contract." However, the particular association and legitimacy of racialized social sorting with Islamophobia, or anti-Muslim racism, in the post-9/11 period, can be understood to have particular roots in the Israel/Palestine context.

Palestinianization, however, arises in relation to the hegemonic state that depends upon its construction. Notably, we argue that a parallel "Israelization" of surveillance and social sorting has developed in the same liberal democratic states that have relied on Palestinianization. While Israel has commonly been identified as an exceptional state without comparison, in the post-9/11 context there has been a shift. Now the US, and by association other liberal democracies in the global North, have come to identify the need for uniquely repressive measures in the face of a perceived "terrorist" threat similar to that faced by Israel since its inception as a state.

To demonstrate this argument, we suggest a reframing of the post-1948 period of Israel's historical narrative to illustrate how the Israeli military state came to rely on the figure of the "Palestinian terrorist," and how this now serves as a microcosm for the "war on terror." As such, we argue that the racialization of security that defines Israel's apartheid-like system has moved in the post-9/11 period further from the local to the global, as have the actual and potential sites and forms of resistance to surveillance and social sorting. We present an interpretive chronological reading based on an understanding of contemporary "terrorism" as a racialized category, derived significantly from the context of Israel/Palestine. We demonstrate how this has become more firmly entrenched in security responses in liberal democratic countries of Europe and North America, feeding policies and practices which bypass liberal norms of racial and ethnic neutrality, due process of the law, and human rights. Israel's surveillance practices and its particular form of social sorting have influenced, in the terms of Agamben (2005), "exceptional" responses in existing liberal democracies wherein provisional measures (a state of emergency) are transformed into a technique of governance.

The argument proceeds in six parts. In the first section, we address the non-democratic character of the Israeli state, and theorize both the limits and utility of the applicability to Agamben's notion of a "state of exception" in the case of Israel/Palestine. We contextualize and challenge the claim to exceptionality of the state of Israel, and frame its particular form of racialization in the context of Mills' notion of the racial contract.

The next four sections cover specific time periods: the establishment of the state of Israel in 1948 to the end of the 1967 war; 1967 until the end of the Cold War in 1991; the Oslo and post-Oslo contexts between 1992 and 2000; and the contemporary post-September 11, 2001 period. Through this periodization we demonstrate how the move from the local to the global has been signficantly buttressed not only by technological developments that may enable greater means for social sorting ("Israelization") but through an aggressive ideological campaign constructed around the notion of the

Palestinian "terrorist" ("Palestinianization"). This ideological construction is shown to posit Israel, artificially, as a victim state, therefore justifying the use of violent measures which subvert human rights norms and normalize US and Western patriotism, security, and exceptional measures in relation to the ascribed threat of "Islamic" and/or "Arab" terrorism. This political assertion of Islamophobia (or anti-Muslim racism), in conjunction with security and the war on terror (Razack 2008; Mamdani 2004; Fekete 2004), impacts the nature of social sorting, affecting both non-citizens and citizens.

The sixth and final section considers sites of resistance, which persist despite the extreme repressive apparatus that maintains Israel's racialization and oppression of Palestinians.

Israel as a state of exception? Theorizing race, and racial contracts

Agamben's concept of the "state of exception" rests ambiguously with regard to its applicability to the Israeli state. At issue is the implication of Israel's unproblematic membership in the community of Western liberal democracies (see Zreik 2008 on its applicability; and Pappe 2008 for the critique). As Pappe notes, if Israel is conceptually included in this community, it would be the only so-called "democracy" where citizenship is overtly defined through ethnicity and religion (Pappe 2008: 160). Put differently, apartheid regimes are normally counterpoised rather than equated with liberal democratic systems of governance. Moreover, as Pappe continues, since 1948 violence has characterized the Israeli state's relations with Palestinians (whether holding Israeli citizenship or not), and therefore violence is the norm rather than, as implied in Agamben's understanding, the exception in an otherwise liberal consensual model (Pappe 2008: 165).

This exchange is useful in illustrating an important aspect of exception not actually considered by Agamben: namely, the specific manner in which Israel has been treated as "democratic," despite considerable evidence to the contrary (see, e.g., Rodinson 1973; Zureik 1979; Davis 2003; Cook 2006; Yiftachel 2006). This we term *mythologized exceptionalism*. Israel is commonly identified as a state without comparison, framed in international politics as the only "Jewish" state, and one that is claimed to be exceptionally "democratic" in the context of the Middle East (Cook 2006; Rose 2004). There is also a mythologized history subsumed in the notion of a "chosen people," and a specific framing in the origins and current hegemonic positioning of Zionist ideology that emphasizes this exceptionality (Noble 2005; Siegel 1986). This mythologized exceptionalism serves to render practices otherwise considered unacceptable in international law and basic human rights practices to be legitimate, and legitimated – that is, beyond normative challenge.

This artificially elevated exceptionality is complicated (and sustained), however, by other conditions. There is in fact, in historical terms, a unique origin to the state of Israel, as a modern state envisioned in the United Nations (through its Partition Plan) and, after 1948, recognized by powerful states and brought into the UN system. Moreover, Israel holds a unique place in terms of its high rate of per capita support from the United States, a fact that has increasingly become the subject of contested debate (Mearsceimer and Walt 2007; Ruff 2007).

The elements of mythologized exceptionalism and its sustaining conditions introduce distinct complications into the study of Israel/Palestine, with implications for how we might think about surveillance, social sorting, and racialization. In particular, Israel's close association with Zionist ideology has created an informal atmosphere of surveillance in the Western academy, where any explicit comparison between Israel and other states is uniquely subject to challenge (Abu-Laban and Bakan 2008: 638). More to the point, those advancing criticisms of Israeli policies or practices can face intense scrutiny of their motivations, underscoring what Virginia Tilley calls "Zionist exceptionalism" (Tilley 2005: 134), a dimension, we would argue, of the mythologized exceptionalism of Israel studies generally. This unique form of exceptionalism has therefore limited the capacity of modern scholarship to identify patterns in the settlement, conquest, and violence directed at Palestinians in the establishment and ongoing conduct of the Israeli state.

We maintain that mythologized exceptionalism needs to be considered as part of an ideological construct, belying an underlying commonality in the origin of the modern state of Israel as a settler-colony, blurring the reality of racism in the context of Israel/Palestine today, and compromising the legitimacy of theorizing "race" in fully comparative terms. Given these important questions regarding the appropriateness of Agamben's concept in relation to Israel, we instead draw on Agamben's idea of exception to highlight how, within Western liberal democracies today, being profiled or labeled a "terrorist" carries with it a high probability of "being taken to a place of law without law" (Razack 2008: 34). It is, we suggest, the racialization of Palestinians as "terrorists" that demands critical attention both in the context of Israel/Palestine and, as we argue below, for its implications in other locales where Agamben's concept of exception may be more readily applied, including the United States, Canada, and countries of the European Union.

From such a vantage point, Israel is unique in its deep ideological claim to exceptionality, but in other respects it is notably, and importantly, comparable. Moreover, in the post-9/11 era, evidence suggests that similarities with liberal democratic states are increasing, specifically in terms of a generalization of a racialized regime which distinguishes "terrorists" on the basis of ascribed characteristics which legitimate extreme state surveillance. We situate our own approach to the question of surveillance in Israel/Palestine in the context of an emerging multidisciplinary literature that challenges both mainstream Western and Israeli scholarly traditions, in legitimizing attention to processes of racialization in the context of Israel/Palestine (see Lentin 2008: 7–11; Abu-Laban and Bakan 2008: 638; Goldberg 2009).

At the same time, we recognize that in the absence of a normalization of discussions of racism in Israel, such a perspective often provokes challenges to the legitimacy of voice, and is often over-determined by such provocations. Here a note on method of presentation is in order. While we do not generally endorse essentialist, identity-based analytical frameworks, in writing on Israel/Palestine we explicitly position ourselves as authors on each side of the Jewish (Bakan) and Palestinian (Abu-Laban) binary (Abu-Laban and Bakan 2008: 639). We adopt an analytical approach which draws from the work of political theorist Charles Mills, who highlights how "whiteness" is the unnamed system of dominance characterizing the creation of the modern world. The racial contract – originally embedded in such processes as slavery and settler-colonialism, but continuing in conditions of liberal democracy – suggests varying forms of understood agreements between those who "count" over those who do not, and thus "whiteness" is not about color but about power (Mills 1997). "Race" (like "whiteness") is a contested concept, with different connotations across time and space. Rather than ignoring "race," or exchanging it with "culture," "religion," "ethnicity," or "class," we utilize the term to illustrate how racism is connected to power in the settler context of Israel/Palestine. Indeed, in many settler contexts (including Canada) it has not only been the more critical scholars and NGOs that have taken up race, racism, and anti-racism, but the choice of concepts is profoundly linked to being able to name lived experiences. The difficulty in actually naming the contemporary experience of racism in Israel/Palestine has been evident in the controversies surrounding the 1975 UN General Assembly resolution calling Zionism a form of "racism and racial discrimination," and, more recently, two world conferences on racism sponsored by the UN (in 2001 and 2009), specifically around discussions of the treatment of Palestinians by the Israeli state.

The racial contract, and the metaphor of whiteness, provides a way of being able to name, at least analytically, what is so often bypassed in real world politics. Applied to Israel/Palestine, the focus on the racial contract makes explicit Israel's core features, as a state grounded on the absenting or subordination of the Palestinian "other." This essential racial contract has, since 1948, constructed Palestinians as non-white, and the subjects of extreme repression and statelessness (Abu-Laban and Bakan 2008). Attention to the Gramscian notion of hegemony can place the racial contract framework in a larger context of class and ideological dominance. Such a context indicates that the racial contract is inherently unstable, and can be either supported or challenged in various ways and locations, not least in Israel/Palestine (Abu-Laban and Bakan 2008; Bakan and Abu-Laban 2009). In sum, it is useful to think of "race" in relation to power and to be attuned to challenges to the status quo; such a framing is applicable in the case of Israel/Palestine.

What David Theo Goldberg calls "racial Palestinianization" is, in his estimate, "among the most repressive, the most subjugating and degrading, the most deadly forms of racial targeting, branding, and rationalization not least in the name of racelessness" (Goldberg 2009: 130). Gargi Bhattacharyya argues further that the Palestinian struggle today has become a cipher for both the "clash of civilizations" and "the war on terror" in ways that reverberate outside of Israel/Palestine. As such, "Israel offers a model for transforming the justified demands of the racialized other into evidence that this otherness is innate, impassable and can only be contained and disciplined in the interests of the enlightened western state and its (full) citizens" (Bhattacharyya 2008: 49).

In what follows, we trace the development of Israel's particular form of social sorting, and how the Israelization of surveillance has entailed a Palestinianization of the racial contract outside of the Israel/Palestine context.

1948–1967: Ethnic cleansing, the making of a military settler state, and the construction of an enemy

As Ilan Pappe has demonstrated, the state of Israel was established through a process of forced exile and transfer of Palestinians, and occupation of Palestinian land, consistent with recognized definitions of "ethnic cleansing" (Pappe 2006: 1–29). This is the foundational element in a process of social sorting defined through the construction of the indigenous Palestinian as the "enemy," and resistance to this process treated as an existential threat to the Jewish-only territory redefined as Israel. The Zionist vision of an ethnically exclusive "Jewish" state coincided with a European political project associated first with imperial Britain and then with US interests in the Middle East. These imperial projects included the demographic transfer of Arab Palestinians. The "colonization of Palestine" was explicit in the visioning of early Zionist thinkers. As Leo Motzkin summarized in 1917: "Our thought is that the colonization of Palestine has to go in two directions: Jewish settlement in Eretz Israel and the resettlement of the Arabs of Eretz Israel in areas outside the country. The transfer of so many Arabs might seem at first unacceptable economically, but is nonetheless practical" (Bein 1939, cited in Pappe 2006: 7–8).

Despite efforts to bury and distort the history of the origins of the state of Israel as an ethnically defined, colonial settler state, and to absent indigenous Palestinian culture and history, the records are clear. Pappe summarizes the early chronology and course of events:

> The [United Nations] Partition Resolution was adopted on 29 November 1947, and the ethnic cleansing of Palestine began in early December 1947 with a series of Jewish [Zionist] attacks on Palestinian villages and neighbourhoods in retaliation for the buses and shopping centres that had been vandalized in the Palestinian protest against the UN resolution during the first few days after its adoption. Though sporadic, these early Jewish assaults were severe enough to cause the exodus of a substantial number of people (almost 75,000). On 9 January, units of the first all-Arab volunteer army entered Palestine and engaged with the Jewish forces in small battles over routes and isolated Jewish settlements. Easily winning the upper hand in these skirmishes, the Jewish leadership officially shifted tactics from acts of retaliation to cleansing operations. Coerced expulsions followed in the middle of February 1948 when Jewish troops succeeded in emptying five Palestinian villages in one day. On 10 March 1948, Plan Dalet was adopted . . . About 250,000 Palestinians were uprooted in this phase, which was accompanied by several massacres, most notable of which was the Deir Yassin massacre . . . The British left on 15 May 1948, and the Jewish Agency immediately declared the establishment of a Jewish state in Palestine, officially recognized by the two superpowers of the day, the USA and the USSR.
>
> (Pappe 2006: 40)

Though it is beyond the scope of this chapter to repeat the full chronicle of the case, a new school of historiography has advanced this analytical starting point, building on and reflected in the work of both non-Arab and Arab scholars (see Khalidi 1987 [1971]; Davis 2003; Pappe 2006; Rose 2004; Tilley 2005; Said 1992; Karmi 2007; Abu-Lughod and Sa'di 2007). Our intent here is to emphasize the violence behind the process of social sorting, where occupation, transfer, and the denial of the right of displaced Palestinians to return to their land were grounded on a differentiation between the ascribed Jewish settler (and eventually Israeli national) and the constructed security "threat" of the Palestinian Arab (and eventually Palestinian refugee or Arab Israeli). Put differently, Palestinian Arabs were perceived and treated as a threat irrespective of whether they held Israeli citizenship, defining a specific racialization in this foundational social sorting.

Beginning under the British Mandate in the 1930s and 1940s, the arming of the Zionist military organization Hagana by Britain (Ben-Gurion 1963), the arming of illegal armed organizations (Irgun and the Stern Group) (Anglo-American Committee of Inquiry 1946), and the covert operations smuggling Jewish refugees to Palestine in contravention of British quotas (Kimche and Kimche 1955) laid the basis for the military and intelligence apparatus of the Israeli state, specifically the Israeli Defense Forces and Mossad. In the lead-up to the establishment of Israel, a pattern emerged where initial settlement was met by local resistance, which was in turn described as an "enemy" attack meriting militarized retaliation on a scale far greater and more violent than the provoking incident, and culminating in the forced exodus of Palestinians (Childers 1961).

This pattern of violent occupation, followed by local resistance, only to be met by immeasurably greater and more violent "retaliation," has characterized Israel's pattern of continued expansion in Palestinian territory. This process demanded a highly militarized state on one side, associated with the newly established state of Israel, and the concomitant perception of a blameworthy (Said and Hitchens 1988) and dangerous indigenous, racialized Palestinian population, sometimes supported by enemy neighboring Arab states. The establishment of militarized borders, heightened monitoring of Palestinian activity at every level of social interaction, and regulated movement to prevent return readily became a normalized feature of Israel's existence. Suspicion, surveillance, and sorting through state identification systems in order to prevent the return of Palestinians to their homes (as Zureik 2001: 213–218 shows in his discussion of "present absentees" in the 1948 Israeli census; see also Chapter 12, this volume), along with more general forms of racial profiling, became standard features of Israel's treatment of displaced Palestinians. Israel continued to maintain, for example, the legislative "emergency status" developed under the British Mandatory government, creating a "permanent war footing" and allowing violence to be used in controlling Palestinian resistance (Cook 2004). Additionally, in its first decade the Israeli state passed a series of laws premised on "security" and the need to "cultivate" the land, which effectively removed more land from Palestinian Arabs inside Israel (Adams 1977: 27–28).

The established pattern of interaction with the state of Israel for Arab Palestinians became clearly differentiated from that experienced by and normalized for Jewish "nationals" (Zureik 1979). For the former, "the main, and perhaps the only, contact of Israeli Arabs with the state was through the army, the police and the criminal justice system" (Korn 2000: 159), sites of the modern state that tend to rely upon both surveillance and repression. Korn finds three principal features that can be understood to characterize relationships between Jews and Arabs in post-1948 Israel: Arab Israelis are separated and distinct from the dominant Jewish Israelis as a group, geographically and socially; Arab Israelis are subjected to differential access to resources, power, and status relative to Jewish Israelis; and Arab Israelis are subject to heightened levels of political and social control relative to the Jewish majority (Korn 2000: 161).

The necessity to hold conquered territory by force, and to maintain a militarized system of regulation and control to ensure power over an indigenous population, followed from the original settler character of the Israeli state. The process of racialized social sorting associated with the original *Nakba* (catastrophe) and the later extended occupation of Palestinian territory during the 1967 war can be understood as part of a continuum in the maintenance of a militarized settler state with a clear racial contract. The permanent acceptance and institutionalization of this level of separation between the Jewish/European national as the normalized, "democratic" citizen and the Palestinian/Arab non-national as the normalized, threatening "enemy" other has become inscribed in the reality of Israel/Palestine. "Israel," and hence Israelization, demanded the subordination of Palestine, and hence Palestinianization. The initial boundaries were sustained through extensive processes of surveillance, borders, and policing, and these boundaries were extended in the periods that followed.

1967–1991: expansion, occupation, and the construction of the terrorist threat

If 1948–1967 was characterized by Israel seeming to solve what Usher (2005: 10–11) calls its "native problem" by ethnic cleansing, violence to prevent the return of Palestinians, asserting control over the remaining Arab population of Israel, and settling new Jewish immigrants as preferred citizens, 1967 marks the start of the period when the "native problem" returned via occupation. Moreover, its return created new public relations issues for the Israeli state, both in relation to its own citizens and regarding the global community. It is in this context that the threat of the "Palestinian terrorist" became more firmly embedded in Israeli discourse, with international reverberations.

"Terrorism" as a discourse has its roots in the French Revolution, and was advanced primarily in relation to resistance in European colonies (such as Algeria) after World War Two (Bankoff 2003: 418). Of course, as David Lyon notes, the term "terrorism" is "notoriously slippery, not least because one person's 'freedom fighter' is another's 'terrorist'" (Lyon 2003: 49); he cites the Israeli–Palestinian conflict as one among several cases in point. Consequently, "terrorism," as Noam Chomsky has argued, can be read into the 1948 foundation and ongoing actions of the state of Israel, as well as prior in the lengthy record of bombings, massacres, and expulsions targeting civilians committed by Zionist groups (Chomsky 1986: 110–113). Yet, until recently there has been a condition of virtual immunity in these acts of violence in Western and especially American elite opinion (Chomsky 1986: 113). In dramatic contrast, by the 1980s the categories of Palestinian/Arab/Muslim were frequently conflated, and the Palestinian/Arab/Muslim "terrorist" came to be treated as a central risk to America and, by extension, the whole of the West (Said 1994: 310). Rather than simply reflecting an uneven application of the terms "terrorism" and "terrorist" in both the American mainstream media and government (Kapitan and Schulte 2003), we suggest the significance of understanding how these terms are racialized, and work in accordance with the racial contract.

The fixation on the "Palestinian terrorist" may in part be attributed to the transition that occurred in Israel/Palestine through the 1960s, when the despised other could not be simply depicted as a regional military enemy. The 1967 war symbolized a turning point in the perception of Israel in many Western countries and especially in Europe; it also heightened awareness of the Palestinian case. The rapid and decisive victory that led to the capture of the Golan Heights, the Sinai peninsula, the West

Bank, East Jerusalem, and the Gaza Strip, coupled with the military occupation of Palestinians, resulted in a new questioning of which side was most appropriately characterized as the "David" and which as the "Goliath." At the same time, the power and validity of the national claims of Palestinians for recognition and statehood were given a boost with the creation of the Palestine Liberation Organization (PLO) in 1964, and the observer status accorded to it in the United Nations in 1974. Not least, as Usher (2005: 12–13) points out, "unlike the 1948 territories, in and from which the transfer of Palestinians had been hidden and/or justified by the imperatives of war and Jewish survival, there was no Israeli consensus, post-1967, over the fate of the newly acquired territories."

In practical terms, however, the situation was unambiguous. When it came to the occupied territories, the Israeli state was able to exercise violence more bluntly, as the Palestinian inhabitants were not formally considered to be Israeli citizens. A regime of military governance reigned supreme, and with it came detentions without trial, deportations, destruction of homes, and curfews (Adams 1977; Aruri 1989). Other forms of collective punishment were also institutionalized, including militarized checkpoints controlling the mobility of Palestinians, with identity cards coming to occupy "the symbol of surveillance *par excellence*" (Zureik 2001: 224).

In short, against key elements of the 1978 Camp David Accords (Carter 2006: 224–228), throughout this period what Neve Gordon calls the "colonization principle" (Gordon 2008a: 27–29) came increasingly to the fore, openly recognized and institutionalized. This colonization involved the management of the lives of Palestinian subjects and the extraction of resources – including water and land – for the use of growing numbers of Israeli settlements in the occupied territories. Nonetheless, Palestinians engaged in forms of resistance to surveillance and colonization, most notably in the first Intifada, which brought to the world the image of Palestinian children challenging the Israeli military with nothing but stones.

Moreover, the military became increasingly integrated into the economic fabric of the state of Israel. It is widely acknowledged that from 1967, and accelerating after 1973, military production, often with American technical, financial, and corporate assistance, was a major engine of growth in the Israeli economy (Pieterse 1985: 20; Maman 1999: 96; Hanieh 2003: 8). As one example, in 1977, and perhaps not coincidentally foreshadowing the "separation barrier" (also dubbed the "apartheid wall"), an electrified wall was built by Israeli technicians at the border of Namibia and Angola to deter SWAPO resistance forces from gaining entry into Namibia (Pieterse 1985: 18). Thus, by the 1980s, Israel had assumed an important place in "all the dimensions of the global counter-insurgency business" (Pieterse 1985: 9), a feature also related to its interface with the PLO. As the PLO came to occupy a position as a national liberation organization committed to armed resistance, as well as the government-in-exile for the Palestinians both in historic Palestine and in the diaspora (Rubenberg 1983), successive Israeli leaders termed it a "terrorist" organization. In the United States and the Western world, "Palestinians became the premier terrorists" (Bovard 2003: 7).

The 1979 Jerusalem Conference on International Terrorism was a significant event in the internationalization of responses to Israel's discourse on terrorism (Ralph 2006: 273), and serves as a marker in the Palestinianization of racial contracts. The conference was convened, in the words of future Israeli Prime Minister Benjamin

Netanyahu, to "begin the formation of an anti-terror alliance in which all the democracies of the West must join" (Netanyahu 1982: 2). This position was echoed by future American President George H.W. Bush, who argued: "Terrorism must be combated . . . by the free nations of the world" (Bush 1982: 335). The common element underlying this perspective, also evident in US government definitions, "is that only private citizens and private groups can be guilty of terrorism," not state actors (Bovard 2003: 228).

The racialized construction of "terrorists" emerging from the context of Israel/ Palestine also laid the basis for a new American focus on "international terrorism" in the 1980s under President Ronald Reagan, which was also steeped in the rhetoric of the Cold War (Bovard 2003: 8–30; Chomsky 1986: 1–10). In its most obvious policy application outside Israel/Palestine, the focus on terrorism made its way into the treatment of non-citizens via immigration and refugee discussions and legal applications in Western countries (Macklin 2001: 391–392; Huysmans 2000), a pattern reasserted after September 11, 2001 with greater resilience.

1992–2000: from Oslo to the second Intifada

By the late 1980s and early 1990s, a number of factors converged to shift the dynamic between Israel and the PLO, including the end of the Cold War, the 1991 US-led Gulf War, the diminished support of the PLO by Gulf states, and renewed questions about the morality of the occupation engendered by the first Intifada. In 1988, the PLO under the leadership of Yasser Arafat effectively abandoned the earlier call for armed struggle and a secular and democratic Palestine, moving to a strategy where Israel's "right to exist" was recognized and a two-state solution became the goal. This helped lay the basis for the 1993 news that "shocked" the world: Israel and the PLO had held secret negotiations in Oslo designed to bring a peaceful resolution to the Palestinian–Israeli conflict. On September 13, 1993, Prime Minster Yitzhak Rabin and Yasser Arafat famously shook hands after a signing ceremony in Washington hosted by US President Bill Clinton. The Oslo process and the Oslo Accords – that is, "The Declaration of Principles on Interim Self-Government" – fostered a series of agreements in the 1990s which led to Israeli withdrawal from parts of the West Bank and Gaza, and the creation of the Palestinian Authority.

Much could be said about the shortcomings of both the Oslo process and the Accords when it came to the roles of both the United States and Norway (Sanders 1999), as well as failing to deal with Palestinian refugees, Palestinian statehood, and other "final status" issues. As critically, Gordon (2008a: 35) points out that abstracted from the discourse of being about a "peace process," "the overarching logic informing the different agreements is straightforward: transfer all responsibilities relating to the management of the population to the Palestinians themselves while preserving control of Palestinian space." As such, the Oslo Accords cantonized Palestinian spaces in the West Bank and Gaza, and introduced new paradoxes into constructions of paradigms of surveillance. The social sorting process that had established Israel, and expanded in the 1967 war, was now to be embedded in the vision of a permanent "peace." Israelization in the Middle East now earned international recognition, including a defined responsibility of a section of Palestinian society in enforcing the social sorting process. For example, implicitly in the agreements, Palestinian police had as a main duty to ensure "the protection of Israeli security and colonial interests in the Occupied Territories" (Lia 2006: 2–3).

In May 1996 Israeli Prime Minister Benjamin Netanyahu declared a localized war on terror, and simultaneously declared war on the Oslo Accords. With no repercussions from the United States, it is not surprising that attempts to revive the Oslo process failed, including the Camp David 2000 Summit orchestrated by US President Bill Clinton. Nor is it surprising that at the same time there was greater violence, with massive increases in the destruction of Palestinian homes and the extrajudicial killing of Palestinians. This process coincided, necessarily, with increased surveillance via military satellites and, for example, unmanned armed drones (Gordon 2008a: 37; Gordon 2008b: 202–203). In 2000 the Al-Aqsa Intifada ushered in a new spiral of desperation and violence involving Palestinian suicide bombers. This "ignited the cultural imagination of Western societies" (Naaman 2007: 941) in combining perceptions about religion (specifically, Islam), as well as the perceived role of women, in so-called "traditional' societies. These constructions – of ostensibly dangerous suicidal men and now women who were driven by religion to destroy the innocent – were foundational in the later construction of post-9/11 moral panic about both non-citizens and citizens well beyond Israel and the Middle East (Razack 2008). The pieces were now all in place for the Israelization of surveillance, and the Palestinianization of the racial contract, a tinderbox to be lit by the events of 9/11.

2001–2008: the "victim state" model and liberal democratic expectations

Since September 11, the representation of the Palestinian/Arab/Muslim terrorist has assumed greater trans-historical and even transnational proportions. In the context of Israel/Palestine, the website of the Israeli Ministry of Foreign Affairs depicts "Arab and Palestinian terrorism against Israel [*sic*]" as "predating" the establishment of the state in May 1948 (Israel Ministry of Foreign Affairs 2002: 1). Its transnational characteristics are contained in the manner by which notions like "sleeper cells" have made their way into the popular lexicon of Western countries. As Bankoff notes, "just as the non-Western world was previously portrayed as disease-ridden, poverty-sricken and hazard-prone, more or less the same regions are now depicted as 'terrorist-spawning'" (Bankoff 2003: 418).

Such representations have been aided by a new ideological framing of the West, and concomitantly Israel's place in this framing since 9/11. This marks a moment of redefining hegemony in the international racial contract. In shaping the response to 9/11, the United States under the presidency of George W. Bush presented the crisis in terms that identified America and American "values" as victims of a global enemy that was neither a state nor the policy of a state. Rather, the "enemy" was perceived to be specifically Arab or Muslim "terrorism," later elaborated as the values of a perceived system of extremism, sometimes bearing the term "Islamofascism." As Sunera Thobani notes, "[t]he Bush Administration has described Western societies as gravely threatened by the murderous violence of the Islamists, and in effect, whiteness has been recast as vulnerable, endangered, innocent and the subject of irrational hatred of this fanatic non-Western Other" (Thobani 2007: 169–170). Among those who accepted various elements of this basic, and racialized, framing of the

9/11 attacks were a number of leading North American and European mainstream feminists (for a critique, see Thobani 2007; Razack 2008: 83–106).

The mythologized, exceptional character of Israel as victim state, rooted in the original Zionist colonial project, has been extended to encompass the US and the West as a whole. The social sorting that constructs the need for violent measures to secure a constructed and settler non-Arabic and non-Islamic public from the threat of "terrorism" is elevated in this framing of the events of 9/11. As Phyllis Chesler (2003: 1) expresses it, "now, we are all Israelis." Moreover, the analogy of victimization is extended and enhanced with a parallel analogy, developing associations first between "extreme" Islam and a "new anti-Semitism" which challenges the legitimacy of Israeli state policies. This in turn draws further parallels with Hitler's Nazis (Chesler 2003: 192). This view of Israel as a victim state comparable to a post-9/11 United States claimed greater ideological space particularly throughout the two terms of the George W. Bush administration. This reframed global context was matched, and in turn supported, by the further entrenchment of the Israeli state's resolve to manage the "conflict" with Palestinians according to a racialized hegemonic project.

The period following 2001 was one of the most violent in Israel's history of apartheid-like practices against indigenous Palestinians. The restrictions on mobility rights of Palestinians, endemic in the original forced settlement and establishment of the state of Israel as a "Jewish-only" territory (Korn 2000), intensified, justified on the grounds that there were heightened security risks associated with the second Intifada (Cook 2006).

Israel's refusal to adhere to international law continues to be, after 9/11, virtually ignored by the major powers in global politics. While this pattern was in place before 9/11, it is perhaps more notable in recent rulings. For example, the continued extension of the "separation barrier" was ruled illegal by the International Court of Justice (ICJ) in 2004; this ruling was affirmed by the United Nations General Assembly in the same year. Yet the construction of the illegal wall continues, with no consequences or sanctions for the violation (Abu-Laban and Bakan 2009; Dolphin 2006). Moreover, the massive Israeli attack in the West Bank in March 2002 (cynically dubbed "Defensive Shield") is, according to Neve Gordon (2008b: 205), paradigmatic of a new form of control wherein "the occupying power adopted more intense and remote mechanisms of violence" while destroying Palestinian civil and administrative institutions. The same parameters of violence and destruction – in contravention of international law, according to Justice Richard Goldstone and the United Nations mission he headed – can also be seen in the December 2008 Israeli attack on Gaza (cynically dubbed "Operation Cast Lead") (United Nations Human Rights Council 2009).

The global accommodation to the Israelization of surveillance and the accompanying violent enforcement of social sorting, and to the Palestinianization of the racial contract and the accompanying dehumanization of the ascribed "terrorist," have apparently enabled the Israeli state to assume a wider remit in its actual oppression of Palestinians. It is therefore unsurprising that Mbembe calls Israeli occupation "the most accomplished form of necropower" in its creation of death worlds (Mbembe 2003: 27). As Mbembe notes, the use of increasingly advanced surveillance technologies – from unmanned air vehicles to satellites – makes occupation of the skies a prelude to more targeted killing (Mbembe 2003: 29).

Post-9/11, the assertion of the (Muslim/Arab) terrorist as the common enemy of both Israel and Western liberal democracies entails in the latter even more aggressive immigration laws and practices, border controls, and forms of increasingly digitalized surveillance over non-citizens (Razack 2008: 31; Broeders 2007; Fekete 2004: 16–17; Cole 2002–2003). It has also entailed a reconstruction of the threat of "foreigners" such that not only non-citizens but "suspicious" citizens may be viewed as dangerous and treated differentially (Bigo 2005; Abu-Laban 2004; Fekete 2004; Dhamoon and Abu-Laban 2009). For example, a new legitimacy for overt racial profiling was established as a feature of advanced security measures, technologically advanced surveillance, and formally responsible democratic governance (Lyon 2003: 49–60; Abu-Laban 2004, 2005; Razack 2008). This contrasts with the post-World War Two and pre-9/11 period, when such practices were commonly considered a relic of an archaic past, and when discriminatory practices were assumed to be readily overcome with the expansion of modernity (Cairns 1999). At the extreme, after September 11, citizens of liberal democracies may even be subject to rendition to torture, as suffered by dual-Canadian and Syrian citizen Maher Arar, whom American authorities accused of being a member of al Qaeda and deported to Syria, where he was imprisoned between 2002 and 2003. While an independent Canadian commission cleared Arar of any wrongdoing, and the Canadian government under Prime Minister Stephen Harper offered an apology for any role Canadian officials may have played as well as C$10.5 million compensation, this case shows the relevance of Agamben's concept of exception even in Canada (Abu-Laban and Nath 2007). Combined, these post-9/11 practices, often advanced through anti-terrorist legislation, speak to the Palestinianization of the racial contracts of liberal democracies. Such practices are differentially directed at non-citizens as well as citizens in the name of security and combating "terror," resting upon a deep, and racialized, acceptance of the unnamed Islamic/Arabic, dangerous other.

In the heightened climate of anti-terrorism surveillance following 9/11, the Israeli state has increased its international profile as an "expert" in "resisting" the threat of the constructed "Muslim terrorist." The results of this expertise – a clear feature of the Israelization of surveillance – were tragically indicated in the response of the London police to the July 7, 2005 attacks on the city's transport system. Fifteen days later, a twenty-seven-year-old man, Jean Charles de Menezes, was shot and killed by police in the Stockwell underground station on suspicion of terrorism. De Menezes was innocent of the crime, but police officers shooting to kill on suspicion of terror was not accidental. De Menezes, a Latino of color and hence already treated as an other in the British/European racial contract, became a suspected suicide bomber on site, perceived as such by police trained in anti-terrorist activity by the Israeli state (Studemann 2005; McCulloch and Sentas 2006). Indeed, McCulloch and Sentas (2006: 5) maintain that Israeli training "directly influenced the development of the firearms tactics that led to the death of Jean Charles." This example illustrates the changed context of post-9/11 security, surveillance, and social sorting. The capacity of Israel to present its colonialist occupation of the indigenous Palestinian population as a defensive posture against "Arab terrorism" was enhanced in the framing of the US and the West in general as victims of 9/11.

Israel has seen fit to market its services in training of police in the aftermath of 9/11 more aggressively on the grounds that its expertise in the science of controlling

"Palestinian terrorists" is applicable to those responsible for the events of 9/11. Police training missions to Israel have been organized by Ontario police in Canada, and across the US. This has included tours of Israeli commanders to US cities to train federal and local law enforcement officials, as well as direct training visits to Israel. According to a 2005 statement by US Capitol (Washington, D.C.) Police Chief Terrance W. Gainer, "Israel is the Harvard of antiterrorism" (Mouammar 2005; Horwitz 2005).

The ideological framing of Israel as a victim state, now apparently comparable to the United States on the world stage, and under siege from purportedly dangerous and collectively suspicious citizens who "look like" Arab/Palestinian/Muslim terrorists, has moved an historic "conflict" once noted for its acclaimed exceptionality into a realm of heightened normality. Naomi Klein has identified the manufacture and export of the Israeli security industry in the aftermath of 9/11 as not only ideologically opportune but profitable for Israeli capitalism. Notably, the infamous separation barrier has become identified as a prototype for increasing surveillance in other parts of the world in the post-9/11 era (Klein 2007: 528). This builds on Israel's contemporary global economic strength in high technology and strategic relations in the region (Hanieh 2003: 14).

Israel's ascribed commonality with the US as a post-9/11 victim state has, however, also had contradictory ramifications. While serving to hide the racialized and settler character of the state of Israel and thereby cultivating global tolerance and even sympathy for its apartheid-like policies, this image also challenges the historic notion of Israel as a peaceful and democratic haven in an otherwise barbaric Middle East Orient (Said 1992). The close association between Israel and a besieged post-9/11 US, in other words, has also served to expose the mythologized exceptionalism that has historically surrounded Israel's aggressive and racialized practices towards the Palestinian people.

A recent international campaign by the Israeli state to "rebrand" its public image testifies to the challenges and contradictions of the post-9/11 moment. Cities targeted by this campaign include Toronto, Tokyo, London, Boston, and New York (Brinn 2008). This effort entails a $20 million, multi-year plan "to re-brand Israel and to improve its image" in a bid to make it a place attractive to foreign investors and tourists (*Israel Today* 2006).

However, while the surveillance and racialized social sorting targeting Palestinians have continued and indeed are intensifying, potential sites of resistance to Israel's oppressive practices have also arisen.

Conclusion: sites of resistance

Throughout this discussion, the power of the Israeli state *vis-à-vis* the indigenous Palestinian population has been apparent. We conclude by considering the ways in which the current conjuncture is one where new forms and locations of resistance to Israel's oppressive practices have also come to the fore.

The ongoing daily struggles of Palestinians on the ground indicate a pattern of continual resistance. This is expressed in multiple ways, including through the words, images, and stories of children living with the consequences of the separation barrier, and navigating the surveillance and violence to which they are subject in this conflict zone (Shalhoub-Kevorkian 2006). It includes the Israeli refuseniks who would rather face arrest for resisting conscription than "dominate, expel, starve and humiliate an entire people" (Grossman and Kaplan 2006: 189). It includes the Israeli women of Machsom Watch who go to checkpoints to monitor the operation of the army and in some cases intervene (Naaman 2006).

Not least, these new sites of resistance have developed outside of the conflict zone of Israel/Palestine in response to the united call that has arisen from Palestinian civil society organizations for a comprehensive movement of boycott, divestment, and sanctions against the Israeli state for its continued illegal military occupation of Palestine, and for its repressive policies. This is now what could be called an international social movement, which brings together Jews and non-Jews, Arabs and non-Arabs, spanning countries of Europe and North America and reaching to nations in the global South, including post-apartheid South Africa (Bakan and Abu-Laban 2009). It is notable that in this movement the analogy between contemporary Israel and apartheid South Africa has become a standard point of reference. In articulating this comparison – one that is making its way into scholarly research as well as such popular works as former US President Jimmy Carter's *Palestine: Peace Not Apartheid* (2006) – the mythologized exceptionalism of the Israeli state is implicitly challenged. Instead, the racialized nature of that state is suggestively, and strategically, compared to the racialized apartheid state of South Africa, a state which is now seen to be on the other side, as it were, of a particularly heinous expression of social sorting and the accompanying processes of surveillance.

While the implications of the 2008 election of US President Barack Obama for the Middle East crisis is a subject of continuing debate, the 2009 election of Israeli Prime Minister Benjamin Netanyahu does not inspire confidence in an era of "hope" and "change." Indeed, the sites of popular resistance that have emerged tend to focus more on transformation at the level of civil society than on official channels of power. Another potential contribution of the apartheid analogy regarding sites of resistance is related to the construction of the racialized Palestinian as the classic, post-9/11 "terrorist." The processes we have referred to as the Palestinianization of the racial contract and the Israelization of social sorting and surveillance depend largely on a particular set of stereotyped constructions that conflate ascribed religious, racial, and cultural identities within a security framework threatened by "terrorism." During South Africa's apartheid period, the African National Congress was similarly treated as a "terrorist" movement, and its leader, Nelson Mandela, was imprisoned. The fact that South Africa has moved into a post-apartheid phase, during which Nelson Mandela was not only released from incarceration but became the first democratically elected president of the country, could perhaps inspire a more optimistic outcome to the current conjuncture in Israel/Palestine.

Bibliography

Abu-Lughod, L. and A.H. Sa'di (eds) (2007) *Nakba: Palestine, 1948 and the Claims of Memory*, New York: Columbia University Press.
Abu-Laban, Y. (2004) "The New North America and the Segmentation of Canadian Citizenship," *International Journal of Canadian Studies*, 29(1): 17–40.
—— (2005) "Regionalism, Migration and (Fortress) North America," *Review of Constitutional Studies*, 10(1): 135–162.

Abu-Laban, Y. and A.B. Bakan (2008) "The Racial Contract: Israel/Palestine and Canada," *Social Identities*, 14(5): 637–660.

Abu-Laban, Y. and N. Nath (2007) "From Deportation to Apology: The Case of Maher Arar and the Canadian State," *Canadian Ethnic Studies* 39(3): 71–97.

Adams, M. (1977) "Israel's Treatment of the Arabs in the Occupied Territories," *Journal of Palestine Studies* 6(2): 19–40.

Agamben, G. (2005) *State of Exception*, trans. Kevin Attell, Chicago, IL: University of Chicago Press.

Anglo-American Committee of Inquiry Regarding the Problems of European Jewry and Palestine (1946), report, reprinted in Walid Khalidi (ed.) (1987 [1971]) *From Haven to Conquest: Readings in Zionism and the Palestine Problem Until 1948*, Washington, D.C.: Institute for Palestine Studies: 595-600.

Aruri, N.H. (ed.) (1989) *Occupation: Israel over Palestine* (2nd edn), Belmont, MA: Association of Arab American University Graduates.

Avnery, U. (2003) "The Prisoner of Ramallah," *Counterpunch*, August 5: 1–13.

Bakan, A. and Y. Abu-Laban (2009) "Palestinian Resistance and International Solidarity: The BDS Campaign," *Race and Class* 51(1): 29–54.

Bankoff, G. (2003) "Regions of Risk: Western Discourses on Terrorism and the Significance of Islam," *Studies in Conflict and Terrorism*, 26: 413–428.

BBC News (2005) "Tube Bombs 'Almost Simultaneous,'" July 9. Available HTTP: <http://news.bbc.co.uk/2/hi/uk_news/4666591.stm>.

Bein, A. (ed.) (1939) *The Mozkin Book*, Jerusalem: World Zionist Publications.

Ben-Gurion, D. (1963) "Britain's Contribution to Arming the Hagana," reprinted in Walid Khalidi (ed.) (1987 [1971]) *From Haven to Conquest: Readings in Zionism and the Palestine Problem until 1948*, Washington, D.C.: Institute for Palestine Studies: 371–374.

Bhattacharyya, G. (2008) "Globalizing Racism and the Myths of the Other in the 'War on Terror,'" in R. Lentin (ed.) *Thinking Palestine*, London: Zed Books: 46–61.

Bigo, D. (2005) "From Foreigners to 'Abnormal Aliens': How the Faces of the Enemy Have Changed Following September the 11th," in Elspeth Guild and Joanne van Selm (eds) *International Migration and Security: Opportunities and Challenges*, London and New York: Routledge: 64–81.

Blair, A. (2006) "Speech to the Los Angeles World Affairs Council," August 1. Available HTTP: <http://news.bbc.co.uk/2/hi/americas/4785065.stm>.

Bovard, J. (2003) *Terrorism and Tyranny: Trampling Freedom, Justice, and Peace to Rid the World of Evil*, New York: Palgrave Macmillan.

Brinn, D. (2008) "Israel's Rebranding Efforts to Focus on Toronto," *Jerusalem Post*, March 16.

Broeders, D. (2007) "The New Digital Borders of Europe: EU Databases and the Surveillance of Irregular Migrants," *International Sociology*, 22(1): 71–92.

Bush, G.H.W. (1982) "The US and the Fight against International Terrorism," in Benjamin Netanyahu (ed.) *International Terrorism: Challenge and Response*, New Brunswick, NJ: Transaction Books: 332–337.

Cairns, A.C. (1999) "Empire, Globalization, and the Rise and Fall of Diversity," in A.C. Cairns, J.C. Courtney and P. MacKinnon (eds) *Citizenship, Diversity and Pluralism: Canadian and Comparative Perspectives*, Montreal: McGill-Queen's University Press: 23–57.

Carter, J. (2006) *Palestine: Peace Not Apartheid*, New York: Simon and Schuster.

Chesler, P. (2003) *The New Anti-Semitism: The Current Crisis and What We Must Do About It*, San Fransisco, CA: Jossey-Bass.

Childers, E.B. (1961) "The Other Exodus," reprinted in W. Khalidi (ed.) (1987 [1971]) *From Haven to Conquest: Readings in Zionism and the Palestine Problem until 1948*, Washington, D.C.: Institute for Palestine Studies: 795–803.

Chomsky, N. (1986) *Pirates and Emperors: International Terrorism in the Real World*, New York: Claremont.

Cole, D. (2002–2003) "Their Liberties, Our Security: Democracy and Double Standards," *Boston Review*, December–January: 1–17.

Cook, J. (2004) "'Democratic' Racism I," *Al-Ahram Weekly On-line*, July 8–14. Available HTTP: <http://weekly.ahrem.org.eg>.

—— (2006) *Blood and Religion: The Unmasking of the Jewish and Democratic State*, London: Pluto Press.

Davis, U. (2003) *Apartheid Israel: Possibilities for the Struggle Within*, New York: Zed Books.

Dhamoon, R. and Y. Abu-Laban (2009) "Dangerous (Internal) Foreigners and Nation-Building: The Case of Canada," *International Political Science Review*, 30(2): 163–183.

Dolphin, R. (2006) *The West Bank Wall: Unmaking Palestine*, London: Pluto Press.

Fekete, L. (2004) "Anti-Muslim Racism and the European Security State," *Race and Class*, 46(1): 3–29.

Goldberg, D.T. (2009) *The Threat of Race: Reflections on Racial Neoliberalism*, Maldon, MA: Blackwell.

Gordon, N. (2008a) "From Colonization to Separation: Exploring the Structure of Israel's Occuption," *Third World Quarterly*, 29(1): 25–44.

—— (2008b) *Israel's Occupation*, Berkeley: University of California Press.

Greene, R.A. (2006) "Bush's Language Angers US Muslims," BBC News, August 12. Available HTTP: <http://www.number-10.gov.uk/output/Page9948.asp>.

Grossman, G. and R. Kaplan (2006) "Courage to Refuse," *Peace Review: A Journal of Social Justice*, 18: 189–197.

Hanieh, A. (2003) "From State-Led Growth to Globalization: The Evolution of Israeli Capitalism," *Journal of Palestine Studies*, 32(4): 5–21.

Harman, C. (2006) "Hizbollah and the War Israel Lost," *International Socialism Journal*, 112: 8–41.

Hitchens, C. (2007) "Defending Islamofascism: It's a Valid Term and Here's Why," *Slate*, October 22.

Horwitz, S. (2005) "Israeli Experts Teach Police on Terrorism: Training Programs Prompt Policy Shifts," *Washington Post*, June 12.

Huysmans, J. (2000) "The Euorpean Union and the Securitization of Migration," *Journal of Common Market Studies*, 38(5): 751–777.

Israel Ministry of Foreign Affairs (2002) "Which Came First – Terrorism or Occupation – Major Arab Terrorist Attacks against Israelis Prior to the 1967 Six Day War." Available HTTP: <http://www.mfa.gov.il/MFA/Terrorism-+Obstacle+to+Peace/Palestinian+terror +before+2000/Which+Came+First-+Terrorism+or+Occupation+-+Major.htm>.

Israel Today (2006) "Israel to Re-brand Itself in the World," September 12. Available HTTP: <http://www.israeltoday.co.il/default.aspx?tabid=178&nid=9460>.

Kapitan, T. and E. Schulte (2003) "The Rhetoric of 'Terrorism' and Its Consequences," *Journal of Political and Military Sociology*, 30(1): 172–196.

Karmi, G. (2007) *Married to Another Man: Israel's Dilemma in Palestine*, London; Pluto Press.

Khalidi, W. (ed.) (1987 [1971] *From Haven to Conquest: Readings in Zionism and the Palestine Problem until 1948*, Washington, D.C.: Institute for Palestine Studies.

Kimche, J. and D. Kimche (1955) "The Mossad Machine – Confounding Military Intelligence 1946–1947," reprinted in W. Khalidi (ed.) (1987 [1971] *From Haven to Conquest: Readings in Zionism and the Palestine Problem until 1948*, Washington, D.C.: Institute for Palestine Studies: 615–623.

Klein, N. (2007) *The Shock Doctrine: The Rise of Disaster Capitalism*, Toronto: Alfred A. Knopf Canada.

Korn, A. (2000) "Military Government, Political Control and Crime: The Case of Israeli Arabs," *Crime, Law and Social Change*, 34: 159–182.

Küntzel, M. (2007) *Jihad and Jew Hatred: Islamism, Nazism and the Roots of 9/11*, New York: Telos.

Lentin, R. (2008) "Introduction: Thinking Palestine," in R. Lentin (ed.) *Thinking Palestine*, London and New York: Zed Books: 1–22.

Lia, B. (2006) *A Police Force without a State: A History of the Palestinian Security Forces in the West Bank and Gaza*, Reading: Ithaca Press.

Lyon, D. (2003) *Surveillance after September 11*, Cambridge: Polity Press.

—— (2007) *Surveillance Studies: An Overview*, Cambridge: Polity Press.

Lyon, D. and E. Zureik (1996) "Surveillance, Privacy and the New Technology," in D. Lyon and E. Zureik (eds) *Computers, Surveillance and Privacy*, Minneapolis: University of Minnesota Press: 1–18.

Macklin, A. (2001) "Borderline Security," in R.J. Daniels, P. Macklen and K. Roach (eds) *The Security of Freedom: Essays on Canada's Anti-Terrorism Bill*, Toronto: University of Toronto Press: 383–404.

Maman, D. (1999) "The Social Organization of the Israeli Economy: A Comparative Analsyis," *Israel Affairs*, 5(2): 87–102.

Mamdani, M. (2004) *Good Muslim, Bad Muslim: America, the Cold War, and the Roots of Terror*, New York: Pantheon Books.

Mbembe, A. (2003) "Necropolitics," *Public Culture*, 15(1): 11–40.

McCulloch, J. and V. Santas (2006) "The Killing of Jean Charles de Menezes: Hyper-Militarism in the Neoliberal Economic Free-Fire Zone," *Social Justice*, 33(4): 1–13.

Mearsheimer, J.J. and S.M. Walt (2007) *The Israel Lobby*, Toronto: Viking Canada.

Mills, C. (1997) *The Racial Contract*, Ithaca, NY: Cornell University Press.

Mouammar, K. (2005) "Khaled Mouammar's Complaint Re: Ontario Provincial Police's Trip to Israel," address to the Professional Standards Bureau, Ontario Provincial Police, August 11. Available HTTP: <http://www.montrealmuslimnews.net/khaled.pdf>.

Naaman, D. (2006) "The Silenced Outcry: A Feminist Perspective from the Israeli Checkpoints in Palestine," *NWSA Journal*, 18(3): 168–180.

—— (2007) "Brides of Palestine/Angels of Death: Media, Gender, and Performance in the Case of the Palestinian Female Suicide Bombers," *Signs: Journal of Women in Culture and Society*, 32(4): 933–955.

Netanyahu, B. (1982) "Foreword," in Benjamin Netanyahu (ed.) *International Terrorism: Challenge and Response*, New Brunswick, NJ: Transaction Books: 1–2.

Noble, D. (2005) *Beyond the Promised Land: The Movement and the Myth*, Toronto: Between the Lines.

Ong, A. (2006) *Neoliberalism as Exception: Mutations in Citizenship and Sovereignty*, Durham, NC: Duke University Press.

Pappe, I. (2006) *The Ethnic Cleansing of Palestine*, Oxford: Oneworld.

[em[em] (2008) "The *Mukhabarat* State of Israel: A State of Oppression is Not a State of Exception," in R. Lentin (ed.) *Thinking Palestine*, London: Zed Books: 148–169.

Pieterse, J.N. (1985) "Israel's Role in the Third World: Exporting West Bank Expertise," *Race and Class*, 26(3): 9–30.

Ralph, D. (2006) "Islamophobia and the 'War on Terror': The Continuing Pretext for US Imperial Conquest," in Paul Zarembka (ed.) *Research in Political Economy, Volume 23: The Hidden History of 9-11-2001*, Amsterdam and San Diego: Elsevier: 261–298.

Razack, S.H. (2008) *Casting out: The Eviction of Muslims from Western Law and Politics*, Toronto: University of Toronto Press.

Rodinson, M. (1973) *Israel: A Colonial Settler State?*, New York: Pathfinder.

Rose, D. (2008) "The Gaza Bombshell," *Vanity Fair*, April.

Rose, J. (2004) *The Myths of Zionism*, London: Pluto Press.

Rubenberg, C. (1983) *The Palestine Liberation Organization: Its Institutional Infrastructure*, Belmont, MA: Institute of Arab Studies.

Ruff, A. (2007) "Do Zionists Run America?," *MRZine*, May 28. Available HTTP: <http://www.monthlyreview.org/mrzine/ruff280507.html>.

Said, E. (1992) *The Question of Palestine*, New York: Vintage.
—— (1994) *Culture and Imperialism*, New York: Vintage.
Said, E.W. and C. Hitchens (eds) (1988) *Blaming the Victims: Spurious Scholarship and the Palestinian Question*, London: Verso.
Sanders, J. (1999) "Honest Brokers? American and Norwegian Facilitation of Israeli–Palestinian Negotiations (1991–1993)," *Arab Studies Quarterly*, 21(2): 47–70.
Shalhoub-Kevorkian, N. (2006) "Negotiating the Present, Historicizing the Future: Palestinian Children Speak about the Israeli Separation Wall," *American Behavioral Scientist*, 49(8): 1101–1124.
Siegel, P.N. (1986) *The Meek and the Militant: Religion and Power across the World*, London: Zed Books.
Studemann, Frederick (2005). "Shoot-to-Kill Tactics Accepted in Israel and Russia," *FT.Com*, July 25. Available HTTP: <http://www.ft.com/cms/s/0/9fb1e632-fd30-11d9-b224-00000e2511c8.html>.
Thobani, S. (2007) "White Wars: Western Feminisms and the 'War on Terror,'" *Feminist Theory*, 8(2): 169–185.
Tilley, V. (2005) *The One-State Solution: A Breakthrough for Peace in the Israeli–Palestinian Conflict*, Ann Arbor: University of Michigan Press.
Todd, P. and J. Bloch (2003) *Global Intelligence: The World's Secret Services Today*, London and New York: Zed Books.
United Nations Human Rights Council (2009) *Human Rights in Palestine and Other Occupied Arab Territories: Report of the United Nations Fact Finding Mission on the Gaza Conflict*, Twelfth Session, Agenda Item 7, September 15.
Usher, G. (2005) "The Wall and the Dismemberment of Palestine," *Race and Class*, 47(3): 9–30.
Whitaker, R. (1999) *The End of Privacy: How Total Surveillance is Becoming a Reality*, New York: New Press.
Yiftachel, O. (2006) *Ethnocracy: Land and Identity Politics in Israel/Palestine*, Philadelphia: University of Pennsylvania Press.
Zreik, R. (2008) "The Persistence of the Exception: Some Remarks on the Story of Israeli Constitutionalism," in R. Lentin (ed.) *Thinking Palestine*, London: Zed Books: 131–147.
Zureik, E. (1979) *The Palestinians in Israel: A Study in Internal Colonialism*, London: Routledge and Kegan Paul.
—— (2001) "Constructing Palestine through Surveillance Practices," *British Journal of Middle Eastern Studies*, 28(2): 205–227.
Zureik, E. and M.B. Salter (2005) "Global Surveillance and Policing: Borders, Security, Identity: Introduction," in E. Zureik and M.B. Salter (eds) *Global Surveillance and Policing: Borders, Security and Identity*, Cullompton: Willan.

Part VII

Territory and population management in conflict zones

15 British and Zionist data gathering on Palestinian Arab landownership and population during the Mandate

Michael R. Fischbach

Britain's ability to govern Palestine during the period of the Mandate (1920–1948) and Zionism's stated goal of establishing a Jewish state in the country both ultimately rested on their ability to control two key features of life there: land and people. Taking the title of Richard Saumarez Smith's (1996) book about British rule in the Punjab, both the British and the Zionists needed to "rule by records" if they were to succeed, for controlling land and people in the modern world requires detailed records of both. By the end of the Mandate, British authorities and various Zionist bodies systematically had collected a wealth of detailed information about Palestinian landownership and population, both for their own purposes.

Records and data are not "neutral." They reflect their creators' imaginings about the things that they report. Data gathering and social sorting therefore represent a powerful sense of agency able to transform the people and the society they detail. Despite this potentially transformative nature of records like census data and land records, British Mandatory authorities ultimately were not able to impose, by colonial diktat, their own imaginings of bodies and property on the land and people of Palestine through record-keeping. New conceptualizations of persons, and new understandings of the nature of land and its ownership, did not in fact come into being by virtue of the Mandate. The nature of British rule and Palestinian resistance to both the Mandate and the Zionist project worked against this. By contrast, the voluminous records on Palestinian land and population collected by the British, and those gathered by Zionist bodies, proved of immense transformative value to Zionist officials and military forces during the "state of exception" offered by the first Arab–Israeli war of 1948, and thereafter in the new Israeli state.

"Rule by records"

For millennia, governments have used writing and records as means of social sorting, taxation, and population control. Richard Saumarez Smith (1996) has coined the apt phrase "rule by records" to describe this process. Taking the Yemeni highlands during the Ottoman and republican eras as a case study, Brinkley Messick writes of the imamate as an example of the "calligraphic state." He describes this state as follows: "[as] both a polity and a discursive condition, the calligraphic state was a phenomenon anchored in the complex authority relations of a spectrum of writings and associated institutions . . . Where the sword served to threaten or coerce, the authority of the pen concerned the conveyance of 'ruling ideas'" (Messick 1993: 251).

In other words, records do not merely enable states to control their populations. In pointing out that the calligraphic state was "both a polity and a discursive condition," Messick articulates a key point: beyond the state's ability to wield writing and records as an instrument of rule, the act of record-keeping and the use of language and words themselves have strong ideological underpinnings that allow the state to create and categorize the society being governed. Data such as population censuses, tax lists, land records, survey maps, and so forth do not merely dispassionately represent a world – in this case, a population that the state governs – that is "out there" in a pristine, positivistic sense. The processes of sorting, categorizing, and describing help create the very population that is being observed and recorded. This represents not merely the need for simplicity dictated by bureaucratic need, but the wider "imaginings" (Anderson 1991) about the nature of society.

The power to create the very categories of persons being enumerated and studied extends even beyond the state. For example, the modern concept of an encyclopedia by which actors within civil society list entries by the "neutral" method of alphabetization in fact stems from a quintessentially and highly ideological European Enlightenment theory that proposed deconstructing the conceptualization of knowledge that helped underpin the *ancien régime*. Eighteenth-century French author Denis Diderot's famous *Encyclopédie* was revolutionary in his time not only because of his belief that all classes in society should be able to access knowledge (and revolutionary Enlightenment era knowledge at that) but because Diderot listed the articles alphabetically – a process representing the egalitarian, equalizing mentality of Enlightenment thinkers keen to overthrow the hierarchical structures then reigning (literally) in Europe.

More than two hundred years later, one must not fall victim to the assumption in the post-Enlightenment world that the scientist and the bureaucrat merely categorize and describe in neutral fashion what is actually "out there." Indeed, the positivistic notion that by conducting a population census, for example, a state is merely counting real persons who are "out there" belies the fact that a census is, instead, an ideological construct every bit as powerful as Diderot's assumptions about knowledge and categorization. Ian Hacking notes:

> There is a sense in which many of the facts presented by the bureaucracies did not even exist ahead of time. Categories had to be invented into which people could conveniently fall in order to be counted. The systematic collection of data about people has affected not only the ways in which we conceive of a society, but also the ways in which we describe our neighbour. It has profoundly transformed what we choose to do, who we try to be, and what we think of ourselves.

(Cited in Zureik 2001: 207)

Even in the modern era, when the printed word began replacing the calligraphy of scribes and the beginnings of mass education threw open the doors of literacy to those outside the bureaucracy and clergy, governments still have used their ability to gather and manipulate data as an instrument of social control. Record-keeping obviously has helped modern states keep track of their growing populations. Another way that modern record-keeping has served the national project in myriad settings is through the creation of the individual citizen as replacement for an undifferentiated mass of subjects. Modern states have done this by recording people and property in population censuses and tax records as individual units, outside of wider social connections such as families (or "tribes"), castes, and hierarchical orders. As Messick writes of Yemen, "In the process [of increased modern bureaucratization], the social basis of the polity is shifting from reckonings by status and kinship . . . to the imagined simultaneity and homogeneity of a national citizenry" (Messick 1993: 254).

In the modern era, "Questions of identity are central to surveillance, and this is both a question of data from embodied persons and of the larger systems within which those data circulate . . . The central social question is again that of social sorting and classification" (Lyon 2003: 3). Censuses are one of the basic methods by which states, particularly modern states, gather data on the identity of populations under their control. But once again, censuses do not merely count people who are "out there." Rather, they are innately political processes that categorize and sort people according to various criteria that are themselves the product of the political imaginings of the state. As Dominique Arel notes,

> Census categories are not neutral. The use and meanings of categories such as "immigrant," "permanent population," and "language" are the results of what is essentially a political process involving state agents, census takers, scholars, and social groups. Census decision-making is shaped by inertia (past practices) and by evolving national interests.
>
> (Arel 2003: 823)

One way in which censuses are political agents is how they categorize the ethnic and/or linguistic identities of those being counted. By enumerating populations according to identity, the state is able to create, through its categorization criteria, the very identity of persons it is enumerating. Indeed, when it comes to ethnic identity, in particular, Arel notes that such "realities" do not always exist outside the mind of the census taker and his/her enumeration of them:

> [T]he determination of identity is a subjective assessment that is endogenous to the very process of categorizing. Primordialism, or the notion that ethnic identities are permanent, has little currency in the social sciences. Yet scholars in general, and demographers in particular, tend nevertheless to the fiction that, somehow, identities have an objective existence outside the process of counting them, that is to say, outside of the social and political circumstances that make them salient.
>
> (Arel 2003: 801–802)

Bernard Cohn has noted how the British conceptualized and actually institutionalized social conflict in India via their censuses: "The British assumed that the census reflected the basic sociological facts of India. This it did, but through the enumerative modality, the project also objectified social, cultural, and linguistic differences among the peoples of India" (Cohn 1996: 8). He also points out that this strengthened their belief that only the colonial power could keep the peace: "The panoptical view that the British were constructing [through censuses] led to the reification of India as polity [*sic*] in which conflict, from the point of view of the rulers, could only be controlled by the strong hand of the British" (Cohn 1996: 8).

Records of land registration and taxation, as well as survey maps, similarly are agents of both surveillance *and* transformative power. They, too, involve considerable power of agency and do not merely record information about land "as it is." They are tools by which the government's logic about land and rights to land can be imposed, sometimes changing existing social conceptualizations of land in the process. In the context of British land registration in imperial India, Smith notes this transformative power:

> But in the process [registration] the principles of shareholding were altered and forms of village organization changed. This change can be stated most concisely, I think, as a change in the idiom in which agrarian relations had been expressed. Shares had been reckoned locally in ploughs, a key term in agriculture with many connotations. When formal weight was given to one particular usage and this was tied to a notion of property in fixed parcels of land, the semantic field was disturbed. Correspondingly the integrity of the old system of shareholding, which had centred on balancing economic resources within a village, was undermined.
> (Smith 1996: 17)

This was particularly true of the British propensity, based on Roman concepts of unqualified possession and Enlightenment era physiocratic notions of private property, to register individual parcels of land throughout Britain's imperial domains. This was done in lieu of registering collectively controlled land. Smith notes: "And I think that everywhere the business of mapping and measuring, of registering holdings as discrete, separately negotiable parcels of land, and of fitting agrarian relations into a new mould must be considered fundamentally disruptive of an older order" (Smith 1996: 378–379).

Similarly, survey maps did not merely chart land "as it was." As Denis Wood argues:

> This is to say that maps work . . . by serving interests. Because these interests select what from the vast storehouse of knowledge about the earth the map will represent, these interests are embodied in the map as presences and absences. Every map shows *this* . . . but not *that*, and every map shows what it shows this *way* . . . but not *the other*.
> (Wood 1992: 1; ellipses and emphasis in the original)

Thus a map links a plot of ground with an entire set of assumptions, interests, and values that the state brings with it. In so doing, Wood states, "We see that this is what maps do: they mask the interests that bring them into being; this to make it the easier to accept what they say as . . . *unsaid* . . . as . . . *in the air*" (Wood 1992: 6; ellipses and emphasis in the original). Like land registers, survey maps drawn by the British in India reflected European conceptualizations about land and property. Walter Neale notes:

> A moment's thought makes it clear that the European view is not itself objectively real, but is a way of relating a piece of the earth's surface to European methods of astral observation and to a technique of plotting observations on a plane surface . . . The European grid map . . . is a perception of the "natural" world in which people live.
> (Neale 1969: 4)

Benedict Anderson agrees, noting, "[l]ike censuses, European-style maps worked on the basis of a totalizing classification, and led their bureaucratic producers and consumers towards policies with revolutionary consequences" (Anderson 1991: 173).

It is clear that records and the bureaucratic imaginings that underpin them carry tremendous transformative capabilities. Did this occur during the Palestine Mandate, however? To answer this, we first must note the type and scope of data gathering carried out by British and Zionist bodies during that period.

Britsh data gathering during the Mandate

While the Palestinians were no strangers to Ottoman era processes of registering people, land, and other aspects of daily life, it was the period of the British Mandate in Palestine that witnessed the exponential growth of statistics, survey maps, censuses, and other data aimed at enabling British authorities to control many aspects of the lives of Palestinian Arabs. By the time they quit the country in May 1948, Mandatory authorities had produced a horde of documents detailing and quantifying myriad aspects of daily life in Palestine. Britain's ability to govern and control the population obviously stemmed from certain types of data gathered: tax lists and maps, for example. But its colonial project also had the possibility of changing the contours of certain areas of Palestinian life, such as landownership.

Martin Bunton offers a word of caution, however, about the extent to which the British were able to impose their authority on the Palestinians simply and easily through data collection, and unilaterally to change such aspects of life as land-ownership. The British authorities depended upon the cooperation of Palestinian villagers, particularly for the success of its large-scale land registration and settlement-of-title operations. They could not afford to alienate villagers via an expansive and disruptive land program, and in fact worked with them. As Bunton notes:

> While one does not wish to erase the power differential between the colonial settlement officers and the colonized property owners, it is nonetheless important to fully recognize the extent to which, in securing cooperation, colonial officers placed an emphasis on local knowledge and on village structures, such as the *mukhtar*, and on how cultivators themselves defined their rights to the land and its resources.
>
> (Bunton 2007: 201)

Bunton continues, "The recorded representations of the land settlement officers . . . are better viewed as the result of contested negotiations among officials and landholders than the result of externally imposed British transformations" (Bunton 2007: 202) The needs of colonial officials, combined with the passive and active resistance of the population, impacted the degree to which "rule by records" was possible in Palestine.

Given this, to what extent, then, did the British manage to "rule by records" and impose their own colonial imaginings about land and bodies on the Palestinians? As far as records enumerating people, the Mandatory authorities, beginning in 1920, required such events as births and deaths to be recorded with the Palestine government's Department of Health in order to gain a clear idea about the nature and scope of the country's people. Village *mukhtar*s (headmen) were delegated, and remunerated for, the responsibility of recording such events. The Mandatory government also twice conducted a full census of Palestine's population, in October 1922 and November 1931. The first census was carried out specifically in order to determine representation for a proposed legislative council. Thus, it not only served the general need to determine how many people lived in Palestine, and where, but served the British authorities' particular political need to establish a legislative body to assist them in ruling. Because the council was to be based on religion, the census enumerated Palestine's population on the basis of religious identity, as the Ottoman Empire had done previously: Muslim, Christian, and Jewish. (Druze were included in the Muslim category.)

The British claimed that they were doing this in accordance with Ottoman precedent and because of social factors on the ground, not because of any social engineering or divide-and-rule policy of their own. Yet the way in which British officials articulated their alleged adherence to tradition betrays their deep ideological understanding of Palestinian society and the role of religion in it: "The classification by religious communities, viz. Moslems, Jews, Christians and others, has been adhered to throughout the period. It is a classification socially necessary by reason of the complete jurisdiction enjoyed by religious communities in matters of the personal status of their members" (*Survey of Palestine* . . . 1991: 140).

There was no further breakdown by specific sect within each religion, by ethnicity, or by tribal identity in the census, and Bedouin tribes in the southern Beersheba district were not counted at all. Overall, the Superintendent of Census described the population as harboring a "suspicion" about the census, and called it "unpopular" (McCarthy 1990: 28). The 1931 census was much more detailed than that of 1922. This time, "ethnicity" – Jew, Arab, or other – was included as a category, in addition to religion. After 1931's, the British never carried out another census. To keep statistics on population thereafter, the Mandatory authorities made annual adjustments to the country's population statistics based on data they collected on births, deaths, and immigration/emigration until the end of the Mandate in 1948.

Were Mandatory land policies likewise motivated by political concerns? Considerable disagreement has emerged among scholars over the degree to which British land policy was driven by the Mandate's requirement to facilitate the Zionist project. Dov Gavish has described the impetus beyond Mandatory land surveying as follows:

> The [survey] system was formally established in July 1920 with only one objective: to survey and map the lands of the country as demanded by the Zionist Organisation, in order to implement legally binding land settlement and registration of tenure rights. Thus, the land issue was at the core of the mapping of Mandate Palestine.
>
> (Gavish 2005: xiv)

Bunton once again urges a measure of caution in this regard, however. Citing Ernest Dowson, the architect of British land policies in Palestine, he points to the fundamental fiscal and developmental bases of the land program as outweighing the need to accommodate Zionism. In 1938, Dowson noted:

The establishment in Palestine of a national home for the Jewish people accentuated the urgency of the reform and imposed a higher standard of performance than might otherwise have been necessary; but basically the measures that were adopted were evoked by the economic needs of the land and the inhabitants, irrespective of creed or race, and would have been intrinsically just as necessary if the Balfour declaration had never been conceived.

(Bunton 2007: 4)

What is clear is that from as early as 1920 Mandatory authorities began surveying/mapping Palestine and registering land. Various types of map were produced. For our purposes, the most important were those dealing with landownership (cadastral maps). Mandatory officials also began registering land in new English-language registers and issuing deeds. In 1928, they began a massive campaign to ascertain and register title and all other rights to land throughout the country. To help in this process, the Survey of Palestine began drawing up 1:2500-scale topocadastral maps as well, a project that was completed in 1933. By the end of 1946, this campaign to settle all rights to land, known as land settlement, had been completed in 473 villages throughout Palestine, and was under way in an additional 102 villages (Gavish and Kark 1993: 197). According to maps submitted in 1947 to the United Nations Special Commission on Palestine, settlement had been completed in 5,240,042 dunums (1 dunum = 1,000 square meters); fieldwork and the cadastral survey were completed in 533,880 dunums; and survey work only in 599,550 dunums (Gavish and Kark 1993: 198). Land settlement led to new land registers that were much more informative and detailed than those previously used. These indicated specific plots of land and who possessed ownership, mortgage, and other rights to them, and corresponded to maps detailing their precise boundaries.

Survey maps and other documents were also produced to assist Mandatory officials in establishing a new basis for a new land taxation system. In 1928, the Urban Property Tax Ordinance was enacted; this was followed by the Rural Property Tax Ordinance of 1935. To help with determining more precise land taxation obligations, the Survey of Palestine then completed 1:10,000-scale maps of all villages north of the Beersheba district from 1933–1934 (Gavish 2005: 165). These laws did not lead to individualized tax assessments – tax obligations were still determined and collected by village committees and authorities – but they did represent the deepening of state knowledge of, and involvement in, the land regime of Palestine.

By 1948, the British had produced thousands of records relating to landownership in Palestine. By the time that the United Nations voted to partition Palestine in November 1947, the Mandatory government had created a total of 3,616 land registers,[1] in addition to thousands of cadastral and topographical maps and a huge number of records relating to land taxation.

Beyond census and landownership data, the British gathered other types of information about Arab life in Palestine during the Mandate. During World War Two, the British Naval Intelligence Division, for example, commissioned the exhaustive study *Palestine and Transjordan* as part of its Geographical Handbook series. The handbook on Palestine was produced by a team of academics working at a Naval Intelligence sub-center in Oxford. One of the main authors was Albert Hyamson, who had served as Director of Immigration for the Mandatory government in Palestine

(Naval Intelligence Division 2006: 581). "The purpose of these handbooks," reported the Director of Naval Intelligence in 1942, "was to supply, by scientific research and skilled arrangement, material for the discussion of naval, military, and political problems, as distinct from the examination of the problems themselves" (Naval Intelligence Division 2006: iii). As he went on to note, the strategic military value of such "scientific research" that was subject to "skilled arrangement" and was "easily digested" was clear: "the work of the fighting services and of Government Departments is facilitated if countries of strategic or political importance are covered by handbooks which deal, in a convenient and easily digested form, with their geography, ethnology, administration, and resources" (Naval Intelligence Division 2006: iii).

The British produced other handbooks and fact books on the country. The military resurveyed Palestine late in the Mandate period and created another grid system for maps that was slightly different from the civilian grid created by the Survey Department on cadastral maps. As a result, a military *Gazeteer of Place Names* was issued in 1945 to go along with the new 1:100,000-scale maps. This replaced the 1940 book that had been created on the basis of the civilian grid corresponding to the 1:100,000-scale topographical maps. The *Gazeteer* listed all villages and natural formations in Palestine, noting the population and other features, as well as their coordinates on military maps.

After World War Two, the Mandatory authorities also published two detailed socio-economic studies, *Village Statistics, 1945* and the *Survey of Palestine*. A version of the former was first released publicly in 1943, largely to Mandatory government offices, to show how much land was owned in Palestine by Jews and non-Jews as of 1 April 1943. This data first had been gathered pursuant to a request made of the Department of Land Settlement by the Palestine government in 1936 in order to present the data to the Royal Commission (the Peel Commission). When the Anglo-American Committee of Inquiry was established in 1946, the Department of Land Settlement and the Department of Statistics were asked to revise the *Village Statistics* for the committee's use. This became the *Village Statistics, 1945*, which was more detailed than the 1943 version. For example, it included population estimates, and more data on other categories of landownership than just Jewish and Arab (for example, land owned by the government, municipalities, and local councils) (*Village Statistics, 1945* 1970: 12). The book gave detailed statistics on the surface area of each village and town in Palestine, and how much of it was owned by Arabs, Jews, and others.

A Survey of Palestine: Prepared in December 1945 and January 1946 for the Information of the Anglo-American Committee of Inquiry, as its title suggests, was another detailed, multi-volume collection of data on myriad aspects of life in British Palestine compiled "with complete objectivity and without suggestion as to the conclusions which might be drawn from them" (*Survey of Palestine* . . . 1991: iii) It was a virtual encyclopedia detailing the history of British Palestine as well as the situation regarding the economy, population, and society as they stood in early 1946.

From 1920 to 1948, the British Mandatory authorities had conducted thorough social sorting and data gathering activities in Palestine. They were not alone. While they did so for their own reasons, various Zionist scholars and agencies also took pains to study the land and people of Arab Palestine.

Zionist data gathering during the Mandate

Zionist officials, organizations, and scholars also took great pains to study Palestine's land and population during the Mandate. A number of Jewish scholars produced detailed studies of Palestine's Arab population and land-holdings. Writers such as Avraham Granovsky (A. Granott) of the Jewish National Fund (JNF) and Arthur Ruppin of the Jewish Agency (JA) researched and published about land and farming in Palestine. Ya'akov Shim'oni, an agent in the Shai (the underground Hagana militia's intelligence service), produced a detailed work in 1947 entitled *'Aravei Erets Yisra'el (The Arabs of Palestine)*. It offered a wealth of information about Palestinian social structure, and no doubt stemmed from the secret studies he undertook on Palestinian villages for the Shai (see below). Alfred Bonné of the JA's Institute for Economic Research wrote *Erets Yisra'el: ha-Arets ve ha-Kalkala (Palestine: The Land and the Economy)* in 1937. Yitshak-Avigdor Vilkanksy (I. Elazari-Volcani) of the JA's Institute of Agriculture and Natural History wrote about agriculture in Palestine, including his 1930 work *The Fellah's Farm*. Beyond that, a variety of Zionist organizations operated agents, both Jews and Palestinians, to gather information about Palestinian society and politics (Cohen 2008).

The most detailed Zionist data-gathering program involved the Shai (a Hebrew acronym derived from *Sherut Yedi'ot* – Information Service), which meticulously gathered data on land, population, and other features of Palestinian rural life for a massive and secret project entitled "Operation Arab Village." The result was the "Village Files." These were "the most striking example thus far of the application of intelligence activity to defined military ends" (Black and Morris 1991: 28). The origin of the idea apparently went back to Ben Tsiyon Luria, an historian at the Hebrew University of Jerusalem who also worked for the JA's Education Department. According to Shimri Salomon, it was Luria who first suggested to the JNF that a list containing details of Palestinian villages should be drawn up (Pappe 2007: 17). Eventually, Hagana official 'Ezra Danin suggested to fellow Hagana member Re'uven Zaslani (Shiloah) in April 1940 that the Hagana should produce a comprehensive list of Palestinian villages. Shai was given the task of preparing the list. The three Shai officials responsible for the project were Danin, Shim'oni, and Yehoshu'a Palmon. As described by Hagana member David Karon:

> The whole idea behind the Haganah in those days was that all retaliation by us had to be against the right target. In order to know what was the right target, you also needed to know what was the wrong one. So the Shai did an immense amount of work documenting villages, collecting information about their families, their internal conflicts.
>
> (Pappe 2007: 29)

Another Hagana figure, Moshe Pasternak, pointed out another military need: "We had to study the basic structure of the Arab village. This means the structure and how best to attack it … The Arab village, unlike the European ones, was built topographically on hills. That meant we had to find out how best to approach the village from above or enter it from below" (Pappe 2007: 19). From 1945 to 1947, over 600 Palestinian villages (some say as many as 720) were surveyed (Cohen 2008: 188;

Black and Morris 1991: 28; Eyal 2006: 85). Both Jewish Shai agents and Palestinian informers were used to obtain information from the villagers themselves.

The files started out as an index-card system that was functioning by 1943 – large green cards on which Shai agents recorded details about each Palestinian village. The data in the "Green Archive" included items of direct military importance – such as roads, numbers of weapons, presence of fighters in the 1936–1939 Arab Revolt, and the level of "hostility" to Zionism – to political information, such as the names of the *mukhtar*s and who was affiliated with *al-Hajj* Amin al-Husayni and the "councilist" faction in Palestinian politics. Other data about land, water sources, wealth in the village, tribal rivalries, and so forth was also entered on the cards (Pappe 2007: 19–21). Eventually this card system was expanded to include aerial photos and maps.

What was the ultimate effect of these various British and Zionist studies of Arab bodies and land-holdings in Palestine? Beyond helping the Mandate authorities to control, tax, educate, and, in the case of the Zionists, "know the enemy," did these records have a wider impact on Palestinian lives?

Impact of British and Zionist data collection on Palestinian land and population

On a basic level, the data collected by Mandatory authorities obviously had value in assisting the British to rule the country and its Palestinian inhabitants. The ability to assess and collect land taxes was essential for the fiscal viability of the Mandatory administration. Survey maps also assisted the British in imposing security control on the country's inhabitants, which in true colonial style they felt was necessary in order to prevent communal unrest (even though it was their own support for the Balfour Declaration that created most of the communal tension in Palestine). The Mandatory authorities found that their detailed maps of the country's topography, roads, and villages helped their security forces in one specific instance: they greatly simplified the task of the British army and air force during the Arab Revolt in the late 1930s. Commissioner for Lands and Surveys F.J. Salmon noted the connection between the maps his agency made and overall British security needs: "Our maps, of course, have to be designed for a variety of users and so they are not ideal for the Army, but being on the reserve of the Survey Branch of the Corps, I do try to keep Military requirements in view" (Gavish 2005: 253). He also pointed out the usefulness of his department's maps in the particular task of quelling the revolt:

> [I]t was by the greatest luck that I had completed the sheets in the area where most of the troops were – Tulkarm, Nablus, and Jenin – which is the worst country for bandits and raiders. So that as soon as the two Divisions came to Palestine I was able to issue them sheets [maps], and in 1936 my printing staff, with only one machine, working often day and night, produced 30,000 copies for the troops and police.
>
> (Gavish 2005: 253)

Beyond this obvious use of documents to rule, this study has noted the theoretical power of records to transform the very objects they enumerate and/or describe. The question then becomes: beyond the obvious degree to which data and information helped Britain rule Palestine, did such surveillance transform the basic nature of Arab life in Palestine as a result? The two major ways in which data collecting theoretically could have impacted Palestinian society were censuses and land records. Did the way that Mandatory authorities conceptualized Palestinians in census registrations – as religious communities and/or as "Arabs" – affect the actual contours of Palestinian society, particularly Palestinians' own discourse about "self"? Did the ways in which the British surveyed and registered land-holdings impact the way the land was owned and farmed? The record would suggest that they did not; not because of any weakness in the transformative power of the data, but because of Palestinian resistance to the Mandate itself and to the Zionist project, and because the British needed to work with the Palestinians to implement certain policies, which forced them to temper their outside, unilateral decision-making.

For example, the British predilection toward counting Palestinians according to sect failed to lead to permanent rifts among Palestinians of different religions, and failed to change how Palestinian society understood and organized itself. The Mandatory authorities continued the Ottoman practice of dividing and codifying the population of Palestine into "Christians," "Jews," and "Muslims" when collecting data for the 1922 and 1931 censuses, as well as other vital statistics. When trying to establish consultative bodies such as the proposed advisory council in 1920 and the legislative council in 1922, the authorities similarly proposed a system of confessional, not national (i.e., Arab), representation. The British claimed that they were merely maintaining the Ottoman status quo, and claimed that the religious hierarchies of the various religions exercised significant control over the day-to-day lives of their adherents (see above).

To be sure, the British tendency to view the Palestinians as members of separate religious communities to some degree did affect, and symbiotically was affected by, the growing power of religion (Islam, in particular) as a discourse of confrontation. For example, the power and influence of the Supreme Muslim Council (SMC), which the British created in 1921, and its president, *al-Hajj* Amin al-Husayni, continued to grow throughout the Mandate period. So did Islamic discourses of resistance and liberation voiced during the Arab Revolt of 1936–1939, persecution of Christians in some areas, and the marginalization of some Christian nationalist voices. However, the Palestinian leadership, including al-Husayni, continued to assert that the Palestinians constituted a unified *ethnic* polity as Arabs, and not merely a collection of discrete Muslim, Christian, and Druze communities. The shared sense of threat and nationalist grievances shared by most sectors of Palestinian society as they together faced British occupation and Zionist immigration and land purchases fueled a common ethnic Arab identity (although the Druze were a partial exception to this generalization). This attitude helped mitigate the potentially transformative effects of the British "sort-by-sect" and "divide-and-rule" policies.

For example, the main Palestinian nationalist coordinating body from 1920 to 1934 was the Arab Executive, which insisted on including both Muslims and Christians, and which therefore represented Palestinian demands to the Mandatory authorities on a national/ethnic, not a sectarian, basis. Partially as a result, in 1923 the British authorities proposed the creation of an Arab Agency through which the Palestinians as a national/ethnic collective could represent themselves to the Mandatory author-ities, much as the Palestine Zionist Executive represented the Jews. The census was changed too, so the 1931 version included the ethnic categories of "Arab" and "Jew" as well as religion, whereas the 1922 versio had not (McCarthy 1990). Even al-Husayni's influence during the Mandate period stemmed as much from his role as a nationalist politician, including his presidency of the Arab Higher Committee (which included Muslims and Christians) from 1936, as from his religious positions as mufti of Jerusalem and president of the SMC. Despite some of its pronounced Islamic aspects, insurgent leaders during the Arab Revolt used both ethnic Arab and bi-communal Muslim–Christian slogans and symbols as expressions of national unity. They printed stamps for use in areas under their control that bore the slogan "Palestine for the Arabs" and featured both the Church of the Holy Sepulcher and the Dome of the Rock. Meanwhile, Palestinian national flags bearing an emblem consisting of a Christian cross and an Islamic crescent were used by some guerrilla fighters (Graham-Brown 1980: 176).

British census data that counted Palestinians as members of a religious sect and, later, as "Arabs" similarly did not transform the social categories by which Palestinians conceptualized themselves. Counting Palestinians as legally equal, discrete individuals dealing face to face with the state outside the parameters of other social ties did not undermine tribal and regional identities, which remained strong among the Palestinians throughout the Mandate period. In fact, any movement toward the "individualization of the individual" *vis-à-vis* the state was checked by the British reliance upon village-wide structures. For example, recording vital statistics and assessing tax obligations remained in the hands of village tax distribution committees and the *mukhtar*s to reduce cost and political friction. As Bunton notes:

> Entrenched from the beginning of the mandate, the position of the *mukhtar*, and of *musha'* [village-wide, collectively owned land], as well as other structures of daily village life, played increasingly crucial roles in the practical administration of rural taxation, particularly as mechanisms for its assessment and distribution. The corollary of this [British] desire for expedience and convenience at every turn is that the untiring rhetoric of individualizing property rights so as to bring about a direct relationship between government and individual in the collection of taxes became less and less pertinent or appropriate.
>
> (Bunton 2007: 169–170)

British land policies brought with them an entire set of Western capitalist notions about land, its ownership, and its "rational" exploitation, and thus offered the potential to alter patterns of Palestinian landownership. For all the potential to bring about great change, however, the Mandate and its records did not radically alter the character of Palestinian landownership. The basic contours of how land was owned remained the same. Bunton admits to the potential power of British imaginings, but notes the ultimate inability of the British to transform the land regime of Palestine's Arab population:

> colonial manipulation and bias were to some extent inherent in the process: local idioms, relevant on the ground for the definition of property relations, were converted into government categorizations and classifications. However, if the colonial period witnessed a process of registration filtered through the fiscal and

cultural preconceptions of the British government officers who recorded and adjudicated the information, the idea of a systematic programme of trans-formation is difficult to sustain.

(Bunton 2007: 192–193)

He goes on to state:

> The recorded representations of the land settlement officers (more so than the regular courtroom system) are better viewed as the result of contested negotiations among officials and landholders than the result of externally imposed British transformations . . . Where necessary, land registration policies in mandate Palestine transformed local realities, but colonial constructs also clearly over-lapped at times with patterns and structures among the colonized, themselves of course neither static nor rooted in antiquity but constantly responsive to changing circumstances.
>
> (Bunton 2007: 202)

The need to gain the cooperation of the population for the sake of cost and efficiency, combined with the fact that the land settlement program could not be completed because of the outbreak of the Arab Revolt, worked against any transformative effect.

Where records and record-keeping *did* exert a profound impact on Palestine's Arabs came in the ways in which the Zionists utilized the data they collected, as well as that collected by the British, during and after the 1948 war. Pre-war Zionist surveillance greatly facilitated Israel's victory in the war. For example, Hagana (and, later, Israeli army) operations benefited tremendously from maps that had been produced by the British. In the first months of 1948, Shai operatives were able to acquire or photograph, through the agency of Jewish employees, 1:10,000-scale fiscal maps of Palestinian villages and other documents at the Survey of Palestine's offices in Tel Aviv. The Hagana also managed to capture British vehicles transporting maps from Tel Aviv to Ramla and make off with their contents (Gavish 2005: 249). The Hagana purchased, or sometimes stole, larger-scale topographic maps of the country as well. Starting in 1944, its Technical Department began printing its own, Hebrew-language 1:25,000- and 1:100,000-scale topographic maps that were copies of English-language maps produced by the British (Gavish 2005: 254–255). These maps were put to good use during the hostilities, given that the war radically changed Palestinian political, spatial, and socio-economic realities.

The Shai's *Village Files* also proved of immense value during the wartime operations of the Hagana and the Israeli army, and even played a role in Zionist imaginings about the nature of Arab village structures. Like the aforementioned maps, the files assisted Jewish forces during their assaults on Palestinian villages. Further, as Ilan Pappe notes, "In 1948, Jewish troops used these lists for the search-and-arrest operations they carried out as soon as they had occupied a village" (Pappe 2007: 21). The files, as well as informers, were used to detain and even execute wanted Palestinians after villages were conquered. Israel used the files for military needs after 1948 as well. Israeli military intelligence, for example, used them to plan raids on villages in the Jordanian-controlled West Bank during the 1950s (Black and Morris 1991: 129). Moreover, the Israeli government imposed martial law on its Palestinian citizens after establishment of the state. The military governors and others in charge of these citizens utilized the *Village Files* in their work, another example of "rule by records." Finally, Gil Eyal has argued that the basis for the wider, long-lasting Zionist conceptual understanding of the "Arab village" as a unit stemmed in no small measure from the *Village Files* and the imaginings of Shai operatives and Arabists (Eyal 2006: 85; 1996: 389–429).

Israeli authorities also used British data – land and tax records, both those left behind and photographic copies obtained from British authorities in London in 1951 – to assist them in their spatial reorganization of Palestinian land after the war. Israel seized a huge amount of land vacated by the 750,000 Palestinian refugees who fled or were expelled by Jewish forces during and after the war. Over 6 million dunums were confiscated by the Israeli authorities (Fischbach 2003, 2006). In January 1949, and again in September 1950, the Israeli government sold a large portion of this refugee land to the Jewish National Fund. Yet the JNF insisted upon the transfer of these properties' legal titles to it from the Israeli government's Custodian of Absentee Property on behalf of the Development Authority. Israeli authorities were therefore anxious to reconstruct missing British land registers to assist them in the task of transferring title to the now-vacant lands to the JNF so it could settle them with Jewish immigrants. Enter the Mandatory land records.

In May 1951, the Israeli government asked the British government to hand over filmed copies of land registration records that the Mandatory authorities had made in 1947–1948 (the British produced 2,160 rolls of 35mm film).[2] Israel already had the original Mandatory land registers relating to Jewish-owned property that the British had left with the Jewish Agency in 1948. What the Israelis wanted was information on Palestinian-owned land to help them identify the vast amount of land vacated by Palestinian refugees, as the original documents had ended up in Jordanian hands as a result of the 1948 war (Fischbach 2003: 234). Britain turned over the films in stages during the first months of 1952. Thereafter, the Israeli Directorate of Land Registration worked with staff members seconded by the JNF to recreate land registers for the refugees' property in order to transfer title to specific plots of land among the large amount of the property from the state to the JNF. By September 1954, JNF staff members had reconstructed registers for 174 abandoned Palestinian villages, covering about 1.5 million dunums of land.[3] The Israelis also benefited from hard copies of Mandatory land taxation records that the British had left behind in 1948. As a result, title to most of the 2,372,676 dunums of refugee land that the JNF purchased in 1949 and 1950 had been transferred to the Fund by 1958 (Fischbach 2003: 58–68).

A thorough demographic and spatial reorganization of Palestine by Zionist forces had been achieved. One must take great care to note that Zionism's ability to use surveillance data to carry out such sweeping changes, in contrast to Britain's relative failure to do so, had everything to do with the special conditions (the "state of exception") offered by war.

Conclusion

The collection of data about Palestinians and their land by the British Mandatory government and Zionist agencies from 1920 to 1948 was nothing if not thorough. Like other types of intelligence gathering and social sorting, instruments such as censuses and land records stem from the imaginings and ideological biases of their creators.

Beyond aiding states to govern the peoples they control, data and record-keeping can therefore mold and change the nature of the subjects they purport to describe. While the data collected by the British Mandatory authorities in Palestine assisted the colonial project, they did not lead to fundamental changes in the nature of Palestinian Arab land and society. Palestinian resistance was an important factor in this regard, as was the Mandatory authorities' need to cooperate with – not transform – social structures and institutions. By contrast, Zionist data collection, and Zionist usage of Mandatory data, did play a role in the dramatic changes to the demographic and spatial nature of Arab society in Palestine during and shortly after the state of exception created by the 1948 war. These data were essential in the spatial and demographic transformation of those parts of Palestine that became Israel.

This case study of data collection in Palestine during the Mandate therefore both upholds and challenges some of the prevailing theoretical observations about the role played by state data gathering and surveillance. When determining the extent to which states use records to rule and transform societies, care must be taken to situate the analysis of this role within an historical context that takes into account such mitigating factors as popular resistance and state budgetary constraints. Similarly, one must also note the sweeping opportunities for "ruling by records" that are afforded by wartime exigencies and states of exception. I hope that this short study provides the basis for further analysis of data collection and social sorting as they relate to the history of Palestine/Israel.

Notes

1 United Kingdom, National Archives, CO 733/494/3, Appendix II to Memorandum of J.F. Spry (1 October 1948) and Memorandum to Spry (13 October 1948).
2 Ibid.
3 United Nations Secretariat Archives, DAG 13-3, UNCCP, Subgroup: Records of the Land Specialist, Series: Records of the Land Specialist 1951–1952/Box 35/Diary (J.H. Berncastle); Document: Berncastle diary entry (10 August 1952); World Zionist Organization, Central Zionist Archive, KKL5/22273, "Report on the Land Administration System of the State" (5 September 1954).

Bibliography

Anderson, Benedict. *Imagined Communities: Reflections on the Origin and Spread of Nationalism*, rev. edn. London and New York: Verso, 1991.

Arel, Dominique. "Demography and Politics in the First Post-Soviet Censuses: Mistrusted State, Contested Identities." *Population* [English edition] 57, 6 (November–December 2003): 801–828.

Black, Ian and Benny Morris. *Israel's Secret Wars: A History of Israel's Intelligence Services*. New York: Grove Weidenfeld, 1991.

Bunton, Martin. *Colonial Land Policies in Palestine, 1917–1936*. Oxford Historical Monographs. Oxford: Oxford University Press, 2007.

Cohen, Hillel. *Army of Shadows: Palestinian Collaboration with Zionism, 1917–1948*, trans. Haim Watzman. Berkeley, Los Angeles and London: University of California Press, 2008.

Cohn, Bernard S. *Colonialism and Its Forms of Knowledge: The British in India*. Princeton Studies in Culture/Power/History. Princeton, NJ: Princeton University Press, 1996.

Eyal, Gil. "The Discursive Origins of Israeli Separatism: The Case of the Arab Village." *Theory and Society* 25, 3 (June 1996): 389–429.

——. *The Disenchantment of the Orient: Expertise in Arab Affairs and the Israeli State*. Stanford, CA: Stanford University Press, 2006.

Fischbach, Michael R. *Records of Dispossession: Palestinian Refugee Property and the Arab–Israeli Conflict*. Institute for Palestine Studies Series. New York: Columbia University Press, 2003.

——. *The Peace Process and Palestinian Refugee Claims: Addressing Claims for Property Compensation and Restitution*. Washington, D.C.: United States Institute of Peace Press, 2006.

Gavish, Dov. *A Survey of Palestine under the British Mandate, 1920–1948*. London and New York: Routledge Curzon, 2005.

Gavish, Dov and Ruth Kark. "The Cadastral Mapping of Palestine, 1858–1928." *The Geographic Journal* 159, 1 (March 1993): 70–80.

Graham-Brown, Sarah. *Palestinians and Their Society 1880–1946: A Photographic Essay*. London, Melbourne and New York: Quartet Books, 1980.

Lyon, David. "Introduction." In David Lyon (ed.) *Surveillance as Social Sorting: Privacy, Risk, and Digital Discrimination*. London and New York: Routledge, 2003.

McCarthy, Justin. *The Population of Palestine: Population History and Statistics of the Late Ottoman Period and the Mandate*. Institute for Palestine Series. New York: Columbia University Press, 1990.

Messick, Brinkley. *The Calligraphic State: Textual Domination and History in a Muslim Society*. Comparative Studies on Muslim Societies. Berkeley, Los Angeles and Oxford: University of California Press, 1993.

Naval Intelligence Division. *Palestine and Transjordan*, reprint edn: London, New York and Bahrain: Kegan Paul, 2006.

Neale, Walter C. "Land is to Rule." In Robert Eric Frykenberg (ed.) *Land Control and Social Structure in Indian History*. Madison, Milwaukee and London: University of Wisconsin Press, 1969.

Pappe, Ilan. *The Ethnic Cleansing of Palestine*. Oxford: Oneworld Publications, 2007.

Smith, Richard Saumarez. *Rule by Records: Land Registration and Village Custom in Early British Panjab*. Delhi: Oxford University Press, 1996.

Survey of Palestine: Prepared in December 1945 and January 1946 for the Information of the Anglo-American Committee of Inquiry, reprint edn. Washington, D.C.: Institute for Palestine Studies, 1991.

Village Statistics, 1945: A Classification of Land and Area Ownership in Palestine, with explanatory notes by Sami Hadawi. Beirut: Palestine Liberation Organization Research Center, 1970.

Wood, Denis with John Fels. *The Power of Maps*. New York and London: Guilford Press, 1992.

Zureik, Elia. "Constructing Palestine through Surveillance Practices." *British Journal of Middle Eastern Studies* 28, 2 (2001): 205–227.

16 Surveillance and spatial flows in the occupied Palestinian territories

Nurhan Abujidi

After more than sixty years of contestation, the "Question of Palestine" arises as the iconic model of geopolitical spatial dilemmas that has marked both the twentieth and the twenty-first centuries. Even now, over sixty years later, it is difficult to comprehend how, between 1947 and 1948, over 400 Palestinian villages were systematically emptied and bulldozed, and an entire territory was confiscated in creating the new state of Israel (Sheik Hassan 2009). Not only is this conflict over space, and not only has it created new and extreme spatial configurations within historic Palestine; its impact has extended beyond these borders. The Nakba of 1948 and the Naksah of 1967 generated the largest and longest-lasting refugee problems in the world: currently more than 4 million Palestinians are refugees. As the late Edward Said (Said & Mohr 1999: 11) observed, the paradox of living in exile has remained a major element for Palestinians both outside and within the occupied Palestinian territories (OPT) since 1948.

This chapter analyzes contemporary Israeli policy of spatial reconfiguration of the OPT by highlighting the complex and shifting terrain of power and resistance, and the complicity of ordinary people in its everyday violence. It argues that the Israeli military occupation's surveillance network – termed "exclusionary surveillance" by Ariel Handel (Chapter 13, this volume) – is used to reconfigure the Palestinian spatial condition and experience. Consequently, analyzing or reading Palestine or the Palestinians as the condition of Palestinian geopolitical space or unified Palestinian human experience is no longer possible. Palestine after the 1948/1967 wars was dislocated, and was reproduced in new places outside Palestine. Since then it has constantly transformed space as its dimensions drastically expand and contract, and as the identities that constitute it adapt and change. Thus, this changing condition creates ever-new realities and relations that neither fit simple categories nor conform to previously encountered forms. At the same time, Palestinians are no longer categorized under the same living conditions: they are either the Palestinians who reside inside Israel or the occupied territories (*fe Al-dakhl* – interiors) or the Palestinians who reside in exile (*fey el-manfa, fey al-kharej,* or *fey Al-ghurba*).

With special attention to the city of Nablus, the largest city on the West Bank, this chapter details how the Israeli civil and military occupation of the Palestinian territories, through its web of complex surveillance and control techniques, fragmented the OPT into several spatial conditions and experiences. As will be shown, the ultimate goal and consequence of this surveillance and control is the fragmentation of both time and space that consequently makes Palestinian life unbearable. This is achieved, as Ariel Handel argues in Chapter 13 (this volume), by the extensive production of uncertainty as part of spatial control practices, which makes nearly every movement dangerous and problematic. Palestinians, however, have also resisted the military network of surveillance and control.

This chapter takes a fivefold approach. The first section discusses surveillance, exception, and resistance. The second addresses the different forms, patterns, and techniques of surveillance imposed on the OPT, scaling from the territorial to neighborhood level, using Nablus as a case study. The third discusses the impacts of the Israeli cogwheel of surveillance and control on the Palestinian spatial, socio-economic, and mental conditions. Using Foucault's theory of power and microphysics, the fourth section explores an analysis of the Palestinian modus of resilience and resistance. Finally, by critically reflecting on the limitations of Agamben's theory, the chapter articulates and redefines the "state of exception" in relation to the special form of surveillance practiced in the occupied territories.

Surveillance, exception, and resistance in the OPT

David Lyon defines "surveillance" as "[t]he focused, systematic and routine attention to personal details for purposes of influence, management, protection or direction" (Lyon 2007: 14). This definition stresses the technical and human management objectives of surveillance but does not address other non-technical, spatial, time, and socio-economic aspects that this chapter deems essential in order to understand surveillance in a colonial context. The spatial surveillance that this chapter details below marks a major shift in the Israeli surveillance system and its network of installation. This development started to materialize after the Oslo Agreement of 1992 and gained visibility after the onset of the Al-Aqsa Intifada in 2000. This shift can be observed in surveillance architecture and techniques, spatial and time dimensions, and population management. The newly developed surveillance network incorporates such high-technology elements as cameras, small airplanes (drones), checkpoints, inspections using laser technology, and the apartheid (or separation) wall. This surveillance consequently succeeded to manage the Palestinian subject's spatial inclusion or exclusion from Israeli laws and responsibility. It also manages – and sometimes stops – the spatial flows and activities of the Palestinian subject, impacting significantly on aspects of his daily life.

The other shift is observed in the Palestinian subject's experience of the Israeli exercise of power, which is designed to give the impression that power is in Palestinian hands post-Oslo when, in fact, Israel still holds the power. Consequently, this exercise of power and the Palestinians' resistance create several forms and layers of the states or spaces of exception that offer unique spatial experiences. Such spaces of exception, detailed below, go beyond Agamben's definition of exception.

Agamben presents the state of exception in diametric opposition to the normal state of affairs (along the lines of inside/outside, sovereign/homo sacer, normal/abnormal, private/public, and so on). The state of exception, for him, is one in which a sovereign exercises absolute power over the victim, who cannot resist and who has no rights since all laws are suspended and all notions are confused. These conditions are undoubtedly present in the Palestinian state of exception, yet the Palestinian states/ spaces of exception are much broader. They entail all aspects of life, not only the juridical and legal levels, and create multiple levels of exception that continually destroy and regenerate themselves in extreme forms. Thus, as will be shown in the final section of this chapter, there is a strong connection between surveillance and the existence of the state of exception, which are articulated here to be, by default, creations of each other. Combining both theoretical and empirical insights and debate to redefine and connect surveillance with the state of exception and resistance discussions is the main objective of this chapter.

Literature on resistance is mostly theoretical and based on limited anecdotal case studies, most of which are presented from a Western point of view. To explain the complex Palestinian resistance modes and link them to surveillance and the state of exception, Foucault's theory on power production demonstrates how Palestinians generated different modes of resistance to and resilience against the Israeli military exercise of power via the surveillance network. Furthermore, due to their experience of this, Palestinians survive extreme conditions of exception.

Foucault did not relegate power to the dominant class, who then preserve and wield influence in order to secure authority. Instead, power is a force that is constructed, enacted, and transmitted through the institutions, social structures, dominant rhetoric, means of communication, and physical and psychic levels that constitute life (Foucault 1980: 174). According to Foucault, there is no "powerless" or "powerful," no two opposite classes, one with power and one without, for the simple reason that power is not a possession but an action. He draws out the inseparability of the exercise of power and the production of resistance and claims that we cannot speak of power without resistance or the potential of resistance.

Thus, the main conclusion of this chapter will be that the Israeli exercise of power via surveillance and control created several formats and spatial dynamics of the state of exception. These, in turn, urged the production of several modes of Palestinian resistance.

Levels and forms of Israeli military and civilian surveillance (exclusionary surveillance) in the OPT: the case of Nablus city

The Israeli control and surveillance network comprises one part of the larger Israeli occupation machine which also includes several other cogs: the Jewish settlements project, the destruction of Palestinian villages, the military laws, land confiscation, and so on (see Figure 16.1). The surveillance network is a very important element in that it enables Israel to exercise full control over the territory and resources, and at the same time manages Palestinians' activity flows in space and time. It is structured around six interconnected systems of surveillance: the apartheid wall; territorial subdivision and zoning; checkpoints; Israeli-only bypass roads; military bases; and the special set of military laws that support all other systems. (Jewish settlements are presented in this analysis to be deployed partially for surveillance and control purposes, among other functions.) The surveillance network produces fragmented Palestinian spatial conditions and multilayered experiences of exception. This chapter divides the spatial condition into four patterns or forms: states of exile and refuge; states of paradox; states of occupation and siege; and states of urbicide. Through a detailed analysis of the states of occupation, siege, and urbicide, the chapter presents the different forms, spaces, and levels of exception that confront Palestinians.

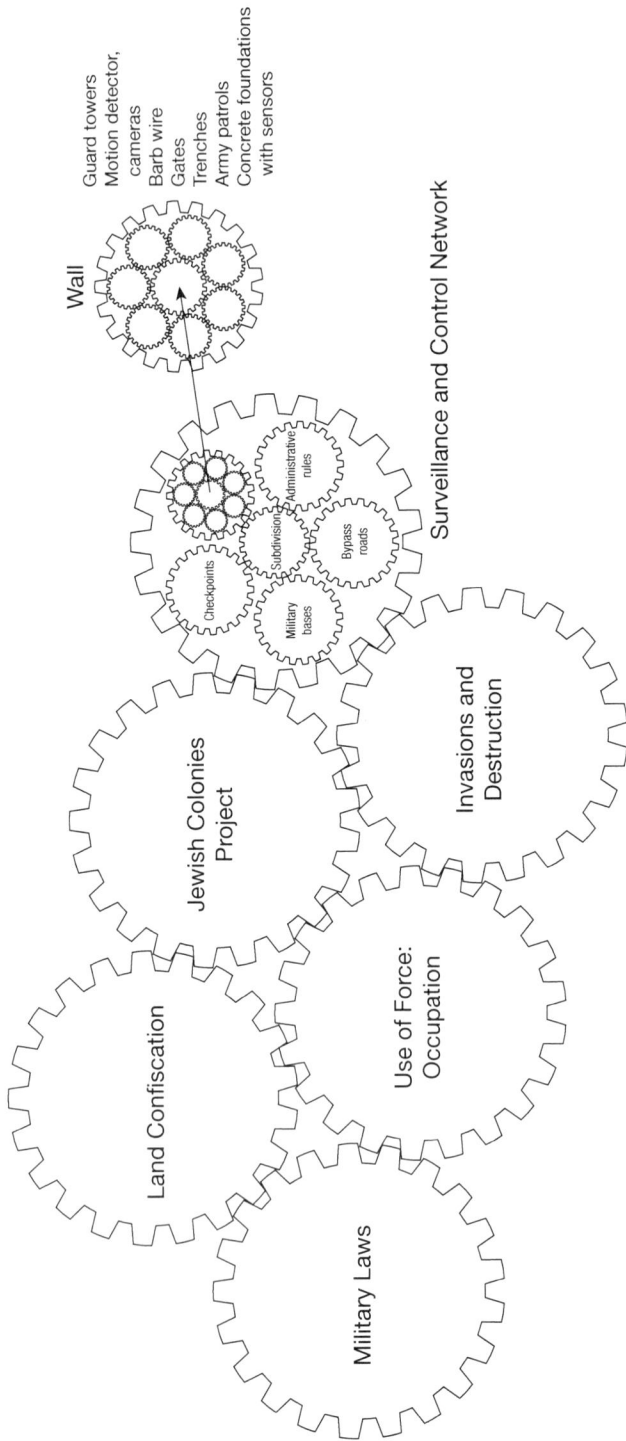

Labels within the figure:

Wall

Guard towers
Motion detector, cameras
Barb wire
Gates
Trenches
Army patrols
Concrete foundations with sensors

Surveillance and Control Network

Administrative rules
Subdivision
Bypass roads
Checkpoints
Military bases

Jewish Colonies Project

Invasions and Destruction

Land Confiscation

Use of Force: Occupation

Military Laws

Figure 16.1 The Israeli surveillance network as part of the occupation machine cogwheels

Source: Author

Since its military occupation of the Palestinian territories after the 1967 war, Israel has actively implemented surveillance networks and techniques to construct control over the OPT. The control is enforced by the Israeli military laws that subjugate Palestinian development and urbanization, and the network of checkpoints, gates, trenches, and military bases that forms the material and spatial matrix which devastates Palestinian urbanity/territoriality. The case of Nablus city illustrates the different scales that the Israeli surveillance and control network touches, and the many techniques and mechanisms that are used.

Nablus is located 65 kilometers north of Jerusalem. It is the largest city in the West Bank, and its strategic location makes it a major focal linkage for a number of Palestinian cities and villages. The city is the trading center for the region and the economic capital of Palestine. Nablus and its environs have been inhabited for more than 5000 years, as far back as Canaanite times. The existing structure of the historic center is characteristic of old Arabic–Islamic cities. This is manifested in the structure and form of its streets, network of alleys, domes, vaulted houses, and souqs (markets). Despite the numerous and substantial social and political changes that have taken place through the ages, the pattern of the Roman city – built in AD 72 – can still be discerned in some sections and buildings. Nablus is also famous for its cultural heritage. Over the past six years, it has suffered the heaviest Israeli military attacks in the Palestinian territories.

Spatial surveillance and control in Nablus

In Nablus, as elsewhere in the OPT, there is surveillance over space. The Israeli authorities have established an surveillance system throughout the occupied territories which penetrates every Palestinian city, village, and camp. This network functions on different scales, from the territorial to the urban, and even extends to the level of neighborhoods and individual houses during times of military invasion.

Since the early 1980s, Israel has developed a strategy of control over key Palestinian spatial and physical structures. A network of strategic "points" was established around the main Palestinian urban areas, manifest in settlements, checkpoints, army bases, and industrial parks. These points are connected by the "lines" of the massive system of highways and bypass roads; the apartheid wall is seen as a border line. One might hypothesize that this wall embodies a permanent state of exception manifested as an exceptional barrier. The eastern edge of the West Bank, declared by the Israeli authorities to be a combat zone and a "closed military area," can be seen as an edging surface of the territories. The layout of this network of points, lines, and surfaces comprises what Jeff Halper (1999) has defined as the "matrix of control." The physical network reflects the visible material layer of the matrix. The other two layers are invisible. These are projected, first, in the military laws imposed on the Palestinian territories since 1967 and, second, in the use of force – the occupation itself (see Figures 16.2 and 16.3).

The physical network is composed of two types of system: permanent and temporary. Although both originate from the same logic and elements of points and lines, the scale, nature, and mechanism differ in each case. The permanent matrix expands from the national, regional, district, and city scale. In addition, it is structured around fixed points and lines represented by Israeli Jewish settlements, Israeli military

Eastern Military Buffer Zone (Under Israeli Control)

Area C, Under Israeli Military Control

Palestinian Built-up Area (and Areas A, B)

Israeli-built Settlments on Confiscated Palestinian Land

Israeli Military Bases

The Israeli-only Bypass Roads

The Separation Wall

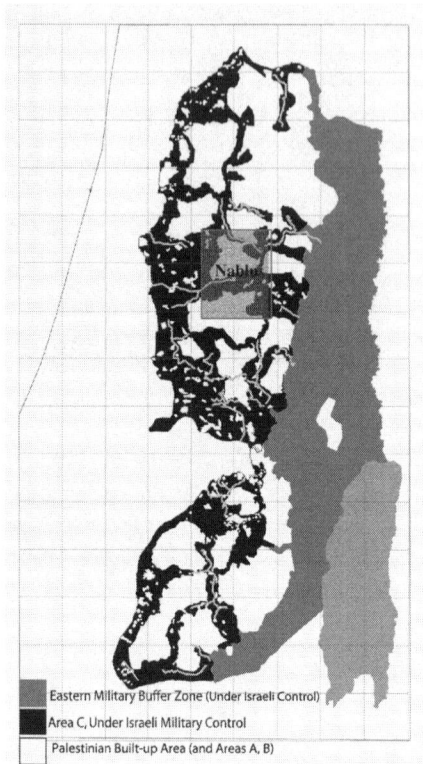

Figure 16.2 An abstract map of the dynamics of control in the occupied Palestinian territories (West Bank) that exemplifies the invisible layer of the Israeli physical network of control; urbicide by control

Source: Adapted by the author from www.btselem.org

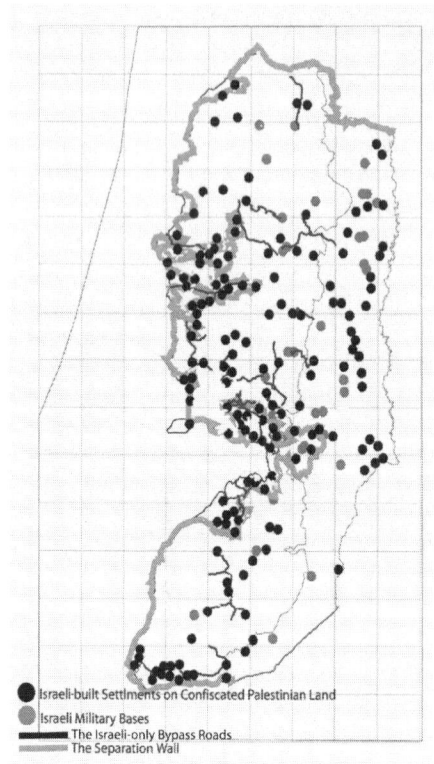

Figure 16.3 An abstract map of the physical elements of the Israeli network of control in the occupied Palestinian territories (West Bank), the settlements, the bypass roads and the apartheid wall; urbicide by construction

Source: Adapted by the author from www.btselem.org

checkpoints, Israeli dumps, Israeli industrial parks, Israeli holy places, Israeli military bases, and Israeli-only bypass roads.

The points of the previously discussed permanent physical network in Nablus operate on several levels. They are intended to control and enclave the main Palestinian centers, and to limit Palestinian urban growth. The process is recognized first by a tight circle of six main settlements, with their master-plans and buffer zones established to enclave the area. These have imposed crucial surveillance and monitoring mechanisms on the Palestinian territories since the 1980s.

The second level is an "iron ring" of 117 full-time and partially manned checkpoints (at the two main city entrances, these are transformed into something more like permanent border crossings), roadblocks, metal gates, earth mounds, earth walls, and trenches that surround the city and its main entrances (UNOCHA 2005).

Some points of the physical network change and damage the Palestinian natural landscape and agricultural land by installing factories and industrial parks within Israeli settlements. Of the seven main Israeli industrial parks in occupied Palestine, Burqan, located to the north-west of Nablus, is the largest.

The lines of the physical network are the apartheid wall and the bypass roads. They are constructed to facilitate access to and travel between settlements without passing through or connecting with the Palestinian-built inhabited areas. Consequently, the bypass roads often block the development of Palestinian communities in the West Bank, creating borders and barriers between communities and routes that were once connected and contiguous. The bypass roads also form clear axes for Israeli control throughout the West Bank. These roads are classified as forbidden: Palestinian travel is restricted or entirely prohibited on forty-one roads and sections of roads within the West Bank, including many of the main traffic arteries (B'Tselem 2005). Nablus is surrounded by three main bypass roads: road 60, road 57, and the road connecting E'bal military base with the Shave Shomron settlement (see Figure 16.4).

The Israeli apartheid wall, another line of the physical network, gouges through the Palestinian territories from the west. Its track constitutes another border that confiscates Palestinian land, reproduces and enforces Israeli control, and limits

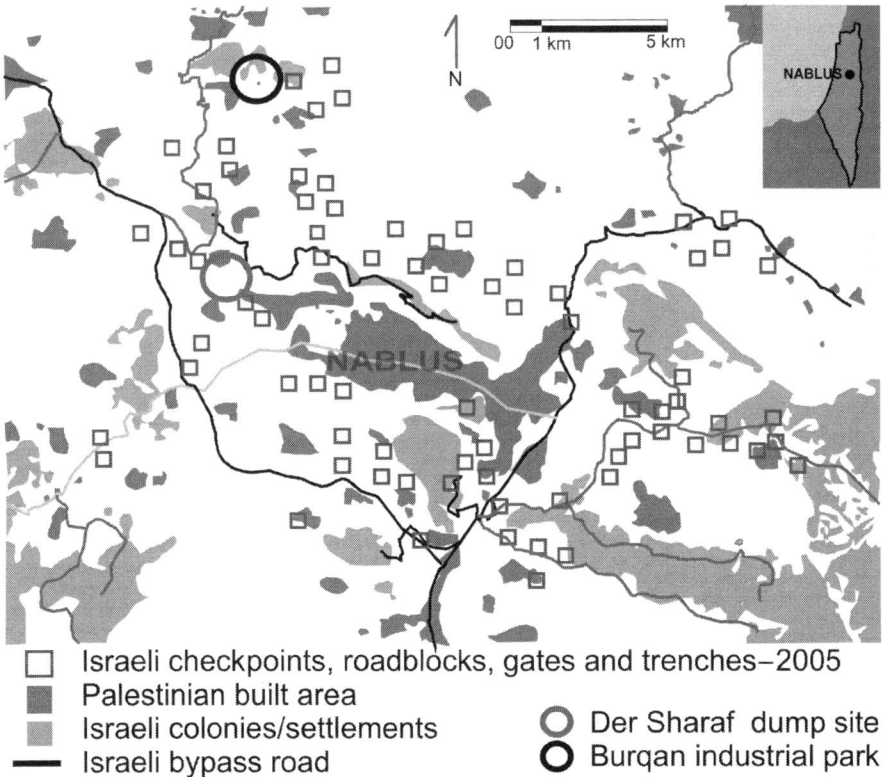

Figure 16.4 Location of the Israeli physical network of control points around Nablus

Source: Adapted by the author from B'Tselem (2005) and UNOCHA (2005) maps

Palestinian urban growth. The wall carves and solidifies the division concept and parallels the other elements of Israeli control, especially the bypass roads and settlements. It can be interpreted as the starkest embodiment, on a material plane, of the logic of a permanent state of exception.

The occupying power reconfigures the urban/neighborhood level during military invasions and special operations. The temporary physical network of control is implemented on the city, sub-district, or neighborhood scale; it is intensified during "temporary" Israeli military incursions into Palestinian cities (in this case Nablus). This network is more often assigned to secure control within target areas; it is made up of military outposts, sniper positions, gates, dividing lines, temporary checkpoints within city borders, and temporary buffer zones. Snipers and military outposts became common during Israeli invasions into Nablus; twenty-eight positions have been registered inside the Old Town alone.

Snipers and forced routes (holes blown through the internal walls of houses to allow access from one building to the next) played important roles as surprise elements in the battle of April 2002; these two techniques were not usually employed during the first Intifada. These strategies enabled the Israeli army to control the battlefield with its heavy machinery, and were an important developmental shift in the Israeli military's strategy inside Palestinian urban areas.

The nexus between the territorial/urban permanent and temporary physical networks of control – discussed earlier – generates a total Israeli military administration of the Palestinian physical and spatial structure. During military invasions special measures are added to the Israeli surveillance and military control network. Between 2002 and 2005, frequent military Israeli invasions occurred in the Old Town of Nablus and the nearby Balata refugee camp. In all instances, the Israeli army used its existing physical network of control to infiltrate and control urban space and dominate the city. During these events new, temporary physical networks of control were super-imposed on the existing networks, consisting of sniper and military outposts, iron gates, temporary roadblocks, trenches, and a dividing system. This system divided Nablus New Town into east and west with a physical demarcation line, called "Tora Bora" by the residents. This comprises a mound of dirt constructed by the Israeli army near the destroyed governorate building (Muqata'a) and the city prison (see Figure 16.5).

My fieldwork and further research reveal four patterns of invasion used during these six years of systematic Israeli military operations (Abujidi & Verschure 2006):

1 *Long-term invasion.* This type of invasion normally lasts several weeks or months. It typically imposes a tight siege and curfew on the Old Town core and on large sectors of the city of Nablus. For example, in April 2002, during an invasion that lasted for two weeks, both the Old Town and the greater Nablus area were under tight siege and a strict curfew. The June 2002 invasion, which lasted for 160 days, was also enforced by means of a continuous curfew imposed on large sectors of the city, besides the Old Town. Such long-term invasions take on some of the characteristics of a prolonged invasion in the more classical sense of spatial domination and control.

2 *Short-term invasion.* This type of invasion lasts from a few days to two weeks. It is accompanied by a curfew affecting different sections of the urban area, besides the Old Town. For example, the December 2003–January 2004 invasion lasted

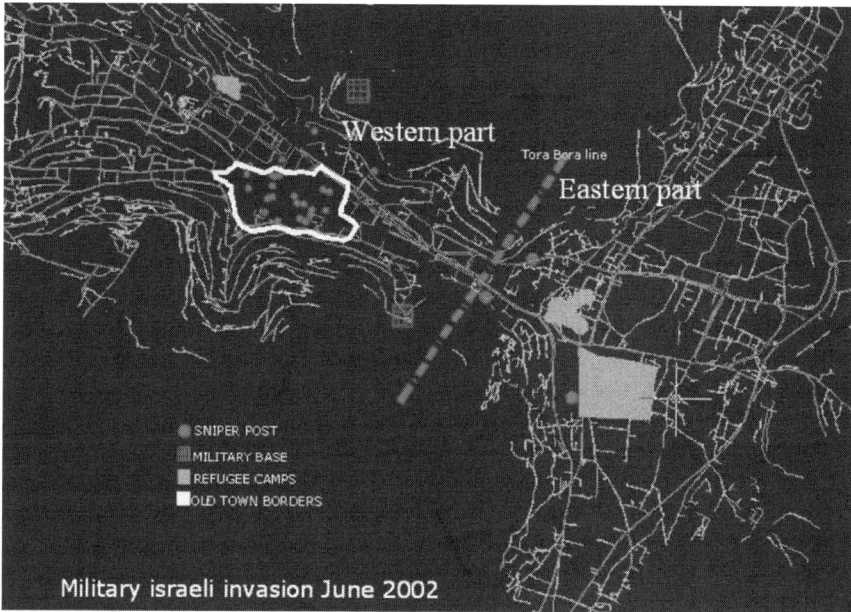

Figure 16.5 Dividing Nablus city into different sections during the Israeli military invasion

for ten days and imposed a strict curfew on the Old Town, although the attack focused only on the Al Qaryun quarter.

3   *Overnight incursion.* This type of operation lasts for just one night, starting at midnight and concluding at dawn. It has become the norm in the night-time existence of the Old Town of Nablus. Since 2004, overnight incursions have followed a regular pattern: no night can pass without the presence of the Israeli army in the narrow alleys of the Old Town, as a permanent incursion feature of this space.

4   *Daylight incursion.* This type of incursion lasts for a few hours during the day. A few Israeli jeeps enter the Old Town, either to apprehend a "suspect" from the Palestinian resistance or simply to create a state of terror among the town's visitors and vendors.[1]

In 2004 the city of Nablus was subjected to two long-term, ten short-term, and countless overnight and daylight incursions. During 2003, it was under curfew for a total of 4,232 hours – a total of almost six months.

Legal and juridical aspects of control in the OPT

The juridical/legal dimension adds another facet to Israeli military and spatial control over the OPT and Nablus. Many laws have been created since the Israeli occupation in 1967 to enforce the occupation machine. Even before 1967, the British "emergency laws" of 1945 were used by them against both the Jews and the Arabs. Of these, Law 124 gives the military governor the right, on grounds of "security," to suspend all citizens' rights, including freedom of movement: the army need only declare a zone forbidden "for security reasons" and Arabs no longer have the right to enter it without the authorization of the military governor. The state of Israel has since used these laws against the Arab population. To justify their retention, the "state of emergency" has not been formally lifted since 1948. Many other laws have been enacted as well, such as planning laws for Palestinian cities and villages, military laws, curfew laws, invasion laws, ownership and construction laws, and other laws that will be discussed in other sections of this chapter.

The innumerable restrictive military laws imposed on the occupied territories give Israel total control and administration of these areas and their inhabitants. They also generate paradoxes in everyday life experience. Siege and mobility laws, for example, have made life unbearable in the OPT since 2000 and the installation of the new checkpoints system. The network of surveillance and control, supported by the elastic and numerous military laws, is designed to control the territories spatially and, at same time, to act as a tool to manage the social and economic flows within the OPT.

Several waves of internal migration have occurred at the level of Nablus city and at the regional level – from Nablus to Ramallah and Bethlehem. These waves generated new patterns of socio-economic and spatial flows and mobility within the occupied territories. Thus, a concentration of certain activities (social, economic, religious, cultural, and administrative) can be observed in the OPT. For example, Nablus is no longer the economic center. Rather, Ramallah became the open city that supports most regional activities, and is now the Palestinian business, administrative, and cultural center.

The impact of Israeli surveillance on the Palestinian spatial and human experience

The many levels of Israeli surveillance and control imposed since their inception in 1948 have clear socio-economic implications for Palestinians. In particular, the previously discussed network of surveillance and control installed by Israel since its creation and intensified after the 1967 war has generated several new Palestinian spatial conditions and dimensions related to the experience of "states of exception." These various and changeable Palestinian spatial conditions produce countless documents and images that map Palestine and foster endless mental images of the place and the people (see Figure 16.6). I identify four interrelated states of the Palestinian spatial condition and experience of exception.[2] ("State" here refers more to a state of mind, to a spatial condition, and a human experience, rather than a territorial boundary or geographical and sovereign area, although these latter connotations are also present.) These states are presented in chronological and scale order (see Figure 16.7). This order must also be read to reflect the fact that states are interconnected and frequently renew themselves in different shapes and forms. For example, the state of exile represents the Palestinian refugees forced out of Palestine in 1948 and 1967, but this condition of exile and refuge continues into the present as more Palestinians leave Palestine either by force or self-imposed exile.

The first state can be described as a state of exile and refuge. The 1948 and 1967 Israeli–Arab wars signaled: the expulsion of Palestinians; the destruction of Palestinian cities, towns, and villages; and exile and loss of life. These conclude the chapter that

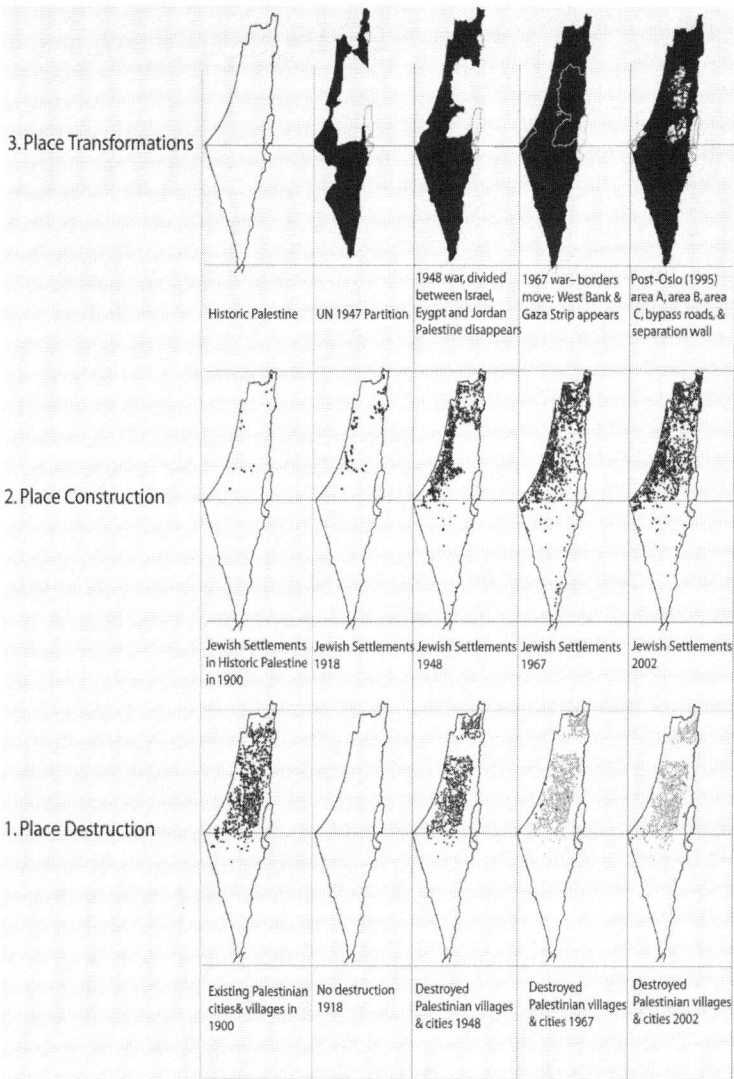

3. Place Transformations

| Historic Palestine | UN 1947 Partition | 1948 war, divided between Israel, Eygpt and Jordan Palestine disappears | 1967 war–borders move; West Bank & Gaza Strip appears | Post-Oslo (1995) area A, area B, area C, bypass roads, & separation wall |

2. Place Construction

| Jewish Settlements in Historic Palestine in 1900 | Jewish Settlements 1918 | Jewish Settlements 1948 | Jewish Settlements 1967 | Jewish Settlements 2002 |

1. Place Destruction

| Existing Palestinian cities & villages in 1900 | No destruction 1918 | Destroyed Palestinian villages & cities 1948 | Destroyed Palestinian villages & cities 1967 | Destroyed Palestinian villages & cities 2002 |

Figure 16.6 Patterns of place destruction, construction, and transformation in Palestine between 1948 and 2002

Source: Author adapted from maps drafted by the Palestinian Academic Society for the Study of International Affairs: <http://www.passia.org/palestine_facts/MAPS/0_pal_facts_MAPS.htm>

describes the disappearance of what was once Palestine. Thus, Palestine (or Filasteen in Arabic) vanished from the geopolitical map of the Middle East. A new emerging state of Israel surfaced; a new history, urbanity, and identity had to be formulated. At the same time, novel Palestinian geo-spaces were constructed and physically manifested inside Palestine and in exile. Thus, Palestine became (at least for Palestinians in exile) an idea, a memory of place.

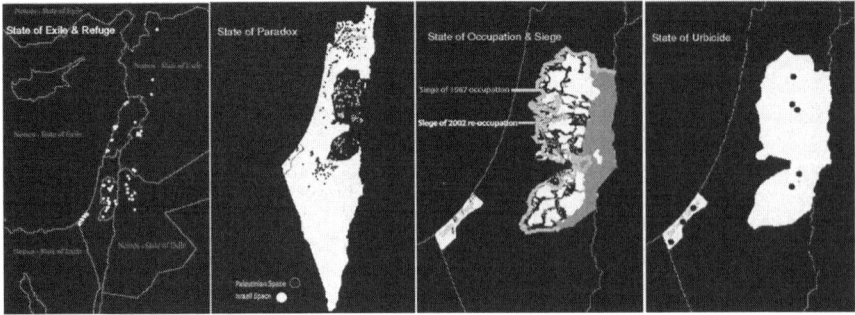

Figure 16.7 The Palestinian states/spaces of exception

This state of exile and refuge became an existential and epistemological condition of the Palestinian experience, as a spatial and temporal state of being, belonging, and becoming, in its material and metaphorical contexts. Edward Said (Said & Mohr 1999: 19) wrote poignantly on this state of exile when noting, "the stability of geography and the continuity of land – these have completely disappeared from my life and the life of all Palestinians."

The second state can be described as a state of paradox. This condition lies within the state of Israel itself. Palestinians who managed to remain in their homes in 1948 acquired Israeli citizenship: they are both Israelis and Palestinians. One Israeli/ Palestinian describes this Palestinian experience as: "Insane. The Jewish Israelis see me as an Arab and enemy despite my papers. Arabs see me as Israeli and enemy because of my papers" (Schulz & Hammer 2003: 79).

The third condition is appropriately labeled the state of occupation and siege, which is experienced by Palestinians residing in the West Bank and Gaza within the "lines" configured after the 1967 war. Different levels, intensities, and scales of siege can be recognized in this state, as discussed in the first part of this chapter. The mechanisms and dynamics generated from this state of siege are materialized in the contiguity/ fragmentation and exclaves/enclaves produced after Oslo and the 2002 reoccupation of the OPT. After the outbreak of the second Intifada in 2000, a strict Israeli military cordon was implemented in the OPT, accompanied by an accelerated process of enclaving Palestinian-built areas. This enclaving is manifest in the existing Jewish settlements (which, after a long process of formation, are now fully developed), Jewish bypass roads, and the newly constructed Israeli military checkpoints, roadblocks, road gates, and the apartheid wall. The Israeli settlement exclaves or islands, in spatial terms, draw the contours of the process of formation and consolidation of Jewish parcels of land in the heart of the Palestinian territoriality. The subsequent enterprise of these exclaves is to expand and multiply, as Falah (2003: 182–183) explains. These Jewish exclaves forcefully and slowly emerged within the Palestinian-built environment, and are connected by a network of bypass roads (and infrastructure) that serves the Jewish inhabitants of the new settlements and is forbidden to Palestinians. The spatial metaphorical reality of these Palestinian enclaves makes them appear as small pockets of land lying outside the main flows and networks that shape the territory.

They are strangers in their own natural setting, yet naturalize the presence of their conqueror (see Figure 16.7).

The fourth state is the state of urbicide, the extreme condition of the state of siege. The state of urbicide represents the permanent state of invasion and strangulation taking place in many Palestinian cities and refugee camps within the state of occupation and siege. The Israeli military invasion and reoccupation (beginning March 2002) of the Palestinian territories, and the destruction of the Palestinian-built environment and infrastructure, aimed at four targets:

1   Palestinian symbols of power (e.g., Ramallah city).
2   Palestinian symbols of resistance – "the myth of Palestinian resistance" (Nablus Old Town, Jenin refugee camp, Rafah refugee camp, and Balata refugee camp are a well-known examples).
3   Palestinian symbols of identity manifested in historic cities and cultural heritage sites. The old centers of Nablus, Hebron, and Bethlehem were destroyed during these invasions.
4   Palestinian symbols of the right of return and the mark of the Palestinian Nakba represented in the refugee camps, which had been the targets of several Israeli campaigns since the 1970s.

The military campaign and regular Israeli military invasions of the OPT (which are ongoing) resulted in the destruction of entire neighborhoods in many Palestinian cities, towns, and refugee camps. Many of these sites – such as the Old Town of Nablus and Rafah refugee camp, to name just two – have been under strict – even permanent – siege since 2000, and experience cyclic military invasions.

The case of Nablus well illustrates the significant socio-economic and socio-cultural impact of the Israeli surveillance network on the Palestinians. Several Nablusi cultural customs have been affected by the frequent invasions and destruction of the Old Town. For example, 60 percent of the interviewed sample[3] in Nablus Old Town pointed out that their social network had been strongly influenced by the continuous siege of the city. Furthermore, their declining economic situation makes it impossible for them to meet the demands of some social activities. For example, many Nablusi families have had to cancel important social festivities. Moreover, social networks have been significantly affected by the insecurity inherent in the frequent overnight invasions and long curfew periods. Organized and informal family, neighbor, and friend visits are disappearing from the Old Town's social fabric. Other cultural and economical patterns are also changing, and sometimes diminishing, there. Ramadan shopping traditions have been missed in the last five years; "Al-Souq Nazel," the daily Ramadan traditional bazaar organized by the municipality in the main square for hundreds of years has been canceled for the above-mentioned reasons. Palestinian cultural identity has lost essential elements, manifested in the destruction of cultural artifacts and the built environment. This deprivation extends to the loss of important cultural and social customs and traditions.

Nablus was the main hub linking the northern governorates of Jenin, Tulkarm, and Qalqilya with the central governorates of Ramallah and Jerusalem. Until 2001, one public transportation center in Nablus provided services to and from all of the northern governorates, as well as to Ramallah. In 2001, the implementation of heightened closure policies made it difficult for travelers from the north to reach Nablus. After January 2002, according to a UNOCHA report (2005), it was more difficult to leave Nablus for Ramallah. The bulk of the movement restrictions – aggravated by the presence of fourteen Israeli settlements and twenty-six outposts around Nablus – continue, and in some cases are tightening. A system of permits and restricted roads continues to limit the movement of people and goods. The West Bank barrier has also made access to Israeli markets for Nablus goods more difficult. In addition, "flying checkpoints" appear at unexpected times and places, with the result that travelers are either delayed, sometimes for hours, or find it impossible to reach their desired destinations at all. On average, the time required for travel has tripled – and this does not even include the delays created by the checkpoints and the sections of road that are now passable only on foot.

To cope with the strict closure of Nablus city, some services and businesses have relocated to smaller towns and rural communities so as to improve access for those outside the city. New shops and services in rural communities reflect the greater reliance on local agricultural activities and offer, for example, seeds and fertilizer, veterinarian services, and fuel and freight transportation. Haulage problems have also motivated businesses to open warehouses outside the city.

The strict siege, invasions, and continuous destruction have forced Nablus residents to adopt economic and trade coping mechanisms. However, they have also transformed Palestinian perceptions of self, other, and place. These events have changed what has come to be considered "normal" since the beginning of the Israeli occupation. Since the 1948 and 1967 wars, Palestinians both within and outside the Palestinian territories live in a permanent state of exile from what was once "Palestine."

This experience of estrangement is further reinforced by the state of emergency imposed since the establishment of the state of Israel. Originating from the British laws of 1945, this regulates and subjugates the Palestinian people's notion of normal life, which hinders their differentiation between normal and emergency, civil and military, and public and private space. During times of invasion, the exception of occupation in the Palestinian territories since 1967 becomes "normal" in comparison to the newly imposed exception established by Israeli army incursions, curfews, and the resulting destruction. This new, extreme, and exaggerated exception is evident in the collective experience of detention, death, and long periods of curfew, house raids, shelling, and demolition. It is realized in the presence of an existence of bare survival, living on the edge, where human rights and dignity no longer exist and profound "existential humiliation" is a recurrent experience:

> When all is said and all is done, sovereign power is the control of bare life: the authority over the citizen's life and death, a concept expressed in the state of exception . . . Hence the sovereign power not only upholds the law, but also, and above all else, maintains the right to suspend the law and declare the state of exception.
>
> (Agamben 1998, cited in De Cauter 2005: 156)

The Palestinian body is regulated in both the "normal" state of exception (created by the 1967 Israeli occupation of the Palestinian territories) and the "extreme" state of exception (during Israeli military incursions and prolonged invasions). It is systematically rendered vulnerable by the presence of surveillance and domination that penetrate all aspects of daily life. During invasions, curfews confine people to inside their houses, regulating the use of public space and extending to the most intimate private space, which is also invaded and redefined:

> Go inside, he ordered in hysterical broken English. Inside! I am already inside! It took me a few seconds to understand that this young soldier was redefining inside to mean anything that is not visible, to him at least. My being "outside" within the "inside" was bothering him. Not only is he imposing a curfew on me, he is also redefining what is outside and what is inside within my own private sphere.
>
> (Khoury 2004)

In these times of emergency, the city is forced to surrender its urban tools and imitates the life of a refugee camp, transformed into an enclave beyond any juridical sphere. Spatial normalcy and legal structuring are, in effect, "suspended" within the temporal frame created by an invasion.

Palestinian private space has been intruded upon and targeted, not only to destroy people's sense of place and privacy, as Falah and Flint (2004) have argued, but as part of the larger Israeli–Palestinian struggle over land and water. Sovereignty over space is an important element in achieving geopolitical aims intrinsic to the longer-term policy imperative within the geopolitical colonial imaginary that guides the Israeli nation-state.

The permanent siege around Nablus city since the year 2000, along with mobility restrictions, has made many Palestinians – especially the young generation – prisoners in their own city. Many leave the city seldom, if at all. The impact of such forcible confinement on the younger generation's perception and imagination of external spaces, cities, and the world is abstract. What for young people elsewhere are non-issues are sources of uncertainty for Palestinians. Lina Jamoul (2004) calls this phenomenon the "colonization of the mind" that results from the repeated experience of stop, search, check ID, wait for hours, have abuse hurled at you, get roughed up, and maybe, eventually, pass through. There is no other way to travel. This colonization of the mind occurs when people lack control over their own space. It becomes so naturalized that people cannot even imagine an alternative:

> A few days later I will be explaining to a Palestinian boy, who is desperate to emigrate to Syria, how we don't have to stand in line, how the soldiers don't search us, how they never turn us back. I will never forget the look on his face as I tell him we just flash our passports and are let through unhindered. "They don't stop you?" he asks, completely unbelievingly. I am ashamed to tell him that, as a foreigner, I am allowed complete free passage into every nook and cranny of his country, given that permission by an occupying military force, while he is completely prohibited from any free movement in his own country by that same occupying military force.
>
> (Jamoul 2004: 584)

The surveillance network and restrictions on mobility also impact the young generation's dreams, which do not extend beyond visiting another Palestinian city, arranging a recreational activity, and so on. Mosa, a young student from the Gaza Strip, told me:

> I can admit that I no longer possess a dream or big expectations. Till now most of what I look forward to are small decisions that I take every year and hope I can fulfill. Because whenever I have a big dream the occupation devastates it. My only dream now is to visit the West Bank (specifically Hebron), and it seems an impossible dream to realize.

Such uncertainties and doubts are strongly reflected in the comic drawings of Amal Kawaash, whose work shows how Palestinian children and youths are no longer certain of anything. One image asks, 'Are you still REAL?', while another employs the picture frame itself to evoke the infinite restrictions that Palestinians must endure (see Figure 16.8)

Palestinian resistance dynamics

Drawing on Foucault's (1984) analysis of power relations in reference to the production of knowledge and resistance, Palestinians' practices of resistance can be mapped. Through long years of occupation, the Israeli military has developed knowledge about

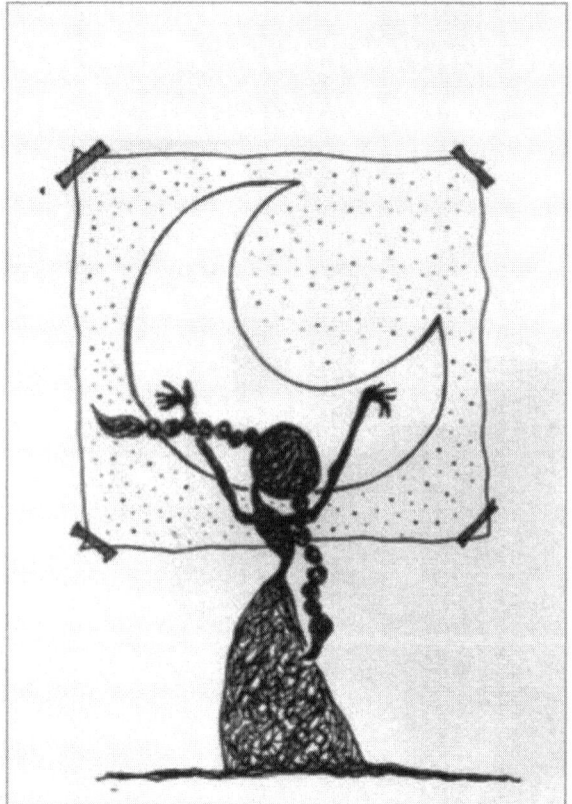

Figure 16.8a Are you still REAL?

Source: Courtesy Amal Kawaash; http://meiroun. blogspot.com/search/label/ Meiroun

Figure 16.8b In the frame

Source: Courtesy Amal Kawaash; http://meiroun.blogspot.com/search/label/Meiroun

the OPT and its inhabitants. This knowledge allowed Israeli military planners to install the previously discussed network of surveillance. This extreme and ubiquitous experience of power generated a collective experience of the occupation and its impacts on Palestinian daily life. It can be said that the experience of power reached into the very core of Palestinian individuals, touching their bodies and inserting itself in their actions and attitudes, discourses, learning processes, and everyday lives, according to Foucault's approach on this issue (Foucault 1980: 39). It also facilitated Palestinians' understanding of the mechanisms of the Israeli network of control, and produced a counter-knowledge to the Israeli military control and occupation practices. Consequently, Palestinians can break through this network of surveillance, thus affirming Foucault's argument that no power exists without knowledge, every power is knowledgeable, and knowledge is one of the cogwheels.

This is evident in the several forms of resistance encountered by the Palestinian social resistance practices of survival. Palestinians unconsciously mentally map the patterns and rhythms generated by the control network, thus formulating strategies or tactics to infiltrate the particular system of control (e.g., a checkpoint or the apartheid wall). This knowledge can be used for empowerment, creativity, and resistance, as well as suppression. Palestinians living around the Israeli apartheid wall, or those for whom the wall created an obstacle, acquired knowledge of how it operates. They were then able to pass through without triggering the alarm system or encountering a patrolling jeep. This practice is illustrated in Avi Mograbi's (2005) documentary about the wall and the checkpoints, and demonstrates Palestinians' in-depth knowledge of the wall and how it works – knowledge that rivals that of the Israeli general who oversees it. One man interviewed in the documentary explains exactly how he passed through sections of the wall several times without being caught. He knew how every element would react if he touched it, and he counted how many patrols took place each hour. This Palestinian knowledge is not merely about scientific techniques, but about how the system of surveillance operates. By trial and error, by experiencing the power of the wall, the checkpoint, and other elements of the surveillance system, the counter-action to break through can be developed.

Another example of knowledge and counter-knowledge is Areej Hijazi's experience of the paradox of living with the strict siege and surveillance system on daily basis, which paradoxically enabled her to break through to Israeli cities to enjoy some normalcy:

> I go to one of the Jerusalem checkpoints and try to pass. Why, I don't know. It could be that at those times you need to do something crazy to regain some of your internal balance, and in my case the craziest thing ever is to challenge the so-called "Israeli security and checkpoints system." Success is 100 percent: each time I tried to pass, I passed not only to Jerusalem, but to Tel Aviv, Jaffa, Haifa, and Nazareth. My passport was my curly hair and the Giorgio Armani sunglasses that I bought only for the checkpoints, and guess what? I believe the $300 investment was worth it. It is so funny that I cannot see my family in Gaza for years, while I spend most of the summer swimming in Tel Aviv or having fun in Jerusalem. What a brilliant security system! In case you feel like knowing more about this issue, please let me know.
>
> (Quoted in Levey 2008)

Civil resistance takes on many different forms in Nablus. For example, during the 2002 Israeli military operation dubbed "Defensive Shield," six out of the nine schools in and around the Old Town were destroyed. Rejecting and resisting the destruction of their city, many teachers held classes in the streets, to show that the power of life is much stronger than the machine of destruction and death, as Salem Hamdi put it. Rabab AbdulHadi (2004) describes how schoolchildren also challenged the 100 days of curfew from July to December 2003: "Children (including my own nephew Ibrahim and nieces Widad, Noura, and Nada, who live in the eastern part, beyond Tora Bora) have been risking their lives to get to school to take their final exams."

Clearly, then, regardless of their harsh experiences of invasion, destruction, and curfews, Palestinians keep a firm grasp on education as a means to struggle against occupation. This is also evident in Irene Siegel's report from the Nablus refugee camp of A'skar:

> An 11-year-old friend of mine named Shifa' described her classroom as a tiny room that crammed in about 40 students. There were no seats; most students

either stood or sat on the floor for the entire 3-hour session. Only a fraction of the usual subjects are taught, without textbooks (which either haven't been able to be completed, or to be delivered, from Ramallah). The students often study without notebooks or pencils as well, as their families are too impoverished by the choking, endless curfew–siege to buy them.

(Siegel 2003)

Palestinians in Nablus also express resistance through memory and commemoration. The remembrance of the impact of occupation and destruction is reflected in the Palestinian martyrdom discourse that extends to everyday activities and social rituals. Inhabitants of the Old Town celebrate and commemorate the tragic outcomes of the invasion and the killing of Palestinian resisters, converting the city into a huge graveyard, a macro-space of struggle and national identity. Locations of the assassinations of key resistance fighters are symbolically converted into commemorative monuments. Commemoration stones inscribed with poetry of sorrow and heroism are etched on the façades of buildings; posters depicting martyrs cover almost all the Old Town's walls. The city, which typically celebrates life, becomes the embattled arena for continual commemoration of seemingly ceaseless instances of death.

The Palestinian states of exception, resistance, and the Israeli military surveillance network

This chapter has shown that Agamben's understanding of the state of exception partially explains the conditions experienced in the Palestinian states of siege and urbicide. His approach, however, is not the only or necessarily the most appropriate tool to map and explain Palestinians' spaces of exception. Agamben's juridical definition of the state of exception hinders the explanation of the other forms and exceptions Palestinians experience in other spaces/state of paradox, exile/refuge, occupation/siege, and the state of urbicide. At the same time, limiting the discussion to a legal and juridical perspective blocks the analysis of other forms and levels of exception that might be generated within the different state/spaces of exception. As discussed above, the experience of exception is present in every aspect of the Palestinian spatial condition that goes beyond any juridical discussion. The experience of exception is revealed in the Israeli military surveillance network and the reconfiguration of Palestinian spaces and socio-cultural and economic dimensions; it even encompasses personal experiences and perceptions of self, other, and space.

The other limitation of Agamben's state of exception is its distinction between two actors (i.e., victim versus victimizer, powerful versus powerless). The current discussion ascribes to Foucault's principle of power: there is no such thing as two opposite classes, one with power and one without, for the simple reason that power is not a possession but an action. This chapter thus rejects the frame of the all-powerful sovereign and the powerless victim. Palestinians, through politics and civil or armed struggle, have shaped the realities of the conflict, and their resistance has been powerful and effective. Thus, analyzing or reading the Palestinian spatial condition only through Agamben's juridical definitions of the state or space of exception simplifies and limits the Palestinian condition to a single level of analysis, ignoring other dimensions and ultra-exceptions that Palestinians experience on a daily basis. At the same time, it hinders the analysis of the impact of the Israeli colonial machine on Palestinians' spatial condition and their lived experience of the exercise of such power.

Drawing on other theories and methods to understand the Palestinian colonized spatial condition is therefore crucial. Foucault's theory of power and microphysics provides a very interesting and powerful technique that deconstructs the Israeli cogwheel of occupation into its various components, and clarifies its mechanisms and impacts. When applied to the Israeli military surveillance network, it reveals six cogwheels that are designed and incorporated to guarantee full military control over the territories (see Figure 16.1). The apartheid wall is a component cogwheel of the larger surveillance and control network cogwheel, and it is considered to be the largest piece of architecture. It is composed of a network of barriers, including ten-foot-high walls topped with barbed wire, guard towers, motion detectors, and video cameras. This wall often prevents Palestinians from participating in activities of daily life, such as tending crops, attending school, going to the hospital, or visiting family members who happen to live on the other side of the Israeli-constructed barrier.

The post-Oslo Accords territorial subdivision into zones A, B, and C comprises the second element of territorial management that is designed to control and manage resources and population. This zoning stresses the occupation project machine: the fragmentation of space and time reaches even the smallest space. Although they are interwoven, every space, enclave, or cell has unique rules of movement, construction, military laws, checkpoints, and so on. The exercise of power is thus experienced in myriad ways. This type of fragmentation also follows the arbitrary Israeli military laws during times of invasion and urbicide.

The third cogwheel is made up of checkpoints, and the fourth is the Israeli-only bypass roads. The fifth cogwheel comprises the military bases, including sniper towers, that are found throughout the OPT, while the final one represents the administrative rules that have been imposed on the OPT. These rules add enormously to the arbitrariness that affects the lives of Palestinians and makes their daily routines or life projects impossible. There are countless examples: prohibiting work on the land for "security reasons"; the rule that states that if land such as an olive grove is not harvested for two years, it becomes state (i.e., Israeli) land; and the seemingly random decisions made at checkpoints which determine whether a traveler may pass through or not. After the 2000 Intifada, the objective of the Israeli military surveillance apparatus became movement prevention rather than movement regulation.

The theoretical discussion in the first section of this chapter called for a redefinition of the surveillance discourse in a colonial context, a definition that accounts for the different dimensions of surveillance and its interconnectedness to the state of exception and resistance. The analysis demonstrated that surveillance in a colonial context (such as the Israeli occupation of the Palestinian territories) develops high-technology knowledge of surveillance and control. This makes it possible for Israel to control Palestinian territory, space, and resources, and manage the Palestinian subject and his activities in space and time. The installation of this sophisticated surveillance network aims at both direct discipline and indirect control. According to Lyon (Chapter 2, this volume) these functions "coexist, layered the one on the other." In this case, they created four forms and layers of the state or space of exception that offered unique spatial, human, and mental experiences.

The intended effect of the Israeli military surveillance network, together with the long-practiced strategies it implemented, is to fragment time and space in such a way that it becomes impossible to lead a normal life. Consequently, a shift in the Palestinian modes of resistance can be observed: from non-violent resistance in the first Intifada of 1987, to guerrilla-type military resistance accompanied by other modes of civil resistance in the second Intifada. Resistance in the latter instance is practiced on a daily basis, in forms not necessarily readily recognizable, such as the Palestinian conception of steadfastness (*sumood*), going to school or work, bringing up children, and so on. These forms of resistance have been made possible by the spatial transformation of the Israeli surveillance and control techniques after the second Intifada. While the West Bank and Gaza Strip have been transformed into Israel's frontiers in the sense of institutional thinning, from a spatial perspective they have become hermetic ghettoes (see Gordon 2008: 39). Palestinians, in their struggle to regain normalcy in their everyday lives, have developed several survival techniques in the form of direct and indirect resistance to the Israeli exercise of power and control.

To conclude, the theoretical discussion and case-study analysis have aimed to demonstrate the complex interconnections between specific forms of surveillance used in the OPT, the creation of an ultra-state of exception that goes beyond Agamben's definition, and the modes of resistance Palestinians exercise in their daily lives.

Acknowledgment

For helpful comments on an earlier draft, I thank Ismea'l Sheik Hassan and Benedikt Zitouni. For financial support of this research project, I thank the Cosmopolis Research Center at Vrije Universiteit, Brussels.

Notes

1   This was reported repeatedly in our interviews. People complained of such invasions hindering the commercial activities and normal life inside the Old Town, and thus discouraging people from shopping there. During our survey, we witnessed ten such invasions. The soldiers in their jeeps would damage the goods displayed in front of shops; more often, they would start shooting for no apparent reason. The survey was carried out principally by the author.
2   Ismea'l Sheik Hassan (2005) used similar categorization of the Palestinian spatial condition for a different purpose.
3   During my fieldwork I interviewed 143 people in Nablus Old Town between 2003 and 2005.

Bibliography

AbdulHadi, R. (2004) "Appeal from Nablus: Lift the Siege of Nablus, Balata and Beit Foreek," *Arabic Media Internet Network*. Available HTTP: <http://www.amin.org/look/amin/en.tpl?IdLanguage=1&IdPublication=7&NrArticle=14150&NrIssue=1&NrSection=3> (accessed August 2006).

Abujidi, N. & Verschure, H. (2006) "Urbicide as Design by Construction & Destruction Process: The Case of Nablus/ Palestine," *Journal of Arab World Geographer*, 9(2): 126–154.

Abu Shmais, W. (2004) "Soldiers in My Home," *Zajel*. Available HTTP: <http://www.zajel.org/article_view.asp?newsI D=922&cat=2> (accessed June 27, 2005).

Agamben, G. (2004) "Life, a Work of Art without an Author: The State of Exception, the Administration of Disorder and Private Life," *German Law Journal*, 5: 609–614.

B'Tselem (2005) "Statistics on Checkpoints and Roadblocks." Available HTTP: <http://www.btselem.org/english/Freedom_of_Movement/Statistics.asp> (accessed May 2006).

De Cauter, L. (2005) *The Capsular Civilization: On the City in the Age of Fear*, Rotterdam: NAi.

Falah, G. (2003) "Dynamics and Patterns of the Shrinking of Arab Lands in Palestine," *Political Geography*, 22: 179–209.

Falah, G. & Flint, C. (2004) "Geopolitical Spaces: The Dialectic of Public and Private Spaces in the Palestine–Israel conflict," *The Arab World Geographer*, 7: 11–134.

Foucault, M. (1980) *Power/Knowledge: Selected Interviews and Other Writings, 1972–1977*, ed. C. Gordon, New York: Pantheon.

—— (1984) *The Foucault Reader*, ed. P. Rabinow, New York: Pantheon.

Gordon, N. (2008) "From Colonization to Separation: Exploring the Structure of Israel's Occupation," *Third World Quarterly*, 29(1): 25–44.

Halper, J. (1999) "Dismantling the Matrix of Control," Search for Justice and Equality in Palestine/Israel. Available HTTP: <http://www.searchforjustice.org/articles/10.00.99.html> (accessed April 2005).

Jamoul, L. (2004) "Palestine – In Search of Dignity," *Antipode*, 36(4): 581–592.

Khoury, N. (2004) "One Fine Curfew." Available HTTP: <http://www.miftah.org/Display.cfm?DocId=3119&CategoryId=20> (accessed September 2005).

Levey, G. (2008) "Twilight Zone/Free Passage," *Haaretz*, August 8.

Lyon, D. (2007) *Surveillance Studies: An Overview*, Oxford: Polity Press.

Mehrag, S. J. (2001) "Identicide and Cultural Cannibalism: Warfare's Appetite for Symbolic Place," *Peace Research Journal*, 33(3): 89–98.

Mograbi, A. [director] (2005) *Avenge but One of My Two Eyes* [documentary], Israel/France.

Ophir, A. (2002) "A Time of Occupation," in R. Carey and J. Shainin (eds) *The Other Israel: Voices of Refusal and Dissent*, New York: New Press: 51–66.

Said, E. (1979) "Zionism from the Standpoint of Its Victims," Social Text, 1: 7–58.

Said, E. & Mohr, J. (1999) *After the Last Sky: Palestinian Lives*, New York: Columbia University Press.

Sheik Hassan, I. (2005) "Charting a Palestinian Strategy of Exile: Burj El Barajneh Refugee Camp", Master's thesis, Catholic University, Leuven, Belgium.

—— (2009) "An Urbanity of Exile," *A1 Magazine*, 27: 60–62.

Schulz, H. & Hammer, J. (2003) *The Palestinian Diaspora: Formation of Identities and Politics of Homeland*, London: Routledge.

Siegel, I. (2003) "A Report from Nablus – Sunday, September 22, 2002." Available HTTP: <http://orias.berkeley.edu/2003/peace/nablus.pdf> (accessed July 30, 2010).

UNOCHA (2005) "605 Closure Barriers in the West Bank," *Electronic Intifada*. Available HTTP: <http://electronicintifada.net/cgibin/artman/exec/view.cgi/11/3817> (accessed August 2006).

17 Territorial dispossession and population control of the Palestinians

Rassem Khamaisi

Introduction

From the outset, control over territory has been a central component of the Arab–Israeli conflict. Processes of territorial control first emerged towards the end of the nineteenth century with the nascent Zionist project, which aimed to establish a Jewish homeland/nation-state in Palestine. These processes are still very much at work today (Kimmerling 1983). The Zionist project was facilitated by a vision and narrative of a return to the Jewish "Promised Land" in Palestine, known in Hebrew as *Eretz Israel* (Land of Israel). Reviving the Jewish people meant fusing Jewish religious and national identities, and focused on the historic territory of Palestine and the ingathering of "Diaspora" Jewry in the Holy Land. Actualizing this new–old Jewish dream required the creation of an activist elite, the generation of new terminology, the development of new institutions, and the acquisition of a national territory. Consolidating the new Zionist territory, in turn, required the appropriation, control, possession, and purchase of land (Sandberg 2007), as well as the development of legal and administrative mechanisms and tools. Together these functioned as a matrix of control and surveillance, a fundamental precondition for the success of the Zionist project.

Despite similarities between the Zionist colonial project and other colonial regimes and ethno-national states, most supporters of Zionism have emphasized its uniqueness, thereby creating a narrative of exception. This narrative has endowed the project with a foundation of morality and legitimacy in the eyes of its proponents, enabling them to accept and support the expulsion of most Palestinians, and the control and surveillance of those who remain.

In order to acquire possession of the territory after the establishment of the state in 1948, Israel deployed four mechanisms of control: purchasing land, occupying land outright, confiscating Arab land, and undermining the legality of traditional rules of inheritance (Forman and Kedar 2004). These mechanisms helped achieve territorial de-Arabization, landscape transformation, and a discourse of the morality and legitimacy of conquest, control, and territorial and population engineering. All this took place in the shadow of a Zionist political discourse that presented Arabs and Palestinians as an existential threat to Jewish existence in the country (Bystrov and Soffer 2008), despite the grossly asymmetric Jewish–Arab power relations within the Jewish state. This discourse gives Israeli state institutions and Jewish agencies "legitimacy" to develop various surveillance mechanisms and instruments to control the mobility of Arab Palestinian citizens of Israel (referred to here as "Palestinian citizens").

Prior to the establishment of Israel, the Zionist movement acquired land in Palestine by purchasing it on the open market. However, by 1948, Jewish landownership in Palestine accounted for only 6 percent of the country's land area. After the establishment of the state, under the aegis of military government and with the power of sovereignty (Kretzmer 2002), Israel made use of the four above-mentioned methods to maintain control over Israel's Palestinian citizens.

Israel established a Jewish state by directly controlling the land, expelling the population, and containing the remaining Arab Palestinian minority (Abu Sitta 2000). These mechanisms, which together functioned as a matrix of control and later a base for state surveillance, brought about changing patterns of landownership and land administration (through a series of basic laws such as the Israel Lands legislation of 1960), and discriminatory application of zoning laws aimed at ensuring Jewish Israeli majority control over the territory.

Land and population control and surveillance shaped the geographic and occupational mobility of Palestinian citizens. They created a mentality of siege and dependency (Jiryis 1966), which in turn guided the thinking of Israeli political elites and how they related to the land and to others. This reality evolved in the context of a specific form of colonialism in which national–religious belonging and landownership rested on a particular religious interpretation: that is, "God" had promised the land to one particular ethnic group (the Jewish people) and denied it to others (Palestinian citizens in 1948).

This chapter documents the tangible and intangible mechanisms that together constitute the surveillance instruments and their matrix of control and territorial dispossession which Israeli authorities have applied to Palestinian citizens of Israel since 1948. It also documents the deployment, modification, and (in some cases) abandonment of these mechanisms in the context of the relationship between the state of Israel and its Palestinian citizens, on the one hand, and between Israel's Jewish and Palestinian citizens, on the other. I argue that these policies and surveillance activities have emerged from a conceptual framework that relies on particular notions of dispossession which justify control over land and natural resources as exclusive to one ethnic group. Such notions necessarily exclude competing ethnic groups, depriving them of their basic natural right to belong to, use, shape, and produce public space. The results are tension and conflict that threaten peaceful coexistence.

This chapter first presents a general theoretical framework for understanding territorial and population control and engineering, and applies this framework to the Israeli–Palestinian conflict. It continues by presenting, analyzing, and discussing some of the primary tools and mechanisms of territorial surveillance, as well as their implications for the relationship between Jews and Arab Palestinians in Israel. It concludes with a number of general recommendations for change aimed at bringing about the peaceful climate necessary for resolving the Israeli–Palestinian conflict.

General overview: state power and territory – control and surveillance

The concept of surveillance developed as one way to address the mobility of individuals or collectivities, such as ethnic or minority groups, and in the process collect information about them (Lyon 2006). Surveillance is part of social and spatial control

(Lianos 2003). Thus it can, for some, create the perception of unhampered mobility; at the same time, however, the government and other institutions can track people and control space (Gray 2003). The concept and study of surveillance emerged in and tended to focus on Western liberal democratic states, where individual privacy is highly prized. In Western states, especially since September 11, 2001, growing attention has been paid to certain ethnic and immigrant groups (Savitch 2008; see also Chapter 14, this volume). These nation-states and communities aim to protect the cities and territory within their borders. In general, creating a nation-state goes hand in hand with the development of a bio-ethnic group, which either changes national identity or shapes a new one (Alatout 2006). This bio-ethnic group, or nation, strives to put its components of identity into practice as a collective group living in a common territory. Acquiring this territory requires power (Gottmann 1973). Defining the territory that belongs to the nation is the result of a process of border demarcation, which is based on the existence of people belonging to the nation in the territory in question. Within this territory, the dominant bio-ethnic group gains sovereignty and builds institutions of government which control and surveil this territory and its borders (Cote-Boucher 2008).

Creating borders is not simply a technical and functional process. Rather, it involves extremely complex actions that take place before, during, and after the establishment of nation-states. The process of creating borders can be broken down into two main components: the first revolves around the demarcation of borders between two closed neighboring states, while the second involves the establishment of internal borders. In the absence of conflict between the neighboring states, marking external borders is clear and stable. External borders determine sovereignty and may also facilitate bilateral cooperation and coordination. Internal borders are more complex, particularly in states with various ethno-national groups. In such states, the bordering process is dynamic, multi-dimensional, and functional (Zureik and Salter 2005). It is an internal geopolitical process used to regulate resource allocation, spatial control, and territorial belonging. Bordering, within and between states, takes place in the context of inter-group power relations. In order to ensure its power and secure its interests (including the control of territory), the national majority creates a matrix of control and imposes it on the national minority. Systematic control and surveillance over borders implicitly tell the unwanted that they are being watched, and can be excluded, prohibited, followed, managed, and directed in the name of protecting the public interest and community from their possible actions and activities within and alongside borders (de Lint 2008).

A matrix of control functions as a system based on a country's power regime, and develops and uses a variety of mechanisms for surveillance. It includes all formal and informal institutions of the regime, which are mobilized to advance the regime's agenda. The power regime, which is shaped by the governing elite, creates an atmosphere that ensures majority support for their interests and agenda. This atmosphere is supported by visions, narratives, goals, and discourses, and includes activities aimed at shaping the public agenda and public opinion in democratic countries, and legitimizing elite decisions in undemocratic ones (Luz 2007). The atmosphere lends legitimacy to surveillance over population mobility and territorial uses. A matrix of control can be easily modified, transformed, and applied as a system of apartheid in instances of majority–minority geopolitical and ethno-national conflicts within states; in accordance with the internal territorial distribution of ethno-national groups, the matrix of control includes urban surveillance (Gray 2003).

Regimes which use matrices of control and surveillance have created and developed various physical, spatial, territorial, legal, and socio-economic mechanisms. These mechanisms are supported by narratives and discourses which legitimate majority control of the minority, whom the former perceives as an actual or potential threat (Yiftachel 1998; Yacobi 2004; Wesley 2006). One component of this system of control is the minority's exclusion from the production of public space, and from public space itself (Lefebvre 1991). Matrices of control and surveillance also make effective use of the different status of individuals and ethno-national groups within states. Such status has a direct impact on minority groups, which suffer from discrimination and inequality that limit their mobility and access to resources and positions of power. Due to their status, the minority will be much weaker, socio-economically, than the majority.

In reference to Israel, Jeff Halper (2008) has defined the matrix of control as an interlocking series of mechanisms that allow Israel to control all aspects of Palestinian life in the occupied territories. The matrix, Halper explains, works like the Japanese game Go. Instead of defeating the opponent (as in chess), a player of Go wins by immobilizing the opponent by gaining control of key points of a matrix so that every time the opponent moves, she or he encounters an obstacle. The matrix of control in Israel emerged during and immediately after the 1948 war with the imposition of an Israeli military government on the Arab Palestinians who remained in the new Jewish state, despite the fact that they were formally citizens of that state. The military government functioned as an effective mechanism for controlling and surveilling Israel's Palestinian citizens.

Other institutions of the new Jewish state also used this security mechanism to control and supervise Palestinian citizens, and to ensure their dependency on the state (Jiryis 1966; Lustick 1980; Khamaisi 1990; Kretzmer 2002; Bauml 2007). This included such steps as concentrating the remaining Arab Palestinian residents of such cities as Haifa and Jaffa into specific urban neighborhoods, and concentrating the Negev Bedouin within a small region known as the *Sayag* Zone. Such control mechanisms allowed Israel to develop and implement a system of land confiscation and spatial de-Arabization. The official end of military government in 1966 did not signal an end to the implementation of mechanisms of control. Rather, the tools simply changed, particularly with regard to land. The end of military government over Palestinian citizens within Green Line Israel in 1966 was quickly followed by the imposition of a similar system upon the Palestinians of the occupied territories, beginning the following year. The system functioned similarly in the occupied territories, but differed in accordance with the different geopolitical reality of the post-1967 occupied territories. One main difference had to do with Israeli sovereignty over territory and population. In the West Bank, where the matrix of control evolved into a system of apartheid which still exists today, Israel did not officially annex the territory and did not grant the population citizenship. In effect, Israel has implemented a dual-control system.

For East Jerusalem, however, Israel annexed the territory and placed it under full Israeli sovereignty. Technically, the Palestinians of East Jerusalem can apply for Israeli passports and citizenship, within the limitations and restrictions of the Israeli citizenship law and policies. However, Israel refrained from offering Palestinian Jerusalemites Israeli citizenship, and instead granted them the special status of "permanent residency." Thus the Israeli central and local government systems imposed all their rules on the territory and the population, while depriving East Jerusalem Palestinians of citizenship in the state which governs them and holds power and sovereignty over the land. This fragmented status of territory and population has been imposed on West Bank Palestinians by the power of the state, and functions as a component of the matrix of control. Despite this official fragmentation, some Israelis still believe that all Arab Palestinians share one common view and pose a threat to the Zionist project and the Jewish state. Differing statuses and the reality of the different Palestinian groups mean little to these Israelis. This way of thinking justifies the policies of the Israeli government and the Jewish Agency, which jointly use the power of the state to apply the matrix of control to different Palestinian groups, in accordance with the status and reality of each.

Inside Green Line Israel, this matrix of control is constituted by different components which divide and allocate territory through regulations on local government, zoning, land purchase, and land administration and inspections (e.g., of buildings, land, and natural resources) to surveil the mobility and activities of Palestinian citizens. This chapter concentrates on the components of this matrix of control and surveillance that pertain to territory and land and population mobility. Needless to say, we remain aware of the direct relationship and mutual impact of geopolitical and socio-cultural factors, demographic management, government institutions, and territorial control.

Israel's territorial matrix of control and surveillance over Palestinian citizens

The Israeli matrices of control and surveillance over Palestinian citizens have evolved in stages: first, Palestinians were pushed out and prohibited from returning (as with the Nakba and the establishment of the Israeli state in 1948); later came land occupation and the imposition of military governors to surveil and control the remaining native Palestinians; later still came mechanisms of spatial control and surveillance over the population and territory, which still exist in various modes and strengths.

One dimension of the matrix of control for managing territory and population is spatial control. Spatial control mechanisms include utilization, confiscation, and dispossession of private land. Aspects of land and territorial management include closing land for public use and restrictive statutory conservation planning. The surveillance matrix uses local, district, and national building inspectors, in addition to new Jewish settlements called *metzbem* (observation points). Consequently, spatial control has been deployed as a strategic policy to protect specific areas. Many states (regardless of their level of democratization) experience varying degrees of ethnic, national, socio-economic, geopolitical, and spatial conflict. Conflicts are often a product of socio-cultural and geopolitical tensions between the minority and the majority. The majority, which has the power to practice spatial control in order to achieve spatial domination, employs strategies and public policies to ensure their continued existence and to gain strength. Such spatial conflict is prevalent in countries characterized by national conflicts and communities divided along national or religious lines, as is the case with Israeli Jews and Israel's Palestinian citizens. The majority national group uses public policies to guide such spatial policies as land allocation and expropriation for public use; territorial management according to geopolitical considerations; and spatial planning and zoning as a means of controlling land use. The so-called public interest in these policies reflects the interests and hegemony of the majority (Stein 1984; Sandberg 2007). This hegemony is part of a paradigm that holds the public interest to be intrinsically linked primarily to the interest of the ethnic majority.

Majorities and minorities have very different – often opposing – explanations for and understandings of the causes of spatial control. Majorities feel that they have the right to demand public policies and spatial control strategies; minorities suffer from these policies and strategies and feel no civic attachment to them. Majorities often limit the development of minorities, ensuring their dependence on the majority. Each community presents its position and narrative so as to convince the members of the other group of its prevailing right.

Transformation from majority to minority as the context for an imposed matrix of control

The 1948 war and the establishment of Israel transformed the Arab Palestinians who remained in the new state from a majority into a minority. At that time, most Arabs lived in small agriculture-based villages located on the periphery of the new state. The Arab Palestinian communities continued to function according to traditional patterns (Khamaisi 1990; Golan 1995), while the pre-1948 Arab towns were depopulated and gradually transformed into Jewish or so-called "mixed" cities (Yacobi 2004). The Arab Palestinian village populations continued to experience natural increases unrelated to migration to Arab villages (Kipnis 1976). The absence of exclusively Arab cities meant the absence of Arab upper and middle classes, which would otherwise have naturally emerged from the process of urbanization (Khamaisi 2005).

Instead, the new situation resulted in a truncated urbanization process among Arab Palestinians in Israel (Gonen and Khamaisi 1992). With the exception of Nazareth, all Arab localities remained as small villages. After the 1948 war, the country's urban Arab core was missing, and the new Israeli government imposed military rule over Arab Palestinian citizens in order to limit and control their movement, and facilitate the confiscation of their land. The imposition of military government, which lasted until 1966, sparked a geopolitical conflict between the new state and its Arab Palestinian citizens. From the outset, the state confiscated land from this sector (Masalha 1997). The Jewish majority retained control of political authority, thus determining resource allocation and ensuring land control, restricting mobility among Palestinians, and limiting their spatial expansion (Jiryis 1966; Kretzmer 2002; Bauml 2007).

The relationships between the central government, Palestinian citizens of Israel, and Israel's Jewish communities were characterized by geopolitical and socio-cultural conflict. This had a direct impact on Israel's Palestinian communities generally, and particularly on their psychological health and self-perception. Ultimately, traditional structures and planning policies were preserved within Palestinian communities in

Israel. Palestinians' identification with the state and the central government was limited, at best. This encouraged the preservation of local, traditional social structures based primarily on kinship and religious affiliations. Devoid of a sense of national belonging (which is typically influenced by the state and the central government) and in order to manage their everyday lives, Palestinians in Israel intensified their sense of "local patriotism" through *hama-il* (the plural of *hamula*: an extended clan group) and villages as traditional social structures.

Although Palestinians are citizens of Israel, they also belong to the broader Palestinian collective, which is currently working to establish its own state. Arabs in Israel thus have a dilemma of identity or "belonging." This dilemma has intensified and come into sharper relief with the growth of Israel's Arab population. Palestinian citizens currently account for approximately 17 percent of the state's population, and they continue to suffer from resource scarcity, state domination, and discrimination in comparison to Jewish citizens. Their dilemma of identity and belonging also intensifies as the Israeli state continues to define itself in law as a "Jewish state." This ethnic definition (and the reality it produces) results in restricted Palestinian access to resources and positions of power, and Palestinians' dependence on Jewish citizens. The feeling of citizenship being imposed on Palestinians in Israel is accentuated by Israel's self-definition as a Jewish state and, ultimately, by Palestinians' sense of political, economic, and social disenfranchisement at the hands of Jewish Israel. From this perspective, Israel's continued existence as a Jewish state endangers Israel's claim to be a democratic state and a civil society. In the meantime, this situation could also force Israel's Palestinian citizens to pursue political reorganization as self-defense.

The domination and spatial control of Palestinians in Israel has frustrated many opportunities for development and mobility. Their location in Israel's geographic periphery has affected Israel's planning and development policy, which aims to prevent any possibility of Palestinian autonomy within the Israeli state. Their location has also sidelined them economically and politically. Discrimination in the realms of politics and policy, as well as confiscation of land and other resources, has reinforced structures of repression and control that were present in the 1950s and 1960s (Forman 2005). This state of affairs has hindered the development of a sense of "belonging" to the state. Palestinian citizens' current state of economic marginalization, lack of opportunities, and political weakness within a formally democratic political system have meant that Israel's small Palestinian population has been unable to transcend its feelings of dislocation and develop a political agenda for territorial separation.

The above description offers an indication of how Palestinian citizens of Israel suffer from four main problems. First, in terms of both numbers and power, they transitioned from majority to minority status after 1948. Second, in transitioning from a majority to a weak minority, Palestinians could not access their historic resources or political power. Third, Palestinian citizens in Israel suffer from discrimination, exclusion, and de-legitimization, particularly since most Palestinian citizens of Israel do not share the state's visions, priorities, and narratives. And fourth, as a result of living in small villages, Palestinian citizens experience physical limitations and reduced opportunities for development. On the whole, Israel's Palestinians tend to live in traditional communities.

Furthermore, since becoming a minority, the Palestinians of Israel have experienced four chronological periods which have affected their sense of identity and belonging.

The first was the transformation from a minority to enforced citizenship after the war of 1948. The second was a waiting period between 1948 and 1957, during which their future was both unclear and unstable. The third was a period of "accommodation" between 1957 and 1988. The fourth, which began in 1988 and is ongoing, involved the selective participation and inclusion of Palestinians with Israeli citizenship in Israeli state and societal institutions.

In the context of the continued state of internal conflict between Israel's Palestinian minority and the Jewish majority, Israeli authorities continue to manage the situation through spatial control policies and surveillance. Such policies limit the expansion and dispersal of Palestinian residential areas, and limit migration of Palestinians to Jewish villages and towns by using "selection committees" to filter and surveil Palestinian citizens who seek land and housing in Jewish localities. Authorities justify these policies by invoking environmental and "anti-sprawl" arguments, which coincidentally bolster ethnic segregation.

Surveillance and Judaization of the land as a component of the matrix of control

The process of transferring Palestinians' land to Jewish hands began in the late nineteenth century and continues to this day (Stein 1984; Masalha 1997; Forman 2005). This transfer has been part of a broader colonial process of Judaization. Before the establishment of Israel, Jewish and Zionist work in Palestine focused on purchasing land from Arabs. Since the establishment of the state, Israeli governments and Jewish settlements have made a determined effort further to decrease the area of land under Palestinian control, with the ultimate aim of transferring most of this territory to the Israeli state. After occupying the land and imposing its rules, Israel developed various surveillance instruments. The following discussion of the instruments implicated in this process highlights the spatial control policies applied to Palestinian citizens in Israel.

Shrinking Palestinian territory in Israel

Since the establishment of the state of Israel, the private and collective spaces of Arab Palestinians in Israel have shrunk (Falah 2003), primarily through land confiscation. Between 1948 and 1966, the military government enforced powerful new Israeli laws and regulations that closed territory and prohibited Palestinian refugees from returning to their lands, villages, and towns. The result was the confiscation of Palestinians' land (Jiryis 1966). After the 1948 war, Israel held sovereignty over approximately 77 percent of Mandatory Palestine. Within this territory, all public and state land that had hitherto served the country's Arab population was transferred into Jewish and Israeli hands. During this process, such legal categories as *mewat*, *miri*, and *matruka* (according the Ottoman Land Code of 1858) were converted into state land and placed under Jewish Israeli control.

With the Israeli land legislation of 1960, state officials placed the vast majority of land under the administration of a central agency known as the Israel Land Administration (ILA), which continued to purchase and appropriate private Arab land. As a result, approximately 93 percent of land came under state ownership. Since then, the ILA and the Jewish Agency have continued to purchase private land from Palestinian citizens.

Although Palestinians represent 17 percent of the total Israeli population, the transfer of land from Palestinian Israelis to Jewish Israelis has reduced the area owned by the indigenous population to just over 3.5 percent of all land. The ultimate aim of this process is to bring all land in Israel under Jewish Israeli ownership or direct control.

The process of Judaization of the land – through purchase, expropriation, other forms of appropriation, and land-swapping between the ILA and the KKL – continues in Israel, even though the Jewish state enjoys sovereignty over all state territory. The

Table 17.1 Ownership, administration, and spatial statutory planning control of land in Israel: from Palestinian to Jewish-Israeli control

	% of total	Area (dunams)
Total area of Mandatory Palestine	**100.0**	**26,323,000**
Division according to the Partition Plan of 1947, UN General Assembly Resolution 181		
Jewish state	57.99	15,261,648
Arab state	41.35	10,885,848
Jerusalem (special international zone)	0.66	175,504
Area of Israel according to 1949 Armistice Agreements	**77**	**20,325,000**
Area of Palestine not incorporated into Israel (West Bank and Gaza Strip)	23	5,998,000
Jewish-owned land prior to 1948	6.4	1,681,586
Of this, land owned by Jewish National Fund	–	1,449,958
Musha' purchased by Jewish citizens	–	56,628
British-owned land	–	175,000
Land belonging to the Palestinian citizens of Israel (not including land with disputed ownership)	–	1,465,414
Refugee land and Islamic *waqf* land	–	5,178,000
Mewat land and land disputed by the state and the Negev Bedouin	–	12,000,000
Pre-1948 Jewish land purchases	–	1,681,586
Total area of the state of Israel	**100.0**	**20,325,000**
according to the official Annual Report of the ILA		
State land and Development Authority Land[1]	74.8	15,205,000
Jewish National Fund (KKL[2]) Land	18.4	3,570,000
Private Land, Jewish-owned	3.7	750,000
Private Land, Arab-owned	3.1	730,000[3]

Notes: [1] According to the annual ILA report from 1997, the ILA holds 19,028,000 dunams, which is greater than the area held in 1962 (18,775,000 dunams). One dunam equals 1,000 square meters or .247 acre.

[2] Before 1948, the Jewish National Fund, called "Keren Kayemet for Israel" (KKL) (a Jewish institution founded in the beginning of the twentieth century to purchase private land for Jewish use in Palestine), owned about 936,000 dunams. In January 1949, the Israeli government sold 1,101,742 dunams to KKL, and in October 1950 it sold another 1,271,734 dunams to KKL, which included a large area of Palestinian refugee land and land previously held by Arab Palestinian citizens of Israel. Today, the ILA continues to substitute KKL land for state land for the sake of Judaization.

[3] This figure does not include approximately 700,000 dunams in the Negev Desert, which is still the subject of a dispute between the government and the Negev Palestinian Bedouin.

Source: Khamaisi 2003

result has been a continued reduction in land owned by Palestinians and the shrinking of their territory. Ultimately, this leads to heightened territorial, functional, and economic dependence on the state. Dependency, as we know, is an effective tool for surveillance and control over populations and territory.

Controlling territory by demarcating municipal borders

Municipal jurisdiction is another aspect of land and spatial management policy and surveillance of populations. Demarcating local government jurisdiction is a common civil act within Jewish localities, but it has important national and ethnic dimensions in the context of Palestinian localities in Israel. The Israeli Minister of the Interior holds complete authority to demarcate municipal borders. Demarcating the municipal borders of Palestinian localities in Israel is borne out of a spatial management strategy guided by three principles (Kipnis 1987): first, reducing the area under the jurisdiction of Arab localities; second, preventing territorial continuity between Arab localities in order to preclude claims to any kind of autonomy, particularly territorial autonomy; third, preventing the establishment of a demographic Arab majority in any region of Israel, particularly in peripheral regions such as Galilee and the Negev.

These three principles inform Israel's policies of spatial surveillance and control, which were (and remain) an important dimension of Israeli national security policy (Shachar 1993). Demarcating the jurisdiction of Arab localities in Israel is neither a neutral nor a professional activity. Rather, it is influenced by political, military, and security considerations (Falah 1996; Razin and Hasson 1994). Today, approximately 3 percent of Israel's land falls under the jurisdiction of 82 Arab localities and is administered by Arab local governments; 83 percent is controlled and administered by Jewish regional councils. The map of local government jurisdiction and municipal boundaries crystallized in the 1950s, causing the fragmentation of Arab localities and a significant decrease in the area under direct Arab local government administration and control. One result has been the current shortage in land for Arab development and an ever-intensifying sense of siege among residents. The small area of land that remains under Arab jurisdiction means reduced opportunities for development and reduced local government revenue. Moreover, the Jewish regional councils use inspectors to surveil Palestinian citizens' use of territory or building within the council borders.

In many cases, such as Kafr Kana and Arrabah, the new municipal borders of Arab localities encompassed only a third of their pre-1948 traditional village lands, and included very little state land. Smaller areas under Arab municipal jurisdiction created a sense of restriction among local Arab leaders and residents and resulted in requests to expand municipal borders to include traditional village lands. Needless to say, not all land under the jurisdiction of Arab local governments and municipalities is private land. My examination of landownership patterns in 2006 reveals that approximately 50 percent of all land under the jurisdiction of Arab local governments is neither private (see Table 17.2) nor planned (see Table 17.3).

Tables 17.1 and 17.2 reveal that about 60 percent of Arab-owned land in Israel is located outside Arab municipal jurisdiction. It should also be noted that centralized territorial management and spatial Judaization have caused Arabs to feel and behave differently within areas under Arab municipal jurisdiction than they do outside. The area controlled by local Arab municipalities is perceived as belonging to Arab residents. However, since all public areas are technically controlled by the state, the

Table 17.2 Distribution of landownership under the municipal jurisdiction of Arab localities, 2005

Ownership	Area (dunams)	% of total	Comments
Private	310,763	50.4	Most land owned by Arab Palestinian citizens
ILA	104,315	16.9	
ILA and others	130,839	21.3	"Others" refers to KKL and government agencies
Claimed and disputed	65,574	10.6	Land claimed by private owners and the ILA
Local Arab authorities	5,520	0.9	Includes roads and land allocated for local public utilities
Total	617,011	100.0	

Source: ILA website (www.mmi.gov.il)

Table 17.3 Municipal jurisdiction, type of ownership, and residential developed land area for Arabs versus Jewish-controlled areas

Variable	Total for Israel	Total for Palestinian Arab citizens of Israel	Comments
Area (sq. km.)	20,325	0.617	This area includes the municipal jurisdiction of Arab localities, constituting about 3% of Israel
2007 population (in millions)	7.0	1.2	Palestinian citizens of Israel comprised 17.1% of Israel's population in 2007
Land control and ownership (sq. km.)	19,690	0.730	Arab-owned land makes up 3.1% of Israeli territory
Land cover for residences (2003, in dunams)	840,714	150,222[1]	About 23% of the municipal jurisdiction of Arab localities (0.7% of Israeli territory) is used for housing

Note: [1] About 160,000 dunams (or 0.8% of the country's land area) are planned and zoned for development.

Sources: Kaplan *et al.* 2007; ILA website (www.mmi.gov.il); and *Statistical Abstract of Israel*, no. 60, Central Bureau of Statistics, Jerusalem

government can and has used these areas for purposes other than the immediate needs of the Arab population.

Control by spatial planning

Spatial planning has provided another effective mechanism of control and surveillance of the Arab population and territory. It has also promoted the Judaization of Israeli space and is integral to the concept of Israeli national security (Shachar 1993). This mechanism is used by a variety of Israeli institutions to confine and limit Arab development and territorial expansion. The Israeli planning system was based on the British Mandate system and is therefore part of the British legacy (Khamaisi 1997). It is still characterized by a centralized and hierarchal structure (Hill 1980; Alexander, Alterman, and Law Yone 1993).

Spatial planning in Israel has two components: proactive and development planning, and regulatory and statutory planning (Gertel and Law Yone 1991; Yiftachel 1998; Khamaisi 1990, 1993). While both types of planning are undertaken for Jewish localities, Arab localities are generally the subject only of regulatory planning. The ideology of the ruling regime determines both the process and substance of the planning system. The central government defines the public and national interests, as well as the goals and tools of the planning system. It also determines its activities, designates land use, and allocates resources. According to Israeli regulatory planning, public interests take precedence over private interests, and various tiers of planning committees on the national, district, and local levels approve plans and crystallize goals.

Overall, the planning system advances the regime's political and national ideology. This ideology differs greatly from – and often directly contradicts – the narratives, ideologies, and needs of Arab Palestinians in Israel. For instance, the main goal of National Plan 35 was to "develop Israel as a Jewish and Democratic state." This resulted in a number of statutory spatial planning tools to control Palestinian citizens. These include the preparation and approval of sectoral and functional national plans (roads, nature reserves, archeological sites, agricultural use, open space, forests, etc.) managed by governmental agencies. These agencies establish special units for surveillance and zoning. The 39 national plans in Israel prohibit development and building on approximately 13.5 million dunams of land – fully 71 percent of the land administered by the ILA (a total of about 19 million dunams). They also limit development and building on about 9 million dunams. All in all, Israeli national plans impose government limitations on approximately 17.5 million dunams, about 92 percent of the land administered by the ILA (ILA n.d.).

Understandably, many countries create national and regional zoning plans that prohibit and limit land development and secure land reserves for future use. However, in Israel, uniquely, such plans are used to control development based on ethnonational affiliation. Among other things, Israeli land reserves are used for governmental initiatives to establish new Jewish settlements, such as the Misgav project in the Galilee region. The same is true in the Negev, where the Israeli government established new *metzbem*. On the national and regional levels, the Israeli government generated planning and development policies aimed at maximum dispersal of the Jewish population in the peripheral regions of the Negev and Galilee, as well as in the Jerusalem area. This population dispersal policy has promoted "ethnic occupation" of the periphery, which is home to most Palestinians in the country. This policy also resulted in a phenomenon known as the "officially unrecognized Arab villages." There are approximately 50 such Arab villages in Israel, representing approximately 70,000 residents. The official planning system includes a special unit which has inspectors who surveil and seize any building constructed without a permit. They may then demolish the building, having obtained a court order.

The Israeli authorities have imposed urbanization on the Arab Bedouin population, and have allocated a minimal amount of land for development based on a policy of blocking the expansion of built-up areas. One component of this urbanization policy includes higher-density (usually high-rise) buildings. High-rise towers, however, are culturally foreign to Arab villagers, whose traditional communities are based on horizontal development. Palestinian citizens of Israel regard this planning tool as yet another way to confiscate their land and negate their control over it.

The status of some Arab localities has been changed from "local council" to "municipality" (usually an autonomous body, independent of regional councils). Despite this change, their planning functions remain part of regional planning committees, which are directed primarily by Jewish Israeli appointees (committee members and employees). The authority to change the planning status of a locality lies with the Minister of the Interior, who opposes providing Arab municipalities with additional authority and independence and has instead chosen to remind them of their dependency upon Jewish planners, policy-makers, and politicians in the realms of spatial planning and administration. Overall, the centralized planning of domination and control ignores Arab needs. About 22,000 buildings standing today were constructed outside authorized local plans and without building permits. Fifty percent of these illegal structures are located in the Jewish sector and 50 percent in the Arab sector. Government planning policy considers illegal building in Arab areas as a national, political, and security problem, while illegal construction in Jewish areas is regarded merely as a civil matter. Limited land allocation for housing development is an important factor spurring illegal building among Arabs. Changing land use planning could immediately alleviate this problem.

All land in Israel is classified as "agricultural," aside from that which is specifically designated for different use by the Committee for Protection of Agricultural Land (CPAL). In 1996, CPAL, which was established by the Planning and Building Law of 1965, added the words "open spaces" to its name, to become CPALOS. This committee currently plays an extremely effective role in preventing urban and rural sprawl in Israel and engages in surveillance of the expanding planning area and land allocated for Palestinian development through the planning process. Although CPALOS operates according to the law, its strategies and policies are guided by an ideological agenda. In Israel today, approximately 3,391,000 dunams are used for agriculture. However, according to the Planning and Building Law, and its later amendments, all areas with no officially authorized CPALOS plans (approximately 8 million dunams) are still technically "agricultural." In addition, the KKL has secured land by planting forests – planting has become part of this organization's guiding ideology (Kliot 1992). In 1995, in cooperation with the Ministry of the Interior, the KKL designed the National Master Plan 22 for Forests and Afforestation, allocating approximately 1.5 million dunams of land to this use. This plan serves to control space and develop it according to central government officials' and institutions' (Jewish) needs and narratives. In this case, competition between Western afforestation and indigenous olive-tree planting reflects the competition between the government and the KKL, on the one hand, and Israel's Palestinian Arab citizens, on the other. The struggle over open space, afforestation, and olive-tree planting is part of an historic conflict of narratives related to control of land.

At first, national spatial planning policies and strategies were designed to move the Jewish population from the center of the country to the periphery through population dispersal based on geopolitical, demographic, and territorial considerations.

Subsequently, the establishment and development of new Jewish settlements facilitated this dispersal. Still later, population growth and economic development triggered urban and rural sprawl, leading to the adoption of spatial planning policies to protect open spaces and agricultural lands through new approaches to sustainable planning. Today, built-up urban and rural areas account for only 7 percent of the country (Kaplan *et al.* 2007). These tools are applicable to the entire territory of the country, and officially apply to all its cities. In practice, however, they function entirely differently, and are dependent on the ethno-national affiliations of different areas.

By law, the National Comprehensive Plan guides master plans on district, regional, and local levels. Statutory planning is restrictive by nature, and the scope and nature of intervention depend on government policies and strategies. Does planning intervention restrict development or facilitate it? In the case of Israel, the central government uses plans to achieve spatial control over Arab citizens. While statutory plans limit the expansion of Jewish localities, they also develop and expand other localities to which the Jewish population may move. Palestinian citizens of the country regard spatial planning – particularly the allocation of land to agriculture, open space, and forests – as limiting their development, and they therefore react to them quite negatively.

National and regional planning policies are implemented on the local level in Arab localities by highly restrictive planning policies. In order to limit the development and expansion of Arab villages, local outline plans have been prepared for every recognized village. In effect, this has resulted in their rapid urbanization. Local plans impose modern, Western, urban planning on traditional Middle Eastern village communities, with the official goal of improving the standard of living among Arabs. Implicitly, however, they have reduced the territory under the jurisdiction of Arab localities and controlled their development and growth. Officials have taken advantage of the positive connotations of urbanization by appropriating land from owners while at the same time purporting to help them. Moreover, in urban localities the government has increased concentrations of people, reduced expenditure on infrastructure development and maintenance, and increased housing density. Finally, urbanization limits population increase, advancing the national goal of maintaining a Jewish demographic majority.

The current reality of development in Palestinian towns and villages in Israel is far removed from the official plans prepared and approved by the country's planning institutions. The predicted migration from villages in the periphery to cities along the central coast did not take place. Villages in the process of developing into towns suffered from a lack of public facilities due to a shortage of land for public purposes. Housing needs were met by each family constructing its own home on a private plot. Some landowners built houses without permits because their land was excluded from the officially planned area and was therefore not eligible for building permits. Others built houses on areas planned as roads to protest against planning institutions that had rejected their appeals.

Such realities are the direct result of planning policies, and have culminated in a severe housing shortage within Arab localities. Unrecognized villages, such as those in the Negev and Galilee, have been ignored by national and regional plans, and official policy sought to relocate the residents of these villages and to concentrate them in urban centers. In mixed cities such as Lod (Yacobi 2004), land use plans have been implemented to achieve national, ethnic, and demographic goals by allocating insufficient private and public land for development. A second strategy has been to limit building rights on private land, thus making it impossible to acquire housing permits and encouraging either population reduction or increased migration.

Over the past decade, the Israeli government has proposed addressing this housing shortage by allocating state land for housing. However, issuing high-density building permits for state land only increases false urbanization, contradicts the current socio-cultural housing norms in Arab communities, and renders the self-building approach impossible. Affected areas include villages in the north (such as the recently "recognized" localities of Kamane, Hosines, and Ein Hawd) and areas in the Negev, where the Bedouin population is largely traditional. Government representatives have justified this policy of urbanization directed exclusively at Arab localities in terms of sustainability, by arguing that Israel suffers from a land shortage. However, most Jewish localities are villages. Between 1961 and 2007, the number of Jewish localities increased from 771 to 941; during the same period the number of Palestinian localities only increased from 109 to 129. To be clear, however, even this small increase is purely statistical, stemming from the recognition of some previously unrecognized Arab villages in the 1990s. In fact, no new Arab villages have been built. Meanwhile, about fifty Arab villages still go unrecognized.

In this way, the government policy of urbanization is applied differentially according to ethno-national affiliation. Planning institutions and relevant government ministries ask local and national representatives to decrease the land allocated for development available for Arab localities. They are then encouraged to promote high-rise building, and to hinder development and expansion in various ways. Although national and district-level plans suggest slight differences in building densities between small and large Arab localities, local outline plans apply the same building densities, effectively converting villages into urban localities. Urban planning policy encourages a move from agriculture to industry and services. This economic policy is echoed in local outline plans and intensifies Arab dependence on the central government, which is controlled by the Jewish majority.

In summary, ideological and geopolitical goals in Israel animate spatial planning and urbanization policies (Kipnis 1987; Gertel and Law Yone 1991). These policies aim to reduce the territory occupied by Palestinian citizens, and decrease those citizens' mobility to Jewish Israeli localities. These policies have developed and crystallized into a situation of national conflict between Arabs and Jews, which has territorial, geographic, demographic, cultural, and political dimensions and implications. The joint vision of the Zionist movement and the Israeli government to transform the country's demography, geography, and culture continues to encounter Arab Palestinians' resistance. The allocation of land and resources is part of this larger conflict (Zureik 1978; Yiftachel 1992, 1997; Falah 1989). As a consequence, the matrix of control and population and territorial surveillance based on spatial planning and management secures the domination and hegemony of the Zionist project.

Conclusion

Israel's self-definition as a Jewish and democratic state has meant that, in theory and in practice, the Israeli state has functioned (and continues to function) as an ethnocracy (Yiftachel 1997): for the Jews, it is a democratic state; for the Arabs, it is a Jewish state.

The project of Judaization during the long geopolitical conflict between Jewish Israelis and Arab Palestinians in Israel has been advanced by the implementation of a matrix of control and surveillance. This matrix is dynamic and changes its mechanisms in accordance with the formal status of Palestinian citizens. The spatial policies applied to Arabs in Israel control their development, and are part of the overall spatial policies of the state. These include the transfer of ownership through land confiscation and the reduction of Arab territory through spatial planning and urban management.

Palestinians in Israel reject and resist the spatial limitations and restrictions Israel imposes on them. On the whole, their identification with the state is minimal, prompting them to resist the various mechanisms implicated in the matrix of control, which they understand as being implemented selectively, according to ethno-national criteria. For example, the appearance of the color green in plans conjures feelings of anger since, in Palestinians' eyes, every new environmental consideration is a potential source of suffering and resource reduction.

Despite internal discussions over spatial planning and land policy in Israel, which aspire to reflect the global economic and environmental discourse, the new Israeli discourse relates to Jewish citizens alone and implicitly ignores Israel's Arab citizens. The dilemma faced by Israeli government agencies is whether to relate to Arab Palestinians as potential enemies (sleeper cells that need to be controlled) or officially, practically, implicitly, and explicitly as equal citizens who enjoy the right to use and produce space and territory.

This chapter has highlighted the reciprocal relationship between control and surveillance, illustrating how they depend upon and nourish each other. Both have used a systematic matrix in action. Some components of each matrix concentrate on collectivities or individuals; others concentrate on the territory/space and land. In both cases, the Israeli state uses its power to control and surveil the minority population in its territory under the claim of protecting the "public interest" – namely, the Zionist project. In effect, Palestinian citizens are specifically excluded. The definition of Arab Palestinian citizens as potential enemies with limited loyalty to the state gives a moral legitimacy for those citizens to be surveilled by state officials and their (Jewish Israeli) co-citizens. Land use, planning, and land management are therefore powerful mechanisms to secure state and ethnic-majority interests and goals over those of the indigenous landowners.

Bibliography

Abu Sitta, S. (2000) "Confiscation of Palestinian Refugees Propriety and the Denial of Access to Private Propriety," report submitted to the United Nations Social, Economic and Cultural Rights Committee, October.

Alatout, S. (2006) "Towards a Bio-territorial Conception of Power: Territory, Population and Environmental Narratives in Palestine and Israel," *Political Geography*, 25: 601–621.

Alexander, E., Alterman, R. and Law Yone, H. (1993) "Evaluating Plan Implementation: The National Statutory Planning System in Israel," *Progress in Planning*, 20: 97–102.

Bauml, Y. (2007) *A Blue and White Shadow*, Bardess, Haifa [in Hebrew].

Bystrov, E. and Soffer, A. (2008) *Israel: Demography and Density 2007–2020*, Chaikin Chair in Geostrategy, University of Haifa, Haifa.

Cote-Boucher, K. (2008) "The Diffuse Border: Intelligence-Sharing, Control and Confinement along Canada's Smart Border," *Surveillance & Society*, 5(2): 142–165.

De Lint, W. (2008) "The Security Double Take: The Political, Simulation and the Border," *Surveillance & Society*, 5(2): 167–187.

Falah, G. (1989) "Israeli Judaization Policy in Galilee and Its Impact on Local Arab Urbanization," *Political Geography Quarterly*, 8: 229–253.

—— (1992) "Land Fragmentation and Spatial Control in Nazareth Metropolitan Area," *Professional Geographer*, 44: 30–44.

—— (1996) "The 1948 Israeli–Palestinian War and Its Aftermath: The Transformation and De-signification of Palestine's Cultural Landscape," *Annals of the Association of American Geographers*, 86(2): 256–285.

—— (2003) "Dynamics and Patterns of the Shrinking of Arab Lands in Palestine," *Political Geography*, 22: 179–209.

Forman, G. (2005) "Israeli Settlement of Title in Arab Areas: 'The Special Land Settlement Operation' in Northern Israel (1955–1967)," unpublished Ph.D. dissertation, University of Haifa.

Forman, G. and Kedar, A. (2004) "From Arab Land to 'Israel Lands': The Legal Dispossession of the Palestinians Displaced by Israel in the Wake of 1948," *Environment and Planning D: Society and Space*, 22(6): 809–830.

Gertel, S. and Law Yone, H. (1991) "Participation Ideologies in Israeli Planning," *Environment and Planning C: Government and Policy*, 9(2): 173–188.

Golan, A. (1995) "The Transfer to Jewish Control of Abandoned Arab Lands during the War of Independence," in S.I. Troen and N. Lucas (eds) *Israel – The First Decade of Independence*, State University of New York Press, Albany, 403–440.

Gonen, A. and Khamaisi, R. (1992) *Trends in the Geographical Distribution of the Arab Population of Israel*, Floersheimer Institute for Policy Studies, Jerusalem.

Gottmann, J. (1973) *The Significance of Territory*, University Press of Virginia, Charlottesville.

Gray, M. (2003) "Urban Surveillance and Panopticism: Will We Recognize the Facial Recognition Society?," *Surveillance & Society*, 1(3): 314–330.

Halper, J. (2008) "The 94 Percent Solution: A Matrix of Control," *Middle East Report*. Available HTTP: <http://www.merip.org/mer/mer216/216_halper.html>.

Hill, M. (1980) "Urban and Regional Planning in Israel," in R. Bilski (ed.) *Can Planning Replace Politics? The Israeli Experience*, Martinus Highoff, The Hague, 259–282.

Israel Land Administration (ILA) (n.d.) Report. Available HTTP: <http://www.mmi.gov.il/Osh/Aspx/DownloadTofes.aspx?Maarechet=71&TofesId=7&UserId=-1&RO=true> [in Hebrew].

Jiryis, S. (1966) *The Arabs in Israel*, El-Ittihad, Haifa [in Arabic].

Kaplan, M., Dvrshem-Drom, L., Haklay, R., Vetman, N., Bokvlde, S., Dyan, H. and Kasbe, S. (2007) *Patterns in the Utilization of Constructed Land in Israel*, Jerusalem Institute for Israeli Studies, Jerusalem [in Hebrew].

Khamaisi, R., (1990) *Planning and Housing among the Arabs in Israel*, International Center for Peace in the Middle East, Tel-Aviv.

—— (1993) *From Regulative Planning to Developing Planning*, Florshimer Institute for Policy Research, Jerusalem [in Hebrew].

—— (1997) "Israeli Use of the British Mandate Planning Legacy as a Tool for the Control of Palestinians in the West Bank," *Planning Perspectives*, 12(3): 321–340.

—— (2003) "Mechanism of Land Control and Territorial Judaization in Israel," in M. Al-Haj and U. Ben Eliezer (eds) *In the Name of Security*, University of Haifa, Haifa, 421–449 [in Hebrew].

—— (2005) "Urbanization and Urbanism in the Arab Localities in Israel," *Horizons in Geography*, Special Issue, 64–65: 293–312.

Kipnis, B. (1976) "Trends among the Minorities Population in the Galilee and Their Planning Implementation," *City and Region*, 3(3): 54–68.

—— (1987) "Geopolitical Ideologies and Regional Strategies in Israel," *Tijdchrift Voor Economishe en Social Geography*, 78: 125–138.

Kliot, N. (1992) "Ideology and Forest in Israel: Man Forest Plantation by Keren Kayemet Lysrael," *Studies in the Geography of Israel*, 13: 87–106 [in Hebrew].

Kretzmer, D. (2002) *The Legal Status of the Arabs in Israel*, updated edn, Institute for Israeli Arab Studies and the Van Leer Institute, Jerusalem.

Kimmerling, B. (1983) *Zionism and Territory*, Institute of International Studies, University of California, Berkeley.

Lefebvre, H. (1991) *The Production of Space*, trans. D. Nicholson-Smith, Basil Blackwell, Oxford.

Lianos, M. (2003) "Social Control after Foucault," *Surveillance & Society*, 1(3): 412–430.

Lustick, I. (1980) *Arabs in the Jewish State*, University of Texas Press, Austin.

Luz, N. (2007) *Land and Planning Majority–Minority Narrative in Israel: The Misgav–Sakhnin Conflict as Parable*, Floersheimer Institute for Policy Studies, Jerusalem [in Hebrew].

Lyon, D. (ed.) (2006) *Theorizing Surveillance: The Panopticon and beyond*, Willan Publishing, Cullompton.

Masalha, N. (1997) *Maximum Land and Minimum Arabs: Israel Transfer and Palestinians, 1949–1996*, IPS, Beirut.

Razin, E. and Hasson, S. (1994) "Urban–Rural Boundary Conflicts: The Reshaping of Israel's Rural Map, *Journal of Rural Studies*, 10: 47–59.

Sandberg, H. (2007) *The Land of Israel, Zionism and Post-Zionism*, Hebrew University, Jerusalem.

Savitch, H.V. (2008) *Cities in a Time of Terror: Space, Territory and Local Resilience*, M.E. Sharpe, New York.

Shachar, A. (1993) "Spatial National Planning in Postindustrial Societies: France, Japan and Holland," in A. Mazor *et al.* (eds), *Israel 2020: Master Plan for Israel*, Report no. 1, Technion, Haifa, 37–65 [in Hebrew].

Sharon, A. (1951) *Physical Planning in Israel*, Ministry of the Interior, Jerusalem.

Shmueli, D.F. (2008) "Environmental Justice in the Israel Context," *Environment and Planning A*, 40: 2384–2401.

Stein, K.W. (1984) *The Land Question in Palestine, 1917–1939*, University of North Carolina Press, Chapel Hill and London.

Wesley, D.A. (2006) *State Practices and Zionist Images: Shaping Economic Development in Arab Towns in Israel*, Berghahn Books, New York.

Yacobi, H. (2004) "In-between Surveillance and Spatial Protest: The Production of Space of the 'Mixed City' of Lod," *Surveillance & Society*, 2(1): 55–77.

Yiftachel, O. (1992) *Planning a Mixed Region in Israel*, Avebury, Aldershot.

—— (1997) "Israeli Society and Jewish–Palestinian Reconciliation: 'Ethnocracy' and Its Territorial Contradictions," *Middle East Journal*, 51(4): 505–519.

—— (1998) "Planning and Social Control: Exploring the 'Dark Side,'" *Journal of Planning Literature*, 12(2): 395–406.

Zureik, E. (1978) *The Palestinians in Israel: A Study in Internal Colonialism*, Routledge and Kegan Paul, London.

Zureik, E. and Salter, M.B. (2005) "Who and What Goes Where? Global Policing and Surveillance," in: M.B. Salter and E. Zureik (eds) *Global Surveillance: Borders, Security, Identity*, Willan Publishing, Cullompton, 1–10.

Part VIII

Social ordering, biopolitics, and profiling

18 The Palestinian Authority security apparatus

Biopolitics, surveillance, and resistance in the occupied Palestinian territories[1]

Nigel Parsons

We are here, in Palestine, facing them.

(Yasser Arafat, cited in Usher 2004)

Momentum continues to gather behind application of Foucault's concept of biopolitics to Israeli surveillance and management of the Palestinian population. From land acquisition to the separation wall understood as "spacio-cide" (Hanafi 2005), through agency in a "state of exception" (Lentin 2008), to the closure regime (Parsons and Salter 2008) and policing (Parsons 2010), conceptual and empirical foundations have started to settle. This chapter builds on them by engaging the Foucauldian injunction to seek out the motive forces opposed to, as well as providing for, control. Important ground has been broken, as Zureik notes, by anthropologists documenting quotidian resistance to occupation (Chapter 1, this volume). Further insight is gained in this collection by Abujidi's treatment of resistance in Nablus through knowledge, quotidian practice, and commemoration (Chapter 16). This chapter shifts up a level to examine resistance among two sets of Palestinian institutions: the Palestinian Authority (PA) security apparatus, and the two leading political factions that have variously commanded and dismantled parts of it – the nationalist Fatah movement and the Islamist Hamas.

The argument is organized into two parts. In the first part, I address the conceptual issue of what Israel *is*. I begin by revisiting the Foucauldian concept of biopolitics and relate it to the occupied Palestinian territories (OPT). I then argue that a racialized biopolitical understanding of Zionism reinforces Pappe's case against the application of Agamben's "state of exception" – as a model of comparative government – to Israel. Two buttresses are utilized. The first is Weinberger's Deleuzean analysis of the Oslo era, in which the PA is said to constitute a shift toward a "control society" in the OPT. Weinberger meets Michael Hardt's call for comparable cases outside of Europe to be identified in the "principles of population management that were employed in accordance with the particular guiding national or social vision of other states" (Weinberger 2006: 46). The study of Zionism unfolds accordingly. The second buttress is Khan's exploration of Israel's "security first" policies, in which security becomes a euphemism for eternal political delay as a means of managing the Palestinian demographic threat. This is a goal whose "origins . . . can be traced back to the very foundation of the state . . . to achieve the military and political capacity to manage the problem" (Khan 2005: 70). In its attention to long-term population management, Khan's analysis concords with a biopolitical reading and generates an ideal scenario for the comparative alternative to a "state of exception." Advocated by Pappe, this is the "*mukhabarat*," or intelligence-agency state, said here to reflect better Israeli institutional reality because it is better placed to implement and protect Zionism's intrinsically racialized biopolitical remit.

In the second half of the chapter I consider the conceptual and practical implications for institutional resistance to Israel thus conceived. I begin with analysis of the Oslo canon's remit for Palestinian demobilization. The PA security apparatus emerges as a torn Palestinian nationalist doppelgänger of Zionism's *mukhabarat* state, a tormented replica mandated to police indigenous pockets in the OPT. But as John Scott observes: "The exercise of power and the possibility of resistance to it establish a dialectic of control and autonomy, a balance of power that limits the actions of the participants in their interplay with each other" (Scott 2001: 3). In what ways did the PA security apparatus find ways to limit the scope of Israeli action? This question is explored by examining three of the more politicized branches of the PA security apparatus: Palestine's own *mukhabarat*, General Intelligence (GI, *al-mukhabarat al-'amma*); the Preventive Security Apparatus (PSA, *jihaz al-amn al-wiqa'i*); and Force 17 (*quwwat al-sab'atash*), the latter now merged into the Special Presidential Guard (SPG, *haras al-ra'is al-khas*). The exercise of agency is manifest in bureaucratic and military resistance, the latter variously facilitative and proactive, organized and individual. Patterns of resistance are seen to draw on a rich tradition, long nurtured by Fatah, and more recently carried forward by Hamas.

Israeli biopolitics

For Foucault, biopolitics mark the culmination of a swing in the purpose of government: sovereign juridical power over territory, negative and manifest in rules of prohibition, gives way to positive power exercised through the biopolitics of population regulation. Population constitutes an aggregate subject to demographic measurement. It has "a birth rate, a rate of mortality . . . an age curve, a generation pyramid, a life-expectancy, a state of health" (Foucault 2007: 161). Surveillance in the form of demographic measurement generates knowledge and expedites manipulation. For Foucault, the biopolitical "technology of power" that results is distinguished by three features: processes, phenomena under consideration, and mechanisms of control. Processes are demographic and measured through statistics: these are "biopolitics' first objects of knowledge and the targets it seeks to control." The phenomena resulting are relevant on a mass scale and over time. Mechanisms of control aspire "to establish an equilibrium, maintain an average, establish a sort of homeostasis, and compensate for variations within this general population and its aleatory field" (Foucault 2003: 243–246).

In former-Mandatory Palestine, Zionist ideology compels the state to regulate and "improve" the Jewish population in the interests of maximum presence and productivity. But the implications for Palestinians outside of that project are limiting. Israeli agents of state resemble the European colonizers of North America; legitimized by a particular reading of John Locke, "improving" Europeans entitled themselves to Amerindian property, while resistance to encroachment increased colonial entitlement by way of reparation (Dean 2002: 48–49). For Amerindians, so for Palestinians, resistance to Zionism routinely amplifies the colonial right to dispossess. Witness the consistent expropriation of West Bank land and property in the name of Israeli "security." Settlements spawn adjacent outposts to commemorate or preclude Palestinian attack: Maaleh Rechavam and Migron are illustrative (Americans for Peace Now 2006; HaLevi 2006). In response to the violence of the al-Aqsa Intifada, the separation wall cuts deep to the east, not the west, of the 1948 armistice or "Green Line"; the fates of Qalqilya, Tulkarm, and Bethlehem, discussed in this volume by Bowman (Chapter 3) capture the process. Settlers in Hebron seize neighbouring properties in defence of their bridgehead, as in Tal al-Rumayda.

Racialized biopolitics in perpetuity: contesting the "state of exception" paradigm

Racialized biopolitics in perpetuity point away from the "state of exception" as a model of comparative government for Israel. Related in Chapter 1 (this volume) by Zureik, Pappe argues convincingly that three key criteria are not met. First, Zionist sovereign power has not migrated decisively from legislature to executive. We might note too that for the Jewish population, elections are still meaningful and specifically evince a lively debate on how best to manage the biopolitical issue of Palestinian population growth. It is also likely that shifts in Jewish sovereignty would have little or no bearing on the Palestinian citizen or non-citizen under occupation. Furthermore, in Palestinian nationalist discourse (and notwithstanding the formalization of Israel Defense Forces (IDF) military orders through the Oslo canon), the exercise of Zionist sovereignty over the OPT is widely deemed illegal. Second, Israel's constitutional order has not been upended or transformed in the dark; on the contrary, the constitutional basis of racialized discrimination and oppression has been consistent, subject to public scrutiny and general approval. Third, Zionist law accurately shapes Zionist reality. Liberal Zionist disquiet arises from a breakdown in cognitive dissonance, not a breakdown in mythical Zionist liberalism (Chapter 1, this volume; Pappe 2008: 155–159).

Pappe's objections are reinforced by the racialized, quantitative, and temporal qualities of Zionism highlighted in a biopolitical reading. Palestinian demographic heft has loomed as an existential threat from the concept stage forward. It is an ever-present variable necessitating constant attention; this puts it at odds with the departure required of a country on the slide toward a "state of exception." Zionist circles – some with distaste – debated the "transfer" of Palestinians prior to independence (Morris 2004: 39–64). But the threat still loomed large upon statehood in 1948. Through a combination of intent and circumstance, and in an atmosphere officially recorded as informed by "a general feeling of contempt for the life of Arabs" (McGreal 2003), the Palestinian refugee issue was born. Ironically, demographic imbalance threatened again with successful military expansion to the east in 1967. Early intentions to hand territory (and, more to the point, the Palestinians who lived on it) back to Jordan are consistent with the biopolitical imperative to re-establish racial equilibrium. The Gaza withdrawal of 2005 can be seen in the same light. The idea has re-emerged, after a fashion, in the Israel Our Home Party of Avigdor Lieberman. This Moldovan immigrant, resident of West Bank settlement Noqdim and post-2009 electoral power-broker advocates a smaller, ethnically pure Israel to a larger, binational one. To that end he would give up heavily populated Palestinian areas of the West Bank and – much more controversially – seek to redraw the border so that Arab areas of pre-1967 Israel become part of a Palestinian state. In other words, those who are now Palestinian citizens of Israel will find themselves living in their same homes – but under the jurisdiction of another country.

(Freedland 2009)

The alternative, in which state power continues to expedite colonization to the east, exhibits biopolitical logic even as it complicates the balancing act required within the Zionist realm. The settlement blueprint of 1978 specifically identified colonization as a means of breaking up Palestinian demographic solidity. Blueprint architect Matityahu Drobles, then chief of the Jewish Agency's Settlement Division, counselled: "state land and uncultivated land must be taken immediately in order to settle the areas between concentrations of [Palestinian] population and around it . . . being cut apart by Jewish settlements, the minority [*sic*] population will find it hard to create unification and territorial continuity" (Weizman 2002).

Throughout the Oslo period, sovereign power backed settlement with remarkable consistency: no major difference pertained in the building records of Labour- or Likud-led governments. It is also worth recalling that the Oslo framework expressly maintained extension of Israeli sovereignty to the settler population, bestowing upon them the mobility and protection required to flow eastward. In the meantime, disempowered Palestinian authorities – barely sovereign at all – continue to draw on separate penal codes for the West Bank and the Gaza Strip (with the add-on of the PLO's Revolutionary Penal Code of 1979; see Human Rights Watch 2001), reflecting the indeterminate status of the campaign for indigenous sovereignty.

The biopolitical impulse is apparent again in Israeli constitutional and legislative history. It is reflected in various laws that define the nature of the state, including the 1948 declaration of a "Jewish state," the June 1950 Law of Return that granted Jews worldwide the right to apply for citizenship, citizenship laws made retroactive to independence and to immigrant advantage, the post-1948 disposal of Palestinian assets by the Custodian of Absentee Property, the Absentees' Property Law (1950), the Jewish National Fund Law (1953), the Israel Lands Law (1960), and the Law of Agricultural Settlement (1967); together they provide for the legal proscription of "the selling, leasing, sub-letting and owning of land by 'non-Jews,' for which read 'Palestinians'" (Lentin 2008: 9). In Israel, racial discrimination is *ipso jure*. It is not, as "state of exception" pioneer Carl Schmitt would have it, consequent of a "suspension of the entire existing juridical order" (Agamben 2005: 32). Liberal hand-wringing not-withstanding, Zionist law usually does determine Zionist reality. In this respect, Lieberman's "no loyalty, no citizenship" policy also merits attention. Failure to comply with an oath of loyalty "to Israel as a Jewish state" is intended to result in a loss of the "right to vote or be in the Knesset" (Freedland 2009). Draconian, certainly, but hardly a radical departure from the constitutional or legislative development outlined above. In sovereignty, historical constitutionalism, and law, a racialized biopolitical reading helps contest the idea of a democratic interruption upon which the "state of exception" – as an appropriate model of comparative government for Israel – would have to be predicated.

The case against is buttressed from another direction by Peter Ezra Weinberger's sophisticated analysis of the Oslo process. Emphasis on the racial and temporal continuities of Zionism, continuities in the race-based predispositions and motive forces driving Israel forward, render this analysis similarly consistent with a biopolitical reading. Following Amnon Raz-Krakotzkin, Weinberger posits a Zionist national consciousness that fundamentally does not wish to *see* Palestinians, much less accord them equal rights. From this perspective, Israel–PLO recognition in Oslo and the resulting construction of semi-autonomy reveal continuity over departure. Importantly, Oslo did not constitute some "crafty act of diplomacy" or even "a grand conspiracy" on the part of Israel's policy-making elite (Weinberger 2006: xi). Rather, in advent and atrophy, it reflected a psychological predisposition toward indigenous Palestinian rights that had long been deemed subordinate and amenable to reduction (Weinberger 2006: 71). There was no discrepancy "between the asymmetrical power structure of the Oslo Accords and the vision of peace in the Israeli narrative" (Weinberger 2006: xii). Historical precedents shore up the point, including the Camp David provisions for Palestinian autonomy realized without PLO input, and subsequent attempts at a re-engineered political association with Jordan. In Oslo, psychological and political history played out again to generate a new form of government, an advanced means of dispensing with Palestinians short of statehood.

This is the "control society" of Gilles Deleuze, a more flexible, distant, and efficient means of achieving old ends, in which "subjection to dominant forces" actually increases "by allowing for greater perceptions of emancipation, and then by contrasting these new systems to the preceding, more restrictive forms of governance. But even in the midst of this process of improvement, the key traits of prior systems of order are only ostensibly transmuted and do not completely disappear" (Weinberger 2006: 114–115).

Empowerment is illusion; reality a more efficient "modulatory" governance characterized, among other things, by "subcontracting" (Weinberger 2006: 107). Enter the PLO, with an Oslo-issued remit to deliver Israeli security through the PA. Subsequent modulation of expectations was made possible by the asymmetry at the heart of the original agreement: three letters of mutual recognition and the Israel–PLO Declaration of Principles (DoP) of 1993. It becomes evident in the maceration of the PLO and Fatah through endless (end-less) negotiations. The modulation of governance is managed through the PA's limited and retractable responsibilities for quotidian affairs. But beyond that stands a complex – and ideally distant – network of IDF macro-control. The "control society" first expedites cheap Palestinian population management by proxy, and then, through negotiation, expectation management on the "right of return." In each case, Zionism's racialized biopolitical agenda is advanced.

The logic of modulatory governance is elaborated indirectly by Mushtaq Khan. The burden of Khan's analysis is Israeli insistence on "security" as a prerequisite of political progress: this is the "security first" doctrine (Khan 2005: 60–61). If perpetuation of Israel as a Jewish state necessitates creation of an independent Palestine, how to explain the drag on momentum caused by repeated invocation of the "security first" mantra? Khan's answer is that Palestinian statehood is *not* compatible with Israeli strategic priorities when considered in full demographic context. Independent Palestine *per se* will have ripple effects within the Palestinian demographic pool. Inside

Israel, Palestinian citizens with raised political consciousness will challenge the constitutional and legislative order. Beyond Mandatory Palestine, refugees in diaspora will be mobilized by recognition of the "right of return" that must be an integral component of *any* final status agreement. In Foucauldian terms, independent Palestinian statehood constitutes an avoidable roll of the dice; it brings new scenarios into the "aleatory field" and may well destabilize an already tricky racial "equilibrium". Thus, for Khan:

> security measures that indefinitely delay the emergence of a sovereign Palestinian state can enhance Israel's capacity to manage Palestinian aspirations in areas *outside* the West Bank and Gaza Strip, which is critical for the sustainability of the Jewish quasi-constitution of Israel . . . If this is understood, both "security first" and the associated facts on the ground become explicable as part of an Israeli strategy of long-term management of its "Palestinian problem" through conditional, partial and reversible transfers of governance responsibilities in densely populated parts of the Occupied Territory.
>
> (Khan 2005: 61)

The post-DoP flexibility identified by Khan echoes the "modulation" of the "control society" explored by Weinberger. The impulse to manage population in the interests of racial "homeostasis" is intrinsically biopolitical.

If the "state of exception" model does not quite capture Israel, Pappe borrows from John P. Entelis to offer a comparative alternative, the *mukhabarat* state. The defining features are security agencies with enduring political centrality, institutional persistence, consistent aggressiveness towards the population (in this case Palestinians), and external dependence on foreign sponsorship. For Pappe, this "authoritarian, rentier militaristic state" best captures "the state within the State of Israel: the state of the Palestinians within the Jewish state" (Pappe 2008: 166). The operational default of any *mukhabarat* is surveillance. Biopolitics anywhere is dependent on demographic statistical data: the population must be known before it can be managed. But the intrinsic racialization of Zionist biopolitics and the consequent discrimination in Palestinian experience more or less guarantee indigenous resistance. It follows that successful pursuit of this remit necessitates both data and force. The *mukhabarat* state is ideally placed to deliver both. In the following section, I consider the implications of this for Palestinian institutional resistance through the construction and reconstruction of the PA.

Remit for counter-resistance: the Oslo canon and PA security

The Oslo canon (1993–1999) devolved to the PA limited responsibility for the more direct forms of surveillance, such as policing and imprisonment. But this was conditional on an end to anti-colonial resistance. In the opening letters of mutual recognition, PLO Chairman Arafat assures Israel that:

> In light of the new era marked by the Declaration of Principles (DoP), the PLO encourages and calls upon the Palestinian people in the West Bank and Gaza Strip to take part in steps leading to the normalization of life, rejecting violence

and terrorism, contributing to peace and stability and participating actively in shaping reconstruction, economic development and co-operation.

To that effect, PA security is to constitute the only legitimate indigenous armed element in the territories. The Gaza–Jericho Agreement (1994) then provided for Palestinian assumption of "responsibility for public order and internal security of Palestinians" in the two enclaves. Besides the nascent PA and the IDF, "no other organization or individual" is to "manufacture, sell, acquire, possess, import or otherwise introduce . . . any firearms, ammunition, weapons, explosives, gunpowder or any related equipment." The PA is required to advise Israel directly of "a terrorist action of any kind and from any source" and to "prosecute individuals who are suspected of perpetrating acts of violence and terror." This is not confined to operations across the Green Line. The PA is mandated to "take all measures necessary to prevent . . . hostile acts directed against the Settlements, the infrastructure serving them and the Military Installation Area." Insofar as a person residing in the OPT may be "suspected of, charged with or convicted of an offence that falls within Israeli criminal jurisdiction . . . Israel may request the Palestinian Authority to arrest and transfer the individual to Israel." A Joint IDF–PA Security Committee and a series of district coordination offices (DCOs) expedite cooperation in practice. The Interim Agreement (1995) then extended PA security through the West Bank beyond Jericho and into most remaining urban centres. Major towns and cities such as Ramallah fell into Area A, the outlying neighbourhoods and villages into Area B. The remaining territory outside Jerusalem was categorized as Area C. Differential degrees of PA autonomy pertained in Areas A and B, and full IDF authority in Area C. The Hebron Protocol (1997) extended PA security to the last major Palestinian population centre outside of Jerusalem, but again excluded Jews from PA jurisdiction. As the strains began to tell, the Wye River Memorandum (1998) lent renewed emphasis to the counter-resistance theme, declaring: "The struggle against terror and violence must be . . . continuous and constant over a long term, in that there can be no pauses in the work against terrorists and their structure." The final item in the canon, the Sharm al-Sheikh Memorandum (1999), calls on the PA to collect "illegal weapons" and apprehend "suspects," as well as to forward a "list of Palestinian policemen" to Israel for vetting. Framing Oslo with Israeli sovereignty, the DoP had ensured that Israel would continue "to carry responsibility for defending against external threats, as well as the responsibility for overall security of the Israelis to protect their internal security and public order."

At least 40,000 Palestinians were employed in the new services (Friedrich 2004: 48–50). The branches most heavily involved in political policing were GI and the PSA (Parsons 2005: 153; Riley *et al.* 2005: 38–39). Local knowledge and political capital were brought to bear. Steeped in Palestine's culture of rebellion, and typically serious political cadres, officers knew where to look for recalcitrant agents of resistance. Political history and hope in the future lent them capital in pursuit of their duties. Equipped with the transferred prison infrastructure that previously passed through British, Jordanian, Egyptian, and Israeli hands, the PA greatly augmented carceral capacity, just as it distanced Israel from the more intimate requirements of occupation. Indicative of formative experiences in Israeli custody, officers were known to use Hebrew in interrogation, relating to it "as the language of power and intimidation" (Parsons 2005: 162). The transition from liberation movement culture to institutional procedure was fraught: the Palestinian Human Rights Monitoring Group recorded just under forty deaths in custody as of 2008 (PHRMG 2009). Efforts to subvert Hamas rule in Gaza following the Islamist movement's 2006 election success spawned more torture, particularly by the PSA (Rose 2008). On the other hand, some attempts were made to reduce friction and improve performance. For example, GI acknowledged sending relatives to expedite an arrest: "There are some examples of using family members to make an arrest; we prefer to send a relative because it is easier, he gives guarantees: 'you won't be beaten, don't be afraid, it is just for an hour' and so on. But if we are given an order, the arrest will happen" ('Abd al-Hafidh 2006).

West Bank PSA chief Jibril Rajub allowed human rights trainers access to his staff. The less politicized Civil Police were known to be especially amenable to training (Mujahid 2006).

Bureaucratic and military resistance within the PA security apparatus

The Oslo-issue remit left PA security conflicted: mandated to provide counter-resistance in pursuit of an illusory state-building aspiration as Zionist colonization accelerated around them. In consequence, avenues for bureaucratic and military resistance were sought and developed. Bureaucratic resistance encompassed counter-intelligence, technical non-compliance with the Oslo framework, prevention of private land sales to colonial agents, and "unauthorized" prisoner releases. Military resistance could be facilitative or proactive: the former included an operational distinction between Israel proper and the OPT, as well as logistical support for guerrillas; the latter involved semi-organized confrontation with the IDF, as well as decentralized, individual martyrdom.

History suggested that surveilling resistance as settlements advanced would not sit comfortably with many intelligence officers. Palestine's new *mukhabarat* drew directly on two distinguished diaspora services: the PLO's Unified Security Apparatus (*jihaz al-amn al-muwahad*), under Salah Khalaf; and Fatah's Central Security Apparatus (*jihaz al-amn al-markazi*), commanded by Hayil 'Abd al-Hamid. Both intelligence chiefs were killed by an Iraqi-sponsored assassin on the eve of Operation Desert Storm. The two services were unified some three years later on establishment of the PA, and relaunched as GI. The service was led in the first instance by veteran intelligence officer Amin al-Hindi (commonly associated with planning for the Munich Olympics operation), and subsequently by Tariq Abu Rajab. The latter had originally worked for 'Abd al-Hamid; his deputy, Tawfiq al-Tirawi, for Khalaf. The surveillance remit afforded the *mukhabarat* comprised four rings of domestic protection: of the political programme initiated in Oslo; of the PA as an institution; of the Palestinian people; and of the land. If the first and second could set them at odds with the Palestinian opposition, the third and fourth squarely confronted Israel. Here, then, was scope for resistance: the people had to be protected from collaboration; the land from sale to Israelis. GI's near operational ally (and rival), the PSA, had the same priorities. *Mukhabarat* officer 'Isa 'Abd al-Hafidh saw a functional overlap: "Frankly, when it was created, it was in parallel with the *mukhabarat*, the same job." The real difference came in senior officers: whereas GI drew on the diaspora for leadership, the PSA drew on Fatah insiders Rajub and his Gazan counterpart, Muhammad Dahlan. During seventeen years in Israeli jails Rajub had forged networks with the Fatah *tanzim*, the network of serious cadres who usually had prison records: "All of his assistants were *tanzim* people from jail; their relationship was more than professional" ('Abd al-Hafidh 2006). Dahlan had five years' prison experience, roots in Khan Yunis refugee camp, and a comparable network in Gaza. The presidential service Force 17 had more in common with the *mukhabarat*, having been formed during the Beirut era to protect the Fatah leadership. Deployment through Oslo put Force 17 on the checkpoints that defined PA territory. Renewed confrontation with Israel would cost them dearly by default. In each case, the more politicized branches of PA security drew on a history and culture of politicized resistance fundamentally at odds with Israeli colonization.

Perhaps the most natural avenue of bureaucratic resistance was in counter-intelligence, and the PA enjoyed real success in turning collaborators, thousands of whom had been on the Israeli payroll for years. Rajub, in particular, has been cited in this regard (Usher 1996: 25). The discernible drop in Israeli intelligence – a reversal of at least one flow of knowledge and power in the OPT – prompted major Israeli concern (Lia 2006: 148, 165). This concern eventually led former chief-of-staff Ehud Barak to lobby against expanded CIA assistance to the PA (Black 2000). Technical non-compliance saw the quasi-extradition clause in Oslo largely ignored: requests for the transfer of wanted Palestinians to Israel were met with intransigence. Regime legitimacy precluded the transfer of security prisoners; the deadly charge of collaboration would quickly have followed. However, as a gesture of goodwill, the PA did hand over a suspected child-murderer and sex-offender in early 2000 (Kjorlien 2000: 117). In another example, new requirements set forth at Wye River prompted the PA to act against car theft, reflecting the cost of Israeli insurance premiums, now among the highest in the world. The agreement prompted a brief crackdown on trade in Israeli vehicles recycled through refugee camp workshops. But public disorder ensued, highlighting deep socio-political tensions between centre and periphery. The initiative was quietly shelved (Wahdan 2000). In respect of the land, real estate sales to Israel were universally equated with treason. Deterrence probably extended to extra-judicial killing, with Force 17 suspected and other services likely complicit. For bitterly contested East Jerusalem, in which Oslo did not grant the PA an official role, Palestinian officers maintained a non-uniformed presence. The booming population of Shu'fat refugee camp provided one source of cover within municipal borders. In dealing with the Islamist opposition, suspects were routinely rounded up for questioning, and fatalities were quickly recorded. But discreet release could also be expedited in the interests of social cohesion. The assassination of Israeli minister Rehavam Ze'evi prompted innovation to keep the prisoners in Palestinian hands: the US and UK helped supervise detention in Jericho for several years until Israel stormed the compound in March 2006, ostensibly to preclude the prisoners' release.

PA military resistance could be facilitative or proactive. Consistent with the PLO's commitment to a two-state solution, a distinction was drawn between operations across the Green Line and those within the OPT. For example, in order "to protect Oslo," GI frequently arrested West Bank Hamas chief Hasan Yusif. GI's 'Abd al-Hafidh (2006) recalled:

> We always arrested suspects after a suicide bombing. We would ask them: "Who supported/organized/carried it out?" It is to show our commitment, part of

protecting our political programme. Many times you find yourself obliged to arrest someone in order to stop these operations, which were never accepted by the outside world.

On the other hand, resistance in the OPT, particularly as settlements and second Intifada casualties mounted, was a different matter; no service escaped unharmed as Israel exacted a heavy toll for an ambivalent stance on the uprising. Resistance could also be facilitated by logistical support for colleagues in or out of uniform and back in the field. Officer cadres from the *tanzim* were well placed to channel equipment and intelligence to colleagues in Fatah, its Islamic franchise the al-Aqsa Martyrs' Brigades, and other factions.

More proactive or direct resistance was also known – occasionally organized, more usually individual. Confrontation between uniformed officers and the IDF had been widespread in September 1996. Nationwide protest at the opening of Israel's Hashmonean tunnel in Jerusalem led to escalating civilian casualties and popular pressure on the PA to respond. In one notable incident, an IDF military post near Nablus was overrun (Mansour 2001: 85; Parsons 2005: 269–272). The concentration of fighting around Israel's colonial transport grid brings to mind Salamanca's (2008) characterization of infrastructure as the nexus of geo- and bio-political pressures. Tasked with manning PA checkpoints, Force 17 found itself very much in the firing line. Force 17 officer 'Isa Maraqa recalled:

> Historically Force 17 was known to be very protective of presidential decisions, so we were very protective of our borders. It was hard, when the confrontations started, to leave our posts; our only choice was to confront Israeli forces as they began reinvasion. Force 17 was hardest hit because it was at the checkpoints. We were on the borders, on the frontline, as at Rachel's Tomb [near Bethlehem].
>
> (Maraqa 2006)

The dilemma confronting the soldiers was recalled by a young lieutenant, now in the SPG:

> Many times Force 17 came and did not intervene, while people were dying in clashes. You hear this, and see the IDF coming, and know they will kill you. Sometimes Force 17 stayed and fought, and many were killed as a result. It is a lose/lose situation. My AK47 is not going to stop a tank; but if you don't shoot, you lose respect in front of the people. And if you do shoot, but end up marked, the IDF will get you later.
>
> (Special Presidential Guard 2008)

Direct resistance was more commonly decentralized and sporadic, a result of personal initiative. Some officers simply resigned their commissions before resuming the role of guerrilla. Uniformed officers continued to die at IDF hands after the second uprising wound down; personnel were still routinely celebrated as martyrs several years after the Roadmap was launched in mid-2003. Posters in public spaces and security service foyers carefully recorded the branch and rank of the martyr. The phenomenon recalls Abujidi's attention to commemoration as a form of resistance (Chapter 16, this volume).

In its recalcitrance, the PA security apparatus drew reprisals from land, sea, and air. Resistance figures in the security services, like those outside it, were targeted for assassination. Population movement was paralysed and mass detention by Israel reintroduced. This left Arafat's successor Mahmud 'Abbas with a West Bank security apparatus that was largely in ruins. The weakened Gazan facilities would fall out of his hands altogether when Hamas seized power in June 2007. The transformed security infrastructure in Gaza would then be obliterated between December 2008 and January 2009 as Israel pursued Operation Cast Lead.

Fatah, Hamas, and the dilemmas of resistance

The calamitous course of the Oslo process put enormous stress on the PA security apparatus, prompting reappraisal and adjustment within the services, the predominantly Fatah personnel that staffed them, and within the Hamas movement that had mostly been on the receiving end of PA surveillance.

Extensive international intervention saw the security apparatus reorganized in accord with a "three-tiered Egyptian model of police, intelligence and army" (Friedrich 2004: 17). The political branches discussed here were allocated to one of each. The PSA linked with the Civil Police and answered to the prime minister through the Ministry of the Interior, although it seemed likely in the long run to be disbanded altogether and merged with GI. The latter remained as the *mukhabarat*, the core of intelligence. Force 17 dissolved into the SPG as part of the PA's quasi-army, the National Security Force. Both GI and the SPG answered to the presidency. The new arrangements were undoubtedly streamlined and more efficient, but the question remained: to what end?

Former PSA officer Ibrahim Ramadan (2006) had asked himself the same question, and concluded that security was premature, and political remobilization in order:

> There is no need for security now. We need Fatah now, just Fatah. If we are in a state, then we need this apparatus. What is the security of a leader if he's in his office and there is an IDF tank outside it? Security is a silly thing right now. The state comes first, then the security; we come with the state. Otherwise, it's security for whom: Israel instead of my people? I think the world is laughing at us.

The aspiration to statehood and Fatah's flagging aspiration to lead it were increasingly understood to require a new position on resistance. To the regret of many, this option seemed to have been ruled out *in any form* by 'Abbas. Fatah Revolutionary Council member and former PA minister 'Abd al-Rahman Hamad (2008) was clear: "Fatah does not have one policy. It is split between those with Abu Mazin and those against him. There has to be an alternative, to resist an Israeli–US imposition." The imperative was all the greater for Fatah in light of Hamas's resonant combination of Islam and resistance.

> Hamas is trying to adopt a policy, and to play a role, in front of the Palestinian people, Arab people, Israeli people, that they are the only people still fighting Israel. Fatah should adopt that policy, not just accept peace talks only. Resistance,

this is one of our policies; without adopting that, it's not easy to get the Palestinian people's support.

(Hamad 2008)

For the US-educated and essentially moderate Hamad, relentless colonization underlined the case: "Don't believe any of this about American pressure on Israel to stop settlements. Underneath the table, the US has accepted what Israel is doing" (Hamad 2008).

Considering the same theme, former Fatah legislator and senior *tanzim* leader Qaddura Faris (2008) alluded to the "modulation" of practice and expectation identified by Weinberger: "The president, the prime minister, and the security apparatus are engaged in peace *coordination*, not peace negotiation." He felt the lack of political progress required a new approach: "The Palestinian people hit a wall, and the resistance also hit a wall, reduced to a few missiles from Gaza. This is not a complete strategy. Palestinians need a new leadership with a new approach: one strategy, and one language, before the outside world." He went on to identify settlement as a target, and to call for a specific type of resistance to it: "I want to see Abu Mazin at the head of a march to al-Aqsa. I want to see Sa'ib 'Urayqat lying down on a bypass road, blocking the way for the settlers. Everyone needs a shock." Here, then, was scope for agency through civil protest – in Scott's formulation, "subaltern resistance that is exercised as a counter-mobilisation to the existing structure of domination" (Scott 2001: 28). But 'Abbas seemed an unlikely figure to take any such initiative; if it were to come at all, the sixth general conference and a renewal of Fatah leadership were probably required.

In the meantime – and with banner of resistance held aloft – Hamas entered the PA. Local election success led to legislative triumph in January 2006, and the prospect of executive power beckoned. It generated new dilemmas in Palestine's surveillance–resistance dialectic. The Islamist movement refused to recognize Israel and the Oslo canon, or to renounce the right to armed struggle. But this may have been a more nuanced position than it first appeared. Refusal to recognize Israel resulted less from dogma than from "witnessing the 'Fatah' experience." In contrast to Oslo, Hamas's "recognition of Israel would come at the end of negotiation, not at the beginning" (Husseini 2009). Similarly, textual analysis of election and post-election documentation points to marked evolution away from the rhetoric of the movement's charter: by way of example, Hamas's proposal for a national unity government spoke of resistance only as a "legitimate right *to end the occupation*" (Hroub 2006: 17). To recall Weinberger, by avoiding "asymmetrical recognition," Hamas appeared to be resisting the "modulation" of expectations that so exhausted the PLO and Fatah. In refusing to police the occupation, Hamas was resisting the "control society" net in which PA security officers had found themselves ensnared. In the meantime, the articulation of resistance as a right subverted another surveillance technique identified by Holoquist and discussed by Zureik: "the collection of information for the purpose not just of reporting the population's collective mood but of managing and shaping it" (Chapter 1, this volume). Hamas generated a "collective mood" of defiance that Israel struggled to modulate; it seems, in the short run at least, that the ultra-violent Operation Cast Lead may only have reinforced it.

Entering a framework predicated on the demobilization of resistance to Zionism, Hamas faced predictable institutional opposition from the PA. First left to govern (and fail) alone, then brought into a short-lived national unity government from February 2007, the Islamist movement confronted a security apparatus on which it could gain little purchase. Gaza-based Interior Minister Sa'id Siyam (the most prominent casualty of Operation Cast Lead) responded by transforming elements of Hamas's military-wing, the 'Izz al-Din al-Qassam Brigades, into the new Executive Force (*quwwat al-tanfidhiyya*). He had cause, as 'Abd al-Hafidh (2006) acknowledged:

> Hamas created its own intelligence service because it has no confidence in our intelligence services; we have different political programmes. So when they are elected and form a government they see that it is their right to form a special intelligence service from Hamas personnel, directed by Hamas to carry out Hamas's orders . . . They cannot carry out their programme because all of the intelligence services are Fatah or Fatah supporters.

The US State Department reinforced dynamics by instructing 'Abbas to retain "independent control of key security forces" and "avoid Hamas integration with these services, while eliminating the Executive Force or mitigating the challenges posed by its continued existence" (Rose 2008). Hamas eventually secured Gaza in two stages: first, a pre-emptive coup in June 2007; second, beginning with Operation Cast Lead in December 2008, "a campaign of abductions, deliberate and unlawful killings, torture and death threats against those they accuse of 'collaborating' with Israel, as well as opponents and critics" (Amnesty International 2009). In the meantime, by September 2007, politicized PA security units in Gaza had been dissolved and replaced by a new Hamas intelligence service, the Internal Security Force (ISF, *quwwat al-amn al-dakhili*). The Executive Force then merged with the core of the Gazan Civil Police (Human Rights Watch 2008).

Conclusion

Zionism is propelled by an inherently racialized biopolitical impulse: to secure Jewish demographic hegemony within the boundaries of Mandatory Palestine. In design and function, the state of Israel has worked consistently toward those ends. Racialized biopolitical continuities – evident in the constitutional and legislative record – call into question Agamben's "state of exception" as an appropriate model of comparative government for Israel. The paradigm seems to work rather better in capturing the "bare life" condition of the individual Palestinian subject to Israeli sovereign power. Confronting and monitoring an obdurate indigenous population and variously hostile Arab neighbours, Israeli institutional development has been marked by the centrality, longevity, and aggressive disposition of its military and intelligence services toward Palestinians. This is the Zionist *mukhabarat* state put forward by Pappe; it is also the source of the "security first" mantra discussed by Khan. The Oslo process produced a conflicted replica of the *mukhabarat* model in the Fatah-dominated PA: restricted in jurisdiction and territorial scope, it was intended to serve as a more intimate and efficient mechanism of surveillance, granting Israel distance from the task. This is the "control society" put forward by Weinberger. But surveilling resistance amid colonization strained PA tensile strength to the limit. The arrangements buckled as bureaucratic resistance expanded to facilitative and even proactive military confrontation. In failure, colonial military power reactivated to devastate the PA. Hamas stood out amid the ruins, focused, and, when pushed, ready to claim Gaza. The Islamist movement then looked to dissolve and replace the more politicized branches of PA security with institutions upon which it could rely in pursuit of a policy of resistance. Nuance within the theme was lost and Gaza was collectively reminded of the fearsome cost of confrontation with Zionism. On the West Bank, Fatah contemplated its options, PA security was reformed to surveil better, and Israel debated how best to expedite racialized biopolitical balance.

Note

1   Portions of this chapter appeared in earlier form: Parsons, N. (2010) "Israeli biopolitics, Palestinian policing: order and resistance in the occupied Palestinian territories," in L. Khalili and J. Schwedler (eds) *Policing and Prisons in the Middle East: Formations of Coercion*, London and New York: Hurst and Columbia University Press.

Bibliography and author interviews

'Abd al-Hafidh, I. (2006) Interview with the author, Ramallah, 20 June.

Agamben, G. (2005) *State of Exception*, trans. Kevin Attell, Chicago and London: University of Chicago Press.

Al Husseini, H. (2009) "They're all with Gaza . . . who is with Hamas?," *asharq alawsat* [English edition], 17 February. Available HTTP: <http://www.asharq-e.com/news.asp?section= 2&id=15407> (accessed 20 February 2009).

Americans for Peace Now (2006) "Why are outposts front page news, yet again?," *Settlements in Focus*, 2. Available HTTP: <http://www.peacenow.org/policy.asp?rid=&cid=3066> (accessed 2 March 2009).

Amnesty International (2009) *Palestinian Authority: Hamas' Deadly Campaign in the Shadow of the War in Gaza*, AI Index: MDE 21/001/2009, 10 February. Available HTTP: <http://www. amnesty.org.uk/uploads/documents/doc_19169.pdf> (accessed 17 February 2009).

Black, I. (2000) "Playing the security game, with CIA as referee," *Guardian*, 20 October. Available HTTP: <http://www.guardian.co.uk/world/2000/oct/20/israel> (accessed 2 March 2009).

B'Tselem (2006) *The Gaza Strip: Israel's Obligations under International Law*. Available HTTP: <http://www.btselem.org/English/Gaza_Strip/Israels_Obligations.asp> (accessed 20 September 2007).

Dean, M. (2002) "Liberal government and authoritarianism," *Economy and Society* 31: 37–61.

Faris, Q. (2008) "One year proposal for stopping both negotiations and violence," paper presented at the Conference of Local and International Experts Reviewing the Peace Process: Towards a Sustainable Peaceful Solution, Center for Democracy and Community Development and Al-Quds University, Abu Dis, 27 November.

Foucault, M. (1977). *Discipline and Punish: The Birth of the Prison*, trans. A. Sheridan, New York: Vintage.

——— (2003) *Society Must be Defended: Lectures at the Collège de France, 1975–76*, ed. Mauro Bertani and Alessandro Fontana, New York: Picador.

——— (2007) "The meshes of power," in J.W. Crampton and S. Elden (eds) *Space, Knowledge and Power: Foucault and Geography*, Aldershot: Ashgate.

Freedland, J. (2009) "A toxic force rises in Israel," *Guardian*, 11 February. Available HTTP: <http://www.guardian.co.uk/commentisfree/2009/feb/11/israeli-elections-2009-israelandthepalestinians2> (accessed 20 February 2009).

Friedrich, R. (2004) *Security Sector Reform in the Occupied Palestinian Territories*, Jerusalem: Palestinian Academic Society for the Study of International Affairs.

Hamad, A.R. (2008) Interview with the author, Cairo, 3 May.

HaLevi, E. (2006) "Feature: outpost residents faithful amidst threats of destruction," *Israel National News*, 5 July. Available HTTP: <http://www.israelnationalnews.com/News/News.aspx/103341> (accessed 2 March 2009).

Hanafi, S. (2005) "Spacio-cide and bio-politics: the Israeli colonial project from 1947 to the wall," in M. Sorkin (ed.) *Against the Wall*, New York and London: The New Press.

Hroub, K. (2006) "A 'new Hamas' through its new documents," *Journal of Palestine Studies*, 35: 6–27.

Human Rights Watch (2001) *Justice Undermined: Balancing Security and Human Rights in the Palestinian Justice System*, 13–14 November. Available HTTP: <http://www.hrw.org/reports/2001/pa/> (accessed 18 August 2010).

—— (2008) *Internal Fight: Palestinian Abuses in Gaza and the West Bank*, 29 July. Available HTTP: <http://www.hrw.org/en/node/62090/section/1> (accessed 1 March 2009).

Israel–PLO agreements of the Oslo process: *Letters of Mutual Recognition*, 9 September 1993; *Declaration of Principles on Interim Self-Government Arrangements*, 13 September 1993; *Israeli–Palestinian Cairo Agreement*, 9 February 1994; *Agreement on the Gaza Strip and the Jericho Area*, 4 May 1994; *Interim Agreement on the West Bank and Gaza Strip*, 28 September 1995; *Protocol Concerning the Redeployment in Hebron*, 15 January 1997; *Wye River Memorandum*, 23 October 1998; *Sharm al-Sheikh Memorandum*, 4 September 1999.

Khan, M.H. (2005) "'Security first' and its implications for a viable Palestinian state," in M. Keating, A. Le More and R. Lowe (eds) *Aid, Diplomacy and Facts on the Ground: The Case of Palestine*, London: Chatham House/Royal Institute of International Affairs.

Kjorlien, M. (2000) "Peace monitor: 16 November 1999–15 February 2000," *Journal of Palestine Studies*, 29(3): 114–129.

Lentin, R. (2008) *Thinking Palestine*, London and New York: Zed Books.

Lia, B. (2006) *A Police Force without a State: A History of the Palestinian Security Forces in the West Bank and Gaza*, Reading: Ithaca Pres.

Mansour, C. (2001) "Israel's colonial impasse," *Journal of Palestine Studies*, 30: 83–88.

Maraqa 'I. (2006) Interview with the author, Bethlehem, 21 June.

McGreal, C. (2003) "Israel learns of a hidden shame in its early years," *Guardian*, 4 November. Available HTTP: <http://www.guardian.co.uk/world/2003/nov/04/israel1> (accessed 16 February 2009).

Morris, B. (2004) *The Birth of the Palestinian Refugee Problem Revisted* (2nd edn), Cambridge: Cambridge University Press.

Mujahid, R. (2006) Interview with the author, Ramallah, 22 June.

Palestinian Human Rights Monitoring Group (PHRMG) (2009) *List of Deaths in Palestinian Custody*. Available HTTP: <http://www.phrmg.org/phrmg%20documents/Death%20in%20Custody/Tables/death%20in%20custody%20english.htm> (accessed 1 March 2009).

Pappe, I. (2008) "The *mukhabarat* state of Israel: a state of oppression is not a state of exception," in R. Lentin (ed.), *Thinking Palestine*, London and New York: Zed Books.

Parsons, N. (2005) *The Politics of the Palestinian Authority: From Oslo to al-Aqsa*, London and New York: Routledge.

—— (2010) "Israeli biopolitics, Palestinian policing: order and resistance in the occu-pied Palestinian territories," in L. Khalili and J. Schwedler (eds) *Policing and Prisons in the Middle East: Formations of Coercion*, London and New York: Hurst and Columbia University Press.

Parsons, N. and Salter, M.B. (2008) "Israeli biopolitics: closure, territorialization and governmentality in the occupied Palestinian territories," *Geopolitics*, 13: 701–723.

Ramadan, I. (2006) Interview with the author, Dhaysha refugee camp, 20 June.

Riley, K.J., Jones, S.G., Simon, S.N. and Brannan, D. with Timilsina, A.R. (2005) "Internal security," in RAND Palestinian State Study Team, *Building a Successful Palestinian State*, Santa Monica, CA: RAND Corp.

Rose, D. (2008) "The Gaza bombshell," *Vanity Fair*, 50(4). Available HTTP: <http://www.vanityfair.com/politics/features/2008/04/gaza200804?currentPage=all> (accessed 18 August 2010).

Salamanca, O.J. (2008) "Life-support systems, bio-power and resistance: insights from the West Bank," paper presented at the States of Exception, Surveillance and Population Management: The Case of Israel/Palestine Conference, Larnaca, 6–7 December.

Scott, J. (2001) *Power*. Oxford: Polity Press.

Special Presidential Guard (2008) Interview with the author, Ramallah, 3 December.

Usher, G. (1996) "The politics of internal security: the PA's new intelligence services," *Journal of Palestine Studies*, 25: 21–34.

—— (2004) "Not Red Indians," *Al-Ahram Weekly*. Available HTTP: <http://weekly.ahram.org.eg/2004/715/re17.htm> (accessed 10 February 2009).

Wahdan, H. (2000) "Refugee Robin Hood," *Palestine Report*, 26 July.

Weinberger, P.E. (2006) *Co-opting the PLO: A Critical Reconstruction of the Oslo Accords, 1993–1995*, Oxford: Lexington.

Weizman, E. (2002) "The politics of verticality," 25 April. Available HTTP: <http://www.opendemocracy.net/conflict-politicsverticality/article_802.jsp> (accessed 18 February 2009).

19 Behavioural profiling in Israeli aviation security as a tool for social control

Reg Whitaker

9/11, besides ushering in what former US President Bush termed a "Global War on Terror," served to focus attention on what has been for many years the most eagerly sought-after target for international terrorists: commercial airliners. Beginning in the late 1960s with hijacking, continuing through a phase of planting bombs on flights, to the 9/11 tactic of suicide bombers assuming command of aircraft converted to weapons of mass destruction, the attraction of high visibility and high death counts has proved irresistible to groups seeking to advance political agendas through acts of violence against civilians. Fascination with air travel continues post-9/11, as the thwarted plot to attack a range of international flights simultaneously in the summer of 2006 and the failed "underwear bomber" on Christmas Day 2009 demonstrate. As a consequence, counter-terrorist security measures have focused disproportionately on civil aviation as a primary vulnerability, as every air traveller for the past few years can ruefully attest.

As so often in the field of counter-terrorist discourse, the Israelis claim special, if not superior, expertise in countering threats to aviation that they insist is the result of longer and tougher experience on the front line of defence against terrorism than anyone else can boast. Specifically, Israeli security officials claim to have developed the most effective approach to airport security against persons attempting to board aircraft with intent to wreak violence. They tend to characterize their approach as a security technique – even sometimes a "technology" – that is politically neutral and universally applicable, and can thus be exported abroad. Indeed, evangelists for the Israeli approach have fanned out throughout North America and Europe, spreading the word of a "better way" to secure air travel from terrorism – with considerable success.

Conventional security approaches stress the identification and interdiction of dangerous *objects* on passengers or their belongings. The Israeli approach stresses the identification and interdiction of dangerous *persons*. Some journalists have seen this as a magic bullet that will not only guarantee air security but reduce if not eliminate the inconvenience and hassle of conventional screening. Security professionals are less sanguine about the latter, but many have nonetheless responded positively to the Israeli model as offering a superior methodology. Looked at strictly from a security perspective, Israeli claims clearly have some validity. There are, however, serious ramifications, social, legal and political, to focusing screening on "dangerous" persons. Above all, particular practices such as security screening cannot be assessed simply in their own terms, but must be looked at in the socio-economic and political contexts within which they have been devised, approved, and applied. Seen in this wider frame, it becomes evident that a "technical" practice like screening serves multiple purposes, not all directly related to the specifics of air travel. The genesis and operation of the Israeli screening model is deeply rooted in the specificity of the Israeli experience, in particular the question of exercising political and social control over Palestinians and Israeli Arabs. Thus it cannot be detached from its origins and presented as a universally applicable technique that will have no unanticipated consequences.

The most controversial consequence of adoption of the Israeli model is the prospect of ethnic, religious, or racial profiling as an official security policy tool of Western governments. Some see this as a threatening spectre of communal division; others as a welcome antidote to the excessive "political correctness" they see growing in Western societies. Neither side, however, objectively assesses the actual security value of the model. I would like to begin with a discussion of two of the various security discourses at play in this debate.

Two discourses

The official security discourse is that of *risk analysis*: resources are limited; 100 per cent security is impossible; the rational response is to analyse the risk levels of potential threats and deploy resources proportionately. In screening for the potential risks posed by individuals, a multitude of risk factors should be brought into play. Among leading risk indicators, national and ethnic origins and/or religious beliefs may be included. In a climate in which the principal terrorist threat after 9/11, Madrid, London and so forth is believed to emanate from those espousing an extreme Islamist ideology, it is perhaps not surprising that at points of entry to Western countries, say, young males of Arab and/or Muslim origin should be seen as posing a potentially higher risk than other categories of people whose identities pose relatively lower risk, as measured in both cases by a number of indicators, such as gender, age, travel patterns and so on. But the implications of this higher-risk factor for screening procedures are quite limited. To put the matter simply: even if most of the terrorists who threaten Western society today are inspired by Islamist ideology, only a tiny proportion of Muslims pose any sort of terrorist threat; therefore, any profiling programme that flags persons as risky solely on the basis of religion would be catastrophically inefficient and ineffective. Adding an FWA ("Flying While Arab") offence to aviation security would be as foolish from a purely practical point of view as the justly condemned DWB ("Driving While Black") offence in urban policing – and equally repugnant from a human rights standpoint.

Members of the targeted communities and civil libertarians are concerned about *any* consideration of race, ethnicity, or religion being included in risk calculations. When visible minority air passengers, for instance, find themselves persistently picked out at airport security or immigration control points for special attention not given to non-visible minority passengers, it is hardly surprising that humiliation, frustration, and anger result. The official risk discourse offers little solace in such situations: one is no less humiliated for being treated as a statistical threat construct than as a target of old-fashioned racism. Of course, unwarranted attention may in practice be the result of front-line personnel interpreting risk more crudely than the model permits, or letting personal prejudice rule in situations in which there is considerable scope for arbitrary officiousness. But this too is a challenge to the official risk discourse. If front-line implementation of security cannot implement the theory properly, there is clearly a problem with the theory.

Inevitably, even with the best of intentions and monitoring of administrative practice, persons from Muslim and/or Arab backgrounds will, in the present global context, find themselves picked out for security attention disproportionately to persons who are neither Muslim nor Arab, and as a result there will be a perception of the violation of their human rights.[1] The official position is that risk analysis justifies this otherwise disproportionate attention. After 9/11, the London Underground and Madrid train bombings, and the terrorist plots allegedly uncovered in the US, UK, and Canada, it would be irresponsible for authorities to ignore this crucial, if limited, risk factor. It is hard to argue with the logic of either of these seemingly contradictory positions. Both are right, but in the sense that they begin from different premises.

There may not be any clear way out of this impasse. Profilers will continue to profile because, to them, that makes more sense than not to profile. And those who are profiled will continue to complain about the practice. From time to time egregious examples of profiling-related injustice will impinge upon the public consciousness, but such instances will be matched by the evidence of religious-based terrorism threatening public safety, with attendant calls for better security measures, including more and better profiling of high-risk persons. Yet even if the impasse remains, it is still worth casting more light on what profiling can reasonably be expected to do, as well as its limitations as a security measure.

Profiling as a risk-management tool

What exactly is profiling? If we look for an officially sanctioned definition, we search in vain. Not surprisingly, officials are reticent about laying down markers to attract complaints of rights violations. Of course, there is no codification of the practice into legal language. A critical definition has been offered by the Ontario Human Rights Commission: "any action undertaken for reasons of safety, security or public protection that relies on stereotypes about race, colour, ethnicity, ancestry, religion, or place of origin, or a combination of these, rather than on a reasonable suspicion, to single out an individual for greater scrutiny or different treatment" (Ontario Human Rights Commission 2010). Useful as this may be for the purposes of human rights litigation, it does rather load the dice with the reference to "stereotypes." There are, however, practical statements about how to apply the procedure in specific contexts. From these we may distil a neutral definition. Profiling refers to the observation, recording, and analysis of selected characteristics of individuals or groups for the purpose of predicting future behaviour. There are a number of key elements involved in this process. The collection of personal data is the necessary, although not sufficient, condition for compiling profiles. Less obvious and less frankly admitted by practitioners is a further assumption: the selection of what data to compile, and the analysis of this data, presupposes *prior guidelines*, or pre-existing models – what to look for and why it matters. Finally, there is a crucial assumption that the past, as revealed in the collected data, can be predictive of the future. If, for example, a set of characteristics (x) has in the past been highly correlated with a certain behaviour pattern – say, paedophilia – then it follows that if a particular individual exhibits a high correlation score with x, he may represent a high risk as a potential (or actual but as yet undetected) paedophile. In other words, he exhibits the profile of a potential offender.

The forensic investigation that followed the 9/11 attacks in the United States, unprecedented in its scope and depth, revealed detailed transactional trails, both paper and electronic, left by the terrorists as they planned and executed the acts that cost the lives of close to 3,000 people. These trails retroactively yielded patterns, or profiles, of what a potential al Qaeda terrorist threatening the United States *might* look like – assuming, of course, that future attacks will mirror the patterns established in 9/11. The promise of this investigation for the future was its apparent potential for predicting, and interdicting, other terrorist plots by identifying the kinds of individual who posed a high threat risk, and offering direction to the kind of personal data that could pick out such individuals from the crowd.

Profiling is nothing if not predictive. The first two elements (data collection and prior modelling) are crucial to determining the predictive capacity of any profiling exercise. If the data is inadequate or if the analysis is faulty, predictive capacity is dubious – and the possibility of false negatives, as well as false positives and potential violations of individual rights, rises sharply. We should be clear that high accuracy in prediction is not the required standard from a security and policing perspective. What is being measured is *risk*, itself a matter more of statistical probability than of certainty. Security screening, for instance, does not indicate culpability but rather seeks to identify levels of risk and to screen out those who might potentially pose a threat (according to agreed risk indicators), those who match or approximate the profile of a risky individual. False positives are an inevitable by-product of any risk-based approach. Of course, this standard, far lower than that required in criminal justice, begs the question of the impact on individuals falsely identified as high risk, or the impact on entire communities that are, in effect, singled out as suspect on the basis of the correlation of high risk with a minority of individuals from that community. Once again, we have two parallel discourses, each yielding very different results.

Let us stay for a moment with the official discourse and, for the sake of argument, grant its tacit assumption that the production of false positives, even in limited proportions, and the resultant collateral human damage are the regrettable but inevitable results of risk-based security. Let us look closely at the profiling process, in its own terms, and attempt to assess its usefulness and its limitations as a security measure.

First, data collection. In the past, finding sufficient information might have been a problem. Today, in the midst of the information technology revolution, with the emergence of a surveillance society in which transparency (also known as the end of privacy) is as much or even more characteristic of the private sector than of the public sector (Whitaker 1999), the problem is the opposite. There is the "Sorcerer's Apprentice" syndrome: how to contain and manage the relentless flow of data. To some enthusiasts, this is not a problem but an opportunity. Most notorious was the Bush administration's "Total Information Awareness" (TIA) programme under the direction of bureaucratic impresario John Poindexter, who spoke glowingly about command and control of the global "transaction space" where terrorists leave "an information signature. We must be able to pick this signal out of the noise"(Whitaker 2006: 157). The TIA programme was so egregiously oversold and roused such antipathy even from conservative supporters of the administration that it was scrapped.

However, a multitude of TIA-like programmes under other names have followed. The Poindexter theory – vacuum up all the "noise" and you will find the "signal" – remains in some respects the ruling guide to American anti-terrorist surveillance practice. After recent intelligence failures, such as 9/11 and the London Underground bombings, others have questioned whether too much information impedes rather than facilitates finding the signal. "Connect the dots" seems like a wise admonition, but not when there are too many dots for any analyst to connect sensibly and instructively.

This brings us to the second element in the profiling process: prior modelling. The prior model contains the expectations that the analyst brings to the collected data. Raw mined data need to be structured. The model tells the analyst which questions to address, on which data to focus, what kind of signal is to be sought out of the noise. Put so baldly, this may sound like prejudice (literally, pre-judgement) at work. Certainly there is enormous scope for prejudice and the application of ideological blinkers. The intelligence literature is rife with warnings about the analytical pitfalls that await those trying to deduce the intentions and future actions of adversaries from the information collected on their past and present behaviour (9/11 Commission 2004: 339–360).

Yet there is no escaping the obligation of the analyst to have a pre-packaged model to apply; otherwise all is drift and confusion. Even hard scientists do not devise testable hypotheses from indiscriminate innocent observation. They pick and choose what they observe and how they measure it from predetermined ideas of what might be interesting and useful. Far down the food chain of knowledge, lowly security analysts grappling with the more intractable difficulties of observing adversaries who are deliberately setting out to conceal their tracks and baffle investigators are in even more need of sharp-edged models that will cut through the noise with some prospect of success.

The issue, then, is not that the analyst is "prejudiced," but rather how well, or badly, the pre-judgment directs that analyst in separating signal from noise. The full returns on the so-called Global War on Terror are not yet in. However, we have the example of counter-espionage from the Cold War that preceded the present security focus on terrorism. The example is not encouraging.

In the early Cold War years a series of British defections to the USSR uncovered high-level penetration of the UK by Soviet intelligence (the so-called Cambridge Ring that ultimately proved to include at least five Britons, all with senior roles in the UK diplomatic and intelligence services). The shock waves from this development struck all the Western capitals, especially Washington, where the Cambridge case quickly became a paradigm for Cold War counter-intelligence. In various ways the Cambridge spies had all been ideologically motivated by sympathy for communism conceived in the 1930s while at university. The model of the "ideologically-motivated traitor directed attention away from betrayals based on non-ideological motives, while instead sending counterintelligence experts chasing after mythical hares. The Cold War paradigm developed abstract profiles of *spies who might have been* and then set out to match real public servants to these hypothetical profiles to find cases of risk." By the early 1970s reckless internal "mole" hunts had been unleashed in the US, UK, and Canada. This "hunt had become, in the hands of true believers, a methodology that admitted of no disproof and turned self-destructively inward" (Whitaker 1997: 25; emphasis in original). Rooted in the ideology of the early Cold War, the profile of the likely spy for the Soviet Union was itself deeply ideological. By the 1970s, money had

Reg Whitaker

become a much likelier motivator for betrayal than ideology had been for the 1930s generation. In short, the Cambridge profile turned out to be a diversion that resulted in counter-intelligence failure, not to mention considerable collateral human damage.

The Cold War example provides a cautionary tale. It does not disprove the value of profiling, but it does caution against placing too much weight on the past to predict the future. To some extent, this lesson may have been taken to heart by at least some in the security world post-9/11. Warnings abound concerning the dangers of fixating too literally on the profiles of the 9/11 bombers. Richard Reid, the would-be "shoe bomber," was not of Arab or Asian origin (although he was a convert to Islam); the perpetrators of the London Underground bombings were born in Britain; and the majority of the Toronto group charged under the Anti-Terrorism Act are Canadian-born (although in all cases Islamist ideology continues to be a common thread). Women have been used as suicide bombers by Hamas in Israel, overturning certain preconceptions of Israeli security. It is not rocket science for terrorists facing security measures designed to block 9/11 profile conspirators to see the advantages of designing different, less suspect, profiles for front-line *jihadi* soldiers of the future. Nor has this possibility escaped the minds of security officials who urge wide vigilance against new and unanticipated terrorist methods – former US Defense Secretary Donald Rumsfeld's famous "unknown unknowns." If there is one post-9/11 cliché to match "connect the dots," it is: "think outside the box."[2]

That said, while appeals to think outside the box and imagine the unimaginable may have some play in the more rarefied atmosphere at or near the top of security intelligence agencies, it is much less likely to be on the plate of street-level, front-line workers doing the daily business of screening individuals in, say, the busy airports of the world. Here adherence to one-size-fits-all guidelines and narrow rule-based decision-making, backed by the usual bureaucratic "cover-your-ass" mentality, will tend to force thinking strictly *within* the box. In one close examination of the US, UK, and Germany since 9/11, the point is made that "the law enforcement agencies of all three states . . . have regularly used terrorist profiles that are based on stereotypical group characteristics such as 'race,' 'ethnicity,' national origin and religion to select the targets of their preventive powers" and have done so "mainly out of political convenience" (Moeckli 2006).

Air passenger profiling: the Israeli case

In this context, I would like to turn to a case study of a proposed innovation in profiling in aviation security. I recently served as chair of an advisory panel reviewing Canadian aviation security that reported to the Minister of Transport and Parliament (Advisory Panel . . . 2006). In the course of our review we examined screening practices and performance across Canada and abroad and we looked at various suggestions for improvements in the system. Featuring prominently among these suggested reforms were recommendations to shift focus away from screening for *dangerous objects* (the focus of the current mandate) toward screening in the first instance for *dangerous persons*.

There has been an undercurrent of support for this latter approach since 9/11, with much of it inspired by Israeli methods of passenger profiling, as implemented at Ben Gurion International Airport in Tel Aviv. But support appeared to gather momentum following the shock to the existing screening system generated by the discovery in

August 2006 of an alleged terrorist plot to target a series of transatlantic flights simultaneously, and the sudden imposition of bans on carry-on liquids and gels at all European and North American airports. Yet more interest followed in the wake of the failed "underwear bomber" on a flight to Detroit on Christmas Day 2009. Each case generated a spate of media commentaries favourably citing the Israeli experience, arguing that it was a waste of time to screen unthreatening people's bags and persons for potentially dangerous objects when such objects will only be employed by the tiny percentage of passengers who intend to wreak havoc. The latter category, it was suggested, would fit the profile of air terrorists and could be screened out, thus enhancing security while at the same time improving the efficient flow-through of peaceful passengers from ticket counter to aircraft.

One response to the admonition to look for dangerous people rather than dangerous objects is to recall the dubious slogan of the US gun lobby: "Guns don't kill. People kill." In fact, people kill much more efficiently with guns than without them. Screening for dangerous passengers while relaxing controls over dangerous objects would invite resourceful terrorists to evade screening with enhanced access to weapons or improvised explosives once on board.

In any event, passenger profiling is only one (albeit important) part of an impressive, multilayered system of security at Ben Gurion. It is this multilayered approach (if a threat makes it past one layer, chances are high that it will fail to penetrate the others) that has made Israeli practice the alleged gold standard in civil aviation security, according to most aviation security experts. Ben Gurion's predecessor, Lod Airport, was hit in 1972 by a terrorist attack by three arriving passengers, members of the Japanese Red Army, who opened fire with automatic weapons and threw hand grenades at people in the airport, killing 26 and injuring 78. Ben Gurion possesses elaborate protection against such an attack, which has never been repeated. In fact, Ben Gurion was planned and built with security "designed-in" from the start, something permitted in Israel's hyper-security environment, but something that has not been repeated in the design of any other international airport, including those coming into operation since 9/11. Ben Gurion offers an architecture of security unique in its multidimensional complexity. The priority accorded security in Israel affords a dedication of resources that no other country can match.

The Israeli approach focuses on reducing the primary emphasis on screening for objects without removing that requirement. As the former head of Israeli air security explained to an American congressional committee, it is impossible to do a thorough check of all passengers (Ron 2002):

> These checks consume a long time (about one hour for a single passenger with one checked bag), they are very intrusive and considered by most passengers as a very substantial hassle. It became clear that it will be impossible to provide this type of procedure to all passengers and therefore [there was] a need to develop a method that will allow an intelligent decision as to who is more eligible for this thorough search.
>
> The answer to this need came in the development of a systematic, real-time, investigation of the passenger profile. This well-designed procedure allows the security officer to make a decision, based on identifying the level of risk, as to the level of checks to be performed before the passenger is allowed to board the aircraft.

This real-time investigation can be as short as ninety seconds or last as long as twenty minutes. It involves the checking of documents (ID, flight tickets etc.) and questions that relate to the passenger's journey and background.

This profiling method has been used very successfully for the last thirty-two years by the state of Israel.

If, when interviewed, a passenger exhibits, for instance, high levels of stress, or reveals contradictions in their story, this will result in intensive scrutiny. The precise criteria flagging for further checking are not publicly available as this is considered sensitive information, but advocates for the Israeli system have always argued strenuously that this procedure is not based on such simplistic categories as race, ethnicity, or religion. Israeli profiling claims to be *behavioural*, looking for anomalous patterns that send warning signals that something may not be quite right with regard to a particular passenger.

The Israelis cite as the primary success of their system the detection of an explosive device on an El-Al flight from London to Tel Aviv in 1986 – an attempted terrorist attack that involved a naïve (and pregnant) young Irish woman. A suspicious El-Al security officer, noting anomalous aspects in the woman's story, discovered that she was carrying a bag she had been given by her Palestinian "boyfriend." A thorough search of the bag found Cemtex and a sophisticated altimeter detonation device disguised as an electronic calculator. The Israelis cite the absence of any further such attempts at El-Al as evidence that their system acts as an effective deterrent.

There is much to be said for Israeli-style passenger profiling purely from a security standpoint. The bombing of an Air India plane in June 1985, in which 329 people (most of them Canadian nationals) were murdered, could have been averted if Israeli-style behavioural profiling had been practised at Canadian airports at the time. When passenger "M. Singh" showed up at the Canadian Pacific ticket counter in Vancouver demanding that his bag be interlined to Air India Flight 182 departing from Toronto Pearson, even though he had no confirmed ticket for that flight, a series of warning flags should have started waving. The expensive ticket had been purchased at the last moment in cash; the passenger name had subsequently been changed; and "M. Singh's" manner was aggressive and bullying. All of these points should have singled out "M. Singh" and his bag for close inspection. Should that have happened, the lives of 329 people would have been spared. Tragically, the harried Canadian Pacific ticket agent, against her better judgement, against airline rules, and to her lifelong regret, gave in and allowed the fatal bag to proceed. But at this time airline employees received no training in behavioural profiling; staff had no authority to question passengers about their personal circumstances; and no intelligence warnings had been given to front-line employees about the security threat posed by Sikh extremists.

Another point is rather more unsettling. While the behavioural anomalies surrounding "M. Singh" would have constituted the core of any passenger profiling exercise that might have identified him as a potential bomber, his Sikh background was hardly marginal, either. Rather, his apparent racial/religious background would be an important factor in a context in which Sikh extremists were issuiing threats against Air India flights. In other words, behavioural profiling does not, and cannot, rule out taking into consideration racial and religious factors as components of the larger picture, even though profiling all Sikh passengers as constituting risks would have been neither appropriate nor acceptable.

Many of the same points could be made about the Christmas Day 2009 bomber, Umar Farouk Abdulmutallab. This young Nigerian, apparently radicalized abroad and given some training in terrorist action by al Qaeda in Yemen, tried to blow up a Northwest Airlines plane by igniting explosives concealed in his underwear. Considerable embarrassment in US official circles greeted the public revelation that Abdulmutallab's father, a wealthy banker, had warned the US Embassy in Nigeria the previous month that his son might be involved with Islamist militants. Abdulmutallab's name and passport number were placed on two separate terrorist watch lists, but not on the "no-fly" list. This intelligence failure was then matched by a security failure. Circumstances surrounding the would-be suicide bomber's boarding in Amsterdam of the flight to the US should have set off several alarm bells. His age, name, abnormal and illogical travel route, high-priced ticket purchased at the last minute, the fact that he boarded without luggage, and other anomalous behaviour signs should have been sufficient to warrant closer examination. Nor should his Islamic religion, in conjunction with his recent stay in Yemen, a country with a high terrorist risk, have escaped the attention of airport security. But none of these warning flags were recognized, and the would-be martyr was able to board the aircraft with concealed explosives.

To make matters even more embarrassing, the company handling security at Amsterdam's Schipol Airport is ICTS International, a firm established in 1982 by former members of the Israeli security service, Shin Bet, and El-Al security, and run largely by Israeli managers. "Two decades ago, ICTS adopted the system used in Israel, namely of profiling and assessing the degree to which a passenger is a potential threat on the basis of a number indicators (including age, name, origin and behaviour during questioning)" (Melman 2010). ICTS has also developed the Advanced Passenger Screening system used by most North American airlines. Yet, in practice, the Israeli-style behavioural profiling championed by ICTS failed the test that it was set by Abdulmutallab.

It is thus paradoxical that the Israeli approach to passenger profiling is increasingly finding support outside Israel, and this has gained further momentum since the Christmas Day fiasco. Although ICTS screening concepts were already widely in place at many European airports, following the August 2006 plot, European ministers decided to consider the formal adoption of Israeli-style passenger profiling (*Times* 2006). Boston's Logan Airport has introduced the SPOT (Screening of Passengers by Observation Techniques) programme having been directly inspired by Israeli advisors (Donnelly 2006; Jacoby 2006). SPOT is now being promoted by the US Transportation Security Administration (TSA) for adoption by other American airports. The TSA today deploys "behavioural detection officers," who utilize "non-intrusive behavior observation and analysis techniques to identify potentially high-risk passengers," although the agency hastily adds that suspect passengers will be referred for closer examination "based on specific observed behaviors only, not on one's appearance, race, ethnicity or religion" (TSA 2010).

In the wake of the Abdulmutallab incident, and under pressure from the United States, Canada introduced its own "passenger behaviour observation programme."

> This additional layer of security to Canada's aviation system focuses on identifying
> irregular or suspicious behaviour and not racial or ethnic profiles. The emphasis

is behaviour-based, for example, wearing heavy clothes on a hot day or sweating profusely. Screening officers trained in passenger behaviour observation screening may ask simple questions about the passenger's identity and reasons for travelling to alleviate any security concerns . . . Canada uses a multi-layered approach to aviation security that benefits from a variety of tools and methodologies. These include technologies, intelligence assessments and cognitive-based indicators. While no single layer of aviation security may defeat terrorism, together the layers of security provide a robust defence.

(Transport Canada 2010)

Earlier, our Advisory Panel's (2006) report on Canadian aviation security paid careful attention to programmes that "rely upon observation of atypical behaviour patterns to identify suspicious persons who are flagged for closer attention. It is important to note that these programmes do not attempt to extrapolate presumed intentions, but merely observe anomalous external behaviour." However, despite the clear advantages promised by such approaches, we were cautious about moving quickly in this direction:

We have some concerns about the application of this approach in Canada. However interpreted, it implies a degree of discretion assigned to frontline personnel to make judgments about passengers – judgments that might have serious impact on individuals. We note that the threat environment in some other countries greatly exceeds anything experienced in Canada; consequently there is widespread acceptance in Israel, for example, of security measures that might not be as acceptable to Canadians. We would note as well the danger of such a system of passenger analysis being misunderstood as "profiling," which in its ethnic, religious and racial forms is generally seen as inappropriate, if not illegitimate, in Canada. In fact, these implications are neither necessary nor inevitable if such an approach is planned and implemented properly. However, there would certainly be public perception and civil liberties issues that must be taken seriously.

Despite our reservations about the introduction of the behavioural analysis method as an additional type of screening tool, the Panel recognizes that its application is being both tested and adopted in a few other countries. Before the adoption of such a technique is considered for Canada, it would be necessary to review international experiences with this method and to carry out carefully planned and controlled pilot projects in Canada in order to assess such things as the accuracy of the behavioural analysis process, the competencies and training required, and the impact on the overall efficiency and effectiveness of screening.

(Advisory Panel . . . 2006: 160–161)

While preparing our report, I was given a behind-the-scenes tour of Ben Gurion by the Israeli security service, Shin Bet. While impressed by the depth and scope of the many layers of security, I had reservations about the profiling. Very young security officers were making quick visual judgements as passengers entered the airport, judgements that could shunt someone into the high-risk stream. My own contacts in Israeli universities had told me that students doing their compulsory military service, who were assigned duties as airport profilers, sometimes received what they considered less than adequate training and admitted that their judgements were often arbitrary. A recent probe by an Israeli newspaper has claimed that security personnel at Ben Gurion are often undertrained and underprepared (Blumenkrantz 2010), Given these concerns, I could not but wonder to what degree Arab Israeli passengers might receive differential, if not discriminatory, treatment – hardly surprising, perhaps, in the high-risk and volatile security situation in Israel.

In fact, Israeli Arabs and Israeli human rights groups have been making such claims for some time (Derfner 2007; Stern 2007a). Israeli spokespersons explaining their system in other countries have in the past tended to dismiss these claims, stressing the behavioural focus of their profiling, while occasionally acknowledging that since their main security threat comes from Palestinians, there is an additional risk factor associated with Israeli Arabs that is taken into consideration in profiling. Yet, in one editorial, the Israeli newspaper *Haaretz* (2007) commented:

> Every traveller passing through Ben-Gurion International Airport recognizes the scene: Arab passengers, citizens of Israel, are automatically pulled aside for security checks, some of them degrading, which sometimes last for hours. There is no dispute that security checks are essential to ensure the safety of flights and passengers. But there are ways to carry them out without besmirching an entire community by suggesting that every Arab is a suspect unless proven otherwise . . . There is no reason to discriminate against Israeli Arabs, in airport terminals or anywhere else. A community of one million people, the vast majority of whom have never participated in terrorist activities against the country, does not deserve to be automatically considered suspect.

Examples abound of clearly discriminatory and humiliating treatment routinely meted out to non-Jewish air travellers, especially Arab Israelis, Palestinians, and non-Israeli Arabs. Take the case of the first-ever Israeli Arab cadet, or diplomatic intern, in the Israeli Foreign Ministry, the daughter of an Israeli Supreme Court justice, who, despite her eminently respectable credentials, was taken out of the passenger line and subjected to intrusive and humiliating questioning both on departing and when arriving back in Israel from her trip to Europe. The reporter who brought this story to light acutely added: "It bears understanding that if ethnic profiling can't be helped, the ethnics being profiled can't help the way they take it" (Derfner 2007). There was also the example of an Israeli Arab member of the Law Faculty at the Hebrew University, who attempted to board a flight to Tunis to participate in an academic conference. She was detained and prevented from boarding when security screeners discovered she resided in East Jerusalem (Silverstein 2006).

It is therefore of considerable interest that Shin Bet has accepted that there is some substance to charges of discrimination, and has publicly stated its intention to revamp its system to minimize such discriminatory treatment:

> The Shin Bet security service is to acquire a security system based on new technology in order to prevent the need for separate personal checks of Arab passengers in airports, Shin Bet chief Yuval Diskin said . . . Once the new technology has been introduced, identical checks will be conducted for Arab and Jewish passengers and will no longer include body searches for Arabs . . . Diskin

said that, in some instances, those conducting security checks have already been instructed to ease their checks of Arab passengers.

(Stern 2007b)

Like Arab passengers, independent observers will be somewhat sceptical of these claims of reform. For instance, much was made about reforming the system of highly visible coloured tags that were attached to baggage, corresponding to the three levels of risk determined in the initial checks at Ben Gurion. The bags of Arab passengers were allocated red tags, which meant that they received the maximum and most intrusive special interrogations and searches further down the security line. In the reformed system, all passengers, of whatever origin, were to be allocated identical white tags (Blumenkrantz and Stern 2007). However, it soon became apparent that nothing had changed. Luggage belonging to Arab passengers still undergoes a more thorough security check than that of Jews: it is sent to an X-ray scanner with higher resolution than is used for Jewish luggage. Moreover, the "identical" white tags are not identical: the Jewish white tags have the number 1 printed on them, while those of Israeli Arabs have 2 and those of non-Israeli Arabs have 5 (*Tikkun Olam* 2007).

The Israeli authorities explained that the new system was intended to end "visible discrimination" (Blumenkrantz 2008). Did they honestly believe that the targets of continuing discriminatory practice would not notice the slightly less visible tagging? Or, more likely, was the whole process merely a public relations exercise with no intention of transforming the existing system? Ariel Merari, an Israeli aviation terrorism expert and an advisor on terrorism to former Prime Minister Yitzhak Shamir, insists that ethnic profiling in airport screening is both effective and unavoidable:

> It's foolishness not to use profiles when you know that most terrorists come from certain ethnic groups and certain age groups. A bomber on a plane is likely to be Muslim and young, not an elderly Holocaust survivor. We're talking about preventing a lot of casualties, and that justifies inconveniencing a certain ethnic group.
>
> (Associated Press 2008)

However, the notoriety of discriminatory practices at Ben Gurion has even reached the US State Department, which has issued travel advice to Palestinian Americans planning on flying to Israel (*Haaretz* 2008). And the complaints made by human rights groups within Israel have risen in recent years (Yoaz and Khoury 2007). We may thus expect that further visible changes will be made, without actually eliminating the crucial element in the behavioural profiling approach, which is to identify the risk level associated with those coming from particular groups, along with other, non-ethnic risk identifiers.

Conclusions

I would like to make some observations after this brief consideration of the "Israeli system." First, it must be said that security at Ben Gurion is truly impressive. As a multilayered, designed-in security system, Ben Gurion is unmatched in the civil aviation world. Its incident-free record, situated as it is in an extremely high-risk environment, speaks for itself, as does the matching security record of the national airline, El-Al.[3] However, neither the dense security architecture of Ben Gurion nor the elaborate security system operating on El-Al flights everywhere in the world is exportable as a complete package, since neither such high-risk perceptions nor such generous funding levels are attained anywhere else. Nevertheless, elements of the Israeli system are eminently exportable, with passenger profiling certainly being one of them.[4] As an export product it has so far had limited but significant success in North America and Europe, and it appears to be on an upward trajectory of acceptance and implementation.

Looked at strictly as a security measure, Israeli passenger profiling has a number of strengths. Even its critics acknowledge that *it works*. However, looking at it simply as a socially and politically neutral security technique misses a great deal that is critical to grasping the significance of passenger profiling in its specific Israeli context. Passenger profiling arose out of a very specific social and political context: an embattled state confronting hostile internal and external forces that challenge the state's very definition. Within a context of a society hierarchically constructed with a privileged Jewish majority, an Arab Israeli minority of decidedly second-class status, and, since 1967, occupied territories with subject Palestinian populations, in a situation of persistent tension, conflict, and violence between Israelis and Palestinians, it would be delusional to expect that any security screening process for Israel could escape the constraints of national ideology and attain a neutral, scientific impartiality.

It is no surprise, then, to find that the system reproduces in its own workings the same ideological colour of the larger society that gave rise to it. In theory, passenger profiling could focus on anomalous behaviour patterns as risk identifiers; but in practice, racial, ethnic, and religious profiling, with all the discriminatory implications of such techniques, have always been central to the approach, too. Passenger profiling serves a dual function: as an effective security measure and as yet another part of a system of domination and repression that works consistently to discriminate against persons of Arab and Muslim background. It therefore serves not only security but the pervasive requirement for social control of the non-Jewish population, which is especially crucial as it operates as a sorting system at Israel's entry and exit points. Nor can these two elements be disentangled. In a specific context of unresolved Palestinian–Israeli conflict, targeting Arabs is a scientifically sound aspect of passenger profiling, and yet it is inherently and irredeemably discriminatory and repugnant to human rights.

In the wider world to which Israel exports its techniques, behavioural profiling remains a viable if controversial tool from the point of view of security in an age of terrorist threats to public safety. Profiling is also inherently dangerous from a human rights perspective inasmuch as it inevitably impacts differentially on different groups. Tensions between the two discourses will continue, and no doubt resulting conflicts in the real world will continue to simmer and occasionally boil over. In countries where community tensions are less fundamental than they are in Israel, the racial and religious elements of behavioural profiling must be handled with extreme caution and circumspection, within a framework that insists upon respect for human rights and non-discrimination. With this caveat, profiling may prove to be a risk-management device that offers some additional security. But it would seem that in the country that gave birth to the technique, there is little if any likelihood of the balance between security and human rights being negotiated successfully unless there is a fundamental transformation of the nature of that society.

Notes

1 The problem was highlighted when an RCMP criminal intelligence brief (RCMP 2001) was subjected to close scrutiny by a lawyer at a public hearing of the Commission of Inquiry into the Maher Arar affair (Commission of Inquiry . . . 2005). The document had identified the "type of adversary we are up against" by describing what was known at the time about the 9/11 hijackers, identified by a number of behavioural characteristics. Under questioning, an RCMP anti-terrorism officer was asked if this description would not apply to "many, many North American Arab/Muslim men who have adjusted and integrated into Canadian . . . society" and that this description constituted "an express invitation to racially profile people when you have a mandate, sir, as you had, which is to turn over every stone." The officer was reduced to mumbled agreement, captured in the transcript as "Mm-hmm."

2 In a document prepared by the New York Police Department Intelligence Division, the authors note that while homegrown radicals exhibit a "remarkable consistency in the behaviors and trajectory across all the stages" of their radicalization into terrorists, there is no "useful profile to assist law enforcement to predict who will follow this trajectory of radicalization." "Ordinary" people may be sought out by extremists "because they are 'clean skins'" (Silber and Bhatt 2007: 82, 85).

3 El-Al's exemplary security record does not carry over into an equally impressive record in aviation safety. The US Federal Aviation Administration in late 2008 downgraded Israel's aviation safety rating to Category 2, which is "commonly assigned to developing countries" (Blumenkrantz 2009).

4 Another example is that of the highly trained and armed air marshals who fly on all El-Al international flights. This was an Israeli innovation copied by airlines in a number of Western countries, including the United States and Canada.

Bibliography

9/11 Commission (2004) *Final Report of the National Commission on Terrorist Attacks upon the United States*. New York: W.W. Norton & Company.

Advisory Panel on the Review of the Canadian Air Transport Security Authority Act (2006) *Flight Plan: Managing the Risks in Aviation Security*. Available HTTP: <http://www.tc.gc.ca/tcss/CATSA/toc_e.htm>.

Associated Press (2008) "Israel's airport security challenged: Arabs complain they face racist treatment when boarding planes," 19 March.

Blumenkrantz, Z. (2008) "Mazuz moves to limit racial profiling at Ben-Gurion Airport," *Haaretz*, 4 June.

—— (2009) "El-Al plane nearly crashed close to Jerusalem hills," *Haaretz*, 4 February.

—— (2010) "*Haaretz* probe: Israel airport security often carried out by untrained employees," *Haaretz*, 11 January.

Blumenkrantz, Z. and Stern, Y. (2007) "Coloured tags for Arabs' luggage at Ben Gurion Airport discontinued," *Haaretz*, 7 August.

Commission of Inquiry into the Actions of Canadian Officials in Relation to Maher Arar (2005) "Transcripts of testimony," 30 June. Available HTTP: <http://epe.lac-bac.gc.ca/100/206/301/pco-bcp/commissions/maher_arar/07-09-13/www.ararcommission.ca/eng/11e.htm>.

Derfner, Larry (2007) "Stereotyping security," *Jerusalem Post*, 22 March.

Donnelly, Sally B. (2006) "A new tack for airport screening: behave yourself," *Time*, 17 May.

Haaretz (2007) "Clipping El-Al's wings," 20 September.

—— (2008) "Palestinian Americans warned of security profiling at B-G Airport," 20 March.

Jacoby, Jeff (2006) "What Israeli security could teach us," *Boston Globe*, 23 August.

Melman, Yossi (2010) "Israeli firm blasted for letting would-be plane bomber slip through," *Haaretz*, 10 January.

Moeckli, Daniel (2006) "Terrorist profiling and the importance of a proactive approach to human rights protection," paper presented to the Annual Conference of the Association of Human Rights Institutes, Vienna, September.

Ontario Human Rights Commission (2010) "What is racial profiling?" Available HTTP: <http://www.ohrc.on.ca/en/resources/factsheets/whatisracialprofiling/view>.

Ron, Rafi (2002) Remarks to the Aviation Subcommittee, Committee on Transportation and Infrastructure, United States Congress, 27 February.

Royal Canadian Mounted Police (RCMP) (2001) "Law enforcement requirements to combat terrorism," report, 18 September.

Silber, Mitchell D. and Bhatt, Arvin (2007) "Radicalization in the West: the homegrown threat," report.

Silverstein, Richard (2006) "Israeli-Arab Hebrew University professor harassed, denied permission to attend academic conference," *Tikkun Olam*, 25 November.

Stern, Yoav (2007a) "Rights group wants to monitor Arab travellers' airport checks," *Haaretz*, 11 January.

—— (2007b) "Shin Bet new system will ease checks of Arabs at airport," *Haaretz*, 28 February.

Tikkun Olam (2007) "Flying while Arab: Israeli airport security harassment," 7 August.

Times, The (2006) "Muslims face extra checks in new travel crackdown," 15 August.

Transport Canada (2010) "Backgrounder: passenger behaviour observation screening," January. Available HTTP: <http://www.tc.gc.ca/eng/mediaroom/releases-2010-h002e-5794.htm>.

Transportation Security Administration (TSA) (2010) "Behavior detection officers (BDO) layers of security." Available HTTP: <http://www.tsa.gov/what_we_do/layers/bdo/index.shtm>.

Whitaker, Reg (1997) "Spies who might have been: Canada and the myth of Cold War counterintelligence," *Intelligence and National Security*, 12(4): 25–43.

—— (1999) *The End of Privacy: How Total Surveillance is Becoming a Reality*. New York: New Press.

—— (2006) "A Faustian bargain? America and the dream of total information awareness," in Kevin D. Haggerty and Richard V. Ericson (eds) *The New Politics of Surveillance and Visibility*. Toronto: University of Toronto Press.

Yoaz, Yuval and Khoury, Jack (2007) "Civil rights group: Israel has reached new heights of racism," *Haaretz*, 16 December.

Index

392   *Index*